CRUISE SHIPS

CRUISE SHIPS

AN EVOLUTION IN DESIGN

PHILIP DAWSON

CONWAY

MARITIME PRESS

Dedication
For Ingrid, my wife, whose love, understanding and moral support
have contributed so vitally to this work

First published in Great Britain in 2000 by
Conway Maritime Press,

A member of the Chrysalis Group plc

9 Blenheim Court, Brewery Road,
London N7 9NT
www.conwaymaritime.com

Distributed in the United States of America in
2000 by Books International
P O Box 605, Herndon, VA 20172

British Library Cataloguing in Publication Data
A record for this title is available upon request
from the British Library

Library of Congress-in-Publication data
A record for this title is available from the
Library of Congress

ISBN 0 85177 660 4

Designed by Peter Champion

Printed and bound
in Spain

CONTENTS

FOREWORD 6
    by Stephen M Payne
    Senior Naval Architect and Project Manager
    Carnival Corporation Technical Services

INTRODUCTION 7

1 GENESIS
    The early cruise yachts 9

2 DUALITY
    Influence of British dual-purpose
    and tropical liners 24

3 ADVANCEMENT
    Towards the creation of the modern
    cruise liner 38

4 THE SUPERLINERS
    Special dual-function express liners 58

5 THE SUN VIKINGS
    Norwegian-style cruising comes to
    America 79

6 LINEAGE AND NATIONALITY
    Liner operators adapt to full-time cruising 96

7 PROGRESS OF SCALE
    Larger cruise ships for greater economy
    and luxury 115

8 REBUILDING AND CONVERSION
    Cruise ships shaped out of refits and
    other surgery 135

9 CONFIDENCE OF PROGRESS
    New ideas in the medium-tonnage range 154

10 TOWARDS SIX FIGURES
    Progress towards the 100,000-ton ship 174

11 ALTERNATIVES OF SCALE
    Ascendancy towards the 20,000-ton yacht 195

12 CLASSICAL RENAISSANCE
    Inspirations anew from the liner era 215

EPILOGUE 234

Appendix A
SHIPS' SPECIFICATIONS 237
Appendix B
NAVAL INTERIOR ARCHITECTS 256

BIBLIOGRAPHY 262
INDEX 265

FOREWORD

There is nothing quite like the tingle of expectation and excitement quayside as passengers eagerly await to board their ship. After tickets are inspected and checked, passengers, now largely defined by the trade as 'guests', swarm on board to find their cabin and explore their new, temporary home. As sailing time nears, deck rails become crowded with passengers as the ship signals her intention to sail. The whistle sounds out, echoing about the surrounding buildings and startling those amassed at the railings and on the pier below. The ship casts off and slowly edges away from the shore, passengers' streamers making a last link to the quayside before being inevitably broken. The euphoria is palpable, with the realisation of an adventure of a voyage just begun. The passenger ship, like no other form of mass transportation, is able to convey its charge around the world with all of the comforts of a grand hotel; it is truly a city at sea. It is therefore, perhaps, not so surprising that cruising is one of the fastest growing sectors of the leisure market.

To the casual observer the modern cruise ship may not seem too different to the classic ocean liner of the past. Look closer and the subtle differences begin to appear, showing the two types to be quite distinct. Look again, this time a little more in depth, and compare particular vessels of the past and present, and new similarities inevitably begin to become apparent. In many cases it is the proverbial 're-inventing of the wheel'. Atriums, popular with liners of the first quarter of the twentieth century had become unfashionable during the 1950s, only to be rediscovered and incorporated into almost every cruise ship design in the 1980s and onwards.

This book by Philip Dawson chronologies and explains the evolution of the cruise ship from her ancestry linked to the point-to-point ocean liner. From the very early cruises run in the nineteenth century to the present day, the book skilfully guides the reader through the various facets of ship design and operation. Celebrated cruise liners past and present are analysed and their place in history expertly described, both from the technical and passenger points of view. We find old favourites such as the 'Green Goddess' – Cunard's *Caronia* (1947), the early 1960s *Canberra* and *Oriana* – line voyages pressed into cruise service for survival when their trade elsewhere ceased to be profitable, and the unusual but very relevant *Wilhelm Gustloff* (1938) and *Robert Ley* (1939). And who better to act as our guide than Philip Dawson, author of the acclaimed *British Superliners of the Sixties* and *Canberra: In the Wake of a Legend*. Philip can be described as a knowledgeable and informed enthusiast, who has an eye for the important without getting carried away with the mundane and tedious, which is a common fault of some so-called liner experts. Here is a book which makes fascinating reading and will certainly come to be regarded as the official history of cruising. It is definitely a most welcome voyage of discovery.

Stephen M. Payne
Senior Naval Architect and Project Manager
Carnival Corporation Technical Services

London, August 1998

INTRODUCTION

The development of modern cruise shipping is no doubt one of the greatest transport and lifestyle phenomena of our time. Since the first notions of floating hotels and state yachts took root in the nineteenth century, deep-sea ships have been viewed as being capable of providing round-trip pleasure voyages as an alternative to their original role of offering swift and reliable passages across the world's oceans and seas. Although some notable early ships were specifically fitted out for cruise services alone, sometimes only on a seasonal basis, the mainstream of passenger shipping activity continued to stress line services. Cruising was seen by many as essentially a diversion to keep ships and crews busy during the off-season of their regular trades.

Some lines went as far as to design liners which could convert by combining their accommodation into a single class for the cruising season. Two ships built during the 1930s in Germany exclusively for providing workers' holidays, produced a remarkably standardised approach to all-one-class accommodation which was well ahead of its time. For the most part, however, passenger tonnage continued to be built until the late 1960s with multiple passenger classes and hold space for heavy baggage, mail and at least a small amount of special cargo.

Even as the great liners *Normandie*, *Queen Mary* and *Queen Elizabeth* were being built in the 1930s, visionaries were already looking to the skies and the future role of commercial aviation. As the first jet airliners took to the airways in the 1950s, it became generally accepted that the days of the ocean crossing were numbered. What could not be foreseen, as the well-known and much-loved Cunard *Queens*, *United States*, *Nieuw Amsterdam* and even such modern ships as *Michelangelo* and *Raffaello* were withdrawn from service and disposed of in the late 1960s and early 1970s, was that incredibly large numbers of even greater ships would follow in the coming three decades to meet a then totally unforeseen demand for pleasure cruises.

The airlines, which were popularly credited with bringing about the demise of sea travel, would assume a new role as cruise-line partners, swiftly bringing millions of passengers across whole continents to ports near the world's most sought-after tropical cruising areas. The wide-bodied Boeing 747 airliner, which could speed half a ship-load of passengers between London's Heathrow Airport and New York's JFK in little more than six hours rather than six days, is more likely these days to be viewed by shipping people in terms of its capacity to bring cruise passengers from their homes to the ship and back again.

However, as much as aviation's role has evolved from competitor of the old steamship companies to partner with the cruise lines, so too have ships themselves changed dramatically. *Normandie*'s legendary double- and triple-height interiors served only the privileged and well heeled who could afford to travel first class. The vast majority of ordinary mortals who 'crossed' aboard these ships did so in the adequately comfortable, although far less spectacular, surroundings of the lower classes.

Apart from the cinemas featured in ships such as *Normandie*, *United States* and *Michelangelo*, there was little provision made for professional entertainment and other diversions such as health spas, conference centres, electronic amusements and casino gaming, which are now part of our lifestyle ashore, let alone on the high seas. Even dining in the liner era was limited, almost exclusively, to the three formal meal services offered in the dining room each day.

At the time *Queen Elizabeth 2* was commissioned as an ostensibly dual purpose liner/cruise ship, many argued that if Cunard and other lines had thought earlier of providing her style of modern and diverse facilities, line services, on the North Atlantic in particular, might have been kept going longer. There were even suggestions of Atlantic liners with ferry-style roll-on/roll-off decks which would allow passengers to take their cars with them. It is probably unlikely that such things would have made much of a difference, since for the person who has to cross for whatever reason, the convenience of a daily flight schedule is impossible to beat.

In fact, developments of the present cruise era were rooted

not so much in the liner image, but in the far more modern approach of the smaller Scandinavian car-passenger ferries of the 1960s. As these have inevitably progressed to larger sizes, so too have their accommodation and public facilities become more spectacular. However, while there are some remarkable recreations of liner-era spaciousness and opulence, these are rendered on entirely more up-to-date designs which are more apt to find their origins in contemporary hotel and resort architecture.

The features which make each ship described in the following chapters a unique facet of the story, are as diverse as the character of these vessels themselves. I have endeavoured to describe them by overall type and in the order of their significance and impact. Chapters One to Four examine products of the deluxe steam-yacht and classic liner era through to the modern examples of *Rotterdam*, *Canberra* and *QE2*, the lifestyles they supported and their influence over later developments. Chapters Six to Twelve follow the diverse paths of modern cruise ship development from the Scandinavian-ferry-inspired *Sun Viking* type to other developments such as the All Outside Cabin cruise liner, Carnival's Fun ships, new adaptations of the original cruising yacht idea, sail, the Clubship and, inevitably, the greater-than-100,000-ton megaship.

The arrangement of this material avoids the monotony of a catalogue-style presentation, where the attributes of each are presented in a chronological sequence. Many of these strains of development have evolved concurrently as a diversification of the cruise 'product'.

While it is probably best to read Chapters One to Four in sequence, the remaining sections can be delved into random-ly without too much loss of continuity. Statistics and figures are, for the most part, given in the appendices, with tonnage, dimensions and other figures only being quoted in the text where needed. To avoid fiendish editing on my part at the last minute as ships may be converted, withdrawn from service or renamed, they are all discussed in the past tense.

Although this is primarily a look at the subject from a design and building perspective, it also endeavours to capture something of the changing ocean-going lifestyles over the years and their influences on the ships themselves. This has generally taken the form of a shift from passengers amusing themselves during long stretches at sea, to them now expecting to be professionally entertained virtually around the clock. The passenger role has, in some areas such as entertainment, shifted from active participant to passive spectator. Yet in areas such as sports, health and fitness, modern-day cruising has brought about new diversions and opportunities which invite active participation. While the megaships, with their emphasis on the personal privacy of electronic-entertainment-centre-equipped veranda staterooms, may offer the anonymity or a large resort or community ashore, *Aida's* creators have striven to re-introduce the traditional type of shipboard camaraderie from *Prinzessin Victoria Louise's* day, through an adaptation of the modern-day sport and health resort.

Company histories and the biographies of the personnel responsible for the design and building of these ships are dealt with here only as far as these have had any direct impact on what was actually planned and built.

ACKNOWLEDGEMENTS

No book such as this is possible without the generous and whole-hearted assistance of those individuals and organizations who are willing to share their valuable time, knowledge and resources. Many of the designers, shipyards, suppliers and cruise lines, along with their officers, engineers and crews have been most enthusiastic and encouraging in their support. Of these I am especially grateful to Stephen Payne of Carnival Corporation Technical Services, to Kvaerner Masa-Yards and Meyer Werft, as well as to Stephen Rabson of P&O Group and Rich Steck at Royal Caribbean International, who are among my longest-standing contacts.

There are a great many others who have helped in some very special ways. Of these I am especially indebted to Klas Brogren of ShipPax Information in Halmstad, Sweden, for having opened so many doors to me within the industry through my work with his publications, *Designs*, *Guide*, *Statistics* and *Cruise & Ferry Info*, as well as the great personal hospitality shown to me during several visits to Sweden. My thanks also to Gordon Turner, editor of the Canadian quarterly cruise newsletter, SeaFare, and friend, neighbour and fellow shipping enthusiast, for the loan of so much material from his personal collection. I also owe him a great deal for the benefit of his knowledge, advice and keen editorial skills, and his very special role in making a pre-inaugural cruise aboard *Disney Magic* possible. I am likewise most grateful to John and Diana Lang for their friendship and the great benefit of their perception of the business and personal side of cruising, and for the opportunities they too have made possible through The Cruise People in Toronto. A special thank you to Yoshitatsu Fukawa for the wealth of information and many fine photographs from Japan, which may otherwise never have been available to me. Finally, and by no means least, to the many others whose names are indeed not forgotten, but, alas, for which space does not permit, my earnest and heartfelt thanks.

I sincerely hope that this look at the world's burgeoning stock in the cruise shipping trade will bring the reader as much pleasure as, for the most part, its creation has given me.

GENESIS

The early cruise yachts

I n 1845 the following advertisement for a luxury cruise appeared in the *Leipziger Illustrierte Zeitung*:

AN OPPORTUNITY FOR TAKING PART IN A VOYAGE AROUND THE WORLD

The undersigned Hamburg shipowner proposes to equip one of his large sailing vessels for a cruise around the world, to start this summer, during which the passengers will be able to visit the following cities and countries, *viz* Lisbon, Madeira, Tenerife, Cap Verde Islands, Rio de Janeiro, Rio de la Plata, Falklands Islands, Valparaiso, and all the intermediate ports of call on the Pacific coast of South America as far as Guayaquil (for Quito), the Marquesas Islands, Friendly Islands (Otaheite) and other island groups in the Pacific, China (Choosan, Hongkong, Canton, Macao, Whampoa), Manilla, Singapore, Ceylon, Ile de France or Madagascar, the Cape of Good Hope, St Helena, Ascension Island, the Azores, and back to Hamburg.

The cruise is not intended for business purposes of any kind; but the whole equipment and accommodation of the vessel, the time spent at the various ports of call, and the details of the whole cruise, are to be arranged with the sole object of promoting the safety, the comfort, the entertainment, and the instruction of the passengers.

Admission will be strictly confined to persons of unblemished repute and of good education, those possessing a scientific education receiving preference.

The members of the expedition may confidently look forward to a pleasant and successful voyage. A first-class ship, an experienced and well-educated captain, a specially selected crew, and a qualified physician are sufficient guarantees to ensure a complete success.

The fare for the whole voyage is so low that it only represents a slight addition to the ordinary cost of living incurred on shore. In return, the passenger will have many opportunities of acquiring a first-hand knowledge of the wonders of the world, of the beautiful scenery of the remotest countries, and of the manners and customs of many different nations. During the whole voyage he will be surrounded by the utmost comfort, and will enjoy the company of numerous persons of culture and refinement. The sea air will be of immeasurable benefit to his health, and the experience which he is sure to gain will remain a source of pleasure to him for the rest of his life.

Full particulars may be had on application to the undersigned and a stamped envelope for reply should be enclosed.
Rob M Sloman
Hamburg, January, 1845
Shipowner in Hamburg[1]

Apart from its date, changes in a few place names and some other details, this could be from a present-day cruise brochure. The requirement that passengers be 'of unblemished repute and of good education' has, in most market sectors, been replaced by the need to simply be in possession of a valid credit card. The route is generally familiar, being similar to the winter world-cruise itineraries of today's *Rotterdam*, *QE2* or *Europa*, taking into consideration that the Suez and Panama Canals had not been built at that time. The promise of an unforgettable experience, the opportunity to visit strange and exotic lands, of being enlightened and to enjoy the company of similarly-minded shipmates continues to be made today in the glossy cruise brochures on your travel agent's shelves.

During the intervening century and a half, cruising has grown and diversified into one of the world's major leisure industries, bringing its pleasures to people in all walks of life. From the standpoint of social history, the democratisation of society brought about through the Industrial Revolution and the machine age placed many once elitist privileges within the reach of the average citizen. As greater numbers of ordinary working people began to enjoy larger disposable incomes and more leisure time, they too sought the diversions of discovery, self-enlightenment and pure enjoyment which modern-day travel affords. Industrial and technical advancement has helped in various ways, both directly and indirectly, to making the means of such mass mobility practicable, attainable and comfortable.

The prestigious Anglo-French Concorde supersonic airliner, South Africa's superlative *Blue Train*, revitalisation of the Venice-Simplon *Orient Express*, as well as elite-class cruise ships such as *Europa* and a number of the smaller yacht cruisers, show that the wealthy and discerning continue to be well served. This is also supported by the fact that private yachts are being built in unprecedented numbers. However, simultaneous developments such as the Boeing 747 jumbo jetliner and its capacity to provide cheap mass air travel, the proliferation of the private automobile and the phenomenal success of Carnival's huge fleet of modern and spacious 'Fun Ships', show that the remaining market sectors are in their own right equally well catered to. At the same time, the financial and social gap between the way the two halves live has narrowed.

Most of us can, if we want to, afford at least once in our lives to travel on the *Orient Express* or to cruise aboard ships such as *Europa* and *Seabourn Pride*. Social and economic class barriers do still exist, but they are far less formidable than they once were. A passenger's social and cultural background may still engender feelings of self-consciousness in unfamiliar territory, but he or she is today unlikely to be denied service, ridiculed or made to feel unwelcome. Even during the years of apartheid in South Africa, the 'international' status accorded the *Blue Train* exempted her passengers from racial segregation while they were aboard. Indeed, much has changed since Herr Sloman advertised his voyage.

Early cruise expeditions were usually organised by tour operators or other specialist societies. Britain's world-renowned Thomas Cook travel and tour company is generally credited with being the first company to arrange escorted group excursions by sea as early as 1841. These used regular steamship services to the Mediterranean, with sightseeing excursions arranged exclusively for the cruise party at various ports of call. The whole tour would, in fact, involve travel in several ships, allowing the ports of greatest interest to be visited in a timely fashion. The Peninsular and Oriental Steam Navigation Company, now known as P&O, entered the field early as one of the first shipping Line's to offer similar 'group tours' on their then newly extended Mediterranean services. They went a step far-

ther by occasionally sending one of their ships on a purely recreational voyage. Among the first of these was a round trip from London to the Black Sea aboard the paddle steamer *Tagus* in 1843. William Thackeray described one of the excursions of this period in his *Diary of a Voyage from Cornhill to Grand Cairo*, published in 1846.

Other organisations arranged various excursions during the mid-nineteenth century using chartered tonnage. As a passenger on the *Quaker City's* 1867 Mediterranean voyage from the United States, Samuel Clemens recorded his impressions under his better-known pen-name Mark Twain in *The Innocents Abroad*. Voyages of this sort were often advertised on the contingency that 'the number of passengers be sufficient to defray the expenses'. Only if enough bookings were made ahead of time would the ship be outfitted for the one excursion. Afterwards, the ship usually was returned to her normal commercial trade.

ST ROGNVALD AND ST SUNNIVA

While the classic tours of the Mediterranean and the Orient, as the Middle East was then called, were often of two or three months' duration, shorter excursions by sea began to emerge in the more northerly latitudes. The foremost pioneer of these, and in many ways of modern-day cruising, was 'The North Company' of Aberdeen. Their unwieldy full name, The North of Scotland & Orkney & Shetland Steam Navigation Company, reflected nearly a century of amalgamation and name changes since being founded in 1790 as The Leith & Clyde Shipping Company. By the 1880s, The North Company had developed reputable regular services from Leith and Aberdeen northwards to various destinations in the Orkney and Shetland Islands, before setting their sights on the broader horizons of Norway and cruising.[2] The first pleasure excursion was publicly announced by a newspaper advertisement carried in the Tuesday, 8 June 1886 issue of *The Scotsman*, saying:

> … fast and commodious steamship *St Rognvald* is intended to make a special trip with a limited number of cabin passengers on Thursday, June 24 ex Leith and Aberdeen to Bergen and some of the principal fjords and places of interest on the west coast of Norway.

Ninety passengers booked, at a price of £10 each, for the nine-day cruise, making it an immediate success. *St Rognvald* sailed first to Stavanger, then on to Bergen where two calls were made during the cruise. A major attraction was the 24-hour shore excursion from Bergen, with an overnight stay ashore before rejoining the ship the following day in the Sognefjord. This voyage marked the beginning of cruising in one of the most spectacular scenic regions of the world. Its comparatively short duration and modest cost were within the reach of a great many more people than could afford the Mediterranean excursions of the day.

While *St Rognvald's* first excursion of 1886 had been run

St Sunniva: At anchor, possibly in Hoy Sound, with her steam excursion launch and a lifeboat alongside for tendering passengers ashore.

(P&O Group, London, neg PO-1-3868)

on a purely trial basis, The North Company's management were far-sighted enough to realise that they had just written the formula for success on their new venture. A second cruise was announced the day of *St Rognvald's* first departure for Norway, with three more subsequently scheduled for the 1886 summer season. All were of similar duration, but with slightly varied itineraries.

The 984-ton *St Rognvald* was chosen for these voyages, as she was then the line's largest and newest ship. She was an iron single-screw vessel with length and beam of 73.45m and 9.44m respectively, built in 1883 by Hall Russell and Company of Aberdeen. Her layout was fairly typical of the larger coastal steamers of her day. Passengers were accommodated in two classes on the main deck, and cargo was carried in the lower deck. It was essentially without major modification that *St Rognvald* undertook her first cruises. While she was plying between the shores of Scotland and Norway fully booked, her owners were already laying plans for a new vessel to be designed exclusively as a cruising yacht, ready for the following summer's programme.

Named *St Sunniva*, this unique ship was delivered by Hall Russell in time for the 1887 summer cruising season. At 864 tons, with a length of 71.62m and 9.14m beam, she was marginally smaller than *St Rognvald*. The new ship was powered by a triple-expansion steam engine, yielding 141kW of power at a shaft speed of 96rpm. When she ran her sea trials in the spring of 1887, *St Sunniva* achieved a speed of 15.5kts.[3]

Externally, *St Sunniva* presented a striking appearance befitting her role as a luxury cruise yacht. She had a clipper bow, with bowsprit and figurehead, and a spoon-shaped stern with a deep counter revealing the upper part of her spade rudder. The sheer lines of her hull, along with the visual balance of her two raked masts and single funnel, were a perfect picture of the yacht aesthetic at its very best. Among the neat rows of boats carried beneath her davits, there was a steam-powered launch port side for ferrying the passengers ashore at places where the ship would be unable to go alongside a pier or quay.

St Sunniva differed from the earlier ship in that she provided first-class passenger accommodation only, with the exclusion of all cargo spaces except those needed for stores and passenger baggage. She had space for 142 passengers, mainly in two- and four-berth cabins arranged throughout the main and lower decks. There was a spacious saloon located aft on the main deck, with seats for 132 persons at its six long tables, allowing for meal service at a single sitting. Other public spaces consisted of the stairway entrance, a ladies' sitting room and the men's smoking room, arranged as three cubicles within a small teak deckhouse above the saloon. In those days it was still customary for a ship's saloon to be the main venue of all social activity on board. Ladies' lounges and smoking rooms merely provided the separate male and female retreats demanded by Victorian social protocol. Apart from the saloon, a ship's open decks were the only place where ladies and gentlemen could mix socially.

Other creature comforts of *St Sunniva's* passenger accommodation included electric lighting throughout, as well as push-button electric call bells in the cabins and a piano in the saloon for the passengers to entertain themselves. In this regard the older *St Rognvald* actually had the upper hand, being outfitted with both a piano and an organ.

St Sunniva went into service on Thursday, 26 May 1887, on the first in a series of ten-day Norwegian cruises running until the month of September. It soon became clear that even this handsome new ship could not meet the growing demand for cruises that season. *St Rognvald* was quickly pressed back into cruise service to handle the overflow of bookings. With her accommodation still virtually unaltered, the older ship's capacity was limited to fifty passengers, thereby according her clientele a reasonable semblance of *St Sunniva's* superior services and amenities. After the season had closed on 15 September, its phenomenal success was studied with a view to still further expansion. The North Company's directors agreed then that *St Rognvald* would be refitted along the new ship's lines, and that both vessels would operate on a far more ambitious cruise programme the following summer.

St Rognvald was brought up to the new ship's higher cruising standards in two stages. The first step was to enlarge the accommodation by enclosing the aft well deck. Cargo access to the hold below was retained via a trunkway passing through the accommodation to the upper deck, which this change had turned into a continuous promenade running from the ship's stern to her bridge. Forward of the saloon and original first-class cabins, the enclosed main-deck area below was fitted with twenty-two new, two-berth rooms amidships. The two cabins farthest aft were removed to increase the saloon's seating capacity to eighty. The enlarged accommodation provided a total of one hundred berths for cruising. Later modifications carried out between 1894 and 1898 extended the upper-deck enclosure farther aft, to include a Music Salon in addition to the original smoking room and two existing six-berth cabins. This change also created an added promenade space atop the deckhouse. *St Rognvald* still retained her forward well deck and cargo holds, enabling her to function both as a cruise yacht and in the regular cargo and passenger trade.

The cost for a ten-day cruise aboard *St Sunniva* ranged from £10 10s (approx $50) per person, sharing a cabin with more than two berths, to £15 for single occupancy of a room. On some of the longer cruises which were offered later the fare was set at £35, on the basis of one cabin for each passenger. The reservation could be secured with a deposit of £3, with the remainder of the fare being due six days before sailing. Shore excursions at the major places of interest in Norway could be purchased on board for a modest additional outlay.[4] Passengers could also book point-to-point passage on cruises. Later, cruise passengers were given the option of leaving the ship at any port and rejoining her on a later voyage at no additional cost. These arrangements were, then, within the reach at least of the middle strata of society, though still beyond the means of the working masses, both in terms of time and disposable income.

It is only comparatively recently that entertainment has been provided as a ready-made part of shipboard service. Aboard the venerable Cunard *Queens* and the lavish *Normandie* of Compagnie Générale Transatlantique (French Line), let alone lesser vessels, during the heyday of transatlantic travel, it was the passengers themselves who played the active role in amusing their fellow travellers to pass the time. Traditionally, ships' concerts were organised around whatever passenger talent happened to be aboard during a particular voyage, with perhaps some help from an obliging artistically-gifted member of the crew.

In *St Sunniva's* time, before the advent of motion pictures, radio and recorded music, passengers were left to their own devices to keep themselves amused and entertained. They tended to be far more resourceful and versatile at passing the hours aboard ship than are the majority of today's cruise clientele, who belong to a spectator society which demands virtually around-the-clock professional entertainment at the touch of a button. Apart from drawing on the skills which Victorian cruise passengers might be able to collectively muster in the performing arts, they were creative at devising all manner of deck games and elaborate shipboard tournaments. This was all accomplished without props and with no special equipment other than whatever surplus items might be borrowed from the crew.

In the relatively small groups which travelled together on ships like *St Rognvald* and *St Sunniva*, it was almost axiomatic that all but the most disagreeable shipmates would soon find themselves drawn into an informal fraternity or club for the duration of the voyage. A popular pastime on a number of such cruises was to produce a newspaper of sorts as a jointly-created souvenir of the voyage. Such productions were more or less scrapbooks containing writings and pencilled sketches from various passengers, maybe a photograph or two, along with perhaps newspaper clippings, extracts from the ship's log and so on. The first of these to come from *St Sunniva* was a creation by passengers on her maiden voyage, entitled the *St Sunniva Chronicle*. Perhaps one of the most outstanding of these was a manuscript produced on a later Eastern Mediterranean cruise in the spring of 1896. This was later reissued as a printed and bound book bearing, in both Greek and English, the title:

THE DEEDS OF THE ST SUNNIVITES
being the
NEWSPAPER PUBLISHED
ON BOARD SS ST SUNNIVA

Not only had these passengers produced this magnificent record of their dream voyage, as this must certainly have been, but they had also named their select little shipboard society.

Despite the occasional production of such an elaborate work, the pleasures of life aboard those early cruises were fairly basic. The order of the day was very simple, requiring no distribution of daily programmes or broadcast announcements. Meals, which were the only routinely scheduled events of the days at sea, consisted of:

Tea or Coffee	7–8am
Breakfast	9am
Dinner	2pm
Tea	6pm

This schedule was annotated with 'Tea to include substantials', meaning that it was high tea. Later programmes showed the now more familiar lunch at 1pm, dinner at 7pm followed by 'late Tea or Coffee'. The quality of cuisine was advertised as being equal to that of a first-class hotel, no doubt a Victorian equivalent for the present-day euphemism 'gourmet dining'. Liquor was available at passengers' expense from the stewards from 8am until 11pm 'when all lights are extinguished and the pantry closed'.

Meagre, to say the least, by the standards of today's *Sea Goddess* or *Seabourn* yacht-style cruise ships, these facilities were on a par with the best deep-sea liners of their time.

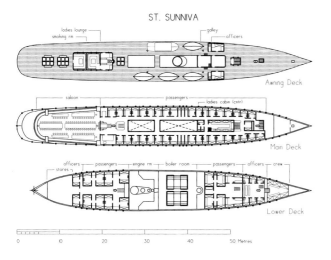

St Sunniva: **Accommodation plan.**

(Author)

Unlike those in first class on P&O or Cunard's liners of the day, *St Sunniva*'s passengers could also enjoy the run of virtually the whole ship, without being restricted by areas belonging to other classes, cargo or mail. As though aboard a private yacht, they had the added intimacy and security of travelling exclusively in the company of a relatively small number of compatibly-minded shipmates.

From 1888 onwards, The North Company expanded their cruising horizons to include, first, the Baltic and the North Cape, and, later, the British Isles and Mediterranean. *St Rognvald* was first to cruise to the North Cape on a 21-day excursion that year, with principal calls at Bergen, Molde, Trondheim, Tromso, Hammerfest, Lofoten, Christiansund and Geiranger. *St Sunniva* closed her 1891 season with a three-week Baltic cruise to the Northern capitals of Christiana (Oslo), Copenhagen, Stockholm and St Petersburg (Leningrad until recently). In 1896, *St Rognvald* was among a number of ships that made cruise expeditions to view a solar eclipse which was expected to be visible in the northern latitudes. While her passengers and those of the other ships which had anchored off Vadsoe were disappointed by local cloud cover, those aboard *St Sunniva*, much farther south near Bodo, had a perfectly clear view of the eclipse.[5]

After being laid up during her first few winters, *St Sunniva* started operating in the Mediterranean under various charters during her off season. The first of these was a private six-week cruise organised by Baron Rothschild. This was followed, in early 1894, by a Thomas Cook cruise to Alexandria, Jaffa (for the Holy Land) and Piraeus. Other Mediterranean charters were organised by Dr Lunn and Mr Perowne, who had previously run group tours aboard the ship's regular cruises and had arranged the 1896 eclipse expedition. During the winter of 1895/6 they ran six cruises from Marseilles to Naples, Piraeus, Constantinople (Istanbul), Jaffa (Haifa) and Alexandria. By the end of this engagement, *St Sunniva* had turned a profit for her owners of £25,500, almost as much as her original building cost. Later, the summer cruise season was extended by offering one or two circumnavigations of Britain. These ran clockwise from Tilbury, calling at Torquay, Dartmouth, Isle of Man, Greenock, Rothesay, Oban, Skye, Stromness, Aberdeen and Leith.

As the twentieth century dawned, The North Company began to strain under serious competition from other Lines with more opulent ships. Rivals were not an altogether new phenomenon. The Wilson Line of Hull had offered three-week North Cape cruises aboard their steamship *Domino* as far back as *St Rognvald*'s first season. Then, *St Sunniva* had quickly proven herself as the right measure of defence against this challenge. However, the later arrival of larger, and better-equipped, tonnage from the fleets of the leading deep-sea Lines presented a far more formidable threat to the Line's market position. By this time Orient Steam Navigation, P&O, Royal Mail, French Line, North German Lloyd and HAPAG (the more convenient universal acronym for

Garonne: This ship was switched from Orient Line's London – Melbourne service to cruising in 1889.

(P&O Group, London, neg PO-1-502)

Vectis: Built in 1881 as P&O's *Rome*, she was adapted as a cruise yacht in 1904.

(P&O Group, London)

Hamburg Amerikanische Paketfahrt Aktien-Gesellschaft) were all offering regular summer Scandinavian and North Cape cruise programmes in addition to tropical cruising elsewhere.

Orient's *Chimborazo* and the first *Garonne* were switched from their London–Melbourne service to cruising in 1889.[6] At slightly less than 4,000 tons each, and with lengths of about 90m, these grossly outclassed *St Rognvald* and *St Sunniva*, even without significant modification for cruising having been made. P&O's 1881-built *Rome* was converted as the cruising yacht *Vectis* in time for the 1904 Norwegian season. At 5,545 tons she was more than five times *St Sunniva*'s size, which in consideration of her only slightly larger passenger capacity of 150 persons, placed her far ahead of the pioneer cruise yacht in terms of comfort and luxury.[7]

In 1908 Royal Mail transferred their liner *Amazon* from her regular service to Brazil, Uruguay and Argentina to a programme of summer cruises in Norwegian waters. The Line's advertising claimed that these voyages were to be run 'in the belief that there is a great desire among tourists to spend a Norwegian holiday at a moderate price in greater comfort and luxury than has hitherto been possible'.[8] By that time Royal Mail Lines had already built up a good reputation as cruise operators elsewhere, with the northern summer cruises becoming a regular part of the Line's diverse leisure excursion offerings.

Royal Mail's successes started with the 2,000-ton *Solent*, their second ship to bear that name, which entered service exclusively for cruising in the West Indies during 1905. She operated out of Barbados, where passengers travelling by regular Royal Mail steamers from Southampton or New York would transfer aboard her. She quickly become eminently successful, and was joined two years later by the slightly larger *Berbice*. These two ships appear to have originated the trend for the hulls of cruise ships to be painted white.

From a very early stage, the Norwegians themselves were eager to exploit the opportunities for cruising and tourism that their own homeland could offer. A Royal cruise to the North Cape was made by King Oscar II in 1873, to show off the pristine natural beauty of his kingdom to an invited entourage of European journalists and photographers. It was in fact one of these guests, Paul de Chaillu from France, who coined the expression 'land of the midnight sun', after this and several subsequent voyages. Originally used as the title of a published account of his experiences and impressions, the phrase has outlived the popularity of his literary work as an internationally-known advertising slogan.

For a while Thomas Cook chartered various Norwegian coastal vessels for cruise excursions into these northern latitudes. Finally, in 1883, a regular series of North Cape cruises from Trondheim was organised jointly by the two foremost companies in the domestic Hurtigruten coastal service. The Nordenfjeldske Dampskibsselskab and Det Bergenske Dampskibsselskab both trace their origins back almost as far as Cunard, P&O and Holland America. In 1851 and 1857 respectively, these private family-owned concerns were born into the rivalry of establishing cargo and passenger services in the early Norwegian coastal trade. With this new interest in Norwegian tourism they were drawn first into operating these seasonal cruises, and in the longer term to building up a steadily growing holiday clientele year-round on the famed Hurtigruten route itself. Indeed both companies would go on to become partners in worldwide deluxe cruising, starting in the early 1970s.

Regular coastal steamers were used for these and for later cruises farther north to the Spitzbergen archipelago, or Svalbard as it is known in Norwegian. However, each spring the ships to be used for cruising were beautified and readied with their black salt-streaked hulls painted white, awnings rigged and portable cabins assembled in their cargo holds. Once the season had finished, the cruise trappings disappeared and the holds once again became filled with mail, dry cargo, fish and livestock.[9]

In 1900 The North Company suffered the loss of *St Rognvald*, thankfully without casualties. While on a regular crossing to Orkney the ship struck Burgh Head, Stronsay, in dense haze during the early morning hours of Tuesday, 24 April. Her sixty-eight passengers and crew of thirty-eight were safely landed at a nearby farm before the ship foundered. *St Sunniva* continued cruising until 1908, when she was converted for the Line's regular mail and passenger services. She continued to operate in this capacity on the weekly Lerwick run from Leith and Aberdeen until 1930, when she too was lost.

A fitting tribute to those early ships, and the seamanship of their times, was given in 1971 by Alastair and Anne Cormack in *Days of Orkney Steam*:

Nowadays it may seem strange to look back and find so many wrecks and strandings of ships in waters familiar to them. We must remember, however, that without the benevolent guidance of a radar screen, our forefathers at the exposed helm of the old boats must have had little to guide them towards their island havens. In times of storm the low lying land would be invisible under a cloak of spray. At times this garb would

be changed for a shroud of mist. A moment's relaxation on the part of the crew could mean disaster, or at the very least an inconvenient stranding.

The sturdy construction, and the experienced navigation of 'North Co' steamers must surely be responsible for the fact that in the past hundred years no company steamer has been lost or seriously damaged due to heavy weather. In the wild waters around our islands this is a remarkable record. It shows that our trusty seafarers have a healthy respect for the sea, and can judge when it is more prudent to remain in harbour.

The twenty-two seasons of North Company cruising, marked perhaps the greatest period of this noble company's history. As far as the story of cruising is concerned, *St Rognvald* and *St Sunniva* were the first ships to offer sequences of cruises with similar itineraries. These were of both moderate duration and cost, reflecting a market approach not unlike that adopted on a far larger scale by many cruise lines today. A later plan to reintroduce cruising to Norway in 1952, aboard the Line's second *St Ninian*, unfortunately failed to materialise owing to poor demand.[10] The North Company itself remained as an individual trading entity until being absorbed into the P&O group in 1971 as P&O Ferries (Orkney and Shetland Services).

PRINZESSIN VICTORIA LUISE

Among the most exclusive cruises of the late nineteenth century, were those offered under the Imperial German flag by the HAPAG and North German Lloyd (Norddeutscher Lloyd) Lines. The first of these was a three-week excursion from Bremerhaven to the North Cape aboard North German Lloyd's 6,990-ton *Kaiser Wilhelm II*. The voyage commenced on 24 June 1890 with 215 passengers aboard, and was a complete success thanks not only to the ship, but also to the fine weather and calm seas enjoyed from start to finish. A chance meeting with the German Imperial yacht *Hohenzollern*, which was taking the Kaiser on a state visit to the King of Norway, lent an unexpected element of excitement to the voyage, which was long remembered.

In hot pursuit of their share of this lucrative and prestigious market, HAPAG were quick to announce their own cruise programme. On 22 January the following year, the 7,661-ton HAPAG ship *Auguste Victoria* departed from Cuxhaven on a lavish 58-day round-trip voyage to the Mediterranean and Orient. There were thirteen ports of call arranged with ample time for shore excursions and sightseeing, interspersed by long enough periods at sea for the mind to relax and digest the experiences of each shore visit. There were altogether 241 passengers aboard, of which only sixty-seven were ladies. The passenger list was predominantly made up of Germans, with forty-nine foreigners representing ten other nations.[11]

The Line's indefatigable managing director Albert Ballin

Prinzessin Victoria Luise: This was probably taken in Europe directly before her maiden positioning voyage to New York and the Caribbean.

(Hapag-Lloyd Aktiengesselschaft, Hamburg; courtesy of Graham Stallard, Vancouver)

was himself aboard to ensure the complete success of the cruise. In this capacity he assumed the role of the charming and gallant host to his passengers. Ballin succeeded in establishing a special feeling of shipboard ambience, derived from top-class service and comfort, superb international cuisine and meticulous organisation, which set the standard for HAPAG and Hapag-Lloyd cruises to come. Tempered over the years by changing lifestyles and travel patterns, as well as developments in ship and hotel design and operation, it is a standard in essence still maintained aboard the present Hapag-Lloyd's *Europa*.

Both German Lines engaged in year-round cruising operations, with their ships following the warm weather during the winter months. At the conclusion of the Norwegian and Baltic cruising season, these and other ships normally in North Atlantic line service would be repositioned either to the Mediterranean or the Caribbean for winter pleasure voyages.

Convinced of the long-term prospects offered by cruising, Ballin proceeded to build a ship specially designed for pleasure voyages alone. Kaiser Wilhelm, who took an active interest in

Ballin's work, himself had a hand in this ship's design. The Kaiser sent Ballin a sketch based on the example of his own royal yacht *Hohenzollern*, along with notes making suggestions for the outfit and equipping of such a vessel.[12] Ballin found this material interesting and of considerable practical value, introducing a number of his sovereign's suggestions into the design of the exclusive new HAPAG ship. An order was placed in 1899 with Blohm & Voss for *Prinzessin Victoria Luise*, as the ship was to be named. She was a handsome yacht-styled vessel of 4,409 tons, similar in conception and appearance to the 1893-built *Hohenzollern*. The two ships compared as follows:

	Hohenzollern	Prinzessin Victoria Luise
GRT	4,228	4,409
Length oa (m)	122.00	121.92
Beam (m)	14.00	14.33
Draught (m)	4.23	5.03
Complement/passengers	313	180
Power (kW)	6,710.4	2,684.2
Propellers	2	2
Speed (kts)	21.5	15.0

The philosophy underlying *Prinzessin Victoria Luise*'s design

Prinzessin Victoria Luise:
Accommodation plan.

(Author)

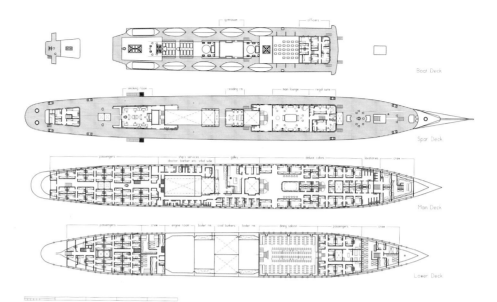

Boat Deck

Spar Deck

Man Deck

Lower Deck

Prinzessin Victoria Luise: **Dining saloon looking aft, showing the light shaft, main staircase and lounge above.**

(Hapag-Lloyd Aktiengesselschaft, Hamburg; courtesy of Graham Stallard, Vancouver)

and outfitting was that she should give her passengers the feeling of being aboard one of the yachts belonging to the ruling monarchs of Germany, Britain, Norway or Russia. Indeed, this was conveyed by the ship's external appearance: the rake of her masts and twin flat-topped funnels, along with the graceful lines of her hull and low superstructure, imparted a strong impression of a regal yacht, yet without merely replicating *Hohenzollern*'s lines. The new HAPAG yacht's profile was more graceful than that of her regal prototype. However, what was not readily apparent on viewing the ship afloat was her additional displacement of some 1,500 tons, accounting for her much deeper draught.

Operationally, *Prinzessin Victoria Luise* was a miniature ocean-going commercial passenger ship, fully equipped to provide luxury accommodation and service to a small number of premium-fare passengers. As such, she replicated, on a more human scale, the finest first-class travel that HAPAG's most prestigious transatlantic liners of the day could offer. Lacking the size of her line-service fleetmates, as well as their second- and third-class accommodation, cargo and mail facilities, *Prinzessin Victoria Luise* was in effect the first pure-bred deep-sea cruise ship to be inspired by a combination of liner experience and the romantic notion of a luxury steam yacht. The lavishly decorated public rooms were designed to convey the ultimate expression of opulence in the ornate styles of La Belle Époque. These were arranged in the then typical German manner, with the dining room being located beneath a wide light shaft passing through the centre of the main lounge, in this case two decks above. These rooms and the adjacent main stairway, with its spacious deck lobbies, were both surmounted by crystal-paned domes, themselves protected from the elements by outer casings of strong marine glass. The dining room's decorative scheme was in old-gold hues embellished by gilded detail work. The lounge was in ivory tones, with red silken wall coverings, and furnished with blue-green upholstery matching the carpet colours. A contemporary description of these spaces was given at the time of the ship's completion in the German engineering journal *Vereins Deutscher Ingenieure (VDI):*[13]

> The stairway is brilliantly illuminated by a skylight in opalescent glazing. Due to the blue tone of the walls this area, which primarily serves the purpose of general passage, also acquires an elegant atmosphere. For recreation and the quietness needed for letter

Prinzessin Victoria Luise: **Smoking room looking aft, separate from the lounge and other rooms on Spar deck, but like the lounge and lobby, with its own ornate dome.**

(Hapag-Lloyd Aktiengesselschaft, Hamburg; courtesy of Graham Stallard, Vancouver)

writing, the tastefully appointed and cosy library offers an appropriate retiring room which will certainly help to make a journey aboard Prinzessin Victoria Luise highly enjoyable. The room's ceiling is cream coloured and the oak walls are blue-green, the panels in warm leather tones, and the upholstery green. The little writing tables are equipped with pretty standard lamps and ample ceiling lights ensure sufficient brightness.

This description illustrates how the prevailing lifestyles of the times bear upon the design of human habitats, be they afloat or ashore. The importance that was attached to the library and reading room in turn-of-the-century ships was far greater than it is today. In that era, when the art of conversation flourished, educated people tended to be avid readers as well as adept letter writers, diarists and sketch artists. Shipboard pencillings and writings served to record a passenger's impressions and experiences then, in the way that cameras and video equipment are used today. Although *Prinzessin Victoria Luise*'s library and writing room was one of the ship's smaller public spaces, it was certainly as well appointed as the main lounge and smoking room. Its location amidships on the spar deck, between the lounge and smoking room, was at the centre of onboard social activity. Yet, thanks to the location of the funnel casing separating the room from the main stairway, a degree of seclusion and quiet sanctity was assured by its discreet accessibility from the outside deck rather than the central foyer. As the St Sunnivites of 1896 had done, no doubt *Prinzessin Victoria Luise*'s passengers penned many a word in these surroundings to preserve their own and the ship's exploits.

Prinzessin Victoria Luise was outfitted with accommodation

Prinzessin Victoria Luise: **Lounge looking aft, showing the crystal dome and light shaft to the dining room below. The lobby and main staircase were beyond the double doors at centre.**

(Hapag-Lloyd Aktiengesselschaft, Hamburg; courtesy of Graham Stallard, Vancouver)

Meteor: The cruise yacht which took *Prinzessin Victoria Luise*'s place after her loss in 1904.

(Hapag-Lloyd Aktiengesellschaft, Hamburg; courtesy of Graham Stallard, Vancouver)

of unprecedented luxury for 180 cruise passengers. The ship's twenty-two *chambres deluxe*, fifty-two double and forty-nine single standard cabins were of a commensurate standard with the Line's most prestigious North Atlantic liners of the day. All passenger bedrooms were fitted with lower berths exclusively, there being no upper bunks or pullman beds. A number of the deluxe rooms on the main deck were arranged around a spacious quadrangle surrounding the main stairway and light shaft between the lounge above and dining room below.

As a crowning touch, Ballin provided a state suite which would be available to the Kaiser himself, should he have wished to cruise aboard the ship or to charter her. This accommodation was located on the spar deck forward of the public rooms, affording it a considerable sense of privacy and seclusion. There were two large state bedrooms, each with its own adjoining bathroom and drawing room. The layout allowed for them to be booked as two separate suites, or for the drawing rooms to be used separately as additional public rooms.

Prinzessin Victoria Luise ran her sea trials in Kiel Bay on 19 December 1900, before being handed over to her owners. The Kaiser himself inspected the ship in great detail before her maiden voyage and was impressed, not only by the cruise yacht herself, but by the quality of workmanship on Blohm & Voss's part. He was satisfied that apart from *Prinzessin Victoria Luise*'s inevitable success, her builders would convey a worthy impression of German engineering and craftsmanship overseas on her worldwide exploits.

When *Prinzessin Victoria Luise* made her positioning voyage to New York in January 1901, she had the misfortune to encounter the winter North Atlantic at its very worst. The ship was baptised in waters she was never designed to take, leaving her miserably seasick passengers and crew with little praise for her. All this was soon forgotten, however, when she sailed south to the West Indies on her inaugural cruise in tropical waters. *Prinzessin Victoria Luise* quickly gained great popularity, catering to German- and English-speaking clientele from both sides of the Atlantic. Unfortunately, this ship's career was tragically short, as she was lost in 1904 after running aground near Jamaica on a reef created only days earlier by an underwater earthquake.

By the time of *Prinzessin Victoria Luise*'s loss a second HAPAG yacht had been built for cruising. Named *Meteor*, this smaller vessel of 3,613 tons was designed to carry 220 passengers in somewhat less palatial surroundings. She was delivered in 1904, also by Blohm & Voss, and served two owners for more than forty years. In 1921 she passed into Norwegian hands when bought by the Bergenske Dampskibsselskab, or Bergen Line, as it was becoming better known to the international cruise market. Her new owners paid the remarkably low price of only £30,000 for her, spending nearly as much again to modernise her and convert her accommodation to suit their own needs as a cruise ship. The original name was retained, 'meteor' being a body of the sky in keeping with Bergen Line nomenclature.[14]

LATER CRUISE YACHTS: *PRINS OLAV* AND *STELLA POLARIS*

While *Prinzessin Victoria Luise* endeavoured to replicate the style of a regal yacht, the former *Alexandra* of Britain's King

Alexandra: Underway in 1912.

(National Maritime Museum, Greenwich, London, neg 4611)

Prins Olav: **After her conversion as a cruise yacht, with her flying bridge enclosed and superstructure extended, she is seen here under tow by the paddle-wheel Cambrian and another unidentified tug.**

(National Maritime Museum, Greenwich, London, neg N36508)

George V actually became a cruise ship. This triple-screw turbine steamer of 2,500 tons was purchased by Nordenfjeldske, and renamed *Prins Olav*. The ship was built in 1907 by A & J Inglis of Glasgow as a smaller rendition of HMY *Victoria and Albert*, for King Edward VII and Queen Alexandra's private use. The ship was unused during the subsequent reign of King George V. After the outbreak of World War I she apparently remained laid up until her sale to Nordenfjeldske was confirmed by Buckingham Palace on 27 May 1925. The yacht was given the name of Olav, Norway's then Prince Regent, to whom Queen Alexandra was maternal grandmother, as well as being mother to Norway's Queen Maud.[15] Although registered with the Norwegian spelling as *Prins Olav*, the anglicised version of the name, *Prince Olav*, almost invariably appeared in English-language advertising and publicity material.

Prins Olav's royal apartments remained basically unaltered, as the ship's new owners realised the appeal that the former role of these state rooms would hold for their passengers. The king and queen's state rooms, each with its own bath and dressing room, the smaller prince and princess's quarters and ambassador's room, along with five other original state rooms could be booked. An additional forty-four standard cabins, some of which would have formerly housed the Royal Family's retinue, completed the accommodation, providing for 100 passengers in all. The traditional sailing-yacht plan, with the best private accommodation located aft, still prevailed in the ship's original design, as it did in the majority of private and state yachts of her time.

All *Prins Olav*'s passengers were berthed in 'bedsteads', with a total absence of upper berths as aboard *Prinzessin Victoria Luise*. This former royal yacht's cabin accommodation was generally of the same high standard as the earlier German ship's superlative luxury. Most of the cabins lacked private toilet facilities.

The public rooms, which consisted of a social hall, smoking saloon and dining room were, however, less opulent than on *Prinzessin Victoria Luise*. King Edward VII was himself a man of discerning taste, whose preference for a more appropriate shipboard expression of luxury and comfort over *Victoria and Albert*'s ornateness had been respected by the ship's builders. Indeed, the understated elegance of these rooms was far better suited to commercial luxury cruising in the 1920s.

Prins Olav entered service in the summer of 1926 as a long-overdue replacement for the company's earlier *Haakon VII*, which was unfortunately among many ship losses of World War I. The necessity of first rebuilding their essential commercial services had left Nordenfjeldske without a cruise ship until *Alexandra* was purchased. Her first season's voyages from Bergen as *Prins Olav* included two different itineraries: 13-day midnight-sun cruises to the North Cape, and 20-day excursions via many of the same ports, onwards farther north to Spitzbergen and the polar ice cap. These ranged in price from £35 per person from Bergen on the shorter trip, to £65 for the Spitzbergen cruise from Newcastle. For those travelling from Britain the fare also included the North Sea crossing aboard Bergenske's *Leda* or *Jupiter*.

During the winter months *Prins Olav* undertook various cruises in tropical waters. For these she tended to be promoted, not by her real name, but rather as 'The Royal Yacht'. One such cruise in the spring of 1928 was a 46-day circuit from Marseilles of 'The Mediterranean and its Borderlands'. This was sold to American passengers at prices ranging from $1,700 to $5,500, including round-trip transatlantic passage. Contrary to modern-day cruise pricing, it is a noteworthy fact that both the cheapest and most expensive accommodation was for single occupancy.

By the mid-1930s, however, *Prins Olav* was beginning to concede her popularity to the many larger and newer ships then competing for the luxury cruise market. Among these were many prestigious express Atlantic liners and superbly outfitted tropical ships of various lines which had gone into seasonal cruising operations of one kind and another throughout the year. Quite apart from liner competition, one of her most formidable competitors was Bergen Line's magnificent purpose-built cruise yacht *Stella Polaris*. At double *Prins Olav*'s size, this modern contender of 5,209 tons had vied for the same class of clientele since entering service herself in 1927. *Prins Olav*'s plight was further aggravated by rising crew and operating costs, which had to be recovered through the fares charged for her small numbers of passenger berths.

In 1937 *Prins Olav* was finally withdrawn from cruising. She was converted for full-time operation on the Norwegian Hurtigruten coastal run, then being expanded into a daily service. The ship's superstructure was enlarged, her two funnels replaced by a single stack, and cargo derricks added, altering her profile radically. With a modern raked bow and cruiser stern she looked very much in place and quite modern among the fleet of fourteen Hurtigruten ships. She continued to provide the finest accommodation, although the Queen's State Room was the only one of her original cabins to be retained intact. *Prins Olav* remained in this service until she was sunk off Lofoten in 1940 during World War II.

Built at the Swedish Goatverken yard near Göteborg, *Stella Polaris* was an outstanding example of Scandinavian design and engineering. In her outward appearance she carried the classic lines of form borrowed from *Prinzessin Victoria Luise* and *Prins Olav*, complete with the bowsprit, jibboom, counter stern, and pronounced hull sheer. Yet, at the same time, she embodied an expression of timeless classic modernity, with her white-painted hull, two raked masts, single buff-coloured motorship funnel and the generally clean-lined look of her superstructure and deck fittings. Despite the interruption imposed by a well deck forward, the smoothness of her flowing sheer lines was stressed by carrying the boat deck fully aft above a large expanse of covered space on the promenade deck. This in itself was an early precursor of many later liner and cruise ship designs stressing larger open spaces 'topsides', rather than the traditional series of terraces aft.

Stella Polaris was handsomely appointed to carry 198 passengers in great comfort. Her private accommodation was, for the most part, arranged in the aft part of the ship, following traditional steam-yacht design practice. These comprised four deluxe double suites, each with separate sitting room, bedroom, bathroom and a lavatory, twelve special double state rooms with their own baths and lavatories, with the remainder being standard cabins without private baths and lavatories. Of these, fifty-one rooms were for single occupancy, while the remainder were twin-bedded. The thirty-five bathrooms provided for these cabins were conveniently arranged along the centre of the ship, so that they were, in most cases, directly opposite the two or three cabins they each served.

The dining room, lounge, smoking room, vestibules and two small writing rooms were on the A and promenade decks, predominantly forward and above the majority of sleeping accommodation. Farther aft on the promenade deck, where there were no cabins at all, the suite of public spaces was completed by a second entrance foyer and a small veranda café. The dining room was by far the most spacious room aboard, with enough seats to accommodate all passengers and a number of senior officers at a single sitting. Here, as throughout the other public rooms and on the ship's wide and uncluttered decks, the emphasis was on a feeling of uncrowded spaciousness, and, as contemporary advertising literature had put it, 'limitation of numbers'.

Below decks, a pair of Burmeister & Wain four-stroke eight-cylinder diesel engines yielded the 2,982kW of power needed to propel *Stella Polaris* at a sedate cruising speed of 15kts.[16] From an engineering and technical standpoint she was advanced to the point of being ahead of her time in cruise ship development. All of her auxiliary and hotel services, including the galleys and laundries, were electrically operated. Although originally not air conditioned, *Stella Polaris* was one of the first passenger ships to be fitted with a forced-air heating and ventilation system throughout her accommodation. This was a particularly welcome refinement in cabins, where the much quieter punkah air outlets replaced the noisy fans and bulky electric heaters then still commonly in shipboard use.

Stella Polaris's building price of 4 million Swedish krona came initially as a great burden to her Norwegian owners, since the order had been placed when the exchange rate on Swedish currency was abnormally high. However, by the time most instalment payments had to be made as construction progressed, Norwegian currency was returning to its earlier par value. Expensive though the ship still was, her public acceptance in service soon proved her to be a good investment. Thanks to her superb accommodation and sound construction, the ship retained a remarkably high value for many years.[17]

Four years after *Stella Polaris*'s debut, another significant ship entered Bergen Line's regular North Sea service between Newcastle and Bergen. Built at the Elsinor yard in Denmark, she was the company's second ship to bear the name *Venus*.

***Stella Polaris*: Showing her classic yacht profile in Norwegian waters during the early 1950s.**

(Gordon Turner collection, Toronto)

Plans to build her had been largely motivated by competition from Swedish Lloyd who had inaugurated a new service of their own between Göteborg and Tilbury, with fast rail connections to Oslo. In response to this challenge, the 5,406-ton *Venus* emerged as one of the fastest passenger motorships of her time. She was certainly a ship of considerable technical innovation, having been designed specifically to take the varying sea conditions of the North Sea with minimum loss of headway. Her performance reduced the passage time from 27 to 19 hours, allowing the ship to make two round-trip voyages each week.[18]

Like *Stella Polaris*, *Venus* was a remarkable ship in her own right, offering an unprecedented standard of first-class accommodation and comfort on the North Sea. With 182 first-class, and only 78 second-class berths, she was also a very suitable ship to provide the feeder service to Norway for many of *Stella Polaris*'s cruises. Later, *Venus* too would serve Bergen Line as a cruise ship, in tandem with *Stella Polaris*.

Venus is also historically significant for having launched the distinguished career of a young Danish naval architect named Knud E Hansen, then on Elsinor's technical staff. He later went on to participate in designing the trend-setting streamlined form of the DFDS ferry *Kronprins Olav* in 1937. He is generally credited with the streamlined form of the DFDS ship's superstructure. The deckhouse front was not only widely bowed, as in the express-liner examples of Lloyd Triestino's *Victoria* and French Line's *Normandie*, but was also decidedly raked, the uninterrupted flow of its lines encompassing the bridge front and wings. *Kronprins Olav* thus made an unprecedentedly modern expression of streamlined ship styling. Hansen left Elsinor at about the time of *Kronprins Olav*'s completion, ultimately to achieve worldwide acclaim applying a similar element of design panache to many ferries and passenger ships in the 1950s and early 1960s. After his untimely death in 1962, the Knud E Hansen firm in Copenhagen has remained a major proponent of progressive ship design of all types.

By the time *Venus* took up her North Sea run, *Stella Polaris* had quickly became a round-the-world success, not only for her wide diversity of celebrated cruises in the waters of Scandinavia, Europe and the Americas, but most notably for her annual winter circumnavigations of the globe. These exclusive world cruises, the first of which took place in 1931, were operated by the noted American travel agency

Raymond-Whitcomb. 'Membership', as passage on the more exotic voyages of the day was called, was of course 'limited' to the ship's low-density capacity of only 198 passengers. Fares for the 96-day 1934 cruise were set in the range of $1,775 for a single cabin on B deck to $7,350 per person for one of the deluxe suites. This particular westwards–about voyage commenced in New York on 18 January, finishing in Monte Carlo on 24 April. Its price did not include the return transatlantic passage to the United States. Much of the cruise itinerary was devoted to the South Sea Islands of the Pacific, with one of its highlights being a two-day visit to the Galapagos Islands. Other attractions included extensive sightseeing in Sumatra, Bali and Ceylon (Sri Lanka). The ship then proceeded on to the Mediterranean with brief calls at Aden, Port Saïd, Santorini and Naples.

This enchanted ship lived on through the depression years of the 1930s, the ravages of World War II and Nazi Germany's occupation of Norway when the ship was seized, then onwards to the highly competitive reality of the post-World War II cruise trade. In 1950 she was returned to her original Swedish builders for full reconditioning after her repatriation. She was brought up to the latest international safety standards, and her accommodation was upgraded mainly to the extent of providing all cabins with private toilet facilities and installing full air conditioning.

The resulting reduction of her capacity to 174 passengers, and the need for a larger 163-member crew, left her hard pressed to make a profit. Her refit had cost more than her original building price. New Norwegian labour regulations, enacted in 1949 restricting the hours of labour at sea, had forced the increase in numbers of her crew. Even her world cruise of 1951 failed to realise its anticipated commercial return.[19]

She was finally sold in 1952 to Clipper Line (Rederiaktiebolaget Clipper) of Sweden, realising an equivalent return of about 7.2 million Norwegian krone, which Bergen Line used towards the purchase of a new tanker. Her new owners continued to operate her, primarily in the Caribbean, until well into the 1960s. She was then sold to Japanese interests who have preserved her in their own home waters as a stationary hotel ship.

Cruise yachts such as *Prinzessin Victoria Luise*, *Prins Olav*, *Stella Polaris*, and even the very much humbler *St Sunniva*, influential though they were, were long regarded as rarities. Following these turn-of-the-century purebreds, *Stella Polaris* was the only yacht, in the proper interpretation of the word, to be built in many years.

Nevertheless, these early commercial yachts, along with the cruises organised by various companies and societies aboard other chartered private yachts, seem to have permanently attached the word 'yacht' to cruise ships of all types. As liners went into seasonal cruising during the 1920s and 1930s, and still later when others were permanently converted for cruising in the 1950s and 1960s, the term was widely used to dispel notions of the rigid class barriers and social protocols of liner life. It was intended to convey the idea that class barriers would be opened up and that the lifestyle on board would be relaxed and informal. Various modern liners, ferries and cruise ships have been enthusiastically described by their promoters and others as 'yacht-like.' Certainly this epithet fitted a number of the more sleek-looking Scandinavian liners, along with some of the small cruise ferries of the 1960s, with their white hulls, steeply raked bows and clean lines of form. However, it can hardly be applied to such vast ships as *Sovereign of the Seas* or *Carnival Destiny*, where the term 'ocean-going resort' might be more appropriate. Cruise yachts, in their proper sense, have since reappeared with *Sea Goddess*, *Wind Star*, *Seabourn Spirit/Pride* and others in their class.

1 Bernard Huldermann, *Albert Ballin* , pp 70–71
2 Alastair Wm McRobb, *Fariplay Cruise Review* (1987) p 5
3 Alastair and Anne Cormack, *Days of Orkney Steam*, p 40
4 Gordon Donaldson, *Northwards by Sea*, pp 83–4
5 Cormack, *Days of Orkney* Steam, p 41
6 Charles F Morris, *Origins, Orient and Oriana*, pp 140–141
7 McRobb, *Fairplay Cruise Review*, p 8
8 T A Bushell, *Royal Mail: Centenary History of the Royal Mail Line*, p 243
9 Mike Bent, *Coastal Express*, p 44
10 Donaldson, *Northwards by Sea*, p 84
11 Hapag-Lloyd, *100 Jahre Kreuzfahrten* 1890-1990, p 4
12 Huldermann, *Albert Mallin*, p 197
13 Hans Georg Prager, *Blohm & Voss*, p 69
14 Wilhelm Keilhau, *Norway and the Bergen Line*, p 213
15 Bent, *Coastal Express*, pp 95–6
16 A C Hardy, *History of Motorshipping*, p 66
17 Keilhau, *Norway and the Bergen Line*, p 230
18 *The Shipbuilder and Marine Engine Builder* (June 1931) pp 530-37
19 Keilhau, *Norway and the Bergen Line*, p 303

DUALITY

Influence of British dual-purpose and tropical liners

The development of cruising during the 1920s and 1930s was, to a great extent, an offspring of the flourishing liner trade of that era. It grew largely out of a need to provide off-season revenue from ships which might otherwise be laid up during those months, when bookings for regular services were low. In other instances, cruising allowed steamship lines to make use of older vessels or other misfit tonnage, unable for one reason or another to meet the increasingly competitive demands of speed and service on the routes for which they were originally built. Nonetheless, cruising grew progressively more sophisticated and achieved greater commercial importance as the liner business itself grew and prospered.

In the early years 'designed for cruising' was a claim made of many liners, which often meant only that there had been a little more space allocated to public rooms, a greater number of interchangeable cabins that could be sold at first-class rates and, in later instances, that a permanently installed tiled swimming pool might be available. Ships of this genre often cruised with vast amounts of vacant cargo and tourist- or emigrant-class space on their lower decks. This duality of function usually best suited intermediate-class ships which were comparatively economical to run at their modest service speeds, with consequently reduced fuel consumption and numbers of personnel needed to run their engine rooms.

The global turmoil and upheaval of World War I curtailed the growth and expansion of merchant shipping as a whole, let alone cruising, until well after 1918. It was only then that wartime losses of tonnage could begin to be indemnified, and the essential line services of many seafaring nations and individual shipping companies could be reinstated. The cruising business was a non-essential commercial sideline which would have to wait its turn.

One of the very few exceptions was the war-damaged Royal Mail Line's steamer *Asturias* (of 1907), which was rebuilt in 1918 exclusively for cruising as *Arcadian*. She was in fact a replacement for the Line's earlier cruise ship of the same name, which at the time of her introduction was claimed to be the largest ship outfitted exclusively for cruising. *Arcadian* proved to be a very successful ship in the British market over the following twelve years, during which she was constantly in demand for regular commercial cruises as well as numerous charter engagements. No doubt this ship helped to sustain an interest in cruising, at least in Britain, until other lines began returning to the trade.

While *Arcadian* was at least to some extent internally restyled for cruising, she was followed by countless misfit and redundant liners which were pressed into cruise service with minimum adaptation of their facilities. Among the list of those to be sent cruising at various stages were Cunard's *Lancastria*, White Star Line's *Homeric*, *Doric*, *Laurentic* and *Calgaric*, along with numerous other British and foreign-flag vessels. Many of these were comparatively new ships built since World War I, which had either turned out to be unsuitable for their intended trades, or were falling victim to the world economic decline which precipitated the Great Depression.[1]

Quite apart from the aspirations of any Lines towards cruising, ship design in the 1920s benefited from an overall improvement in passenger accommodation. This reflected not only the generally higher living standards prevailing ashore, particularly in the United States, but also the worldwide influence of modern American hotel design. Many Americans, who had been given their first look at Europe while in wartime military service, returned with their families in peacetime as tourists. Whether travelling in first class or tourist class (as the old second and third classes then began to be known), visitors from the New World expected the same standards of accommodation and sanitation as they had by then become used to at home, both during the crossings and whilst in Europe. Likewise, Europeans travelling in the opposite direction to America, either on business trips or holidays, began to demand similar standards.

While it was quite acceptable in the 1880s for a passenger to be berthed with three total strangers in a minuscule lower-deck cubicle, the traveller of the 1920s expected privacy and much greater personal comfort. This, along with improved standards of safety, greatly increased the cost and complexity of new tonnage. No longer were shipowners able to profit from carrying large numbers of passengers in small vessels which were inexpensive both to build and operate. The economics of running these more expensive ships, where only four passengers might be accommodated in the space allocated for twelve 30 years earlier, depended on the owner's ability to sell passengers on the prestige value of the added safety, comfort and service at premium rates in all classes.

There was, however, economic relief for the owner to be derived from other developments. Higher service speeds and shorter turnaround times at the terminal ports permitted a greater number of voyages during a ship's operating season. Reduced turnaround times were thanks mainly to the switch from coal to oil fuel. Not only was oil bunkering of a ship much faster, but also far cleaner than the filthy ordeal of manual coaling, reducing also the time needed for cleaning the decks and accommodation. The other saving to be realised from oil was the economy of fewer engine-room crew being needed, since the legions of stokers, trimmers and firemen were eliminated.

Other advances in marine engineering were to gain long-term economies over the expected lifespan of a ship, despite their greater initial costs. Geared steam turbines and high-compression superheat boilers realised considerable improvements in operational efficiency. Far more compact machinery installations were achieved than had been possible in the days of direct-drive turbines and coal-fired watertube boilers. At the same time, the marine diesel was fast gaining favour for powering large deep-sea ships. Among the first of these were the new Royal Mail Line motorships *Asturias* and *Alcantara*, along with the *Kungsholm* of Svenska Amerika Linien (Swedish American Line), all of which were completed in 1927.

While the operating economies of shorter turnarounds and reduced engine-room staffing were of substantial benefit to the owner, the basis of competitiveness would, in the eyes of prospective passengers, depend on what they could see and readily comprehend: accommodation, service and speed. It was through these tangibles that one ship or line would be favoured over another, regardless of the class being considered. The importance of providing for North German Lloyd's tourist-class passengers, for example, was explained by the Line's technical director, Paul Biedermann, with regard to *Bremen*'s design in the late 1920s:[2]

Priority also has to be given to the standard of comfort in the Second Class where in post-war service the former Second and Third Classes have more or less amalgamated into a new class, namely Tourist. So must the entire arrangement of cabins in this class be assembled together into a suitable accommodation block above the bulkhead deck in a similar manner to that of the First Class on the decks above.

Hitherto the accommodation for Tourist and Third Classes in medium- and larger-size liners on the North Atlantic service were arranged entirely aft and forward on the lower decks. However, Norddeutscher Lloyd believes that the design of their new ships must take into account the social conditions of the post-war period in providing these two classes with well-planned and well-appointed accommodation. It is correct to think that the potential clientele of these two classes is unlikely to be content with cramped accommodations in the lowest and least comfortable parts of the ship having poor light and ventilation.

The general trend in cabin design which emerged in this period was for virtually all passenger rooms to have at least washbasins with hot and cold running water. Private lavatories and bathtubs became standard equipment in first class, with some tourist-class rooms likewise having either their own or connecting toilet and shower spaces. The fixed upper and lower bunks of previous generations generally gave way to the hotel-like side-by-side arrangement of beds, which the larger rooms could readily accommodate. Where upper berths were fitted, mostly in tourist class, they tended to be of the pullman type, improving the room's appearance and functionality when folded away against the wall or deckhead during daytime hours. Passenger cabins of the period, particularly in first class, had in many instances become miniature hotel rooms, replicating on a shipboard scale the amenities of the best modern hotels ashore.

While steamship companies had touted their top liners to be 'floating hotels' ever since Cunard's *Umbria* and *Etruria* were built in the 1880s, it was the 1929 debut of *Bremen* which introduced the most real and complete semblance of modern, urban hotel accommodation aboard ship. Her remarkably standardised cabins throughout first class and much of tourist class came perhaps closest to resembling contemporary American hotel standards. Unfortunately, *Europa*'s completion, which was to have coincided with that of *Bremen*, was delayed due to a disastrous fire aboard the ship while fitting out.

Bremen's bedrooms were spacious and rectangular in shape, with fully equipped en-suite bathrooms, built-in wardrobes and full-size beds arranged parallel to each other. These rooms were also furnished with dressing/writing tables and easy chairs, extending their use for merely sleeping and personal grooming, to function as daytime retreats from the public rooms and decks. The functional and straightforward layout of *Bremen* and *Europa* was also most successful in

Orion: One of the most exquisitely-designed modern British liners of the 1930s.

(Orient Line, London)

providing direct cabin access from the main fore-and-aft passages. Their hotel-like simplicity of overall layout, in eliminating the myriad sideways passages of so many ships, set a standard of design which is now universally required as a matter of safety in cruise ship and ferry design.

The accommodation in _Bremen_ and _Europa_ was perhaps ahead of its time by a decade in setting the standard for other ships. A common perception in the deep-sea liner trade that passengers needed a great diversity of cabin types continued to influence liner design in many nations. Consequently, functional modern hotel-style accommodation remained the exclusive preserve of the uppermost first-class cabin grades. In the examples of _Empress of Britain_, _Normandie_ and _Queen Mary_'s individual rooms and suites were indeed of hotel standard, but more representative of traditional Grand Hotel style. Their overall layout lacked the conception of simplicity and straightforwardness which the North German Lloyd prototypes promoted so well, along with their understated modern comfort and elegance. Many of the countless other liners built until the 1960s continued to also offer vast quantities of the far simpler accommodation considered necessary for emigrant, student and other minimum-fare clientele. Usually lacking private toilet facilities, these utilitarian rooms were often designed to berth three or four people in almost Dickensian fashion. Standardisation of passenger cabins and rationalisation of their layout on _Bremen_ and _Europa_'s scale were not to become widespread until the end of the 1930s.

In the case of Orient Line's _Orion_, which was one of the most exquisitely-designed British liners of the 1930s, a great deal of ergonomic research on cabin design and outfitting was done at the earliest design stages, before a building contract was negotiated. This addressed issues of optimising space usage as well as improving the attractiveness and comfort of the rooms as seagoing hotel accommodation.

Key items included the following:

Careful measurements were taken of the various things the average passenger carries, so that the dimensions of drawers, wardrobes and dressing tables could be adjusted, as closely as possible, to the needs of both sexes.

The lee rails of the sides of the cabin beds were treated solely as a rough weather fitting; they were therefore specially designed to fold away.

Special stabilisers were fitted on all cabin doors, so that they could be held in any degree of openness without rattling.

Large pantries were provided on each deck for serving light breakfasts in the cabins.

Thermos jugs were fitted in each cabin so that iced water would be available in the middle of the night.

Large numbers of portable tables were provided for letter writing, to cope with the rush of the day before arrival at port, when everyone wanted to write eleventh-hour letters.[3]

While the sleeping accommodation was being radically improved, changes were also taking place in the public rooms. The general trend here was towards the expression of a more informal lifestyle, as explained in a 1935 issue of _Shipbuilding and Shipping Record_:[4]

Passengers must always feel perfectly free to act as the mood of the moment dictates: consequently each apartment has to be planned accordingly, and many rooms serve a dual purpose. The dining saloon has a dance floor and light meals are served at tables grouped conveniently around the walls of the ballroom or dancing space. The deluxe cabins have a disappearing bedstead so that the bedroom by night serves as a sitting room by day. The smoking room card tables have reversible tops for card playing and the card room has a grand pianoforte, bookcases, writing tables and a games cupboard. In practice each of the public rooms – no matter what its original designation may have been – is regarded and used as an informal lounge.

This was achieved in a number of progressively designed ships, including _Scharnhorst_, _Ville d'Alger_ and _Kungsholm_, through the widespread use of open planning and the adaptation of various rooms to suit the needs of a variety of shipboard functions. _Orion_'s ultra-modern open-plan interiors, designed by the young New Zealand architect Brian O'Rorke, demonstrated a degree of modernity and informality through the use of modern materials and

Malolo: **Seen here leaving Honolulu early in her career. Although still in her original exclusively first class configuration, Matson Line's livery had already been changed to white.**

(Matson Line, San Francisco)

furnishings in their interior decoration. Unique among these examples was the Canadian Pacific ship *Empress of Britain*, whose interiors combined strong elements of both modern art-deco and traditional period-revival shipboard styling.

All of these ships, along with a good many others from the world's leading seafaring nations, sailed in line service as well as cruising. In most cases the owners claimed that these ships had been designed specifically for such duality of function. Certainly from the design and outfitting standpoint, at least of accommodation for the uppermost two classes, such claims were in some cases well founded.

In *Kungsholm*, for instance, the public rooms belonging to both classes were of similar quality in their interior design and furnishing. The first-class lounges occupied the full length of the promenade deck. Those of tourist class were located below and aft on B deck, according to the traditional liner plan. However, the proximity of the B-deck lounges to the highest-grade cabin accommodation forward at the same level, facilitated the seamless amalgamation of these two additional lounges and their entrance lobby into a single-class cruising arrangement. The change was easily effected by simply opening the connecting doors at the aft ends of the B-deck first-class cabin corridors.

The Americans went a step farther in designing the Matson liner *Malolo* of 1927 as an exclusively first-class ship. The Line's regular service between San Francisco and Honolulu, for which *Malolo* was specifically built, was in fact largely booked for holiday voyages. It was thought that this

clientele would sustain the ship's exclusive all-first-class operation year round. *Malolo* was followed in the early 1930s by the larger Matson sister ships *Mariposa* and *Monterey*, which were designed for two-class service, on a similar plan to *Kungsholm*. These differed from the earlier Swedish ship in that additional public spaces were included in first class to accommodate their needs as cruise ships, with the cabin-class lounges two decks lower, intended for use only in line service.

Apparently the line had found that its regular services demanded the flexibility of a two-class operation, offering a greater range of passage fares. When refitted as *Matsonia* only a few years later, *Malolo*'s accommodation too was rearranged for first and tourist classes. However, like the elite North Atlantic express liners of that era, Matson's ships spent their off-season months on lavish, exclusively first-class, cruise circuits.

Other well-known American ships of the period, such as the Grace Line *Santa Rosa* class, catered largely to holiday travellers in their regular point-to-point services. Although of shorter duration and less prestigious standing than, for example, Matson's 'Millionaire's Cruises', these voyages also served to introduce a great many Americans to a consistently high standard of leisure sea travel.

Similar in overall design concept, particularly to the Matson examples, were the fine British-flag liners *Monarch of Bermuda* and *Queen of Bermuda*, of Furness Withy & Co. They were built for a weekly service between New York and Bermuda. Although designed essentially as liners with two-class passenger facilities and a limited cargo capacity, they catered largely to a holiday clientele. Their accommodation in both classes was comparable to the high standard of the *Mariposa*, *Monterey* and other new American tonnage.

During the 1930s, the range if services offered in cruising was becoming more diversified. In North America a variety of coastal and Great Lakes services, which were once vital domestic services, were becoming more oriented towards seasonal leisure travel. For these operations this was a means of survival against the growth of the continent's road and railway networks, which would have otherwise rendered them redundant far sooner. Although these ships are generally not within the scope of this book, their contribution to the development of cruising is nonetheless notable.

Various other excursions were offered for those with special interests, such as golf and personal health. For instance, an around-the-world voyage, organised under the auspices of the American Osteopathic Foundation, was scheduled for December 1932 aboard the Cunard liner *Scythia* as a health cruise. With admission limited to 400 passengers, this was to feature inclusive medical care provided by a team of doctors, interns, nurses and lab technicians who would travel with the group. The announcement claimed that, since osteopathic medicine had originated in the United States, passengers would have a unique opportunity to travel the world with care that might otherwise not be available overseas readily at hand.[5]

Although less specialised than the health cruise, Cunard began at the same time offering golf and bridge instruction on some of their America-based cruises. In 1932 George Ferrier, a well-known professional golfer of the day, was aboard *Aquitania* on her Mediterranean cruise of 3 February, following his successful engagement aboard *Mauretania* during the previous Christmas cruise. These were the beginnings of a variety of diversions offered by various Lines to attract cruise passengers. As sound motion pictures became popular aboard ship, a commonly used line in cruise advertising of the day was 'equipped for talkies'.[6] What this often amounted to was that a projection screen, portable 16mm sound-projector and loudspeaker would be set up in the main lounge or ballroom for film shows.

In other developments, particularly during the depression years of the early 1930s, cheap overnight 'cruises to nowhere' aboard out-of-work liners provided at least enough revenue for owners to maintain these ships in a service-ready condition. These excursions defined the lowest common denominator of mass-market cruising, affording many ordinary people the opportunity to sample ocean travel, a luxury then otherwise beyond their means.

ATLANTIS AND ARANDORA STAR

Despite such diversity, then as now, it was the luxury sector which attracted the greatest interest. Apart from the elegant *Stella Polaris*, there were relatively few other ships which had been fitted out exclusively for full-time cruising in the elite sector. Following its proven success with *Arcadian*, Royal Mail Line had its 1913-built *Andes* converted for cruising. Her original three-class accommodation for 1,330 passengers was rebuilt to cater to only 450 cruise passengers in first-class luxury. Renamed *Atlantis*, she started her new career in 1929, serving cruise clientele on both sides of the Atlantic.

A similar conversion was carried out on the much newer *Arandora*, the last of a four-ship class of combination cargo

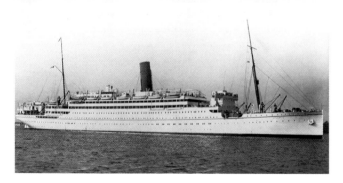

***Atlantis*: Built in 1913 as *Andes* here she is underway in 'cruising white', probably around 1930.**

(National Maritime Museum, Greenwich, London, neg P18211)

***Arandora Star*: Originally the passenger and cargo liner *Arandora*, here she is underway near Cape Town in 1934, following her rebuilding for full-time cruising.**

(National Maritime Museum, Greenwich, London, neg P14991)

and luxury passenger ships completed for Blue Star Line's London – La Plata service in 1927. After a very extensive transformation, carried out by Fairfield, she emerged ready for full-time luxury cruising in 1929 under the new name of *Arandora Star*. The rebuilding had involved the complete conversion of her former refrigerated cargo spaces for passenger accommodation, as well as substantial lengthening of her superstructure decks both forward and aft. This more than doubled her original passenger capacity to 354 berths in luxury twin and single cabins.

In this regard *Arandora Star* came perhaps closer than any of her contemporaries to achieving *Stella Polaris*'s uniqueness of function as a cruise yacht, albeit on a considerably larger scale. The Blue Star ship's lengthened superstructure allowed for the addition of a number of public spaces, including a ballroom, garden lounge, gymnasium and tiled swimming pool, making her amenities comparable to those of any liner whose multi-class public rooms had been amalgamated for cruise service.

Her fairly conventional internal layout, like that of *Atlantis*, still reflected the character of the tropical line services for which both ships were originally designed. Each featured large and airy public rooms with deep promenades surrounding them, as well as premium-grade first-class cabins, nearly all of which had either windows or portholes. These rooms had been extended as far as possible for the cruising market.

Arandora Star was particularly suited for cruising as she had been built with exclusively first-class accommodation for her original passenger capacity of only 168 people. The Blue Star ship also offered intrinsically better cabin accommodation, in that she featured large rectangular bedrooms as opposed to

Arandora Star:
Accommodation plan.

(Author)

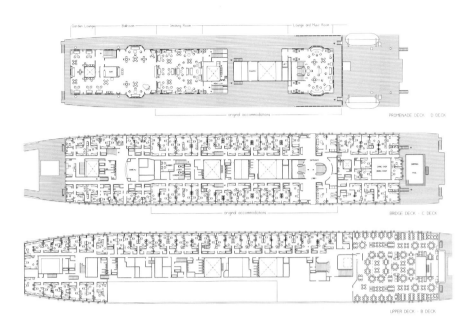

Atlantis's greater prevalence of L-shaped Bibby-style cabins. The ubiquitous Bibby-plan room gave access to a porthole at the ship's side from an otherwise inner space by way of a narrow passage, bypassing the adjacent outer cabin. The equally ingenious layout of *Arandora Star*'s cabins was derived from a virtually uniform room width, determined in effect by the width needed to place a passenger berth lengthwise against the inside of the hull. This bore only a distant relationship to the ship's structural arrangement of hull frames and supporting columns, and produced great complexity of layout prescribed by the placement of entrances and toilet facilities. However, the scheme produced some very attractive, and otherwise eminently functional, passenger living spaces.

Nonetheless, both ships ranked among the best of their time. What *Arandora Star* offered in her superior cabin accommodation she lacked in her external appearance. Although a most attractive ship as built, the extensive modification of her superstructure was done with apparently little regard for exterior aesthetics. The ship underwent almost constant change, with the massive forward extensions of her upperworks becoming progressively more overpowering in appearance every time the ship went into dry-dock for her annual overhauls. Still her popularity held, as she developed a steady and loyal following; perhaps she was first to establish the apparent 1970s and 1980s axiom that a cruise ship does not necessarily have to be outwardly attractive to make money.

Ships such as *Atlantis* and *Arandora Star*, along with *Empress of Britain*, *Bremen*, *Europa* and *Kungsholm* and their legendary cruises, belonged in reality to a dying era of *grande luxe* style and service. These, together with the Orient Express, Rheingold and various elite 'limited' American trains, as well as the old-world luxury of the Ritz-style Grand Hotels were in a class of their own. They catered

largely to the established wealthy. The term 'members' continued to be preferred in reference to the cruise passengers. Despite the addition of various recreational and technical amenities such as radio and 'talkies', these voyages continued to foster the refined arts of conversation and writing among their patrons. It was still customary in many cases for a book to be put produced to record the events of many such voyages. Often these would be published in hard-covered editions by the Line and then made available, both to the members of that trip and prospective clientele for their forthcoming cruises. Some of the finest of these were produced by the Swedish American Line for *Kungsholm* and *Gripsholm*'s cruises.

Empress of Britain's memorable circumnavigations of the globe, and *Normandie*'s celebrated excursions to Rio de Janeiro, were no doubt among the best examples of a variety of such epic voyages which have created the still enduring mystique of luxurious cruising in this opulent era. It was there that the rich and the famous of the day rubbed shoulders aboard magnificent ships bound for exotic places. The fact that these experiences occurred against the historical backdrop of the Great Depression, and the gathering storm clouds over Europe as prelude to yet a second world war, contributes only more to their mystique.

These great liners themselves have tended to hold far less influence on the design of modern-day cruise ships than their exploits had in fostering the mystique and sense of romance which continues to be associated with cruise travel. Apart from the largely unseen advances in engineering below decks and the refinements of hull forms which have benefited all types of shipping, the concepts of their accommodation and passenger services were becoming increasingly dated. It was thanks largely to the availability of cheap labour that these ships, with their decentralised and often duplicated services, could continue to operate profitably on pleasure voyages where their cargo, mail and least attractive accommodation spaces remained unused.

However, a number of the more forward-thinking shipping men of the era had their eyes fixed on a more distant horizon, one which lay beyond yet another world war. The increasing demand for cruises worldwide during the 1930s led to the introduction of several noteworthy dual-purpose intermediate-class ships with specific provision for cruising, more or less along *Kungsholm*'s lines. Perhaps most outstanding among these were the new *Andes* of Royal Mail Line and Cunard's *Caronia*. Although the Royal Mail ship was in fact delivered in 1939, it was not until well after the conclusion of World War II that she entered commercial service. She and the *Caronia* of 1949 were in fact among the first ships to offer luxury cruises in the post-World War II period, an epoch which would drastically and irrevocably change the patterns of passenger travel the world over, and ultimately spawn the development of cruising on a scale whose vastness could then hardly have been envisaged.

ANDES

The Royal Mail Line's *Andes* was among a number of notable passenger ships which were prevented from entering commercial service by the outbreak of World War II. She, along with French Line's *Pasteur*, was scheduled to make her maiden voyage to South America in September 1939. Messageries Maritimes's *Maréchal Petain*, later to be renamed *La Marseillaise*, and the Rotterdamsche Lloyd *Willem Ruys* were at various stages of building, with their deliveries delayed still longer.

The detailed planning of *Andes* started four years earlier in 1935, at about the same time as the conceptions of *Pasteur*'s design were beginning to solidify in France. The two ships were in fact to have run as opposite numbers, competing in the same market as Hamburg Südamerika's well-established and prestigious *Cap Arcona* of 1927.

When tenders were invited for the construction of a single new ship in 1935, Royal Mail's specifications were for a 21kt vessel, designed basically for the South American service, although also to 'permit her to be used for cruising purposes when found necessary'.[7] First and foremost, she was to be a passenger liner equipped for regular South American mail and special cargo service. This meant that, in addition to the usual postal facilities needed in that era before regular airmail service, large volumes of refrigerated hold space were required for carrying commercial cargoes of meat, mostly from Argentina. Known as the 'A boats', the prestigious passenger liners of this trade were among the fastest ships on the route, despite their comparatively modest speeds in relation to North Atlantic standards. In terms of superb first-class passenger accommodation and service, the best River Plate ships were a formidable match to their northern

Andes: **Seen here in her original livery, this pleasing view clearly shows her superbly balanced structural proportions and the visual effect of her deep promenades on E and F decks.**

(Fotoflite Ltd, New Romney, Kent, neg 9658)

counterparts. Certainly the innovative design of Germany's *Cap Arcona* and France's tragically short-lived *L'Atlantique* were key to establishing the high standards that passengers could expect on this route.

Against the background of such outstanding tonnage, the standards to be expected of a new ship such as *Andes* were high for line service alone, even before taking into account the expectations of an increasingly sophisticated cruise market. Planned at a measure of 26,000 tons, *Andes* was originally to have carried only 607 passengers, allocated as 403 first class and 204 tourist class. Third-class passengers would not be carried at all, leaving that part of the trade entirely to the Line's older *Alcantara* and *Asturias*. By way of comparison, these smaller sister ships of 22,181 tons each carried 330 first-, 220 second- and 768 third-class passengers, following changes made to their engines in 1933.

The building contract was awarded to Harland & Wolff, who had previously built the line's motorships *Alcantara* and *Asturias*. During the early months of construction in 1937, P G Milne Mitchell, then managing director of Royal Mail Line, insisted that the tourist-class accommodation be built to a higher standard than the second-class facilities of *Alcantara* and *Asturias* to 'enable the company to meet foreign competition'.[8] His plans were also to sell this accommodation at minimum first-class rates for cruises, where *Andes* would be operated as a one-class ship.

The accommodation was spacious and well planned, even by today's cruise ship standards. All cabins in both classes were at the ship's sides, with their own portholes or windows. Those in first class were for the most part rectangular hotel-style rooms with their own en-suite bathrooms. They were arranged throughout the two lower superstructure decks and uppermost hull deck. The overall plan was as simple and straightforward as it could be, with all rooms opening directly from the two parallel passages extending the length of each deck. The tourist-class cabins for the most part lacked private lavatories, and generally followed the well-proven but none-too-attractive Bibby plan.

Andes was noteworthy for her dining arrangement, which resolved two important design issues. The first-class dining room itself was made large enough to seat all passengers at a single sitting, avoiding the need for dividing passengers into 'early' and 'late' meal times. This, of course, was easily achieved thanks to the remarkably low passenger capacity for a ship of her size. Also, there was the practical addition of a spacious reception room adjacent to the first-class dining room, with its own American-style bar at the foot of the main stairway and opening directly into the dining room.

It was still common practice for the dining rooms of a liner to be located low within the hull in the interest of stability and comfort. Consequently there was the inherent design pitfall of them being distanced from the lounges and other public areas by as much as four or five decks. All too often passengers were forced to trek down numerous flights of linoleum stairs, with nowhere comfortable below to await the opening of the dining room. The descent often had about as much appeal as entering a Paris Métro station. In the design of *Andes*, consideration was given to providing passengers with a convenient rendezvous point immediately adjacent to the restaurant itself. It was a place where diners could enjoy an aperitif in spacious and comfortable surroundings, rather than having to stand in a sparsely furnished foyer or on the lower flights of stairs, as was so often the case.

One of the first ships to introduce this idea was White Star Line's *Olympic* of 1911, coincidentally also built by Harland & Wolff. Similar aperitif lounges were also incorporated into the plans of Furness Withy's *Monarch of Bermuda* and *Queen of Bermuda*, built a few years earlier than *Andes*, as well as their later *Ocean Monarch* of 1950. In a number of other notable European examples of the 1930s, such as *Cap Arcona*, *Victoria* and *Oceania*, dining rooms were located in the superstructure, overcoming the problem of adjacency to the main run of public rooms.

All things considered, *Andes* was regarded at the time of her building to be a fairly advanced ship. However, there was nothing particularly sensational or radical about either her physical and technical design or her aesthetic expression. Had her intended European counterpart, *Pasteur*, gone into service as planned, *Andes* might well have been perceived as being less modern by comparison. The French ship exhibited *Normandie*'s style of modern design rationale and unique internal layout whose panache, in the eyes of many, so outclassed *Queen Mary*'s.

As a ship of timeless classic elegance, *Andes* embodied the ultimate expression of the traditional British tropical liner aesthetic as perhaps no other ship has done. The visual balance of her hull, superstructure, funnel and masts, along with the disposition of lifeboats, cargo gear and other visible equipment, was as though she had been created by an artist. The forward wall of the superstructure was rounded and stepped back at the upper deck levels. A sense of modernity was also carried by the rake of the broad motorship funnel and the two masts.

Modern as she was, *Andes* retained the practical feature of deep covered decks, both at the level of her first-class public rooms and of the strata of cabins immediately below them. These upper and lower promenades were important in

Andes: **Accommodation plan showing E and F decks with their deep covered promenades.**

(Author)

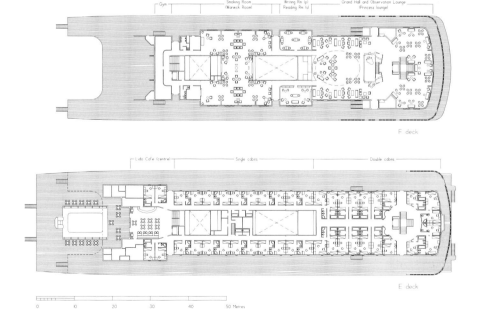

providing shade and air circulation to keep the ship's interiors bearably cool in the heat of her long trans-equatorial voyages. Only the foremost end of the lower deck, and the forward third of the level above were glass enclosed. Otherwise their open sides were divided only by stanchions positioned below the lifeboat davits, with the teak-planked decks contained behind standard metal ships' railings with teak handrails. These unusually broad decks contributed a greater sense of spaciousness. Their depth was sufficient to also obscure the windows and other deckhouse details from view, giving the ship an exceptionally clean-lined appearance when seen from even relatively short distances away.

Indeed the aesthetic appeal of *Andes* put her in the elite class of a number of remarkable classic liners, whose lines of form were of enduring and ageless appeal. Among the best of these are *Canberra*, *Conte di Savoia*, *Caronia* (1949), *France* (1962) and *Rotterdam* (1959).

In the opinion of many of her admirers, *Andes* looked her best as originally built, with her hull painted black, although in 'cruising white' she was also attractive. However, the two excursion launches added to her deck equipment in 1960 were thought by many to be somewhat an eyesore. The artist Howard Jarvis, who painted many fine pictures of *Andes* for brochures and other publicity, disliked the launches so much that he simply omitted them from two of his brochure paintings. In his later work he would endeavour to hide them, perhaps behind the sails of a Chinese junk in Hong Kong, or would portray the ship from an angle which would make them as inconspicuous as possible.[9]

After finally being discharged from her wartime service, *Andes* was returned to Harland & Wolff for a post-trooping refit in 1947. This work included a number of improvements to her passenger accommodation which lowered her capacity to 528, with a reduced proportion of first-class cabin space and improved crew accommodation. This was achieved mainly through the appropriation of a block of less desirable tourist class cabin, below the dining room, as crew space. Otherwise the ship's interiors were unaltered from their original condition at delivery in 1939.

Andes took up her regular commercial service between Britain and the River Plate in January 1948. Although for the next few years she was engaged solely in line service, Royal Mail made the first concessions to cruising by reserving 100 first-class berths for passengers making the full round trip. These people were also given the option of living aboard during the week that the ship spent at her southern terminal of Buenos Aires. The per-person fare for such a round trip in those days was from £330 to £610, including a £10 charge for use of the ship as a hotel in the Argentinean capital.

It was not until 1955 that cruise voyages as such were offered aboard *Andes*. Until that time she had sailed on the River Plate service virtually booked to capacity. The need for passenger space on this route, and indeed the popularity of *Andes* herself, had materialised far beyond her owners' expectations. The first break in her regular routine came

when *Andes* participated in the Coronation Naval Review at Spithead in 1953, with 404 passengers and special guests aboard. During those few days the guests and, perhaps more significantly, the ship's officers and crew, got their first impression of *Andes* in her future cruising role.

In the meantime she had been fitted with Denny Brown fin stabilisers, the work being done in two stages, during her annual dry-dockings in 1952 and 1953. The first stage involved fitting the hull recesses, with the fins themselves and their hydraulic machinery being installed the following year. This work brought *Andes* up to the standards of the latest P&O and Cunard ships, which had already been built with stabilisers.

From 1955 onwards, *Andes* became engaged primarily for cruising in the Mediterranean and West Indies, with the ship making only a couple of voyages to South America each year. Two years later she ventured into Norwegian coastal waters on her first Scandinavian itinerary since a voyage to Oslo in 1945, when she repatriated the exiled Norwegian government during her wartime service career. By the end of 1958, as these and other itineraries gained popularity in the luxury British cruise market, the line voyages to South America were dropped altogether. However, as Royal Mail had a retinue of passengers who regularly made round trips to South America to escape the dreary English winters, longer-than-usual cruises were run during these months. The 1958 offering was a 17,000-mile voyage to Rio de Janiero and Cape Town of some six weeks' duration. The per-person fares for these voyages ranged from £380 to £1,010 plus, of course, the added cost of shore excursions, incidentals and gratuities. Some of the more exotic shore excursions could themselves each run to more than £100 per person.

The fact that *Andes* was operating in the premium sector of the cruise market meant that her owners were obliged to keep her up to date and abreast of the latest developments in ship design. By the late 1950s there were already a number of outstanding new ships in service, including *Gripsholm*, *Rotterdam* and *Leonardo da Vinci*. In addition to these, P&O's futuristic *Canberra* and French Line's elegant *France*, were scheduled to debut during the early 1960s. Each of these was planned with at least some provision being made for cruising, and any of them could well have been expected to compete directly with *Andes*.

Faced with this challenge, Royal Mail were forced, in 1959, to spend nearly one-third of what it had cost them to build the ship twenty years earlier to bring *Andes* up to the latest standards. The work was contracted to NV Koninklijke Mij De Schelde in Flushing, the Netherlands. Much of the job dealt with completely rebuilding the old Tourist cabins to first-class standards. The extra space needed to achieve this without further reducing the ship's capacity was found by extending the superstructure both forward and aft at D deck, its lowest level. Fortunately this was achieved without serious compromise of the attractive appearance of *Andes*. Forward, this extended into the well-deck space, while aft it had the

Andes: **Seen here in 'cruising white' after her refit when the superstructure was extended fore and aft at D deck and the excursion launches, which Howard Jarvis so disliked, were added.**

(Fotoflite Ltd, New Romney, Kent, neg C-1123)

added benefit of greatly extending the swimming pool lido area.

The new cabins themselves were spacious and attractive in their modern, clean-lined, functional European styling, with coromandel, zebrano and teak panelling and furniture, flat white ceilings and walls, and pleasant lighting. These became known as the 'Dutch cabins', to distinguish them from the ship's original first-class rooms which, although thoroughly refurbished, generally retained their original character.

Nonetheless, the passenger capacity was still reduced to a nominal figure of 470, a number which could be increased to 500 when all fold-away upper berths and children's cots were used. The capacity was, to some extent, influenced by the owners' insistence that all passengers should be able to dine in a single sitting. This was itself made possible by extending the dining room forward into the original foyer area and by completely refurbishing the room to increase its seating density. The tourist-class dining room disappeared, only its inboard centre part being retained as a grill room, used almost exclusively for private parties. The remainder of the room was converted into new cabins.

Other major work included the construction of a superb cinema-theatre aft in what had previously been cargo hold number 4. A new automatic lift was also installed to give easy access to this addition deep within the bowels of the ship. The lido lounge was enlarged, with its curved bar being moved back into space originally occupied by two cabins. Air conditioning was extended throughout the entire

passenger accommodation, with the exception of the lido bar adjacent to the pool. It was felt that passengers would not want to go directly from the outdoor pool in hot weather into the chilled air of the bar.

Andes was probably among the first cruise ships where public room naming was carried beyond merely descriptive designation to something more fanciful. It was thought that this would make passengers' orientation to their ocean-going resort easier. The names chosen were attractive, and mostly relevant to the Royal Mail Line history. The smoking room, which was the ship's only period-style interior, became the Warwick Room, in honour of the Line's chairman, Walter C Warwick. The dining room's name, Atlantis Restaurant, recalled the name of the Line's earlier cruise ship *Atlantis* of the 1930s. The open-plan Grand Hall and observation lounge were renamed as the Princess Lounge, for a spontaneous visit made by Princess Margaret in Lisbon during 1959, when the ship hosted a cocktail party for her. The four deluxe private suites were named after Royal Mail's well-known South American 'A-boats' *Araguaya*, *Alcantara*, *Asturias* and *Almanzora*.

With the enormous task of conversion completed, *Andes* truly emerged into the modern cruising world. She was a fully integrated single-class ship equipped for cruising alone, with none of her original cargo capacity remaining. Those hold spaces which had not otherwise been used for installations such as the cinema, housed the air-conditioning plants and other auxiliary equipment needed for the comfort and wellbeing of her clientele.

By the time *Andes* returned to service in mid-1960, her character was changed. The leisurely pace of her long River Plate voyages, with a full week in Buenos Aires, had quickened to meet the commercial vicissitudes of operating a succession of three-week cruises, with scarcely more than a 24-hour turnaround between voyages. These were changes which demanded as much of the many long-serving members of the crew as they had done of the ship herself. Nonetheless the refit had prepared *Andes* for a further decade in her long and successful career.

However, towards the end it was becoming increasingly difficult for *Andes* to turn a profit for her owners. Although every effort had been made to keep the ship herself up to date, she was in reality an enormous luxury yacht belonging to the pre-war era of *grande luxe* travel and service. Her passenger capacity was little more than double that of *Stella Polaris*, but measuring at 25,895 tons following the refit, *Andes* was some five times the Swedish cruise yacht's size. Her passenger-to-crew ratio was about one-to-one, making her operation as a cruise ship extremely costly. The profitability of *Andes*, and for that matter the entire Royal Mail Line passenger fleet, in their original line service, had depended significantly on the revenues they could earn by carrying the mail, and large consignments of meats from Argentina, in their spacious refrigerated cargo holds.

Advancing age was also beginning to take its toll, with various engineering and technical problems occurring during her later cruises. She was finally withdrawn and sold to Belgian shipbreakers at Ghent in May 1971. At the same time the sun also set on the entire Royal Mail Line operation, which was wound up as the last hull plates were being cut from *Andes*, their greatest and best-loved ship, by the breakers' torches.

CARONIA

Cunard's most progressive move towards cruising prior to *Queen Elizabeth 2* was taken only after World War II, with their second *Caronia* in 1949. In terms of size and speed, the ship was, in fact, a slightly smaller post-war rendition of the 35,738-ton second *Mauretania*, which had been completed in 1939 by Cammell Laird of Birkenhead. The *Mauretania* was built with a considerably larger passenger capacity to augment the motorships *Britannic* and *Georgic* on their London – New York service, as well as to be able to stand in for *Queen Mary* if need be.[10] She had also been nominally equipped for cruising out of New York during the winter months, reflecting the 'designed for cruising' denominator of her day.

Conversely the 34,183-ton *Caronia* was primarily designated for transatlantic service in tandem with *Mauretania*, but with a strong emphasis on cruising. When the ship was ordered from John Brown & Co (Clydebank) Ltd, Sir Percy Bates, then chairman of Cunard White Star Line, said with typical British understatement:

We are paying much attention to making our new passenger ship at Clydebank rather attractive for cruising without detracting from her usefulness for service on the North Atlantic.

As explained in Cunard White Star publicity literature released when *Caronia* was completed, her duality of purpose required her designers to achieve:

> ... (a) blending of the massive proportions of the Atlantic liner with the feminine grace of a cruising yacht. Not only did this mean that the exterior appearance of the Caronia should not be bizarre, but that the attention due to the special needs of the North Atlantic trade should not make it difficult to include those features of design essential to the perfect cruise liner.[11]

In this regard, *Caronia*'s appearance differed greatly from that of her closest British rival, Royal Mail's *Andes*, which was designed as a tropical ship to fill a similar double role. *Caronia*'s appearance was very much more that of the solid North Atlantic liner, with her high freeboard and fully glass-enclosed promenade decks. As such, she was more the harbinger of things to come, as the design of later purebred cruise tonnage would emphasize fully enclosed and air-conditioned interior spaces in preference to the rationale of the classic open tropical liner as had been so well epitomized by *Andes*.

Caronia's exterior appearance showed the same advances in naval architecture, since the second *Mauretania*, as *Queen*

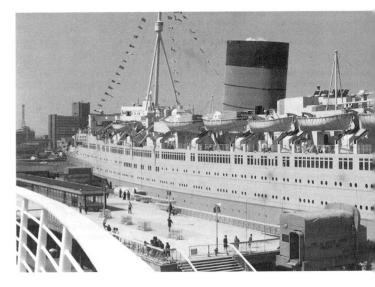

Caronia: **A detail showing the gentle sheer of her classic North Atlantic superstructure and her vast single funnel, as seen from the deck of another ship in port at Yokohama during her 1967 World cruise.**

Elizabeth had exhibited over *Queen Mary*'s design of only a few years earlier. Both of the newer ships had a far more clean-lined appearance to their upper decks, thanks to the use of internally reinforced funnels needing no outside cables for support. The topsides clutter of ventilator cowls, fan houses, and so on was also greatly reduced, with ventilation and air-conditioning intakes, exhaust fans, emergency generators and other top-deck equipment neatly housed in an upward extension of the superstructure proper at the funnel's base. In *Caronia*'s case, the deck spaces thus cleared and opened up for passenger use were vitally important for tropical cruising. Atop her superstructure, as on the larger *Queen Elizabeth*, this primarily took the shape of a large sports deck flanked at either side by the lifeboats.

Terracing of *Caronia*'s Sun (boat) deck and the promenade decks was extended considerably farther aft than would have been done aboard purely North Atlantic ships, making room for the essential outdoor swimming pool and lido areas. The only unfortunate consequence of this was that the two decks immediately below were brought to a rather abrupt end, almost one above the other, atop the rather uninspired lines of the ship's cruiser stern. This aesthetic shortcoming was the more noticeable as being the opposite expression of *Caronia*'s clipper bow and fine forward hull lines.

What was most surprising about this ship, which otherwise was a sturdy example of Clyde-built Cunard tonnage, was that she broke completely with the usual company livery of black hull, white superstructure and red-and-black funnels. *Caronia* was painted in four shades of pale green, chosen rather than cruising white to give the ship her own distinctive identity. Of the usual Cunard colours, only a white ribbon line above the waterline boot topping and the identifying funnel colours were retained. Three shades of pale green, stepping up from darker to lighter, were used, darkest for the hull, intermediate for the main part of superstructure and lightest for that part of the superstructure above the boat deck, along with the mast, boat davits and other deck equipment. The fourth shade, darker than the others, formed a thin riband line around the hull between the main-deck and A-deck rows of portholes.

To make sure that the shades chosen would not be prone to fading or discolouring in prolonged exposure to tropical light and heat, those finally selected were each applied to sections of ships' shell plating and sent to sea aboard various Cunard ships for a period of eighteen months. This field testing subjected the paint samples to prolonged exposure to the actual sea and weather conditions *Caronia* would encounter in her normal service life. Some of these made repeated North Atlantic crossings while one panel made five crossings of the equator aboard the foredeck of a cargo ship.

The accommodation fitted aboard *Caronia* was of a uniformly higher standard than those aboard any other Cunarder, including the *Queens*, and, for that matter, without peer in the entire cruise industry of the day. There was no tourist class, as aboard the regular North Atlantic liners, with

the only remaining segregation being the less-formidable barrier between first and cabin classes. Thus the number of large rectangular outside-facing first-class rooms greatly exceeded the proportion of small inside cabins usually prevailing aboard Cunard's Atlantic fleet. The lower grade cabin-class accommodation on B and C decks, of which many were inside rooms, were intended mainly for Atlantic service. The original intention was that they could be closed off and unoccupied when cruising.

Caronia's main block of cruise accommodation centred around the hotel-style rooms above the dark green riband underlining her A-deck portholes. These cabins was remarkably standardised, considering British shipbuilding practices of the time which generally stressed a more tailor-made approach. They were arranged in mirrored pairs of near-identical layout, throughout the full length of the accommodation spaces of both decks. Access to each pair of rooms was by way of doors facing each other across the ends of short beamwise alleyways. These semi-private passages, extending from the main passages past the cabin bathrooms, allowed each pair of rooms to be combined by a use of a third door at the secondary passage's head. Additional connecting doors in the cabins themselves allowed greater numbers of rooms to be likewise joined. However, considering that *Caronia*'s wealthy clientele was made up mostly of elderly couples travelling without children, it seems unlikely that this feature was widely used.

The comfort of side-by-side beds and generously upholstered easy chairs, convenience of abundant wardrobe and drawer space and luxury of spacious en-suite bathrooms with full-sized bathtubs, were ideally suited for the long-duration worldwide cruising that was to become the ship's virtually exclusive role. Compared with these vast rooms, even the usually prestigious Sun deck location offered comparatively small spaces, which were sold at prices usually lower than those on the lower decks, despite their location. *Caronia*'s luxurious main- and A-deck cabins eventually became the prototype of a widely replicated first-class adaptation aboard *Queen Elizabeth 2* twenty years later.

The layout of public rooms, almost exclusively located on the promenade deck, was a somewhat scaled-down rendition of *Queen Elizabeth*'s corresponding spaces. No matter what ship they were adapted to, Cunard promenade-deck plans were mostly adaptations one way or another of the venerable *Aquitania*'s A-deck layout, with the main lounge amidships and smoking room aft. In later manifestations, the exclusively feminine sanctuary of the forward ladies' lounge or music room of Edwardian times was replaced by a heterogeneous observation lounge and cocktail bar overlooking the bow. As lifestyle became still more sophisticated, a cinema was added aft of the smoking room, which by then was liberated from its former male exclusivity. The whole arrangement was basically functional and usually considered to work well up until *Queen Elizabeth 2*'s planning got underway during the 1960s. In its *Caronia* rendition, the promenade deck also took in the cabin-class lounge, which in effect had been pushed up through the strength deck plating to new heights, both in consideration of its use during cruises and due to the extra indoor space created by the Sun deck's extension aft.

Above, there was a veranda café aft on the sports deck, resembling the famed grill rooms of the *Queens*, but lacking their catering facilities. Below, the cabin-class smoking room was left to its solitary self, astern on the main deck. Still deeper, the two dining rooms were arranged in the usual fore-and-aft liner style on B deck. These were both inside rooms with a passage and row of cabins along either side, increasing the ratio of outside to inside accommodation. The fact that these rooms were named as Balmoral and Sandringham restaurants, rather than being merely designated as first- and cabin-class dining rooms, itself bore clear indication of the ship's intended use in an open-class arrangement for cruising.

Caronia's architectural styling adopted a downscaled and rather downplayed adaptation of the ocean liner eclecticism borrowed from the *Queens'* outsized North Atlantic interiors. Restraint was obviously the underlying design theme, as there was also to be nothing bizarre about the ship's insides. Her designers were instructed to play it safe, pandering to *Caronia*'s moneyed, elderly clientele with a strong sense of tradition, which was allowed only mild flirtation here and there with elements of frivolity and whimsy. There was to be none of the 'mild vulgarity' which some architectural critics of the day had ascribed to *Queen Mary*'s interiors. Those vast expanses of highly polished exotic veneers, outrageous geometric carpet patterns and those visually bewildering, indirect ceiling lighting schemes nonetheless held fast, as the vestigial remaining bastions of Cunard corporate ocean-going architecture.

Much was written in the technical, artistic and popular press about *Caronia*, 'Britain's wonder ship of 1949', as her building was completed and she entered service. Still more was written in the design and artistic journals of the 1960s as plans were being laid for *Queen Elizabeth 2*, much of it deriding and ridiculing her interiors in support of a case for a more up-to-date standard of design aboard the new flagship. The merit or effectiveness of architectural and industrial design of a ship's interiors and fittings is difficult to quantify accurately in terms of ultimate commercial success. John Maxtone-Graham's comments on the effectiveness of *Caronia*'s lounge, as perceived through the eyes of her passengers, puts the whole matter of ships' interior design into practical perspective in his outstanding book, *Liners to the Sun*:

> But in truth it is doubtful that any of the thousands of passengers who remember the Caronia with such consistent fondness ever scrutinised that room critically. If perhaps a little startling it was the way steamship lounges were meant to look, sort of art-deco, like the WPA post office back home or Radio City Music Hall. And that veneer radiated only good

Caronia: **The subdued, late art-deco interior of the main lounge, despite its visually bewildering mix of direct and indirect lighting and reflective polished veneers, still had endearing nostalgic qualities of liner design eclecticism.**

(Cunard photograph, Gordon Turner collection, Toronto)

subliminal vibes; it was faultlessly maintained, it cocooned one in comfort and luxury, as it took one to nice places. In McLuhanese, the lounge was the longing; decorative nitpicking was secondary and probably nonexistent.[12]

After setting out on a single, round-trip, North Atlantic maiden voyage on Tuesday, 4 January 1949, *Caronia* immediately made the transition to cruising with a Southampton departure on 29 January, calling at Cherbourg and Bermuda *en route*. This voyage gave a number of Britons the opportunity to cruise to their winter holiday resorts in Bermuda aboard the world's newest and most luxurious cruise ship. Others remained aboard for the first of a series of four Caribbean cruises, which American passengers would be joining in New York on Saturday, 12 February. These, and all of *Caronia*'s cruises, were carefully scheduled to coincide with the line's North Atlantic sailings, making them conveniently available to clientele in both Europe and North America.

Caronia quickly settled into a regular year-round routine.

This commenced each January in Southampton with a four-week Caribbean cruise, followed by her annual three-month world cruise, returning to New York in May. The spring Mediterranean cruise would bring her back to Southampton *en route* to pick up British passengers. At its conclusion, Americans would return home aboard one of the *Queens*, as *Caronia* would bear northwards into Norwegian waters bound for the North Cape and the land of the midnight sun, and then return south to make an eastwards circuit into the Baltic and to the Scandinavian capitals, on a spectacularly scenic six-week voyage. In the autumn she would retrace her path back to the Mediterranean for two more long and leisurely circumnavigations throughout the cradles of western civilisation, with the second circuit taking her farthest east to the Dardanelles, Egypt and Israel. By the time the last of her Mediterranean passengers descended the gangways into the morning chill of an early December day in England, it would once again be time for *Caronia*'s annual overhaul and dry-docking, before repeating the cycle the following year.

All of these were longer than usual cruises, taken at a leisurely pace, with stopovers of more than a day in their most attractive ports. Elaborate shore-excursion arrangements were available, which often involved overland travel in foreign lands where passengers would leave the ship in one port and rejoin her at a later stage of the cruise. Later on, as *Andes* entered a more competitive phase of her career, with shorter turnaround times and protracted cruise itineraries, *Caronia*, or the *Green Goddess*, as she was known, continued to retain an exclusivity somewhat akin to that of *Empress of Britain*'s pre-war cruises.

Caronia had developed a steadfast and loyal following on both sides of the Atlantic, who sailed with her year after year, in a favourite cabin, or perhaps in the care of a particular steward, regardless of the cruise itinerary. The ship developed somewhat the atmosphere of a London gentlemen's club (with ladies permitted of course), propagated for the benefit of all by the legions of her regulars. In the progress of her career over nearly two decades, the average age of her clientele steadily increased to the point that she was known to her crew as 'God's waiting room'. Indeed in the course of her worldly duties, *Caronia* had dispatched more than a few of her aged patrons to meet their creator by way of the deep.

Caronia, like *Andes*, finally fell victim to the harsh economic realities of doing business in the late 1960s. She was by then becoming too expensive to operate, not only from the standpoint of fuel costs, but also on account of her low passenger-to-crew ratio and unused lower-deck spaces. In *Caronia*'s case this shortcoming was particularly apparent, as she was built only a few years ahead of the precedent set in 1953 by Swedish American Line with *Kungsholm*, for planning a luxury two-class ship in which *all* cabins had portholes or windows and private toilet facilities, qualifying them from the outset as suitable for cruising.

Sadly, a far less dignified end awaited *Caronia* than that accorded to her Royal Mail counterpart. She was sold to Universal Line SA of Panama as part of Cunard's fleet rationalisation of 1968, in preparation for taking delivery of *Queen Elizabeth 2*. This came only three years after the ship had undergone an extensive life-prolonging modernisation. Renamed *Caribia*, and hastily pressed into mass-market Caribbean cruising, she did not prosper, her reputation being compromised in part by a boiler-room explosion in which a crewman was killed. Yet, with capital costs amounting to only the $3 million paid for the ship, and the reduced staffing expenses achieved through convenience-flag registry, the ship still proved too costly to operate. She was eventually laid up in New York until finally being sold to Taiwanese interests for scrapping. Whilst under tow on her way to the breakers she broke loose off Guam, where her tow cables snapped and she committed herself to the deep in the pounding waters of a severe tropical storm.

Caronia was a handsome, traditional ship whose contribution to the history of cruising was that, rather than breaking any new ground in naval architecture, she established a still-surviving gold standard of top-quality deluxe cruising. Some elements of her influence were to transcend to *Queen Elizabeth 2*'s planning. In Cunard's negotiations over the purchase of the Norwegian America's *Sagafjord* and *Vistafjord* in 1983, long after *Caronia* was gone, she was cited repeatedly as an example of what was to be expected of the new acquisitions. Her name appears again as a point of reference in articles describing later ultra-deluxe cruise ships such as Hapag-Lloyd's new *Europa* of 1982 and Royal Viking's *Royal Viking Sun* a few years later.

1   'The Cruising Liner', *Sea Breezes* (February 1950) pp 84-5
2   Der Schnelldampfer Bremen, *Der Zeitschrift des Vereins Deutscher Ingenieure* No 21 (1930) p 10
3   'The Traveller and his Stateroom', *Shipbuilding and Shipping Record* (26 December 1935) p 716
4   'Informality in Ship Furnishing', *Shipbuilding and Shipping Record* (26 December 1935) p 711
5   'Health Cruise Planned', *The Gazette* (Montreal, 2 January 1932)
6   'Golf Talks on Liner', *The Gazette* (Montreal, 25 January 1932)
7   'RMS *Andes*: Ship of Three Worlds', *Ships Monthly* (March 1971) pp 90-91
8   'RMS *Andes*: Ship of Three Worlds', *Ships Monthly* (March 1971) p 92
9   'RMS *Andes*: Ship of Three Worlds', *Ships Monthly* (June 1972) p 217
10 Commodore C R Vernon Gibbs RN, *The Western Ocean Passenger Lines and Liners*, p 36
11 *Caronia: Britain's Wonder Ship of 1949*, p 2
12 John Maxtone-Graham, *Liners to the Sun*, p 165

ADVANCEMENT

Towards the creation of the modern cruise liner

Returning again to the 1930s, much of the period dual-purpose tonnage designed still followed traditional conceptions of the British tropical or North Atlantic liner, even if built elsewhere in the world. Modern as they were, *Andes* and *Caronia* were still products of 1930s design thinking, solidly rooted in two-class operation, with such diverse grades of accommodation as apparently demanded by the wide cross-section of society they served. There were always passengers on line voyages who felt the necessity of having bigger cabins, in recognition of their personal wealth or higher social standing ashore. While the best suites and cabins were well-suited both to these passengers and cruise travellers alike, the lower grades were, by virtue of the required diversity of cabin categories, woefully inadequate for pleasure travel.

However, the best cruises of that *grande luxe* era, when the clientele were called 'members' rather than passengers, by their nature prescribed a considerably more egalitarian shipboard atmosphere. The mutual enjoyment of a sensation of discovery and other pleasures offered by cruising called for a greater sense of personal contact on more or less equal terms among those aboard. The plans of *Prinzessin Victoria Luise*, *Stella Polaris* and *Arandora Star* were in this regard more suitable than those of *Andes* and *Caronia*. In those earlier yacht-inspired examples, one or two deluxe suites and the alternative of single-berth rooms offered the only alternative to the twin-bedded rooms making up the bulk of their accommodation.

While cruising had originated primarily as a pastime for the wealthy, its growth and continued prosperity would ultimately rely on the support of a far greater cross-section of modern society. Indeed, this was to be helped along largely by the increased mobility and wealth of a more democratised

society to emerge only after the Second World War. It was to become a society that would cater to the great masses, and, in time, reshape and redefine the development of its own elite market sectors.

The basic idea of large and economical, mass-market passenger-ship operations was originally seen as being realistic and attainable in the 1930s. Huge liners of this type were then taking shape in the minds of creative designers such as Theodore Ferris and Vladimir Yourkevitch. They and others were planning 100,000-ton Atlantic behemoths that would each carry thousands of passengers in uniform all-tourist-class accommodation.[1] These, along with a number of other schemes which would follow in the 1950s, were perhaps too grandiose in scale, particularly in view of the rapid development of post-war commercial aviation.

The first manifestation of this type of thinking, albeit on a less ponderous scale, was to emanate from Adolf Hitler's Third Reich. Superlative industrial design and engineering were key aspects of Nazi ideology and propaganda in asserting an impression of German efficiency and superiority. It was a case where the administration of tyranny opened windows of opportunity, through which a number of worthwhile technological and scientific achievements would ultimately emerge to survive on a worldwide scale, long after the regime's fall. However, the acknowledgement of these sources in their correct historical context remains tainted and stigmatised by the colossal brutality of the despotism which breathed life into them.

WILHELM GUSTLOFF AND ROBERT LEY

The planning, building and operating of these ships was an important facet of the Nazi party's elaborate propaganda scheme, aimed at winning over the hearts and minds of ordi-

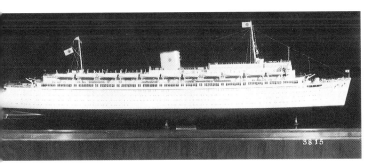

Wilhelm Gustloff: **Builder's model of the ship.**

(Bohm & Voss, Hamburg, neg 3815)

nary working German citizens. By way of its *Kraft durch Freude* (KdF – Strength through Joy) programme, the regime's *Deutsche Arbeitsfront* (German Labour Front) endeavoured to make a number of tangibles available to workers, who otherwise might never have hoped to aspire to such things. Among other offerings was the opportunity of international sea travel on the organisation's own cruise ships. Of course, such a privilege had to be applied for through the *Deutsche Arbeitsfront*, and would be granted only to those who were in good standing with their employers as well as being agreeably disposed towards the Nazi regime itself. The programme gave many Germans, who could otherwise scarcely have afforded to venture beyond their own home towns and villages, the rare opportunity to visit foreign ports in the Baltic, Norway, Spitzbergen, the Atlantic Islands and the Mediterranean. Furthermore, they could do so in the comfort and security of ships of their own nationality.

As to be expected, the benefits of this venture to the Nazi regime compensated handsomely for its apparent gestures of kindness to the working masses. KdF cruises had started as early as 1934, at first mainly as a means of putting laid-up German passenger tonnage back to work, creating desperately needed employment for many seafarers and revitalising the nation's shipbuilding industry. However, it was also realised that, once aboard, the passengers were themselves conveniently within earshot of the Nazi ideology and propaganda which KdF was also responsible for disseminating. There was also a financial reward for the regime, as KdF passengers were not allowed to use valuable foreign currencies. All shipboard expenses and shore excursions had to be paid for in Reichmarks, thereby supporting only the German economy.[2]

Wilhelm Gustloff and *Robert Ley* were the first new ships to be built exclusively for KdF cruising. They were in fact part of an ambitious expansion programme which was also to include use of the new HAPAG Atlantic liner *Vaterland*, then being built by Blohm & Voss. The envisaged KdF fleet was to include thirty ships, capable of providing cruise holidays for 2,000,000 people a year.

The orders for *Wilhelm Gustloff* and *Robert Ley* were placed with Blohm & Voss and Howaldtswerken AG respectively. Of the two, the slightly larger *Robert Ley* was designated

to be the KdF flagship, at least until some of the Third Reich's more grandiose plans were expected to materialise in the early 1940s. *Wilhelm Gustloff* was to be run by the Hamburg Südamerika Line, with HAPAG being responsible for the flagship.

The overall design criteria for both ships were essentially the same:

Accommodation of all passengers in two- and four-berth cabins.

No inner cabins, all cabins to have daylight and to be outfitted with modern functional furnishing.

Spacious public rooms in functional, though appropriately artistic, design (these were to be capable of seating all passengers at one time, without having to use the dining rooms).

Large sports- and sun-decks, gymnasium and swimming pools (open spaces were also to be free of ventilator heads, winches and other deck equipment).

Cabins and public spaces provided for the crew to be of the same standard as those for the passengers.

A moderate speed of 15.5kts, as opposed to the higher speeds generally required for line services, allowing passengers time to fully enjoy each ship's recreational facilities while *en route* from place to place.[3]

Cap Arcona: **An earlier Bohm & Voss–built ship of similar-size which was the prototype for various design features of the KdF ships.**

(Bohm & Voss)

The transformation of these criteria into reality, during 1938 and 1939, produced a pair of very attractive and functional single-funnelled motorships. The exterior appearance of the two ivory-coloured sisters was very similar, with *Wilhelm Gustloff* having a slightly more refined aesthetic. The difference was not so much due to the Blohm & Voss ship's smaller size as it was to the arrangement of her masts, the rake of her funnel and elegant lines of her cruiser stern. *Robert Ley* was of greater depth, accommodating an additional deck. However, it was the enclosed forward part her boat deck, as much as anything else, which gave the latter ship's profile a definitely heavier look, indicative of the additional 1,804 tons measure of her size.

These were quite substantial ships, ranking in size with many larger intermediate-class North Atlantic liners and other principal passenger liners on various long-haul services around the world. In terms of German shipbuilding, they came perhaps closest to the Hamburg-Südamerika *Cap Arcona*.

	Cap Arcona	W. Gustloff	Robert Ley
Length bp (m)	195.00	195.00	190.80
Beam (m)	25.70	23.50	24.00
Depth to strength deck (m)	16.90	17.25	20.70
Draught (m)	8.41	6.50	7.56
GRT	27,561.00	25,484.00	27,288.00
Service speed (kn)	20.00	15.50	15.50
Propulsion power (kW)	17,894.40	7,083.20	6,561.28
No of passengers	*1,434	1,465	1,766

* passengers carried in three classes

Apart from their distinction as the first purpose-built KdF cruise ships, *Wilhelm Gustloff* and *Robert Ley* were also the first ships in the world to be built for carrying a large number of passengers in uniform accommodation, solely for the purpose of cruising. Among many other factors, this meant that the cargo and hold space normally required aboard deep-sea liners of their size could be entirely eliminated. With the exception of a single stores hatch fully forward, there were not the usual obstructions of multiple hatchways, along with the kingposts, derricks and winches on deck necessary to work them. This in effect cleared the way for longer superstructures with wide-open and uninterrupted deck spaces available for passengers' use. Likewise, the internal spaces were remarkably free of the intrusion from the ships' workings. The single funnel casing amidships, with the necessary ventilation trunkways clustered neatly around it, was the only interruption of the midship spaces otherwise completely available for passenger and crew living quarters.

To further ensure that there was enough space to house all passengers and crew with a uniform level of spaciousness and comfort, the height of the machinery installations below the

accommodation on both ships was restricted as far as possible. This was handled in different ways by *Wilhelm Gustloff* and *Robert Ley*'s respective builders.

Blohm & Voss's approach with *Wilhelm Gustloff* was to install a quadruple-engine diesel aggregate, geared to twin propellers. By the time of *Wilhelm Gustloff*'s building, Blohm & Voss already had considerable experience in using this type of machinery in a number of other ships, both for German owners and export. The overall installation's low engine height, small cylinder diameters, and relatively short fore-and-aft length were particularly noteworthy design features.[4]

Howaldtswerken engined *Robert Ley* with electric propeller motors powered by six diesel generator sets, which also satisfied the ship's entire auxiliary and hotel electrical needs. Although diesel-electric propulsion dates virtually from the inception of diesel marine engineering, *Robert Ley* was among the first large passenger ships to use this form of power.

Before direct-reversing marine oil engines were developed, reverse-switchable electric drive offered the only convenient way to obtain astern power. A number of the earliest motor tugs and barges, built at the beginning of the twentieth century, were in fact diesel electric. A more sophisticated 'power station' approach was tried during the 1920s on vessels where there was a high demand for auxiliary electrical power, as in the case of refrigerated cargo ships. An aggregate of diesel-powered generators, similar or identical to the later version was used as the power plant, feeding the propeller motors, refrigeration plant, and all other auxiliary services. The United Fruit Company's *La Playa* of 1923 was among the first deep-sea cargo ships to use this engine arrangement. At the same time diesel-electric propulsion was also found to be ideally suited for the type of rapid manoeuvring needed in short-sea ferries, tugs and various other specialised craft.[5]

The first passenger diesel-electric ship, or 'electroschiff' to use the preferred German terminology of the day, was HAPAG's handsome and well-appointed *Patria*. She was completed by Deutsche Werft of Hamburg only a month earlier than *Robert Ley* for the express cargo and passenger service to South America's Pacific coast ports. As such, she had 1,249cu m of refrigerated cargo space, imposing a high auxiliary electrical load. *Robert Ley*'s design and construction, at virtually the same time, represented a different application of the same overall approach rather than a follow-up to *Patria*.

Robert Ley's power station consisted of six diesel-driven generator sets arranged in two separate machinery compartments amidships. Each unit of three sets was capable of delivering 800kVA of alternating current (AC) electrical power at 2,380V to either the propeller motors or auxiliary services. In normal operation *Robert Ley*'s main motors required the full output of two alternators each, provided by the centre and one outer unit in each engine room. The remaining two outer generator sets handled the entire auxiliary and domestic load. The two centre units were switchable between the motor circuits and the auxiliary distribution system, providing sufficient built-in redundancy so that near normal operation

Wilhelm Gustloff and *Robert
Ley*: Comparison of
machinery arrangements.

(Author)

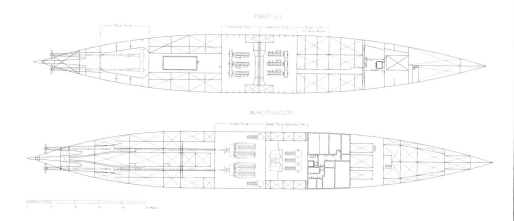

could be continued with any one of the engines out of service, either for regular servicing or on account of breakdown.
This switching flexibility also provided for running at
reduced speed in the event that one or other of her engine
spaces might be incapacitated by fire or flooding. *Robert Ley*
could hold speeds of 14kts and 11kts, running on three and
two generator sets respectively.

The two Siemens synchronous 48-pole AC propeller
motors provided for electrical control of the propeller speed.
Thus a continuously variable service speed of between
14.5kts and 16kts was achievable by regulating the generator
output between 44Hz and 48.4Hz (or cycles per second).
This prevented the inevitable loss of power at lower speeds
that would result if the voltage, rather than the frequency,
were reduced. However, the disadvantage was that this prevented full interchangeability of all six main generators, as all
auxiliary services would have been likewise subjected to the
same electrical fluctuations.

The motors could also be synchronised to keep both
three-bladed propellers turning in a consistent relationship to
each other, with the blades always oriented in the same way, as
would be the hands of two clocks, side by side, set to the same
time. This ensured that the flow of water around the two out-
ward-turning propellers was always constant, improving performance and reducing the possibility of propeller-induced
vibration. Full reverse power was achieved by reverse switching the motor pole windings.[6]

In terms of compactness, *Robert Ley*'s machinery arrangement was certainly as effective as that aboard her earlier-com-
pleted sister ship. Unfortunately, the outbreak of World War II
curtailed the careers of both ships so quickly that there was
hardly the opportunity for the performance of her machinery
to be measured against that of *Wilhelm Gustloff*. Theoretically
at least, she should have been a quieter ship, thanks to the
absence of reduction gearing. Diesel-electric propulsion was
at the time quite widely tried, and has since regained acceptance in a number of large cruise ships, following the example
of *Queen Elizabeth 2*'s re-engining in Germany during the
winter of 1986–7.

The abundance of clear and unencumbered space on the

decks above each ship's compact engine rooms, allowed for
straightforward and uncomplicated accommodation layouts
of unprecedented scale. The overall simplicity of plan was
achieved also as the result of a complete absence of passenger
class barriers. This was also extended, minimising the functional segregation of passenger and crew amenities. The crew
had their own day rooms and mess halls, mainly to serve them
during those hours of the day or night when they would be
off watch. Where separate passages and stairways were provided for the crew, the purpose was to improve accessibility
rather than to entirely segregate the ships' personnel as a separate community. After all, passengers and crew were supposed to be *Arbeitskameraden* (workmates).

The arrangement of public rooms on both ships generally
followed the same remarkably clear and spacious promenade-
deck layout of Hamburg Südamerika's luxury-class *Cap
Arcona*. The KdF ships' promenade-deck plans had the same
simple progression of large rectangular rooms within the
bounds of a wide enclosed promenade. The sequence was
interrupted only by the funnel casing amidships and by two
lift shafts forward. The overall layouts differed from *Cap
Arcona*, mainly in that the dining rooms on the KdF ships
were located one deck below rather than forming the aft part
of the public suites. Two of *Robert Ley*'s social halls, as German
nomenclature would have it, were extended up through the
boat deck above, where there were mezzanines. The most
attractive and unusual of these crowned the immense aft hall,
where the upper Galleria was circular, following the shape of
an enormous polished hardwood dance floor beneath it. This
immense room occupied nearly half the promenade deck's
interior length, giving it probably the largest seating capacity
of any ship's lounge.

The architectural design of the public rooms in both ships
was supervised by Professor Woldenar Brinkmann of Munich.
The expression of his skilful treatment of these interiors was
one of elegance, accomplished through a functional clarity
and simplicity of form and fabric. His work here stressed the
overall character of the ships' own structural design, in a manner which also expressed the unique structural character of
the interior schemes themselves. The ceilings were mostly

Wilhelm Gustloff: **The forward social hall, furnished for use as a club room. Note the portrait of Adolf Hitler on the main wall.**

(Bohm & Voss, neg 38 175)

white or cream coloured, as were those walls not panelled in various polished woods and veneers. The differing dimensions and disposition of public spaces aboard the two ships did, however, demand an individual treatment of each. Although neither vessel was intended to be superior to the other, the original plans and sketches done by Professor Brinkmann for *Robert Ley* did, in fact, reveal a more complete scheme with respect to wall coverings, reliefs, paintings, prints and other decorative accessories.[7]

Both ships were outfitted with remarkably complete medical facilities, with fully equipped operating rooms and dental surgeries. These were each staffed by two physicians and a dentist, along with several nurses and other staff. The ships' hospitals also included dispensaries and several wards for male and female patients, as well as isolation wards.

Another noteworthy addition to *Robert Ley*'s accommodation was an elaborate state suite comprising sixteen rooms for the Führer's own use. It was located on the port side of B deck, with provision so that the whole area could be shut off from the rest of the ship's accommodation. A smaller suite of similar type was also included aboard *Wilhelm Gustloff*.

Perhaps the greatest achievement of those responsible for the interior layout of the two ships, was their ability to render a workable and uncomplicated arrangement of standardised two- and four-berth outer cabins for about 2,000 passengers and crew on each vessel. This remarkable feat was accomplished by an ingenious trick of planning, whereby the larger four-berth cabins were, in effect, wrapped around two sides of the smaller two-bedded rooms. Each cabin consisted in essence of a sleeping alcove and sitting area. The rooms were dove-tailed together in pairs so that the sleeping areas of the four-berth units fitted inboard of their two-berth counter-

Wilhelm Gustloff: **The music room, looking forward at the centre of the room. Note the central doors behind the bandstand which indicate the axial plan of all promenade deck rooms aft of the funnel casing.**

(Bohm & Voss, neg 38 149)

parts. The sitting alcoves, which were of equal width for both cabin types, were arranged at the ships' sides where portholes gave them access to daylight, fresh air, and a view.

The four-berth cabins were accessed directly from the main fore-and-aft corridors, while each pair of two-berth rooms was reached by way of a short crosswise alleyway bypassing the four-berth sleeping alcoves. The pattern was replicated uniformly throughout *Wilhelm Gustloff*'s and *Robert Ley*'s accommodation decks, with only minor variation to handle the narrowing of the decks toward each ship's bow and stern. Apart from a few other minor aberrations devised to get around obstructions of one kind or another, the only exceptions to the whole scheme were a series of deluxe cabins on the port side of each ship and the quarters of the captain. Of the two ships, *Robert Ley*'s overall plan was slightly better articulated, with fewer irregularities and variations of layout.

The expanse of both ships' accommodation plans was unprecedented, with uninterrupted runs of cabins extending the length of the hull, from the steering flat aft to the chain locker forward. This appeared even more extensive on deck plans, as there were none of the grand foyers and wide processional stairways normally associated with passenger liner planning of the day. Each ship's six identical stairways and their adjacent lobbies were ample for the access and circulation purpose they were designed to serve, and no more, giving them an almost diminutive appearance in relation to the vast numbers of cabins surrounding them.

The dimensions of the whole cabin arrangement had also been worked out to coincide exactly with the structural web of the two ships. Structurally a ship is not unlike the skeleton of a mammal. Her hull is constructed around a series of regularly spaced steel frames. These are in essence the ribs of the beast, stemming from the 'backbone' of her keel, and held in place above by the virtual 'breastbone' of the strength deck. The hull shell plating is the hide or skin which encloses and protects the internal organisms of propelling and auxiliary machinery, life support services and accommodation. Rudders, propellers with their support brackets and shaft bossings, superstructure, funnels, masts, lifeboats and deck gear are the appendages which allow the whole body to function.

The regular spacing of the frames determines the pattern, or rhythm, of everything inside. On an ocean-going ship the frames are usually spaced 800mm to 900mm apart amidships, with a shorter interval used towards the extreme ends of the hull where added strength is needed. The position of watertight and fireproof bulkheads, along with the spacing interval of support columns, is determined by multiples of the frame spacing. The locations and sizes of all openings such, as portholes, hatches and sidelights, in the hull's shell plating, along with funnel and hatch trunkways as well as stairwell openings, ventilation and service conduits, are also determined by the same dimension.

The cabin widths for *Wilhelm Gustloff* and *Robert Ley* were determined to coincide directly with the ships' hull-frame spacing. This worked out at four cabins per nine frames aboard *Wilhelm Gustloff* and per ten frames on *Robert Ley*. The reason for the difference between the two ships was that *Wilhelm Gustloff*'s frames were more widely spaced at 900mm. The advantage of this regularity of the cabin arrangement was that the precise positions of the supporting columns could be anticipated throughout a long run of rooms occupying the length of an entire deck. Space was provided inside a double wall between the inner and outer sleeping alcoves, through which the supporting columns would pass predictably in every fourth cabin. This, along with an equally consistent pattern of porthole openings, greatly simplified not only the plan but also the construction of the cabins, in that no special fitting was needed to accommodate the supporting columns or portholes.

Indeed, this approach was a harbinger of the uniformity, modularity, and complete cabin prefabrication schemes of cruise ship and ferry designs more than thirty years later. Standardisation of design elements for manufactured goods, vehicles, industrial equipment, machinery and building components had already begun to emerge as a quintessential strength of German industry and building ashore. While standardisation of ships' cabin sizes and layouts was introduced in the planning of North German Lloyd's *Bremen* and *Europa*, demand for the vast range in accommodation types needed for their three-class line service somewhat compromised its overall effectiveness. Design of the KdF cabins represented the very important step of linking the detailed design and outfitting of the rooms to the hull-frame spacing. This acknowledged, as never before in shipbuilding history, a primal integration of domestic function with structural form of the vessel herself.

The KdF cabin design was in reality a variation of, and vast improvement on, the original idea of Bibby cabins. The added expense and complexity of its construction were compensated for by the potential attractiveness and functionality of the rooms. Indeed, this arrangement was the prototype of its various adaptations used on passenger and cruise ships for many years to come. A variation of the idea was adopted by the Matthias-Thesen-Werft of Wismar, in the former Deutsche Demokratik Republik, for the East German workers' cruise ship *Fritz Heckert* of 1962. This unique 7,200-ton ship, designed exclusively for pleasure travel, probably came closer in its overall conception to the KdF liners than anything else built since their day. *Fritz Heckert* herself represented the prototype of various features later adopted in the design

Cap Arcona: **The first class lounge, showing an earlier and more ornate treatment of spaces similar to those aboard the KdF ships, whose modernity appeared almost stark in comparison.**

(Bohm & Voss, neg 476 7470)

Robert Ley: **Hauptdeck plan showing her efficient and highly standardised cabin layout.**

(Author)

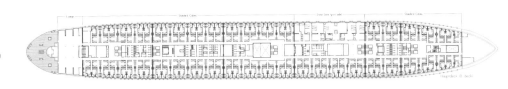

of the larger *Alexandr Pushkin* class liners built by the same yard for the Soviet Union. Original drawings of these ships, released early in their design development, showed a far greater similarity with *Fritz Heckert* than did their later appearance as finally completed. Accommodation on the lower decks of the *Pushkin*-class actually bore a much closer similarity to the original KdF example.

An adaptation of the KdF-style cabin also appeared in an enlarged and considerably more luxurious version, with private bathrooms attached, throughout the luxurious *Stockholm*, being built at the same time as *Robert Ley* for Swedish American Line. In 1969 a very similar scheme was widely adopted in some of the higher-grade tourist-class cabins aboard Cunard's *Queen Elizabeth 2*.

By the time of the outbreak of World War II in September 1939, *Wilhelm Gustloff* had been in service for little more than a year, while *Robert Ley*'s career amounted to only a few weeks. Both ships were withdrawn from service and subsequently came to disastrous ends towards the war's conclusion. *Wilhelm Gustloff*'s name became synonymous with the greatest ever loss of human life aboard a single deep-sea vessel. The circumstances of either ship's tragically short service careers within an alien and belligerent fascist society are generally

unrecorded and little known. No doubt these ships did afford to many ordinary working German citizens, unwittingly swept into the fold of Nazism, one fond and memorable look at a peaceful world, gradually fading into the darkness of a second global military conflict.

ERIC TH CHRISTIANSSON'S SWEDISH AMERICAN LINE SHIPS

Apart from the similarity of her cabin layout, *Stockholm* was to bear a fairly strong overall resemblance to *Wilhelm Gustloff* and *Robert Ley*. Externally, the Swedish ship was almost a two-funnelled adaptation of the German pair's crisp modern lines, differing mainly in that the proportions of her superstructure were less dominant. She was ultimately to share the misfortunes of her KdF contemporaries by falling victim to the ravages of war. Fortunately, both Eric Th Christiansson, her designer, and Swedish American Line survived the war and went on to bring forward many of the same ideas and techniques to the building of three further magnificent Swedish ships in the post-war era.

Preliminary planning for *Stockholm* had started as early as

Wilhelm Gustloff: **Here she is enthusiastically given the Nazi salute during her launch in May 1937.**

(Bohm & Voss)

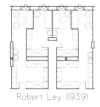

Robert Ley (1939)

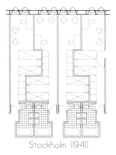

Stockholm (1941)

Alexandr Pushkin (1966)

Queen Elizabeth 2 (1969)

Robert Ley: **The standard cabin plan compared with later examples using a similar design aboard** *Stockholm, Alexandr Pushkin* **and** *QE2.*

(Author)

both as deck and engine ratings on a variety of ships until returning home to Göteborg in 1923, where he then worked at the Lindholmens yard as a plater, while also studying marine engineering. He later joined Swedish American Line's parent company, Brostroms, where he served as their technical director between 1934 and 1965. It was in this capacity that he learned to uphold the progressive approach to ship design, which the Line's first chief executive-officer, Dan Brostrom, had initiated with *Gripsholm* in the mid-1920s. The individuality of Christiansson's approach to the design of *Stockholm* was no less progressive.

Before *Stockholm* could be delivered to her owners she suffered two great misfortunes, firstly a devastating fire on 19 December 1938 while fitting out, and then the loss of immediately-built replacement parts during bombing by British aircraft in July 1944 and again in May 1945. She had, in the meantime, been sold to the Italian government for use as a troop ship, and renamed *Sabaudia*. The final aerial assault on the unfortunate ship's, already half-submerged, remains took place only two months after *Robert Ley* had met a similar fate in Hamburg, and four months since *Wilhelm Gustloff*'s tragic sinking in the Baltic.

Measured at 30,390 tons, the replacement *Stockholm* was the largest ever passenger liner in the Swedish American Line fleet, surpassing their last *Kungsholm* of 1966 by the considerable margin of 3,712 tons. It was not until 1985, when the 33,830-ton Baltic ferry *Svea* was delivered by Wärtsilä that *Stockholm*'s tonnage was surpassed by any Swedish-owned passenger ship. Apart from the KdF ships, the largest and most powerful of *Stockholm*'s immediate contemporaries were the Dutch motorships *Oranje* and *Willem Ruys*. Although of only about 20,000 tons each, they were engined for higher speeds, giving them each, in fact, greater power than the Swedish ship.

Stockholm represented yet a third propulsion alternative to the geared four-engine diesel aggregate and diesel-electric

1935, with Swedish American Line's aspirations towards putting their own transatlantic service on the same prestigious level as those of the leading North Atlantic carriers Cunard, French Line, North German Lloyd and Holland America. Having achieved remarkable success in cruising with their first *Gripsholm* and *Kungsholm*, the line wanted a ship which was designed from the outset for a truly dual-purpose role. The order for *Stockholm*'s construction was placed the following year with Cantieri Riuniti del'Adriatico at Monfalcone, Italy.

Stockholm was the first ship designed by Eric Christiansson, a man of considerable and varied experience for his age. He was born in 1901 and had gone to sea aboard the barquentine *Jonstorp* at the tender age of fourteen. He served

Stockholm: **A builder's model of the first ship, superimposed on a seascape, which clearly shows the distinctive twin-funnelled profile which would become a hallmark of Christiansson's work.**

(G Dividini, Monfalcone, 24 Gen, 1938 neg 8030; courtesy of Brostroms)

machinery of *Wilhelm Gustloff* and *Robert Ley* respectively. When tenders were invited for the building of *Stockholm*, Swedish American Line's specifications allowed for various alternatives of diesel propulsion only. The line were already solidly committed to their preference for the oil engine over steam turbines, thanks to the proven success of their earlier *Gripsholm* and *Kungsholm*. A three-screw direct-drive arrangement, using a trio of Sulzer single-acting two-stroke engines, was finally chosen from among a number of proposals.

A similar decision had been made at about the same time by *Oranje*'s owners, who chose the larger twelve-cylinder variant of *Stockholm*'s ten-cylinder machines. In both cases the choice was based on the compactness and inherent simplicity of the installation as a whole. Christiansson was particularly concerned that the maintainance of the machinery could be continued during the several months of winter, when *Stockholm*'s cruise programme took her out of the reach of the experienced technicians and specialised workshops of her builders and engine makers. While *Stockholm* herself did not live long enough to prove the value of this point, *Oranje* certainly did. After sailing from Amsterdam on 1 September 1939, she endured almost seven years of active wartime service without serious mechanical failure before returning to her home port.

Stockholm was one of the very few passenger ships to be completed during World War II. When she ran her sea trials in the Adriatic during October 1941, she had been fully completed to her owner's specifications, right down to the last details of outfitting and equipment. This was in fact one of the conditions of the ship's sale.

The streamlined profile, two well-proportioned ovoid funnels, raked bow and cruiser stern of this white Nordic ship must have come as a welcome respite from the angular battleship-grey silhouettes of that era. Indeed she was enthusiastically received by the marine press. The American trade journal *Marine Engineering and Shipping Review* noted that:

> The *Stockholm* is the first vessel designed originally as a large cruising ship…. She will, it is true, also engage in transatlantic traffic when circumstances warrant, but even in times of peace it was intended that this should be secondary to her cruising schedule. Probably most of the cruises will be made from New York, and it is understood that one of the main reasons for designing a ship along these lines is the owners' previous ships, the *Kungsholm* and *Gripsholm*, have proven very attractive to cruising passengers.[8]

From the standpoint of either of her two roles, *Stockholm*'s accommodation was of a remarkably high standard. The ship was intended to carry 1,350 passengers in three classes on Atlantic line service between New York and Göteborg. For cruising, the first- and tourist-class facilities were to be totally amalgamated and the third-class areas closed off entirely, reducing the passenger capacity to a mere 620. Among the

Stockholm: **First class cabin interior (probably a mockup) showing the sitting area with vanity unit at the ship's side.**

(Brostroms)

special provisions made for the ship's cruising role were her large open-air swimming pool and spacious decks. All cabins and public rooms to be used in cruise service were completely air conditioned. This, in itself, was noteworthy at a time when many liners designed exclusively for tropical services offered this comfort only in their first-class dining saloons and perhaps one or two other major public rooms.

Stockholm's accommodation was most notable for the 250 large, well appointed first- and tourist-class cabins which would be used in cruise service. Every one of these hotel-like rooms was equipped with full-size twin beds, spacious wardrobes and, in most cases, a separate sitting area. The majority of the en-suite bathrooms had full-size baths and twin washbasins. The overall layout followed sound shipbuilding practice, with the beds and baths all oriented fore and aft in the interest of comfort and safety, despite the use of anti-heeling tanks.

Perhaps the most unusual feature of the cabin arrangement was that virtually all rooms to be used for cruising were arranged either side of a single wide central hallway extending the full length of each deck. Of the bigger passenger ships, whose greater width makes such arrangements difficult, the Compagnie Générale Sudatlantique's *L'Atlantique* of 1931 was the only other example of such a plan being widely adopted. In both cases the designers achieved layouts with almost exclusively outer cabins, each having its own portholes or sidelights. As with the earlier French ship, *Stockholm*'s layout offered the apparent simplicity of a

***Stockholm*: Partial
accommodation plan
showing the axial layout of
cabins and public rooms.**

(Author)

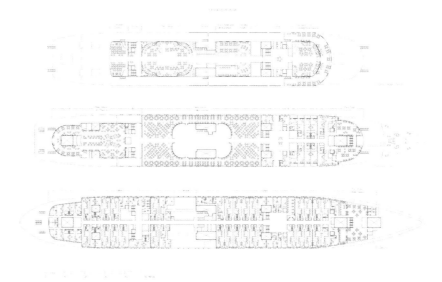

single passage, as in a hotel, rather than the more usual ship-board layout with twin parallel alleyways.

However, a closer look at the plan of either ship reveals that the layouts as a whole were, in reality, extremely complex and rather irregular. The divided funnel casings, stairways and hatch trunkways, which made the central passage possible in the first place, were in effect doubled in number along the two sides. The need to provide separate access routes for the crew as well as for multiple classes in line service, in addition to the inherent complexity of the cabin layouts themselves, served only to compound the complexity. With this in turn driving up the cost of building and maintaining such an arrangement, it seems hardly surprising that schemes of this type were not more widely used, in spite of their apparent functional simplicity and attractiveness.

The layout and outfitting of the public rooms above were equally striking. The promenade deck layout also featured a central passage, creating the same type of centreline circulation axis used in *Bremen*, *Europa*, *Normandie* and *Nieuw Amsterdam*. This type of layout, with its doubled funnel uptakes, lift shafts, stairways and other services, has always worked better in the larger public areas than on the cabin decks. The layout of the dining room, located immediately beneath the main lounge, was also noteworthy in that the space was roughly doughnut shaped, completely surrounding a central service core. The core also contained various concealed sliding partitions, which enabled the dining area to be divided into two or more spaces when on multiple-class Atlantic service, or when smaller private dining rooms might be needed.

The décor of *Stockholm*'s interiors was of strikingly modern Scandinavian design, inspired by the example of the Line's earlier ship, *Kungsholm*, where a similar design theme had received much public acclaim. *Stockholm* was to have been the crown jewel of Swedish American Line's fleet, and accordingly was to be a veritable showplace of contemporary Swedish art and craftsmanship. A number of works were especially commis-

sioned for her interiors. These included, for instance, a charming series of Mississippi riverboat murals produced in enamels, by the Swedish painter Kurt Jungstedt, for the Show Boat Restaurant. In view of the ship's ultimate fate, it was of dubious fortune that most of her artwork had not yet been installed when the first ship was destroyed by fire.

In their book *Damned by Destiny*, David Williams and Richard De Kerbrech commented in detail on *Stockholm*'s interiors:

> In a spirit of competition, most large liners had generally provided not only luxury in the First-Class accommodation, but also a magnificence of décor and standards vastly in excess of the experience and expectations of their passengers, invariably causing admiration but, sometimes criticism. The Orient Company had broken with this tradition in their *Orion* and *Orcades* in 1935 and 1937, but these were for the Australian run. The *Stockholm* provided luxury with greater simplicity and, had she gone into service on the North Atlantic, her accommodation would have produced a sensation. Her designers were, in fact, some years ahead of their time, since these trends only appeared on the route after the 2nd World War.[9]

Stockholm survived in her pristine glory probably just long enough, though, to leave a deep and lasting impression of her outstanding design and aesthetic beauty with her owners, builders and, perhaps most significantly, with Eric Christiansson himself.

Before Swedish American Line proceeded with further plans for large luxury passenger ships and cruising, a third *Stockholm* was built using the proceeds from her hapless predecessor's sale to the Italians. Designed also by Christiansson, this was a modest, single-funnelled combination of cargo and passenger vessel of 11,650 tons, intended to meet immediate post-war needs. Her modern two-class passenger accommodation was pleasant enough, but quite utilitarian by comparison. She emerged from the Götaverken yard in 1948 as the Line's only passenger ship to be built in Sweden, but preceded their remaining three liners in being powered by Swedish-made Götaverken diesel engines.

Christiansson's design work, as Swedish American Line's technical director, went on to span three full decades, from the preliminary planning of *Stockholm* in 1936 until the completion of the Line's last *Kungsholm* in 1966. Through the progressive development and refinement of his unique design approach, the last three ships achieved in full what had originally been expected of *Stockholm*. The later ships were not so much a sensation as were, for instance, the modern profiles of *Rotterdam* and *Canberra*. Instead, they expressed a sedate and traditionally-grounded progression towards the superlative styling, elegance and luxury of 1950s and 1960s cruising at its best.

The exterior appearance of Christiansson's four major passenger ships followed *Stockholm*'s basic form, retaining her clean well-proportioned hull and superstructure lines along with the perfect visual balance of their two funnels and masts. These elements created an image of classic beauty which became a veritable trademark of Swedish American Line's post-war fleet. While the Line remained almost alone in preferring twin funnels, the overall character of their ships was otherwise quite similar to their single-funnelled Norwegian rivals, *Oslofjord*, *Bergensfjord*, *Sagafjord* and *Vistafjord*.

As Christiansson himself explained, in an article published at the time of the second *Kungsholm*'s completion in 1953:

Although the time has passed when one of the most important demands on a new Atlantic liner was that she must be beautiful, there obviously still remains a desire to have a ship as attractive as technical and economical conditions will permit.

This latter point, in fact, contains the key to the conditions under which any ship is designed to-day and explains why it is outside the realm of practical possibilities to tell a naval architect to create a beautiful, a daring, or a majestic exterior and then have him design an interior to fit these lines. It is not even a matter of 'the designer' or of 'his' intentions. An infinite number of detail problems each affecting the central question of the ship's fitness for her purposes, must be considered and decisions made which will stand the test of efficiency. This means that the exterior must always be the product of a long series of careful considerations and compromises.

The 'single mind' idea, and purely aesthetic considerations, are no doubt fine when it comes to the design of items such as a woman's hat or dress, a flat-iron or a coffee pot, a painting or a vase. Then the individual artist may, simply, come into his own. But even when it comes to a chair, there has to be a compromise between technical functions and aesthetic design. Any essentially useful thing must, in the first place, be practical, then, if it is technically right – and a really practical thing will generally appeal functionally to the eye and so acquire attractiveness in appearance ... .

In designing large passenger liners, there are no convenient short-cuts or ways of changing things around once the product is completed. A flat-iron may perhaps be designed from the outside with an attractive, streamlined exterior and then the inside fittings added. A lady's hat that does not turn out exactly as the milliner had visualised it is easily altered. An unsuitable type of car will disappear from the market quickly, the cost of the experiment falling gently on a large number of consumers. Even an unattractive house can be made beautiful by screening trees. The ugly part is called the back of the house, and no one expects it to look as well as the front. But a ship cannot have a 'back'. Nor can she be covered by any protective disguise. Besides, she should, if possible, look as attractive to people 30 or 40 years from now as she does to the present generation. Complications are caused by the frequently incompatible differences in taste among the general public; not all gentlemen prefer blondes.

The second *Kungsholm* and *Gripsholm* were built during the 1950s by the Dutch de Schelde and Italian Ansaldo yards respectively. Each was designed to carry about 800 passengers

Stockholm: **First-class reading room, looking from port to starboard. The wide passage with the lighted display cases, centre right, was part of the centreline thoroughfare connecting the smoking room, veranda cafe, and lobby forward, with the main lounge and second veranda lounge aft.**

(E Mioni, neg 351-10; courtesy Brostroms)

Kungsholm (1953): **A longitudinal section of the ship showing the relationship of machinery location to the funnels.**

(Author)

in a two-class Atlantic service, or a slightly reduced number in single-class cruising. These ships differed from *Stockholm* in a number of details, but not in overall concept. For instance, as these were again smaller ships of about 23,000 tons, Christiansson reverted to the two-engine twin-screw arrangement of the earlier *Gripsholm* and *Kungsholm* pair. However, his retaining of *Stockholm's* exterior appearance was not only in preference of traditional styling aesthetics, but also a significant matter of technical planning, as described in the same article:

> It was considered desirable to place the engines as far aft as possible, partly to reserve for passenger staterooms, public rooms, and dining rooms the midship sections, the most valuable part of the ship. The original intention was, therefore, to place the machinery right aft. Certain difficulties made a modification of this policy necessary, and the engine rooms were moved somewhat forward but remained further aft than is usual.
>
> To avoid wasting too much valuable space by long ducts, exhaust pipes, stacks from boilers, etc, one funnel had to be placed approximately above the forward end of the main engine room. This position is so far astern that, for aesthetic reasons, the ship could not very well have only this one funnel, and another funnel was placed forward to balance her exterior – but also to take certain ventilation exhausts, reserve dynamo and batteries, etc, which would otherwise have called for a separate superstructure.
>
> The quarter-century old tradition in the matter of two funnels carrying the three golden S.A.L. – crowns on the blue discs, introduced by the M.S. *Gripsholm* and the old *Kungsholm* – was another reason why the Swedish American Line, in fact, welcomed the idea of two funnels on the new *Kungsholm*.

Among the technical refinements were a switch to fin stabilisers from the Frahm-type anti-heeling tanks in *Stockholm*. The P&O liners *Chusan* and *Himalaya*, completed in the late

1940s, were among the first merchant ships to adopt this type of stabiliser and to prove its success in passenger tonnage. Another development was the change from incandescent tungsten-filament lighting to extensive use of cold-cathode fluorescent tubes. Altogether *Kungsholm* had some 268 linear metres, or about 1.4 times the ship's total length, of fluorescent lighting throughout her Grand Hall, first-class lounge, first- and tourist-class dining rooms, as well as the cinema and various circulation areas.

In this regard, *Kungsholm* was also noteworthy as being a trendsetter in the move to alternating current (AC) auxiliary power, following the example of Messageries Maritimes triple-screw motorship *La Marseillaise* completed in 1949. While fluorescent lighting offered the advantage of drawing far less current and dissipating less heat, it would not work on direct current (DC), which had previously been standard for most ships. In this regard *Patria* and *Robert Ley* had stood as notable exceptions to the general rule on account of their diesel-electric propulsion. *Kungsholm's* auxiliary plant was designed to generate alternating power at 60Hz (cycles per second) for distribution aboard at 440V, 220V and 24V. The 220V supply, used for lighting and most other hotel passenger services aboard, was compatible with domestic electrical power ashore throughout much of Europe and Scandinavia. This was a consideration which would gain great importance as passengers of the 1950s would themselves start to bring things such as electric shavers, hairdryers, radios and tape recorders aboard ship for their own use.

The lower 24V supply was used mainly for the service call bells and other signalling applications. The higher 440V three-phase supply was used for larger equipment in the engine room and major auxiliary services including air conditioning. Here too, *Kungsholm* was notable as being the most completely air-conditioned ship then to have been built. This took in the entire passenger and crew accommodation, as well as a number of important working areas. Indeed, this was a significant concession to *Kungsholm's* cruising role, which would eventually become her full-time occupation.

The second *Gripsholm*, completed four years later in 1957, may, at first glance, have appeared to be a near-identical sister ship for *Kungsholm*. However, the new 23,214-ton ship brought forward a number of refinements both in her external appearance and interior design. The rake of her bow was more pronounced and her upper decks were extended farther aft than on the earlier vessel. With the extension of the superstructure the distances between the funnels and masts were likewise increased. Upon closer inspection, *Gripsholm* also presented a much smoother appearance, as her shell plating was butt welded rather than being lapped as on *Kungsholm*.

While the interior plans of the new *Kungsholm* and *Gripsholm* were basically similar to that of Christiansson's original *Stockholm* scheme, the later ships' accommodation was arranged around conventional centreline funnel casings. The main run of public rooms again occupied the full length of

Gripsholm (1957): Seen here in an early artist's rendering which showed two continuous sweeps of large windows around an apparently widely-bowed superstructure front.

(Gordon Turner collection)

the promenade or veranda deck, with the same sequence of observation lounge and quieter rooms forward, a large main lounge amidships, followed by a second lounge or smoking room aft with direct access to an open lido deck fully astern. However, the duplication of spaces such as the libraries and smoking rooms, designated forward and aft, rather than first and tourist, indicated the refinement of subtly providing a flexible suite of public spaces for both two-class Atlantic service and integrated cruising.

The promenade deck layouts of *Kungsholm* and *Gripsholm* showed a gradual progression towards integrating the enclosed promenade with the interior plan, rather then leaving it as an

Gripsholm (1957): As built, the same ship showed stiffer and more angular lines, giving her instead a greater impression of North Atlantic liner strength and stamina.

(Gordon Turner collection)

essentially outdoor veranda surrounding the public rooms. *Stockholm*'s classic liner-style veranda promenade was gradually moved into the air-conditioned interior verandas or galleries directly accessible from most of the public rooms as well as the deck lobbies. Christiansson's plan for *Gripsholm*, completed in 1957, carried this progression to its natural conclusion, with the main lounges being extended to the ship's full beam, having principal access via the deck perimeter.

Public room layouts of this type set the standard for the majority of purpose-built cruise ships which would follow in the late 1960s, and on through the 1970s. Similar arrangements were also featured in the design of neighbouring Norwegian America Line's ships which, apart from their own distinctive character, were functionally similar to Swedish American's passenger tonnage. *Sagafjord*, completed in 1966, and her much later sister ship *Vistafjord*, delivered nine years later, featured remarkably well-articulated veranda-deck plans with a wide diversity of functionality and excellent sense of orientation. These two Norwegian ships were also notable for the inclusion of cinema/theatres centre-forward on their veranda decks, a feature which Christiansson added to his last ship, the British-built 1966 *Kungsholm*.

Despite the concession to traditional centreline casings, the feature of all-outside passenger accommodation, as in the KdF examples, was fully achieved in both of Christiansson's 1950s ships. All cabins were arranged along the outboard sides of the two parallel passages, flanking the central line-up of funnel casings, stairways, lifts and other services. The resulting shortened depth of the cabins themselves from the sides of the hull, as opposed to *Stockholm*'s centre-passage arrangement, simplified the overall accommodation layout immensely.

All first-class cabins were rectangular, with their own bathrooms, entrance vestibules and wardrobe spaces at their inner sides. In *Gripsholm* the first-class cabins each had a passage of their own, parallel and immediately adjacent to the main hallway, allowing two or more cabins to be combined via this private secondary hall to form multi-room suites. It was an unusual idea which provided for better soundproofing than the interconnecting doors normally used in the rooms themselves. When cabins were not combined, the space could be used for storing cabin trunks or other luggage during a voyage.

For the tourist class and interchangeable accommodation of both ships, Christiansson reverted to a modified form of his *Stockholm* plan, which was in fact an inspired refinement of the original Bibby-cabin idea. Lacking the hull-side seating areas of their KdF and *Stockholm* prototypes, these were rooms of alternating upright and inverted L-shapes, where the boot of the L formed a sleeping alcove with side-by-side beds, and its stem served as either the access to a porthole in the ship's side or the cabin entrance, where private bathrooms for each pair of rooms were located inboard of the L. Unlike the original Bibby cabins, those rooms with the inner sleeping alcoves had a wide enough access to the ship's side to accommodate

Swedish America Line veranda deck plans showing the progression from the traditional enclosed-promenade layout of *Stockholm*, to the veranda plan of the 1953 *Kungsholm* and the air-conditioned full-beam interiors of the later *Kungsholm,* built in 1966.

(Author)

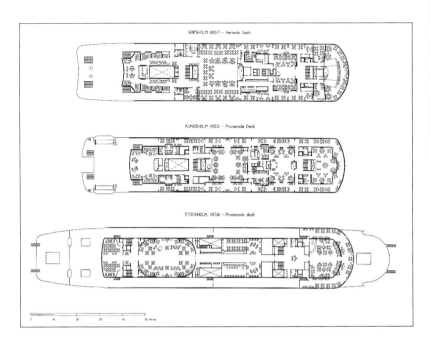

at least the writing table and a couple of easy chairs beneath the porthole.

Although stabilisers and other technological advances had become well developed, Christiansson continued to observe some of the finer points of traditional design. For instance, all beds, baths and stairways were oriented fore and aft, rather than side to side. This was a long-established rule of good design practice to ensure the greatest comfort and safety, particularly for the unseasoned traveller. A ship's tendencies to fore and aft pitching are, by the very nature of the hull's shape, less pronounced than is her likelihood to roll from side to side. Consequently, one is apt to be more comfortable sleeping while oriented in the direction of least movement. It is also safer to ascend or descend stairs which are likewise lined up. Basic fluid dynamics dictates that any shipboard bath be lined up fore and aft, as there is less likelihood of its contents being slopped over the bathroom floor during a North Atlantic storm.

A number of new ships in the 1950s were designed with a single file of deep and narrow cabins between a pair of parallel passages and the sides of the hull. In these circumstances it was generally more convenient to simply place the beds side by side against each room's outer wall, and to trust the stabiliser fins to suppress any excessive rolling. No longer were dining room tables fitted with moveable edges or fiddles, which could be raised to prevent spillage in rough seas. Circular staircases and, alas, sliding doors likewise gained wider acceptability aboard ship. What happens when the stabilisers malfunction or fail, or when the seas are too rough for them to be used at all, for fear of shearing off the fins altogether? It is, perhaps, largely thanks to other technological wonders of satellite weather forecasting and advanced radio communications that such perils can normally be foreseen and avoided altogether.

Among the first modern ships of the 1950s whose design fully exploited the benefits of fin stabilisers in this way were the United States-flag Moore McCormack Line *Argentina* and *Brasil* twins. These 15,000-ton turbine-powered liners were built to provide single-class accommodation for 553 passengers on line services to the eastern seaboard of South America. The very high standard of accommodation provided for these comparatively long voyages, which were sold as round-trip cruises as well as line services, gave them a definitely cruise-oriented character. Although, owing to their small passenger capacities, they proved to be uneconomical in their original form, their design did not go unnoticed.

Eric Christiansson himself finally yielded to the march of stabiliser and other technical progress in the design of his last and finest ship, the third *Kungsholm*. Here, the inherent complexities of earlier cabin layouts were to some extent foregone in favour of a simplified plan resembling that of the Moore McCormack ships. *Kungsholm* was delivered by John Brown and Co (Clydebank) Ltd in April 1966, representing the crowning achievement of Eric Christiansson's distinguished career. She was, without a doubt, the most worthy successor to his original *Stockholm*, and at 26,678 tons, she came closest to the earlier ship's size.

Kungsholm's ultra-luxurious accommodation provided for only 750 passengers on line service and a mere 450 for cruises. The ship's 304 passenger cabins represented a significant departure from Christiansson's earlier accommodation designs. These large and luxuriously-appointed rooms were essentially of two absolutely standard layouts. They consisted of single- and double-bed types as used when cruising. In line service the majority of these converted into two- and four-berth units by way of concealed upper pullman-type beds. Thanks to the superior sea-keeping characteristics already demonstrated by *Kungsholm's* older fleetmates, it was considered satisfactory for beds and baths to be oriented side to side as aboard *Argentina* and *Brasil*. The added degree of flexibility which this afforded to the interior design of the ship was used to good advantage.

The rooms themselves were arranged with their beds at the ship's side, a sitting alcove with two easy chairs, coffee table, writing desk and chair farther inboard. The bathroom and wardrobes were still innermost, where they also furnished a sound barrier against the passageway. Each pair of cabins was entered from a small vestibule, which itself could be closed off from the corridor, effectively combining two rooms to form a suite, again with superior privacy and soundproofing. Unlike the earlier *Kungsholm* and *Gripsholm*, the new ship did have a number of smaller inner cabins located along the centreline between the corridors on each deck. While this was probably a necessity dictated by the added space taken up by the outer rooms, it also extended the range of available accommodation, particularly for families, students and other passengers wanting to travel at minimum fare.

Kungsholm's range of public rooms was extended upwards to include the forward part of the boat deck. The principal veranda-deck spaces were of a similar layout as those on *Gripsholm*, except that the corresponding location of the earlier ship's forward observation lounge was occupied by a large multi-function auditorium. The forward boat-deck plan featured a suite of integrated spaces made up of a central multi-purpose lounge and bar, flanked by enclosed verandas to either side. Forward, large windows offered a commanding view ahead over the ship's bows. This area was equipped for buffet-style dining, thereby serving as an informal daytime restaurant readily accessible from the pool and lido areas farther aft on the same deck. It was also easily adaptable to evening use for dancing and entertainment.

The architectural design of *Kungsholm's* interiors was entrusted to top-rank professionals in the design fields. The noted Swedish industrial designer Count Sigvard Bernadotte was given charge of the forward suite of boat-deck rooms, which were among the ship's most elegant and sophisticated interiors. Co-ordination of the entire ship's design schemes was handled by the Göteborg architect Robert Tillberg, who himself designed the main lounge, forward cocktail bar and library. Tillberg had previously designed interiors for a number of smaller Scandinavian ferries. His much-admired work aboard *Kungsholm* was the starting point of his tremendous success in the later cruise-ship design field.

Christiansson realised that passengers probably still wanted some vestige of the old-style enclosed promenade, not within the entirely climate-controlled ship's interior. The last *Kungsholm* and *Gripsholm* each had an inner promenade on their boat decks, a feature unique to these two ships. The deck space at either side of the ship was divided lengthwise so that there was a glass-enclosed inner promenade within the superstructure itself, leaving only the outer perimeter beneath the lifeboats open. In *Kungsholm's* case the enclosed boat-deck promenades provided access to the lounges forward, the

swimming pool with its adjoining café amidships, and to the open lido aft.

As *Gripsholm* had done in 1957, *Kungsholm* laid claim to having been fitted with the largest and most powerful Götaverken diesel engines produced up to her time. In the latter ship's case these nine-cylinder machines were each of 555 tonnes in weight. The choice of these followed the Line's original philosophy of equipping their ships with uncomplicated and reliable machinery which could be easily maintained by the ship's own engineers during long periods away from the home port.

The appearance of these robustly built behemoths, with their cast-iron bedplates and between-cylinder supporting columns, earned them the nickname 'cathedral engines', for their unmistakeable resemblance to Gothic architecture. Each engine had a brake power of 18,790kW (25,200bhp) and shaft speed of up to 124rpm. The simple direct-drive arrangement of the ship's propellers and the ability of these engines to burn heavy- and low-grade fuel were considered most likely to ensure the ship's trouble-free operation in long-term service. With only eighteen cylinders in total, this two-engine installation also had the advantage of fewer moving parts than there would have been in multiple, medium-speed, geared diesel aggregates.

Kungsholm's exterior profile differed slightly from the earlier *Kungsholm* and *Gripsholm* in that the superstructure was one deck higher, and its lowest deck was extended farther forward beyond the bridge front. Also, the line of lifeboats was interrupted amidships by the glass-enclosed extension of the terraced swimming-pool lido between the funnels. The overall visual balance of the ship, along with the arrangement of her decks with its inner and outer boat-deck promenades, was otherwise most similar to *Gripsholm*.

In their third and second lives respectively, the 1957 *Gripsholm* and 1966 *Kingsholm* were still going strong in 1995, and doing so in the highly competitive America-based cruise market as *Regent Sea* and *Sea Princess* (recently renamed *Victoria*). Had the 1938 *Stockholm* survived the ravages of war, would she still be with us? Being of slightly earlier design thinking, with third class accommodation unused and unsuitable for cruising, she might have belonged more to the era of *Andes* and *Caronia*. She certainly would have prospered as well as them, if not better. With timely modernisation designed by Eric Christiansson, perhaps with some help from Robert Tillberg, she could very well still be going strong!

HAMBURG

Meanwhile, Germany's first large post–World War II passenger liner was taking shape as *Hamburg*. She would represent a remarkably up-to-date rendition of North German Lloyd's contemporary luxury and panache, combined with a dramatically updated KdF-style design rationale and elements of the Swedish American cruising approach. *Hamburg* was to take up service virtually at the end of the liner era. Delivered in 1969, she made her debut at about the time of *Queen Elizabeth 2*. This new European ship reflected a unique, yet characteristically no-nonsense German industrial-design approach.

The late building of a German ship such as *Hamburg* was the result of the rather unusual circumstances of post-war German commerce. North German Lloyd had restored their transatlantic service, with the pre-war *Gripsholm*, renamed *Berlin* in 1954, and *Pasteur*, extensively rebuilt as their fifth *Bremen* in 1959. Meanwhile, HAPAG acquired no tonnage of their own for Atlantic passenger service. Instead, the Hamburg-based line used the Home Lines' *Italia*, for which they were the German agents.

It was, in fact, largely thanks to the energetic Danish-born Home Lines agent, Axel Bitsch-Christiensen, that *Hamburg* was built. Bitsch-Christiensen, or ABC as he was known to many, was keen to revitalise passenger services to New York, with a new Hamburg-based ship. The venture was launched in 1958, with six million deutschmarks start-up capital from Home Lines' Nicos Varnicos Eugenedes and a promise of loan guarantees for 16.5 million marks from the city's mayor Max Brauer.

Named Deutsche Atlantik Linie (German Atlantic Line), this new entity immediately acquired the former Canadian Pacific liner *Empress of Scotland*, which was renamed *Hanseatic* and rebuilt to a similar standard as *Bremen*. With HAPAG's offices serving as its passenger agents, this venture finally restored the two-line German presence on the North Atlantic by mid-1958. Eight years later *Hanseatic* was gutted by fire at her New York pier, and was subsequently written off as a total loss. The planning which had been going on from the Line's beginnings, for the new ship that ABC ultimately wanted, took top priority, while interim tonnage and building capital were also sought. Much of the early design work had been done with Blohm & Voss, who were favoured to secure the building contract. However, with the need to secure loan

guarantees from the city of Hamburg, the order for a replacement ship, to bear the name *Hamburg*, was ultimately placed at home with Howaldtswerke Deutsche Werft AG in December 1966.[10]

In the meantime, an offer was made to the Zim Israel Navigation Company for outright purchase of their modern and elegant *Shalom*, for about three-quarters of her building cost. This was quickly accepted, and the three-year-old ship entered Hamburg Atlantic's service in early 1968. With their own new ship to be completed within the following year, Hamburg Atlantic Line would be on an equal basis with North German Lloyd as a two-ship operation. Negotiations were entered into between the two Lines for an integrated North Atlantic service. After failing to reach an agreement, the Hamburg company then withdrew completely from Atlantic line service, switching to full-time cruising under the new name German Atlantic Line.

The Line had chosen well in their purchase of *Shalom*, since the Israeli ship had been designed for extensive use in cruise service, catering to Western European and American clientele. The 24,950-ton *Hamburg* had likewise been ordered as an essentially dual-purpose ship, but with an increased emphasis on pleasure travel as the company switched to full-time cruising during her building.

Hamburg's structural design and engineering were for the most part fairly conventional, reflecting the German preference for things which are soundly proven and have a good record for long-term reliability. The hull and superstructure were constructed almost entirely of steel, with only a very small amount of aluminium and other light alloys being used. The economy in weight possible in a ship of this size was not considered worthwhile in view of the additional cost of light alloys and in the difficulty and expense involved for working such metals in shipbuilding applications.

By constructing the superstructure of steel it was possible to integrate it more closely with the stress and load-bearing

Hamburg: **Shown underway, her clean straight lines of form and the unusual design of her two-thirds-aft funnel can clearly be seen.**

(Skyfotos Ltd, neg CN 7999)

Hamburg: **Interior views of the spacious sitting rooms (left) and sleeping alcoves (below) of the deluxe suites.**

(HDW, Hamburg)

capabilities of the hull, forming the ship more as a unified structural entity. The concentration of stresses around the corners of windows and shell doors in the vessel's plating was reduced through rounded corners of large radii on all such openings. The number of access openings was restricted to a total of thirteen, twelve of which were square openings of a standard 2m x 2m size, located above the bulkhead level on A and B decks only. The remaining door was a smaller opening, located amidships on the starboard side on C deck, for crew access only. Likewise, through careful planning, the deck openings for stairwells, lift shafts and various casings were widely spaced along the ship's length in the interest of structural strength. For the most part, these were divided either side of the centreline as dictated by the accommodation layout.

Ten bulkheads divided the hull into eleven watertight compartments which were necessary to satisfy the international conventions and standards on damage control and safety of life at sea. The straight vertical line of four of these divisions was extended directly upward, without deviation, to the uppermost superstructure deck, affecting the fireproof division of the accommodation in a simple and absolutely straightforward manner.

As a modern ship *Hamburg* was, however, built around straight lines. The traditional touch of sheer lines turning the decks slightly upwards towards the bow and stern was gone. Beamwise, only the main deck and superstructure decks above were cambered with a modest downward turn towards the scuppers for drainage. All other surfaces were essentially flat. These lines of form were adopted in the interest of structural simplicity and added strength. The effect of sheer needed to satisfy the various safety regulations was met by a linear upward sloping of the hull decks from the superstructure front towards the bow.

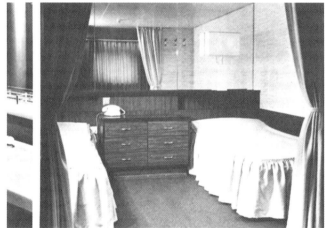

The ship's most striking visual feature, whether one liked it or not, was her unusual funnel. This was one of several innovative designs developed in the 1960s, in an effort to find the ultimate solution for discharging engine smuts and gases well clear of passenger decks. While only some distant variations of its form do perhaps exist in other ships, it has remained as unique to *Hamburg*'s appearance as have *France*'s wing-topped funnels or the latticed mortar-board-topped stacks of *Michelangelo* and *Raffaello*. Only the goalpost stacks of *Rotterdam*, *Canberra* and *Shalom*, along with James Gardner's original design masterpiece atop *Queen Elizabeth 2*, seem to have engendered any sort of following at all.

Hamburg's stack featured three narrow tubes extending up from a smaller than usual, conventional funnel body to a wide, flat, mortar-board-like plate above which the exhaust emissions would be discharged into the atmosphere. The principle of its operation was that the tubes would carry the gases high enough above the air slipstream around the main funnel body, created by the ship's motion, to discharge them into the relatively undisturbed air above. No doubt this funnel worked as well as any of the new types tried by various shipowners. The fact that its design was not repeated probably had more to do with factors such as the construction costs, or perhaps simply that nobody else liked the look of the thing enough to want to copy it.

The two-thirds aft location of *Hamburg*'s funnel coincided with the similar siting of her conventional steam turbine machinery. Following usual modern design practice, the funnel's massif was, to some degree, visually balanced by that of the main mast structure atop the navigating bridge. The overall lines of the superstructure were not unlike those of the 1966-built *Kungsholm*, except that its overall form had a more massive and rectilinear appearance. *Hamburg*'s top deck likewise featured a midships-located swimming pool, whose windscreened terraces extended outwards into the lifeboat line at either side. Full-height glazed windscreens were also used farther aft, inboard of the lifeboats, to provide shelter to the large sports deck located aft of the funnel. The original Blohm & Voss design, in fact, bore a stronger resemblance to *Kungsholm*, particularly with regard to the window arrangement of the upper superstructure decks.

The internal layout and design of *Hamburg*'s accommodation was derived from an exhaustive survey of the plans of all major post–World War II passenger ships. Identifiable with no one ship in particular, the amalgam of this research succeeded in producing a highly original approach, which stressed better-than-average spaciousness throughout the ship. *Hamburg* was intended to carry a maximum of 790 passengers in line service, with that number being reduced to 652 for cruises. As usual, the difference took into account the number of foldaway upper berths generally unused in cruise service.

The owners wanted all cabin accommodation concentrated throughout three decks only, using single centreline passages rather than a conventional parallel-corridor plan. This was thought to provide the simplest layout and most direct access to the three main stairways, located one in each fireproof zone. The use of the Main, A and B decks placed all passenger cabins above the watertight bulkheads, avoiding any additional complication in their layout.

Unlike the earlier *L'Atlantique* and *Stockholm* plans, which featured a single row of outer cabins at either side of their central passages, *Hamburg*'s far more practical layout featured a double row of rooms either side. The outer rows were accessed by short crosswise alleyways bypassing the inner accommodation. Consequently the ship had a relatively high proportion of inner rooms. All 316 cabins were of three virtually standard types, consisting of 188 outside cabins, 108 inner rooms and 20 deluxe suites, of which 8 were also inner units. *Hamburg* was probably about the only ship ever to be built with premium-grade accommodation lacking an outside exposure. The high degree of standardisation and the close relationship of the accommodation layout to the technical design of the ship herself reflected, to some degree, further development in a design rationale stressed in the KdF cruise ships thirty years earlier. Howaldtswerke's own experience in building *Robert Ley* may well have been of some direct influence, at least in the technical details of the scheme.

With the exception of the deluxe suites, which featured twin beds and separate settees, the standard cabins were fitted with full-size sofa beds which converted them to sitting rooms for daytime use. All passenger accommodation was equipped with the, by then *de rigueur*, luxuries of full en-suite bathrooms, controllable air conditioning, telephones, radio and television. The décor was, in reality, stark 1960s modern domestic, and yet functional and quite attractive.

Extremely well articulated as *Hamburg*'s cabin layout was, the inevitable irregularities of plan inherent in a centre-passage plan of its type still had to be contended with. There remained a few awkward dead-end secondary passages needed to circumnavigate the divided boiler uptakes, and various other services which simply could not be avoided. Whatever minor compromises had to be accepted in the layout of cabin accesses, they were more than amply compensated for by the axial arrangement of the public rooms and the highly rationalised planning of the ship's catering services.

The two decks above, comprising the main superstructure levels, were exclusively given over to the public rooms, of which there was a great range and variety. Their layout generally stressed the same centreline orientation used on the cabin decks and use of the uninterrupted forward part of the ship for the larger multi-function rooms. The 290-seat theatre was the only major public space to be located astern of the side-by-side funnel casings. The scheme made good sense as it provided the two main lounges, sited one above the other, with superb locations, offering panoramic views over the ship's bow and to either side. The layout was especially well articulated, with these spacious rooms being reached directly from the forward deck lobby and having immediate access to the smaller bars and lounges farther aft at either side of the ship on the promenade deck.

Centre-axis public-room plans of the type used aboard ships of the 1930s, such as *Bremen*, *Europa*, *Normandie*, *Nieuw Amsterdam* and *Stockholm*, were achieved largely thanks to the lack of upper-deck swimming pools. Centreline lounge-deck plans were possible in the 1960s examples of *Oceanic* and *Eugenio C*, only because the topside pools were two or more decks above. The pool tanks could be fitted in between the double cabin passages on the accommodation decks in between. Since *Hamburg* was planned with centreline passages on all decks and her lounges at the uppermost levels, the required swimming pool presented a problem. This was solved by way of a split-level arrangement making use of the additional height of both lounge decks. The pool tank was, in effect, placed at a level between the two principal levels so that neither was blocked by its presence.

A centrally located night club was cleverly worked into the tween deck, as it was called, surrounding the tank, giving

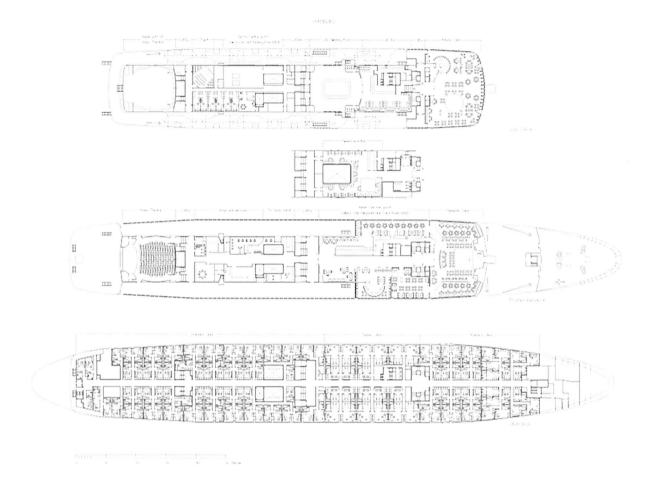

Hamburg: Partial accommodation plan, showing centreline access to cabins and public rooms. Note the partial deck surrounding the swimming pool tank.

(Author)

it a special sense of separation from the other public areas, being in effect on a deck of its own. This location also served the purpose of sound isolation making it highly suitable as a late-night social spot. Thus the promenade deck below had a full-length central circulating artery, while the pool and its adjacent lido bar above were raised slightly above lido-deck level, also with easy central access to the other spaces forward and aft.

Smaller special and fixed-function rooms such as the beauty salon, library, children's nursery, indoor sports centre and chapel were arranged on either side of a wide central passage, in the areas adjacent to the funnel casings and service core. These areas were flanked on the promenade deck by enclosed promenades and on the lido deck by the open expanse of the lifeboat deck at either side.

Planning of the dining rooms and catering facilities for a ship of Hamburg's unique design was a matter of special complexity. During the early planning stages, a midships dining-room location directly beneath the promenade-deck public rooms was considered. Similar in concept to the original

Stockholm plan, this would have consisted of a U-shaped arrangement of three separate rooms surrounding a central service core. One of the main advantages of this was that it offered the possibility of having large windows of the type then being planned for QE2's upper-deck restaurants.[11] Hamburg's one full-beam room, and its two smaller counterparts at either side, would have been serviced from a centrally located galley immediately below on A deck. However, the owners were dubious about this arrangement's effective blockage of fore-and-aft passenger circulation along the two uppermost cabin decks, since the Line had opted for a centre-axis layout throughout the ship to simplify their passengers' sense of orientation. This plan was dropped in favour of a lower-decks dining and catering location.

Compromises of this sort have been an inevitable by-product of any departure from traditional and time-proven layouts. In Stockholm's case, the large core area of her dough-nut-shaped dining room also contained the divided funnel casings, and still could not be made large enough to completely contain the needed catering facilities. Consequently, prime midships cabin space on the deck below was needed to augment the central core. The full-length centre passage was nonetheless still retained on that deck, but with the consequence that the service areas were divided to port and starboard. In order to keep Hamburg's plan as uncomplicated and straightforward as possible, the upper hull decks were allocated exclusively for passenger cabins. These were, in effect, 'sandwiched' between the recreational and sports facilities above, and the catering complex with its adjacent dining rooms below.

The dining rooms ended up being located lower down than usual, partly within the watertight subdivision of the ship's lower decks. Consequently, it was not possible to provide a single large room with the seating capacity normally required for a one-class cruise ship. The main galley and principal dining saloon were given as much space as the designated passenger capacity could afford, amidships on B deck, at the lowest cabin level. With only 294 seats this room had to be augmented by a second dining room and grill room below on C deck, having capacities of 192 and 128 seats respectively. The extent of these C-deck rooms and the galley space between them was restricted by the placement of the watertight bulkheads, a limitation which normally makes such spaces unsuitable for dining rooms or restaurants.

Despite its complexity of being spread over two decks, with the lower level encumbered by the watertight bulkheads, Hamburg's entire catering complex was remarkably well planned. During its planning, colour-coded workflow diagrams were made of the galley and service areas, to maintain the most effective workflow and the least possible interference of one activity or service with another. The main galley, which surrounded the forward stairway and lift core on B deck, was designed also to serve the forward concentration of public rooms on the upper decks. With separate crew lifts, dumb-waiters and a service stairway also worked into the same vertical core as the passenger stairways and lifts, an integrated and extremely effective service distribution pattern was achieved.

In addition to the passenger lounges, bars and pool lido area, this also serviced the officers' mess on the sun deck as well as an amalgamated crew mess two levels below on D deck. The service stairway and lift, along with the dumb-waiters and the individual deck pantries, were all positioned on the port side of the centreline corridors on the passenger decks. Opposite these, from B deck downwards, two stores lifts descended through four decks to the store rooms and cold lockers below. Additional lifts for exclusive crew use, with access to their accommodation and working areas only, were also arranged alongside the forward passenger lifts. The arrangement of these was such that their presence was virtually unnoticeable in the passenger areas.

The interior decoration of Hamburg was handled by Georg Manner, a noted German designer from Munich with considerable experience in passenger-ship work. Among his previous contracts, he had been responsible for interior design of the dining rooms, children's room and first-class public rooms in the rebuilding of Pasteur as North German Lloyd's Bremen.[12] His work on Hamburg's interiors went beyond the mere decoration of already-defined spaces, to having a degree of influence over the structural arrangement and layout, both of the public rooms and the cabins. He was also responsible for selection of all fabrics and soft furnishings, as well as the choice of artwork.

Hamburg was completed by her builders ahead of schedule, after a fitting out period of only thirteen months. She started her service career with two 36-day inaugural cruises from Hamburg to West and South Africa, before making a maiden crossing to New York as a positioning voyage prior to taking up cruising from the United States. Unfortunately, the ship's service to German Atlantic Line was shortlived owing to the Line's later financial difficulties. In 1973 Hanseatic was transferred to Home Lines, becoming their cruise ship Doric. Hamburg's capacity was increased by adding ten more deluxe suites in the enclosed promenade space. She took up the name Hanseatic, but, alas, was laid up in Hamburg later that year. Her idleness was interrupted briefly when she was used for the making of the British film Juggernaut with the false name of Britannic.

She was later mysteriously purchased by Japanese interests who, as it turned out, were acting as agents acquiring her for the Soviet Merchant Marine. In January 1974 she was registered in Odessa as Maksim Gorkij, becoming the flagship of the Black Sea Shipping Company. For several years she returned to North American waters during the summer cruising season, until finally being taken up in long-term charter by the German tour operator Neckermann for exclusive service in their own cruise market. At the time of writing that contract has lapsed and, following the upheaval of the Soviet Union's political dissolution, she is once again successfully cruising on the open international market.

During later years she was very lucky to have survived a near-sinking when she struck an iceberg during an Arctic cruise. It was only due to her high standard of compartmentation that she was saved.

1   David Williams & Richard de Kerbrech, Damned by Destiny, pp 113, 169.
2   Hans Georg Prager, Blohm & Voss, pp 166-7.
3   R Keine, Schiffbau, Schiffahrt und Hafenbau, 1939, p 209.
4   The Shipbuilder and Marine Engine Builder, December 1938, pp 649-51.
5   A C Hardy, History of Motorshipping, p 114.
6   Th Deeg, Schiffbau, Schiffahrt und Hafenbau, 1939, pp 223-4.
7   R Keine, Schiffbau, Schiffahrt und Hafenbau, 1939, p 216.
8   Marine Engineering and Shipping Review, June 1940, pp 59-60.
9   David Williams & Richard de Kerbrech, Damned by Destiny, caption for plates 88-90, pp 130-1.
10 Commodore C R Vernon Gibbs RN, The Western Ocean Passenger Lines and Liners, pp 137-8.
11 Hansa, No 6, 1969, p 391.
12 Hansa, No 33/34, 1959, p 1735

CHAPTER 4

THE SUPERLINERS

Special dual-function express liners

During the 1950s and 1960s, progressive new dual-purpose ships such as Rotterdam, Oriana, Canberra, France and Queen Elizabeth 2 were to be among the last built with provision for regular deep-sea passenger-liner services. The owners of this expensive new tonnage realised fully that their clientele had alternatives, either in the speed and comfort of long-range jet travel for point-to-point service, or in the diversity and sophistication of modern resorts and hotels ashore for recreational travel. Not yet ready to offer leisure voyages exclusively, the most progressive shipping Lines at least recognised that the cruise ship, rather than the liner, would set the standards of line service by sea for as long as such services could be expected to turn a profit. It had become most prudent to follow the examples of Swedish American Line and those others who were making primary provision for cruising. The newest tonnage of this era would sooner or later have to switch to cruising alone to continue making money. Where these ships differed was mainly in the scale, which designated them as superliners.

Although the individual factors of size, speed, luxury and comfort qualified a number of extraordinarily well-designed ships of the 1950s and 1960s as superliners, not all ultimately turned out to be well suited to cruising. For instance, *United States*, which was one of the earliest of the post–World War II super ships was solidly committed by design to the express North Atlantic run, with a traditional, hard and fast division of her accommodation into three classes. This in itself was a highly contentious issue between her principal designer, William Francis Gibbs, and United States Lines who would have preferred only two classes. After being withdrawn from North Atlantic service in 1969, *United States* languished in a state of steady decay whilst various schemes to reactivate her as a cruise ship for one reason or another vaporised.

Likewise, the design of *France* and the later Italian Line sister ships *Michelangelo* and *Raffaello* stressed a traditional, if not elitist, service in line operation, with at best only marginal consideration given to off-season cruise services. *France* was built in essentially the same philosophical mould as her great predecessor *Normandie*, herself the epitome of behemoth North Atlantic *grande luxe*. *France*'s owners themselves later realised that a smaller ship would have been more suited to the dual role into which *Queen Elizabeth 2* was cast. After only twelve years of operation *France* was laid up as being unprofitable, even for her elite North Atlantic service. Following five years of idleness, she was 'rescued' by Norwegian shipping interests, by whom she was greatly refitted and extensively 'Americanised' for cruising, as discussed later.

While *Michelangelo* and *Raffaello* would probably have been much better suited for cruising from the standpoint of size, their internal layouts were far too firmly committed to a rigid three-class Atlantic line service. The amalgamation of public rooms, the majority of which were arranged along each ship's promenade deck, presented no great difficulty.

Alas, it was the layout of the cabin decks below that created the real obstacle.

The cabins were deftly segregated fore and aft of a centrally-located cluster of catering facilities. Dining rooms for all three classes were arranged so that they were only accessible from the cabins and lounges of their own class. Below these, an aggregate of store rooms, garages for passengers' automobiles, engineers' accommodation and, farther down, the engine rooms themselves served in effect to carry this division right down to the keel. With the exception of one corridor on the main deck, it was impossible for passengers to get from one end of the ship to the other, on any level below the promenade deck. Whilst the internal layout of these ships was very sophisticated in its own right, major rebuilding would have been needed to adapt it for open-class cruising.

Difficulties of this type tended to create a far greater obstacle to conversion than the usual concerns about large amounts of cargo space or the need to downgrade machinery to suit the lower speeds, then generally considered desirable for cruising. Indeed, the curse of class barriers has damned many an otherwise suitable ship to early scrapping.

ROTTERDAM

No ship has made the transition from line service to cruising as effortlessly and more gracefully than has Holland America Line's magnificent *Rotterdam*. While her 38,650-ton size may not strictly qualify her as a behemoth superliner, certainly her ambassadorial status as the veritable flagship of the Netherlands would. She was completed by De Rotterdamsche Droogdok Mij NV in 1959, and entered transatlantic service as one of the last ships of her kind. Although her exterior lines and interior styling were contemporary, her expression of

Nieuw Amsterdam: **Representing an ideal of the classic liner, she is seen here against a backdrop of the Manhattan skyline, probably during the 1950s.**

(Holland America, New York, neg 11068)

modernity also carried with it a strong impression of timeless classicism, reflecting the line's long and deep-rooted tradition. The futuristic advance of twin goalpost stacks, situated side by side rather more astern than usual, was aesthetically set against the traditional appeal of the graceful curve of her sheer lines and visual balance of the superstructure against the hull's own impression of elegance, strength and stability.

The overall concept of *Rotterdam*'s design evolved largely through the unique character of Holland America's highly successful and much-loved *Nieuw Amsterdam* of 1938. The earlier ship was considered by many to be the ideal North Atlantic liner. At 36,287 tons, with a combined three-class passenger capacity of 1242, she was neither too large nor too overpopulated as to be awesome and overpowering, retaining instead an important sense of human scale and offering an easily-acquired familiarity of her layout. Rather than ornate period-revival, pseudo art-deco or stark modern, *Nieuw Amsterdam*'s interiors extolled the virtue of refined contemporary comfort, solid top-quality materials and exquisite craftsmanship. Her overall dimensions and draught were sufficient to ensure adequate stability and comfort in even the heaviest seas.

Like their Scandinavian counterparts, Holland America believed that the colossal additional cost of both building and operating vast liners in the *Normandie* and *Queen Mary* class could only be justified in cases where their speed allowed two liners to replace three. There would also have to be a consistently high year-round demand for the greater capacities of such tonnage to make it profitable. With a service speed of 21kts *Nieuw Amsterdam* was able to make the six-day crossing between Rotterdam and New York on an interval of one round trip every three weeks.[1] A suitable running mate was envisaged from the outset of her career in 1938. However, these plans inevitably had to be postponed until well after World War II's conclusion, with the building of such a ship finally announced in July 1952.

In planning *Rotterdam* as an improved and updated rendition of *Nieuw Amsterdam*, her design would incorporate much of the considerable progress in naval architecture, engineering and domestic styling made in passenger shipping over the twenty years since the older ship's delivery. In consideration of post-war lifestyles on both sides of the Atlantic, a fundamental change was made from three passenger classes to two, with an extraordinarily high number of interchangeable cabins. The way in which the ship should be divided between first class and tourist class was rethought, emphasising full amalgamation of both classes for cruising.

Holland America's designers wanted to avoid the inherent pitfalls of a vertical class segregation, with the passengers in one class or the other being restricted to either the forward or stern part of the ship. They also did not want to isolate first class to an island of space on the upper decks amidships, with the rather miserable consequence of tourist passengers having to trudge through long passages to get from one part of their disjointed spaces to another, fore and aft. This was resolved by

Rotterdam: The 'trick' main stairway seen from the first-class landing at lower promenade deck level. Access to the tourist Main Lounge, visible at the top of the stairs to the upper right, would have been closed off in Atlantic service.

(Author)

interleaving the division, with alternating decks allocated to first and tourist classes. In this way passengers in either class would have the impression of being given the run of the entire ship.[2] With the arrangement of lifeboats at two levels, as had been done in the case of *Pasteur*, both classes had their own boat decks and separate enclosed promenades, with the possibility of being able to walk fully around the superstructure.

The feat of quickly segregating or combining both classes was accomplished through the ingenious arrangement of *Rotterdam*'s midships-located 'trick' main stairway. The inspiration for this came to Willem de Monchy, then one of Holland America's directors, some years earlier when visiting the sixteenth-century Château de Chambord in France. The chateau's grand stairway was designed as two separate overlapping spirals, so that the royal family could circulate about the palace independently of other members of their court.

Aboard *Rotterdam* the effect of the double spiral was achieved with straight fore-and-aft interleaved stairways, in a scissors arrangement. Based on the principle of escalator installations in such places as department stores and airport terminals, this fixed-stair plan was adapted to achieve segregation by passenger class rather than by the up-and-down movement of the stairs themselves. Sliding panels, concealed within the staircase housing and vestibule walls, separated the two stairways, providing separate and discrete access to only those decks designated to each class. Rolling back the moveable partitions into their recesses quickly achieved the amalgamation of both classes for cruising. The effect of the 'trick' change was truly remarkable in its mystifying ability to effectively divide *Rotterdam* into two separate ships, one magically separated from the other. Later in her career, when engaged solely in cruising, this system of flexible access continued to be used, albeit less frequently, enabling various parts of the ship to be closed off when

needed for large private functions or various other special purposes.

The staircase itself was surrounded by spacious vestibules on each deck, flanked by rows of lifts to the port and starboard sides. The control system for the lifts allowed them likewise to be switched either to universally access all decks or to independently serve one class or the other. This entire complex of stairs and lifts was fully isolated from the rest of the ship within its own fireproof 'tower', with its own separate ventilation and air-conditioning system. Concealed fire doors on all decks allowed the stair tower to be sealed off from the source of any emergency, providing a safe means of escape.

A similar degree of flexibility and versatility was achieved in the design of *Rotterdam*'s cabins. Apart from the deluxe suites and state rooms amidships on the lower promenade deck, and other special-purpose rooms elsewhere, the majority of *Rotterdam*'s accommodation was virtually interchangeable between classes. The layout and outfitting of these was standardised around three basic plans. The width of the rooms at the ship's side coincided with the spacing of hull frames, with two standard measurements of 3.3m and 4.125m, minus the

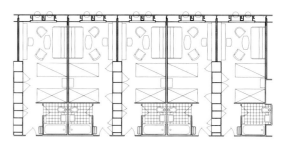

First Class cabins

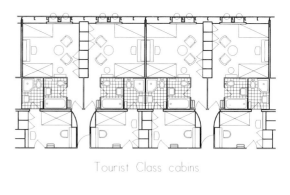

Tourist Class cabins

0   10 Metres

Rotterdam: Standard cabin plans, illustrating the larger First class outer rooms compared with the more compact Tourist plan, featuring inner and outer accomodation in a space of similar depth from the ship's side.

(Author)

thickness of the walls. These cabins were of two standard depths in from the ship's side.

The deeper rooms had direct access from the main passages, with their large individual bathrooms isolating them from any source of disturbance from corridor traffic. The shallower design normally provided for a row of inside cabins between them and the passage, with access to the outer rooms being by way of short passages to the side. Doors fitted at the main corridor ends of these secondary halls allowed the outer rooms to be effectively joined to form two-room suites when needed. Smaller bathrooms arranged side by side between the outer and inner rooms served each, and provided a sound barrier between them.

In most of the outer cabins, of either the larger or smaller type, the wardrobes were arranged so as to dampen sound between adjacent rooms at the ship's side. These were furnished with hotel-style twin beds oriented fore and aft, and a third pullman-type berth being fitted above the innermost bed in some rooms. The inner cabins were fitted with a single lower bed and upper pullman, allowing them to be sold for either single or double occupancy.

The great flexibility provided by *Rotterdam*'s use of a relatively small number of standard cabin designs was quite remarkable. Apart from the interchangeability between classes, it enabled the ship's designers to cope with various dimensional irregularities imposed by such things as the narrowing of the hull fore and aft, divided boiler uptake casings, and the width of the first-class dining room, itself an inside space flanked by cabins at either side.

Rotterdam's designers were also keen to pursue the modern trend towards location of the ship's machinery as far aft as possible. Their main reason for this was that it would allow the dining rooms to be lowered one deck deeper than had been possible aboard the midships-engined *Nieuw Amsterdam*, allowing an entire extra deck to be made available for passenger cabins. The dining rooms themselves would be arranged as aboard the earlier ship, with the first- and tourist-class rooms being directly fore and aft of the main stairway. Service would be from the deck below by way of escalators. This arrangement seems to have had great favour with Dutch shipowners, as, apart from *Nieuw Amsterdam*, it was also used aboard the Rotterdamsche Lloyd liner *Willem Ruys*, completed in 1947.

A conventional twin triple-expansion steam turbine aggregate was chosen for installation about two-thirds aft, with special consideration given to achieving a compact and lightweight installation. The turbine sets, which were of Parsons design and built under license to the British engine-makers by De Schelde, were of relatively compact design, with their overall shape well suited to locations in the narrowing afterbody of the ship's hull.[3] These units, along with the compact gearing of hardened high-loaded steel, also had the advantage of reduced mass, which was essential to the overall weight distribution of a passenger ship with engines aft. The machinery layout was otherwise fairly conventional, with the boiler room forward of the main engine space and the auxil-

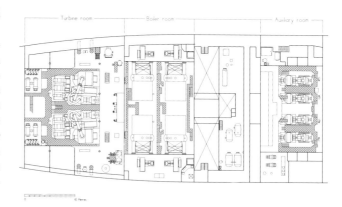

Rotterdam: **Machinery plan showing the turbine and boiler rooms at C deck and the auxiliary rooms at D deck.**

(Author)

iary machinery in a third compartment ahead of the boilers.

As *Rotterdam*'s plans took shape, various modern features of her design, particularly with regard to locating the machinery aft, would have a profound influence over her exterior appearance. Where Eric Christiansson was concerned about balancing the traditional profile of his *Kungsholm* and *Gripsholm* with a dummy forward funnel, concealing the reality of their two-thirds-aft diesel installations, *Rotterdam*'s designers dispensed with traditional funnels altogether. Instead they mounted a pair of tall slender side-by-side stacks atop the superstructure, directly above the twin boiler room uptake casings about two-thirds aft.

Mast-style stacks, or 'macks' as the Americans like to call them, gained popularity in the United States during the 1940s and 1950s. They appeared on Delta Line's *Del Mar*, *Del Norte* and *Del Sud* of 1946-7, as well as the three-ship *President Jackson*-class planned for delivery to American President Line in the early 1950s. This trio was taken over by the government

Rotterdam: **Engine room, the port-side triple-expansion turbine set, with its large low-pressure turbine seen in the foreground.**

(Author)

Rotterdam: The ship's functional modern goal-post funnels, with their connecting strut supporting the aft flagstaff.

(Author)

and completed for military service as troop ships. All six were designed by the prominent New York naval architect George G Sharp. At about the time of *Rotterdam*'s building, the Moore McCormack liners *Argentina* and *Brasil*, which were styled by the noted American industrial designer Raymond Loewy, also featured tall side-by-side macks.

In all of these examples the aft-located working macks were overshadowed by some sort of dummy funnel or funnel-like deckhouse as a stand-in, where a large ovoid steamer funnel traditionally ought to have been. One compelling reason for this was that owners still wanted their ships to prominently display their funnel colours or emblems, considered to be as important an identification as the houseflag. The culture of passenger shipping had long placed considerable emphasis on funnels as symbols of great power and strength. In the period immediately preceding World War I, the 'four stacker' became the ultimate symbol of liner might. During the 1930s the squat motor-ship style became popular as representing the expression of modernity, while *Normandie*'s wide, streamlined funnels became associated with speed. Later, the massive twin streamlined funnels of *United States* stood to symbolise that ship's decisive conquest of the North Atlantic Blue Riband.

In planning a prestigious ship as expensive to build and outfit as *Rotterdam*, any departure from the traditional expression of funnels was, in those days, both unexpected and a considerable gamble on her designer's part. However, Holland America were confident enough of their new flagship's chances of success to opt for a modern expression of profile, having no vestige of the conventional steamer funnel. *Rotterdam*'s tall and slender stacks, known in Dutch to her builders as 'rookkanalen' (smoke channels), were visually balanced against the radio mast and navigating bridge forward. This impression was further strengthened by the absence of traditional tall masts forward and aft of the superstructure. As a final

remnant of the age of sail, masts of this type had long outlived their real purpose in passenger ship design, with their secondary role of supporting cargo-handling derricks having also been replaced by more modern deck equipment. By the 1950s, most passenger ships were being built without conventional fore and aft masts. Their place was usually taken by the single radio mast with its array of necessary antennae and radar scanners, doubling also as the ship's main flagstaff. This last function was duplicated in *Rotterdam* by placing a strut beamwise between the two funnels, supporting a second mast to carry the houseflag.

The top-deck space between these two opposing masses was divided equidistant by a small deckhouse containing the lift and air-conditioning machinery for the main stair tower below it, as well as an additional first-class lounge and an open observation platform. This structure also served the purpose of displaying the Line's insignia and the ship's name. Aesthetically it set a focal point, below which the line of lifeboats was split between the sun and boat decks, and where the enclosed forward part of the upper promenade deck ended.

Whatever misgivings traditionalists of the day might have had about *Rotterdam*'s lack of conventional funnels, they were almost sure to have been soothed by her outstanding interior architecture and decoration. Although the new Holland America flagship's building was a predominantly private enterprise, with only a thirty per cent government-guaranteed loan from the National Bank for Reconstruction in Holland, she was effectively designed as a 'ship of state' to show the world the very best of modern Dutch design and craftsmanship. A team of the nation's most prominent architects, industrial designers, artists and artisans were carefully chosen for the all-important task of rendering the ship's interiors, everything that would be visible and experienced by her passengers, to the same superlative standards as her structural, engineering and technical design.

Altogether, the combined creative signature of more than two dozen Dutch architects, interior and industrial designers, various ateliers and individual artists was written throughout the interior design and decoration of *Rotterdam*'s twenty-one different public rooms, including the dining rooms and indoor pool. The greater part of the ship's architectural work was undertaken and co-ordinated by several principal designers, each responsible for various public areas. The linking element of the main stairtower, along with its various lobbies and vestibules, was handled by J A van Teinhoven of Amsterdam, whose domain also included the dining rooms and the first-class Ambassador Lounge. Apart from these principal areas and some of the first-class suites, the remaining cabins, passageways and all secondary stairways were designed by Holland America's own New Building Department.

The only perceivable difference between the first- and tourist-class public spaces aboard *Rotterdam* was that, although of essentially modern design, the first-class interiors tended to be more formal in character, whereas the design of the tourist-designated rooms on the promenade deck generally

Rotterdam: **The Ritz Carlton Room, looking towards the curved stairway and the forward wall, where a lacquered teak mural by Cuno van der Steen depicts an Aegean scene above the entrance and around the stairs.**

(Author)

displayed a more contemporary appearance through their larger areas and more extensive use of open planning. However, the tourist-class clubroom, with its ivory-coloured lighting fixtures, wood veneer panelling and colourful wall murals, was perhaps more reminiscent of the bygone liner era than any other room in the ship.

The first-class Ritz Carlton and Ambassador rooms were, without doubt, created as two of *Rotterdam*'s most luxurious interiors. As a combined ballroom and lounge, the Ritz Carlton, designed by Mutero NV Interieurarchitecten of Rotterdam, somewhat reflected the character of its earlier namesake aboard *Nieuw Amsterdam*. Like its 1930s prototype, the space was two decks high, with an upper gallery. However, in place of the twin stairways of the earlier ship's plan, *Rotterdam*'s balcony was accessed by a wide curved staircase on the room's port side only. This was one of several instances of asymmetrical layout used in the newer ship.

Van Teinhoven's treatment of the Ambassador Room was for its main use as a night club. The room was actually rectangular, although it was given a circular expression. Its side walls were bowed outwards into the enclosed promenade at either side, and there was a round hardwood dance floor with an inlaid compass rose at its centre. The bar and orchestra stand were arranged around the dance floor in two diagonally opposite quadrants, with the bar facing outwards to the starboard bow. There was a small, indirectly lit dome above the dance floor, surrounded by a panelled-wood canopy of larger diameter above the bar and orchestra stand, concealing the light fittings. The same dark panelling was also used for the bar and other fixtures.

This very functional and compact layout effectively segregated the room's varied activities, yet without losing its sense of intimacy. This was achieved largely as a result of the inher-

ently shortened lines of sight in curved spaces. The room's fine finishing and decoration added greatly to its sense of warmth and intimacy.

Among the upper promenade deck rooms, the smoking room, designed by Carel L W Wirtz, was notable both for its attractive panelling and its unique bi-directional settees. The ceiling and wall were covered with rectangular wood and leather blocks arranged in an irregularly alternating pattern. In typically 1950s style, the ceiling was sloped upwards towards the room's port and starboard sides in a shallow 'V' form. This theme was continued by the aft wall, where a similarly V-shaped partition of solid wood concealed the entrances to the Tropic Bar and Ritz Carlton vestibules at either side. This was cantilevered above the floor and topped off a little short of the ceiling, giving it the 'floating' effect so popular in that era. It added both a sense of depth and spaciousness to the room, which would normally be entered from the centre of its forward side.

The smoking room was flanked at either side by a shallow alcove of floor-to-ceiling windows. A row of wood-clad columns, tracing what would otherwise have been the room's outer walls, was arranged to support a line of swingback settees. The back rests were attached to the columns at each end on a pivot, allowing them to be swung inwards or outwards, facing either towards the sea beyond the windows or inwards to the centre of the lounge itself. A versatile space, intended for either daytime or evening use, the smoking room was particularly appealing after dark when its great expanse of windows would be concealed by full-width curtains, and its plush interior would glow under soft incandescent electric light.

One of the greatest triumphs of van Teinhoven's design work for *Rotterdam* was her magnificent dining rooms located five levels below, on B deck. The two main rooms were

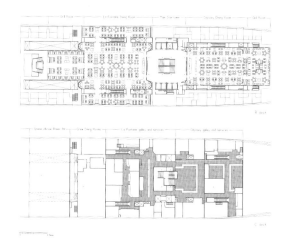

Rotterdam: **Partial plan of B and C decks, illustrating the arrangement of the dining rooms in relationship to the main stair tower and the services below.**

(Author)

located forward and aft of the main stairway, coinciding with the division of the ship for Atlantic service so that the, then-divided, staircases would deposit first- and tourist-class passengers conveniently in front of the Odyssey and La Fontaine dining rooms respectively. In cruising mode, the two rooms would be equally accessible to all, with, as it has turned out, the designation being for the preference of either smoking or non-smoking clientele.

Both were essentially designed as inside rooms, contained between narrow casings housing the service escalators and lifts, accessing the galley complex below. However, the tourist class also had two outer anterooms between these casings and the ship's sides. These were intended for use in line service, when passenger capacity was increased by using the pullman upper berths not normally sold for cruises. Whilst it was not uncommon for the better liners to offer a surcharged grill room alternative in first class, both of *Rotterdam*'s main dining rooms featured en-suite grill rooms.

Rotterdam's dining rooms were of near-identical interior design. Their high, flat ceilings were decorated with Delft porcelain half spheres and four-pointed stars, arranged in a regular pattern on a black background. These were floodlit by upward-facing light fittings in the walls surrounding the domes, with the reflected light being a key source of each room's illumination. Recessed ceiling fittings provided additional light in the peripheral areas of each room, surrounding the domes. These areas were larger in the tourist dining room, where a wider spacing of the service casings provided for a greater seating capacity.

The walls at B-deck level in both rooms were decorated with friezes of rosewood panelling above the table-top level. These were inlaid with bas-relief porcelain sculptures depicting scenes from Homer's *Odyssey* and from the fables of La Fontaine in the respective rooms. The scenes were separated by sections of recessed mirror tile recessed into the rosewood facia. These had the effect of providing an added sense of depth and brilliance to the entire work. The figures themselves were created by Nico Nagler and made by De Porceleyne Fles of Delft, who also furnished tiles for the indoor swimming pool and decorative elements for the theatre.

Rotterdam departed from the Port of Rotterdam's Wilhelminakade terminal on Thursday, 3 September 1959 on her first voyage to New York, via Le Havre and Southampton. This magnificent new Holland-America flagship not only represented the epitome of modern design, but also symbolised the remarkable re-emergence of the Netherlands as a whole, and especially the city of Rotterdam, after the brutal devastation wrought by World War II. *Rotterdam*'s maiden voyage also coincided with the 350th anniversary of Henry Hudson's first arrival at present-day Staten Island aboard his discovery ship *Halve Maan* in 1609, and the establishment of Nieuw Amsterdam, the first Dutch community in the New World. By coincidence, *Rotterdam* passed the same point for the first time exactly 350 years later to the day.

The new ship quickly made her debut in the cruise business, with her first such voyage being a 49-day circumnavigation of South America, departing from New York on 11 December, with calls at sixteen ports. This was followed immediately by the first of *Rotterdam*'s famed world cruises, a 75-day odyssey, visiting eighteen ports on four continents, before commencing her summer North Atlantic season in April 1960. By the close of the 1960s, *Rotterdam*'s summer crossings were replaced by weekly cruises from New York, first to Nassau, and later to Bermuda. With fares as low as $295, these gave a great many Americans of average means the opportunity to experience the luxury and superb service offered by one of the world's truly great modern liners. The winter months were spent in longer Caribbean cruises and the annual round-the-world cruises, which soon became the highlight of *Rotterdam*'s career. These were curtailed for a few seasons in the late 1980s, but were subsequently resumed after Holland-America was taken over as a subsidiary of Carnival Cruises, a powerful corporate entity in the cruise business born some twelve years after *Rotterdam* herself.

The sands of time drifted gently, and with great kindness, over *Rotterdam*'s career and over her emergence into a full-time cruising role. Great changes occurred in her operation which were essential to her survival. Her registry was changed to The Netherlands Antilles, and she was staffed at lower cost by Indonesian personnel from the former Dutch East Indies colony. Working under the command of Dutch officers in the ship's hotel, deck and engine departments, these people were especially trained by Holland America at a facility set up in the Orient. Despite the change in corporate ownership, Holland America remains as a fairly autonomous unit under Carnival management.

The ship herself was functionally modernised to keep pace with the times, yet these alterations, for the greater part, left the beauty of her original design virtually unchanged. The original good taste of *Rotterdam*'s design and decoration and the excellent quality of her finishing and craftsmanship, stood the test of time remarkably well.

Perhaps the reason *Rotterdam* succeeded so well as a cruise ship was through her designers' ability to contemporise the classic *grande luxe* liner atmosphere. This took into account changing passenger tastes and lifestyles of the times, yet without compromising the special sense of occasion that being aboard a truly great ocean liner affords the traveller. The use of rich and traditional materials, and sense of spaciousness accorded to the public spaces was combined with superbly livable modernity and functionality throughout the uniformly attractive private accommodation. The modern versatility and luxury character of *Gripsholm*, *Kungsholm* and other dual-role ships of the 1950s were, in *Rotterdam*'s case, given the larger scale of the elite North Atlantic liners. *Rotterdam*, in essence, brought cruising of a modern style into line with the general public's traditional perception of the great ocean liner they had probably held since childhood. For a substantial part of her cruising career *Rotterdam* fitted the superliner role as the world's fifth largest ship, after *France*, *QE2*, *Canberra* and *Oriana*.

Oriana and *Canberra*

The design of *Oriana* and *Canberra* evolved out of circumstances as different from those of *Rotterdam*'s conception as were the routes they would serve. Long before the planning of these ships was started, P&O and Orient Lines were already looking to the Pacific Rim for new trading opportunities. With the end of the Raj, and the granting of independence to India, Pakistan and Ceylon (Sri Lanka), the roles of both Lines in providing necessary services for government officials, troops and mails moving to and from the motherland was irrevocably changed. While essential services farther afield to the Far East, Australia and New Zealand remained intact, fed largely with a consistent diet of assisted passages for those emigrating to Australia, the trading positions of these Lines were, however, further jeopardised by new and unfamiliar competition.

Rivals emerged not only from the stratosphere and a developing pattern of long-haul international jet air routes, but also at sea level from various neophyte Lines which were conceived into the immediate post-World War II era, with its vast migrations of British and European peoples to all parts of the globe. These newcomers included Home Lines, Sitmar, Chandris and Costa. Later came the added challenge of the Soviet Union's huge passenger fleet. Resourcefulness and flexibility would have to be the way of the future for the long-established lines such as P&O and Orient.

Increased Australian trade with Japan, North America, Indonesia and China helped form the basis of new Pacific routes opened up by P&O and Orient during the early 1950s. Apart from trade and commerce, the Pacific was seen as a vast untapped reservoir of tourism and leisure travel. In addition to the cultural diversity of those nations surrounding the Pacific, there were the veritable tropical paradises Hawaii, Fiji and Tahiti. New services could be built up, not only on the Australian- and New Zealand-based markets, but also on the affluent populations of the United States and Canada, whose western ports also lay on the Pacific Rim.[4]

By the mid 1950s both Lines realised that the type of ships needed for so great a diversity of services, over such vast distances, would have to be considerably faster, and thus substantially larger than the 22.5kt 28,000-ton liners of that era. The most logical increment in speed was to 27kts, which would work out with existing routings, reducing the round-voyage time from England to Australia and New Zealand by a full two weeks.[5] The higher speed would also give the proposed new tonnage the range and flexibility to undertake extensive cruises in the Pacific, within a reasonably short time-span of two to three weeks. This would allow, for instance, a cruise from Sydney and Auckland to Honolulu and back to be completed in three weeks, or a one-way voyage from the same ports to Vancouver or San Francisco, with a stop in Hawaii, in about two weeks.

Research carried out on Orient Line's behalf by Vickers Armstrong showed that the minimum-sized ship capable of running economically at this speed would be of about 40,000 tons. The overall vital statistics of this theoretical ship are shown as follows, in comparison with those of *Oriana* and *Canberra* as actually built.

	Preliminary design	*Oriana*	*Canberra*
Length oa	245.05m	245.05m	249.93m
Length bp	225.55m	225.55m	225.55m
Beam moulded	29.57m	29.57m	31.09m
Draught	9.63m	9.63m	9.91m
Service speed	27.00kts	27.50kts	27.50kts
Trial speed	29.75kts	30.64kts	29.27kts
Maximum power	59,648.00kW	59,680.00kW	63,410.00kW
GRT	40,000.0	41,923.0	44,807.0

The tremendous expense of building and operating such large and fast ships was rationalised through the long-term benefits of their increased passenger capacities and reduced voyage times. This in turn would result in fewer ships of their class being needed to maintain the anticipated annual passenger load and requisite numbers of departures each year, over a projected lifespan of twenty or more years. The added costs of fuelling the high-powered machinery needed to deliver the additional five to six knots would be offset by the reduced overall staffing levels of a two-ship operation. Other economies of scale would also be possible with two larger ships, as opposed to the three 28,000 tonners of the *Oronsay* or *Iberia* class that each Line would have otherwise needed to independently maintain their existing service level. These economies were increased twofold by the decision of P&O and Orient Lines to operate a single joint service with one new superliner of each, rather than to continue running as competitors.

Both ships were ordered independently by their respective owners, with Orient's contract for *Oriana* being placed with

Oriana: Seen here shortly after her completion in late 1960, still in Orient Line's livery with its distinctive corn coloured hull.

(National Maritime Museum, Greenwich, neg D4410)

Vickers Armstrong of Barrow-in-Furness, while P&O's business was taken up with Harland & Wolff at Queen's Island, Belfast. Although the two companies had agreed to build new ships of the same size, capacity and overall performance, the detailed planning, structural design, engineering, interior architecture and outfitting of each ship were executed quite independently of each other. The research figures given by Vickers Armstrong were closely followed with *Oriana*, as completed by the yard three years later. However, those of *Canberra* differed somewhat in consequence of the radically dissimilar approach taken by her designers and builders.

In general terms, the planning of such large, fast and flexible ships for the world's longest line service resulted in some rethinking of the whole concept of the traditional tropical liner. Unlike virtually all previous tonnage serving these routes, cargo would not be carried at all, with the exception of a small amount of 'special' freight. The tight scheduling needed to keep these fast new ships moving profitably would not allow the time needed for handling commercial cargoes along the way. Passengers, lots of them, would have to be the sole source of revenue.

The increased speed, and the added height of the larger ships that would achieve it, called for the planning of open decks, which would be protected from the high-velocity airflows created by the ship's motion and likely to be influenced by prevailing winds. With the help of extensive wind-tunnel testing, this was handled largely by way of full-height glass windscreens along the uppermost decks and refinements in the form of some parts of the superstructure. In *Oriana*'s case the main promenade, located high above the waterline, was fully glass enclosed, more like those of North Atlantic liners or dual-purpose ship such as *Caronia*, *Kungsholm* and *Oslofjord*.

Since cruising was envisaged as an important secondary role, easy amalgamation of first and tourist classes had to be taken into account. This also made a much higher standard of tourist-class cabin accommodation necessary than was to be found in ships even as new as *Oronsay* and *Iberia*, although what was finally achieved still fell short of *Gripsholm* or *Rotterdam*'s standards. Accommodation in *Oriana* and *Canberra* still had to be compact enough to satisfy the need for a high-capacity emigrant trade, and yet sufficiently attractive to appeal to cruise passengers, who would also be occupying the rooms for several weeks.

Accommodation and services would, in effect, have to match those of the latest tonnage on other routes likewise planned with a view to cruising. *Oriana*, *Windsor Castle* and *Leonardo da Vinci*, built for the Australian, South African and North Atlantic trades respectively, turned out to be the three most outstanding new passenger ships of 1960. In an article published late that year, C M Squarey drew attention to this trio's functional universality:

> For instance suppose that the *Oriana* were put on the Southampton – New York run, the *Windsor Castle* on the Australian service and *Leonardo da Vinci* on the

Canberra: **This photograph was taken early in her career before some of her original aluminium lifeboats were replaced with excursion launches.**

(Skyfotos Ltd, neg C1066)

> South African route, is it likely that they would be accepted by the regular passengers on those trades as having the required amenities and in general find favour outside their normal sphere of operation? … All of them are air-conditioned so that trading in tropical waters presents no difficulties. In my view their public rooms and their cabins are perfectly acceptable for any trade.[6]

Certainly universality was evolving out of the higher standards in accommodation and service being demanded on all routes. The expected cruise clientele of the 1960s would settle for nothing short of air conditioning throughout the entire ship. This in itself would do away with the need for deep-shade decks, which had once asserted the individuality of *Andes* and various other ships designed for tropical services. The space could instead be used for revenue-earning cabins, bringing a further expression of the more enclosed North Atlantic look of perhaps *Caronia* or *Gripsholm* to the tropics. Certainly the possibilities of also designing full-width public rooms would warrant consideration in the need to cater for a more diverse and sophisticated passenger lifestyle, both in line service and on cruises. Fully equipped cinemas and other special rooms for various uses, along with a wider range of lounges and bars would have be added to the obligatory Main Lounge, Ballroom and Smoking Room of the 1920s *Viceroy of India* and early 1930s *Straths* examples. Strangely, the elaborate indoor swimming pools of these early ships were not repeated in later P&O liner tonnage.

Oriana's design evolved through a close collaboration between Orient Line's chief naval architect, Charles F Morris, and the builders' design department. This work brought about important technical advances in the large-scale use of aluminium for the superstructure and various internal elements, as well as overall drive for weight economy throughout the whole ship's structure and outfitting. She was also to be the

Canberra: **Machinery plan, showing the tanker-style propulsion arrangement with the boilers fully aft above the propeller shafts.**

(Author)

CANBERRA

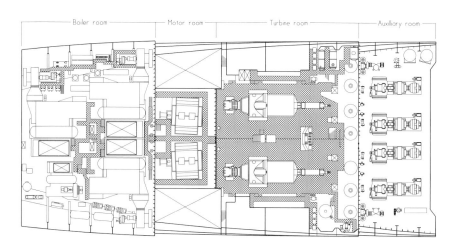

culminating *oeuvre* in Morris's own distinguished career, during which he had supervised the design of a great many Orient Line ships. As *Oriana* was to be a radical departure from anything he had designed before, he had greater latitude to apply his vast experience to numerous refinements of the unique nature and scale of this project.

These dealt with such matters as the superstructure and funnel form, location of mooring decks, machinery layout and lifesaving equipment, all devised to improve the ship's operation, but not necessarily her looks. One point of view concerning her somewhat controversial appearance was given by C M Squarey:

> … the Orient Line have always been adventurous in their design of ships and have never tended to pander to popular appeal, believing that functional efficiency in all departments is more important than mere looks. Likely enough her external appearance will startle some and may even shock some, but at least most will concede that she is in her own right very definitely an outstanding personality.[7]

Meanwhile, working with Harland & Wolff's technical department, P&O's young and energetic naval architect, John West, was working out the details of building a twin-screw ship of similar size, yet with her machinery as far aft as possible. The basic premise underlying this approach was to apply the tanker-design principle of giving the ship's special cargo, ie, the passengers, pride of place aboard, with as much of the machinery and other working parts moved as far aft and out of the way as possible. This would give those responsible for the accommodation design, the freedom to design a veritable floating hotel as a single integral block of space unbroken by the intrusion of funnel and boiler uptakes, hold trunkways

and so on. This too held the promise of creating a ship of great personality and public appeal.

The design approach taken with both ships was similar, in that each was soundly based in well-grounded and proven precedent. Charles Morris and his team had drawn heavily from a vast wealth of relevant Orient Line passenger shipping experience, backed up with the expertise on modern lightweight building and high-performance propulsion provided by Vickers Armstrong's technical department. John West, his colleagues at P&O and the Harland & Wolff people looked as well to developments in other aspects of the shipping world for inspiration in defining their approach. Apart from West's own experience with the design of aft-engined tankers for P&O's Trident subsidiary, the small French-built short-sea passenger ship *El Djezair* had introduced a practical use of aft-positioned machinery to passenger shipping in 1952.

Harland & Wolff's own experience in building the larger Shaw Savill *Southern Cross* a few years later had done much to assert confidence in the same idea in British shipping circles. The special interest in these examples lay in their use of a truly tanker-style machinery arrangement, with the boilers located aft of the turbines in the space above the propeller shafts. This offered a potentially greater extent of uninterrupted passenger space than, for instance, the more conventionally arranged aft engine installations of *Rotterdam* or the Moore McCormack *Argentina* and *Brasil*. Despite the attractive alternative design of modern motor-ships such as *Kungsholm*, diesel propulsion was ruled out as it still remained to be tried in the higher power and speed range. The Dutch *Oranje* was then still the world's fastest motorship.

Canberra's designers were also keenly interested in the latest developments in containerisation of ships' cargoes, for ideas on how to free their brainchild's passenger spaces of the further incumbrances of baggage and stores handling. They (and for that matter Orient Line's people too) also took a close look at new baggage-handling systems then being tried by the airlines, in anticipation of the jumbo jet age. Both shipping Lines faced the potential nightmare of having to handle a thousand pieces of passenger baggage on and off their new ships quickly, during greatly shortened stays in port. In a contemporary rendition of Orient Line's progressive accommodation design approach of *Orion's* interiors in the 1930s, P&O sought likewise to make *Canberra's* as modern and appropriate to 1960s lifestyles as possible.

While the size and performance of both *Oriana* and *Canberra* demanded specially-designed slender and refined hull forms, that of *Canberra* had also to take into account the concentration of about 500 tons of machinery packed into its afterbody. This had to be balanced by the opposing force of added buoyancy forward, despite the need for a narrow V-shaped waterline form to minimise the effects of surface turbulence at speeds of up to 27kts. Also to be considered was that in a passenger ship the machinery represents the major concentration of weight, whereas a tanker's liquid cargo, filling most of the hull interior, distributes a far greater mass evenly along virtually the entire length of the keel. With the relatively light weight of accommodation, and some 2,000 passengers with their belongings, amidships, *Canberra's* arrangement would counterbalance the engine mass against only a small variable volume of fuel, ballast, stores and special cargoes fully forward. With the two principal structural loads distributed so far apart, the ship as a whole would have to endure the additional bending and twisting stresses inflicted by the seas bearing upon a body with widely divided weight distribution.

These circumstances precluded use of the lightweight structural approach adopted in *Oriana's* building. *Canberra* stressed a more traditional, and far heavier, physical construction. The hull was built as a discrete entity, supporting the superstructure atop a strength deck rather than relying on the upperworks as an integral strengthening element of the ship as a whole, as was done with *Oriana*. For whatever *Canberra* may have lacked in this sort of weight economy and structural high-tech, she more than made up for in her sound construction, functionality and outstanding aesthetic appearance.

Canberra's design, with exhaust uptakes aft, took the *Rotterdam*-type profile a step further, by also doing away with the midships deck house appendage displaying the house colours traditionally worn around the girth of a dominant steam-packet funnel. The open top-deck spaces amidships, which were three decks above her fully nested boats, were opened up to the full width of the ship and to the skies above. Forward, this vast ocean-going playground was given protection from the wrath of the elements by the bridge housing, with its built-in wind-deflecting fairings.

Another major difference of philosophy and approach was the wider involvement of architectural design at a much earlier stage in *Canberra's* planning. Having taken a far greater gamble in adopting John West's tanker-style engines aft approach, P&O were acutely aware of the special need to cre-

Canberra: **The tall tanker-style stacks fully aft.**

(Author)

ate a sense of public appeal. The same feature in *El Djezair* and *Southern Cross* was not presented externally with any sense of flare or panache. Visually, both ships had nothing more to recommend them in the eyes of the general public than the, rather more astern than usual, positions of their otherwise rather ordinary funnels.

What P&O wanted their co-ordinating architect, Sir Hugh Casson, to do, in addition to his interior work, was to give *Canberra's* exterior a sense of styling which would, in a marketing sense, promote the idea of an aft-engined marvel of modernity in a way which would fire the imagination of the average traveller. Had Orient Line brought in Brian O'Rorke or their newly appointed professionals, Misha Black's Design Research Unit, at the same stage and with the same authority, *Oriana* could well have ended up with a less controversial external appearance.

The designer influence in *Canberra's* outward appearance helped to define the crisp and clean-lined form of her superstructure. She was thus given an aerodynamically curved forestructure and fully nested lifeboats, which encased all of the ship's total design elements like the shell of a Mercedes-Benz or Ferrari. *Canberra* was thus outwardly shown as belonging to the 1960s – the era of the space race, freedom of expression and the sexual revolution – with her very shape expressing the confidence, optimism and expressiveness of the times.

Canberra: **Promenade deck, beneath the nested lifeboats, surrounds the public rooms, to which it served as a veranda for outdoor employment.**

(Author)

Within the smooth outer shell of her hull and superstructure *Canberra* held numerous innovations. As in *Oriana*, the overall accommodation layout centred around a vertical division between first and tourist classes directly amidships, rather than the traditional British scheme of relegating tourist class to the lower decks. Although lacking the appeal for either class of *Rotterdam*'s interleaved approach, the vertical division also made the amalgamation of all accommodation and facilities for cruising a simple matter of merely opening a few doors, as is done to connect the adjacent coaches of a train. The only drawback of this arrangement was that in-line service passengers of either class had access to only one or other end of the ship and lacked the use of a full walk-around promenade.

The lower position of *Canberra*'s nested lifeboats was exploited to full advantage by locating the main suite of public rooms at boat-deck level. This, in effect, put the main lounges and bars at the vertical centre of the hotel block, with cabins on the two levels above and below. Conversely, *Oriana*'s designers retained the more conventional approach of locating her public rooms on the uppermost decks, two and three flights up from the promenade, beneath her similarly arranged, though semi-nested, lifeboats. While the *Canberra* approach extolled the advantage of integrating the lifeboat space as a walk-around open promenade surrounding the epicentre of social activity, *Oriana*'s plan offered the potential of making the ship's entire beam available for her lounges and bars. However, with the exception of the full-beam Ballroom and Monkey Bar lounge, traditional promenades were retained. In consideration of *Oriana*'s height and speed, her promenades were glass enclosed, though not integrated into the interior architectural scheme as was done three years earlier in *Gripsholm*.

While the interior spaces of *Canberra* were, by virtue of the machinery being aft, opened up and freed of obstructions

such as boiler and hatch casings, the necessary stairways, lift shafts and other services remained lined up along the ship's centreline. This was no doubt done with regard to the special considerations of structural strength bearing on the ship's weight distribution. There is a basic naval architectural axiom that deck openings should be kept as small, and as far from the ship's sides, as possible to maintain the greatest structural strength.

Despite the attractiveness of the *Normandie*, *Nieuw Amsterdam* or *Stockholm* divided-access layouts, these were achieved through at least a theoretical compromise of structural integrity, particularly as far as the effectiveness of the strength deck is concerned. Although *Canberra*'s interior plan may have appeared to be somewhat traditional, compared with these axial examples or with the asymmetrical public-room layouts of her 1959 contemporaries *Argentina* and *Brasil*, it was nonetheless simple and well articulated, as in the examples of *Cap Arcona*, *Wilhelm Gustloff* and *Robert Ley*.

The design of *Canberra*'s cabins showed great resourcefulness and ingenuity in their extensive use of two ideas originally devised in the United States by George G Sharp. The first of these was the 'court' cabin, which Sharp originally patented in 1927, as a means of getting natural light and ventilation to a greater majority of ships' state rooms. The other idea was a radial plan, for making optimum use of the semi-circular plan at the superstructure's forward end around a minimum of corridor space.[8]

Sharp himself used the court-cabin plan with great success in the streamlined *Ancon*-class ships he designed with Raymond Loewy for the Panama Railway Company in 1938. His radial layouts first appeared in his design of the three *Del*-class ships of Delta Line in 1946. The *President Jackson*-class American President Line ships of 1950, which were completed instead as military transports, also adopted a similar plan. Although otherwise not widely adopted in later American

Oriana: **The ballroom was one of the full-beam spaces made possible by the ship's arrangement of public rooms above the lifeboat recess.**

(Author)

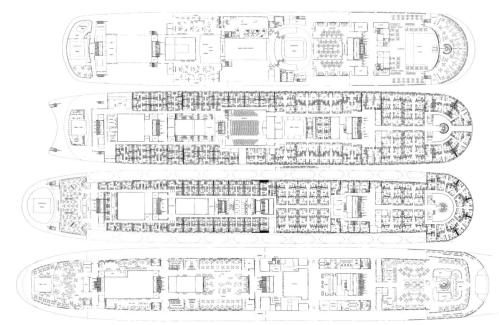

Canberra: **Partial plan showing the four main superstructure decks, with the upper and lower strata of public rooms. Note the regular and radial-plan court cabins on the two cabin decks.**

(Composite from P&O deck plans)

tonnage, similar thinking ultimately went into planning the compact yet attractive accommodation needed for the large passenger capacities of *Oriana* and *Canberra*.

Both the court arrangement and the radial layout were adopted in modified forms for extensive use throughout the first-class accommodation in the forward half of *Canberra*. These groupings were mostly arranged either side of a single centreline passage, on A, C and D decks. The court groupings aft of the first-class main stairway had to be arranged around twin parallel passages due to the use of the centreline space for other services, including the cinema. Perhaps the most ingenious planning of all was that of combining the court arrangement with a radial plan in the forward parts of A and B decks inside the semi-circular front wall of the superstructure. The overall scheme was developed by John West, with the detailed design of the cabins themselves being carried out by Barbara Oakley.

In *Oriana*, court cabins were used far less extensively. With the exception of only one court high up on the stadium deck, they appeared amidships and forward on C deck only. However, *Oriana* did have a number of other court-cabin groupings in her officers' quarters.

Apart from a number of larger deluxe cabins and suites on both ships, the remaining tourist class cabins were disappointing from the standpoint of their layout. They were small rectangular cubicles, albeit well fitted out, for two or four passengers in upper and lower bunks. However, as a concession to the space being used for cruising, many of the four-passenger rooms were designed to be quickly converted into two-berth rooms with private bathrooms. This neat trick, somewhat resembling railway sleeping-car design ingenuity, allowed a three-sided recess surrounding one set of bunks to be turned into a washroom with shower and lavatory. The

berths were folded away, revealing the plumbing fixtures, and a concealed sliding partition, complete with a door, drawn shut to separate the space. The change-over could be made single handed by a cabin steward, all in a matter of only a minute or so.

In an address on the interior design of passenger ships given in London to the Royal Society of Arts in 1966, after *Oriana* and *Canberra* were already well proven in service, P&O's Director Sir Colin Anderson had this to say about the design flexibility and habitability of their cabins:

Today's best cabin has won for itself all modern conveniences, including a private bath and lavatory, and should have even those strangely rare things, a wardrobe long enough to take an evening dress and a full-length mirror. Its furniture is no longer thought of as separate items but will be carefully designed and built in. One's cabin is never so impersonal as an hotel room. Its whole essence is to be neat and ingenious, full of housing places and hanging places for the treasures of its occupant. This is its first purpose. To be a sitting room as well is secondary. But too often in trying to make it look like a smart little 'with it' sitting room, that might appeal to the casual visitor, the designer allows it no comfortable future for the passenger whose bedroom it may be for some weeks. The fact is that, to do the bed-sitter trick well, there must be some loss of comfort for the occupant who must put up with a struggle to get at the dressing table or the bed when the cabin is in its sitting room uniform.[9]

Throughout both *Oriana* and *Canberra*'s vast numbers of cabins, the pitfalls of doing the 'bed-sitter trick' was avoided by restricting convertibility to the use of flush-folding upper berths, and to the four-to-two berth convertible tourist cabins mentioned earlier. The first class, and interchangeable, accommodation on these ships epitomised the careful, and flexible, planning and fitting out of private quarters, for ships' passengers to withdraw from the centres of social activity for sleeping, personal grooming and relaxing.

Architecturally, the modernity of the two ships differed mainly in the approach of the noted British architects separately engaged for each. Professor Misha Black, a senior partner of the firm Design Research Unit, was chosen by Orient Line to co-ordinate the interior design of *Oriana*. The work was shared with R D Russell and Partners, the partnership including Brian O'Rorke himself, already well experienced in designing Orient Line ships. For him, as for Charles Morris, *Oriana* was to be the final achievement in a long and distinguished association with Orient Line's passenger fleet.

Although Brian O'Rorke himself was primarily responsible for the design of cabins, the whole interior scheme reflected a gradual evolution of the approach he had originally adopted with *Orion* in 1935. Through the intervening decades and generations of Orient Line ships, his style had become more refined and sophisticated, keeping pace with developments in Scandinavian, European and American shipboard architecture. To some extent, *Oriana*'s first-class interiors exuded a rich and spacious ocean-liner character not unlike that of *Rotterdam*.

The design of *Canberra*'s similarly attractive and functional modern interiors was co-ordinated by Sir Hugh Casson, working with two other architects, namely John Wright and Barbara Oakley. Sir Hugh himself was responsible for the first-class public rooms, while those of tourist class, along with the first-class Crow's Nest observation lounge, fell within John Wright's jurisdiction. Barbara Oakley was given responsibility for the cabins and the important connecting elements of the passageways, stairways and deck lobbies. The move to an entirely contemporary expression of shipboard interior design was the more dramatic in the case of the P&O ship, whose predecessors had tended more to reflect the Cunard flavour of British post-war liner eclecticism. By comparison with *Oriana*, *Canberra*'s interior architecture expressed an altogether clearer and crisper expression of modernity.

Although in their own right no less luxuriant than the Holland America and Orient Line examples, the clean lines and solidly functional forms of *Canberra*'s first-class architecture were then perhaps more futuristic, expressing an optimistic view to the future rather than even so much as a hint of reminiscence from the past, not even of something as rational as *Orion*. In this regard *Canberra*'s interiors offered a more uniform expression of style between her first and tourist classes.

At first glance the completed *Oriana* and *Canberra* appeared to have some degree of visual similarity. Both ships had long slender hulls, extensive superstructures, nested lifeboats and uniform funnel colours. Internally, there were layout features and some special equipment which were also common to both ships. Perhaps their greatest likeness lay, not with these factors, but rather with the uniqueness of design approach in either ship. Each represented her own alternatives to the realisation of the same special set of circumstances and requirements. The synthesis of ideas, not necessarily all in themselves new ones, produced a unique end product in both ships. They were perhaps at least ten years ahead of their time through their flexible accommodation planning, advanced baggage- and stores-handling systems and various other operational innovations.

Each ship would go on to develop her own loyal following, both among passengers and crew. Those who have piloted and navigated both will quickly attest to *Oriana*'s superior manoeuvrability and lighter handling characteristics. However, despite her added draught and generally heavier construction, it was *Canberra* which survived in service the longer of the two. Certainly as far as the development of the modern cruise ship is concerned, it was also *Canberra*, and the appeal of her design with the machinery aft, that held the greater influence over later ships.

After *Oriana* had quietly slipped into her regular service at the end of 1960, *Canberra* made a spectacular debut, which was probably one of the best-orchestrated pieces of publicity ever accorded to the introduction of a new passenger liner. This was in fact the culmination of a long-haul public-relations exercise which P&O had employed to keep the ship's building progress, and hence an interest in the ship, in the public eye.

After moving first to Southampton, for dry-docking in the King George V graving dock, and then to the Clyde for extensive sea trials and technical testing, *Canberra* was officially handed over to her owners in Greenock on Friday, 29 May 1961. The following day she embarked her first few hundred passengers, special guests invited for the two-day positioning voyage back to Southampton. Scheduled for the Whitsun holiday weekend, this was planned to leisurely take the gleaming new white ship close to shore where she could be seen for the first time by thousands of people in the coastal cities and communities that she passed, and so too captured by the news and television cameras of the nation's media.

Canberra's service career started on Friday, 2 June as she sailed at 16.50hrs, under the command of Captain Geoffrey Alan Wild, for a three-month voyage to Australia, New Zealand, Hawaii and the Pacific ports of Canada and the United States, returning by the same route. The outward voyage was fully booked, her passengers including 750 emigrants going to Australia and another 120 on their way to new lives in New Zealand. *Canberra* took her place as the flagship of the combined P&O and Orient Line fleets, then numbering eighteen passenger ships, which in total served all continents except South America and Antarctica.

For the first few years of her career *Canberra* was mostly engaged in the Australian run for which she was primarily designed, with only occasional short cruises to the Atlantic

Isles and the Mediterranean being offered. However, one notable deviation from her regular routine brought her from Southampton to New York in July 1962. One of the purposes of this voyage was to give *Canberra* a trial for possible North Atlantic service.

With the higher degree of interchangeability amongst various routes made possible with modern air-conditioned ships such as *Leonardo da Vinci*, *Windsor Castle*, *Oriana*, *Canberra* and the then newly completed superliner *France*, a number of Lines were looking at alternatives to their regular services. P&O had approached Cunard, who were then planning replacements for the *Queens*, with a proposal of co-operative joint operation of large liners on their main Atlantic and Pacific routes. Cunard were also considering an arrangement of their own with French Line, whereby a joint weekly service would be offered with each Line operating a single superliner. Neither arrangement materialised, although ultimately *Queen Elizabeth 2* did end up running in a sole partnership with *France* on the North Atlantic until she was taken out of service in 1974.[10]

Although generally well received by the Americans, *Canberra* did not return to New York until 1973. With the Suez Canal closed for the second time in eleven years, and a falling demand for assisted passages to Australia, *Canberra* was dispatched to the ravages of the burgeoning and highly competitive American short-cruise market. However, while the Americans may have been fascinated by her modern outer appearance, and impressed with the contemporary decor of her lounges and bars a decade earlier, most were not prepared to book her numerous tourist-class cabins lacking private toilet facilities.

After running a few lightly-patronised cruises, *Canberra* was laid up, first in the United States for three weeks during the spring in the hopes that bookings would improve, and then indefinitely after returning to British waters in September. At first the signs of doom were ominous, with her owners declaring that, despite earlier optimism over developing Pacific Rim trade and tourism, *Canberra*'s ultimate future in cruising was jeopardised by her deep draught. P&O's policy on ship disposal was opposed to selling redundant tonnage for further trading, preferring to scrap rather than have to compete with surplus ships in the hands of other owners. Having been an expensive ship to build, and then at only about half of her life expectancy, *Canberra*'s prospects were not at all clear for some time.

Canberra was unexpectedly reinstated in 1974 as a replacement for the 1954-built *Orsova* in the British cruise market. Subsequently, *Canberra* gained great popularity in the British market, where the higher standard of accommodation and toilet facilities demanded by American clientele was not as all prevailing. In fact the advantageous pricing of the lower cabin grades consistently attracted vast numbers of ordinary Britons who would otherwise have found cruising to be too expensive. Indeed many of these were people who would book individually in shared accommodation, something seldom

done in the America-based cruise market with its greater demands for luxury and privacy.

Oriana and *Canberra* were converted for full-time cruising in 1974, although the work needed for the transformation was minimal. Both ships' passenger capacities were reduced, with the concealed toilet facilities of their convertible tourist-class cabins being permanently opened up. A number of other rooms with upper berths were also redesignated as single and two-bed rooms. At least in regard to these changes the rationale of their original dual-purpose design stood up well.

By late 1979, when *Oriana* was permanently repositioned to Sydney, *Canberra* remained as the only large ship serving the British cruise market. As such, *Canberra* has remained very British in character, managing to evade the fever of 'Americanisation' which at the time rendered so many ships as sterile clones of the floating Las Vegas stereotype. Indeed *Canberra* retained much of her character as a British tropical liner. Although officially a one-class cruise ship, passengers booked in the more expensive forward cabins and assigned to the former first-class Pacific dining room always tended to gravitate towards the forward public rooms and Bonito Club swimming pool, while those berthed aft continued to prefer the original tourist-class lounges and pools at their end of the ship. There was never any enforcement of such a division, and nor was anyone ostracised for drinking or dancing at the wrong end of the ship, or jumping into the other party's swimming pool. It was just always the way *Canberra* worked. After a long career, *Canberra* was finally withdrawn in 1997.

QUEEN ELIZABETH 2

To a great extent *Queen Elizabeth 2* represented the continuing evolution in modern British ship design which got underway with *Oriana* and *Canberra*. After scrapping their earlier Q3 design of essentially a *Queen Mary* concept, with only express North Atlantic service in mind, Cunard began thinking in terms of a more versatile approach in *Oriana*'s class. Still convinced that the big-ship image was the only way to go, the line envisaged a size of about 50,000 tons. This would have made the new Cunarder about the size of the *United States*, certainly enough to qualify her in the big league, above the class of *Rotterdam* and *Leonardo da Vinci*, although still smaller than *France*. Cunard had no illusions of outclassing their French rivals, having no doubt learned of French Line's realisation that a smaller ship with a shallower draught would have been more suitable for cruising.[11]

Oriana rather than *Canberra* was chosen as the prototype for the new ship's technical design as Cunard did not want to risk trying the engines-aft approach in regular line service. With her machinery fully aft, the effects of the singularly heavy bending stresses that winter North Atlantic conditions can inflict upon the hull, would be increased greatly by the wide separation of weight towards either end of the ship. A compact midships arrangement of *Oriana*'s type, with fuel and

Queen Elizabeth 2: **Waterline model of the ship.**

other high-mass items concentrated nearby, would concentrate the greater structural load nearest to the natural centre of buoyancy. The extent of bending and twisting would be reduced, allowing the ship to absorb these stresses by turning or rotating as a whole about her centre of buoyancy.

Oriana's builders, Vickers Armstrong, were also to have built *Q3* in collaboration with Swan Hunter and Wigham Richardson. Their partnership in the winning bid indeed qualified them ideally for participation in *Q4*, as the revived and revamped project was then called. Cunard's Chairman at the time, Sir John Brocklebank, was further impressed by their proposals for a different type of ship:

> This tender in particular incorporated ideas which may lead to improvements in design as regards the ratio of power to size and speed and which will profoundly influence our thinking in regard to any large ship which may later be built for this service. Quite apart from our adverse profit experience we could, I think, wish to give this shipbuilding group and our experts time to evaluate these ideas further before finally committing ourselves as to the size and performance of the new ship.[12]

Certainly it was this thinking which helped form the basis of the new *Q4* partnership between Cunard and Vickers. Engaged as design consultants, their task was primarily to bring together three essential aspects of the overall design process:

To integrate all that had been learned by both parties from the *Q3* experience.

To optimise the key factors of the size, power and speed relationship for a larger centre-engined *Oriana*-type ship.

to reach beyond the realm of Cunard's North Atlantic world into the realm of worldwide cruising, with particular emphasis on exceeding the stringent American safety regulations by a comfortable margin.[13]

Considerable weight economy was to have been gained in *Q3* through building an aluminium superstructure, and adopting welded hull construction in place of the riveted plating of the old *Queens*. By using lightweight alloys in the deckhouse structures, an additional deck for accommodation would be possible, as in the examples of *Oriana* and *Canberra*. Other reductions were sought by way of using plastic domestic piping, lightweight furniture and fittings, and synthetic deck coverings to replace heavy teak planking. Another development came in the form of extensive perforation of the frames, girders and struts used throughout the ship's structure. Cunard's naval architect, Dan Wallace, had already tested many of these items in the building of *Sylvania* during the mid-1950s.[14]

The *Q3* accommodation layout was also quite advanced for a ship which was otherwise considered to be old-fashioned in overall concept. As aboard *Rotterdam* and *France*, the public rooms for each class were given the full run of a separate deck within the superstructure. This was taken a step further by also locating the dining rooms on these higher decks, primarily to allow greater flexibility in the exclusive use of the lower decks for cabins.

The optimum North Atlantic service speed was determined to be 28.5kts, with sufficient reserve to make up for lost headway when needed. The total power needed to achieve this performance was originally determined to be 89,472kW (120,00shp), but was subsequently reduced to 82,060kW (110,000shp) at the expense of reducing the reserve margin as a building economy measure. The machinery also had to be designed to provide efficient performance at the lower speeds of as little as 16kts which would be used when cruising. To keep the bulk and weight of the propelling and auxiliary machinery as low as possible, a compact installation of PAMETRADA design was developed, occupying only three of the ship's fifteen watertight compartments. One of the greatest advantages of the twin-screw design was that only one engine room was needed, as opposed to two in the case of the quadruple-screw *United States*, *France* and the earlier *Queens*.

Although very much an express Atlantic liner in terms of size, luxury, speed, multiple-class passenger accommodation and hold space for passengers' baggage and automobiles, *Q4*'s design concept was equally based on cruise liner practice. This brought Cunard's own cruise-ship experience with *Caronia* together with the outside influences of various modern dual-purpose liners and cruise-only ships. The arrangement of passenger spaces was centred around, and above, an integral central core of the ship's machinery, air-conditioning plants and auxiliary services, as well as a tight concentration of catering services, stores and crew facilities. The cabins, whose

Queen Elizabeth 2: **A bow-on view of the ship as built, showing the upper deck's forward-facing 'look-out' large windows before the superstructure front was modified in 1971.**

all facilities becoming fully integrated when cruising.

The conception of her passenger facilities was shifted from the notion of an express vessel, with hotel facilities added, to that of a modern ocean-going urban resort, with North Atlantic express speed available when needed. As such, she would provide equally for worldwide cruise passengers as for those whose travels would include an Atlantic crossing as part of a holiday or business trip.[16] With the technical advances of her structural design and powerful twin-screw propulsion plant already rendered into reality, the remaining business of completing the ship would be highly concentrated on appealing to a then elusive new ocean-passenger market which *Queen Elizabeth 2* herself would ultimately help to define and develop.

The matter of design, both of the ship's modern interiors and of her exterior aesthetics, was at last put in the hands of Britain's top professionals. From their viewpoint at least, this move set to rest a long-standing sense of dissatisfaction over the rather backward standards of British shipboard design. Since *Queen Mary's* time, when European and Scandinavian shipping was keeping pace with modern architectural and industrial design trends, British shipowners, Cunard in particular, continued to propagate a bygone Grand Hotel eclecticism, disproportionately cast into vast ocean-going renditions. Even as late as the time of *Q3's* planning, it was once suggested that her interiors might be decorated in Georgian style.

As *Q4* was beginning to take shape on the Clyde, the whole question of interior design had become quite controversial. Sir Basil Smallpiece, who had then recently taken over as Cunard's chairman, consulted privately with Sir Duncan Oppenheimer, chairman of the Council of Industrial Design, to work out the formation of a revised design team.[17] James Gardner, who was first engaged in 1961 to do the exterior styling of *Q3*, was retained and paired up with Dennis Lennon as joint design co-ordinators, working closely with the technical design people under Dan Wallace. Gardner would continue to be primarily responsible for the ship's outside appearance, whilst Lennon would head a team of professionals, approved by Sir Duncan, who would be responsible for the great number of interior spaces in his domain.

Those named to work with Dennis Lennon and his own partnership were, among others, Professor Misha Black and Sir Hugh Casson, noted for their work on *Oriana* and *Canberra*. Each designer was given a fairly free hand in rendering the areas assigned to them, with a sense of harmony or unity being achieved through standardisation of the linking passages, lobbies, stairways, and the perimeter promenades. These vitally important elements, along with by far the greatest number of public rooms and other spaces, were designed by Dennis Lennon and Partners. The captain's quarters were done by Lennon himself as a compliment to Cunard and the ship's master.

Whilst the design team had not been assembled early enough to exercise an enormous influence over the structural

design reflected the cruise passengers' preference for large outer rooms, were thus pushed outwards to the sides of the hull and upwards, well into the superstructure. High up, above these and all of the ship's inner workings apart from the funnel and air-conditioning casings, three uninterrupted strata of public spaces were spread out to the ship's full beam. The required open deck spaces, lidos and open-air swimming pools were laid out atop these, and in a series of long terraces stepping down four decks to the upper layer of cabins.[15]

The *Q4* project proceeded according to plan through the awarding of a building contract to John Brown Shipbuilders at the end of 1964, and on to a fairly advanced stage of building when she was launched as *Queen Elizabeth 2* in September 1967. Following this, the ship's design progressed into its third and final stage since its original conception as *Q3*. With the delivery of the ship postponed by the builders, Cunard took the opportunity of using the six-month delay to drastically rationalise the accommodation design and styling of the ship. One of the key elements of this was an all-important change from the line's venerable three-class North Atlantic formula to a loosely-defined two-class arrangement for line service, with

Queen Elizabeth 2: **Plan of upper and quarter decks, showing the original layout of public rooms and catering services.**

(Author)

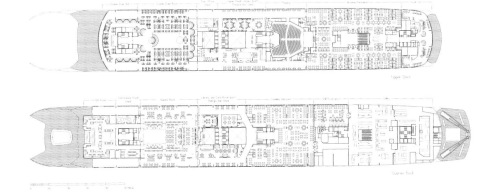

arrangements of their domains, the rationalisation itself and postponed delivery certainly afforded them more flexibility than might otherwise have been possible. It did, however, involve a near-total redesign of the public rooms to occupy the uppermost three decks. Named quarter, upper and boat decks, these were originally to have been allocated to seperate classes, giving first class the full and exclusive run of the quarter deck, with cabin and tourist above on the upper and boat decks respectively. The revised plan essentially combined the facilities of cabin and tourist classes on the upper and boat decks into a suite of rooms complementing its first-class counterpart below on the quarter deck.

A large cruise lounge and show place was created by breaking through the boat deck and combining the original aft-located cabin and tourist main lounges. Aptly named the Double Room, this multi-function area, with its spacious mezzanine, was to serve as the focal point of shipboard entertainment. Its first-class counterpart immediately below would serve as a ballroom, or take second place as an alternative showplace when needed as such. The remaining tourist-class rooms on the boat deck were eliminated, with their space being taken over by a shopping arcade amidships and the universally-accessible night club, coffee shop, gallery and teenagers' room forward of the theatre's balcony level.

The overall plan, which at various earlier stages of its evolution included traditional open and closed promenades, was further reworked as a fully enclosed and climate-controlled arrangement. The promenades were retained within this temperate enclosure as the principal circulation artery, providing side access to the public rooms as aboard the latest Scandinavian liners *Gripsholm*, *Sagafjord* and *Kungsholm*. The promenades bracketed even the largest spaces, such as the Queens Room and the Double Room, at its lower level. Here the promenades could serve as extensions of the rooms themselves when needed. Smaller spaces such as the libraries, card rooms and Theatre Bar were arranged alongside the funnel uptake, stairwells and other service cores. Only the dining rooms and the Look Out Lounge were given the full width of the ship, situated as they were forward of the circulation promenades on the quarter and upper decks.

Queen Elizabeth 2's rationalised plan also took an impor-

tant step towards specifically catering for professional entertainment. Until her time, shipboard entertainment tended to be a rather haphazard affair. A dance floor and small stage or bandstand were all that was provided in spaces still basically furnished as railway-terminus waiting rooms, with numerous groupings of settees, occasional chairs and tables. Dance floors on British ships were often covered by carpets, and yet more furniture, to suit some obscure notion of what the room's principal daytime use might be apart from bingo and afternoon tea.

Since first being introduced into the plans of a few notable ships of the 1930s, cinemas were, for a long time, about the only real special-purpose shipboard entertainment fixture. In 1935 *Normandie*'s magnificent theatre, with its wide stage, tiered auditorium seating and technical facilities, set the precedent for bringing truly shoreside facilities out to sea. Her example was later followed, on a similar scale, aboard *Rotterdam*, and, not surprisingly, her own ultimate successor, *France*. Indeed, many other ships of the 1950s and 1960s were equipped with elaborate cinema auditoria, and *Queen Elizabeth 2* was likewise to be fitted with the latest technical facilities.

Gaby Schreiber, who designed the theatre, adopted the powers of an architectural lighting scheme to set the various moods of this otherwise plain glassfibre-clad room for its uses as a cinema, church, lecture hall and theatre. One lighting scheme was installed for cinema use which was entirely separate from the system designed for the room's alternative uses. In her own words:

My object was to create a background which, when you enter, puts you into a different mood from the everyday world outside: for example, glamorous indirect lighting changes into colours and creates a different atmosphere and mood as the film starts and accordingly to the mood of the film. When people go to a cinema or jazz concert they want to feel different instantly. The approach to the design basically was very simple and almost stark, with white walls, charcoal grey floor and striped seat covers which gave a natural background again for different types of lighting.[18]

Queen Elizabeth 2: **The Double Room, where the small circular bandstand at centre was sufficient for late 1960s and early 1970s professional entertainment.**

(The University Archives, University of Liverpool, neg D-387-JB/31672)

The cinema/theatre was fitted only with concealed indirect fluorescent fixtures in red and white. To this basic scheme 'production' pan-and-tilt spotlights, with automatic colour change, were added for when the room was not used as a cinema. The latest-model Philips film projectors were installed for showing wide-screen 70mm films, as well as separate units for 35mm and 16mm productions. In view of the ship's modern sense of worldliness, facilities were also provided for simultaneous language translation for lectures, conferences and other such events.

Some worthwhile considerations of theatrical planning were also brought out to a number of the other rooms. The Double Room, Queens Room and 736 Club, which were the main entertainment spots, were each fitted with a stage equipped with permanently-installed production lighting and sound facilities. The arrangement and furnishing of these spaces were carefully thought out to offer good lines of visibility from all parts of each room. Peripheral seating areas were raised by two steps, allowing those seated farthest from the stage to see over the heads of others sitting in the front seats as in a theatre or cinema. The chairs and settees were arranged so that no seat had its back towards the stage.

In comparison with the proscenium stages in the Queens Room and 736 Club, the huge Double Room's original minuscule circular bandstand may, in retrospect, appear to have been something of a shortcoming. It was in fact probably quite well suited to the style of popular music of the day, featuring small rock 'n roll groups of the Beatles and Rolling Stones type, or the American-style folk and jazz alternatives. Being the tourist-class main lounge in transatlantic service,

this room was, by its nature, designed to cater to the tastes of a younger clientele.

The design of these rooms placed the emphasis on their evening usage on at least an equal basis with their daytime functions. The cruise passenger of the 1970s could not be expected to be content merely with an after-dinner drink in the lounge and a quick whirl around the dance floor, before retiring to bed for the night as their parents might have done aboard *Aquitania* or *Viceroy of India*. Indeed, the modern cruise experience had to offer its clientele the same type of nightlife to be found in urban hotels and luxury seaside resorts ashore. So too would the modern cruise ship have to swing, rock and boogie her passengers well into the small hours of the morning.

Largely exempted from the rationalisation was the basic design and layout of the ship's cabin accommodation. This part of *Queen Elizabeth 2*'s internal layout does, in fact, reflect the strongest link with the original Q3 design. It was here, on the lower decks, that the greatest amount of detailed design, and part of the outfitting itself, was already completed when the rationalisation was announced. A great deal was learned from *Caronia*'s cabin design and layouts, and from ideas actively solicited from her passengers and crew. The accommodation aboard other new passenger ships, both of British and foreign registry, was also studied, to determine the value of various new design trends.

Queen Elizabeth 2's accommodation featured a high proportion of large rectangular hotel-style rooms arranged with direct access from the main fore-and-aft passages flanking the central service core. These followed the proven design practices of their en-suite bathrooms and wardrobe areas forming a sound barrier between the passageways and the bedrooms proper, and of the beds being oriented fore and aft for maximum comfort in transatlantic service. In most instances the entrances to each mirrored pair of rooms were arranged either side of a small vestibule or passage, which itself could be closed off from the main corridor to form suites, as was done in *Rotterdam* and *Kungsholm*. With a design requirement that seventy-five per cent of all passenger accommodation have an outside exposure, the planning of the lower cabin grades became more resourceful. Many of these smaller rooms were designed around various interleaving L-shape arrangements like those of Christiansson's all-outer-cabin *Kungsholm* and *Gripsholm* of the 1950s.

The many advances in propulsion, weight economy, operational rationalisation, and the near total restyling of the passenger public areas, were each in themselves technically significant, but not enough to create any radically different image in the public eye without some help. What really presented *Queen Elizabeth 2* as something 'significantly new' was

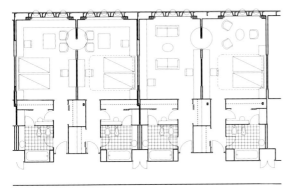

First Class suite rooms on One deck

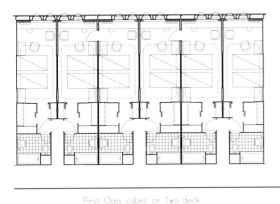

First Class cabins on Two deck

0   10 Metres

Queen Elizabeth 2: Cabin plans showing first class suite rooms and deluxe rooms on One and Two decks.

(Author)

her unique and distinctive external appearance. The importance of this image was considered to be vital to her ultimate success and of Cunard's promotion of her to the public. The rather esoteric appearance of ships like *Oriana* or *Willem Ruys* were confidently accepted by their owners without deference to public appeal. Cunard had too tough a marketing job ahead of them to take such chances. On the one hand there was the image of the great bygone *Queens* to be lived up to in a traditional sense, and on the other, an entirely new concept of a modern dual-purpose ship to promote. Whether depicted in a brochure photograph or magazine advertisement, or seen in reality at the quayside or from the deck of a passing ship, an all-important strong first impression had to make the initial pitch for the ship. If that failed, then it would be the more difficult to get the second chance. As it was explained in *The Architectural Review*:

> A major cruising liner has to attract passengers by force of personality; it has got to be as glamorous as the places it goes to. It must look and feel safe and luxurious, and it must be fun. If the same ship is to double as a North Atlantic packet, one must be convinced that it is safe, luxurious and fast. As a would-be passenger's first contact, the overall appearance of a ship is a vital part of the operators' commercial equipment. And as such it justifies a major design investment. Basically the visual 'feel' of a ship is a problem which rests squarely in the hands of the naval architect. The massing of the 'sit' and the end-to-end coherence, go hand-in-hand with the vessel's technical evolution. At the same time the problems of visual organisation and environmental design, increasingly merged, demand another major input: the employment of specialist designers.[19]

Here James Gardner excelled in his styling of the ship into a thing of beauty, against the seemingly opposing technical forces of shipbuilding and engineering knowledge amassed by generations of Cunard and John Brown people. James Gardner was originally brought into the Q3 design project when it appeared that the classic approach was not going to work in something that was fast evolving to fill the proportions of a colossal floating building. It was Gardner's success in that job which brought his name to the surface again when the Q4 design team was assembled.

What James Gardner succeeded so well in doing for *Queen Elizabeth 2*'s overall shape and appearance was to soften its lines of form and reduce the more severe expression of the traditional North Atlantic packet. He used a dark charcoal-grey colour for the hull instead of traditional black. This would better balance the fine lines of the single slender funnel topsides, itself a masterpiece of functional modern design. He used khaki paint, rather than white, on the deckhouse walls at the boat-deck inset, to effectively 'dodge' the davits and launching gear out of sight. Khaki was also applied to the inset below the bridge to produce a futuristic cantilevered appearance. He also skilfully retained some elements of traditional appearance, adding to the total effect and even going as far as to deceive the eye in concealing such structural expediencies as the flattening-out of traditional sheer lines in the hull form.

Despite the radically different appearance of *Queen Elizabeth 2* from her famed forebears, she still retained the pre-eminently no-gimmick appearance of a Cunard North Atlantic liner. She was definitely sleeker and more refined of line and form than the old *Queens*, lacking their bluffness of appearance. Modern and futuristic as she was, *Queen Elizabeth 2*'s design still reflected the mature experience of the Line's long-standing practical experience.

During the course of her planning, building and eventual entry into service, *Queen Elizabeth 2* was no doubt the subject of more publicity than any other ship ever built. Although controversial and critical publicity was no stranger to all concerned, the potentially most damaging coverage came when her debut in service was yet again postponed. She was originally to have been handed over to Cunard in November 1968. First there was the problem of a great amount of unfinished interior work in the public rooms, and secondly a disastrous turbine failure during a shake-down cruise to the Canary Islands made during the Christmas holiday. While the fitting-out was completed and repairs made to the machinery, which had become severely damaged, the ship's officers and crew were kept aboard on standby so that the ships could get underway as soon as possible. A second set of technical and acceptance trials was run at the beginning of April 1969 with entirely satisfactory results.

Queen Elizabeth 2 finally departed from Southampton under the command of Captain William Warwick on Friday, 2 May, 1969, bound for New York with a stop *en route* at Le Havre. The ship was only three-quarters booked, a figure which was considered surprisingly good in view of the delays and uncertainty surrounding the maiden voyage. The crossing itself was uneventful and little publicised as there were no celebrities aboard and few journalists. It was an inauspicious beginning to a brilliant career, which in retrospect left the foregoing delays and difficulties behind as something of a bad rehearsal.

Queen Elizabeth 2 emerged triumphant as singularly *the* most outstanding ship of the year, focusing the world's attention once again to things British. The 1960s was a decade which had brought mixed fortunes to the United Kingdom's trade and industry in one way and another. *Queen Elizabeth 2* in effect closed the decade on an 'up beat', which reflected a refreshingly more contemporary and 'with it' outlook. This had been a golden decade of British popular art, music and temperament. It had produced the 'mod' look and expression, the mini dress and numerous manifestations of popular artistic expression acclaimed the world over. Indeed the smart, crisp and mod lines of the new Cunard Superliner expressed something of the same sentiment on perhaps a loftier plateau. As

the lyric of one song put it 'Roll over Beethoven and tell Tchaikovsky the news' – this would be *Queen Elizabeth 2*'s time to shine.

Shine she indeed did, for *Queen Elizabeth 2* almost immediately won the public appeal that she had been so very carefully planned to attract. She at once set a superlative standard in design and outfitting for the rest of the cruise industry to follow. Her development and progress in service were carefully watched by a number of Scandinavian shipping men, themselves intent on making their own mark in the luxury cruise market. *Queen Elizabeth 2*'s unique duality of function and, at the time, comparatively large size precluded the likelihood of being copied, although various elements of it appeared in the great number of cruise ships to follow.

Queen Elizabeth 2 herself remained in her pristine condition, as built, for only about three years. As discussed later, she has during her distinguished career undergone more changes and conversions and rebuilding than perhaps any other merchant ship.

1   J H Isherwood, *Sea Breezes*, June 1982, pp 395-6.
2   *Schip en Werf* (Rotterdam souvenir edition), September 1959, Hoofdlijnen van het Ontwerp, p 12.
3   *Shipbuilding and Shipping Record*, 8 October 1959, p 275.
4   Philip S Dawson, *British Superliners of the Sixties*, p 13.
5   *Shipbuilding and Shipping Record*, 31 January 1957, p 146.
6   C M Squarey, *Shipbuilding and Shipping Record*, International Design and Equipment issue, 1961, p 3.
7   C M Squarey, *Shipbuilding and Shipping Record*, International Design and Equipment issue, 1961, p 3.
8   George G Sharp, *Transactions of the Society of Naval Architects and Marine Engineers*, 1947, pp 460-1.
9   Sir Colin Anderson, *Journal of the Royal Society of Arts*, May 1966, pp 479-80.
10 Neil Potter & Jack Frost, *Queen Elizabeth 2*, p 15.
11 Neil Potter & Jack Frost, *Queen Elizabeth 2*, p 15.
12 Lawrence Dunn, *Shipbuilding and Shipping Record*, 28 September 1967, pp 438-9.
13 Kenneth Agnew, *The Architectural Review*, June 1969, p 412.
14 *Shipbuilding and Shipping Record*, 31 January 1969, p 146.
15 Kenneth Agnew, *The Architectural Review*, June 1969, p 412.
16 Neil Potter & Jack Frost, *Queen Elizabeth 2*, p 90.
17 Neil Potter & Jock Frost, *Queen Elizabeth 2*, p 126-7.
18 Neil Potter & Jack Frost, *Queen Elizabeth 2*, p 150.
19 Kenneth Agnew, *The Architectural Review*, June 1969, p 418.

THE SUN VIKINGS

Norwegian-style cruising comes to America

The outstanding examples of *Prins Olav* and *Stella Polaris*, along with the cruising opportunities offered by regular ships of the Hurtigruten, had given the Norwegians an enviable reputation as pioneers of modern cruising. These developments brought to cruising the same high standards of seamanship, accommodation and service which Norwegian America and Swedish American Lines were known for in North Atlantic line services and worldwide cruising. Inevitably the diverse enterprises of Scandinavian shipowners would spread to further development in the cruise field.

A Norwegian conquest of the vast and virtually untapped American cruise market began thirty-three years short of the thousandth anniversary of Lief Ericsson's discovery of the New World in the year 1000. However, this time the Vikings headed directly for Miami and the warm Caribbean, rather than arriving by way of Iceland, Greenland and Labrador as their forefathers had done. Knut Ulstein Kloster was the modern-day Norseman who, metaphorically at least, was manning the 'styrboard' on a new kind of Viking ship. His Nordic cruise vessel was, in its own right and time, as remarkable as the magnificent longships which had borne his forebears of the previous millennium across the Western Ocean.

It was to transform the cruising industry in America forever, building a new clientele from the middle class, who were persuaded away from their habitual holiday destinations to experience this new phenomenon

SUNWARD

It was an unusual turn of circumstances which brought Knut Kloster and his Oslo-based shipping firm, Kloster Rederi A/S, to Miami[1] sooner than they might otherwise have arrived. In 1966 the firm had taken delivery of the 8,666-ton *Sunward*, essentially a Scandinavian-style ferry designed for round-trip voyages of seven days. She was to be based in Britain and run by a subsidiary company in London, named Kloster Sunward Ferries Ltd. A weekly car/passenger service was to be inaugurated, with Saturday sailings from Southampton to Vigo, Lisbon and Gibraltar during the summer, and to Lisbon with either Casablanca or Gibraltar alternating as the southern terminal port during the winter months. Although, in reality, a line service with provision for passengers to take their own cars, the voyages were to be marketed also as round-trip seven-day cruises.[2]

Sunward herself was largely an enterprise of Nordic ship design and building experience. Her structural and technical design was undertaken by the Danish consulting naval architects Knud E Hansen, in collaboration with C Barclay, Kloster Sunward's British managing director. The ship was built in Bergen by A/S Bergens Mekaniske Werksteder, at a cost of £2.5 million (then worth about $5.8 million). Her keel was laid in August 1965 with the completed ship being turned over to her owners only ten months later, on 20 June 1966.

Sunward: Profile view of the ship in the North sea shortly after delivery, showing the typical Knud E Hansen profile of that era.

(Skyfotos Ltd, neg 66/868)

Sunward emerged with the added distinction of being the largest passenger ship to be built in Norway.

Outwardly, she bore the unmistakable characteristics of the Knud E Hansen ferry design approach. Her hull and superstructure stressed a clean-lined modern form, a pronounced rake of the bow and the squared-off transom stern giving access to the vehicle deck. Topsides, she carried diminutive goalpost stacks slightly aft of amidships. These were visually balanced against a low dummy funnel containing an observation lounge atop the deckhouse aft of the bridge. The raked main mast was incorporated into the lines of the dummy funnel, and was complemented by a second mast immediately aft of the stacks. The overall profile was further balanced by pairs of electric cranes on the main deck, forward and aft of the superstructure. The eminently pleasing aesthetic appearance of this handsome ship represented one of best examples of the Knud E Hansen firm's work in that period.

The planning of her interior layout and passenger facilities were largely Barclay's responsibility. As he explained:

> In designing the *Sunward* a major problem was whether to provide accommodation of a standard corresponding to the functional austerity of short-range car ferries, or to adopt the costly luxury of transatlantic vessels. It was not possible to find a happy medium. If planned as a compromise, the ship would compare unfavourably with the larger vessels along the same route. If designed for austerity, the number of passengers would necessitate enormous public rooms so that all could find seats during crossings of the Bay of Biscay on rainy days.[3]

The solution ultimately derived from producing an upgraded variation of the Scandinavian short-sea ferry, rather than a down-scaled deep-sea liner. This approach provided both improved cabin accommodation and a suitable variety of public spaces within approximately the same physical confines of the larger ferries then in service.

Sunward followed the standard Scandinavian ferry layout, with all passenger accommodation, including the dining rooms and galley, located on the upper decks. The main run of public rooms occupied the full length of the boat deck. Here the full-width, forward main lounge afforded views over the bow and to either side of the ship. The layout of the dining room, fully aft on the same deck, was designed for ease of movement between the tables and the central *smorgasbord* buffet. The midship space between these two main rooms was taken up with the galley and *à la carte* grill room lying along the port side, opposite a wide starboard-side gallery used as a veranda lounge.

The open-air pool and lido, along with the adjoining veranda saloon and snack bar/club, were above on the sun deck, where they were far enough from passenger or crew cabins to permit their use as the ship's night club until 2 am. The remaining public spaces, namely the main foyer, shopping arcade, cinema and children's room, were below on the cabin decks. The children's room, originally named Seven Ages Club, was particularly noteworthy for its versatility. It served in the daytime as a playroom for the little ones, being taken over by the teen-agers in the evening, and finally serving as an adult retreat in the small hours of the morning.

All public rooms, other than the dining and grill rooms, were planned to provide seating for sixty per cent of the full passenger complement at any one time. Although it was realised that these rooms would not be so heavily used on summer services and in the more southerly latitudes during the winter season, this was a rainy weather contingency. These seats, augmented by the bed/sitting room arrangement of the outer cabins, were enough to satisfy the passengers during the Bay of Biscay crossing, and on the departure or approach to the English coast when outdoor conditions were likely to be unfavourable.

The noted Danish designer Mogens Hammer was commissioned to handle the interior decoration of all public spaces. These were finished in a bright and airy Scandinavian style, which was both elegant and starkly functional. Hammer was also responsible for the officers' accommodation, which stressed a distinctly Norwegian atmosphere.

With the exception of a few deluxe top-deck suites, cabin accommodation for most of *Sunward*'s 558 passengers was arranged in two, nearly identical, strata on A and B decks, lying between the public rooms above and the car deck below. The plan provided approximately equal numbers of inside and outside cabins, each with private toilet facilities. They would be sold at different fares within a single class of service. The more expensive outside cabins were considerably larger, with enough space to compensate for a slightly reduced length within the fore-and-aft narrowing of the hull. This superior accommodation was designed to work as compact bed-sitting rooms. The two lower beds were fitted as settees with swing-down back rests which, in their daytime arrangement, concealed the already made-up lower beds. Upper berths, where installed, were of the Pullman type, which were folded away into the wall during the daytime. As

Sunward: **An aerial view which clearly shows the wide spacing of the funnels astride the central expanse of the garage deck beneath the accommodation.**

(Skyfotos Ltd, neg C1066)

Barclay explained it: 'Accommodation is reminiscent in disposition, but not in size, of the deluxe compartments of the 'Orient' express or the 'Blue Train.'[4]

The *Blue Train* analogy was quite appropriate. The original British-built train carriage sets from 1946 were then still in service. These, like train sets which followed in 1972, were designed to pamper their passengers with a level of comfort and individual attention commensurate with the traditional luxury of first class aboard the highly-successful Union Castle liners. Far more than mere railway compartments, much of the train's private accommodation took the form of elaborate convertible bed-sitting rooms, with their own en suite toilet facilities. The suite, consisting of separate sitting and bed rooms with twin lower beds, tub bath and built-in bar, would compare remarkably well with accommodation in many of the latest ships.

Indeed, the *Blue Train* example demonstrated the possibilities of creating luxurious accommodation on a compact scale, even within the confines of long and narrow railway coaches. Likewise, the elegant furnishings and decorative schemes of the dining coaches, and particularly the bar, showed a far more imaginative approach than is normally to be expected of train accommodation. The *Blue Train*, more than any other,

could in this respect be seen as coming closest to being a deluxe modern cruise ship on rails.

Despite whatever could be learned from train accommodation and other sources, the approach developed for *Sunward* had to be proven, before being produced several hundred-fold within her hull. The usual mock-up cabins were assembled in a mould loft at the shipyard before any accommodation was actually fitted aboard the ship. However, no doubt to the great amusement of all concerned, members of the Line's sales staff, along with the designers and a contingent of shipyard engineers, were sent off to Bergen, where they were paired up into the sample cabins to test the accommodation's 'livability'.

They all had to go through the motions of unpacking their suitcases, washing and dressing for dinner, preparing for bed, and even spending an hour or two in the berths. At a later stage the experiment was repeated with the owners, designers and others, sharing the same accommodation with their wives. The ladies were even asked to make up the beds before leaving the rooms. These exercises spawned a list of thirty-three changes in the placement of fixtures such as towel rails, mirrors, reading lamps, switches and so on, which were made before work began on the actual interiors of the ship.

The standardised approach to cabin plans greatly simplified the overall layout of the accommodation decks. These were designed around two dead-straight parallel fore-and-aft alleyways running close enough to the sides of the ship so that they gave direct access to the outside cabins. This differed from the traditional British and continental practice of routing the corridors inboard of double or triple rows of cabins, with the outside rooms being accessed by short dead-end crosswise alleyways. All of *Sunward*'s inner cabins were laid out back-to-back in blocks of six each with access from beamwise passages connecting the two lengthwise alleyways. Since the engine casings were divided towards the sides of the ship, this scheme could be carried out without interruption along the full

Blue Train: **A luxury train cabin with fold-away berths, occasional chairs and an en-suite bathroom, which could do the 'bed-sitter trick' in the context of a modern ship, as envisaged by Kloster Rederi.**

(South African Railways)

length of each deck. The arrangement was devised to meet the requirements of the Norwegian registry, which prohibited dead-end alleyways of more than 3m length in ships' accommodation.

Sunward's hull form was developed by the Knud E Hansen firm, following extensive research carried out at the university model-testing tank in Trondheim. Following the similar experience of Sagafjord's hull testing, this work showed that the bulbous bow, common to many ships of her class, would have offered no speed advantage and little improvement in stability. The underwater lines of the bow were pointed, with the stem line being raked like that of an ice-class ship. Above the waterline the rake was increased substantially for the sake of appearance, giving Sunward 'the hungry look' as it was then described. This element of styling was used to diminish the otherwise rather stout and portly car-ferry look.

Aft, the hull was moulded into an ingenious hybrid cruiser stern, with an above-water transom providing access to the vehicle deck. The keel line finished in a tapered fin which normally would have guided the water flow to the rudder. At either side of this, the two fixed-pitch propellers were supported by A-brackets at the ends of their exposed drive shafts. Each propeller was lined up with its own spade-type rudder, giving Sunward the necessary manoeuvrability, without the added expense and complexity of fitting controllable-pitch screws. This arrangement of twin propellers and rudders became virtually standard practice in Hansen-designed ferries and cruise ships for quite some time to follow.

A notable feature of the ship's technical design was that she was provided with two roll-suppressing systems. A pair of Denny Brown-AEG movable-fin stabilisers was fitted for normal use at sea. However, devices of this type are not able to reduce rolling when navigating at low speed in fog or while lying offshore awaiting the pilot launch. These were the wisely-anticipated normal conditions of crossing the Bay of Biscay and sailing in and out of Southampton in winter conditions. To avoid passenger discomfort at such times, a passive system of L-shaped flume anti-roll tanks was incorporated into the hull-forward of the engine room.

Much of the equipment and outfitting of Sunward came from various Scandinavian sources. She was powered by twin Burnmeister & Wain twelve-cylinder diesel engines, manufactured in Denmark. The sprinkler system for Method II fire prevention was manufactured in Norway by Norske Sprinkler A/S, while the air-conditioning system was installed by Witts & Borgen of Bergen. Sound distribution facilities in the accommodation consisted of audio tape players, amplifiers and other equipment from Oslo's world-renowned Tandberg Radio Corporation.

Sunward was comparable in size, and in varying degrees of outfit and service, to a number of other superb car/passenger ferries also completed at about the same time. These too were intended to offer cruising as an alternative source of revenue on their various routes. In Norway Det Bergenske Dampskibsselskab took delivery in 1966 of the 9,000-ton Jupiter and Venus from Lubecker Flenderwerft. These ran under an unusual arrangement which combined a summer North Sea service between Newcastle and Bergen, with the ships switching to cruising between London and the Canary Islands for the Fred Olsen Line during the winter months. Jupiter was renamed as Black Watch for her cruising season, while Venus was renamed Black Prince. Although differing somewhat in appearance and internal layout, these slightly larger ships had many of the same technical features as Sunward, including her dual stabiliser systems. Their continuing popularity kept them in dual-role service for a great many years.

From Britain came Spero, and from Sweden, the sister ships Svea and Saga, which were operated jointly by Ellerman's Wilson Line and Rederi A/B Swedish Lloyd on services between England and Sweden. The Cammell Laird-built Spero was noteworthy as being the only British ship to have a sauna, along with the unusual feature of also providing dormitory accommodation for school children. The Swedish pair's near-sister Patricia entered service on a route between Southampton and also the northern Spanish port of Bilbao, also became very popular with British travellers. Meanwhile, in Finland the trend-setting Baltic ferry Finlandia was taking shape at the Helsinki yard of Oy Wärtsilä AB. She represented an important development in Wärtsilä's rise as a world leader in ferry and cruise-ship design and construction. The following year Finlandia inaugurated the Hansa Route as an extension of the Finska Angfartygs/Oy Finnlines flagship Helsinki–Copenhagen service, onwards to Travemunde in Germany. In the marine trade press this ship was enthusiastically described, not as a mere ferry, but a 'vehicle-carrying passenger liner'.[5]

Although advance bookings for Sunward were brisk, two unforeseen circumstances were soon working against her chances of success. A long-standing dispute with Spain over Gibraltar's sovereignty had erupted anew, eventually forcing the borders between La Linea and the colony to be closed. This effectively wiped out the line trade and its 'floating motorway' to and from Spain and Portugal via Gibraltar. At the same time, the British economy was in the doldrums following, among other things, a disastrous seamen's strike which had crippled the country's foreign trade for six weeks. Currency exchange restrictions were imposed, limiting the exchange allowance for British tourists travelling abroad to a mere £50. Whilst the Norwegians were sympathetic, to the point of one Oslo newspaper calling for them do everything possible 'to help out visiting British friends',[6] there was little that Kloster could do to make his new ship pay. He was stuck with a ship but no passengers to fill her cabins.

In Miami a similar fate had simultaneously befallen Ted Arison, another ambitious shipping man with visions of a thriving cruise operation of his own. He had made arrangements, in 1966, to charter the two newly built Israeli car/passenger ferries Bilu and Nili for short cruises based in Miami. These ships were built for a regular line service between Haifa and the western Mediterranean ports of Naples and Nice for Israel Car Ferries Ltd, part of the privately owned Somerfin SA group based in Geneva.

Nili: **One of the two Israeli-owned car ferries first brought to Miami by Ted Arison for cruising.**

(Michael Cassar, Valletta)

The 6,380-ton *Bilu* was delivered in 1964 by the Belgian Cockerill-Ougree yard, followed by her slightly larger sister *Nili*, of 7,851 tons, two years later from Britain's Fairfield Shipbuilding & Engineering. These were in fact quite similar to *Sunward*, providing modern and comfortable accommodation for 550 passengers and 120 cars on voyages of several days' duration. The accommodation of both ships was attractively designed in contemporary Israeli style, showing a functional elegance not unlike that of Scandinavian passenger tonnage of the day. An unusual feature of this pair was that there were no portholes or sidelights of any kind in their cabin decks, leaving them with effectually all inside cabins. They were promoted as offering 'the first classless sea travel in the Mediterranean'.

Bilu had spent the summers of 1964 and 1965 on her intended Mediterranean route without much success, although she had fared much better on a Miami – Nassau circuit during the intervening winter season. *Nili*, which was to have joined her sister immediately upon completion, went instead to the Baltic at short notice. As *Helsinki Express* she stood in for the fire-damaged *Finnhansa* of Oy Finnlines on their Travemunde–Bornholm–Gotland–Helsinki route during the peak summer season. *Nili* was then positioned in Miami, under charter to Pan American Cruise Line, which suddenly cancelled their agreement with Somerfin, with no explanation. Arison immediately took over the charter and placed the ship in service as *Jamaica Queen*. She was to run four- and five-day cruises to the Bahamas and Jamaica respectively.[7] Arison's troubles were brought about by the financial demise of Somerfin due to difficulties outside its passenger division. Both *Bilu* and *Nili* were seized by United States authorities at the request of Israel's government which had liens against Somerfin's assets. Arison found himself with plenty of passengers but no ships.

Ted Arison learned of the *Sunward* story only through an article published in the trade magazine *Travel Weekly*. He saw the possibility of an immediate opportunity arising from the two seemingly complementary situations, and quickly tele-

phoned Kloster. The Norwegian's response was characteristically concise: 'Give me a guaranteed income of half a million dollars in the next year, and you can have the agency for the *Sunward*.' Done! An agreement was struck, even though Arison did not then have the money to back his commitment. Within two weeks Norwegian Caribbean Lines (NCL) was established as a subsidiary of Kloster Rederi in Oslo, with the Arison Shipping Company as its agency in the United States.

Sunward entered service in the autumn of 1966 on a programme of three- and four-night cruises to Nassau, with Monday and Friday departures from Miami. During each voyage the ship remained tied up in the Bahamas, with cruise passengers living aboard during either the two or three days between overnight mainland crossings. Alternatively, the one-way voyage could be booked in either direction.

Sunward was promoted as 'an air-conditioned floating palace of fun in an incomparable Norwegian tradition'. The brochure claim that, 'There isn't a more magnificent, lavishly furnished ship afloat' was, however, stretching the point more than a little! Nonetheless, *Sunward* was an attractive modern ship in the Scandinavian style, in tune with the times, and with the promise of great things yet to come. With fares for the three-day cruise at $125 per person for a minimum-rate outside cabin, the ship quickly began to gain public favour and confidence.

Kloster and Arison found themselves to be competitively well positioned in a rather new Miami-based cruise market. There were already a number of established regular cruise services which had been run by American operators out of the port since around 1960. *Bahama Star* and *Miami* were on three- and four-day cruises to Nassau, whilst *Ariadne* and *Yarmouth* offered longer West Indies cruises on various itineraries of up to fourteen days. However, these were older ships, albeit some of them with remarkable histories.

Yarmouth and *Bahama Star* had been built by American yards, in 1927 and 1931 respectively, for various short-sea services out of United States ports. *Bahama Star*, which was originally the New York and Puerto Rico Steamship Company's *Puerto Rico*, had even endured several years of North Atlantic service in the emigrant trade as *Arosa Star* under the Panamanian flag. Despite the addition of air conditioning and a few other more or less cosmetic improvements, the accommodation still remained fairly basic, with the majority of cabins lacking private toilet facilities. *Bahama Star* still had a number of six- and eight-berth inside emigrant cabins.

Miami was the newest among these ships, having been completed in 1957 as *Jerusalem* for Zim lines, before being chartered from her Israeli owners in the early 1960s. Although her accommodation was of a higher standard, she too had not been designed with a view to cruising, and thus lacked the range of public rooms and extent of open-deck space offered by the new *Sunward* and her Scandinavian contemporaries.

Ariadne probably came closest to the new standard. She had been built in 1951 as the earlier *Patricia* for Swedish Lloyd and had benefited from extensive refitting for cruising after being sold to HAPAG in 1957. This work had involved considerable rearrangement of her cabins to provide single- and double-berth rooms with private toilet facilities for all of her 249 passengers. The public rooms were likewise upgraded to meet the high standards expected by HAPAG's German and European clientele. Air conditioning was installed throughout the accommodation, and a swimming pool added. The ship's relative luxury was reflected in the wider range and longer duration of the cruises she was capable of offering. *Ariadne* was sold in 1960 to Atlantic Cruise Lines Inc of Miami for Caribbean cruising. She was by far the most luxurious of the Miami regulars of her day, yet she unavoidably remained the product of an older generation of thinking in overall ship design.

By comparison, the altogether more modern profile of *Sunward* was itself something new. The sleek lines of the white hull with its raked bow and smooth all-welded outer shell, the curved form of the upper decks, bridge front and main mast appeared less severe than the old liner or steam-packet look. Once aboard, passengers were immediately struck by the attractiveness of her bright, modern Scandinavian interiors, and the ever-present sense of orientation offered by her open planning and straightforward layout on the cabin decks. The distinctly Norwegian service brought not only the delights of smorgasbord dining, but more importantly, the sense of quiet competence, impeccable housekeeping and superbly professional seamanship, which almost went unspoken in its sense of unobtrusiveness and reassurance. America had discovered the Scandinavian touch!

The task of building an American clientele and expanding on the success of *Sunward* was to be a formidable one. Winning over the competition's passengers would not be enough. Nor could a following be established among the displaced regular steamship patrons, forced up into the air by the eventual demise of their favourite foreign-flag liners. Such a clientele, with its demands for white-glove service in first class, was thought to be a dying breed anyway. Instead, a new market would have to be cultivated from the vast masses of so-called Middle America, most of whom had never even seen an ocean-going ship let alone travelled aboard one. These people, many of whom received only two weeks of vacation each year, would have to be coaxed away from their summer cottages, trailer parks, favourite ski slopes, Las Vegas, Atlantic City, or wherever else they had vacationed, to experience something new.

At the same time the remaining liners, which continued to set the standards for shipboard service, were also a significant factor of competition. These ships were turning more and more to cruising as an off-season diversion from their regular line services. Short and inexpensive cruises, usually from New York, periodically offered the opportunity to sample the superlative accommodation and services of elite-class modern liners such as *France*, *Rotterdam*, and the brand new *Sagafjord* and *Kungsholm*. Another alternative was the attractive round-trip cruise possibilities such as Italian Line's 'Mediter-ranean Go Rounds' aboard *Leonardo da Vinci* or the new *Michelangelo* and *Raffaello*, as part of their regular line services. For those with the time to spare, these voyages could be booked quite cheaply in the lowest of the ship's three classes.

The names alone of these great ships had the power to entice those already accustomed to ocean travel, along with a healthy proportion of newcomers. Once the exquisite French cuisine and impeccable service of *France*'s restaurants, the elegant club-like ambience of *Rotterdam*'s Ambassador Room or the deluxe hotel comfort of *Kungsholm*'s enormous 'standard' cabins had been sampled, even if for only a few blissful days, recollection of these experiences would remain as the unyielding standard against which all later cruises would be judged.

There was also formidable competition in the New York-based trade from Home Lines' new *Oceanic* and the Victoria Steam Ship Company's *Victoria*. Both were comparatively large deep-sea ships, with modern European-style accommodation and service.

Eventually all of these same ships would find their way into the full-time modern cruise market too, while others would be built to offer similar standards of spaciousness and elegance, even in the mass-market sector. From the outset, their examples were duly noted by men of vision such as Knut Kloster and Ted Arison, who saw that there was a bright future in cruising.

Arison had no trouble in meeting his original financial commitment to Kloster. In fact, the only problem seemed to be that there were more passengers than there were berths aboard his ship. *Sunward* had become an instant commercial success and the catalyst for almost immediate plans to expand Norwegian Caribbean Line's one-ship operation into 'The First Fleet of the Caribbean'.

THE FIRST FLEET OF THE CARIBBEAN

Two larger 16,000-ton ships were quickly ordered from AG Weser's Seebeckwerft yard in Bremerhaven, to be named *Starward* and *Skyward*. The building of these was somewhat unusual in that each was constructed in halves, which were only joined together at a rather advanced stage of completion. This was done so that the yard could meet a short delivery schedule for Kloster despite a lack of space owing to other work.[8] Each vessel was completed within an elapsed time of only twelve months. *Starward* entered service from Miami in December 1968, with *Skyward* following almost exactly a year later.

The Knud E Hansen firm was again engaged as consulting naval architects, working with both the owners' and builders' design departments. The plans were for larger renditions of *Sunward*, showing a further development of the uniquely 'Hansenesque' expression of Scandinavian passenger-ship styling. The balance of form from the earlier ship's overall hull and superstructure lines appeared again, easily

Skyward: General arrangement plans of the principal accommodation decks.
Note the centreline galley on Rainbow deck with galleries at either side, and the divided
funnel uptakes remaining from the original prototype's design with a car deck.

(Builder's drawing; courtesy Schiffahrst-Verlag 'Hansa', Hamburg)

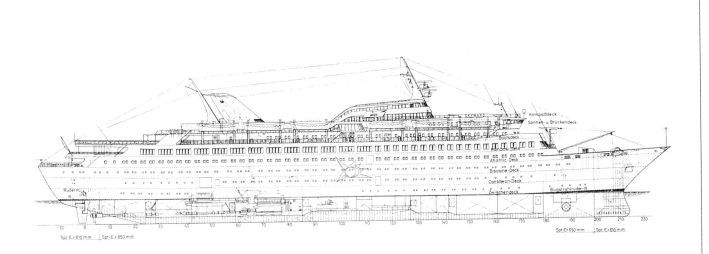

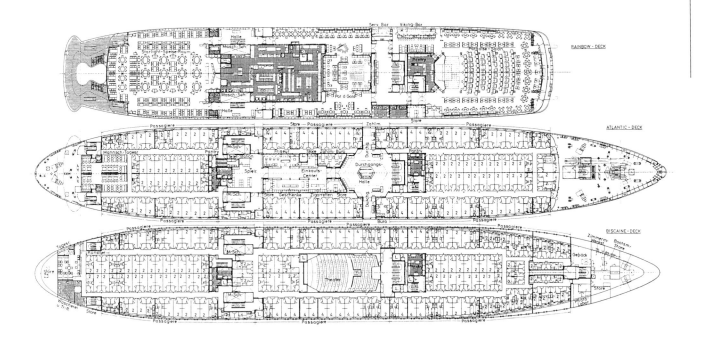

accommodating the additional length and extra deck added in the superstructure.

Below the waterline the bulbous forefoot, thought to contribute little to performance and stability in *Sunward's* case, was incorporated into *Starward* and *Skyward's* hulls. The additional power needed to propel each of these larger ships was delivered by a pair of MAN sixteen-cylinder V-form diesel engines, driving controllable-pitch propellers through single-reduction gearing. This arrangement reflected a general trend in the ferry and cruise ship industry towards geared medium-speed propulsion. The compact design of the V-form engines' alternating arrangement of cylinders, slanted obliquely to either side above the crankcase, made it possible to accommodate the machinery entirely below the vehicle decks included in the original design of these ships.

Showing the aesthetic side of Hansen's work, *Starward* and *Skyward* retained the essence of the dummy funnel, enlarged into a two-tier lido housing a bar and lounge in its lower level, and a covered deck space above. This was left open to the stern, and glass-enclosed forward, to the sides and above. Outwardly this structure bore a greater resemblance to the enclosure of a private cabin cruiser than to a dummy funnel. Nonetheless it provided the right visual balance to the steeply raked twin side-by-side funnels farther aft. Amidships, the lines of the 'cabin cruiser' lido enclosure were carried down a further level to encompass a swimming pool and lido area on the sun deck. This somewhat resembled the arrangement of *Canberra's* Bonito pool and lido, situated high atop the superstructure and protected from the elements by forward deck housings and shielded at either side by glass windscreens. These new ships also adopted the glass-enclosed bays extended out over the boat deck as had been seen in Swedish American Line's last *Gripsholm* and *Kungsholm*, as well as in *Hamburg*. The whole arrangement was very successful in providing an extraordinarily large amount of attractive, usable and versatile deck spaces on ships of comparatively modest size.

Although *Starward* and *Skyward* appeared to be nearly identical sisters, internally there was one major difference in the way the two ships were built. *Starward* was originally fitted out as a ferry, with space for 736 passengers and 168 cars. She had a full-length garage, the double height of which was flanked by two tiers of passenger cabins at the ship's sides on B and C decks. However, within only a few months of her delivery, the ship was switched from her original three- and four-day Nassau run to a seven-day Jamaica itinerary. In the new service the demand would be for passenger space rather than vehicle capacity. *Skyward*, then at an early stage of building, was completed with cabin accommodation in place of the garage, as she too became destined for longer Caribbean voyages. This change increased her capacity to 930 passengers. An additional 108 inner cabins and a cinema were eventually fitted into *Starward's* empty vehicle decks, increasing her capacity to 928, and bringing her up to her newer sister's standards.

As aboard *Sunward*, the layout of the cabin decks was simple and straightforward. Whereas the earlier ship's inner cabins had been arranged in groups and opening onto short crosswise passages, those aboard *Skyward* were arranged in two files, back to back along the centreline. This provided the same direct access from the two parallel lengthwise halls as for the outer rooms. This design has remained the standard cabin arrangement aboard most of the larger cruise ships which have followed. When the inner rooms were added aboard *Starward*, they had to be arranged either side of a central third corridor to avoid the compromise of fire safety and the expense of having to cut numerous doorways, and other openings, through the fire walls either side of the original garage.

When *Skyward* made her maiden arrival at the Port of Miami on 3 January 1970, she was given a tumultuous welcome, second only to that accorded the brand new *Queen Elizabeth 2* the previous spring. Her arrival marked the midpoint of what had then become a $100 million investment in cruising on the part of Kloster Rederi and NCL. Two further ships were planned for completion by the end of the following year. It was estimated that this five-ship operation would bring some $60 million a year into the Miami area, through operational spending by the Line itself and tourist revenues from passengers. With a total of sixteen new cruise ships then under construction for various owners, the future for both the cruise industry and Miami looked very bright.[9]

The Greater Miami Chamber of Commerce decided that *Skyward's* arrival was an appropriate opportunity to celebrate the city's emergence as a major cruise home port. After nearly a week of festivities, while the ship was duly certified by the US Coast Guard and other authorities, she was ready to go cruising. At first she ran the three- and four-day Nassau circuit, and later was switched to a seven-day Puerto Rico and US Virgin Islands itinerary.

Within a year, orders were placed in Italy with Cantieri Navali del Tirreno e Riuniti (CNTR) for the remaining two ships, to be named *Southward* and *Seaward*. They were to meet not only the needs of a growing clientele, but also the challenge of a new and highly competitive rival, Norwegian-owned Royal Caribbean Cruise Line. Knut Kloster's fellow Vikings had recently arrived in Miami with their first two ships *Song of Norway* and *Nordic Prince*, newly delivered from Finland's Wärtsilä shipyards. NCL set out to compete not only on the basis of price and service but in the realm of ship design that would counter the unique features of the new arrivals.

From the Knud E Hansen drawing boards in Copenhagen came an inspired variation on the *Starward/Skyward* design. The position of the lifeboats was lowered three decks to the base of the superstructure, where they were semi-recessed above a shallow deck overhang, as on Orient Line's *Oriana*. Above, the lounge deck was extended outwards over the boats to the ship's full beam. The glassed-in sides of the superstructure here were carried up a further level to shield

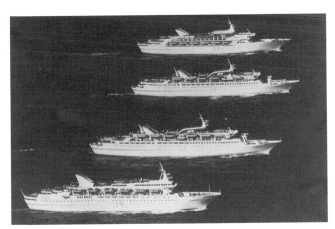

NCL's 'White Ships' with *Starward* and *Skyward* centre, *Southward* above and *Sunward II* (formerly Cunard *Adventurer*, and which replaced the original *Sunward*) below.

(Norwegian Caribbean Line, Miami)

the extensive lido area above on the 'beach' deck, as it was called. Above this the 'cabin cruiser' housing of the earlier two ships was retained forward, extended to the full width of the ship, and reduced to a single deck height. The gently curved topline of this uppermost enclosure was repeated again farther aft in the shape of the beach-deck windscreens. The height of these was tapered at either side of the highly raked funnels, to join with a steeper curve continuing the line down at the aft end of the lounge-deck windows, and closing off the lifeboat recess below. This was reflected by a similar curvilinear sweep at the leading end of the boat recess and in line with the windows above.

The structural arrangement of the hull and superstructure was similar to that of the 12,219-ton *Italia*, built a few years earlier at another Italian yard. Naval architects in that country were ingenious in their use of the lifeboat-davit supports as supporting elements of a ships' superstructure. This approach first appeared in the Dell'Adriatico-built *Oceania* and *Neptunia* completed for Lloyd Triestino in the early 1950s. A later and more sophisticated adaptation of the same basic idea gave the *Oceanic* of Home Lines her distinctive semi-nested lifeboat arrangement and unusual sloped promenade deck enclosure below.

However, execution of this modern Italian shipbuilding practice in the design of Kloster's new ships bore the signature of Hansen's distinctive styling. Their clean-lined plastic quality of form showed a considerable refinement of *Italia*'s overall concept. *Southward* retained the classic balance of form, with a much longer foredeck and gentler terracing of the after decks than would be seen on a number of her contemporaries and a great many later ships. There was nothing frivolous about her styling. It was attractive, functional and, of most importance, aesthetically pleasing in creating an appropriate and unforgettably unique image.

Internally, *Southward* followed a similar plan to the earlier *Starward* and *Skyward*. The major difference was that the dining rooms were relegated to the boat deck, as in *Italia*, beneath the main run of public rooms. Whereas the additional deckhead height required for the lifeboat davits had been given to the dining room ceiling height in *Italia*, the vertical surplus in *Southward* was divided between the dining room and the main lounge above. This allowed the central part of the lounge to be recessed by about 1m, with improved lines of sight for entertainment features. The perimeter of the room, which was at lounge-deck level above the lifeboat recesses, offered a raised vantage point from which to view the stage and dance floor.

Like her earlier fleetmates, *Southward* was propelled by a medium-speed, geared, diesel installation. However, she differed in that four ten-cylinder Fiat diesel motors were used, as opposed to the twin sixteen-cylinder V-form arrangements of the German-built *Starward* and *Skyward*. *Southward*'s screws were thus each turned by a pair of diesels pneumatically coupled to a single-reduction gearbox following the ultra-compact propulsion system used in many modern car ferries. This approach had again started to gain great favour in the design of compact modern passenger-carrying tonnage. Also among the more noted examples of this approach during the period was its adaptation by Wärtsilä for *Finlandia*, completed for Oy Finnlines in 1966.

Another change in technical design made in *Southward* was to eliminate the anti-heeling tanks which had served all three earlier Kloster ships as an alternative stabiliser system. With the line then solidly committed to Caribbean cruising, away from the Bay of Biscay and England's fog, it was felt that these devices could at last be dispensed with.

Southward was delivered on time and went immediately into service at the end of 1971. However, before her sister ship *Seaward* could be delivered, the yard ran into financial troubles. They wanted to renegotiate the building contract for *Seaward* at an increased price. By the time the Italian government was able to intervene and secure the necessary financing, Kloster had already rejected the ship, leaving her to eventually be completed for P&O as *Spirit of London*.[10]

By this time Norwegian Caribbean Line was operating a fleet of four modern cruise ships on weekly cruises from Miami. The phenomenal success of this operation was based largely on promoting a highly standardised offering. Each ship repeated her own identical Caribbean itinerary every week, year round. Repeat passengers wanting a different experience had only to book a different ship, knowing that they could count on the same standards of service and comfort. For the Line this was a case of the Holiday Inn hotel chain's dictum that 'the best surprise was no surprise', in that the costs of running each circuit were constant and predictable. The same menu and entertainment schedule could be used every week, greatly simplifying the task of provisioning, bunkering, staffing and maintenance. Since all four ships were based in the same port there was the advantage of bulk purchasing of consumables for the entire fleet.

NCL were also both innovative and aggressive in marketing their cruises. Borrowing from airline experience, they worked through large national advertising agencies in a manner previously unheard of in the shipping industry. Cruises were advertised throughout the United States in newspapers and magazines, including the glossy publications which airline passengers were offered aboard their flights. The Line even capitalised on the great popularity of the Danish-born musical satirist, Victor Borge, by featuring him in their advertising as their honorary Commodore. Advertisements depicted the amiable 'Clown Prince of Denmark' in a double-breasted officer's blazer and peaked cap, with the caption:

> Victor Borge, 'honorary Commodore of the Fleet', invites you to come aboard for the cruise you will never forget.

In little more than five years Knut Kloster and Ted Arison had created a veritable blueprint for success in cruising. It was a plan which was quickly adopted and applied by the competition, with some particular twist of the same basic formula to assert their own presence.

THE FIRST ROYAL CARIBBEAN AND ROYAL VIKING SHIPS

Perhaps most similar to NCL in their style of operation and targeted clientele were Royal Caribbean Cruise Line. Again, this was a new venture emerging from the collaboration of American- and Scandinavian-based interests. Edwin Stephen, a young hotel executive originally from Wisconsin, saw that there was great opportunity in the field after working aboard Miami-based cruise ships himself. Wisely he sought the financial and technical backing for his own cruise line from Scandinavian sources. In 1967 he flew to Norway where, by way of introductions arranged through the Fearnley & Eger ship brokerage firm in Oslo, he was put in touch with three of Scandinavia's leading family-owned shipping concerns, IM Skaugen A/S, Anders Wilhelmsen and the Gotaas-Larsen Group.

The shipping and related experience of these companies covered a worldwide diversity of operations in cargo shipping, tankers, offshore operations and passenger services. The Skaugen family had commenced its shipping activities under sail in the late nineteenth century. Wilhelmsen had diversified their interests into data processing and support services for the offshore oil industry. Gotaas-Larsen, apart from their other activities, were already experienced in the Miami-based cruise business as owners of Eastern Shipping Corporation.

Stephen's Royal Caribbean Cruise Line was incorporated in 1968 with the three Scandinavian firms as partners. Gotaas-Larsen assumed overall responsibility for business development and shipbuilding aspects of the new Line, while Wilhelmsen handled the administration and accounting roles.

Royal Caribbean were among the first to place orders for larger luxury cruise ships in Finland with Wärtsilä. The yard's already fairly extensive passenger-ship experience, prior to building Royal Caribbean's *Song of Norway*, *Nordic Prince* and *Sun Viking*, had been gained almost entirely with short-haul car/passenger vessels, designed for domestic services in Scandinavian waters. The most notable exception was *Boheme*, a modest 10,328-ton cruise ship looking remarkably like *Finnhansa*, the ferry delivered to the German-based Wallenius Group in 1968. Orders for the three Royal Caribbean ships were signed in tandem with a booking for three cruise ships of similar design for another conglomerated newcomer in the field, namely Royal Viking Line. The sum of these very prestigious contracts secured for the Finnish builder one of the healthiest order books seen in the passenger ship business for a good many years, as well as a sound foothold in the cruise-ship building business.

The design of all six ships originated out of an overall concept developed by Knud E Hansen A/S. With their first NCL designs by that time already proven in service, *Cunard Adventurer* and *Cunard Ambassador* then being transformed from drawing board conceptions into reality, the Danish firm was building up a distinguished reputation in cruise-ship design. When the Royal Caribbean and Royal Viking orders were placed with Wärtsilä, Hansen also had work in hand on the prestigious 20,000-ton *Sea Venture* and *Island Venture* for other Norwegian owners. The smaller *Copenhagen* of 13,750 tons, designed at about the same time for Danish owners, showed a marked transition in Hansen's work towards a more liner-like appearance and exterior aesthetic. Had this ship been completed as originally scheduled, she would have emerged as the pivotal element in the firm's move towards designing larger deep-sea cruise tonnage. Following a similar owner/builder dispute as had befallen Kloster's *Seaward*, *Copenhagen*'s completion was substantially delayed until the ship was finally sold to the Black Sea Shipping Company of the Soviet Union. She was only completed and put in service in 1975, as *Odessa*.

The original and underlying concepts for the six Royal Caribbean and Royal Viking ships were further developed by Wärtsilä's own technical department. This work was done in collaboration with each of the two groups of owners, separately one from the other, to tailor the design to the specific needs of each. What was retained from Hansen's work were elements of the hull and superstructure lines along with the overall scheme of internal layout and accommodation plan. These influences also provided some sense of identity with Hansen's designs for *Sea Venture* and *Island Venture*, and in so doing contributed to asserting a prototype image of the luxury cruise-ship aesthetic.

It was in the realm of propulsion and engineering that Wärtsilä exercised their greatest influences. Here the builders applied the same geared four-engine, twin-screw approach which they had successfully developed for *Finlandia* a few years earlier. The origins of quadruple-engined diesel propulsion can be traced to the 13,600-ton *Monte Sarmiento*, built by

Blohm & Voss in 1924 as the first of five ships designed to each carry 2,470 emigrants and seasonal farm workers to South America. While the minimal height requirements for an installation of this type paid off in terms of space freed for accommodation on the decks above, its rationale was also attributed to the yard's apparent surplus of submarine engines after World War I.

However, a modernised adaptation of basically the same approach was to become virtually standard practice for Wärtsilä in the great many cruise liners and ferries to come from Helsinki and Turku over the following two decades. The machinery for most of these ships was also made in Finland at Wärtsilä's Vasa factory under license from the Swiss engine maker Gebrüder Sulzer of Winterthur.

These medium-speed Z-series engines were then a new development, designed by Sulzer to be produced in either two- or four-stroke versions for various purposes. Their small size and low mass were ideally suited to being fitted beneath a drive-through car deck or an uninterrupted block of passenger cabins. The Z-40/48 machines used in these ships were each only about three-quarters the size of a London double-decker bus and of about 55 tonnes mass, or approximately the weight of ten African bull elephants. By comparison, the twin low-speed engines used in the slightly larger 1957-built *Gripsholm* were each of some 550 tonnes mass and a full three decks in height. Despite the progress in diesel engineering represented by developments such as the Sulzer Z engines, it must be remembered that the Swedish ship was also intended for North Atlantic service, and was therefore of considerably heavier construction throughout.

As in the smaller *Finlandia*, the propulsion plants of the Royal Caribbean and Royal Viking ships were each made up of four nine-cylinder, two-stroke, Wärtsilä/Sulzer Z40-type engines. Since the output of the engines had been somewhat downrated below their design values for prototype installation aboard *Finlandia*, the necessary performance could be had from these same machines in the larger cruise ships. Again, as on the prototype ship, the engines engaged the two propeller shafts in pairs through flexible rubber couplings connecting them by way of single-reduction gearboxes. The Pneumaflex flexible coupling devices, chosen originally for *Finlandia* and retained in the six cruise ships, allowed for the simplest construction of the reduction gear involving the fewest moving parts.

Apart from its inherent space-saving characteristics, Wärtsilä's propulsion approach offered other worthwhile economies of building and operation. In addition to their lower installation costs was the added operation flexibility of being able to shut down any one engine for maintenance while underway without serious loss of headway. This alone was a feature that virtually no other passenger ship propulsion system could then offer. Certainly *Monte Sarmiento*'s fixed couplings offered her engineers no such convenience. Indeed this feature would become increasingly desirable as the service schedules for both ferries and cruise ships alike would become ever more demanding, with the barest minimum of

port time being allowed for maintenance and overhaul. In the builders' opinion at least, the advantages of the medium-speed four-engine approach seemed to clearly outweigh its inherent shortcomings of having up to twice as many cylinders as a comparable low-speed twin-engine alternative, of needing increased exhaust valve maintenance and of requiring a higher grade of fuel.

The six Wärtsilä cruise ships also used *Finlandia*'s arrangement of twin bow thrusters, incorporating it with the Hansen-style twin-rudder arrangement for optimum manoeuvrability. What was also retained from Hansen's work and the experience of building under 10,000-ton passenger vessels in general was a comparatively narrow hull frame spacing, of only 650–700mm. In deep-sea passenger tonnage of comparable size, such as *Gripsholm*, *Kungsholm* and *Sagafjord*, midships frame intervals tended to be from 800–900mm, depending on the practice of individual builders. Following their own experience in building generally smaller passenger ships, Wärtsilä continued to favour a frame interval of only 630mm.

To the original Hansen design and to Wärtsilä's technical and engineering experience, the two groups of owners each added the influences of their own designers. Royal Caribbean's house naval architect, with overall project responsibility, was Martin Hallen of IM Skaugen. He was teamed up with Gier Grung, who was responsible for the exterior styling of the ships in somewhat the same role that James Gardner had been given in *Queen Elizabeth 2*'s creation. Mogens Hammer, whose cruise ship work had started with *Sunward*, was also engaged to handle the design of the passenger accommodation in *Song of Norway*, *Nordic Prince* and *Sun Viking*.

What had originally emerged from the contract specifications were plans and renderings for a class of vessel looking rather like a deep-sea rendition of *Finlandia*. To this Grung added his distinguishing touch, which went beyond merely imposing a sense of styling upon a new ship, to creating an entire corporate fleet image which through later generations of the Line's ships would 'carry the RCCL theme'. He made extensive use of scale models to try various ideas and configurations of detail elements which he carefully studied from every possible angle. Grung realised, as had Swedish American Line's Erik Christiansson, that a ship must look good from all sides at sea level and above, and that she has no hidden backside where the ugly seams and edges can be concealed from scrutiny.

Gier Grung's work was, however, tempered by two other persons involved in the RCCL fleet building project. The Line's distinctive 'crown and anchor' logo emanated from an inspired piece of notepad doodling done by Sigurd Skaugen in the early stages of the Line's inception. Grung incorporated its final form into his design scheme, along with the name 'ROYAL CARIBBEAN', spelled out in huge sans-serif block letters at the base of the funnel, infusing the Line's corporate identity into its fleet livery in accepted airline style. This was one of the first instances of an America-based cruise Line identifying itself with its ever-important link to the airlines.

Sun Viking: **Seen here at Vancouver in 1995, she shows the Viking Crown Lounge pod on her funnel and the relationship of its shape with the curved glass-enclosed deck overhangs aft and amidst the lifeboats.**

(Captain Jack McCarthy, Vancouver)

For the passengers themselves this would be an important, though perhaps subliminal, psychological link, associating Royal Caribbean in the same way as the already well-known air carriers which would bring most of them to the ship from thousands of miles away and take them back home again.

The other factor to influence Grung's work and the Line's unique identity was Edwin Stephen's own ideas about funnel design. He wanted to have an observation room high up in the funnel with a commanding view over the entire ship's decks. Indeed, passenger vantage spaces had already been put inside a number of dummy funnels. Among the earliest of these was Raymond Loewe's original designs of Moore McCormack's *Argentina* and *Brasil* of 1959.

What Stephen wanted was something far more extraordinary, incorporating in essence the revolving restaurant pod of the Space Needle tower built for the 1962 Seattle World's Fair and the tripod-style funnel of the German Atlantic liner *Hamburg*. Certainly no such thing would be technically workable within the scale of the 18,000-ton ships then being planned. What Martin Hallen and his colleagues had to do was rework the whole idea, to incorporate a circular gallery into a more conventional motor-ship funnel. The first 'workable' approach to be drawn up was too timid, with only a small viewing gallery cautiously protruding out of the oblique lines of a conventional streamlined funnel. With the later help of Gier Grung and part-owner Gjert Wilhelmsen, himself also a practising naval architect, the concept was given the strength of form that Stephen wanted. It took shape as a circular pod impaled on the aft lines of a broad stack rising obliquely from a wide pyramid-shaped profile. The whole structure had a boldly three-dimensional form, the likes of which had never before graced the lines of any ship's superstructure. Again this carried a sense of jet- if not space-age imagery, which would further serve to identify the modern

cruise ship more with the future than with past ages of ocean liners and steamship travel.

The Royal Caribbean logo and name were prominently displayed on the white funnel sides diagonally forward and below the lounge pod, where they could clearly be seen from afar at sea and at closer range from the quayside wherever the ships called. These, along with all other elements of hull, superstructure and funnel, were carefully 'sculpted' by Grung into a single balanced and cohesive composition of form. To these elements he added the distinctive touch of a wide blue riband surrounding the base of the superstructure and encircling the uppermost row of cabin windows. This stripe also helped to 'carry the RCCL theme' in a manner until then not widely used in ship design. Its airliner-style camouflage, obscuring a whole row of identical cabin windows from view, helped to diminish the impression of freeboard height as well as superimposing a strong visual delineation of hull and superstructure.

All three Royal Caribbean ships were essentially identical, except that in *Sun Viking*, the last-built of the trio, the forward mooring deck was raised to the level of the public rooms, with the blue riband being carried fully around the heightened forward plating. Apart from a slight increase in internal space, this gave the ship a more clean-lined external appearance than her two earlier sisters. When *Song of Norway* and *Nordic Prince* were returned to Wärtsilä for lengthening in 1980, the gusset plating was extended upwards to also provide the same visual effect.

Like RCCL, Royal Viking Line was formed by a trio of established Norwegian shipowners, namely Nordenfjeldske Dampskibsselskab, AF Klaveness & Co A/S and Det Bergenske Dampskibsselskab. Nordenfjeldske and Bergenske had already gained cruise experience in the luxury market of the 1920s and 1930s with *Prins Olav* and *Stella Polaris*. Both lines had also remained as co-operative partners in the Hurtigruten service until the late 1980s. Apart from providing an

Royal Viking Sea: **The third of Royal Viking's original trio seen here at the time of her completion in 1973.**

(Wärtsilä, Helsinki, neg WHT73-546R)

essential domestic service, this route offers a breathtaking natural beauty and unspoiled charm which draws passengers from all over the world to travel side by side with ordinary Norwegians going about their normal daily lives.[11] These owners have catered to the needs of both types of passenger throughout virtually all of their careers. Away from Norwegian waters, the Bergenske company, or Bergen Line as it is better known, developed international services between Bergen and Newcastle, with many of their North Sea ships also widely used for cruising. Among the best known of these were the streamlined 1932-built *Venus* and her later running mates *Leda* and *Meteor* dating from the 1950s.

The new Viking Line venture was organised on the same principle as the Hurtigruten fleet, in that each partner would order one of the three planned ships. These would be nearly identical sisters of 21,500 tons, costing about $23.4 million each, with each partner company retaining ownership of their own investment. As a fleet the ships would be planned jointly, with their management and operation in service being a co-operative venture. The three building contracts were signed with Oy Wärtsilä's Helsinki yard:

Royal Viking Star –	Bergenske Dampskibsselskab, Bergen, for completion May 1971.
Royal Viking Sky –	Nordenfjeldske Dampskibsselskab, Trondheim, for completion July 1973.
Royal Viking Sea –	AF Klaveness & Co A/S, Oslo, for completion December 1973.

Unlike NCL and RCCL, whose operations were then based entirely in the seven-day Miami market, the Royal Viking fleet would cruise worldwide. Their programme would be run on a 'rolling schedule' of seven- to twenty-one-day voyages, often beginning in one port and ending at another. These would encompass Europe, the North Cape, Scandinavia and Russia, the Mediterranean, Black Sea, Atlantic islands, American eastern seaboard and Caribbean, Panama Canal, Mexican Riviera, Pacific, California and Alaska within a single year's cruising. The cruises were organised as segments with no consecutively repeated itineraries so that longer voyages would be possible for passengers wanting to combine cruises. The fare range for the first season of *Royal Viking Star*'s operation worked out at $60 – $160 per day, depending on the grade of accommodation. The price for the ship's top suites on her first sixty-six-day circle-Pacific cruise was set at $10,230 per person.

In planning their fleet, the owners made a careful study of some fifty liners and cruise ships already in service. They paid particular attention to the design features and service amenities of the Swedish American 1957-built *Gripsholm* and *Kungsholm* of 1966, along with the Norwegian-flag *Sagafjord*, all of which represented the epitome of modern Scandinavian ocean-going elegance and luxury. They also took note of other modern trends, particularly from Italy and Britain.

In the examples of *Oceanic* and *Eugenio C*, the interior and outdoor spaces sited above the lifeboat line, with their protection from the elements and their commanding views, were greatly admired. This trend had followed some progressive British thinking in ship layout, resulting from *Canberra*'s successful use of nested lifeboats. The layout of *Queen Elizabeth 2*'s upper-deck catering arrangements with the restaurants and galleys located fully forward were likewise duly noted.[12] This was seen to offer a worthwhile improvement over the original conception of upper-deck dining facilities located aft, as in Hamburg Süd's *Cap Arcona* and Lloyd Triestino's *Victoria* of 1927 and 1931 respectively. The new Cunarder's layout offered the advantage of direct access to the open afterdecks from the public rooms astern of the restaurant and galley. This approach was also less cumbersome than the *Sunward*-style Scandinavian ferry practice of locating the restaurant and galley amidships where a passage or promenade, usually on the starboard side, was needed to give passengers the full run of the public rooms. The *Queen Elizabeth 2* arrangement needed no such passage since passengers would not have access to the galley and forward deck areas in the

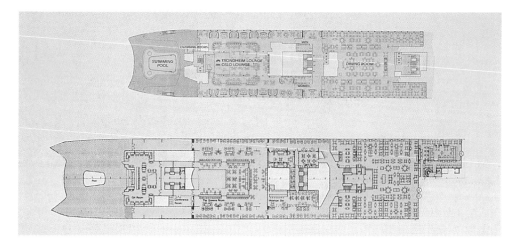

Royal Viking Sea/Sky: Scandinavian deck layout compared with the quarterdeck plan of QE2, showing a similar arrangement of public rooms, with the dining rooms and galleys (not shown) forward and a perimeter circulation scheme for the rooms farther aft.

(Author)

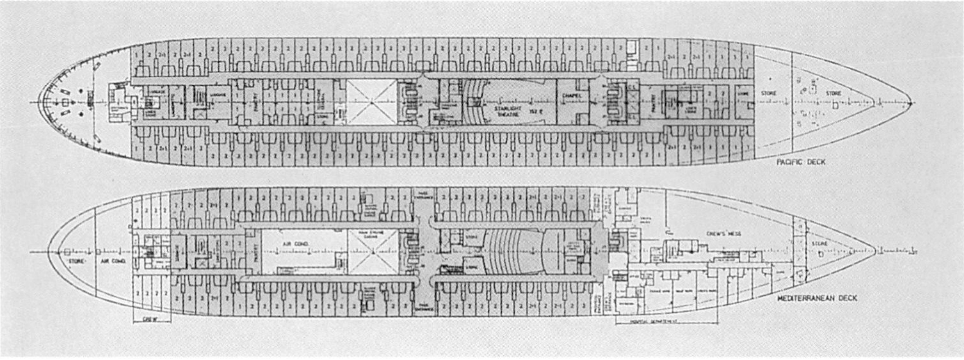

Royal Viking Sky: Discovery
Room, providing a
panorama of passing
scenery in greater space
and comfort from atop
the bridge rather than a
funnel pod as in the
Royal Caribbean ships.

(Author)

first place. It also made the full width of the ship available for
both the dining room and its service areas.

Both *Queen Elizabeth 2*'s overall catering arrangements
and the emphasis of top-deck passenger recreation spaces
from the Italian ships were incorporated into Royal Viking's
plans. From the elite Scandinavian liners came the general
approach to public room layout, with suites of full-width
lounges leading from aft of the dining room to spacious and
wide open pool lidos fully astern. The three tiers of luxury-
class cabins arranged throughout the decks below, although
smaller on average than *Kungsholm*'s extraordinarily big
cabins, were similar in concept. Each of the Royal Viking passenger rooms nonetheless met the same remarkably high standard in outfitting and finishing. The majority of interior
architectural work was done by Finn Nilsson of the Norwegian design firm FS Platau. His reputation in the field had by
that time already been established through his interiors for
Sagafjord.

Unlike the successors to *Sunward* and their opposite numbers from Royal Caribbean, the Royal Viking ships featured a
wider variety of generally larger cabins, including rooms
designed specifically for single occupancy. In this regard they
adhered more to the liner tradition of Swedish American and
Norwegian America, rather than the standardisation adopted
by the followers of Scandinavian ferry-design rationale. This
in itself accorded passengers a degree of individuality in their
accommodation, which the owners believed would be appre-
ciated by the top-market clientele that they sought. Royal
Viking's ships had a considerably lower passenger density,
with berths for only 559 persons as compared with 870 in the
RCCL trio, or 767 each in *Sea Venture* and *Island Venture*. This

alone served to establish for Royal Viking Line an elite position among the newcomers to the cruise market.

Likewise, the exterior appearance of the Royal Viking
ships was less radical, conveying an understated sense of
modernity, progressive in its own right, although more akin
to the deep-sea liner than the Scandinavian ferry idiom. The
funnels were of a more traditional appearance, in comparison with the raked side-by-side stacks on the Kloster ships
or Royal Caribbean's progressive Viking Crown arrangements. They helped to convey the less flamboyant expression
of understated luxury and taste that the owners wanted. As
with the whole design process for these ships, the funnel
form was derived from painstaking research. Various adaptations of the tapered and ovoid type were tested for their
smoke dispersion characteristics. None of these proved satisfactory for the two-thirds-aft stack location and the expanse
of open deck astern. Finally, it was the example of *Queen
Elizabeth 2* which provided a solution. Her inspired combination of a slender uptake, encased within a wider cowling
surrounding its sides and rear, mounted atop a wide wind
scoop at its base, solved the problem. Although its functional
elements were essentially the same as on the Cunard flagship, the Royal Viking funnels were not as tall, and appeared
broader and more squat in form. Their black-and-white livery, no doubt inspired by the original funnel colours of
QE2, provided yet another visual suggestion of the superlative luxury-liner design which inspired these up-scale white
Vikings in the first place.

One of the most distinguishing features of these ships
when they were new was the dominance of their superstructures. They then seemed as oversized perhaps as those of

Wilhelm Gustloff and *Robert Ley* must have appeared in their day, some thirty-three years earlier. The Royal Viking super-structure was extended a full two decks above each ship's lifeboats, with the uppermost glass-enclosed level housing an observation lounge forward atop the bridge, a sports deck amidships and side-screened sun deck aft. The impression of height was further strengthened by the substantial air-conditioning housing at the base of the funnel, which also incorporated the wind scoop. This was visually balanced by a similar structure forward at the base of the mast. The juxtaposition of these elements made perhaps the strongest impression then seen of the balanced mast-and-funnel profile form developed from the examples of *Rotterdam*, *Canberra* and *Hamburg*.

In this respect the appearance of Royal Viking's fleet was also carried by yet two more new Norwegian ships, then also in quest of the top market sector, namely *Sea Venture* and *Island Venture*.

SEA VENTURE AND ISLAND VENTURE

This pair of sister ships was built for yet two more Norwegian owners, Fearnley & Eger and Oivind Lorentzen, who joined forces under the name Norwegian Cruiseships A/S. For financial and economic reasons the ownership of the two vessels was vested under separate holding companies, Kommandittselskapet Sea Venture A/S & Co and Kommandittselskapet Cruise Venture A/S & Co, for *Sea Venture* and *Island Venture* respectively. The operation of the ships was placed under a Bermuda-based company Flagship Cruises Ltd, which would be represented in the United States by Flagship Cruises Inc. The board of directors for the owning and managing companies was made up of representatives from the two Oslo firms, Fearnley & Eger and Oivind Lorentzen.

Original specifications and plans for two luxury-class cruise ships were drawn up as early as in 1968 by technical representatives of the two founding companies, in collaboration with the Knud E Hansen office. Tenders were invited from a large number of European and Scandinavian yards, with contracts finally being awarded at the end of that year to the German builders, Rheinstahl Nordseewerke GmbH of Emden.

Sea Venture and *Island Venture* were at first to have been placed in Pacific-coast service on one- and two-week cruises, with San Francisco as their home port. After construction had been started, plans were changed, with the ships finally to run out of New York to Bermuda during the summer and on longer Caribbean itineraries for the winter months.

Despite similarities to the Royal Viking Line fleet in exterior appearance, propulsion arrangements and some aspects of their layout, *Sea Venture* and *Island Venture* brought along a number of differences and design innovations of their own.

While the glass-enclosed the sun deck on each ship featured the same type of forward-facing observation lounge as *Royal Viking Star's* equivalent space, far better use was made of the area amidships. Here, a swimming pool was fitted beneath a retractable glass roof of the type first used aboard the Home Lines' *Oceanic* in 1966. The plan of this deck had to some extent evolved out of the change from West Coast- to New York-based operation. Designer Knud Yran restyled the entire deck from its original tropical plan into a suite of far more versatile all-season spaces. The forward area, which was originally to have been no more than a veranda, was elevated to the status of a fully-fledged observation lounge with its own bar. The sliding Magrodome roof, along with extra saunas and massage rooms aft, completed the revised scheme at this level. Above, where the Magrodome track and handling mechanism were fitted, and on some of the other decks below, the amount of open space was increased so that these changes would not diminish the outside recreation and sunbathing areas available in fine weather.[13]

The arrangement of open decks was otherwise quite similar to that of the Royal Viking ships. The major difference

Island Venture: **Here she can be seen later in her career as** *Island Princess*. **The Royal Viking-style arrangement of her upper decks, with the added flexibility offered by the sliding Magrodome roof over the swimming pool area, can clearly be seen.**

(Princess Cruises)

Sea Venture / Pacific Princess: **Standard cabin interior, showing the compact arrangement of the settee bed and fold-away canister berth.**

(Princess Cruises, Los Angeles)

was that the open boat-deck promenade did not encircle the superstructure, as the cabin accommodations forward of the boats themselves extended out to the ship's full width. The observation veranda overlooking the bow, which could only be accessed from the ship's interior, was otherwise disconnected from the open spaces aft. These ships did, however, feature the diminished *Sagafjord*-style pool and lido area aft of the main run of public rooms. The lounge, which opened onto the lido, was extended up through the deck above, where, between the two arms of the boat deck flanking the pool area, it was fitted with double-height folding glass doors. The overall arrangement of these two adjoining areas was similar to that of the Moore McCormack's 1959-built *Brasil* and *Argentina*.

Interior planning of *Sea Venture* and *Island Venture* differed from the majority of other new cruise ships in that their dining rooms were relegated to the bulkhead deck. However, this apparent throwback to liner design practice produced an exceptionally well-articulated layout of lounges and other facilities above on the lounge deck of each ship. Here the arrangement of the lido lounge, midships-sited auditorium-cum-lounge and a second entertainment lounge facing forward, was laid out around the two main stair lobbies, which themselves were extended to the full width of the ship. These two lobbies gave access at their outer extremities to the main suite of rooms, linking the vertical access to other parts of the ship with the lounge deck's perimeter circulation pattern. In this regard, the lounge-deck plan was a close adaptation of Dennis Lennon's inspired approach to integrating *Queen Elizabeth 2*'s indoor promenades into her public-room layout.[14]

The central lounge was ingeniously designed to serve also as a cinema. In concept its plan resembled that of *Queen Elizabeth 2*'s Queens Room which could be closed off into a smaller space.[15] Here, too, the change could be easily effected by means of concealed sliding wall panels. These could be drawn shut, like curtains, to close off and darken the centre part of the room, leaving its peripheral areas undisturbed as two attractive veranda lounges overlooking the sea. The auditorium, or cinema, was fully equipped with a projection booth, large screen, stage, production lighting and audio facilities. For cabaret-style evening entertainment, or daytime use for bingo and other activities, the area could again be opened up to its full size incorporating the veranda areas at either side.

A noteworthy technical feature of this space, and of the dining room three decks below it, was that both were built without the need for supporting columns. This was accomplished as a result of the yard's experience in building large freighters where the roll on/roll off (ro/ro) cargo decks had to be free of obstruction. The use of heavy 525mm frames spanning the full 25m width of *Sea Venture* and *Island Venture* above the dining room and below the lounge floor, was based specifically on Rheinstahl Nordseewerke's then recent experience in building the *Atlantic Crown*-class freighters for the Atlantic Container Line.

The resulting deeply-serrated structural texture of the dining room deckheads on both ships was skilfully concealed by the interior architects. Finn Nilsson and his Swedish partner Robert Tillberg 'dressed' the crosswise frames as cross-members in a series of gently curved ceiling vaults. The indirectly lighted vaults themselves stretched only across the centre part of the room, with the ceiling being flat along either side where the floor was slightly raised. The line of each beam was traced fully across the room to its outside walls, where its cladding served also to conceal air-conditioning and ventilation ducts.

The dining room, cinema/lounge and lido lounge, along with the two-deck-high lobby containing its own spiral staircase on the decks in between, were the most tastefully designed interiors of these ships. These areas reflected the quieter colour schemes and restrained expression of luxury and elegance characteristic of Tillberg's earlier work on *Kungsholm* and of Nilsson's *Sagafjord* interiors. In addition to these noted Scandinavian designers, Miss Mildred Masters of New York was brought in to lend expertise on American taste in general hotel design, colour schemes and so on. Consequently, the first vestiges of Las Vegas panache began to find their way aboard ship, in touches such as the gold 'palletted' ceiling of *Sea Venture*'s Bermuda lounge.

OTHER DEVELOPMENTS

By the close of 1973 the last of Kloster's *White Vikings* had been delivered and was successfully in service. RCCL, Royal Viking and Flagship Cruises had by then all fully realised their own fleet-building plans. These ships were accompanied by yet more Hansen-designed tonnage vying to serve a steadily growing America-based market. These included the Dutch-built *Cunard Adventurer* and *Cunard Ambassador* of 14,150 tons, completed in 1971 and 1972 respectively. Within five years these were superseded by the larger 17,500-ton *Cunard Countess* and *Cunard Princess*, built in Denmark and delivered to their British owners in 1975. These later Cunard sisters, along with their Royal Caribbean, Royal Viking and Flagship Cruises counterparts, came close to establishing the 20,000-ton, 20kt ideal of the intermediate-class liner as a prototype of cruise ship development.

Despite the inevitable progression to cruise tonnage of ever increasing size in the years to follow, the cruise ships of this era have remained among the most commercially successful passenger vessels of all times. With the single exception of *Cunard Ambassador*, which was badly damaged by fire and subsequently rebuilt as a livestock carrier, all were still in service at the time of writing.

Five of the six Wärtsilä ships were lengthened by the early 1980s to keep pace with the march of cruise-industry progress. *Song of Norway* and *Nordic Prince* were returned to the Wärtsilä yard in Helsinki, where a 27m midship section was inserted into each ship, increasing the passenger capacity by forty-four per cent. Royal Caribbean decided not to so modify *Sun Viking* in the interest of fleet diversity. The more intimate atmosphere of the smaller *Sun Viking* would be retained for longer duration cruises. Royal Viking Line had all three of their ships similarly enlarged in Germany by AG Weser, with the addition of 200 passenger berths each. The Royal Viking ships were subsequently redeployed after Kloster's acquisition of the Line in the late 1980s. *Royal Viking Star* and *Royal Viking Sky* became *Westward* and *Sunward* respectively in the NCL fleet, its initials by then standing for Norwegian Cruise Line. *Royal Viking Sea* went to Royal Cruise Line, also acquired by Kloster, and renamed *Royal Odyssey*.

Sunward, the little ship which had started it all, was sold in 1973 as she could no longer meet the stringent United States Coast Guard regulations. The previous year Knut Kloster and Ted Arison had parted ways in a dispute over business matters. Arison and his long-standing assistant Meshulam Zonis along with other key executives of the agency were soon to rise again to even greater strengths in the cruising field. As for *Sunward* herself, she has subsequently returned to Florida, joining the SeaEscape fleet under Liberian registry as *Scandinavian Song*.

1 Tony Newman, *The Naval Architect*, September 1988, p E259.
2 *Shipping World & Shipbuilder*, August 1966, p 236.
3 C Barclay, *Shipping World & Shipbuilder*, 19 January 1967, p 247.
4 C Barclay, *Shipping World & Shipbuilder*, 19 January 1967, p 249.
5 *Shipping World & Shipbuilder*, September 1967.
6 Barbara Ovstedal, *Norway*, p 28.
7 Colin F Worker, *The World's Passenger Ships*, p 157.
8 Dipl-Ing. A Schlenker, Ing F. Künker, *Hansa*, No 10, 1970, p 851.
9 Peter T Eisele, *Steamboat Bill*, No 114, Summer 1970, p 86.
10 Tony Newman, *The Naval Architect*, September 1988, p E259.
11 Mike Bent, *Coastal Express*, p 27–31.
12 Philip S Dawson, *British Superliners of the Sixties*, p 131, 140.
13 *Hansa, Sea Venture/Island Venture*, special issue, p 11.
14 Philip S Dawson, *British Superliners of the Sixties*, p 117.
15 ibid, p 125

CHAPTER 6

LINEAGE AND NATIONALITY

Liner operators adapt to full-time cruising

The impact of cruise-ship developments through the 1960s and 1970s had originated largely out of new Scandinavian and European ferry and short-sea experience, rather than from an ocean-liner background as might have been expected. Cruise Lines such as Norwegian Caribbean, Royal Caribbean and Royal Viking had all made a strong market impression with the elegant new tonnage which they had introduced. Of the few remaining liner operators, P&O and Cunard retained their market positions with Oriana, Canberra and QE2, all of which, by 1980, were still foreseen to have a number of years' service left. Both Lines were also engaged in cruising with smaller 1970s-generation tonnage. P&O had entered this market with the purchase of Stanley McDonald's successful Princess Cruises, which the Line retained as an operational subsidiary. Cunard had ventured into American-style cruising with smaller new-style cruise ships of their own.

While the proponents of modern cruising were undaunted in their enthusiasm, there was also much scepticism about its long-term prospects. Many believed that the spate of activity might be short-lived, and that the ships being built at that time would be positively the last. It was then thought that when the time came for the big liners to be withdrawn from service, they might be replaced with smaller and cheaper vessels of the *Cunard Countess* or *Sea Princess* type. For a long while nobody believed that ships as large as *Oriana* and *Canberra*, let alone *QE2* or the then laid-up *France*, would ever be

built again. After the completion of *Royal Viking Sea* and *Cunard Countess*, cruise-ship building activity seemed to have quietened for a while.

In 1979, Knut Kloster purchased *France* for conversion as a cruise ship, and it was perhaps this, more than anything else, which jolted others into the realisation that the growth of cruising was sustainable, and that maybe large ships did have a future after all. Other long-established shipping Lines such as Germany's Hapag-Lloyd and Holland America had already begun to consider investing in new passenger tonnage. As plans were first laid in the late 1970s, the right time had come for these owners to consider larger ships of the size and scale they were already accustomed to, rather than the smaller Norwegian Caribbean or Royal Caribbean vessels of the age. A number of younger companies, including Costa, Home Lines and Sitmar, which were rooted in the post-World War II emigrant boom, had also sustained their livelihoods by switching to cruising.

Of these, Hapag-Lloyd and Home Lines were the first to consider new tonnage, while the others would respond later, in some cases much later.

EUROPA

In 1973, *Hamburg*, which was then laid up, came close to being purchased as the fifth *Europa*. HAPAG and North German Lloyd had merged in 1970, forming the single entity Hapag-Lloyd AG. Two years later, North German Lloyd's *Bremen*, which had emerged out of an extensive 1959 rebuilding of the French liner *Pasteur*, was sold to the Chandris, becoming *Regina Magna*. Hapag-Lloyd was than left with the single passenger ship *Europa*, formerly the Swedish American Line *Kungsholm* of 1953. Apart from their diverse worldwide cargo operations, the newly formed Hapag-Lloyd Line found themselves to be in an elite German-speaking cruise market, requiring but a single ship. However, at the age of twenty, the existing fourth *Europa* was considered in need of replacement with more up-to-date tonnage to maintain the Line's high-prestige cruise image.

At the time, *Hamburg* was only some four years old, and embodied the type of progressive German design, spaciousness and luxury which made her very attractive to the home market. These same characteristics had featured prominently in the pre-World War II *Bremen* and *Europa*, and had re-emerged with a new sense of panache and modernity aboard *Hamburg*. Although her high percentage of inside cabins would have been somewhat of a throwback to North Atlantic liner design from the fourth *Europa*'s still-intact exclusively outer-cabin plan, the newer German ship still had a great deal to offer.

Unfortunately, no agreement was struck for *Hamburg*'s sale to Hapag-Lloyd, and the ship was sold eventually to the Black Sea Shipping Company of Odessa, becoming their flagship *Maksim Gorkij*. With no other suitable tonnage available to meet their specific needs, Hapag-Lloyd were forced to design and build from scratch. Planning was started for a completely new ship to replace the fourth *Europa* and uphold her deep-rooted tradition of worldwide cruising excellence, effectively taking up her name, crew and her devoted (more than fifty per cent repeat) clientele.

From their own vast cruising experience and their perception of modern lifestyle and ship-design trends, Hapag-Lloyd decided on a number of overall qualities which they thought would best uphold the existing *Europa*'s tradition and character within the context of modern shipbuilding progress. The new ship would have to be large enough to accommodate 600 passengers, as opposed to the mere 482 for which the fourth *Europa*'s cruise accommodation was then arranged. An exceptionally stable and seaworthy liner-style of ship would be needed to run longer-duration worldwide voyages often of twenty-one days or more, and up to three months for round-the-world voyages. She would also have to provide an eighty-five per cent proportion of outer cabins, and have an individual cabin floor area of 21sq m. Also, in special consideration of the Line's exclusive market sector, suppression of machinery, propeller and other noise sources was to be maximised, to levels of at least −60 decibels.

In broad terms of technical and operational consideration a number of criteria were given as essential:

maximum safety and stability plus greatest economy;
longevity of operational life;
optimal workflows for stores handling and servicing;
sustained economical operation at full and part loads;
low noise and vibration levels throughout living and sleeping quarters;
minimal wear and minimal maintenance overhead.[1]

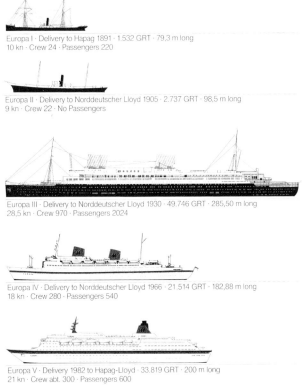

Europa I · Delivery to Hapag 1891 · 1.532 GRT · 79,3 m long
10 kn · Crew 24 · Passengers 220

Europa II · Delivery to Norddeutscher Lloyd 1905 · 2.737 GRT · 98,5 m long
9 kn · Crew 22 · No Passengers

Europa III · Delivery to Norddeutscher Lloyd 1930 · 49.746 GRT · 285,50 m long
28,5 kn · Crew 970 · Passengers 2024

Europa IV · Delivery to Norddeutscher Lloyd 1966 · 21.514 GRT · 182,88 m long
18 kn · Crew 280 · Passengers 540

Europa V · Delivery 1982 to Hapag-Lloyd · 33.819 GRT · 200 m long
21 kn · Crew abt. 300 · Passengers 600

Europa: The fourth ship to bear the name, she was originally Swedish American Line's 1953-built *Kungsholm*.

(Skyfotos Ltd, neg 72/6221)

Europa's lineage: The five *Europa*s, from the 10-knot steamer of 1891 to the new ship built between 1979 and 1981.

(Hapag-Lloyd, Aktiengesellschaft, Hamburg)

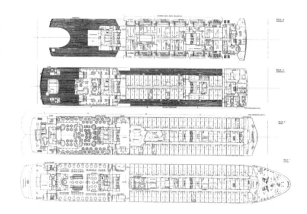

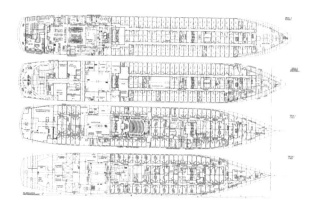

***Europa*: General arrangement plans of the ship.**

(Schiffahrts-Verlag)

By 1977, builders' tenders were invited on the basis of these concepts without any specific prototype, leaving the yards free to develop and promote their own ideas. The winning proposal came from a consortium of Bremer Vulkan and A G Weser, based on an adaptation of the layout of the then recently completed Finnish superferry *Finnjet*'s. This stressed a vertical separation of the cabin block from the public rooms, rather then the more usual horizontal plan with entire decks allocated to either sleeping accommodation or public areas. Although not an entirely new idea, this approach offered some rationalisation of services which were considered important to the design of the Finnish ferry. The Bremer Vulkan/A G Weser bid also involved the rather unusual practice of building the hull in two halves, one at each of the yards. The hull would only be joined together at the graving dock once all other parts were complete. However, the building contract was ultimately signed with Bremer Vulkan alone, after A G Weser's withdrawal from the project.

The ship was designated Bremer Vulkan hull number 1001. Hapag-Lloyd took this to be a good omen for her success, based on the number's more romantic connections with the 'Thousand and One Nights' tale. However, in a tacitly more commercial context, the more explicit designation *Die neuwe Europa* quickly took root. In terms of layout *Die neuwe Europa* offered none of the structural daring, such as divided uptakes and spectacular double-height axial spaces, prominent in her pre-World War II forebears. These features were not repeated even in more starkly functional manifestations, as on *Hamburg*. Instead, *Europa*'s designers looked to the more low-key rationale of the *Finnjet*-style layout for that element of innovation seemingly essential to German ship design.

In consideration of the larger cabin sizes and greater diversity of public spaces needed for long-range ultra-deluxe cruising, the original *Finnjet* innovation of vertical segregation between the cabin block and public rooms required substantial reworking. The 316 cabins and suites needed for *Europa*'s nominal capacity of only 600 passengers would have to occu-

py the forward half of five decks in the superstructure and upper part of the hull. Conversely, the smaller cabins needed in *Finnjet* for her 1,500 berthed passengers were all accommodated in her three superstructure decks alone.

Europa's layout stressed a less rigid vertical separation of public rooms and services from her integral cabin block than had been applied in *Finnjet*. The wider range of communal facilities needed in a long-range cruise ship made it both necessary and desirable for these to be extended fully forward on the decks both above and below the cabin block. The glass-enclosed swimming pool and lido, with their retractable Magrodome-type roof, along with the spacious forward-facing Belvedere Lounge, occupied the full length of the cabin block two decks higher up, above the officers' accommodation and navigating bridge. This intervening layer of officer cabins permitted sufficient flexibility to be worked around the centreline swimming pool tank without interfering with the centre-passage plan of deluxe boat-deck cabins.

Europa's designers also took the sensible and practical approach of locating those public rooms where views of the outside world are neither necessary or desirable below the cabin block. The ship's elaborate auditorium, complete with its multi-media projection room and language-translation booths, was situated forward of the main stairways in a centre-line space flanked by the entirely separate milieu of crew accommodation. Two decks beneath this, and coincidentally below the waterline, were the indoor swimming pool, with its attached saunas and health spa, and the nightclub. Both areas were directly accessible from the foot of the forward stairs and lifts. Although the night club was two full decks beneath the lowest strata of passenger cabins, enough attention was given to soundproofing throughout the ship to make even the crew cabins on the intervening deck sufficiently isolated from noise.

Aft of the main stairtower and central deck lobbies, which formed the division between the cabin block and public spaces, the plan generally followed that of *Finnjet*. Of the public rooms, the dining room was at the lowest level, on the *Hauptdeck* (main deck), vertically at the middle level of the five strata of cabins forward. The Europa Salon, or main lounge was directly above, occupying about the same area as the dining room, while the smaller and more informal Clipper Bar was situated two decks higher up. On this uppermost level of the aft-sited public rooms, a swimming pool astern of the bar was ingeniously encased within the deckhead space above a pantry situated aft of the Europa Salon on the deck below. This trick was made possible by a special quirk of *Europa's* planning to provide a sense of spaciousness.

To achieve the necessary effect of roominess and luxury in the main public rooms, their ceiling heights were increased above those of the cabin areas forward on each deck. Starting with the dining room flush at main-deck level, an increasingly pronounced split-level effect prevailed above, where the Europa Salon was four steps higher than the *Oberdeck* (upper deck) lobby, and the Clipper Bar was eight steps above its adjacent lobby on the *Sonnendeck* (sun deck). Although arguably a nuisance for anyone confined to a wheelchair or with other mobility difficulties, this arrangement otherwise produced extremely effective results, without the structural complexities of clerestories or other such devices to achieve the needed airiness.

This scheme was carried off without spoiling the outer appearance of the ship with disjointed window arrangements. The location of the open stretches of deck beneath the lifeboats was also used to delineate a change in the window arrangement of the public areas aft. Groupings of three panes were used at the dining room and Europa Salon levels below. At the Clipper Bar level and that of an enclosed sports deck area above, continuous ribands of panes were used, giving a softened appearance which de-stressed the impression of differing deck heights. This topmost row of windows in fact fell slightly below the long run of windows surrounding the domed pool lido and Belvedere Lounge forward. The visual effect suggested an uninterrupted riband of windows at this uppermost deck level, with the impression perhaps of extreme deck camber accounting for the slightly lower position of the windows in the full-beam superstructure wall aft of the lifeboats and beneath the funnel. Below the dining room there was no need for visual stylising, as the relatively few openings in the service areas aft generally fell in line with the cabin windows or sidelights forward.

The galley, bakeries, serveries and other catering services were located immediately below the dining room, with table service by way of twin sets of escalators. The necessary dry store rooms, larders and cold lockers were immediately below these, with direct access to the galley complex and to additional stores farther below by several service lifts. These service areas, along with a small block of catering-staff accommodation, made full use of the spaces aft of the engine-room headspace. There was thus no need to provide passenger access to any part of the ship positioned aft of the main stair-tower and below the main deck.

The main stores area was given quayside access through shell doors on port and starboard, as well as by way of an aft hatch designed to accommodate a standard 20ft stores container beamwise. This, and a similar hatch forward giving access to the hotel stores, were each fitted with twin 5-ton electro-hydraulic cranes with a 12m reach, capable of handling palletised or containerised loads over either side of the ship. Although these represented an updated approach to the conventional fore and aft hatches of the liner era, their purpose for the cruise ship *Europa* was for ships stores alone, with no additional provision for baggage or other cargoes.

Europa's cabins were beyond a doubt one of her most outstanding features. At a size of 33,819 tons and a nominal passenger capacity of only 600, the ship offered the potential for the most spacious and luxurious passenger accommodation of any ship built thus far. In catering to the individuality of their loyal and well-established regular clientele, Hapag-Lloyd avoided much of the rigid cabin standardisation applied in the *Sunward*-style approach of most new cruise ships.

Particularly noteworthy in *Europa's* plan was the presence of genuine single-berth cabins at various rate categories, as the Line recognised the needs of the single traveller within their clientele. This is not to say that there are not those who wish to travel by themselves aboard cruise ships of other Lines. However, the operators of the majority of other cruise ships prefered to stress their own preference for letting all space aboard exclusively to couples, whose combined capacity to buy more drinks, shore excursions, shop goods and casino tokens better suits their on-board revenue-earning potential. Apart from the handful of single cabins offered on the original Royal Viking Line ships, *Europa* and the new Home Lines' *Atlantic* would be among the exceptionally few cruise ships of the 1980s to offer the real ocean-liner flexibility of being able to book proper single cabins.

The single traveller aboard most other cruise ships is forced to retain a double cabin, usually at a heavily surcharged per-person double-occupancy fare. Where an unused sofa-bed or fold-away upper pullman berth would have once discretely obscured a cabin's intended double occupancy, the preference for hotel beds in modern ships leaves the unoccupied bed standing in the single traveller's quarters as a constant reminder of the hefty premium he or she has paid for it to remain unused. (Whenever forced into this situation myself, I am greatly tempted to spend the nights in one bed and use the other for my afternoon naps. It is only out of regard for the already hard-working cabin stewardesses that I desist.)

The range of accommodation consisted of 316 cabins and suites, with a total of 600 lower beds and 158 additional pullman berths, in eight overall categories ranging from deluxe suites to inside single rooms. All of these, of course, came with their own private toilet facilities.

Despite their variations of internal layout and outfitting, 409 of *Europa's* 499 passenger and crew cabins were built using Bremer Vulkan's standardised bcd-Programm ships' accommodation system. This was an approach developed by the yard since 1965 for supplying top-quality, fully assembled and outfitted cabins, ready to be installed aboard a ship as complete ready-to-use units. Unlike the mass-produced utilitarian image of 'prefab' worker-housing schemes originating out of early Bauhaus-type experiments ashore, the bcd-Programm was clearly aimed at using the manufacturing techniques of, for instance, a Mercedes-Benz or Leica plant, to produce premium-quality finished products.

The idea was that by custom-building ships' cabins and state rooms in a factory environment, far better working conditions, improved supervision and closer quality-control could be maintained than in the often damp, noisy and poorly illuminated milieu of a ship's hull in a graving dock or alongside a fitting-out pier. Erection of ships' cabins usually had to be started at a fairly early stage of building, under onboard working conditions basically unsuitable for the necessary finishing trades. The finishing and decorating of public rooms, passages and other circulation areas would usually be left to a much later stage of building, when the working conditions aboard were much improved.

Each bcd-Programm cabin would be delivered to the building berth with a finished ceiling, carpeted floor, completed bathroom unit, all furniture, fittings including soft furnishings, bed linen, and finally an installed and locked passage door. Each could then be lifted and positioned aboard ship in much the same way as a cargo container is stowed. The module would be slid into position using rails installed in the deck, and finally secured in place at its proper location. Connection of the necessary plumbing, ventilation ductwork and electrical services would be the only tasks to be carried out on board before the corridors and other linking elements would be finished.

Europa's cabins were based on a module size of 3.05m wide by 7.45m deep, which was about twenty-two per cent longer than a standard 20ft cargo container. The ship's hull and superstructure were built, with four strategically-placed deck openings positioned along the centreline, which allowed the cabin modules to be lowered aboard in their correct beamwise orientation. Starting at the lowest deck, the first modules at each location would be slid along centreline rails and then moved towards the sides of the hull, sliding in between the vertical supporting columns at each fourth frame, and positioned against their already-completed windows or portholes. The inner cabins were next positioned along the centreline, with the remaining supporting columns being erected as the cabins were set in place. The last step was to plate over the delivery openings, either positioning the final cabins to be installed over them, or later completing the stairways, lift shafts or other vertical services designated to their locations.

Apart from reducing *Europa*'s overall construction time and minimising the numbers of workers needed on board the ship, her completed bcd-Programm accommodation had the look and feel of unsurpassed shipboard quality and elegance. As an entirely separate free-standing enclosure within its own supporting frame, each cabin module was resiliently secured in place, structurally free of the ship's hull and deck, minimising the effects of structure-borne noise and vibration. The

Europa: **Double-bedded outer cabin mockup showing the superlative standard of outfitting and finish.**

(Hapag-Lloyd; courtesy Peter Kohler, Washington D C)

double walls, with integral acoustically-dampening voids formed between adjacent modules and alongside the finished corridor walls, yielded remarkably good soundproofing throughout the entire hotel block. The readily-discernible wall thickness also served to give the entire hotel block the impression of a solidly constructed building on land rather than the customary feel of a lightweight metal-built ship's interior.

Only the six deluxe suites, some of the senior crew rooms and a few other irregularly sized cabins were custom-built aboard. These too were constructed with the same resilient floor, wall and ceiling mountings, double walls and high-quality workmanship of the modularised rooms. Thus there was a consistent sense of quality and craftsmanship throughout the entire hotel and crew accommodation aboard *Europa*. The connecting corridors, stairtowers and other circulating spaces were completed later, with cushioned raised flooring throughout corresponding to the height of the floors of the cabin modules themselves.

Hapag-Lloyd were reluctant to publicise the use of modularised or manufactured accommodation, for fear of raising the spectre of mass-produced 'prefab' worker housing in the minds of would-be passengers. This point has been carefully avoided in a lavishly illustrated book about *Europa* produced with the cooperation of the Line. In addition to its coverage of the completed ship and her extensive worldwide cruise destinations, there were some remarkable construction photographs of the ship. The selection of these shipyard images was such that they gave absolutely no hint as to the use of ready-made cabins. Nonetheless, as one of the first large passenger ships to use such an accommodation building approach, *Europa* bears strong testimony to the effectiveness of this approach when done properly, without any apparent compromise either of luxury and comfort or of flexibility and individuality.

The cabins themselves were exceptionally well planned and outfitted. The twin- and double-bedded rooms, which made up the bulk of *Europa*'s accommodation, were laid out in order to separate their sleeping and daytime functions, with about half the floor space of the cabin proper being allocated to each. Beds were oriented fore and aft in the outer rooms and beamwise in the inner units along the centreline. The sitting areas, with their sofas and occasional chairs, were also equipped with full-height tables, allowing for meals to be taken with complete dining-room comfort in the cabins. In addition to the ample wardrobe and other storage capacity, separate hanging space was also provided near the entrance of each room for outdoor apparel, pool and sportswear and so on. Rails were even fitted out of the way near the entrance for the hotel staff to hang the bedcovers away at night time. In addition to fully-controllable air conditioning, a flexible lighting scheme and telephones, the technical outfit of each room included a television set, a three-channel stereo radio and a digital alarm clock controlled by the ship's master-clock system.

The toilet facilities were also well thought out and of premium quality. Each bathroom module, with its neatly built-in fixtures and stark white tiling, represented the epitome of characteristic German neatness and attention to detail. *Europa* was among the first cruise ships to offer built-in hand-held hair dryers. The inclusion of double washbasins was a thoughtful touch in consideration of the need of cabin-mates to do their pre-dinner toilette at about the same time. The specially-designed compartments for towels in various sizes, wash cloths, tissues and toilet rolls in the washbasin console, along with such extras as a retractable clothes line above the shower or bath, added to the pullman-like functionality and versatility of these remarkable spaces.

Whether or not one wants to acknowledge the manufactured or 'prefabricated' origins of *Europa*'s accommodation, they have nonetheless set a superlative standard in the cruise industry which few have since surpassed or matched, even with individually custom-made cabins. Since *Europa*'s construction, prefabricated accommodation has become more widely used. The art has steadily progressed towards the higher end of the luxury scale, with much of *Europa*'s appearance of quality being achieved.

Suffice it to say that the wide use of so elaborate a modularised accommodation system as this came at a considerable overhead in terms of extra space taken up and the added weight of such large structurally integral modules. The amount of interior space lost to the structural expediency of building modules sliding into place between the necessary structural columns was arguably wasteful. However, given that the overall size of the ship allowed for individual cabin areas of about 21sq m despite this extravagance, it was not nearly as critical to make the fullest possible use of interior space as it would have been for a ship of comparable size designed to serve the mass market, with perhaps twice *Europa*'s passenger capacity. The extra few hundred millimetres in cabin widths which could have been achieved by custom building walls with the supporting columns in-line was simply considered as not being worthwhile, either in terms of increased usable space in the cabins themselves, or in relation to the cost of building.

Following the early decision to use bcd-Programm accommodation modules throughout *Europa*, some very careful structural planning was needed in consideration of the added weight. A unified structural approach was adopted, similar to that of the 1960s-built *Oriana* and *QE2*, where the hull and superstructure would form integral strengthening elements of the ship as a whole. In *Europa*'s case this would be somewhat simplified by building an all-steel structure, without the complicated bi-metallic joints needed in the earlier British examples. This solution was arrived at through exhaustive calculations of the static and dynamic strength characteristics of the ship's structural elements. Also resulting from this extensive exercise in theoretical mathematics was the integration of such, usually ancillary, elements as the stairways and periphery seating banquettes in public areas as additional structural load-bearing and strengthening elements.

While the accommodation layout allowed for a relatively narrow beam with better than average stability, a design decision was made nonetheless to increase the waterline form. Consequently *Europa* was built with the traditional feature of a tumblehome or narrowing of the hull above the waterline, in the region of the uppermost three hull decks. The extent of this inward slant of the hull shell was, in the case of *Europa*, only a modest 250mm, far less than the readily discernible tumblehome of the earlier Dutch motorships *Oranje* and *Willem Ruys*.

Structurally, *Europa* retained a fairly strong sense of traditional liner design, although her hull form was developed from a container ship hull. At a waterline length of 170m, top speed of 22kts and draught of 7.85m, she was capable of worldwide cruise service, including comfortable crossings of the largest oceans with adequate speed reserve. These characteristics essentially kept her in the same class as her predecessor, which had been built for the dual role of Atlantic line service and cruising for Swedish American Line. Although close to the new *Europa*'s size, the 32,336-ton former *Bremen* was of considerably greater draught, having been originally built as Compagnie de Navigation Sud Atlantique's *Pasteur* of 1939 for express passenger and cargo service to South America.

	Bremen (1959)	Europa (1965)	Europa (1981)
GRT	32,336.0	21,141.0	33,819.0
Length oa	212.00m	182.27m	199.92m
Beam moulded	26.80m	23.47m	28.50m
Draught	9.33m	8.02m	7.85m
Speed	23.00kts	19.00kts	22.00kts
Maximum power	44,110.00kW	13,048.00kW	21,280.00kW
Passengers	1,207	802	758
Crew	545	418	295

As the first in a number of larger cruise ships completed in the early 1980s, *Europa* initiated a trend towards the continued use of the large low-speed diesel engines which had so well served her immediate predecessor, as well as countless other liners of the 1950s and 1960s. Two-stroke engines were again specified since, despite being potentially less efficient under the partial load conditions often used in cruising, they could burn an economical lower-grade fuel of up to 600 centiStokes. This fuel was a thick tar-like substance, needing to be heated to make it ductile enough to be piped to the engine cylinders at about the temperature and consistency of porridge.

Of course, the inevitable march of progress in marine engineering had brought along a number of refinements, most notably the reclaim of by-product energy, to meet the various auxiliary needs. Foremost among these was the need to economically generate electrical power. With the great dependency on electricity in virtually every facet of modern living, the demand for electrical power aboard modern cruise ships had risen to as high as thirty or forty per cent of the installed propulsion power.[2] Supplying such vast amounts of power by way of conventional auxiliary engines burning higher-grade fuels was simply becoming too expensive.

The evolving philosophy was that less energy would be needed to generate electricity, domestic steam and fresh water from the reserve capacity and waste by-products of the main engines, than would be necessary to power separate auxiliary engines and boilers. *Europa* (with *Tropicale* following in 1981) was among the first cruise ships to extensively adopt this type of operational economy. Prior to her building Hapag-Lloyd had already become familiar with the approach through its application in their HDW-built container ship *Frankfurt Express*.

One of the major developments in this approach to designing the whole machinery plant as a total-economy package was to capture the reserve power of the main engines so that electricity could be generated. This was done by driving a 2,000kW PTO (power take-off) generator from the opposite end of each main engine's crankshaft. The generators were thyristor-controlled to produce a constant output at engine speeds of above 100rpm up to their maximum continuous rated speed. Thus the PTO equipment was able to provide full auxiliary and domestic power while the ship was underway at speeds of 17kts and above. This system was backed up by five auxiliary diesel alternator sets with a combined generating capacity of 8,500kW, or slightly more than double the output of the PTO units. While the economy of shutting down the auxiliaries could be achieved while underway on the high seas, they had to be capable of meeting the ship's entire service loads at lower speeds, as well as providing the extra power needed to run the bow thruster when manoeuvring in and out of ports.

Additional economy of operation was also achieved through recovering engine waste by-products. Hot exhaust gases from the engine uptakes were captured to produce domestic steam and to distil fresh water. These were sufficient to meet most service needs, but could, when necessary, be supplemented by two auxiliary boilers. With *Europa*'s generation of ships, the once spacious funnel casing of cathedral-like height, with its skylights admitting light and fresh air to the engine room below, had became a thing of the past. This space was taken over for the intricate complex of tall boiler cylinders, condenser units and piping of the steam plant. The resulting power needs for forced-air engine-room ventilation could easily be offset against the extent of reclaimed energy. More importantly, the power potential of those gases, which were once discharged wholesale through the funnel, were being harnessed on their way up to the higher decks to provide the necessary steam for cooking, laundry and other domestic purposes.

Additionally, the engine heat transferred to the jacket cooling water was reclaimed to distil the necessary quantities of potable water. Once spent in this auxiliary function, the engine coolant and the water produced from the air-conditioning condensers were collected for non-potable purposes such as deck washing. This helped to save on the use of fresh water for these purposes as well as reduce the amount of waste water needing to be disposed of. Indeed, with regard to the economy of operation incorporated into her engineering, *Europa* was among the first of a trend-setting new generation of highly economical passenger tonnage.

Europa was also built as one of the most environmentally friendly or 'green' ships of her time. It was partly a requirement of Hapag-Lloyd's that *Europa* should be capable of travelling to environmentally sensitive areas of the world, such as Spitzbergen and perhaps even the Galapagos Islands. Engine-room exhaust emissions were, as already discussed, reduced to an absolute minimum. Apart from this, there were three other classes of waste disposal to be considered. These included:

Solid material such as domestic waste and refuse along with oil sludge from the engine room, burned in high-temperature incinerators yielding a minimum of smoke and exhaust fumes. (The remaining ash and waste from the twice-daily firings were ground into a fine powder and stored in a bunker space for disposal ashore at each voyage's end).

Used domestic water, biologically treated and stored in holding tanks for later disposal ashore.

Bilge water, and other liquid waste from the engine room, likewise collected into separate tanks for later discharge ashore.

The design on the accommodation decks above *Europa's* up-to-date energy-efficient power plant, expressed the ship's modernity in ways that were more tangible to the passengers.

Europa's modern ambience was tempered by the same understated sense of timeless elegance and understated luxury which had become characteristic of the 1930s *Bremen* and *Europa*. The historical relationship was similar to that of Holland America's 1959 *Rotterdam* with her earlier Atlantic running mate *Nieuw Amsterdam* dating from 1938. Indeed *Die neuve Europa's* similarity with her forerunners in accommodation design was intended to draw upon the enduring strengths of Hapag-Lloyd's vast cruising experience, which in essence began with North German Lloyd's ornate *Prinzessin Victoria Luise* of 1900. A more appropriately modern expression of design continuity was assured by the Line's choice of Joachim Buchwald and Wilfred Köhnemann as *Europa's* principal interior designers, with academic advice and counsel being rendered by Professor Arno Votteler of the Akademie der Bildenen Künste (Academy of Applied Arts) in Stuttgart.

Joachim Buchwald's previous experience with German passenger-ship work had entailed the rather prestigious design of the former *Bremen's* new interior scheme in her 1957–59 conversion. The modern public spaces he then created for North German Lloyd were a fine example of elegantly low-key 1950s contemporary chic at its best. Buchwald's style was well complemented by Wilfred Köhnemann's classic approach in furniture and industrial design. *Europa's* interiors were shared between the two men, with Buchwald being responsible for all passenger cabins and suites, the Clipper Bar and its adjacent lido area, along with the crew accommodation. Köhnemann's areas included the remainder of the passenger public spaces as well as the stairways, lobbies, entrances and the various ship's offices. In modest explanation of his overall approach, the architect said: 'I strive for discreet harmony throughout all of the spaces which I design, where one plays the star theatrical role for which these are created.'

Hapag-Lloyd's design brief called for the interior architecture and decoration to stress the luxury and home comforts of the best contemporary German resorts and urban hotels, with consideration given also to the special character of the ship's own modern structural and technical design. *Die neuve Europa* was to emphasise a uniformly luxurious appearance throughout the entire ship, within the limitations of space usage and choice of materials imposed by the strict regulations for safety of life at sea and fire prevention. The interior spaces and furnishings were thus given the same functionality of form, cleanness of line and emphasis on top-quality materials as had gone into other outstanding interior schemes, such as those of *Rotterdam*, *Canberra* and in the original design

Europa: **Interior of the Delfter Krug (a small and intimate bar adjacent to the main lounge) which shows an understated sense of the timeless elegance and good taste which has traditionally been the hallmark of Hapag-Lloyd's forebears.**

(Hapag-Lloyd)

of *QE2*. Sir Hugh Casson's dictum that 'Ship's interiors demand simple forms, clean surfaces and good serviceable materials left to speak for themselves'[3], prevailed with its corollary that the constant movement of people aboard the ship, and ever-changing panorama of the natural elements beyond her enclosures, should play the active role.

Empty, except perhaps for the ship's cleaning staff, in the dark pre-dawn hours, the elegant Europa Salon, with its rich mahogany wall panelling and the solid colours of its carpeting and soft furnishings, may well have appeared a little austere. Indeed it lacked the vivacious Scandinavian colour schemes of other ships' lounges seen at the same hour of the morning. Yet later in the day, when illuminated by a tropical sky and seascape or perhaps the hues of Norway's magnificent fjords, or at night with players and dancers on stage and filled with passengers, the room took on a remarkable sense of hospitable warmth and '*Gemutlichkeit*'. The scheme was an inspired embodiment of the rationalist 'less is more' idiom which, as far back as the *Bremen* and *Europa* of the 1930s, had set an unostentatious yet impressive sense of well-tempered richness and comfort aboard North German Lloyd's liners. In *Die neuve Europa* the same basic theme was brought forward with its inherent sense of classicism which, at the same time, left one in no doubt of its appropriately contemporary chic.

The indoor swimming pool and health centre at waterline

Europa: **The Sportdeck pool, shown here with its glass roof open, extended *Die Neuwe Europa*'s versatility for indoor/ outdoor activities well beyond her predecessors, an improvement in line with modern lifestyle trends.**

(Author)

level on C deck perhaps conveyed the strongest impression of the new ship's great predecessors of the 1930s. In its size and scale the area was quite similar to that of the 1930 *Bremen*, although with a lower ceiling and on a more open plan with its adjoining exercise spaces. The potential oppressive lowness of the ceiling was visually overcome with the inclusion of three shallow vaults above the pool tank, which, along with the four stainless-steel supporting columns at the corners of the pool itself, gave the whole area a significant architectural centre of focus. The wall murals by artist Alfred Klosowski, '*Europa reitet auf dem Stier*' (*Europa* rides upon the bull) endowed the area with a distinctive classic mythological touch within the otherwise modern context of its surroundings.

Throughout the other public areas, including the superstructure-sited dining room and the various lounges, all in the modern safety- and space-conscious rationale of single deckhead heights, the overall ambience was more quietly contemporary. Yet in the many linking elements of passages, lobbies and vestibules, the walls were hung with framed original posters from the early days of North German Lloyd and Hapag cruising, keeping one ever mindful of the Line's rich history.

Upon her completion *Europa* was actually handed over to the firm Breschag Bremer Schiffsvercharterungs AG, a holding company from whom she was chartered by Hapag-Lloyd on a long-term basis. Functionally and operationally she was entirely a Hapag-Lloyd ship, for whose specific purposes alone she had been so carefully designed and built.

Europa would be to Hapag-Lloyd as *Caronia* had been to Cunard some thirty years earlier. She, too, was to exclusively serve the regular and seasoned clientele, the carriage trade so to speak, of a great shipping Line, which likewise traced its corporate roots almost as far back as the very inception of the

steamship era itself. Apart from the inevitable progress in ship design over the intervening decades, the new German ship's operation would also take into account the significant social and lifestyle changes experienced the world over. Although she would follow many longer voyage itineraries similar to those of the earlier Cunarder, passengers would also have the option of purchasing two- or three-week segments of the trip with connecting flights to and from Germany.

Since the days of *Caronia*, and indeed of Hapag-Lloyd's own cruise operations of the 1930s *grande luxe* era, the emphasis on leisure activities had shifted towards the needs of a considerably younger clientele. This in itself brought about a far greater emphasis on sports and keep-fit activities, as well as on a high standard of live professional entertainment, in addition to first-run cinema shows and telecast media. These were foreseen and specifically addressed in the design of the ship herself, to suit the lifestyles of a generally younger crowd. Again, *Europa*'s spacious cabins were notable in that they provided the individual passenger with an almost totally self-contained, on-board living environment, in line with the ever increasing general demands for personal privacy and security. With a television camera located in the main mast to broadcast interesting voyage segments – such as cruising the Norwegian fjords or passage of the Panama Canal – throughout the accommodation, satellite ship-to-shore telephones and provision for meals to be served in the cabins and suites, passengers could virtually keep to themselves for an entire cruise if so inclined.

Above all else perhaps, *Europa* was most notable for the distinct German character of her service, and indeed her entire being. This singularly classed her as a ship with a national identity, a rare distinction in the largely American-

Europa: **The elegant and superbly equipped theatre was designed to serve the needs of experienced passengers on longer cruises wanting first-run films, extensive port lectures, musical performances and religious services. The facility was equipped for three-language simultaneous translation.**

(Hapag-Lloyd)

Europa: **The Club Belvedere, seen as a spacious observation lounge worthy of the ship's varied excursions into such spectacular regions as the Spitzbergen and the Norwegian Fjords, was also fully equipped for live entertainment and dancing.**

(Author)

flavoured international cruise field of the post-liner era. In much the same way that an essentially American standard has prevailed over the worldwide luxury hotel market, the Norwegian Caribbean and Royal Viking type of operation had engendered its own 'international' image. More accurately expressed, this was a multi-national style of enterprise, with vessels of Scandinavian ownership and construction, designed to American tastes in resort styling, staffed by multi-national crews from as many as fifty-seven countries of the world, and in some cases registered under the flags of yet other nations. Gone were the days when going to sea offered the opportunity to sample the culture, languages, cuisine and culture of the nation whose ship one had chosen to sail aboard, with *Europa* and a select few others as noted exceptions.

Aboard *Europa*, beds were made up with the duvet-style '*bettdecken*' and large square-shaped pillows preferred in German homes and hotels ashore. Cuisine emphasised a characteristic Germanic preference for fowl and game served in generous portions. A beer always was served in a '*steinkrug*' (beer stein) bearing the Hapag-Lloyd logo. Other traditional touches of high-class continental service included the privilege of leaving one's shoes in the corridor upon retiring for the night so that they could be cleaned by the establishment's attentive staff. This final point was, in fact, only made possible by special consideration shown to *Europa* by the unions representing her crew at their own request.

In contrast to the 'American international' idiom, *Europa* offered a less ostentatious type of entertainment in favour of variety shows and music-hall-style features. European shipboard audiences enjoy a closer and more personal contact with their entertainers. For instance it is quite likely that after

their main show of the evening the star vocalists or musicians will descend to the night club, where they will entertain the late night revellers in a far more intimate and personal club-like atmosphere.

A sense of continuity in service was assured by the transfer of the fourth *Europa*'s crew to the new ship, virtually as a complete and intact entity. Many of these, officers, deck crew and most importantly, the hotel staff, had been in the service of Hapag-Lloyd and its predecessors for many years. When cruising aboard *Europa* myself in 1985, I met a number of people who had served as far back as the days of the fourth *Bremen*, the early 1950s *Berlin*, and even one steward who was familiar with the third *Europa* before World War II. The long-standing relationships which these people have formed with *Europa*'s many repeat passengers over the years have proved to be an important ingredient in the remarkably personal and club-like atmosphere which this ship alone engenders.

One of my own fondest recollections of that cruise aboard *Europa* was the group of ship's hostesses who gathered at the end of the railway platform at Bremerhaven's Columbuskai in their smart airline-style blue uniforms and high-heeled shoes to wave farewell to us as our special 'boat train' departed from the port at the voyage's end. This is no doubt part of their job, but the gesture is nonetheless a pleasing invitation for old friends to return.

ATLANTIC

Home Lines had likewise started considering a new cruise liner in the early 1970s, at about the time Royal Caribbean and Royal Viking's first-generation tonnage was being completed in Finland. The Line was, in this regard, well ahead of the times through their successful experience with their earlier ship *Oceanic*, essentially of liner design, adapted for full-time cruising in the course of her construction.

As a family-run concern of great individuality, Home Lines was founded in 1946 by Eugen Eugenides, with Greek, Italian, Swiss and American financial backing, as well as a link with the Swedish Broström Group. The name Home Lines was itself an anglicisation of the Swedish word '*holm*', taken from Swedish American Line passenger ship nomenclature. In fact one of the early Home Lines ships was the former *Drottningholm*, renamed *Brasil* upon her acquisition in 1948. The 1928-built *Kungsholm* also joined Home Lines, after having served the United States in wartime as the troop ship USS *John Ericsson*, becoming their well-known *Italia*.[4]

After running successful line services, first from Italy to South America, and later from the Mediterranean, northern Europe and England to the United States and Canada, a complete transition to year-round cruising was made between 1960 and 1963. The move to leisure travel also coincided with planning of the first ship to be built for Home Lines. This was accordingly transformed into a full-time cruise vessel, at least in the minds of her designers and Home Lines management.[5]

Atlantic: **The ship making her maiden arrival at New York in April 1982 before she began cruising in tandem with *Oceanic*.**

(Home Lines, New York)

What actually emerged on the drawing boards was another dual-purpose liner, similar in design concept to *Rotterdam* and *Canberra*. The new Home Lines flagship offered a similar degree of adaptability, with her easily combined first- and tourist-class accommodation and provision for a limited amount of special cargo, including automobiles. In addition to the especially well-articulated layout of her tastefully designed modern public rooms, the ship's indoor/outdoor dual top-deck swimming pools, with their retractable sliding glass Magrodome roof, were well suited to a modern cruise lifestyle.

Apart from her cruising role, she would be suitable for line service, not only on the routes which had been served by Home Lines themselves, but in other trades such as those served by *Windsor Castle*, *Oriana* or her Italian contemporary *Eugenio C* if need be. For anyone building a passenger ship in those times of change, adaptability was an especially important consideration in the event of having to transfer or sell the vessel later.

Nicos Varnicos-Eugenides, who was then the Line's president, had insisted on only the best in design, construction, outfitting and performance for his new ship. Completed in 1965 by Cantieri dell'Adriatico as *Oceanic*, she became an immediate success, setting a high standard of luxury and service for her owners. *Oceanic* was extremely popular in the New York-based market, which she served with distinction for two decades until being sold to Premier Cruises in 1985.

Her original running mate on her year-round cruising programme was the former Matson liner *Mariposa* of 1932, which following extensive rebuilding by her original owners, was sold in 1955 to Home Lines who renamed her *Homeric*. After a disastrous galley fire in 1973 she was withdrawn and eventually scrapped. She was replaced the following year when Home Lines purchased the *Hanseatic* from Hamburg Atlantic Line, renaming her *Doric*. Built originally as *Shalom* for Zim Lines, this ship was an ideal companion for *Oceanic*, having likewise been built for a dual-purpose function as liner and cruise ship.

The good experience Home Lines gained in cruising *Oceanic* and *Doric* clearly influenced the planning done in the 1970s for a new cruise ship. A building contract was signed in April 1979 with the French builders Constructions Navales et Industrielles de la Méditerranée (CNIM) of La Seyne sur Mer for a 1,200-passenger motor-ship of 32,000 tons. When finally completed in 1982 as *Atlantic*, the new ship would, to a great extent, represent an amalgamation of design features from both earlier ships.

As a cruise liner, *Atlantic* generally followed the pattern of *Oceanic*'s passenger facilities, stressing a wide diversity of public rooms and other communal spaces. As in the earlier ship, an extensive main run of lounges, bars and other spaces was originally to have occupied the full length of the principal superstructure deck. However, at a fairly advanced stage of planning, the forward part of this deck was appropriated for additional cabins. On the deck immediately above, a near adaptation of *Oceanic*'s much-admired twin Magrodome-enclosed swimming pools was planned. However, one of *Atlantic*'s swimming pools had to be eliminated when the extra cabins were added to the lounge deck below, forcing a relocation of the main lounge to the midships space below the lido area. In *Oceanic*'s plan the two levels of public spaces were interspersed with a cabin deck made necessary by her lower lifeboat location, giving her designers greater freedom from any such obstructions.

Atlantic's lifesaving outfit more closely followed the example of *Doric* in that the lifeboats were atop the superstructure rather than being semi-nested as in *Oceanic*. In both *Doric* and *Atlantic* the lifeboat davits were arranged without the customary open promenade space beneath them as in most modern ships. In *Doric* there were fully enclosed promenades on the deck below the davits, which provided for lifeboat embarkation through shell ports incorporated into the superstructure window arrangement. The corresponding enclosed deck in the new *Atlantic* was conveniently arranged around her *Oceanic*-style pool lido. The boats were thus above these facilities rather than below them as in *Oceanic*. The periphery area of the midships-located lido, along with its adjacent cafés and bars, could thus be used for lifeboat embarkation. In *Oceanic* this function was filled by the enclosed promenades surrounding her main public rooms on the deck below her nested lifeboats.

Unfortunately this style of lifeboat arrangement, with the

Atlantic: Lifeboats were fully atop the superstructure, as on *Doric*. The enclosed Lido-deck promenade beneath the lifeboats similar to that on *Oceanic* provided circulation about the pool lido and an informal daytime space, as well as protected emergency muster stations.

(Author)

davits rooted unusually high up atop the superstructure, contributed nothing to *Atlantic*'s exterior appearance. Lack of the usual inset to the superstructure side beneath the lifeboats served to strongly emphasise the featureless slab-sided structure of the ship as a whole. The only dimensional relief to the unbroken monotony of five rows of portholes and two tiers of larger windows above them was an enclosed overhang projecting from the belvedere deck aft of the funnel. Otherwise there was not so much as a painted riband to break the vertical expanse. The diminutive bow deck (which to me always looked as though it were a deck lower than it should have been) unfortunately also contributed to the ship's visual impression of height. In my own mind *Atlantic*'s aesthetics would have been vastly improved if she had been given the inner/outer boat deck promenade arrangement of Christians-

son's last *Gripsholm* and *Kungsholm*.

However, *Atlantic* was at least given an attractive spoon-shaped counter stern, somewhat resembling those of *Oceanic* and *Doric*. She was in fact one of the few modern ships to be so endowed, as the rationale of new cruise ship design was beginning to favour transom sterns due to their easier fabrication as well as the greater internal and deck space they offered. Carnival's *Tropicale*, Hapag-Lloyd's *Europa* and, later, Holland America's *Nieuw Amsterdam/Noordam* sisters were all to follow with transom sterns.

The example of *Doric*'s layout also prevailed in *Atlantic*'s cabin accommodation. In this regard *Oceanic* had still represented pure North Atlantic liner design practice, with a great many small and inside cabins as well as a diverse range of room categories to suit the various needs and expectations of point-to-point travellers. Alternatively, *Doric*, with regard to her originally intended cruising role as *Shalom* for Zim Lines, offered a high standard of accommodation more akin to Swedish American Line's superlative standards. Indeed *Atlantic*'s cabin plan as a whole, along with the layout of the rooms themselves, could clearly be seen to have originated with the former Israeli ship as her prototype.

Like *Europa*, *Atlantic* offered a fairly wide range of cabin types, and was among the last of her generation to do so. Apart from the six deluxe suites, with their separate bedroom and living areas, there were 180 luxury cabins with separate sleeping and sitting areas similar in overall conception to the majority of *Europa*'s rooms. Additionally, there were smaller inner and outer cabins with the *Sea Venture*-style L-shaped bed arrangement, where the beamwise-oriented bed folded away into a sofa for daytime use. *Atlantic* also offered a num-

Atlantic: Styling of the ship's single bulkhead-deck restaurant reflected a liner tradition, since its design whose expression was somewhat akin to *Rotterdam*'s dining room.

(Author)

ber of proper single rooms, in most instances located fully forward and aft where the narrowing of the hull reduced the space otherwise needed for the L-shaped bed layout. Unlike *Europa*, there was no provision made for double-bedded accommodation aboard *Atlantic*.

The single dining room, which was designed to serve *Atlantic*'s passengers in two sittings, was located two decks lower than those aboard *Oceanic* and *Doric*. The new ship's designers were not tempted to follow the examples of *QE2*, and the great majority of Scandinavian cruise ships, by locating the dining room in the superstructure, preferring to go instead towards a bulkhead-deck location. However, with all passengers to be served in a single saloon, the traditional mid-ships-galley liner plan could be reworked with the usual location of the second dining room being allocated instead to crew catering and recreation facilities.

This allowed all those aboard to be efficiently served from a single catering complex, without compromise to the layout of passenger facilities on the decks above. Stores were arranged immediately below the galley on the bulkhead deck, where shore access was conveniently provided through shell doors at pier level. The overall layout of *Atlantic*'s catering facilities was in fact not unlike that of Matson's *Malolo* of 1927, in her original configuration as a one-class ship. By the time that ship had been acquired as Home Lines' first *Atlantic* in 1953, a second dining room and separate galley for tourist class had long since been added on the deck below her original crew catering facilities, which were retained in their original location.

Although giving a strong visual impression of a modernised deep-sea liner of the Home Lines fleet, *Atlantic* differed in a number of key operational and technical characteristics. Apart from having a single accommodation class and lacking conventional baggage holds, *Atlantic*'s class of cruise liners introduced an altogether lighter and less robust construction which was considered adequate for the less demanding vicissitudes of full-time cruising.

	Oceanic	Doric	Atlantic
GRT	27,645.0	25,338.0	30,262.0
Length oa	235.00m	191.70m	204.70m
Beam moulded	29.30m	24.80m	27.35m
Draught	8.60m	8.20m	7.38m
Speed	26.50kts	22.70kts	23.50kts
Maximum power	44,500.00kW	18,389.00kW	22,064.00kW
Passengers	1,200	1,098	1,306
Crew	560	469	490

In comparison with her earlier fleetmates, generally of similar size, overall dimensions and capacity, *Atlantic* differed most significantly in terms of her considerably shallower draught. While the reduced underwater depth allowed for quayside docking at a greater number of attractive cruise ports, there was at least a theoretical compromise in perfor-

mance and comfort by traditional ocean-liner standards. The reduced depth was gained partly at the expense of dead-weight capacity, in other words, the quantity of fuel, stores and consumables carried in compartments and holds in the bowels of the ship below the waterline. Also, with no cargo or passenger hold baggage capacity and generally smaller and more compact machinery installations, *Atlantic* and other cruise ships of her generation had potentially lower margins of vertical stability against possible rolling and pitching.[6]

In this regard *Atlantic* perhaps fell between the application of two different design philosophies. Her hull lines retained much of the fineness of form which was characteristic of her liner fleetmates, affording no compensation in deadweight for her shallower draught. Later cruise ships of her class, based on an 'economy-of-scale' design approach, would, to some degree, offset this compromise with a fuller hull form, and consequently the stabilising influence of a larger displacement. In other words, a greater volume of space would be immersed in the water for a ship of given length and breadth, lowering the effective centre of gravity and reducing the propensity to roll and pitch.

What is not as readily apparent from general specifications is the tendency towards an altogether lighter type of construction in modern cruise ships than could be permitted in, for instance, a North Atlantic liner. Unlike the quest for weight economy exercised in building Orient Line's original *Oriana* or Cunard's *QE2*, the modern cruise-ship approach was towards an entirely lightweight steel construction from the keel up. The hulls of *Oriana* and *QE2* were built with the strength and stamina to withstand sustained long-haul service at high speed on the Atlantic and Pacific Oceans, with full consideration of wave lengths and heights experienced on these extremely wide and deep bodies of water. The weight economies achieved through their extensive use of aluminium in the superstructures, internal structures and other measures was directed at reducing topsides strains on already heavy-duty hulls.

Since cruise ships of *Atlantic*'s type would not be expected to encounter anything like the same constant bending, twisting, slamming and hogging stresses in service, an altogether less robust hull structure could be quite safely accepted. Consequently, the hull frames and deck beams could be lighter and of a shallower profile, and thinner all-welded shell plating could be accepted without undue compromise of security and stability for the anticipated service conditions. In the same way that architectural practice ashore had led to new buildings being designed to actual environmental and usage conditions, rather than being over-built to some arbitrary and outmoded rule of thumb, so too did the modern cruise ship adopt a designed-for-actual-service approach.

None of these characteristics was viewed as a source of any real discomfort or inconvenience, but rather an inevitable consequence of operating in an aggressively competitive market against the adversities of high capital, fuel and labour costs. While maintaining a regular seven-day cruise circuit based in

Atlantic: **Interior of the Observation Lounge forward on Lido deck.**

(Author)

Miami, restricted fuel and stores capacities posed no difficulties as bunkering and victualling could be carried out during the weekly turnaround period between cruises. Likewise, any compromise of seakeeping and stability, as perceived against North Atlantic standards, was reconciled in terms of sustained service under mild and friendly tropical navigating conditions. Thanks to the universal reliance on stabilisers, the effects of most adverse sea conditions encountered in regular service could be dampened to comfortable levels without serious loss of headway. Despite severe damage to *Atlantic*'s bow during an Atlantic storm early on in her career, abnormally serious conditions such as hurricanes and typhoons would be avoided altogether thanks to adequate weather forecasting.

Although essentially a 1980s-generation cruise ship, *Atlantic* nonetheless retained a couple of notable traditional features. As she was planned for regular cruising between New York and Bermuda, she was engined for a service speed of 21kts, which accorded her sufficient reserve power to make up for lost headway under the unfavourable weather conditions sometimes encountered on the open seas between New York and Bermuda. In this regard she differed somewhat from a number of her near contemporaries in Caribbean service, which had been designed for optimum running efficiency at downrated speeds of between 17 and 19kts. *Atlantic* was also distinguishable for exclusively retaining the use of conventional portholes below the lounge-deck windows. Apart from its traditional appearance, this feature also contributed to the ship's structural strength by eliminating the stress points around the corners of straight-sided ships' windows, hatches and other shell openings.

After running successful sea trials off the coast of France, *Atlantic* made her New York debut on schedule in the spring of 1982. She started cruising from New York in tandem with

Oceanic on 17 April. Home Lines had negotiated a five-year contract with the government of Bermuda to secure prime berthing space alongside Front Street in Hamilton for their new ship. *Atlantic* joined the regular New York summer cruise fleet of *Rotterdam*, *Statendam* and *Volendam*, all of which sailed on Saturdays on varying seven-day itineraries to Bermuda and the Bahamas.

Throughout her service life with Home Lines, *Atlantic* retained the essentially Italian flavour of the entire Line's operation. She was running in league with *Oceanic* which had started cruising in the last days of the liner era, at a time when deep-sea passenger ships still tended to represent microcosms of the nations which had put them to sea. Despite coming from multi-national origins with foreign-registered ships, Home Lines had retained the predominantly Italian national identity of their crews throughout the Line's entire operations right from the beginning. Being based in New York rather than Miami, the competitive influences coming from the opposite sides of the Big Apple's piers were then essentially still of the international liner era. Home Lines operated against the competition of Holland America, which had been in North Atlantic service, until the early 1970s. Until the mid-1970s, Home Lines ships would dock from time to time across the pier from *France*, or from the Italian line *Michelangelo* and *Raffaello* whose characters they were most naturally similar to.

After *Michelangelo* and *Raffaello* had sailed off to their unhappy eventual fate as military accommodation ships in the Middle East, and *Leonardo da Vinci* had been destroyed by fire, many of the Italian officers and crew of these ships found their way into the fleets of Carnival Cruises and Home Lines. While English was the language of Carnival's multi-nationally staffed operation, Italian remained the working language of the Home Lines fleet. Right through to the final days of Home Lines in the late 1980s, to sail aboard their *Oceanic* and *Atlantic* and eventually the last *Homeric*, which replaced *Oceanic* in 1986, was to re-live something of the lifestyle of the final 1960s heyday in Italian passenger shipping.

NIEUW AMSTERDAM AND NOORDAM

Europa and *Atlantic* were soon followed by Holland America's first new ships since their 1971-built *Prinsendam*, which burned and sank off Alaska in 1980. Orders were placed with Chantiers de L'Atlantique at St Nazaire, in October 1980, for two 1,200 passenger motor-ships of 32,000 tons, at a fixed price of $150 million each. The French yard secured the contract largely as they were the only builders willing to quote a fixed price in dollars. Holland America might in fact have done better if they had negotiated their price in French francs, in view of subsequent currency devaluation which could have given them their ships as much as thirty per cent cheaper.[7]

Chantiers de L'Atlantique's past laurels in passenger-ship work were gained with the building of such famed North Atlantic liners as *Normandie* and *France*, along with other French-flag notables such as *L'Atlantique* and *Pasteur*. Since delivering French Line's prestigious second *France* in 1962, Zim Line's *Shalom*, Compagnie Française de Navigation's *Renaissance* and the China National *Yao Hwa* were completed as the last traditional liners to be built at St Nazaire.

In response to the decline in passenger shipping during the 1960s, Chantiers de L'Atlantique tooled up to concentrate on building supertankers for the then booming oil industry. The yard's building berths were extended to accommodate hulls of up to 400m in length and 64m beam. The hull fabrication shops were doubled in size and equipped with computer-aided drafting and production facilities, rendering these

among the world's most advanced facilities at the time. New gantry cranes were also installed, allowing hull sections of up to 750 tons to be prefabricated and lifted into place in the giant new building docks. The yard managed to retain some presence in the passenger field, and thereby also to hold on to its skills in the necessary finishing trades, through building ferries for various domestic and other Euro-Scandinavian owners. Among the largest and most prestigious of these were the three *Svea Corona*-class ferries built in 1975/6 for Silja Line's Stockholm – Helsinki service.

In 1976, Chantiers de L'Atlantique merged with the Alsthom group, bringing them also together with the Dubigeon and Ateliers et Chantiers de Bretagne shipyards, and forming France's fifteenth largest industrial entity, with a total workforce of 45,000.[8] At the time of the St Nazaire yard expansions and modernisation probably nobody could have foreseen these advanced facilities ever being used for the construction of great passenger ships ever again.

By the time the new Holland America building contracts were signed in 1980, French passenger shipbuilding was beginning to re-emerge at La Seyne where CNIM already had construction of Home Lines' *Atlantic* in hand and were negotiating with Sitmar for the building of a new cruise ship. As Chantiers de L'Atlantique's seventy-sixth passenger ship, *Nieuw Amsterdam* would re-establish the yard's presence in deep-sea passenger-ship building, albeit for cruise ships rather than traditional liners.

The new Holland America design, which called for maximum passenger comfort and luxury to be achieved with maximum operational efficiency, evolved as a collaborative effort between the owners and builders. The building techniques that were used involved sectional construction derived from the yard's extensive supertanker experience. Hull and superstructure sections of up to 680 tons would be assembled by the fabrication shops before being lowered into place in the building dock.

In terms of their size and capacities, the two new ships would fall slightly below the overall specifications of the 1959 *Rotterdam* and the earlier *Nieuw Amsterdam*. The greatest individual difference, would be in the considerably shallower draught and the lower speed used for cruising by each of the new ships.

	Nieuw Amsterdam (1938)	*Rotterdam* (1959)	*Nieuw Amsterdam* (1982)
GRT	36,287.0	38,650.0	33,930.0
Length oa	231.19m	228.12m	214.65m
Beam moulded	26.82m	28.65m	27.20m
Draught	9.60m	9.00m	7.40m
Speed	20.50kts	20.50kts	18.00kts★
Maximum power	25,350.00kW	28,332.00kW	21,680.00kW
Passengers	1,232	1,456	1,374
Crew	650	776	599

★ optimised cruising speed

Nieuw Amsterdam: **Nearing completion at Chantiers de L'Atlantique's St Nazaire yard in France.**

(Holland America)

Nieuw Amsterdam's overall layout stressed an inspired adaptation of the vertical *Finnjet* accommodation approach. While the catering services were essentially concentrated aft as in the Finnish ship, the main run of public rooms was extended to the full length of the the promenade deck. This effectively divided the forward hotel block near its vertical midpoint, as opposed to the *Europa* variation with public spaces above and below the hotel block.

Nieuw Amsterdam also differed from *Europa* in that her plan emphasised a concentration of open air recreational facilities aft rather than above. Instead of emphasising a glass-enclosed pool and lido atop the cabin block, a series of terraced open decks was stressed. Holland America had found favour with this approach since they started cruising *Rotterdam* and *Statendam* as well as with the two former Moore McCormack ships.

Although lacking the continuity of *Europa*'s full-length topsides amenities, with the forward-facing Belvedere Lounge, *Nieuw Amsterdam* and *Noordam* nonetheless retained the separate Holland America-style observation lounge. An above-the-bridge room of this type was first introduced in the intermediate liner *Statendam*, as built in 1956. It appeared again in *Volendam* and *Veendam*, as those ships were acquired, and was repeated in the Line's first purpose-built cruise ship *Prinsendam*, an 8,000-ton luxury mini cruise liner intended for cruising in the East Indies. In fact the overall distribution of private and public accommodation elements in the 1983 *Nieuw Amsterdam* can be clearly seen as a developed and much enlarged adaptation of *Prinsendam*'s layout.

In achieving their objectives of passenger comfort and luxury, as would be expected of them, Holland America also retained design elements from their highly regarded North Atlantic experience, as embodied in the former *Nieuw Amsterdam* and then current flagship *Rotterdam*. The double-height main lounge of the new ship, with its mezzanine, bore the influence of her earlier namesake's Grand Hall, despite being rendered in a more contemporary form. From the example of *Rotterdam* came the main lobby plan, with its area completely encompassing wide central staircases, along with a great expansion of the asymmetrical planning introduced in parts of her public rooms layout. From *Rotterdam*'s 1969 cruising refit came the influence of her highly successful Lido Restaurant. This was an indoor/outdoor space with full-function buffet catering facilities which had been created out of the ship's original tourist-class Café de la Paix aft on the promenade deck.

While it was relatively easy to incorporate the best elements of layout from the Line's existing ships, the question of decoration and outfitting was far more onerous. Ultimately, Holland America would like to have also replicated at least some of the unique design elements and fine craftsmanship of *Rotterdam* and the former *Nieuw Amsterdam*. After two decades of service, *Rotterdam*'s virtually unaltered interiors were still as great an attraction for repeat and new passengers alike as they had been when the ship was new in 1959. However, despite

Nieuw Amsterdam: **The double-height main Stuyvesant Lounge and Minnewit Terrace which, although recalling Rotterdam's elegant 1950s modernity, was one of the last rooms of its type to use the traditional mezzanine arrangement typical of so many earlier liners.**

(Holland America)

the advanced building techniques developed by Chantiers de L'Atlantique and their retention of the essential passenger-ship finishing trades, many of the materials and much of the craftsmanship which had gone into *Rotterdam* would have been scarce at any price.

A clever solution to this dilemma was worked out by the Dutch firm, De Vlaming, Fennis, Dingemans – Interiors BV (VFD) of Utrecht, who were awarded the contract for interior decoration of *Nieuw Amsterdam* and *Noordam*. Their approach was to decorate the public spaces simply, using understated and generally plain wall coverings of quality hard-wearing materials, and to furnish the lounges and bars mainly with quality stock, contract furniture. Appropriate works of art, including sculptures, paintings and various artifacts were to be used to accent these otherwise relatively unadorned schemes. With the proper use of architectural lighting these items would be further enlivened to create a sense of far greater richness and luxury. Although the initial cost of the art was itself considerable, it could be expected to accrue greater value in the future. Also, as a readily moveable asset, it could be transferred to newer ships in the future as needed.[9] The decorative theme for *Nieuw Amsterdam* was created around the history of the Dutch West India Company, while that of *Noordam* would centre instead around the history of early Dutch settlement in America.

Indeed the whole idea worked very well, as the interiors

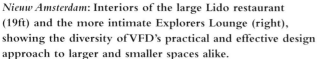

Nieuw Amsterdam: Interiors of the large Lido restaurant (19ft) and the more intimate Explorers Lounge (right), showing the diversity of VFD's practical and effective design approach to larger and smaller spaces alike.

(Holland America)

of both ships won immediate favour with the American cruising public. They offered something different from the 'Americanised' interiors of so many US-based ships. While this might have been a pleasantly unexpected change for neophyte cruise passengers, to those who already knew Holland America Line, it was no doubt something to be expected of them.

The other feature which was developed from VFD's work was the asymmetrical plan introduced in *Rotterdam*'s promenade deck public rooms. In both *Nieuw Amsterdam* and *Noordam* the promenade-deck rooms were, for the most part, arranged around a wide thoroughfare which started near the centreline forward and gradually undulated towards the port side and then back again towards the centreline, where it finished up at the main lounge. This unique departure from normal shipboard symmetry allowed the designers to create a varied array of rooms with different sizes and shapes to add an element of interest and diversity. It also had the effect of giving passengers the impression of being aboard a considerably larger ship.

The refinement of *Nieuw Amsterdam*'s interior design was, not reflected in her external styling. This tended more to bespeak Holland America's wish for economy of operation. The superstructure lines were quite angular and rectilinear, more in line with the square-all-over look of *Finnjet*, *Silvia Regina* or a number of other then recent ferries. There was no curvature to the superstructure front as in *Atlantic* and no cantilevered sun decks topsides to visually 'tidy up' the

appearance of the lifeboats and their associated paraphernalia. The bow lines were similarly modern and functional and the hull lines came to an abrupt halt aft at the transom stern. Forward, the juncture of the curvilinear bow flare and flat plane of the slab-sided midbody formed a definite oblique chine crossing three rows of cabin windows and portholes beneath the forward end of the superstructure. This particular feature gave the hull a solid look of massive strength, reminiscent in character, if not in form too, of the new ship's great North Atlantic predecessors.

Nieuw Amsterdam's external look was in its own right quite attractive. There was no appearance of excessive superstructure height, thanks largely to the more traditional arrangement of the uppermost decks within the confines of the lifeboat davits. In his book *Liners to the Sun* John Maxtone-Graham describes *Nieuw Amsterdam* and *Noordam* as having 'a kind of Bauhaus superstructure reminiscent of *Prinsendam*'.[10] Indeed these ships did appear as proportionately enlarged renditions of *Prinsendam*'s uniquely rationalist styling. Their exponentially greater size was somewhat belied by the dark paint scheme of the hull, which largely obscured the lower row of large windows for the dining room from sight in daylight.

Holland America chose twin, low-speed, diesel propulsion for this their first *Nieuw Amsterdam* to be preceded in name with the initials MS (motor ship) rather than SS (steam ship). The arrangement of *Nieuw Amsterdam*'s dining room farther amidships fairly high up, with the galley and its related facilities aft on the same deck rather than below, allowed the additional headroom for the higher main-engine blocks. The Sulzer R-type engines chosen for *Nieuw Amsterdam* were a more advanced version of the 1978-developed RND-M crosshead engines fitted aboard Carnival's *Tropicale*, which was

Nieuw Amsterdam: **Here she is in the care of a Moran tug on her maiden arrival in New York. The austere angular lines of the ship's superstructure, though not unattractive, bespoke the cost-effective rationale of new economy-of-scale planning.**

(Holland America)

completed some months earlier. *Nieuw Amsterdam*'s RLB machines, first introduced by Sulzer in 1980, featured a longer stroke and larger bore, giving them better performance at lower running speeds. The new RLB-type engines were able to maintain maximum cylinder pressure at their full-load rating over a greater range of actual load conditions.[11] These were thus ideally suited for downrated running at 135rpm, yielding 10,800kW each, at the ship's optimised cruising speed of 18kts.

As in *Europa*, *Nieuw Amsterdam*'s machinery installation was designed around the integrated power-plant principle. The main engines also provided the primary source of auxiliary and domestic electrical power while at sea. Each main engine drove a 2,400kW Alsthom-Unelec generator by way of Lohmann & Stolterfoht step-up gearing in the propeller lines. Since *Nieuw Amsterdam* was designed with controllable-pitch propellers, the main engines could be run at a fairly constant speed, eliminating any need for the expensive thyristor generator controls required in *Europa*'s case. *Nieuw Amsterdam*'s backup electrical service or additional power, when needed for manoeuvring with the bow and stern thrusters, was provided by two additional 2,200kW generators, both driven by a single RLB diesel, itself a smaller four-cylinder version of the seven-cylinder main engines.

The machinery layout was noteworthy in that the third engine was tucked into a space aft of the main machines,

between their power take-off gearboxes and shaft couplings. The auxiliary generators were situated aftmost, between the propeller shafts.

Although *Nieuw Amsterdam*'s maiden Atlantic crossing in 1983 was postponed due to an unfortunate electrical blackout just before sailing from Le Havre, she and her propulsion plant have since proved extremely reliable in service. The following year she was joined by *Noordam*, which slipped quietly into service without incident. As *Atlantic* and her crew had sustained the Italian nationality of Home Lines operation at the opposite side of the Hudson river piers which were her new-world home, so would *Nieuw Amsterdam* and *Noordam* continue to uphold Holland America's distinctly Dutch tradition, by then of some 110 years' standing. Commanded by Dutch officers and staffed with a large proportion of personnel from the former colonies of the Netherlands East Indies, Holland America's new generation of cruise ships continued to uphold service traditions similar to those of Britain's P&O Line.

In fact, Holland America's transatlantic liners were originally staffed almost entirely by Netherlands nationals due to Union problems. It was only in the latter years, after the Line had become heavily engaged in cruising, that multi-national crews from the Orient began to be employed aboard these ships. This brought aboard a P&O style of Dutch internationalism actually originating from the Nederland and Rotterdamsche Lloyd lines which had served the Dutch colonies in the Far East. Indeed this has been an important ingredient in preserving the distinct sense of nationality which has made 'the dependable Dutch' so famous in the world of shipping. Even today, on a later and more prestigious generation of Holland America cruise ships, Dutch remains the ship's working language, and the same courteous service is offered under

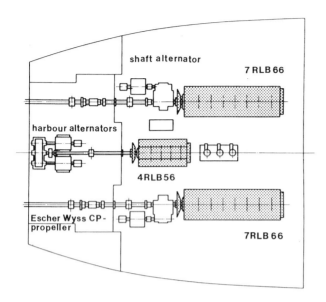

Nieuw Amsterdam: **General arrangement plan of the main machinery, with the two main engines augmented by a third, smaller, unit of the same class driving the two harbour alternators in the adjacent compartment.**

(Gebruders Sulzer, Winterthur)

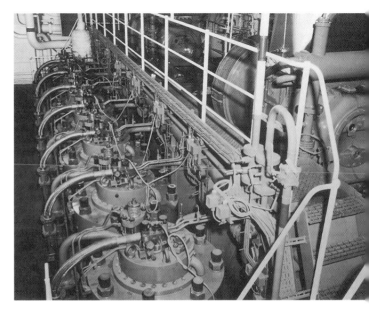

Nieuw Amsterdam: **View of the starboard main engine looking forward along the cylinder heads.**

(Gebruders Sulzer)

the leadership of each ship's Dutch captain and senior officers.

Apart from the sense of individuality which is preserved by the crew's nationalistic and language identity with the Line, *Nieuw Amsterdam* and *Noordam* also had the benefit of the distinctly Dutch approach in terms of their design. This came not only from the progressive influence from earlier generations of Holland America tonnage, but also from the choice of her Netherlands-based interior designers, who have shown a special understanding of Holland America history, and of outstanding design in their own work. In my own opinion it is also greatly to the Line's credit that they have avoided the trite nomenclature of so much modern cruise shipping with its *ad nauseam* vague references to monarchy and royalty. Thank goodness we have been spared the ultimate absurdity of 'Royal Dutch Princess' in favour of a continued use not only of traditional Holland America names, but also in their indigenous Dutch spellings.

These sister ships, along with *Europa* and *Atlantic*, as well as the later *Tropicale*, and *Song of America* represented a turning point in passenger-ship thinking, from the viewpoint both of those long-established shipping Lines which were prepared to adapt fully to cruising, and of the more visionary newcomers to the trade. Both could by then see the great potential for business growth which cruising had to offer in the long term. This was a point beyond which owners gained the confidence to build more new tonnage of still greater individuality and, in most cases, of prodigiously larger scale.

Atlantic was chartered in 1988 to Premier Cruises as

Starship Atlantic following the demise of Home Lines. *Europa*, which is being replaced by a new Hapag-Lloyd ship of the same name, has been sold to Star Cruises. The two Holland America ships remain in the line's service at the time of writing.

1   *The Naval Architect*, January 1982, p E9.
2   H Schmidt, *Versatility with Economy for Cruise Ship Propulsion*, 1986, p 5.
3   Philip S Dawson, *British Superliners of the Sixties*, p 63.
4   C R Vernon Gibbs, *Western Ocean Passenger Lines and Liners 1934-69*, p 142-3.
5   Stephen Berry, *Guide 87*, pp 25-6.
6   Stephen M Payne, *Cruise & Ferry Info*, No 2, 1994, pp 16-17.
7   *Fairplay*, 14 July 1983, p 11.
8   *Hansa*, No 9/10, p 646.
9   Stephen Payne, *Grande Dame*, p 68.
10 John Maxtone-Graham, *Liners to the Sun*, p 47.
11 David T Brown, *A History of the Sulzer Low-Speed Marine Diesel Engine*, pp 39-4

CHAPTER 7

PROGRESS OF SCALE

Larger cruise ships for greater economy and luxury

The confidence in the future of full-time cruising already declared by Home Lines, Hapag-Lloyd and Holland America through their new ships in the early 1980s, along with Kloster's introduction of the immense *Norway*, set a general trend towards larger ships. The business rationale for this trend was implicit in the term 'economy of scale' which was universally applied to the description of this upward migration in size, passenger capacities and service diversity. Ships such as *Atlantic* and *Nieuw Amsterdam* were able to realise a lower per-passenger cost in operating the same cruise over the smaller ships built a decade earlier. It was much the same phenomenon which the airlines had experienced with the decrease in seat/mile expenses of carrying greater numbers of passengers in wide-body aircraft such as the Boeing 747, Lockheed L-1011 and Douglas DC-10.

Historically, Home Lines' new *Atlantic* was first to surpass the KdF *Wilhelm Gustloff* and *Robert Ley* as a ship designed exclusively for cruise service. While being registered at between 2,000 and 5,000 tons more than *Robert Ley*, she and other new economy-of-scale ships had only slightly more than two-thirds the passenger capacity of the earlier German prototype. Although planned for the middle-to-upper market sectors, the new Home Lines and Holland America examples each reflected the modern lifestyle trends towards far greater personal privacy and luxury. Nonetheless, these also represented the smallest and slowest ships which would fulfil their

owner's performance requirements. Albeit on a less elitist scale than the design of *Europa*'s facilities for a mere 600 passengers, the amenities provided by these new cruise vessels set a very high standard as the basis of further economy-of-scale developments.

TROPICALE

After parting ways with Knut Kloster, Ted Arison lost little time in starting up all over again. He first made arrangements with the Boston firm American International Travel Service Inc (AITS) to realise their cruising aspirations based on purchase of the laid-up Cunard intermediate liners *Carmania* and *Franconia*. When these were found to be in poor condition, Arison instead purchased the Canadian Pacific liner *Empress of Canada*. She was brought to Miami and readied for cruising with much the same rapidity that had brought *Sunward* into the American cruise market in 1966. The Canadian Pacific 'multimark' logo on the funnel was ingeniously repainted into a large stylised letter 'C' which became the trademark of the new entity, Carnival Cruises. Within six weeks the ship was in service as *Mardi Gras* on a weekly Caribbean circuit based in Miami. She commenced her new career virtually 'as was', with only essential maintenance work being done. The addition of new cabins and upgrading of others to include private toilet facilities was carried out piecemeal while the ship was in service.

Despite running aground on her first cruise, *Mardi Gras* quickly became a popular ship with a strong mass-market appeal. It was learned from members of the original *Empress of Canada* orchestra, who had remained in the service of the new owners, that this had always been a remarkably happy ship for both passengers and crew alike. Although originally dubbed the first ship in the 'Golden Fleet', it was from these comments that the famous Carnival slogan 'Fun Ship' was coined by Bob Dickinson, who became senior vice-president of sales and marketing in 1979. However, Arison and his business colleagues realised that Carnival could not ultimately succeed as a 'one-horse show'. There would have to be more Fun Ships.

Unable to find suitable tonnage at a price they could afford, Carnival approached the Goulandris family, owners of Greek Line, to try and negotiate a joint operation running their *Queen Anna Maria* in tandem with *Mardi Gras*. When this failed, Sun Lines was approached, and finally an arrangement with Holland America was explored in some depth for joint operation of *Mardi Gras* and *Statendam*; but, alas, the Dutch were not then interested in Carnival's fledgling operation. As things finally turned out, Arison was able to purchase *Queen Anna Maria* after the Greek Line went into receivership in 1975, and her owners were anxious to sell at a much lower price. Formerly *Empress of Canada*'s 1950s-built running mate *Empress of Britain*, she was once again reunited with her newer sister ship, becoming *Carnivale* in early 1976. By that time Arison had also concluded his business arrangement with AITS, giving him the independence he had always wanted.

During Carnival's early years, both ships underwent little alteration other than marginal upgrading and expansion of their cabin facilities. The extent of this work had been limited to whatever could be accomplished at sea while the ships were in service. It was not until the acquisition of their third ship that the luxury of a more extensive refit could be considered and that the owners could experiment with new ideas gained through their experiences with both *Mardi Gras* and *Carnivale*.

In October 1977, Union Castle Line and Safmarine terminated their passenger service between Britain and South Africa, putting *Windsor Castle* and *S A Vaal* (originally *Transvaal Castle*) up for sale. Meshulam Zonis, who was on holiday in Israel with his family, was quickly dispatched by Arison to make an inspection of *S A Vaal* in Southampton at the conclusion of her final line voyage. He was immediately captivated by the possibilities which this ship offered for Carnival's operation. Her vast amounts of cargo space offered great possibilities for increasing the cabin capacity and extending the public facilities well beyond whatever could have been possible with the two former Canadian Pacific ships. After spending twelve hours aboard the ship, Zonis telephoned Arison late at night, telling him that this ship could not be passed up, but that they would have to move fast to purchase her as there were other interested parties, including Sitmar Cruises. The senior man agreed and, without seeing

Mardi Gras: **Arriving at San Juan in May 1975 she appears unchanged from her time as Canadian Pacific's** *Empress of Canada*.

(Author)

the ship for himself, the sale was concluded along with an option on *Windsor Castle*. Unfortunately, Arison allowed his broker to sell the second ship, believing the buyer to be Sitmar, with whom Carnival had a friendly relationship. He was somewhat disappointed when he learned that the ship had instead gone to The Latsis Group for use as an accommodation vessel in Bahrain.

Before entering Carnival's service as *Festivale* at the end of 1978, *S A Vaal* was extensively remodelled in Japan at the Kobe shipyard of Kawasaki Heavy Industries. The conversion was somewhat simplified by the ship's original design for one-class operation. The passenger capacity was increased from 723 to 1,430, with the number of cabins rising from the original 353 to 580, including 10 deluxe suites with their own private verandas. Much of this added accommodation was housed in the redundant cargo holds and superstructure extensions both forward and aft. These additions also enclosed the greatly extended and enhanced public facilities on the upper decks. Interior design of the remodelled ship was handled by the Miami-based husband-and-wife partnership Joseph and Carole Farcus, initiating a long-standing and virtually exclusive relationship with Carnival.

One of the most noteworthy operational innovations in the ship's rebuilding as *Festivale* was the inclusion of a huge goods-handling area in one of the former cargo holds. This space was fitted with shell doors at pier level and arranged so that it could be closed off from the rest of the ship. It allowed for stores and passenger baggage to be quickly loaded during the turnaround time between cruises, without stevedores and other shoreside personnel having to find their way around the ship's interior. Luggage could be distributed and provisions stowed instead by the ship's own crew after sailing. Upon return to home port at the end of a cruise, this facility also proved to be of great benefit as it allowed for speeded-up on-board customs inspection of incoming baggage and its quick discharge to the pier.

Despite whatever concerns anyone might have had about the baggage-handling area being a possible loss of revenue-earning space, its operational success was such that it was incorporated into all later Carnival tonnage. Surprisingly, this remained a unique feature of the Fun Ships alone until being incorporated also into the Holland America *Statendam*-class ships, the first new tonnage to be built for the Dutch line after its acquisition by Carnival.

Festivale was also significant from the standpoint of Kawasaki and the entire Japanese shipbuilding industry as it was their first involvement in modern western cruise-ship work. With the almost instant commercial success of *Festivale* it was hoped that follow-up orders, particularly the building of new cruise tonnage from scratch, would be placed in Japan. Once *Festivale* was in service, Carnival became the major competitor of Ted Arison's former business partner Knut Kloster. The Norwegian owner's purchase of *France* in 1979 put Carnival in the position of having to act quickly in order to retain their own market position. There was no other suitable tonnage on the second-hand market with which to compete against the world largest cruise ship, as *France* would become through her rebirth as *Norway*. Carnival would simply have to build.

Despite the high quality of their work in *Festivale*, the Japanese builders were unable to offer the extremely attractive subsidised financing arrangements for new building available from a number of European and Scandinavian builders.[1] Indeed, even as work on *Festivale* progressed, planning was started in Japan for a possible new ship to follow her into Carnival's service. Joseph Farcus had discussed various features of a then somewhat ethereal new ship with Micky Arison, who in 1979 was to take over from his father Ted as president and chief executive officer of Carnival.

As chairman of the board of directors, the elder Arison remained in charge of new ship construction and continued to operate a catering subsidiary to the line. It was under this working structure that the first order for a new Carnival ship was placed with Aalborg Wærft in Denmark. Carnival was able to build the ship without a major capital outlay through a lease-purchase arrangement. The ship would be owned by AVL Marine Inc, a holding company set up by the builders, and leased on a bare-boat charter basis to Carnival for five years. At the conclusion of the lease in November 1987, ownership of the vessel would be transferred to Carnival.

To be named *Tropicale*, the new ship was to a great extent derived from the Line's own experience with their existing ships. Apart from the direct involvement of Ted Arison and Meshulam Zonis, the British firm of consulting naval architects Technical Marine Planning (TMP) were retained to work with the owners and Aalborg Wærft's technical department. TMP had done the initial surveys on *Carmania* and

Franconia back in the days of AITS, and had later participated with Carnival in the acquisition of *Carnivale* and the *Festivale* conversion. Also included in the design team were Joseph and Carole Farcus, whose interior designs for *Festivale* had contributed so much to that ship's great public appeal.

As part of infusing the lifeblood of his Fun Ship phenomenon into the new ship's design, Ted Arison also wanted the thoughts and ideas of the key people who would actually run the ship and be responsible for her day-to-day operation. Once an initial design had been worked out by Aalborg and TMP, *Tropicale*'s already-designated captain and chief engineer, along with Carnival's catering superintendent and operations manager, were sent to Denmark to help work out the details. Each met separately with the yard's design team to discuss their own particular areas of interest and concern. After these meetings they met with Arison in the evenings to review each day's progress and identify and work out various details and issues. At the end of this process the specifications were finalised, with the contribution and agreement of those people who ultimately have to live by the consequences of their choices.[2]

What emerged from this amalgam of knowledge, experience and creative daring was a ship of basically sound proven, and even somewhat traditional, conception, yet with the inspired flare of some remarkably new and forward-thinking features. As Joseph Farcus later explained:

> Carnival demonstrated the most creative and innovative ideas, in order to achieve a result, which fully implements what I would call the most meaningful and successful philosophy in leisure time marketing - the 'Fun Ship' concept. This is not an empty slogan, but rather a credo, which is the life blood within the entire Carnival Cruise Lines organisation. Planning meetings were organised where all departments gave their best ideas. The best of the past was also examined and used as the basis for next-generation ideas, but nothing of the past was cast in stone or beyond scrutiny.[3]

The overall layout of *Tropicale* was similar to that of *Atlantic* in that, like her Home Lines contemporary, she followed a classic liner layout with the dining room low in the hull, accommodation throughout the decks above and, atop these, the public rooms on the uppermost superstructure decks. Despite her arguably old-fashioned layout, the ship's external appearance and the ambience of her interiors were anything but traditional. An expression of aircraft styling in the funnel shape and superstructure form, along with other modern elements such as the fully enclosed bridge and transom stern, were no mere styling frills. The function of these forms was in fact carefully devised to improve one aspect or another of the ship's operational efficiency.

One of the primary technical questions facing Carnival was the basic choice of machinery type for this, their first new

Tropicale: **The ship that started a lineage for Carnival which has since progressed through three generations of progressively larger tonnage.**

(Carnival Cruise Lines, Miami)

ship. Steam was at first considered, as the Line's existing fleet was all turbine powered, thus use of a similar installation aboard the new ship would make exchange of engine-room personnel possible among all four ships. This was an option which Sitmar chose a year or so later in planning their own first-ever new ship, *Fairsky*. Alternatively, diesel propulsion offered the further choice of low- or medium-speed plants, both of which had their own staunch followings in cruise shipping.

The choice finally made was for twin, low-speed, diesel engines each direct-driving its own controllable-pitch propeller. This was based on the same type of regard for simplicity and reliability as had prevailed in the design of Swedish American Lines' six diesel-powered liners. Certainly *Tropicale's* greater size alleviated the concerns for space saving which had largely precipitated the widespread use of multiple-engine medium-speed plants in the many cruise ships built during the 1970s.

Since *Kungsholm's* completion in 1966, however, the demands made of the modern passenger ship's power plant had changed considerably, following the fuel crises of the 1970s and the great increases in building and operating costs. Economy of operation was to be a major engineering concern, especially on the scale of the larger passenger ships envisaged at the beginning of the 1980s. Carnival wanted a highly versatile arrangement which would make maximum use of main-engine power, to also serve the ship's electrical power needs as well as to achieve the economy of using a single heavy-oil fuel source, both for main and auxiliary engines. The difference between the ship's nominal service speed of 21kts and actual in-service cruising speeds of 18kts or less provided a power margin which could economically be absorbed if the main engines given the added duty of generating electrical power.[4] It was found that this type of arrangement would, in *Tropicale's* case, allow the main engines to also satisfy this entire hotel and auxiliary load while at sea.

In addition to directly driving the propellers at 150rpm,

the twin, seven-cylinder, Sulzer crosshead engines were each coupled to a 3,310kVA Siemens alternator. Step-up gearing attached to the propeller shafts engaged the alternators at their required running speed of 720rpm. This arrangement was dependent on a constant engine speed to maintain the supply of electrical power. The ship's cruising speed was thus controlled by adjusting the pitch of the propeller blades rather then the engine revolutions. Electronic speed governors and cylinder misfiring sensors were used to automatically bring an auxiliary generator on line when full-speed headway was needed, during dead-slow manoeuvring with the shafts turning below 80rpm or in case of engine failure.

Tropicale was equipped with a complete auxiliary power plant consisting of three additional 3,310kVA alternators, each driven by a heavy-oil medium-speed diesel engine. Apart from taking over from the main shaft-driven generators when needed in service, the auxiliary system was also capable of meeting the ship's needs in port. The auxiliaries could also be used to supplement the shaft alternators under special circumstances, such as when additional power was needed run the 1,100kW bow thruster when docking or undocking.

With the machinery and other technical systems chosen and their spaces allocated, the remainder of the ship's layout generally followed a direct development of Carnival's *Festivale* conversion. The large-scale extension of the earlier ship's original well-planned one-class accommodation had enabled Carnival to adapt her to specifically suit their own unique operational needs. This, along with the stores and baggage area, was carried forward, more or less intact, to the design of the new ship despite a, no doubt merely coincidental, similarity to the general plan of Home Lines' new *Atlantic*.

Tropicale's galley and dining facilities for both passengers and crew were located one deck higher than their corresponding position in *Festivale*. *Tropicale's* bulkhead deck was thus made available for an unobstructed adaptation of *Festivale's* on-board stores- and baggage-handling facilities. A full-width main handling area, with shell doors at pier level, was located aft of the funnel casing, immediately below the main galley areas. The main storage areas, cold rooms and freezers were in the aft compartments directly beneath on deck 3, with access by way of a large platform lift. These facilities were designed to be worked by the ship's own electric fork-lift trucks, allowing stores and baggage to be handled as much as possible on pallets. Two nearby service lifts, adjacent to a crew stairway, were used for transfer of goods as needed to the galley above as well as to the shops, bars and other services on the higher decks.

Passages wide enough for fork-lift access also gave direct access to the passenger and service lifts at all three main stairways to facilitate rapid baggage handling to and from the passenger accommodation. A secondary baggage handling area at the forward stairways was arranged to be also used for passenger transfer to launches or tenders when necessary at shallower ports of call. The remainder of *Tropicale's* bulkhead deck was, for the most part, occupied by crew accommoda-

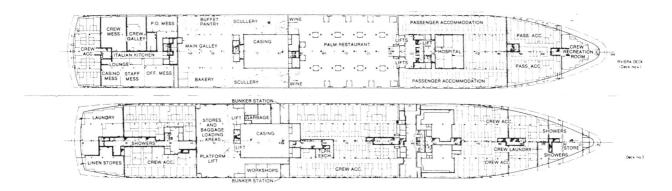

Tropicale: General arrangement plan of decks 3 and 4, showing the pier side accessible stores and baggage-handling area aft of the casing, and its relationship to the main galley directly above. The platform lift allows pallets to be lowered to the provisions stores on deck 2 beneath.

(Builders' drawing)

tion, along with a large ventilation plant room, a group of workshops, port- and starboard-side fuelling stations and the ship's laundry, and it's accomodation located as usual fully aft.

At the time of *Tropicale*'s planning, a number of Italian Lines were winding down their passenger operations, thereby displacing many highly qualified and well-experienced officers from their jobs. Ted Arison very astutely tapped this resource to meet the growing staffing needs of his steadily expanding fleet. Consequently, provision was made to provide this important and prestigious crew community aboard *Tropicale* with the cuisine of their homeland. This type of domestic consideration was of course not entirely new aboard ship, as Chinese laundry crews have usually prepared their own meals in their accommodation on vessels of all nationalities, and separate kitchens have long been provided for Indian and Asian deck and engine-room ratings aboard ships belonging to P&O as well as other British- and Dutch-flag Lines.

Above the dining-room level, there were two and a half strata of passenger cabins, comprising a virtually integral hotel block accommodating the bulk of *Tropicale*'s 1,200 complement. Following on from the preceding decade's spate of Scandinavian cruise ships, these were of a rigidly standardised design, comprising only three basic alternatives of plan and outfit. There were 324 outer cabins with rectangular windows, 187 inside rooms back-to-back along the ship's centreline and 12 deluxe suites three decks higher up, above the public rooms. However, Carnival took the application of modular functionality a step farther by improving the versatility and liveability of the private living spaces for their passengers. To start with, the greater overall size of *Tropicale* allowed for larger standard cabin sizes in addition to increased capacity. At 14.5sq m each, standard rooms were generally of the same area as the luxury-market Royal Viking ships built ten years earlier.[5] As each new generation of

North Atlantic greyhounds had offered its tourist class clientele living standards approaching those of first class in the ships they superseded, so too was Carnival bringing mass-market standards of the modern cruise age up to the former deluxe-sector standard.

Carnival also considered that perhaps the many younger couples making up their clientele might prefer to sleep in double beds rather than to be berthed against the opposite walls of a cabin as their grandparents might have been in, for instance, *Bremen* or the original *Kungsholm*, back in the 1920s. The usual design solution to this concern would have been to fit some cabins permanently with doubles and others with twin beds. However, the obvious pitfall was that the singles-versus-double question for passengers had to be contested at booking time, with the distinct possibility of there being insufficient accommodation of one type or empty cabins of the other by sailing day. Many shipowners over the years simply avoided this problem by not offering their passengers the choice. To the best of my knowledge, there had never been a double bed aboard any Swedish American Line ship up to the time of the 1966 *Kungsholm*.

The problem was solved in *Tropicale*'s cabins by having one of the berths moveable so that it could be easily shifted alongside the other to form a double. Thus the change between the twin- and double-bedded arrangement could be made at will, even by the passengers themselves, if need be. The ship's standard outside rooms used the familiar L-shaped plan of the NCL and RCCL fleets, with the possibility of pivoting the beamwise bed to lie alongside its mate beneath the windows to form the double. The inner cabins, which used a parallel layout with the beds normally against opposite side walls, allowed for one bed to be moved against the other. In both cabin types a locking device was used to secure the moveable bed in one position or the other. The problem of reading lights was solved by using focused lamps installed in the ceilings. A third fixture with its own wall switch was provided to serve the alternative location of the moveable bed.

Another noteworthy feature of *Tropicale*'s accommodation was a comprehensive closed-circuit video system, with television sets in all passenger cabins as well as many crew rooms. *Canberra* and *France* were among the first ships to offer TV in the early 1960s, although it was available only in premium-grade first-class cabins and suites. Use of these early systems was confined to closed-circuit distribution of live programming either from the public rooms or a minuscule on-board studio, and to taped material, greatly limited by the capabilities of the cumbersome open-reel videotape machines of the day. However, the advent of compact video cassettes suitable for telecasting full-length films and the development of text-based video information systems has since made TV systems far more attractive for shipboard use.

Tropicale's Philips video entertainment and information system was among the first of its kind to be installed aboard a cruise ship. It was able to supply three channels of material, one for films, another for text-based information such as the ship's daily programme, restaurant menu information, and shore excursion offerings, and the remaining channel for miscellaneous use such as live telecasting aboard the ship and continuously running information and promotional features. With the capability of being able to show films via the cabin television sets, it was possible to drop the once-obligatory cinema from the assortment of public rooms.

Forward from the topmost strata of standard cabins and for the full length of the promenade and boat decks above, the vast bulk of *Tropicale*'s superstructure enclosed her diverse array of public rooms. A first glance at deck plans seemed to reveal an almost old-fashioned liner layout, with the lounges and bars being flanked by traditional North Atlantic-style enclosed promenades. However, the plan was in reality quite advanced, particularly with regard to the design and layout of those spaces intended for live entertainment.

The enclosed promenades were in fact an adaptation of the *QE2* perimeter-access approach for the public rooms. In terms of Carnival's own experience, they reflected the modified layout of *Carnivale*'s promenade deck from her original cruising refit as Greek Line's *Queen Anna Maria*. *Tropicale*'s promenades allowed the then largest-ever ocean-going casino to be strategically placed amidships amidst the main show lounges forward, the discotheque aft and other more informal spaces above. They provided the necessary bypasses for the few hours of the day when the casino would be closed at sea or when in port. It was also necessary to separate the casino to some degree as a primary through-access route for the sake of keeping children and under-age passengers away from the gambling tables and slot machines. However, for all other purposes the casino's prime location ensured that the lure of its pleasures could hardly be escaped by anyone.

Fully appreciative that American holidaymakers tend to be avid gamblers, given the opportunity, Carnival was set to oblige them to the fullest. It was planned that the large casino, operated by a staff of forty, would generate a major part of the ship's operating income.[6] In this regard Carnival had learned from the shoreside examples of Las Vegas, Atlantic City and Freeport of the great trading value offered by strategically placed, if not outright unavoidably located, casinos. *Tropicale* was a pioneer in applying this type of thinking to cruise-ship

design. Despite her casino's prime location, however, other commercial services, such as the shops and hairdressing salons, remained inconspicuously tucked away amid the cabin decks below. Despite the attractive arrangement and outfitting of these spaces in a gallery above the ship's main lobby, they could still escape being noticed for the entire length of a cruise. The handsome curved stairway connecting the gallery with the lobby might be seen when boarding the ship in Miami and then not again until disembarking a week later. Certainly the success of *Tropicale*'s casino showed the way to resolving this shortcoming, and likewise increasing the onboard spending opportunities for passengers on later cruise ships for Carnival and other Lines.

Adjacencies have become an important consideration in planning the public areas of cruise ships. As explained in a later interview by the British designer John McNeece, whose work has featured prominently in a number of later cruise ships:

> It's like the high-street shopping district in a town, where the best retail properties are along either side of the main road on the ground floor. Those on the floors above, below in the cellars or up side streets are less suitable to selling their product.

In the two principal entertainment lounges the quest for improved visibility was taken beyond the traditional, and seldom satisfactory, use of a mezzanine balcony or the more modern raised periphery areas, as used aboard *QE2* and other ships. Instead theatre-style terraced floors were used to surround the stage. *Tropicale* was in fact among the first modern cruise ships to use this approach for multi-function rooms other than sole-purpose cinemas or auditoria. Film shows

Tropicale: **An artist's rendering of the Tropicana Lounge, showing the terraced seating in a rather exaggerated rendition of scale and in the unusual state of the room's concealed cornice lighting being on during a lightly patronised performance.**

(Carnival Cruises; Gordon Turner collection, Toronto)

were in fact the one thing that *Tropicale*'s show lounges were not equipped for, as that function was to be filled entirely by the cabin video system. The main show lounge Tropicana, intended mainly for dancing and cabaret entertainment, had a tiered floor rising in three levels towards the back of the room. These inclines, which were bowed to follow the geometry of the stage front, were carried across the ship's full width in the style of a cabaret lounge ashore.

The viewing experience this afforded for passengers in 1982 was probably about the finest available aboard any ship since *Normandie*'s theatre and its more contemporary successors aboard *Rotterdam*, *France*, *Michelangelo* and *Rafaello*. Certainly it was *Normandie* which was first to offer facilities of this type for stage performances and films. While the raised periphery alternative was a practical and workable shipboard adaptation of theatre design, the mezzanine has, for various reasons, never been satisfactory. By the time *Tropicale* was completed, the upper gallery of *QE2*'s multi-function Double Room had long since been appropriated for, of all things, the shopping arcade. However, nearly a year before *Tropicale*'s debut in the Caribbean, the style of greater things to come had already been set with the elaborate double-deck terraced Röda Nejlikan (red carnation) show lounge aboard the Swedish short-haul ferry *Kronprinsessan Victoria*, which was completed in 1981.

Larger terraced lounges of the Röda Nejlikan type were soon to follow on later Carnival ships. However, aboard *Tropicale* the additional headroom needed for the two lounges, one above the other, was cleverly achieved through a split-level arrangement ahead of the forward stairway. The dance floor of the main lounge was at the same level as the cabins aft on the same deck, with the two higher terraces rising by some 300mm and 400mm each above this. The added ceiling height needed here resulted in the second show lounge's floor above being slightly higher than promenade-deck level. Named 'Islands in the Sun', this alternative show place was arranged around a circular dance floor and bandstand, recessed by two concentric tiers in the room's floor. The room's lowered-centre effect was conveniently accommodated within the contours of the Tropicana Lounge's sloped ceiling below.

Intended both as a daytime lounge and a night-time venue for late dancing and music, the Islands in the Sun room was given a commanding outlook over the ship's bow. Eight large rectangular windows in the obliquely raked superstructure front afforded *Tropicale* the distinction of having the only outlook of this kind on any new ship built for Carnival until *Fantasy* was completed at the end of the decade. The observation lounge function was set apart from the room's other uses for music and dancing by way of an oval bar arranged beamwise between the forward window bay and the bandstand. The bar was in its conception and scale not unlike the original Double Up Bar in the mezzanine of *QE2*'s enormous Double Room.

However, it was *Tropicale*'s aesthetics which made the greatest impact with the public. The ship's rather radical external appearance clearly bespoke the essence of Carnival's by then already well-established Fun Ship image. Although clearly a liner in terms of size compared with the previous decade's new cruise tonnage, there was none of the traditional ocean-liner severity of form and detail in *Tropicale*'s lines. This effect was accomplished by way of such elements as the superstructure front's oblique slope reflecting the rake of the bow below. The transom stern, a feature which could easily have created a freighter-like end to the ship's lines aft, was angled inwards toward the waterline to give a more pleasing appearance. The impression of height was diminished by a riband painted beneath the lower row of superstructure windows.

Tropicale's lines were further softened by the irregular grouping of rectangular promenade-deck windows beneath the lifeboats. Other superstructure windows were either of an elongated circular shape or were actually enlarged portholes. Those of the Tropicana Lounge were of the porthole type and were cascaded at three levels, following the floor lines of the lounge itself. Although far less pronounced than its earlier manifestation in *Kronprinsessan Victoria*, this unusual quirk of modern ship design certainly took some getting used to in the eyes of many. However, the 'crooked line of windows' became something of a Carnival trademark, which was faithfully reproduced in two succeeding generations of larger cruise ships which followed. *Tropicale* was also noteworthy in that all outside cabins, right down to those forward of the dining room on deck 4, were fitted with large rectangular windows rather than portholes. This in itself contributed significantly to her overall expression of a light and bright tropical pleasure ship, as opposed to the more severe expression of an Atlantic liner.

The most outstanding element of *Tropicale*'s exterior profile was undoubtedly her distinctive funnel. This decidedly aerodynamic, gull-winged structure was of some considerable practical value too. It worked on the same basic principle as *France*'s modernistic, finned funnels of nearly twenty years earlier. The original French idea was to discharge engine-room exhaust gases through the tips of the airfoil-shaped wings near the tops of the otherwise conventional, streamlined steamer funnels. This was probably as good a solution as anyone had then found for keeping these emissions clear of the open decks below. Similar ideas, although of considerably more daring shape, had also been proposed by *Canberra*'s designers in the late 1950s, but were ultimately rejected as being too outlandish. Carnival felt that their image would indeed permit so daring a funnel shape. In their adaptation of the original French idea, the entire top of the funnel was divided into a huge swept-back gull-wing arrangement. To this was added a large circular air intake, looking more like the mouth of an aircraft jet-engine pod than anything else. Its purpose was to force an airstream through the wings while the ship was in motion and, in theory at least, force the exhaust stream yet farther away from the ship.

Any challenge to the purely technical merits of *Tropicale*'s funnel design would in all certainty be outweighed by its enormous success as a veritable icon of Carnival's fleet identity. Its shape was unique and unmistakable. The crescent-shaped letter C in white, with red forward and blue aft, was carried not only on either side of the raked funnel, but also a third time on the curved top surface formed by the wide gull wings. As one observer put it at the time of *Tropicale*'s introduction in Miami, 'The funnel has a strong sense of aircraft imagery linking the ship with the airlines and their essential role in conveying so many cruise passengers to and from their ships'. Indeed there is a reasonable resemblance to the empennage of the well-known 'T-tailed' Boeing 727, Lockheed L-1011 or Douglas DC-10 airliners. Since then the same funnel form has been faithfully reproduced in progressively larger manifestations for three successive classes of Carnival cruise ships.

Tropicale's interior design and decoration, by Joseph and Carole Farcus, ran from the bold to the outlandish. An informal lounge and café area surrounding the base of the funnel on the boat deck, called the Boiler Room, was decorated as a somewhat whimsical representation of the ship's inner workings. The ceiling steelwork was left open with its various wiring runs and pipes fully exposed to view. The effect was enhanced with addition of dummy pipes and fittings painted in bright colours. The theme was continued to the walls which were adorned with various gauges, valves and other engine-room fittings. Even the table tops of clear perspex were inlaid with such items as lag bolts, hex-nuts and washers to further carry the effect.

Below on the promenade deck the discotheque featured a snowflake-shaped translucent fibreglass dance floor, illuminated from beneath with lights of various colours controllable by the room's sound system. This was complemented by a ceiling array, including strobe lights set at various angles, mounted in an open framework above the dance floor. Additional coloured lighting was also used in the perimeter of the room, where seating was arranged into a number of bays surrounding the basically hexagonal plan of the central dancing area. The room was further enlivened with a strong emphasis on mirrored surfaces and wet-look upholstery in blue trimmed with pink, creating an animated high-tech ambience devised to appeal to the younger passengers. As explained by Farcus, the scheme was supposed to 'create the sense of sitting on an island watching the waves roll in on a moonlit night'.[7]

Perhaps a little less outlandish in the overall effect of their styling, the remaining public rooms nonetheless still stressed bold forms, bright vivid colour schemes and highly imaginative lighting. The circular dance floor in the Islands in the Sun lounge was made of black glass to resemble an island raised above the room's recessed centre area. Four decks lower down, the dining room's central buffet area had a pink marble floor, with the same material also used as trimming elements in the room's columns and in the ceiling itself. Here an imaginative lighting scheme with incandescent fixtures and strobe units was arranged among coloured glass diffusers to give the impression of sunlight filtering through the leaves of palm trees. As in the example of *Canberra* and a number of American ships, the dining room had no windows or portholes, relying entirely on its architectural lighting scheme both day and night.

The essence of Farcus's work was to make the public areas of the ship work as a sort of theatrical setting for passengers to enjoy themselves or, so to speak, live the Fun Ship experience. Indeed his work on *Festivale* and *Tropicale* formed the substance of this philosophy, of which *Holiday* and later ships would be refinements and diversions. Farcus explained this in an article written when completing *Holiday*:

> My approach is very simple. I design a facility which I would enjoy using for the purpose intended. My definition of a cruise is an experience in which the passenger can indulge in his or her fantasy that is enhanced by the mystery of the sea. Of course, this is a very romantic definition, but it provides insight into my philosophy and approach to this design. The ship should provide many atmospheres as well, which result in varied opportunities and modes of escape. Passengers should not be boxed into the monotony of uniformity. They have not come aboard for a week's languishing in subdued sameness, but rather for a sensual experience which provides them with elegance, charm, excitement, relaxation and awe. They should debark with a maximum feeling of being recharged and exhilarated, a feeling which I would liken to experiencing a thrilling and fulfilling movie in which you are both a member of the audience as well as the cast. Such is the environment I have attempted to create.[8]

The Farcus approach, which came as quite a shock to some of the more traditionally minded, was intended to stir the mode of living from merely passive to active. Rather than merely being backdrops for 'people providing their own constantly changing pattern of colour and movement',[9] as Sir Hugh Casson had designed *Canberra*'s elegant first-class interiors to be, *Tropicale*'s interiors already had most of the colour and a good sense of animation already built in. These were to be places which would entice people to play games of chance, move on the dance floors and buy rounds of drinks at the cabaret shows.

It seems somewhat ironic, however, that this approach was in reality directed squarely towards the intrinsically passive 'society of spectators', which appears to stereotype modern lifestyles in the world's most affluent nations. By the early 1980s, cruise passengers expected to be perpetually entertained rather than to amuse themselves as their forebears might have done aboard *Mauretania* or *Kaiser Wilhelm der Grosse*. While the art of conversation once flourished in ships' lounges and the smoking-room card tables were always busy after dinner, modern-day passengers have no doubt become blasé about the constant stream of professional entertainment which flows endlessly into their daily lives by way of television, video, recordings and so on.

Arguably the *Mauretania* and *Kaiser Wilhelm der Grosse*'s owners were trading in an essential point-to-point liner trade, where it was speed and frequency of sailings which were most important. However, the fierce competition for those passages forced rival shipowners to also compete on the basis of the highest standards of luxury and service as set by the hotel standards of their day. As the modern cruise era has picked up from where the liners left off, the urban resort complex has tended to fill the trend-setting role of the earlier Grand Hotel. As in Las Vegas, Miami, Honolulu or Nice the ship as floating resort must provide a sufficient sense of occasion to entice her passengers to partake of her pleasures. The perhaps reserved or timid passenger may actually need to be enticed into an 'active' role in what the ship has to offer. Whether as cabaret spectators or as participators in the discotheque or casino, imaginative, and in this regard, provocative interior design and decorative schemes can themselves perform as the needed catalyst.

Tropicale's designers got it right because they understood clearly that Carnival's clientele were the great continental melting pot of middle-income wage-earners and their families, known euphemistically as 'Middle America'. Joseph and Carole Farcus did not try to beguile these heartland folk with anything pretentious, bourgeois or trendy, and nor did they sell them short with mere floating adaptations of Las Vegas glitz. Bold and even brash colours and expressions of form were used with conviction and confidence on a scale never before seen aboard an ocean-going ship. Yet these schemes were also limited to those areas where they would be appropriate. The library and card room reflected a more needed sense of quietness. The main lobby and shopping arcade, which were geographically quite far removed from the main run of public rooms, had a more business-like appearance with their dark, panelled wall coverings, concealed spotlighting and brass handrails. The cabins, which would be the actual living quarters of the ship's passengers, were of an appropriately more subdued sense of modern shipboard styling.

The instant success of *Tropicale* in service stood as reason enough for Carnival's immediate progression to more, and larger, ships derived from the same design. Had the same sort of progressive thinking, bold ingenuity and unpretentious realisation of the modern-day passenger market and its real expectations, prevailed more abundantly back in the 1960s, one wonders what might have been its effects on the liner trades of those times. Could there have been a greater number of successful dual-purpose ships such as *Rotterdam*, *Canberra*, *Eugenio C* and *QE2*? Could the North Atlantic express trade at least have been kept alive, and maybe even developed in the way of *Tropicale*? Could this and other deep-sea trades have continued to flourish in the style of the modern and progressive Scandinavian ferry trades?

HOLIDAY

The limelight of publicity surrounding *Tropicale*'s inauguration was also used to announce the further building of still larger cruise ships. Called 'superliners', no doubt to identify with the same prestige value of *Norway*'s origins as a liner, an order for the first of these had been placed again with Aalborg Wærft. In addition to *Tropicale*, this, and two additional ships in their class later booked with Kockums in Sweden, amounted to a billion-dollar fleet expansion programme. The first of these, to be named *Holiday*, would in fact follow P&O's introduction of their trend-setting *Royal Princess*, yet another 45,000-ton ship, by some six months. This once elitist size range was on its way to very quickly becoming the economy size of the cruise industry, with still more ships to follow later.

The design rationale of *Holiday* and her two Swedish-built sisters *Jubilee* and *Celebration* was based on an enlarged and updated conception of the original *Tropicale* plan. With the addition of 17m in overall length, 1.7m in beam and a deeper draught by 0.5m, it was possible to include an additional accommodation deck, increasing the passenger capacity by 398 berths. *Holiday*'s increase in length was determined by the amount of space needed for the two additional lifeboats necessary for her greater payload. With a further addition in length of but a cabin's width, the two later Kockums-built ships offered an even more impressive increase of 500 berths. At a thirty-six per cent increase over *Tropicale*'s capacity, this represented a good exercise in economy-of-scale building.

Celebration and *Jubilee*: The two larger Swedish-built ships are shown here in drydock at the Kockums yard in Malmö.

(Kockums, Malmö, neg 596-1346 F)

Holiday: In the turning basin at the Port of Miami showing the progression of Tropicale's overall form to a larger size.

(Carnival Cruise Lines)

	Tropicale	Holiday	Jubilee/ Celebration
GRT	36,600.0	46,052.0	47,262.0
Length oa	204.00 m	221.56m	224.80m
Beam moulded	26.30m	28.00m	28.00m
Draught	7.00m	7.50m	7.50m
Speed	21.00kts	19.50kts	19.50kts
Maximum power	19,832.96kW	23,520.00kW	23,520.00kW
Passengers	1,396	1,794	1,896
Crew	491	660	670

Apart from the necessary increases of main machinery power, auxiliary electrical and steam outputs, air-conditioning capacity, and other technical services, a number of significant changes were also introduced in the passenger facilities. Indeed, these were not merely enlarged renditions of Tropicale's already well thought out design, but entirely new ships derived extensively from her building experience and also taking into account the latest developments from other sources. Tropicale in fact had yet to prove herself in actual service conditions while much of the critical planning for the Holiday generation was being done.

Some of the key accommodation detail was worked out among the owners, designers and builders at the end of 1980, a full year before Tropicale's delivery:

With the increased number of passengers over Tropicale's capacity, two dining rooms would be needed, and in line with modern trends, these would be located in the superstructure.

The two forward show lounges in Tropicale had proven to be a duplication of each other, with neither having sufficient seating capacity or adequate production facilities for the type of live entertainment features envisaged. In the new ships these would in effect be combined into a double-height facility with a large stage, tiered seating and improved sight lines capable of seating a far greater proportion of each ship's passengers.

Following the example of NCL's Norway, where the former enclosed promenade decks were revitalised as 'streets' giving primary access to the public rooms, Carnival wanted to use a similar scheme, although with a wider single 'street' on the starboard side only.

The sheer logistics of feeding nearly as many passengers as carried aboard Oriana or Canberra called for a return to the proven liner design of these earlier ships, using two separate dining rooms served by a single galley between them. However, in Carnival's scheme of doing things, the lower-deck location these facilities normally occupied had already been appropriated by the centralised stores and baggage-handling facilities. While these working spaces could be located below Festivale and Tropicale's catering facilities, the additional dining room and larger galley, not to mention also the increased baggage-handling space, needed in the new ships could have greatly complicated their entire layout. Holiday's liner-style dining room plan was moved up to the space aft of her double-height show lounge's lower level.

The overall approach for Holiday's design was to combine all public spaces, including the dining rooms, in the two principal superstructure decks. The cabins were allocated to the full lengths of the four decks below. Thus passengers had full end-to-end access along all levels except America deck (deck 8), where the lower level of the Americana Lounge and the dining rooms were. It was felt that this would present no difficulties to passenger circulation and orientation, as the use of this deck was such that there would normally be no need for circulation along its length. The three main stairtowers each provided direct access to one or other of the dining rooms, with that at the forward-most end also attached to the show lounge's lower level. Passengers would have no need to circulate along its length, and outside meal times would normally merely pass through this level on the way to and from the public rooms and deck spaces above.

This solution avoided the confusion of divided cabin blocks at various levels, dead-end alleyways and partial-height stair and lift runs. Any of these shortcomings can make a ship's layout difficult to comprehend for the seven days most passengers stay aboard. The layouts of some liners, even comparatively modern ones such as Leonardo da Vinci, tended to be notoriously complicated when they were opened up for single-class cruise service. From the crew standpoint the traditional middle-galley layout is usually preferable to the various arrangements tried with galleys below, and table service being made by way of lifts or escalators. Apart from its practical and operational benefits, Holiday's arrangement met with the public's perception of being entirely up to date in offering passing panoramic vistas of tropical seascapes from one's dinner table. This image continues to persist, despite the fact the only meal many passengers take in the main dining rooms is dinner, at a

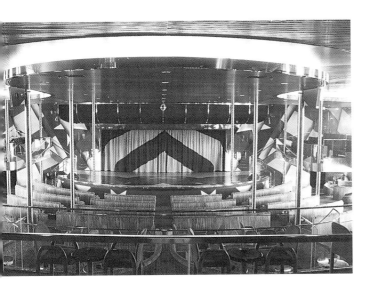

Holiday: **The Americana Lounge looking forward from the upper level towards the stage, showing the terraced seating which so effectively combines the two deck levels.**

(Author)

time which is invariably after nightfall in tropical cruising latitudes.

Carnival's *Holiday*-class design had the great distinction of finally delivering an effective double-deck show lounge plan suited for professional entertainment to the world of cruising. The plan was conceptually similar to that of *Kronprinsessan Victoria*'s Röda Nejlikan mentioned earlier. Considering the very early timing of *Holiday*'s planning, it would be difficult to determine if the Swedish ferry really did have any influence over Carnival's initial design work. However, once in service, she was no doubt noted in the later planning stages. As in Röda Nejlikan's example, *Holiday*'s Americana Lounge was successfully dissolved into the two decks it shared. Upon entering the room at either level one soon lost the impression of being on one deck or the other, becoming instead conscious of the lounge as a whole, integral space seemingly independent of the two levels it connected with outside its domain.

The effect was achieved by way of the tiered central seating arrangement which joined the two decks in its continuous unbroken sweep from America deck up to and slightly above promenade-deck level (decks 8 and 9 respectively). The entrances at both deck levels brought one directly into the tiered seating, either at its base on America deck, or near its top from the promenade deck. The theatre-style upper seating galleries to either side of the room and the double rows of Carnival's 'trade-mark' cascading windows clearly showed off the room's double-deck height.

However the double-height dimension was merely secondary to the impression of an entirely integral space set by the tiered centre seating mass and the volume of the stage area forward. Periphery points of reference to the individual decks

had little bearing on the overall plan's cohesiveness. Larger renditions of this space, which ultimately appeared in Carnival's *Fantasy*-class ships and Holland America's *Statendam* class, had a definite division between lower- and upper-level seating somewhat reminiscent of *Rotterdam* or *France*'s theatres. In these later manifestations the sense of integrity from *Holiday*'s plan was compromised in that the connection between the lower and upper levels was by way of conventional stairways, both inside the lounge itself and its adjoining deck lobbies.

Apart from the functionality of its seating arrangement, the Americana Lounge featured a wide proscenium stage with excellent sight lines from virtually every seat in the house. The large front area of the proscenium was arranged to serve also as a dance floor, with the orchestra performing on the raised rear part of the stage. As in *Tropicale*'s case, the only function the show lounge was not intended to serve was that of a cinema.

The function of *Tropicale*'s Islands in the Sun lounge as an alternative entertainment venue was filled by the Blue Lagoon lounge on *Holiday*'s promenade deck, at its opposite end to the Americana Lounge's upper level. The corresponding space within *Tropicale*'s proportionally shortened superstructure was occupied by the discotheque. In *Holiday* the two show lounges bracketed the full length of the ship's wide indoor 'street'.

The precedent for this had been set in Scandinavia, with the Silja Line ferries *Finlandia* and *Silvia Regina*, delivered in 1981 and 1982 respectively. Both ships featured wide single interior promenades along the starboard side of their lounge decks. Again the building of these ferries was concurrent with *Holiday*'s formative planning, yet Carnival had the opportunity to observe these in actual service before their own adaptation of the idea was finalised. When brought aboard *Holiday*, the same basic idea was given a special sense of liveliness at the hands of Joseph Farcus.

Norway's example, where the enclosed deck spaces had been named Champs Élysées and Fifth Avenue, was the original inspiration for Carnival's single promenade. With its additional width over *Norway*'s promenades, Farcus was given the latitude to develop a far more realistic looking streetscape. The breadth of this space gave it the latitude to function not only as an attractive thoroughfare but also a public gathering place in its own right.

Named 'Broadway', this wide promenade was a wonderful shipboard adaptation of a real street, with its floor tiled as a brick street, complete with drain gratings, as well as authentic New York street signs and with pillars rendered as old-fashioned cast-iron lamp posts. The centrepiece of the scheme was a fully-restored vintage Bedford bus, strategically located at the Bus Stop Bar outside the casino. Zonis was horrified at the 300,000 Danish kroner bill he received for the bus's restoration, and asked Farcus why he could not have made a replica vehicle. As the flamboyant designer explained: 'We definitely could have fabricated a bus for a lot less money, but I feel if we tried to copy it we would end up with just that – a copy of an old bus.'[10]

Holiday: The bus stop on the Broadway promenade, featuring the beautifully restored Bedford bus with a 1930s period-dressed mannequin in the driver's seat.

(Author)

The bus was hoisted aboard and mannequins dressed for a day at the seaside were placed in a number of its upholstered leather seats and the name 'Coney Island' was put on the destination board above the vehicle's windscreen. The rear part of the bus had been fitted out with opening windows enabling it to be used as a snack service bar alongside a raised 'sidewalk'. Farcus did not restore any more buses or trams for use aboard cruise ships, and had to be content to fabricate copies for his later interior schemes. Although these had a whimsical charm of their own, their effect was not quite the same as *Holiday*'s genuine bus.

A nearby coffee bar was decked out as a pavement café, belonging to the street itself, while larger spaces such as the casino and discotheque were given the appearance of street-front properties with plate-glass windows, each an enticement to the pleasures of entertainment and service it offered. The ship's library and an additional lounge were located on America deck immediately below, where they flanked a short central passage connecting the forward dining room with the forward stairs and lifts. These rooms were far enough 'off Broadway' to escape its whirl of activity, yet not too widely removed from the centre of things as to be difficult to find. In view of Carnival's perennial advertising claim 'We've got the fun', it is noteworthy that their realistic sense of passengers' diversity in cultural background, age, and lifestyles was reflected in providing a great amount of quiet space too. The three *Holiday*-class ships along with the larger *Fantasy* vessels each offered the largest libraries in virtually the entire industry.

Joseph Farcus's overall design theme for *Holiday* was 'Americana', boldly pronounced by the enormous stars-and-stripes supergraphic on the stage-front wall of the Americana lounge. The theme was carried by the Broadway promenade, cast in its role as a make-believe New York street. Elsewhere, sculptures, paintings and murals paid homage to America's

Holiday: The discotheque, with such high-tech effects as its illuminated dance floor, was one of several rooms located along the ship's promenade 'street', Broadway.

(Author)

various holiday destinations ashore, tying the ship's name into the theme. Among the most notable of these were ten large tiled murals by San Francisco artist Helen Weber, depicting such places as New England, New York, the Mississippi, the Southwest and Pacific coast. The largest of these adorned a 7m stretch of wall in the starboard-side forward America-deck lobby. Named Union Square, this area served as one of the lower-level foyers to the Americana Lounge.

Times Square, on the opposite side of the deck, was decorated with a mural of similar size rendered by father-and-son Miami artists Gene and Barry Masson. This featured nearly life-size cut-out figures of performing artists made of polished stainless steel. These were interspersed with smaller figures cut from coloured acrylic and set against back panels of the same steel as the larger characters. The embellishment of transparent acrylic marquees, signs, and posters added a sensation of Times Square excitement and ambience as a prelude to the entertainment features to be enjoyed in the Americana Lounge beyond the lobby itself.

Another quintessential aspect of 'Americana', the movies, was also acknowledged in the decoration of Rick's Café. This was a creation straight out of the film *Casablanca*, with its ceiling fans and piano bar. The plaster arches, dark wooden ceiling beams, stocky round columns and an iron spiral staircase, leading to the casino on the deck above, were of the same Moroccan style as the studio sets used in the film. A frieze of dummy piano keys was set into the top of the bar wrapped around the raised grand piano, and a microphone on a long cord was included, as perhaps the vestigial beginnings of shipboard karaoke.

Another room which warrants mention, although one of those not specifically carrying the Americana design theme, was the Blue Lagoon lounge. The room was planned as both a daytime lounge and night spot, beneath an undulating ceiling of formed glassfibre giving the impression of some mythical underwater garden. The ceiling and walls, of similar contour, were inlaid with coloured mosaic waves and sea creatures, and festooned with coloured Tivoli lights. During daylight hours passengers could enjoy the passing seascape through its large round-ended windows set into the billowing texture of the glassfibre wall cladding. After dark, when the electric lighting scheme would take over, the room assumed the mystical and surrealistic sensation of an underwater garden illuminated by rays of simulated sunlight filtered through the waters of, perhaps, a garden pond.

Holiday: **A corner of Rick's Cafe, where the iron spiral staircase was inspired by the production sets for the film** *Casablanca*.

(Author)

As in *Tropicale*'s interiors there was nothing pretentious about the designs. They were devised to appeal to the sensations of 'Middle America'. The Americana theme was clearly articulated, with ideas and images which people from all walks of life would readily appreciate and enjoy. For instance, Rick's Café would recall the film *Casablanca* to any living soul with access to a TV at home. Yet, these themes were never mundane or tiresome thanks to Joe Farcus's special talents for rendering them as a sort of theatre for people to take full advantage of the Fun Ship experience, either as active player or passive observer.

Farcus's interior design theme of *Jubilee* was of a more traditional character, while that of *Celebration* stressed a far more futuristic character. In both of these later ships, the effect of the designer's work was as varied and attractive as that of *Holiday* in its own right. Although Carnival was not as heavily committed to repeat business as Hapag-Lloyd, the diversity of design did take into account the idea of satisfied Fun Ship clientele returning to the Line for different itineraries without feeling a sense of *déja vu*.

Again building on the in-service success of *Tropicale*, cabin accommodation in the new superliners represented only a slight refinement of design and outfitting. The sizes of the rooms, which were again of three basic layouts, were optimised to make best use of the hull's greater dimensions. The additional overall lengths of all three ships allowed more cabins per deck, based on their standard width prescribed by multiples of the frame spacing. However, the extra 1.7m in beam also had to be considered to determine the best sharing of crosswise dimensioning among the two files of both outer and inner cabins and the obligatory two passageways. These dimensions had to be carefully considered to allow for the best possible usage of space and furniture arrangements in each room. It was important in Carnival's approach to accommodation planning not only to offer the maximum amount of space per passenger possible, but to impart the greatest possible illusion of roominess.

Apart from some fine adjustment to actual room dimensions, the basic layout of *Tropicale*'s rooms was ultimately found to be very difficult to improve upon. Certainly one of the key elements of the earlier ship's sense of cabin luxury was the use of large rectangular windows and the feeing of brightness and airiness which they created. These were, of course, retained and their effectiveness was improved with the use of ceiling cladding in a light metallic finish which would better reflect light around the room. The electric lighting was also improved to give a higher level of ambient light, again enhancing the impression of spaciousness. While colour and lighting were used to gain the greatest impression of space, at approximately 18sq m each, Carnival's *Holiday* cabins were in reality only about fifteen per cent smaller than the ultra-deluxe *Europa*'s standard room size.

The outfitting of *Holiday*'s cabins included a surface-mounted anodised metal duct at chair-back height along the walls, carrying all electrical wiring for the room. This was also

Holiday: One of the suites, showing a custom built appearance in which the cabling runs are concealed behind both the headboard on the bed and the backs of the settees in the lounge area beyond.

(Carnival Cruise Lines)

used as a support for the bedside reading lights and the necessary outlets, switches and other controls. Telephones, which aboard *Tropicale* had been wall mounted, were fitted as moveable table-top sets to eliminate sound and vibration from their ringers being transmitted through the cabin structures. The manufactured bathroom units were again supplied by the German company H W Metallbau. Carnival liked the swing-out washbasin assemblies in these, which permitted access to the plumbing for servicing from within the cabin rather than in the corridors where such work could be an obstruction. This point of view is the complete opposite of the marketing

Jubilee: Seen underway from astern, the lower location of her stern mooring deck and absence of the hull fins as fitted on *Holiday* are clearly visible.

(Kockums, neg 596-1776)

position taken by Wärtsilä and other accommodation makers, who promote the advantage of their corridor access in allowing maintenance work to be done without disturbing passengers in the privacy of their cabins.

In the all-important areas of propulsion and power, Carnival again opted for the low-speed diesel as they had done for *Tropical*. The engines chosen for the larger *Holiday* were the Sulzer 7RLB66, the same machines as used aboard *Nieuw Amsterdam* and *Noordam*. The RL series was a more efficient long-bore version of the units fitted aboard *Tropical* three years earlier, clearly showing the technical progress in marine engineering which had been made in the post-1970s oil-crises era.

Holiday's main engines were of course also integrated into a power-station type of propulsion-and-generating aggregate as had by then become standard practice for passenger ships. Carnival chose the *Europa*-style approach of running the generators directly from the forward end of the engines, rather than through step-up gearing as had been done in *Tropicale*. This simplified the overall setup by reducing the number of moving parts, namely the gearboxes, along with their inherent power loss and possible source of vibration. Since *Holiday* had controllable-pitch propellers, sufficiently high engine revolu-

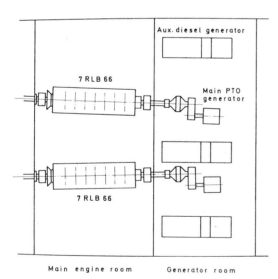

Holiday: General arrangement plan of the main machinery, showing the main engine-driven generators located forward in the auxiliary engine room between the auxiliary diesels.

(Gebruders Sulzer, Winterthur)

tions could be kept up over a wide range of cruising and manoeuvring speeds. So-called 'combinator' settings of propeller thrust and pitch allowed for the ship's speed to be widely varied while maintaining a constant engine speed of 136rpm, sufficient for operation of the generators. *Holiday's* calculated combinator settings effectively eliminated the need for the thyristor controls which were needed for *Europa's* fixed-pitch propeller installation.

SONG OF AMERICA

While *Tropicale* was taking shape as Carnival's first-ever new ship, Royal Caribbean Cruise Line were looking at building on their already proven success with purpose-built cruise tonnage of ten to twelve years earlier. Constantly near-capacity sailings and often long waiting lists seemed to bear out the predictions being made for the sustained long-term growth of cruising. Like Carnival, one of their chief competitors, RCCL would also have to face the formidable challenge of competing against Kloster's vast *Norway* in the 1980s.

An unexpected opportunity for fleet expansion arose in 1975, when A F Klaveness & Co opted out of Royal Viking Line, offering their share of the enterprise, namely *Royal Viking Sea*, for sale. However, adapting the then practically brand new ship for RCCL service would have been a complicated and costly endeavour, involving lengthening the hull to increase her passenger capacity from 559 to *Song of Norway's* figure of 870. It would also have been necessary to completely rebuild the funnel to incorporate the line's trademark Viking Crown Lounge. The whole scheme finally fell through as Klaveness' Norwegian partners finally purchased the ship jointly, retaining her under the Royal Viking Line houseflag.[11]

Lengthening was ultimately adopted as a means of increasing capacity, with two of the original RCCL ships,

Song of Norway and *Nordic Prince*, being stretched in 1978 and 1980. The one-third increase in overall fleet capacity which this realised would meet the Line's most immediate needs, while longer-term planning was directed towards a larger fourth ship. Early design studies for this were started in September 1978, with RCCL being the first owners of purpose-built 1970s tonnage to place an economy-of-scale order. To be named *Song of America*, the new ship was planned as a larger and more economical rendition of the proven original *Song of Norway* prototype. Most of the same designers were once more engaged, and the building contract was again signed in Helsinki with Wärtsilä.

The continuity of approach from the earlier ships can be seen from the following points in the design brief:

Passenger capacity to be about double that of *Song of Norway* as built.

Overall size of the ship to be optimised for seven-day Caribbean cruises, with draught and hull dimensions being optimised for the ports to be regularly visited.

The owners' policy towards their chosen market sector to be maintained in regard to providing functional cabins of moderate sizes and limited variations in plan, with all necessary facilities, including the option of combining single beds to form doubles.

A wide variety of public rooms to make the best possible use of available volume, with special emphasis on easy orientation and direct traffic flows for passengers and services.

Minimised manning and maintenance work, to be achieved through efficient bunkering, catering, hotel services, baggage-handling and refuse-disposal systems, as well as optimum use of standardised and reliable machinery and materials.

The ship's external appearance to retain RCCL's distinctive styling despite differences in size and layout over the original *Song of Norway* design.

By the time *Song of America* was being planned, Wärtsilä had already gained the valuable experience of designing the 31kt superferry *Finnjet*, completed in 1977, as well as the two conventional-speed Baltic ferries *Finlandia* and *Silvia Regina*, delivered in early 1981 and 1982 respectively. These examples had shown how well passengers accustomed to a modern lifestyle ashore could be accommodated and catered to in relatively high-density accommodation at sea. The incredibly short port turnaround times demanded by *Finnjet's* 24-hour rolling schedule had caused the whole area of service and workflow aboard ship to be rethought and greatly rationalised.

Song of America: **Not merely a larger version of the** *Song of Norway* **class but a substantially redesigned ship, which managed to also retain a strong sense of fleet identity with the earlier generation.**

(Wärtsilä, Helsinki, neg WHT82-757)

Song of America's turnaround time between cruises would be eight hours rather then *Finnjet*'s two hours, and her passengers would be aboard for seven rather than one or two nights. Although of similar passenger capacity, at 37,000 tons *Song of America* would also be considerably larger than the latest Scandinavian ferries. The additional space would, in fact, amount to the barest minimum needed to support the additional staffing and services needed for her seven-day voyages. While the newest ideas in ferry planning could in principle offer much for cruise-ship design, they would of necessity have to be somewhat reworked for deep-sea vessels making longer voyages with far less dependency on shoreside support facilities, particularly for hotel services.

The design of *Song of America* in effect started with her cabins and evolved outwards to encompass the complete ship. Following the proven success of the Line's earlier generation of ships, cabins were to be essentially no greater in area, and again of only three types: standard two-berth, with or without window, and a small number of two-berth deluxe rooms.

The standard cabins were essentially of the same layout as on the original *Song of Norway* generation of ships. The outer rooms again featured an L-shaped arrangement of berths, with a convertible bed-settee beneath the window and a fold-away canister bed built into the side wall at a right angle. The inner rooms were likewise a repeat of the *wagon-lit*-style arrangement, with two parallel bed-settees against the opposite side walls. A major refinement here was that one of the beds in each cabin was moveable, allowing it to be shifted over alongside its mate, forming a double bed as needed. One or two additional fold-away upper berths were fitted in a number of inner and outer rooms, raising the ship's nominal 1,414 lower-berth capacity to 1,575.

While the standard cabins themselves were clearly derived from the earlier generation of RCCL's fleet, their arrangement on *Song of America*'s decks differed considerable. The new ship's cabin plan, and hence her higher capacity, was largely accommodated by way of a 4.4m increase in the hull's midbody breadth, making a high-density cabin layout, similar to that of *Finnjet*, possible. This mainly affected the grouping of inner cabins, which were arranged beamwise in blocks of twelve, rather than in two files back to back along the centre-line, as in the narrower *Song of Norway*-generation's hulls. While this type of layout, with its inherent need for additional beamwise passages for access to the inner rooms, remains a fairly constant feature of ferry design, RCCL are virtually its sole proponent in cruise tonnage. They have continued to feature the same plan in two succeeding generations of cruise ships.

Along with the general arrangement of cabins, Wärtsilä also applied much of *Finnjet*'s rationale to the catering, hotel services, baggage handling and refuse-disposal systems in order to minimise workload and manning efficiency aboard *Song of America*. Here, as in the latest Baltic ferries, these services were arranged around two vertical cores, one forward and one aft. *Song of America*'s aft core, with two service lifts

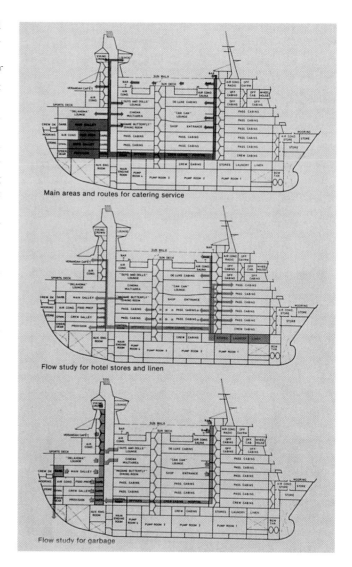

Main areas and routes for catering service

Flow study for hotel stores and linen

Flow study for garbage

Song of America: **Schematic diagrams showing the flow of catering, hotel and linen services to the accommodation, and of waste removal from them by way of the two service cores and horizontal paths.**

(Wärtsilä)

and an adjacent crew stairway immediately astern of the engine casing rose through eight levels, from C deck to the sun deck, at the base of the funnel. It directly connected the provisions stores on C deck with the crew galley on B deck, bakery and other food preparation areas on A deck, passenger galley at the dining room level on the main deck and the majority of lounges and bars on the four remaining decks still higher up. On the lower three decks, disposal facilities were provided immediately adjacent to the lifts for the incineration, compacting, grinding and storage of both regular and refrigerated refuse.

The forward core, also comprising two lifts, was designed to primarily serve the needs of the hotel department. Based on D deck close to the laundry and hotel stores, this had direct access to the major concentration of passenger cabins forward on six levels from B deck to the boat deck, as well as to crew and officer cabins on C deck and bridge deck respectively. Both cores were connected on C deck by a wide working alleyway capable of handling fork-lift trucks, which, as aboard *Tropicale*, were part of the ship's equipment. This allowed for sharing of the hotel and catering functions where necessary between the two service cores as well as giving access to various working parts of the ship such as stores, baggage-handling areas and the engine room. Following *Tropicale's* similar bulkhead-deck arrangement, shell hatches forward and aft at this level accommodated, baggage handling and refuse removal during the turnaround time between cruises.

The influence of *Finnjet's* layout stopped short of also imposing a strict vertical division between *Song of America's* cabins and public spaces. The layout of *Song of America's* principal lounges and bars emerged as being more akin to *France's* plan, with approximately the forward-most third of the lounge decks being occupied by cabins. The additional height given to *Song of America's* dining room and lounges, on the main and cabaret decks respectively, allowed for the insertion of an additional mezzanine deck ahead of the public areas, increasing the accommodation density in the forward part of the ship. Below, on A and B decks, the lines of outer cabins at the ship's sides were extended fully aft, increasing more passenger rooms with a view than would have been possible with a strictly *Finnjet*-type plan. However, on these decks the blocks of inner accommodation extended only as far astern as the engine casing and aft service core. Farther astern, the inner reaches of those decks were occupied by the galleys and catering complex.

The essence of *Finnjet's* vertically oriented plan was in effect retained, but considerably 'softened', as had been done by Holland America with their *Nieuw Amsterdam* and *Noordam*, to meet the needs of a cruise ship where a greater diversity of easily accessible amenities are essential. Even in the examples of *Berlin* and *Europa*, whose designers had more closely adhered to *Finnjet's* segregation of functions, communal areas such as lounges, swimming pools and other recreational features were extended farther forward both above and below the tightly integrated multiple-deck cabin blocks. While *Song of America's* inspired amalgamation of *Finnjet's* newfound design rational with more traditional horizontal planning has ultimately had a far greater influence over the design of larger cruise ships, the Finnish superferry's influence has remained stronger in the emergence of a new generation of smaller 'superyacht' cruise tonnage, as discussed later.

In designing their new ship RCCL took little for granted, even from their own experience. Among the things reassessed was the question of propulsion machinery. After carrying out extensive research, a four-engine, medium-speed, diesel aggregate was again specified for *Song of America* in preference to following the trend towards low-speed machinery. This

choice was rooted in both RCCL's service experience with the Sulzer Z80 engines, and in Wärtsilä's own proven building experience since a compact four-engine geared diesel plant was first placed beneath *Finlandia's* car deck in 1966. Apart from the additional revenue-earning space made possible by the low headroom of this type of plant, its use aboard *Song of America* also worked well into the scheme of the ship's other services. The main engine spaces were accommodated in a two-deck-high space beneath the aft service core, following the example of *Finnjet*.

However, a change was made from the Sulzer Z40 two-stroke engines of the earlier ships to the ZL40, a four-stroke version of the same basic machine. Although intrinsically more complex than their two-stroke counterparts, these engines were reputed to offer good reliability under the varying power requirements typical in cruising, as well as being able to best cope with the high vanadium content of heavy fuels used in the Caribbean. RCCL chose to keep the generation of electrical power as an entirely separate entity by not fitting take-off generators to the main machinery. Five auxiliary generator sets were located in a separate compartment aft of the main engine room.

In view of the quest for maximum operational efficiency, these were fuelled with the same heavy oil burned by the main engines. This in itself greatly simplified the arrangement of fuel tanks in *Song of America* as only one grade of bunker oil needed to be carried. The tanks themselves were arranged in a tight configuration amidships, requiring a minimum of ballasting adjustments to keep the ship in proper trim as their contents were used.

Song of America's aesthetic design, both inside and out, showed a marked progression to greater sophistication over *Song of Norway*. Gier Grung and Mogens Hammer, who had been the sole architectural and industrial design professionals for the earlier ships, were again brought together as part of an expanded team alongside Njål Eide and Finn Nilsson.

Grung was once again responsible for the exterior styling of the ship, including detailed layout and design of the top-deck swimming pool area, along with its lido and other such appendages. He succeeded in transforming the bland lines and forms in the contract design into a unique expression of the RCCL fleet image. This was achieved, not by merely enlarging his previous scheme to suit the proportions of the bigger ship, but through distinctive rendering of her greater bulk into a pleasing aesthetic form of functionality and grace.

The most striking change in *Song of America's* styling was to extend the original Viking Crown funnel fixture into a larger structure completely encircling the funnel. This called for substantial reshaping of the funnel itself as well as its integration into the topside of the superstructure. Again relying on numerous scale models, which he studied from all conceivable viewpoints, Grung developed precisely the right balance of mass and form. The funnel itself was proportionally taller, with its height being bisected approximately midway by the Viking Crown's doughnut shaped pod. The line's 'crown

Song of America: The Viking Crown Lounge pod, never seen before, which completely encircled the funnel, looking somewhat like a stylised airport control tower.

(Wärtsilä)

and anchor' logo, which had been beside the lounge windows on the earlier funnels, was appropriately placed beneath *Song of America*'s larger Viking Crown. The lines of the funnel itself were stiffened, expressing the strength of a much steeper rake over the more oblique lines of the *Song of Norway* prototype.

The three-quarters-aft location of *Song of America*'s funnel allowed for extensive 'deckscaping' of the superstructure top into a vast swimming pool and lido area, spread out full-beam above the lifeboats. Here Grung skilfully managed to avoid an overpowering or boxy appearance by varying the sundeck overhang of *Song of America*'s glass-enclosed lidos, reducing more the impression of bulk than the amount of actual usable space sacrificed. In effect this approach took the original glassed-in lido bays, tucked in among the lifeboats of the

Song of America: Progression of the ship's exterior styling from the contract design with a narrow riband below the superstructure, to Grier Grung and Mogens Hammer's modification of the funnel structures, addition of the forward verandas and the widened riband surounding both rows of large windows.

(Wärtsilä, negs WHT79-819R and WHT082-158V)

earlier ships, and elevated, enlarged and duplicated them above the larger ship's lifeboats. Continuity of line with the funnel was achieved by joining the lido glazing and its topside railed walkways with the forward edge of the funnel trunking. Aft of the funnel a permanent canvas awning, standing in for the earlier generation's pyramid-form base, brought the eye gently down to the deck below. A smaller awning of similar geometry in the lea of the forward raked mast added an appropriate element of balance to the overall profile.

The blue riband which girdled the *Song of Norway*-generation's superstructures was widened aft of the small cabin windows which it encompassed on the main deck, to surround both rows of large windows along the aft two thirds of *Song of America*'s main and cabaret decks. This diminished the impression of the ship's added height, and served to mask visual discordance between the three rows of cabin windows forward and the two-tier fenestration of the public rooms aft. Grung also added open verandas to the superstructure front in an effort to diminish the impression of height created by the triple-deck cabin block housed within its forward end. This turned out to be an extremely effective touch, with the navigating bridge front and compass platform above it also being worked into the pattern of steeply terraced forward porches or verandas.

Early renderings of the ship's original concept design, with the enlarged Viking Crown fixture in place but before the distinctive signature of Grung's stylistic creativity was added, showed a perhaps somewhat stylised interpretation of modern Scandinavian ferry design. In particular, the lines of the glass-enclosed upper-deck lido were not as well articulated, with only a minimal straight-lined overhang above the boat deck; and the blue riband was a finer line scribed beneath the superstructure. In overall form, the superstructure's forward end, with its three rows of small cabin windows, had a measure of *Finnjet*'s severity, yet lacked the boldness in expression of the earlier Finnish superferry's absolutely rectilinear lines.

The remainder of the architectural design team was responsible for *Song of America*'s interiors. Following the examples of such notable liners as *Rotterdam*, *Canberra* and *QE2*, RCCL believed that the greater range of amenities of their new ship called for a wider diversity of creativity than could be expected from a single designer. Mogens Hammer was given charge of co-ordinating the work of all three designers as well as execution of the linking elements of passages, deck vestibules and stairways. The remaining interiors were allocated as follows:

Mogens Hammer	Can Can (main) show lounge Cinema/lecture room Piano Bar Inside and outside cabins with parallel bed plan
Njål Eide	Oklahoma (aft) show lounge Guys and Dolls night club Viking Crown lounge
Finn Nilsson	Main entrance lobby Dining rooms Outside cabins with L-shaped bed plan

What these Scandinavian designers were asked to do was retain the modernity of approach from their previous passenger and cruise ship work, but also to give it a distinctly American style. 'Americanisation', as this concession in ships' interior design to the North American contemporary hotel stereotype is usually called, was itself the most singularly identifiable feature of this collaborative effort. While the *Song of America* interiors were attractive, livable and quite popular in their own right, they lacked the diversity of interest and richness of character to be found in the examples of *Rotterdam* or *QE2* or indeed of much of the European work already done by the same individual designers. Nonetheless, it was an idiom which, even if the cruising public was not wildly enthusiastic about it, they at least did not find, objectionable enough to complain about. Consequently the style found its mark in the field, and was replicated in various schemes aboard many other new cruise ships completed throughout the remainder of the decade.

The overall theme for *Song of America* was derived essentially from the shoreside-proven formula of Las Vegas hotel

Song of America: **Oklahoma Lounge, which served as an alternative entertainment spot, featuring a mood-lighting scheme which could be changed from day to day throughout each cruise.**

(Wärtsilä, neg WHT82-1079)

design experience. The bold expressions in form, direct lighting and bright colour palates of earlier Scandinavian-inspired interiors were subdued into a more chic contemporary, of a lower ambient light level with emphasis on selective spotlighting, less vibrant colour schemes and the widespread use of smoked glass surfaces and bright metal accents.

In the two main show lounges, theatrical lighting schemes were used not only to meet the needs of the professional evening entertainment, but also to provide changeable mood lighting for the rooms themselves. The Can Can show lounge amidships was specially designed for cabaret-style entertainment, with a wide proscenium stage and extremely good sight lines thanks to the complete absence of columns or stanchions in its central area. The ceiling height of nearly two decks permitted sufficient space for an upper-level balcony at the rear of the room for theatrical lighting, projectors and other such technical facilities. As a secondary entertainment centre, the Oklahoma Lounge was more versatile, being intended for daytime use as a veranda lounge and as a venue for pre-dinner cocktails and so forth. The entertainment outfitting here consisted of a smaller bandstand and dance floor. This room's lighting scheme allowed for a different mood to be set for each evening of a seven-day cruise by illuminating its interior in different colour hues. In its daytime role the Oklahoma Lounge took its mood and ambience from the daylight and panorama of the world beyond its windows along both sides and astern.

On *Song of America*, the design approach was less original than Farcus's work with *Tropicale*. Being derived from an existing shoreside prototype, great care had to be taken in adapting it to work properly at sea, particularly with regard to maximising spending opportunities for its inhabitants. In *Song of America*'s spacious discotheque, for instance, smoked glass was used in the large windows overlooking the boat deck, potentially keeping the visual centre of attention focused within the room, even during daylight hours in the tropics. Through devices such as this, passengers would be less likely to be distracted from the entertainment being offered and its encouragement to, for instance, buy a round of drinks, or perhaps lay out for the entertainer's latest recordings in the ship's shops. The effect achieved is similar to that derived from the many windowless commercial schemes used ashore in department stores, shopping centres, restaurants and casinos. However, in its rendition within the microcosm of a cruise ship, this approach needs to be less pronounced so as not to be perceived as overpowering or inescapable. Aboard *Song of America*, the interior design scheme's first priority was to do justice to the special environment which only a ship can offer, before attempting to make any other statement of itself, commercial or otherwise.

Where *Song of America*'s passengers might have been encouraged to open their wallets more often through any subliminal coercion by way of the design scheme, the message had to be subtle enough to escape the conscious notice of even the most jaded passengers. After all, a cruise usually rep-

resents a greater financial outlay than many other holiday excursions, and a good deal more is expected in return. If passengers are allowed to feel that they are being conned into a lot of extra spending, they may well resist and consciously try to part with as little extra money aboard as possible.

While it would be difficult to accurately quantify the commercial effectiveness of this approach, a rough idea of its potential was later given by the builders. In a paper on passenger-ship profitability presented by Wärtsilä to the Hellenic Institute of Marine Technology at Athens in 1982, the statement was made regarding shipboard money-making potential that, 'In passenger shipping the profitability increases more if we can get each passenger to spend $5 a day extra than if we can save ten per cent in bunker costs'.[12]

1 Lawrence Miller, *Fairplay Cruise Review*, p 20.
2 Carnival Cruises, *The SuperLiner Holiday*, p 20.
3 Ibid, p 49
4 H Schmidt, *Versatility with Economy for Cruise Ship Propulsion*, p 5.
5 John Maxtone-Graham, *Liners to the Sun*, p 243.
6 *The Motor Ship*, March 1982, p 54.
7 *The Motor Ship*, March 1982, p 54.
8 Carnival Cruises, p 51.
9 Philip S Dawson, *British Superliners of the Sixties*, p 63.
10 Carnival Cruises, p 79.
11 John Maxtone-Graham, *From Song to Sovereign* p 49.
12 Kai Levander, *Increased Profitability for Passenger Ships*, p 9.

CHAPTER 8

REBUILDING AND CONVERSION

Cruise ships shaped out of refits and other surgery

The phenomenon of cruise-ship conversions probably traces its origins to such early adaptations as *Vectis*, and other liners which were taken over for full-time cruising in the late nineteenth century, as discussed at the beginning of this book. Ship design of that period was far less sophisticated than it is now, with the changes necessary to adapt any vessel from one type of service to another being fairly simple and direct. Cabins would be erected in the cargo spaces and perhaps a makeshift swimming pool would be assembled above-deck or in a redundant cargo hatch. HAPAG's *Deutschland* was one of the earliest large-scale conversions to be carried out. This once prestigious record-breaker had ultimately proved to be quite expensive and rather troublesome for the express North Atlantic run. Still too new and valuable to be scrapped outright, she was adapted exclusively for cruising and renamed *Victoria Luise*. The work involved re-engining the ship for a down-rated service speed of 17.5kts and extensively rearranging her accommodation to a one-class standard for 487 passengers only. Then having the distinction of being the world's largest cruise ship, *Victoria Luise* remained in this service until the outbreak of World War I in 1914.

Prins Olav and *Arandora Star* were notable examples of cruise-ship conversions of the *grande luxe* cruise era between the two world wars. It was not until the 1950s, when large numbers of liners started falling victim to irrevocably changing trading circumstances, that more sophisticated cruise-ship conversions started to be undertaken in greater numbers. Typical of these were the modifications made to *Andes*, as her trade switched from liner service to cruising. Some of the conversions done during that era were particularly remarkable for the way in which the aesthetic character of the ships involved was retained, with structural additions normally being confined to extensions of the lower superstructure and closing in of well decks forward and aft.

However, not all conversions were as conciliatory to existing design. Those ships such as Union Castle's *Dunnottar Castle* and Messageries Maritimes' *Cambodge* were so completely rebuilt that their new personalities left virtually no recognisable vestige of their former selves. However, there have been many other make-overs which were not nearly as well executed as these classic examples. For example *Amelio de Mello*, renamed *Ithica*, rebuilt for cruising, and later becoming *Dolphin IV*, lacked in her extensive modification even so much as the finesse of a consistent alignment and styling of windows both in the original and added parts of the superstructure. She suffered the drawbacks of a contrived and unduly complicated internal layout. When the *Ryndam* and *Maasdam* passed out of Holland America's hands, *Ryndam*'s ultimate restyling as the cruise ship *Atlas* was bizarre to say the least, particularly as compared with her sister ship's far more elegant treatment as *Stefan Batory*.

VICTORIA

A near contemporary of *Andes* likewise underwent a life-extending refit in the Netherlands a year prior to the Royal Mail ship. While the ship in question certainly lacked the pedigree of *Andes*, her modernisation was far more complete, structurally bold and more aggressively modern in conception. Built by Harland & Wolff in 1936 as Union Castle Line's intermediate-class *Dunnottar Castle*, this ship had served the London – Cape Town run and was later switched to a round-Africa service from her British home port. The 15,008-ton, 17kt ship was originally designed to accommodate 258 first- and 250 tourist-class passengers in addition to a large volume of refrigerated and general cargo. In essence she was a smaller and less glamorous rendition of the basic tropical-liner design, embodied so well in the form of *Andes*. It was by mere coincidence that an earlier Union Castle *Dunnottar Castle* had also found her way into cruising when purchased by Royal Mail in 1912 and renamed *Caribbean*.[1]

The newer *Dunnottar Castle* fared much better. After an undistinguished career in her intended line service, interrupted only by a mandatory stint of government service as both an armed merchant cruiser and troop transport during World War II, the ship was sold in 1958 to Liberian interests for further trading. Her sale was in fact part of an overall rationalisation of the Union Castle fleet in preparation for their forthcoming modern liners *Transvaal Castle* and *Windsor Castle*. *Dunnottar Castle's* new owners intended her for cruise service under their Bahamian-flag subsidiary, the Incras Steamship Company Ltd, where she would run from Miami with the *Nassau*.

However, before taking up her new service in the predominantly America-based market *Dunnottar Castle*, then already renamed *Victoria*, was sent to the Wilton Fijenoord yard at Schiedam, near Rotterdam. Here she was not merely refitted, but extensively rebuilt, altering both her external appearance and internal arrangement virtually beyond recognition. Hardly a single feature remained which could visibly identify the ship with her old Union Castle lineage. After spending 282 days in the hands of the Dutch yard's workers, she emerged in white as a sleek modern cruise ship of remarkable elegance.

In the course of rebuilding, the ship's overall characteristics changed.

	Dunnottar Castle	*Victoria*
Length oa	170.50m	174.50m
Length bp	161.40m	161.40m
Depth to main deck	12.50m	12.25m
Draught	8.50m	7.95m
Service speed	16.0kts	18.0kts
Propulsion power	7,083.2kw	14,017.3kw
GRT	15,007.0	14,917.0
Passenger capacity	508	615

The increase in overall length resulted from rebuilding both the bow and stern to give *Victoria* a more modern appearance. The rake of the bow was increased, giving its stemline a pronounced curvilinear form. The old cruiser-style stern, a style popular in the 1930s, was reshaped into a classic curved form. Above, the superstructure and funnel were completely redesigned, carrying the impression of restrained modernity created by the hull modifications. The lower promenade, or Shade deck as it was called on her original plans, was fully plated in and extended aft in place of the original poop-deck housing and tourist-class open-deck space. The superstructure was also enlarged towards the bow, bridging and enclosing the original forward well deck. Despite the increased size of the passenger accommodation and the addition of full air conditioning and other modern comforts, the ship's draught was slightly reduced.

The major technical feature of the entire rebuilding was the replacement of the original Harland & Wolff twin oil engines with a pair of Fiat two-stroke turbo-charged diesels of nearly twice their power. The ship had in fact originally been designed for engines of greater power than the machines actually installed. This in itself eased the conversion since much of the original mainline shafting could be used. The tail shaft lines, bushings and oil glands, however, had to be replaced with heavier components, matched to the new larger-diameter Lips propellers which were fitted. In the engine room itself structural modifications had to be made to provide for the sturdier bedplates needed by the larger, heavier and more powerful engines. This involved the addition of some 150 tons of steelwork.[2]

The entire process of replacing the main engines and most of the auxiliary machinery, along with fitting of new air-conditioning plants, was carried out by way of the existing

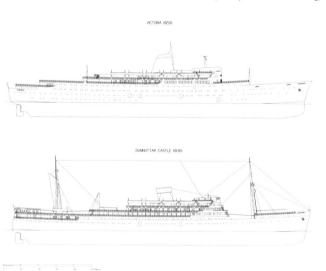

Victoria: **Profiles of the ships in her original form as** *Dunnottar Castle* **and after rebuilding as** *Victoria*.

(Author)

Victoria: **Plan of Sapphire deck with its completely new large staterooms and theatre, compared with the original layout of the same deck as *Dunnottar Castle*.**

(Author)

VICTORIA - Saphire Deck as rebuilt in 1959.

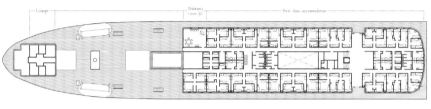

DUNNOTTAR CASTLE - Same deck as built in 1936.

engine and funnel casings. This was an extremely difficult task, rivalling in its own scale that of assembling a model ship inside an Aspirin bottle. The original machinery had first to be disassembled in situ and then lifted out of the ship piece by piece. Similarly, the new bedplate structures, main engines and auxiliary equipment had to be assembled in the engine room after being lifted aboard one part at a time. The crankshaft had to be lowered vertically and manoeuvred into its near-horizontal plane within the limited confines of the engine room, while the engine blocks were assembled from individual cylinder castings, joined together once in the engine room atop the new bedplates.

While the re-engining was in progress the hull was meticulously restored, with some 185 tons of structural framing, shell and bottom plating being replaced, along with the renewal of 25 tons of deck plating. Lightweight aluminium alloy was used in rebuilding the wheel house and superstructure front in modern curvilinear form.

Inside, *Victoria*'s accommodation was stripped down to the bare steel decks and bulkheads. The existing electrical wiring, plumbing and ventilation ducts were also completely removed. All that was kept from the original interior was the forward stairway and passenger lift, along with some parts of the crew quarters. Once cleared of debris, the interior spaces were rebuilt with 214 new deluxe cabins, arranged throughout the four lower passenger decks. Above, in the enlarged promenade-deck superstructure enclosure, a completely new and more extensive suite of attractive public rooms was built to match 1960s-style cruising. A completely new and enlarged dining room was also constructed in the location of the ship's former first-class dining saloon. The space occupied by its tourist-class counterpart had been surrendered to the hotel department for new cabins.

While the main galley retained its original location, it was extensively redesigned and newly equipped to support a

higher level of catering service. Separate spaces were arranged for the coffee pantry, wine pantry, pastry and ice-cream shop, cutlery room and vegetable-washing area. New oil-fired ranges and electric grills, ovens, salamanders (iron plates) and stock pots were installed in the main cooking area. Located centrally in the ship, this facility was equipped to cater for snacks and light meals in the public rooms four decks above, as well as room service to the cabins.

The transformation of this ship went far beyond the purely physical aspects of engineering, functional rationalisation, upgrading and revitalisation of her accommodation. *Victoria* was given an altogether different character, appropriate to the tastes and lifestyles of the modern luxury market her owners aimed to capture. The ship had to create an elegant yet informal and relaxed atmosphere conveyed by both the surroundings and their identities. Not only were the public rooms named, as was done for *Andes*, but the decks were redesignated with fanciful new names. The upper promenade, promenade, shade, upper and main decks became the Rendez-vous, Sapphire, Emerald, Coral and Amber decks respectively. Above, the sun and boat decks remained unchanged, as did the lower deck beneath the passenger accommodation.

From *Victoria*'s time onwards the trend for such all-too-often meaningless deck names has continued to flourish, rivalling only the names given to some of the later ships in their absurdity. Granted, passengers should not have to try to deal with such strange nauticalia as tween and orlop decks, or whether the shade deck is above or below the upper deck, or why a tropical cruise ship might have a hurricane deck. However, at least 'boat deck' leaves little room for doubt as to the most probable location of the lifeboats, and promenade, veranda or lounge deck are logical names for meeting places for onboard social activities. Can a bewildered passenger, confronted by an emergency during the first few hours of a cruise, be expected to know that the lifeboat

Victoria: The auditorium, an entirely new space added forward of the cabin accommodation offered one of the best shipboard facilities of its kind at the time.

(Courtesy of Gordon Turner, Toronto)

Victoria: One of the new cabins built on Sapphire deck, which, like the public rooms, showed the clean-lined modernity of Gustovo Pulitzer's shipboard work.

(Courtesy of Gordon Turner)

muster stations are on Tiffany or Fantasy deck? Although we are told that this is supposed to simplify passenger orientation, the claim appears to be unsubstantiated beyond the whimsy of cruise-line marketing and public-relations departments. To my mind it makes no more sense than naming the floors of an office building in London or Chicago after Ali Baba's forty thieves.

Having far greater significance than the naming of decks, public rooms or the ship herself was the owner's choice of Italy's famed Gustavo Pulitzer to handle the interior layout and design of *Victoria*'s passenger accommodation and public spaces. His eminent career of notable ship-design work featured the sophisticated modern interiors of Lloyd-Triestino's 1931 *Victoria*, surpassed in their own time by his outstanding expression of luxurious modernity in the first-class areas of her much larger Italian Line contemporary, *Conte di Savoia*. His ideas were also behind much of the remarkable interior design of the great variety of Italian-flag passenger ships built during the 1950s.

Victoria represented a superb example of his 1950s work, for its expression of sound modern design rendered in a basically international flavour, executed with a characteristic Italian flare for bold and innovative use of colour and clean-lined modernistic form. This was especially well carried out in the large multi-use Riviera Ballroom on Rendez-Vous deck, with its open planning encompassing an adjacent sit-up bar and lido lounge overlooking the ship's twin swimming pools. The irregular-width wall panelling elements, latticed partitioning of the bar area and plate-glass wall separating the lido seating, along with the imaginative grouping of flush overhead lighting fixtures, were typical of the modern design features to be found in the latest Italian-flag liners. Undoubtedly the architectural centrepiece of the conversion was the auditorium built into the former forward well deck and cargo

hold space. This was furnished with proper tiered theatre seating on two levels and equipped with a fully appointed projection room, production, sound and lighting facilities, proscenium stage and performers' dressing rooms.

The cabins were of basically clean-lined and simple styling, yet with a bright, spacious and cheerful character. The furnishings and fittings were arranged to allow the greatest amount of floor space. All rooms were provided with private bathrooms, themselves ingeniously arranged in pairs, one with a shower cubicle and the other with a bath, also making good use of space and rendering a uniformly high standard of luxury throughout the accommodation. All in all, the character of the state rooms was very similar to that of the latest American ships such as Grace Lines' 1950s-built *Santa Paula* and *Santa Rosa*, as well as the Moore McCormack *Argentina* and *Brasil*.

In December 1959 *Victoria* was handed over to her owners, and departed a few days later on her maiden cruise from Le Havre to Madeira, Morocco, Lisbon and back. It was the beginning of a new career for the old *Dunnottar Castle* which would outnumber the years spent under her original name and house-flag by a considerable margin.

STELLA SOLARIS

Another classic cruise ship conversion of this period involved a similarly comprehensive rebuilding, in which virtually all but the hull and machinery of the Messageries Maritimes' combination cargo/passenger liner *Cambodge* were retained. Like many others of her kind, this was a modern liner completed in 1953 for France's counterpart to some of the colonial Far Eastern services operated by Britain's Orient Line and P&O. *Cambodge* ultimately fell victim to containerisation of cargoes and a falling demand for passenger services to and from the various French territories of Indo-China served on her Marseilles – Yokohama route. She remained in this service until 1970, when she was bought by Greek shipowner Haralambos Kioscoglou for conversion to a luxury cruise vessel. Her two nearly identical sister ships *Viet Nam* and *Laos*, which were also sold at the same time, went into other line services, without such extensive conversions.

Kioscoglou, whose shipping career had started in the Eugenedes-owned Home Lines, founded his own company Sun Line in 1959, on the basis of combining the intimacy and personal service of a private yacht with the luxury and comfort of the larger and more prestigious cruise ships of the day.[3] His design and conversion experience with Home Lines, which included much of *Oceanic*'s planning, laid the groundwork for the highly imaginative work involved in building up his own fleet. His first ships had been a former Canadian frigate, previously converted for Alaska cruising, and a small North German day-excursion vessel. *Cambodge*, which was first renamed *Stella V*, and then *Stella Solaris*, was Sun Line's largest-ever acquisition, now serves under the Royal Olympic house flag.

The conversion of *Stella Solaris*, which was undertaken in Greece at the Parama yard in Piraeus, involved literally stripping the ship down to the bare hull and engines, and building anew within the remaining shell atop the machinery spaces. In essence the two most expensive parts of a total newbuilding were saved as the workings and containment of completely new accommodation, public spaces and topsides deck areas. Above, the locations of the new ship's funnel casing, bunkering ports and a single stores hatch forward of the passenger accommodation would be the only elements prescribed by the *Cambodge*'s original design and layout.

The design concept of *Stella Solaris*'s new passenger cabins was similar to that of *Victoria*, stressing once again a standardised plan, with many of the rooms having the same L-shaped furniture arrangement of other recent cruise ships such as *Sea Venture*. An alternative plan amidships of wider inner and outer rooms featured a more traditional *Rotterdam*-style layout with parallel beds arranged against the inner and outer walls of each cabin.

However, the internal layout of *Stella Solaris*'s superstructure, which was at least three times the length of the original deck house, clearly showed the progress in cruise-ship design since the *Victoria* planning a decade earlier. Most notably, the dining and catering plan generally followed that of the then recently completed *QE2* and of *Royal Viking Star* under construction at the time in Helsinki. As in the Cunard and Royal Viking examples, *Stella Solaris*'s galley was fully forward on her principal superstructure deck, with the dining room immediately aft of it, and most of the remaining public rooms farther astern. The galley, which was equipped with its own stores lift, also served the crew dining facilities on the deck below and had access to stores and other auxiliary facilities on the lower decks. The single remaining cargo hatch allowed for

the loading of consumables aboard the ship by way of two electric cranes. Alternate access was also provided by way of shell doors at opposite ends of a beamwise passage on the bulkhead deck.

The remaining public rooms aft of the dining room on Solaris deck, as it was called, consisted of a combination bar and grill-restaurant to port and promenade gallery starboard, either side of the midships-sited funnel casing and stairtowers, and a large main lounge with separate bar-lounge farther aft. These were all arranged on a remarkably open plan, creating the illusion of a ship of far greater size than *Stella Solaris*'s modest measure of 10,595 tons. Two decks higher up, above a stratum of boat-deck cabins, the lido deck featured an *Oceanic*-style double swimming pool arrangement with surrounding lido extended full-beam out above the open deck below. Thanks to this carefully thought-out arrangement, the boat deck retained the essence of a promenade loop completely surrounding the superstructure without interruption. The discotheque and cinema/theatre, both being spaces where daylight was not a consideration, were relegated to former cargo spaces deep within the stern of the hull in a manner similar to that of the cruise refit for *Andes*.

Apart from the *QE2*-style dining room and galley plan, the overall layout followed the luxury-yacht-inspired formula of Kioscoglou's two smaller ships *Stella Oceanis* and *Stella Maris*. The same ambience appears to have been quite remarkably upheld in the larger ship, despite her intermediate-class liner capacity of 750 passengers. However, with this ship Sun Line was able to expand their sphere of operation beyond the Mediterranean, to the Caribbean, northern European and, even for one season, to the New York markets.

By comparison, the modernisations of *Andes* and *Caronia* were pale and timid efforts which fell far short of what really needed to be done to keep those ships apace with the changing times. The newcomer owners who effected the creation of *Victoria* and *Stella Solaris* were not bound by sentiments of

Stella Solaris: **Seen at Grand Cayman in 1987, more than twenty-five years into her second life as a cruise ship, in a very different form from her original lines as** *Cambodge*.

(Author)

upholding line traditions or past glories of the *grande luxe* era. They looked instead to the horizon before them, to modern ship design and contemporary passenger expectations which would set their course for at least the following twenty years. Instead of trying to catch up with the preceding decade's progress.

Had *Andes* and *Caronia* have undergone such bold and progressive restructuring, granted they would have completely lost their old identities, but perhaps the essential elements of their solid original construction would have survived as long, continuing to pay back their owners on the investments originally made in their building, and giving them a head start in the modern cruise market. At the time of writing *Victoria* and *Stella Solaris* are still in operation. While *Victoria* has changed hands, becoming *Princessa Victoria* for Louis Cruises, *Stella Solaris*, and her similarly converted smaller sister ships *Stella Oceanis* and *Stella Maris*, continue to serve the same luxury market sector which Haralambos Kioscoglou had originally identified back in the 1960s. These ships have become classics of the modern era which continue to hold pride of place in competition with the much newer and more sophisticated tonnage which one might expect to have overwhelmed their positions.

OTHER EARLY CONVERSIONS

Indeed not all conversions were destined to serve the luxury cruise markets, and nor were all ships rebuilt for cruising any more of a likeness than the clientele they would ultimately serve. Two of the more unusual instances involved adapting redundant troop-carrying ships to provide special educational cruises for school children. During the 1950s the British Ministry of Transport had subsidised the building of *Nevasa* and *Oxfordshire* as peacetime troop transports serving the various possessions of the Commonwealth. In addition to open accommodation for soldiers these were provided with cabins for other passengers, mostly military officers and government officials. However, these ended up going into service at a time of rapidly decreasing demand for their rather specialised roles.

The fifteen-year government trooping contracts for both ships were terminated in 1962, little more than five years after the two ships were commissioned in 1956 and 1957 respectively. British India Line, who owned *Nevasa*, and Bibby Line, under whose flag *Oxfordshire* was registered, were free to redeploy or dispose of the ships as they could.

After a short lay-up in the River Fal, British India Line refitted *Nevasa*'s original troop facilities as dormitories for school children to be carried on educational cruises. Other areas such as mess halls and recreation areas were ideal for easy adaptation for school use as refectories, common rooms and even classrooms. The original three-class cabin accommodation was restyled to offer single-class facilities for 307 passengers. These would be available for teachers and faculty personnel as well as other passengers wanting to take the same longer cruise itineraries with the extensive port lectures and sightseeing programmes offered for the children. While the original cabin accommodation was amalgamated to offer a single level of service, the children's accommodation still remained completely segregated, as they had been in the ship's trooping days. Other educational cruise ships had already been successfully converted, including *Dunera* in 1962.

The success of *Nevasa*'s conversion when introduced in 1965 was such that a second British India ship was likewise adapted. The 1961-built *Uganda* was rebuilt to similarly accommodate 1,224 school pupils. However, as *Uganda* had been designed as a traditional two-class British tropical cargo/passenger liner, the dormitories were built into the former tourist-class accommodation spaces and part of the original cargo spaces aft. Consequently, the structural changes to the ship were far greater, altering her exterior appearance far more than had been done in *Nevasa*'s case. The promenade and bridge decks were extended fully aft to house the students' quarters and recreational spaces. At the forward part of the boat deck, the deckhouses were extended out to the ship's full beam, as a means of providing the same proportion of cabin space as available in *Nevasa*. Both ships were operated by P&O for the remainder of their careers. *Nevasa* was withdrawn during the late 1970s, while *Uganda*

Uganda: **The ship seen off Lerwick in the Shetlands during a cruise in 1968.**

(Author)

remained in service long enough to serve in the 1982 Falkland Islands conflict, and for a while thereafter in other government services in the South Atlantic, until finally being decommissioned and scrapped in 1984. School children's cruises have continued, using chartered short-sea tonnage with a fairly basic style of accommodation. While the cruises continue to be successful, the ships used have never offered the same sense of character which was unique to *Nevasa* and *Uganda*.

Meanwhile, at the end of her trooping activities in 1963, *Oxfordshire* was taken up on a six-year charter by the Sitmar subsidiary Fairline Shipping Corporation for emigrant service to Australia. Only a year into the charter *Oxfordshire's* new owners were pleased enough with their acquisition to purchase the ship outright. She was sent to Wilton-Fijenoord in Schiedam for conversion for single-class service for 1,800 passengers. Although the original rather utilitarian centre-island-type cargo ship profile was much improved with substantial lengthening of the superstructure both fore and aft, the attractive and generally functional accommodation within were not of the same luxury standard which prevailed throughout the yard's earlier work in *Victoria*.

Renamed *Fairstar*, the ship's first role was that of carrying emigrants from Southampton to Brisbane. Although some pleasant lounges and other public spaces were created, the rebuilt troop accommodation was very basic, even dated, in its nearly universal lack of private toilet facilities, and in the large numbers of four-berth rooms. As the emigrant trade dwindled the ship gradually shifted into a full-time cruising role, for which she turned out to be ideally suited to the Australian market.

There has always been an elite section of the Down-Under cruise market, mostly older couples who would book the best cabins aboard *Oriana*, *Canberra*, *Rotterdam* and other world-class ships whose diverse itineraries would take them through the southern hemisphere. However, there have always been even greater numbers of younger Aussies to whom comradeship and an informal atmosphere were more important than splendid isolation in a deluxe state room with their own video cassette player and mini-bar. This trade has always been less oriented towards creatures filing 'two-by-two' aboard the biblical ark, emphasising instead the very special importance which Aussies of either sex attach to being together with their friends.[4] While the traditional booking policies of Lines such as Orient and P&O always allowed berths to be booked individually by those of the same sex wanting to share cabins, later attempts by America-based operators such as Princess failed in the Australian trade because they lacked this sort of flexibility.

Consequently, *Fairstar*, with her basic accommodation and great flexibility in booking policies remained the veritable standard bearer of the unique Australian mass-market sector. In this market she flourished alongside the Japanese-owned *Oriental Queen*, the Soviet *Mikhail Lermontov*, various ships of Italian and Greek registry, as well as older Orient and P&O

tonnage, all of which offered large quantities of basic emigrant-style accommodation. When the Sitmar fleet was acquired by P&O in the late 1980s, with their America-based ships all being renamed and taken into the Princess Cruises operation, *Fairstar* remained unchanged. Eventually she was scrapped in 1997.

When *Fairstar's* time for withdrawal finally comes, as inevitably it will, some rather imaginative thinking will be needed to replicate her unique character. However, faced with a somewhat similar, though less acute, set of considerations in planning the new *Oriana* as a possible running mate for their venerable flagship *Canberra*, P&O's planners and designers showed remarkable sensitivity for the actual diversity of their very wide market.

Norway

The design departments of yards like Wilton Fijenoord and owners such as Haralambos Kioscoglou had indeed shown what was possible with one-off conversions of intermediate-size ships. Carnival's transformation of *S A Vaal* into their *Festivale* in Japan advanced the art not only to a much larger ship, but also in helping to form key elements of their extensive later newbuilding programme. However, before *Festivale* was handed over to start her new life for Carnival, some surprising developments in Europe led to the then largest passenger ship in the world being adapted for full-time Caribbean cruising.

Perhaps the first that was known of this was when Knut Kloster dropped in to the Copenhagen office of Knud E Hansen on his way home to Oslo. Speaking with Tage Wandborg, one of the firm's senior partners, he asked a hypothetical

France: **Seen in her original form as an elite North Atlantic express liner with only nominal provision in her design for off-season cruising. The excursion launches were added later.**

(Fotoflite Ltd, neg 73-2204)

question about buying the then laid-up *France* for conversion as a cruise ship. Wandborg's initial reaction was 'Don't do it.' When the visionary Norwegian confessed that he had already bought the ship, Wandborg graciously accepted the greatest-ever challenge in passenger-ship conversion with the reassuring words 'Don't worry, we will make it work'.

The great French liner had been lying in a quiet backwater of Le Havre. She had a skeleton crew aboard her to maintain her in suitable condition for sale, if French Line were to be lucky enough to find anyone who wanted to buy her. It was almost reminiscent of *Normandie*'s state of operational limbo during the early days of World War II. The ship had in fact been sold in 1978 to Saudi financier Akram Ojjeh for use as a hotel off Jeddah. Previously Montréal's energetic mayor Jean Drapeau had wanted to purchase the ship for a similar static role, which in that instance also included a casino, as a means of financing the 1976 Summer Olympic Games. However, Montréal's taxpayers ended up picking up the Olympic expenses, and Ojjeh's own plans finally failed to materialise. Considering the technical and financial difficulties which *Queen Mary*'s upkeep over her years at Long Beach have presented, it would seem most unlikely that the world had room for yet another large Atlantic liner in a similar dormant role for very long. In such a capacity her final fate might well have ended up being far more agonising than *Normandie*'s heartbreaking loss by fire in New York nearly forty years earlier.

Kloster bought the ship from Ojjeh for $18 million. This represented a mere pittance compared with the original building price of around $75 million at 1961 rates of exchange. The additional $40 million to be spent converting her from the elite express liner *France* to the cruise vessel *Norway*, with appropriately downrated power and speed, was relatively cheap for such a large and high-quality ship still in such remarkably good condition. By comparison, the contract price for Carnival's new 36,000-ton *Tropicale*, which was being built at the time *France* changed hands, was $100 million.

France's existing accommodation ranged from tourist-class inner cabins, the vast majority with private toilet facilities, which were at least comparable to the standard-grade rooms aboard ships such as *Sea Venture* or *Royal Viking Star*, to deluxe first-class state rooms and suites that would rival and even surpass the best that *QE2* had to offer. While renewal of soft furnishings and some fresh paint would suffice in these areas, the public spaces of the two classes needed to be amalgamated into a single complex and had to be given a far greater contact with the outside world. In their original form the enclosed promenades on the promenade and veranda decks would be totally unsuitable for cruising, while what was needed would be a vast increase in the amount of open deck space, with swimming pools, lidos, and sports facilities. Furthermore these changes would have to be made without undue compromise to the ship's unique original external appearance. Although Kloster's conversion proposals were

required to meet the approval of the French government, the magnificence of the ship's form itself was inspiration enough for those involved in the planning to preserve as much of her original character as was practically possible.

The original public room plan was similar to that of *Rotterdam*, with a separate set of spaces for each class being arranged, one above the other, on two adjacent decks. Some linkages already existed, in the form of the double-height theatre and a staircase joining the two original night-club bars. Although using separate stairtowers for each class, as opposed to *Rotterdam*'s French-inspired single 'trick' staircase, stair towers allowed some access between the two strata of lounges and halls in the rather limited contingencies made for cruising in the ship's original planning. With her engineering more solidly committed to the speeds needed for five-day Atlantic crossings, *France*'s cruising role tended to be more secondary than that of the slower *Rotterdam* or Swedish American Line ships. While *France*'s aft-located tourist-class swimming pool endeavoured to address the ship's secondary cruising role, its immovable glass roof confined it, along with the enclosed promenades, to being part of an inside world protected against the ravages of the winter North Atlantic, rather than being open to the more hospitable climates to which her extra-curricular cruising activity took her.

With Atlantic crossings no longer a consideration, some of the ship's overall characteristics would change irrevocably.

	France	*Norway*
Length oa	315.52m	315.52m
Depth to veranda deck	28.09m	28.09m
Draught	10.00m	10.00m
Service speed	31.0kts	17.0kts
Propulsion power	119,360.0kW	59,680.0kW
GRT	66,348.0	70,202.0
Passenger capacity	2,044	2,200
Crew	1,044	800

In his approach to restyling the ship's facilities and opening them up to the tropical cruising world of her new life as *Norway*, Wandborg started by extending the superstructure decks aft in a broad sweep of terraces over the ship's slender stern. This was part of a highly integrated approach which addressed both the formation of a new set of specialised and closely integrated public interiors out of the former lounges, smoking rooms and other areas of the original two classes as well as the creation of vastly expanded open deck areas with open-air swimming pools, lido areas and various sports facilities.

The tourist-class pool was pushed up from its original position aft of the cabin accommodation on the upper deck to the promenade deck. At last opened to the skies there, it became the centrepiece of a vast new lido, of roughly rectangular shape, cantilevered out well beyond the finely tapered lines of the upper deck's bulwarks below. The veranda deck above was also extended aft, although less extensively. The original first-class smoking room lost its veranda with a view over the ship's stern due to the extension of the aft-most stair-tower to reach the outdoor restaurant located on the new deck area. While the boat deck remained little changed, apart from an extension of its open area aft, cabins were added above on the sun deck. These effectively filled in a lengthwise step-back of the superstructure at this level, creating an uninterrupted expanse of open deck space above at the base of the funnels on the original observation deck.

The second outdoor pool was added at this level, with its tank filling in *France*'s unique courtyard, around which a small group of inward-facing first-class cabins had been grouped. The accommodation remained, becoming standard inside cabins. The lido surrounding the pool was given added width by extending the deck outwards, creating an overhang above the lifeboat davits. Access to this area was optimised with an extension of one of the main stairtowers into a nearby deck-house, also containing the pool bar, toilets and deck stores.

Collectively these additions and modifications gave *Norway*, then the world's largest ship, the distinction of also having the greatest amount of open deck space, despite her North Atlantic origins. Most remarkably though, was the way in which this was achieved without compromise to the ship's original magnificent appearance and superb balance of profile. The widened expanse of her promenade-deck extension above the stern was perhaps the most alarming concession to the new economy-of-scale shape of things in shipping, but that was most noticeable from the air or at sea level close in to the stern quarters, as seldom seen by most passengers.

The original layout of public rooms on the promenade and veranda decks was similar, with the location of the

Norway: The North Cape Lounge looking aft through its high-ceilinged central entertainment area. This room was completely redecorated, retaining nothing from its original French Line styling.

(Author)

tourist-class main lounge aft and smoking room amidships on the promenade deck being reversed above in first class, where the smoking room was astern and the lounge amidships. These rooms were all of similar size, with the tourist main lounge benefiting from the additional areas of its extension into the enclosed promenades to either side. The forward boundary of the public spaces at both levels was formed by the theatre, which was shared by both classes. Duplicity of function was eliminated in Norwegian Caribbean's permanent amalgamation of the two strata, with the original general-purpose nature of most rooms being made far more specialised. In addition to opening up the former tourist-class main lounge to the new pool lido aft, the midships tourist smoking room became the casino. Above, the first-class smoking room and main lounge became the Club Internationale and Checkers Cabaret Lounge, set up as separate venues for solo or feature acts and night-club entertainment respectively.

The former tourist-class main lounge, whose aft wall had formed a horse-shoe surrounding the forward part of a semi-sheltered deck space around the pool dome, was expanded and opened up to the new lido deck aft via a glassed-in ante-room, featuring a double sided indoor/outdoor bar. Renamed as North Cape Lounge, the lounge itself became a highly versatile space which could serve either as a daytime extension of the newly added lido bar or as a principal entertainment and dancing area for evening use. Proclaimed as one of the most spacious rooms of its kind afloat with the world's largest shipboard bar when completed in 1962, the room remained nonetheless impressive after its restyling as the North Cape Lounge, despite being a rather wide, low-ceilinged space. Below, the space which had originally formed the indoor pool lido area was transformed into a high-tech

Norway: View along the port side of the Club International where the classic French Line styling, with windows looking into the promenade and to the boat deck above, was retained and further opened up to the promenade's revitalised life as the main circulation route.

(Author)

discotheque, complete with portholes looking into the pool which had in effect risen up to the skies above.

Wandborg was not tempted to open up the North Atlantic-style promenades, as Sitmar had done in their conversion of the former Cunard intermediates *Carinthia* and *Sylvania* as *Fairsea* and *Fairwind*. Instead, the veranda-deck promenades were retained and upgraded to serve as the principal circulation arteries of *Norway*'s indoor public areas. Although similar in general concept to Greek Line's approach in *Empress of Britain* as *Queen Anna Maria*, and Carnival's promenade treatment in *Festivale*'s conversion, *Norway*'s size and complexity called for greater sophistication, as these galleries had also to effectively serve the public areas below, created out of the original tourist-class spaces. The two lower enclosed promenades had been appropriated as additional cabin space, leaving the main level of the theatre, the casino, North Cape Lounge and other smaller areas to be dependent on the stairtowers for their integration into the whole scheme of things.

The midships stairway, which also accessed the ship's main foyer and original first-class dining room, and its aft counterpart, which had been extended up to the veranda deck, became designated as the primary vertical cores. Development of the promenades into arterial streets emphasised these and their spacious vestibules as the 'addresses' both of the public rooms immediately below and of the dining rooms and ship's entrances three and four decks farther down. Two additional forward-located stairtowers (one of which was beyond the reach of the promenade anyway) and the remaining two vertical accesses bracketing the aft engine casing were in effect downrated as secondary links. The distinction was made largely by way of the more prominent signage for the two designated principal stairtowers.

The promenades, named Fifth Avenue and Champs Élysées, also served as the only means of access to a number of smaller shops and bars. These were fashioned out of the children's playrooms, teenagers' soda fountain and hairdressing salons forward of the theatre in *France*'s plan. The original combined-class Cabaret de L'Atlantique, starboard side aft, was turned outwards towards Champs Élysées as the upper gallery of a bi-level shopping centre. Deck pantries were revitalised in the service of the Parisian-style cafés which were to add a livelihood to the ship's newfound 'streetscape'.

Ship's services such as the purser's bureau, shore excursion office and cashier's desk were relocated from the entrance foyers to the promenade, where they would be at the centre of activity and most readily accessible. These were arranged as counters facing outwards alongside the theatre, where they would be central between the main stairtowers. Appropriately, these had somewhat the look of information and ticket stations at the airports where most of *Norway*'s passengers would begin their cruise vacations. Strangely, it seems, this approach has remained unique to *Norway*, with other proponents of sophisticated promenade plans such as Carnival still preferring the more traditional entrance-foyer location for their ships' offices and services.

Norway's remaining public spaces on the deck below were notable for being appropriately rendered as inner spaces, for functions where an outside exposure was not needed, and in some instances not even desirable. The original promenades at this level were taken over for additional cabins, effectively cutting these rooms off completely from the outside world. The theatre, which was upgraded for revue-style entertainment productions, the casino and shopping arcades were all areas which would best be served by their architectural and production lighting schemes, regardless of what time of day or night they were being used. The new cabins which were built into the outer spaces at either side made far better use of the natural light and views of the passing world than the inner public areas could ever have done. These were fashioned as some of the most attractive cabins *Norway* had to offer, with each room lying lengthwise against the ship's side and having three of the large original promenade-deck windows to itself.

This example demonstrates that, in addition to the lower-deck-sited dining rooms, there is a surprisingly large proportion of public space in a modern cruise ship which can be confined to the inner reaches of each deck, leaving the periphery areas free for bright and attractive cabins. Considering also the advances in ferry design, where huge garage spaces can be created inside the hull without the need for internal columns, this part of *Norway*'s plan would seem to offer great possibilities for some radically different thinking in cruise-ship design. Appropriately, one of the most compelling precedents for a plan of this type can be found in the example of *France*'s own great and magnificent predecessor *Normandie*. A 100m-long and three-deck-high dining room ran through the centre of this vast ship's hull, flanked by a remarkably high proportion of attractive outer cabins and suites.

Another example which featured an appropriate predominance of windowless public space was the 1989 rebuilding of the ferry *Las Palmas de Gran Canaria* as *Crown Del Mar* for Caribbean cruising. In her case, the dining room, casino and two lounges were arranged throughout the original vehicle deck, below the accommodation. Only a two-level observation lounge and a lido bar and grill were located on the upper decks. While making good use of the already open garage deck area for the large open spaces needed for evening dining and other mainly nocturnal activities, the overall plan allowed for a strong emphasis on attractive cabins with outside exposure on the upper decks.

While the conversion of *France* to *Norway* did indeed change the function and character of many public interiors, as much as possible of *France*'s original design was retained. The first-class Chambord dining room, its adjoining lobby and the first-class library and writing room were retained virtually intact, with the major difference being an increase of seating density and improved lighting in the dining room. The theatre also retained as much of its original character as the technical and production installations necessary for NCL's purposes would permit. Also largely unaltered, with the exception of its

ABOVE *Tagus*: The ship on which William Thackeray made the cruise recounted in his *Diary of a Voyage from Cornhill to Grand Cairo*.

(P&O Group)

BELOW *Rotterdam*: The Ambassador Room, looking diagonally to port across the circular dance floor, with the bandstand and bar behind the bullseye-glazed screens to the left and right respectively.

(Author)

Rotterdam: On an Alaska cruise during the 1980s.

(Holland America Line)

ABOVE *Royal Viking Sea*: Seen here at San Juan after being lengthened in the early 1980s.

(Greg Lynn, Toronto)

BELOW *Europa*: The indoor swimming pool was a modern shipboard architectural feature in a similar size and scale to its predecessors on the 1930 *Bremen*.

(Author)

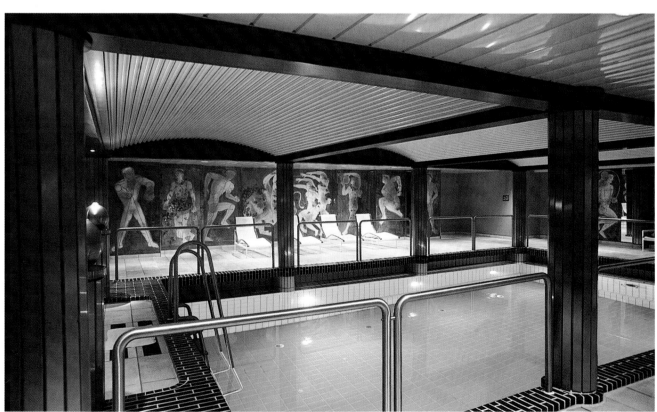

ABOVE *Festivale*: Extensively modified from her original self as *Transvaal Castle/S A Vaal*, she makes an afternoon arrival at Miami's Dodge Island terminal in 1982.

(Author)

BELOW *Holiday*: The Blue Lagoon Lounge, with its undulating fibreglass ceiling creating the impression of an underwater garden.

(Author)

Norway: **Her maiden arrival at New York in May 1980 with a dark blue hull, new funnel colours and the addition of two high-capacity excursion launches on her foredeck as the most immediately discernible changes.**

(Author)

ABOVE *Aida*: Cut-away illustration of the ship showing the layout of her public areas throughout the upper decks above the sleeping accommodation and the nested lifeboats.

(Kvaerner-Masa-Yards, Turku)

BELOW *Aida*: With her distinctive red kissing lips and mascara-highlighted brown eyes hull supergraphics, painted by German artist Feliks Büttner, she is seen here at Tortola in the British Virgin Islands during a Caribbean **cruise.**

(Author)

Aida: Part of the open-plan resort and recreation area which occupied the entire central part of deck 9. The footbridge cleverly disguises the existence of the fire bulkhead which divides the space at its centre.

(Valokuvaamo Saaristo Ky; courtesy of Kvaernaer-Masa-Yards)

Fantasy: The atrium, or Spectrum as it was named, was spectacular not only for its seven-deck height and glass dome (seen here after dark in the upward view), but also for its special high-tech lighting effects.

(Carnival Cruise Lines)

ABOVE *Star Princess*: On her maiden arrival in Fort Lauderdale, after having also lost the 'softening' touch of the Sitmar supergraphics in the change of ownership.

(Princess Cruises)

BELOW *Mercury*: Second of the two larger ships following *Century*, her profile is distinguished by a number of details without appearing noticeably larger overall. Note the second row of cabin verandas beneath the lido area overhang.

(Hero Lang, Bremerhaven; courtesy of Meyer Werft)

Galaxy: Following the same basic design approach as used aboard *Century*, the Orion Restaurant of the second ship emphasises a circular expression of plan by way of its stairway arrangement and polar-projection ceiling map.

(Ingrid Fiebak, Leer; courtesy of Meyer Werft)

ABOVE *Sun Princess*: Representing a refined adaptation of *Star Princess*, without Renzo Piano's styling elements, the ship retained the lines of the prototype's droop-nosed bow.

(Princess Cruises)

BELOW *Sun Princess*: **A photo-realistic computer rendering of the Riviera Spa pool with its hemispherical glass dome. A similar dome was considered for** *Canberra* **nearly forty years earlier.**

(Princess Cruises)

Carnival Destiny: The Universe Dining Room, showing the huge open central space resembling the Holland America Statendum-class's dining room in scale but with the inevitable Farcus touch in its décor.

(Carnival Cruise Lines)

Carnival Destiny: With a change of name from Atrium in the earlier ships to Rotunda aboard *Destiny*, this is one of several awe-inspiring spaces which more dramatically bespeak the ship's great size than does her exterior.

(Carnival Cruise Lines)

OPPOSITE PAGE *Wind Star*: The completed ship making her maiden arrival at Miami under sail in November 1986.

(Author)

ABOVE *Silver Cloud*: Show Lounge, representing a masterful adaptation of the Carnival-style double-deck facility to the scale of a larger Yachtcruiser.

Costa Classica: The reception hall at the floor of the atrium, with the marble-clad sides of its shaft visible above.

(Costa Cruise Lines)

(Silversea Cruises, Miami)

Fascination and *Ryndam*: Although hardly identifiable as
such from the air as seen here, these corporate half-sisters
share a number of operational similarities in their internal
arrangement.

ABOVE *Statendum*: The double-height Rotterdam dining room with its full width windows along three sides at both levels, which introduced this type of plan for the first time aboard a Holland America ship.

BELOW *Oriana*: Lord's Tavern, upholding the theme of *Canberra*'s Cricketer's Tavern in the context of the greater design sophistication demanded by cruise ship design more than thirty years later.

aft veranda being closed off, was the first-class Fumoir, in its adaptation as the Club Internationale. This, *France*'s only double-height space apart from the dining rooms, differed from the rest of the ship's exuberantly modern original architecture in its more art-deco style of decoration, which represented a vestigial reminiscence of her great forebear *Normandie*'s vast interior magnificence. This last link with French Line's rich history has become even more cherished as *Norway* herself has gracefully aged and put half a century between her times and the *grande luxe* age of *Normandie*.

Those interiors such as the North Cape Club, Checkers Cabaret and the Monte Carlo Casino, whose areas and functions were changed, were entirely redecorated. The tourist-class dining room, whose original rather bland French Line styling had little to offer, was also restyled. Although far enough removed from those public areas which did retain the essence of their original character, the restyled interiors were nonetheless in direct contact with the many linking elements of stairways, lobbies and vestibules which, although newly carpeted, still retained their original wall coverings and lighting schemes. The renewed interiors and their co-ordination with the existing infrastructure were rendered in the modern Scandinavian/American style which cruise passengers in the United States had come to expect, their design being intrusted to New York architect Angelo Donghia. He succeeded in producing a livable yet appropriately elegant style which complemented the existing character of the ship, and was at the same time neither overpowering nor pretentious.

While the added deck spaces and pools, along with the necessary changes to accommodation and public rooms, would ultimately have to win for *Norway* the public appeal which would sell her cruises, equally important engineering and technical work was necessary to make the ship function properly. Key among these considerations was the reduction in power and propulsion performance to make *Norway* economically operable at the lower speeds needed for Caribbean cruising. Other major items included installing side thrusters to enable the ship to manoeuvre without tugs and providing sufficient lighterage or tenders to get her 2,200 passengers ashore and back aboard in all but her base port of Miami, owing to *Norway*'s deep 'Winter North Atlantic' draught of 10m. Additional air-conditioning and electrical loads, upgraded sewage and waste-handling facilities and modernised navigational and control systems all added to the vastness of the transformation.

Since *France* had been built with two completely independent sets of machinery, one each driving the inner and outer propellers, the propulsion systems could be downrated to the required 15–17kts by using one set of engines and propellers only. The owners would have preferred to make a complete switch to diesel machinery, but the conversion time frame available would not have been sufficient for such an unprecedented undertaking. The outer propellers were removed, and the forward aggregate of boilers and turbines permanently shut down. The machinery itself was for the most part not removed to preserve stability, while the propeller shafts and their bossings were also left intact. Not only did this serve the expediency of the conversion schedule, but it also avoided having to deal with the immensely complicated issues of redistributed centres of buoyancy and longitudinal balance which would have arisen from the removal of so much structural steelwork and machinery.

Although the forward propulsion plant would cease to function as such, its auxiliary electrical generating capacity was needed to help meet the increased demand of six transverse thrusters, additional air conditioning and other services as well as the increased hotel load from the new cabins and extended public areas. Four of the ship's original steam turbo-alternator sets were retained, with the remaining two being replaced by new 6,000V units. The remaining four were taken off the ship and rewound to also generate the higher voltage, so that all units could serve a common power management system of the type being used in new ships of the day, such as Carnival's *Tropicale* and others. This increased the ship's original 450V main power distribution system to the level of its biggest consumers, namely the five 6,000V transverse thrusters. Transformers were fitted into the forward and aft machinery spaces to step down the voltage to the lower levels needed for hotel services, lighting and various other domestic uses, including passengers' personal grooming and entertainment appliances brought aboard.

The original arrangement of three generator sets in each engine room was retained, with the two new units going into the otherwise largely decommissioned forward machinery space. However, since the adjoining boiler plant would no longer be operative, pipes had to be fitted to deliver steam from the remaining aft boiler room and return exhaust vapours and gases to the aft funnel. The forward starboard boiler was in fact removed to make way for the sewage treatment plant fitted as part of the conversion.

The aft boiler room was capable of easily handling the additional generator load owing to the lower demands made by the propulsion turbines to achieve *Norway*'s sedate cruising speeds of below 17kts. An added margin of efficiency was also gained by replacing the two remaining four-bladed inboard propellers. The new screws were of a smaller-diameter, but optimised, five-bladed type, designed to achieve the required service speeds from less engine power. While the new propellers, which were also fixed pitch, like the originals, would not themselves improve the ship's manoeuvrability, the addition of five thrusters allowed her to turn in her own length and to move sideways. These were arranged three forward and two aft, with a total power of 7,800kW, enough to enable this extremely large and high ship to manoeuvre in wind forces of up to Beaufort 7.

Operation of these and the main propellers was automated for integrated functioning by way of joystick-type controls located in the wheelhouse and on the bridge wings. Thus the 315m-long ship could be independently swung around within the confines of the Port of Miami's turning basin, docked and undocked with the single-handed ease of manipulating a type of device which has since become widely used in aircraft control systems, and even commonplace in the home computer games market. However, *Norway*'s automation was extremely advanced for its day, and was the prototype for much later development in shipboard cybernetics.

Alas, the question of getting 2,200 passengers ashore and back aboard at her cruise stops, which included a private island purchased by the Line, called for some unconventional thinking of its own. The ordeal of landing such great numbers of passengers, a hundred or so at a time, using lifeboats or lifeboat-sized launches would simply have been too tedious. The world's biggest cruise ship was thus given two of the largest and most sophisticated landing craft ever to be carried under davits aboard any ship. These were double-deckers, designed along the lines of military landing craft, each with a capacity of 400. Their catamaran-style forward hull skegs incorporated a ramp which could be lowered directly onto the beach. The aft deck height of these craft was arranged to coincide with the level of shell doors forward and aft on *Norway*'s B deck, through which passengers could step directly to and from the tenders.

However, with a length of 28.4m and weight of 55 tons each, stowage of these enormous 'daughter vessels' aboard *Norway* demanded special considerations. Obviously, the boat deck was out of the question. However the fore deck, whose original design incorporated two hatches aft of its *Normandie*-style whaleback, offered both the space and structural strength needed. The existing kingposts and cargo derricks were removed to make way for the specially designed hydraulic luffing davits and supporting cradles needed to carry the tenders. It was a great credit to the ship's structural stamina and huge reserves of buoyancy and vertical stability that an installation of this type was possible at all. Indeed not all ships, even those designed for express Atlantic service, could have sustained such a huge installation. Those of lightweight construction, such as P&O's first *Oriana* or *QE2*, would never have been able to support such an addition without the costly modifications to the basic hull form itself.

Kloster had purchased *France* in May 1979. Within the following three months all design work for the conversion was carried out and a contract awarded for this, the largest-ever passenger ship conversion to be carried out, in as little as eight months. While there was hope in France that the prestigious job would be done by French shipbuilders, Hapag-Lloyd Werft in Bremerhaven was the only yard which could guarantee a delivery date of 1 April the following year. Tracing its origins back 100 years as North German Lloyd's exclusive ship-repair facility, this specialist yard had since become a wholly owned subsidiary of Germany's vast corporate Hapag-Lloyd entity. Conversions in the early 1970s of *Volendam* and *Veendam*, for Holland America Line, as well as *Caribe* and Kloster's *Sunward II*, had already established the yard's reputation for cruise-ship work on the open market. An extensive modernisation and expansion of Hapag-Lloyd Werft's facili-

ties between 1976 and 1978 was aimed at positioning the yard to take a major position in cruise-ship conversion and rebuilding work on a far greater scale. This investment of some 26 million deutschmarks was key to securing the contract for *Norway*'s conversion, itself establishing the yard's unparalleled reputation in large-scale work of this type. What Wärtsilä had become to the passenger-ship newbuilding field so was Hapag-Lloyd Werft to be in the conversion field.

Norway was completed both on time and on budget. Despite the inevitable teething problems of any technical endeavour of its scale, the conversion was an immediate commercial success, both for the Kloster's Norwegian Caribbean Line and for Hapag-Lloyd Werft. *Norway* has since returned to Bremerhaven for additional work, including the addition of two superstructure decks in the early 1990s. Other work undertaken by the yard, its name since shortened to Lloyd Werft, has included extensive upgrading of several Soviet cruise ships, conversion of the ferry *Begonia* as *Explorer Starship* as well as *QE2*'s re-engining in 1987. The lengthenings of NCL's *Dreamward* and *Windward* and the completion of *Norwegian Sky* are among the yard's most recent work.

QUEEN ELIZABETH 2

Probably no ship has undergone as much change, restyling and retro- and re-fitting as has *Queen Elizabeth 2*. Some of the changes, most notably her re-engining, were essential. Others, such as the addition of a casino in her early years and various changes to the entertainment and catering facilities, were undertaken to keep pace with modern cruise lifestyle changes being reflected in the design of new rival tonnage entering the luxury cruise market. Still others, such as the Magrodome-style pool lido and post-Falklands change in hull

Queen Elizabeth 2: The 1/16 scale plastic and Plexiglas model used by the shipyard and engine maker to develop the solution finally chosen.

(Cunard Line, New York)

livery, have not lived up to expectations and were subsequently either eradicated or further modified.

Modifications were made in an effort to provide the ship with the type of entertainment venue which her vast Double Room unfortunately never could achieve. If the notion of Carnival's cabaret-style show lounges could have been foreseen, probably the whole deckhouse surrounding the Double Room should have been rebuilt during one of the ship's first major refits in the 1970s, to provide a column-less double-deck *Holiday*-style facility with amphitheatre seating and a wide proscenium stage.

The additions of penthouse suites and other deluxe cabins over the years, changes to restaurant configurations and other rearrangements of public facilities have gradually compromised the ship's original integrity of plan. This in itself has produced the need for a total re-evaluation of the ship's function in the most recent refurbishment prior to writing, in which key elements of the original plan have been restored, revitalised and to some degree improved.

From all of this work, certainly *Queen Elizabeth 2*'s epic re-engining was one of the most noteworthy technical accomplishments in the entire history of marine engineering. The Cunard flagship's original steam-turbine machinery, though advanced in its time, was becoming something of the same economic liability which had courted *France*'s withdrawal from service in 1974. Thanks to the British ship's slightly smaller size and lower propulsion power, the problem of survival was not as acute as it had been on the other side of the English Channel. By virtue of having been built seven years later, *Queen Elizabeth 2* was specifically planned with a far greater emphasis on cruising at lower and more economical speeds. Only forty per cent of her service time each year was spent in Line service at a speed of 28.5kts, with the original machinery also having a second optimum setting for 16kts to be used in cruise service. However, despite even these contingencies, the Cunard flagship was becoming prohibitively expensive to operate, both on the North Atlantic and in lower-speed cruise service.

Ships of the 1980s such as *Europa* and *Nieuw Amsterdam* had become far more energy efficient through modern developments in diesel propulsion and application of the power-station principle to total energy management. Yet despite the planning of larger economy-of-scale tonnage which would rival her own size, any new ship of *Queen Elizabeth 2*'s individuality, offering her spaciousness, wide range of cabin accommodation and varied public facilities, would have been prohibitively expensive to build from scratch. It was estimated by Cunard that in 1985 such a replacement could cost over $400 million to build, more than double the contract price for *Sovereign of the Seas*, then recently ordered in France.

With less than fifteen years in service, *Queen Elizabeth 2* was still new enough so that other options could be considered to increase her lifespan by at least another twenty years as well as her earning potential and service efficiency. Using a theoretical diesel power-plant type installation as the basis of

comparison, a possible thirty per cent economy in the ship's then £12 million annual fuel bill was projected. Various alternatives were studied, as a practical means of achieving this optimum result:

Maintaining the original propelling machinery for the remainder of the ship's life, and conversion of the steam plant to burn cheaper fuels such as coal or coal slurry.

Retaining the original propelling machinery and boilers, but replacing part or all of the turbo-generator plant with new diesel alternators to reduce the boiler load and improve fuel economy.

Full or partial conversion to hybrid steam- and gas-turbine propulsion, with various alternatives including diesel for generating electrical power.

Complete re-engining with either low- or medium-speed diesels in a flexible power-station-type installation, offering the greatest operational flexibility for both cruising and liner service.

After evaluating more than fifteen different alternatives from various shipbuilders and engine makers, Cunard finally chose Lloyd Werft's proposal for full conversion to a diesel-electric power plant, using MAN/B&W engines, GEC alternators and drive motors and Lips controllable-pitch propellers. The $115 million contract also included other life-extending remedial structural work and modification to some of the passenger accommodation. This, *Queen Elizabeth 2*'s most extensive refit, and the largest ever re-engining of a passenger ship, was scheduled for a period of only 179 days over the winter of 1986–7.

This would make *Queen Elizabeth 2* the most powerful diesel passenger vessel in the world, surpassing the forty-year records of the Dutch East Indies motor ships *Oranje* and *Willem Ruys*, both planned in the 1930s, although the *Willem Ruys* was not completed until 1947, owing to the Nazi occupation of the Netherlands during World War II. The 20,017-ton *Oranje* had been powered by a trio of low-speed twelve-cylinder two-stroke Sulzer engines yielding 27,960kW, and a service speed of 26.5kts through three direct-coupled screws.[5] *Oranje* had been lost by fire in 1984 as the cruise ship *Angelina Lauro*, leaving her 21,119-ton running mate still in service as *Achille Lauro*. This ship's 28,310kW Sulzer eight-engine medium-speed geared installation was a closer prototype to the *Queen Elizabeth 2*'s re-engining approach, although her record number of eight engines was exceeded by the Cunard flagship's nine alternator sets.

Queen Elizabeth 2's re-engining was also significant as being the largest diesel-electric installation to go into any passenger ship since *Robert Ley*'s completion in 1939. This set the trend for similar propulsion systems in other large cruise ships soon to follow. However, since the time of the KdF ship's early power-plant type installation, and even the later steam turbo-electric propulsion machinery used in *Canberra*, there had been significant technical advancement in solid-state frequency control devices. These allowed full flexibility in controlling the motor speed through its electrical link with the generators while allowing the power generating source to be maintained in a constant state of maximum efficiency. This was of particular importance in *Queen Elizabeth 2*'s case, where various speeds for cruising had to be available in addition to a higher level of performance for Atlantic line service.

In perhaps oversimplified terms, a converter is needed to regulate the generated alternating current frequency, or number of times per second that the AC reverses itself between positive and negative, to a lower rate which will turn a motor shaft at a given speed. In present-day marine engineering this is done with electronic circuitry using the modern solid-state thyristor as a current controlling device. These can be used to make the necessary adjustment in two different ways, known as cyclo- and synchro-conversion. The simpler of the two is cyclo-conversion which in effect slices the alternating electric current into short regular pieces of its continuous transition between the positive and negative phases. Depending on the rate at which this is done the 'slices' of current fed to the motor appear to be at a lower frequency, ie perhaps 16Hz as opposed to the original 60Hz frequency produced by the generators. The motor responds by turning at the speed determined by the 'slicing' rate.

Alternatively, synchro-conversion uses a more complex two-step conversion process where the alternating current from the generator is first converted by a thyristor-bridge supply converter circuit into direct current, which the second-step machine converter changes into a series of electrical power pulses which sequentially power or 'excite' the sequence of synchronous motor windings causing the armature shaft to turn at the speed determined by the machine-converter pulse rate.

Both systems have their own characteristics as well as their own staunch following among marine engineers. Cyclo-conversion is unquestionably the simpler of the two. However, its simulated alternating current characteristics are thought by some to deteriorate to the point of providing less effective control over wider speed ranges. The synchro-system more closely simulates the original mechanical excitation switching used in earlier examples such as *Normandie*, and is thought by others to be too cumbersome and inefficient. It is one of those on-going controversies of technology, which like the debate over four- versus two-stroke diesel engines, never seems to be resolved conclusively one way or the other. It is a question which will probably eventually simply go away as the technology changes and new issues come into focus.

Of the two approaches, synchro-conversion was chosen for *Queen Elizabeth 2*, with its at least theoretical smoothness of control over a wider range of motor speeds being considered advantageous enough to outweigh its greater technical

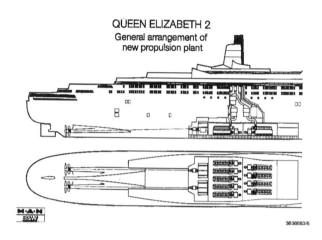

Queen Elizabeth 2: **Outline section and plan of the diesel-electric plant, showing the nine engines and two motors as well as the funnel uptake installations.**

(MAN/B&W, Augsburg)

complexity over the cyclo-system. The new power plant was made up of nine MAN/B&W medium-speed large-bore four-stroke engines each directly driving its own GEC AC generator through a flexible coupling at 400rpm. Each set delivered 10,000kW of electrical power, at the unusually high level of 10kV, to the ship's main switchboard for distribution to the drive motors, transverse thrusters and step-down transformers for other auxiliary, hotel and domestic loads. The new installation was housed within the length of *Queen Elizabeth 2*'s original machinery compartments. The new alternator sets were arranged four and five abreast in the approximate locations of the former boiler and main engine compartments respectively. The two custom-built 44,000kW propulsion motors were lined up with the existing propeller

Queen Elizabeth 2: **One of the nine MAN/B&W medium-speed large-bore four-stroke engines being tested in Augsburg.**

(Cunard Line)

shaft lines in a separate compartment added at the aft end of the machinery spaces.

The conversion also involved replacement of *Queen Elizabeth 2*'s original fixed-pitch propellers with new Lips five-bladed controllable-pitch units of the same diameter. Apart from their added operational flexibility, these had also been designed with a more steeply skewed blade profile, overcoming the vibration induced by the original pressure pulses at the ship's higher speeds. Each propeller was equipped with a new innovation, called a Grim Wheel. This was a second screw of slightly larger diameter designed to spin freely in the wake of the main propeller, reducing the width of the slipstream and thereby providing added thrust. Its function was rather like that of the large 'bypass' turbines of a modern jet aircraft engine. It was expected that this innovation alone would improve *Queen Elizabeth 2*'s performance by as much as

fifteen per cent. In reality the Grim Wheels appeared to have been unsuitable for as powerful an installation as that of *Queen Elizabeth 2*, and were thought to have broken off during astern trials at 21kts. It is clear that they did not appear later in the ship's reborn diesel-electric career and the remaining sections were removed prior to her first commercial voyage after re-engining. Since the new 5-bladed propellers were optimised for use with the Grim Wheels, new blades had to be designed for optimum performance without them.

The re-engining involved a great deal of structural work, which included the relocation of several watertight bulkheads. The division between the former engine and boiler rooms was moved ten frames farther forward at the centreline, where it formed the division between the new forward and aft alternator rooms. The forward machinery space retained its original length, by being extended part-way into the original turbo-alternator compartment, where a new bulkhead was erected at frame 164. A second bulkhead was

also added at frame 118, forming the motor compartment directly astern of the aft alternator room, back to original bulkhead aft of the engine room at frame 105.

This repositioning of the engine compartments was necessary so that the two new alternator spaces could share direct access to the funnel casing above. Previously the domain of the boiler room alone, this trunkway had to contain the exhaust uptakes from all nine engines, along with their in-line boilers, economisers and silencers. The alternator sets were arranged so that their generator and exhaust-manifold ends were closest to the dividing bulkhead beneath the funnel casing, thus minimising the piping and wiring runs. The main electrical switchboard was located centrally in the original engine-room headroom space at Six-deck level in a special compartment aft of the bulkhead between the two alternator rooms. Exhaust-gas-fired boilers, incorporated into the uptake from each engine, were arranged inside the funnel casing space between Five and quarter decks. An additional two

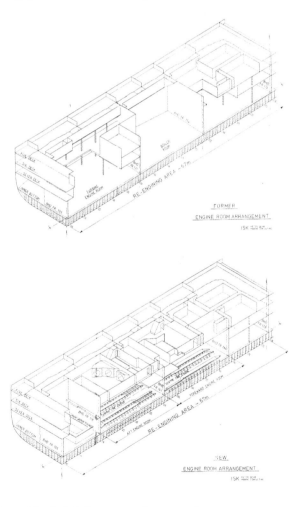

Queen Elizabeth 2: Former and new engine room arrangements, showing the change from the original boiler and turbine room spaces to the new diesel alternator rooms, motor compartment and other auxiliary spaces.

(Lloyd Werft)

Queen Elizabeth 2: One of the new propellers seen here after fabrication by Lips in Holland. Note its size compared with the girl in the foreground.

(Cunard Line)

donkey boilers, needed to provide domestic steam while in port, were also housed in the fennel casing, on a flat erected on Five deck.

The remaining forward part of the former turbo-alternator space was taken over for air-conditioning units and other auxiliary machinery, with the 'switchboard flat' above it on Seven deck becoming the new integrated and automated control centre for the entire ship's machinery, power and other technical facilities. The double bottom in the two alternator rooms was modified and reinforced to accommodate the nine 18.5m-long engine pits and foundation structures for the alternator sets, as well as two additional pits and foundation structures for the propulsion motors. Bulkhead relocations and other rearrangements of tanks required additional work to the double-bottom structure, all of which had to be executed without compromise of the hull's residual strength afloat and underway. Once installed on their vibration-damping resilient mountings, the new alternator sets were covered by an acoustic ceiling built at Six-deck level. This not only helped to suppress engine-room noise levels, but also served as a platform for the electrical switchboard room and the added structural framing of the elaborate funnel uptake installations above.

The only outwardly visible manifestation of *Queen Elizabeth 2*'s re-engining was the replacement of her funnel with a broader one, necessary to house the uptakes from her nine new alternator sets. Wind-tunnel tests on various types of new funnel revealed that the original design was outstanding with its wind scoop base and two converging upper masses. The same distinctive form was retained, although, remarkably, in a somewhat more traditional steamship proportion to the superstructure. The base dimensions were more than doubled, to 3.6m in width and 4m in length. It was decided by the owners that its proportions warranted a re-use of the original Cunard funnel colours which the former funnel had been given during *QE2*'s last years as a steamship. The colours were applied to its afterbody, still leaving the tall forward 'stovepipe' structure in black for its full height.

With the re-engining having secured *Queen Elizabeth 2*'s future mechanically and technically for at least another twenty years, 'Project Lifestyle' was mounted in 1994 to likewise retain the more tangible aspects of the ship's accommodation, amenities and commercial identity. Conceived in essence as the refit to end all refits, Project Lifestyle would bring her more up to date in such things as catering, service and on-board revenue-earning opportunities. The project's sweeping proposals were the combined work of Met Studio and John McNeece. Remarkably, both had connections with *Queen Elizabeth 2*'s origins. Met's managing director, Alex McCuaig, started his design career with James Gardner. John McNeece had been among the group of young and progressive architects chosen to design the ship's interiors before Sir Duncan Oppenheimer proposed his roster of the day's big-name British architects.

Much of the Project Lifestyle work, which was carried

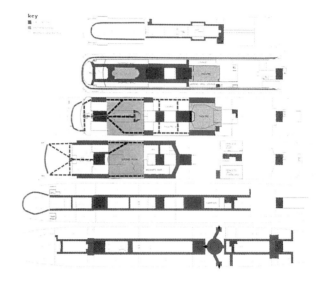

CIRCULATION: EXISTING

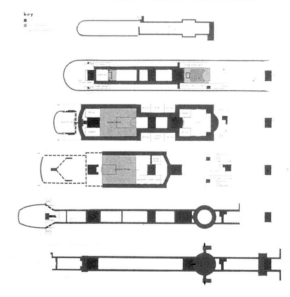

CIRCULATION: MASTERPLAN

Queen Elizabeth 2: Circulation plans showing the existing arrangement and the Project Lifestyle masterplan, not all of which was implemented.

(Met Studio, London)

out in Germany by Bremer Vulkan at the end of 1994, had to do with John McNeece's dictum of getting the infrastructure right. Functional emphasis of the ship's three principal public strata, the quarter, upper and boat decks, was changed from its original notion of first, tourist and 'mixed' use in the North Atlantic class structure. The revised concept stressed instead a day, day/night and night structure of activities and services, with the idea that all areas would be universally available to everyone, even on Atlantic crossings. Within the budget and time limitations of what was actually done, this materialised with the former first-class preserve of the quarter deck becoming the daytime centre of activity and its tourist counterpart above adopting a combined day/night and night focus.

The quarter deck's daytime function was asserted with a complete rebuilding of the Club Lido and Magrodome pool area into a new Holland America-style Lido Restaurant, with its own complete kitchen and extensive permanent buffet fixtures. Opened up to panoramic views either side of the ship and astern, this area was developed as a modern adaptation of the old Winter Garden idea. As such, it provided *Queen Elizabeth 2* with her first fully functional large-scale alternative restaurant venue for the type of informal breakfast, lunchtime and midnight buffet dining which cruise passengers had come to expect. The pool and Magrodome were removed altogether, with the original tourist-class pool farther aft on One deck below being brought more closely into the Lido scheme by way of both inside and outer stairways and a nearby service pavilion.

Above, on the upper deck, the Grand Lounge (originally the Double Room) continued to form the central focus of evening entertainment. A modest extension of the superstructure aft of this was made to extend the Yacht Club lounge (formerly the Double-Down Bar) into a larger and far more versatile facility. This was restyled into a sophisticated multi-use facility, serving as a daytime lido lounge for the extended sports deck aft atop the quarter-deck Lido Restaurant. After dark, the Yacht Club would become a night club, in keeping with the upper deck's principal emphasis on evening activities. Its location aft of the Grand Lounge also supported the intended flow of activities towards the ship's stern as the night would wear on into the wee morning hours.

In an effort to simplify *Queen Elizabeth 2*'s layout, one of the key elements of Project Lifestyle was to revitalise the original peripheral circulation plan in the public areas. In Alex McCuaig's words, '. . . providing the means of encouraging a return to the practice of promenading'. It was also important for this aspect of the work to increase the visibility of various activities offered and of the opportunities for passengers to spend money whilst aboard. While the quarter-deck plan has remained fairly well intact over the years, that of the upper deck has become more fragmented. The arterial promenades on both decks have been substantially improved with the addition of connecting elements turning them into completely surrounding loops, like the enclosed promenade decks of a traditional liner. On the quarter deck, the existing forward connection at D stairtower was complemented with a new beamwise passage aft of the G stairtower, adjacent to the new Lido Restaurant.

On the upper deck the enclosed plan of the casino (added

Queen Elizabeth 2: **A corner of the new Lido restaurant on quarter deck, which shows the higher grade of finishing and furniture than the area had previously featured.**

(Met Studio, London)

in 1972) was opened up to the portside promenade space. A passage similar to that on the quarter deck was added aft, at the entrance to the Yacht Club. The port and starboard promenades were also joined forward for the first time by way of a new aperitif bar worked into the first bay of the dining room. The intention was that the Crystal Bar, as it was called, would provide direct access to all the ship's restaurants. However, the stairways added nearby connected only to the Princess and Britannia Grill Rooms on the quarter deck below, with secondary access to the adjacent Mauretania Dining Room being possible, but obviously not primary. Reworking of the service core behind the Crystal Bar to join up with the Queen's Grill above on the boat deck was not carried out.

Vertical circulation was also improved by extending the G stairtower up to the boat deck. The need for this had become more acute after Jon Bannenberg's steel and glass spiral stairway was removed in the Double Room's adaptation as the Grand Lounge in 1987. This gave the four principal stairtowers, A, D, E and G, complete access between the three principal public levels and the cabin accommodation decks, One to Five, below. The two strata of penthouse accommodation above on Sports and Signal decks remained accessible only by secondary staircases and lifts rooted on the boat deck. While this lent some sense of exclusivity to these premium-grade suites, it remained as a vestigial remnant of the plan's fragmentation. Also a source of difficulty to orientation about the ship since her 1969 debut was the forward A stairtower, which at the three public levels remained segregated from the overall circulation scheme by the location of the restaurants.

Project Lifestyle has, despite its inevitable teething troubles, breathed another twenty-five years' life into the famous Cunard flagship. Its overall scope and range is broad enough to stand as the basis for any future work which will be needed during that time. With the emphasis on broadcasting films aboard ship by way of the cabin TV system rather than showing them on a wide screen, an option still remained to move the casino to the theatre's main level on the upper deck, and turn its boat-deck gallery into a small cinema-cum-lecture hall, more suited to informal modern shipboard lifestyle. A reincarnation of the Look Out Lounge, which in its original situation was difficult to reach owing to its near total segregation forward of the dining rooms, was also proposed. Both the previous *Queens* had forward-facing rooms. The standard should have been upheld, even if it meant appropriation of the officers' communal spaces above on the boat deck, where a better link could have been made with the other passenger spaces farther aft. After all, who was the ship intended to serve, its paying passengers or its officers?

LATER CONVERSIONS

While the mega-conversions of *France* and *QE2* were being carried out, the Italian Costa Line was achieving great success with cargo ships which had been rebuilt for cruising. The British-flag Port Line refrigerated freighters *Port Sydney* and *Port Melbourne* were unrecognisably reshaped into sleek-lined 500-passenger cruise ships. These were rebuilt during 1972 in Greece, at the Khalkis yard, originally for Greek owners. As in *Cambodge*'s example, completely new accommodation and a spacious passenger-ship superstructure were constructed in place of these ships' midships-sited crew accommodation blocks. Eventually named *Daphne* and *Danae* they were chartered in 1979 by Costa Armatori SpA, with options to purchase being taken up in 1985.

Fully satisfied with *Daphne* and *Danae*, Costa went on in the late 1980s to take over the conversion of the former

***Costa Marina/Costa Allegra*: Plans of deck 6 on both ships showing the comparison of *Costa Marina*'s European-style plan with its larger Americanised rendition aboard *Costa Allegra*.**

(Author)

Swedish ro-ro container ships *Axel Johnson* and *Annie Johnson*, built in 1969 by Wärtsilä's Turku yard. The first vessel was originally sold in 1986 to Greek owners who renamed her *Regent Sun*, before reselling her to the Rome-based Navy Club to be converted for cruising under the name *Italia*. However, this venture failed, with the ship changing hands yet again during the process of rebuilding at the T Mariotti yard in Genoa. She was taken over by Costa, with radical changes being made to the ship's styling before her 1990 redelivery as their 25,500-ton *Costa Marina*. Conversion of *Annie Johnson* was also booked with the same yard for completion two years later, emerging as *Costa Allegra*.

The exterior styling of these ships was shaped by the Italian naval architect Mezzani to reflect the character of Costa's larger newbuildings, *Costa Classica* and *Costa Romantica* of the same period. The bright and spacious interiors designed by Guide Canalii were given a likeness of style and elegance to those of the larger fleetmates. However, a noteworthy feature of the two converted ships was the manner in which their squared-off sterns, originally incorporating the vehicle deck ramps were treated.[6] Their former shape remaining somewhat apparent, the combined aft walls of the superstructures and hulls were given a distinctive arrangement of wide bowed windows on the upper decks, with similarly shaped mooring and working deck spaces below.

Although starting their careers as identical container carriers, their conversion to cruise ships was to make a remarkable distinction in serving the specific needs of their divergent Europe- and America-based markets. The first ship, *Costa Marina*, was introduced into her intended European service on the Mediterranean in 1990, before being temporarily transferred to the Line's Caribbean programme in late autumn to fill a shortage of berths there. In Miami it was soon realised that there were some fundamental differences, not only in cuisine, language and service, but also in lifestyle, to be considered.

With an identical second conversion already planned for full-time US-based operation, design changes were made to

***Danae*: The ship, together with her sister *Daphne*, was the first of Costa's successful cargo-ship conversions.**

(Courtesy of Peter Kohler, Washington D C)

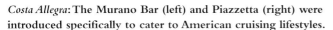

Costa Allegra: **The Murano Bar (left) and Piazzetta (right) were introduced specifically to cater to American cruising lifestyles.**

(Costa Cruise Lines)

the principal suite of public rooms to meet the expectations of the American cruise market, with its higher emphasis on entertainment and onboard passenger spending. The layout of the midships-area public rooms was completely reworked to give greater visibility and enticement to the shops and an inescapable central casino. The large open-plan lounge of the first ship was downscaled to the type of more intimate space preferred by American revellers. The revised plan also incorporated a circular 'Piazzetta' with a bar and pastry shop as a central cog of the shopping area. Also a larger stage and improved production facilities were worked into the main show lounge forward.[7] These alterations were to some degree facilitated by a lengthening of the ship by 13.2m to increase passenger capacity.

There have indeed been numerous other conversions and rebuildings of passenger ships of all kinds; enough to fill a book on their own. These have ranged from the mundane and routine to the highly imaginative. Surgery of this type has spared a number of former liners from premature scrapping, either as totally redundant vessels or as less profitable cruise tonnage, rendering them instead as up-to-date and highly competitive full-time cruise ships. An outstanding example of this was the rebuilding of the *S A Vaal*, formerly the Union Castle Line's *Transvaal Castle*, as Carnival's *Festivale* in 1978 as discussed earlier. The former Greek Line flagship *Olympia* was extensively modified internally for cruising by HDW in Hamburg after having been laid up in Greece for ten years. She re-entered service as *Caribe 1* in 1983 with her exterior profile little changed apart from the replacement of her funnel. However, the near-total internal renovation also included the replacement of her original steam machinery with diesels.

Likewise, the 1960s-built Lloyd Triestino sister ships *Guglielmo Marconi* and *Galileo Galilei* were rebuilt exclusively

for cruising, becoming Costa's *Costa Riviera* and Chandris's *Meridian* respectively in 1985 and 1990. Although carried out by two entirely different yards, and at a five-year interval , both were of a similar nature. However, while the original steam-turbine machinery was retained, extensive structural changes were made involving lengthening of the superstructure both fore and aft. Despite the radical changes in profile, the two conversions were considered to be masterpieces, in retaining and enhancing a strong impression of the ships' original, typically Italian, elegance and grace of line and form. These aesthetic elements were skilfully combined with completely rebuilt accommodation and facilities of the latest standard for her 1,106 passengers.[8]

1   T A Bushell, *Royal Mail: Centenary History of the Royal Mail Line*, p 244.
2   *Shipbuilding and Shipping Record*, 21 January 1960, p 75.
3   David Glass, *Guide 89*, p 67.
4   Bruce R J Miller, *Fairplay Cruise Review*, 1987, pp 31-5.
5   A C Hardy, *History of Motorshipping*, pp 53, 96.
6   *The Naval Architect*, July/August 1990, p E347.
7   Management, *Lloyd's Ship Manager*, Cruise and Ferry Quarterly Review, February 1991, pp S13-4.
8   Peter C Kohler, *Guide 91*, p 6

CHAPTER 9

CONFIDENCE OF PROGRESS

New ideas in the medium-tonnage range

conomy-of-scale cruise ships such as *Atlantic, Nieuw Amsterdam, Tropicale* and *Song of America* not only introduced the trading advantages of larger capacities, better operational efficiency and greater rationalisation of services, but also the beginnings of some fundamental changes in passenger-ship design. Royal Caribbean and Carnival, in particular, had departed from the traditional view of ships' lounges, bars, swimming pools and lidos as merely being pleasant places for people to while away the hours spent at sea. They began to think of these more as an integral revenue-earning infrastructure. Integration of its various parts became vital so as not to compromise the earning potential of the whole ship. While it remained vital for the lines of access to remain direct and simple, things had to be in precisely the right places and follow one another in the proper sequence. To get the infrastructure wrong was to directly lose income and to even render an entire new ship a potential commercial failure. In Carnival's interpretation of the same approach, design with a capital 'D' was an essential ingredient of their success formula. The stimulating lifestyle theatrical backdrop which Farcus's work promoted established the added sense of wellbeing and magic which would entice passengers to enjoy the ships and spending opportunities they offered to the utmost. It was from the standpoint of these ideas that naval architects, shipbuilders, interior designers, as well as cruise-ship owners began to take still bolder steps towards more creative thinking.

All of this was being carefully considered by Finland's Wärtsilä yards who were steadily emerging as a recognised world leader in the field. Much of their design strategy and building approach at the stage of *Song of America*'s building, was concisely explained in several technical papers presented by the yard's then manager of passenger-ship research and development, Kai Levander, at various shipping conferences around the world. The idea of these was to secure further orders for tonnage of progressive design and optimal operational efficiency. Apart from presenting some radically new ideas, and an overview of their marketing intent, these papers also presented a rare insight into the shipbuilder's perspective of the relationship between the processes involved in delivering a product of ultimate commercial success.

From this background Wärtsilä's marketing people were able to in effect offer a product line of standard ship design concepts which could be tailor-made to an individual Line's specific needs. These etherial ships showcased the great individuality and imaginativeness of Levander's own unique creativity, the mark of which was first borne in his involvement with *Finnjet*'s design and building in the mid 1970s. Backed by this type of creativity, Wärtsilä took an aggressive role in actively marketing their product line, directing their attention towards both the mainstream trade or perceived new 'niche' markets.

In a paper describing the development of the *Viking Saga* class of two Baltic ferries for Viking Line in 1980, Levander explained the evolution of the design as a 'Total Economy Programme'. Using computer programmes to evaluate different alternatives of ship configuration and performance, this approach also took into account the owners' economic considerations beyond the initial building costs, onwards through the entire anticipated lifespan of the ships. Capital costs, asset depreciation, crew, fuel and consumables costs, upkeep and maintenance, and earning opportunities, including the ticket price and onboard spending opportunities, were all calculated into the Total Economy formula. This particular paper showed how these factors were translated into a specific tailor-made business solution for Viking Line's overnight service between Helsinki and Stockholm. In other words, the design approach for the two ships themselves was derived largely from the economics of their planned operation over a period of perhaps twenty years. In his concluding remarks in this paper Kai Levander wrote:

> Profitability is ensured by low costs and large incomes. These in their turn derive from good basic design, skilful construction by the yard and efficient operation by the owners.[1]

In a second paper read two years later at the Hellenic Institute of Marine Technology in Athens, Levander illustrated how the same type of approach had been applied in offering *Song of America* as a Total Economy package for cruise service in the Caribbean. Here he pointed out that, given a life expectancy of twenty years, new cruise ships then being considered would in reality have to be planned in anticipation of increased passenger expectations in the year 2000. Those planned in the early 1980s would by the end of the century be in optimum cash-flow situations, with their capital costs having been paid out during the first eight years of operation. Therefore the trends of that time should be anticipated as early as possible so as to keep these ships still attractive in the later and most profitable years of their service lives.

At that time new ships such as *Song of America* were still in fact largely the product of twenty-year-old thinking, despite the industry's direction towards economy of scale and optimised infrastructure planning. What Levander predicted to be necessary were radically new ideas in the overall design of economy-of-scale tonnage as well as the development from scratch of new ship types to fill various perceived gaps in the cruise marketplace. He believed that the trade should be examined as far as possible from the consumer (ie passenger) standpoint, taking into consideration alternative means of travel as well as other leisure and holiday options offered by hotels and resorts. In these instances the comfort and service, activities and spending opportunities offered to the consumer needed to be taken into account.

The development of new cruise tonnage would have to rely heavily on advanced research and development as well as imaginative thinking to the limits of the human mind to find the most attractive and cost-effective solutions. These initiatives would, however, have to contend with the worldwide exigencies of slow economic growth and increased costs, particularly for labour and fuel. Teamwork would also be vital among the naval architects, interior designers, engineers, builders, owners and operators to make these solutions wholly workable in service.

On the subject of design development Levander quoted from the Massachusetts Institute of Technology's (MIT) course in Creative Engineering, four questions aimed at improving some crucial features of industrial design:

INCREASE THE FUNCTION
Can we make the product do more things?

HIGHER PERFORMANCE LEVEL
Can we give the product a longer life, and make it safer, more reliable and easier to repair?

LOWER COSTS
Can we eliminate excess parts, use cheaper materials, and design to reduce manual labour or for complete automation?

INCREASE SALEABILITY
Can we improve the appearance, package and sale points? [2]

To again quote Levander's own words, seemingly as the text of a manifesto:

> If we demand increased profitability we must find creative new approaches to passenger shipping as a whole, looking into all aspects, from the travel business and marine operation to the shipbuilding... . If the objectives are well defined, the team will be able to start the design from a theoretically ideal solution and evolve this into the plan of a technically reasonable and economically attractive passenger ship. Attempts to start with an old ship design and proceed by merely making small modifications and improvements will in all probability give a second-rate result.[3]

The Wärtsilä 'product line' of passenger ships spawned by Levander and his design team, made up then of Pirjo Harsia, Ilkka Penttinen, Birger Trygge and Jan Kingo, included five entirely different prototypes:

AOC   An All Outside Cruise liner – A deep-sea design featuring an outside exposure from all passenger cabins, adaptable for capacities of 500 to 1,500 passengers.

Ferry 85   An advanced vehicle/passenger ferry concept for medium- to long-haul service, aimed at increased profitability through optimised performance, imaginative space usage and increased versatility through new technical design solutions. This design's most alarming feature was the colossal size of its rectilinear superstructure, overhanging the hull at the bow quarters.

SWATH — Small Water-plane Area Twin Hull – A catamaran-style cruise vessel with typically superior seakeeping characteristics. The wider deck areas would allow for unprecedented shipboard architectural possibilities and unusually large deck areas, providing a new scope of activities and amenities both aboard and on the sea surface.

Yachtcruiser — A smaller vessel intended to fill the market gap between the bigger liner-style cruise ship and the smaller private yachts available for cruising. With a capacity of only 120 passengers, this would have a shallow draught enabling it to call at many of the smaller and more exotic destinations not usually served by the larger ships.

Windcruiser — Similar in overall conception to Yachtcruiser, but with the added attraction of sails. This prototype could be either entirely sail-powered or sail-assisted, as well as machinery-powered when called for.

This highly structured and vigorously marketing-orientated conceptual design work was being undertaken by Wärtsilä at a time when a great many other yards throughout the world had reduced their research and development efforts. Levander and his staff were, in fact, the cruise and ferry part of a design 'think tank' which Wärtsilä had invested in to develop new ideas for all types of shipping which the yard was either involved in or interested in. As part of this effort the company also built the first ever arctic test basin for development of ice breakers and new ice-class merchant ship types.[4]

While owners such as Home Lines, Holland America and others ordered new ships in the early 1980s with some trepidation, sustained gradual growth in the cruise industry was soon to prove that they had invested wisely. Buoyed by this newfound confidence in an otherwise fairly bleak shipping market, others were inspired not only to invest in new tonnage, but also to try something at least a little different to attract their share of passengers.

It speaks well of the soundness of their conception that all of these, except Ferry 85, have since materialised. Most of them took shape in tailor-made or customised variations of the original brainchild at Wärtsilä's own Helsinki yard. Windcruiser and SWATH were realised at other yards in France and Finland respectively. Although not rendered into reality as a whole, many of the concepts of the Ferry 85 design have since found their way into other ferry tonnage built by Wärtsilä, their successors, Kvaerner Masa-Yards, and others.

AOC AND *ROYAL PRINCESS*

AOC offered perhaps the best alternative design approach at the time, as it was still based primarily on well-known and trusted liner design concepts. This would be a large ship in line with economy-of-scale thinking, and suited to the existing market rather than an untried niche. Yet despite these elements of the mundane, it offered something radically new in its solution to an age-old problem of ship design, namely that of providing all passenger cabins with daylight and an outside view.

The idea of a large all-outside-cabin ship traces its origins back to the 1930s examples of *L'Atlantique*, *Wilhelm Gustloff*, *Robert Ley*, and later to Christiansson's *Stockholm*, *Kungsholm* and *Gripsholm*. An abundance of other examples can also be found, including a number of large domestic American ships of the 1930s, and more recently the Russian five-ship 1960s class of *Alexandr Pushkin* liners.

While *L'Atlantique* and *Stockholm* were among the first examples of large ships with all-outer cabins, at least in their superior passenger classes, the design approach was itself entirely satisfactory. Indeed these featured some very attractive deluxe accommodation of this type. Later refinements of the same basic approach appeared even as late as the 1950s *Kungsholm* and *Gripsholm*. However, the limited size of portholes allowed on the lower cabin decks and the

AOC: **An artist's rendering of Levander's idea, which in effect put a hotel block on top of a hull to solve the old problem of providing outside cabins for all.**

(Wärtsilä, neg WHT81-841V)

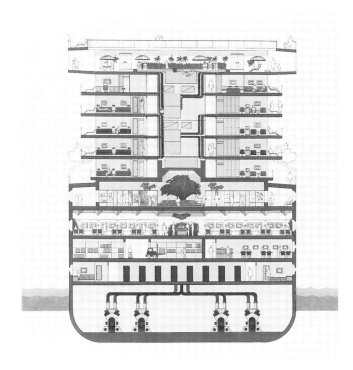

AOC: A cross-section of the concept design, showing the relationship of its cabins, public areas, machinery and the auxiliary electrical and mechanical services in the central casing of the hotel decks.

(Wärtsilä, neg WHT81-841V)

irregular shapes of these rooms tended still to leave their inner reaches in comparative darkness.

Wilhelm Gustloff and *Robert Ley* meanwhile represented significant early examples of single-class cabin standardisation and modularity. However, the interlocking layouts of these rooms, and of those in other ships of similar design, were still unduly complex, making their assembly time-consuming and costly as well as adding to the long-run expense of their cleaning and upkeep. In line with the four questions from the MIT Creative Engineering course quoted by Levander, Wärtsilä wanted a solution that would in effect 'do more things' by

making the rooms more functional and liveable, 'eliminate excess parts...and manual labour' in its construction, and would by its simplicity allow for easier and more efficient upkeep. With these questions satisfactorily answered, the final point of improved 'saleability' could almost be expected to follow as a matter of consequence.

Wärtsilä's AOC concept put into practice the notion of finding creative new approaches to passenger shipping as a whole. By taking an entirely fresh solution to an old design problem, it was possible to arrive at a seemingly obvious solution which had somehow eluded traditional thinking. AOC was derived from in effect turning the whole accommodation arrangement upside down. The full width of the uppermost hull decks would be used, not for hundreds of small cabins, but rather for the large lounges and restaurants for which their cubic volume was more ideally suited. Cabins would be relegated to the decks above, turning the superstructure into a hotel block having only the width necessary to best suit the workable dimensions of absolutely rectangular hotel-style rooms.

Certainly this approach brought the overall accommodation layout closer then ever before to the hotel idiom so often striven for in passenger-ship design. Here, as ashore in perhaps the Ritz, Intercontinental, Hesperia or Caesar's Palace, the cruising 'hotel guests' would go downstairs for dinner, dancing, a cabaret show, or perhaps a flutter in the casino, and return upstairs to retire to their bedrooms and suites. Furthermore, virtually all those private spaces could be uniformly designed with more of the look and feel of real hotel rooms than a more conventional shipboard approach could accommodate.

This scheme allowed for the lifeboats to be lowered by several decks to superstructure's base. The hotel block's sides could, by virtue of there being no need for large public rooms inside, rise sheer within the confines of the lifeboat davits. The only need for wider spaces above would be for the lido and sun decks, which could be easily cantilevered outwards, well above the lifeboats. While achieving something of the same functional effect as a *Canberra*-style nested lifeboat arrangement, the AOC approach would be far less costly to construct. Theoreti-

AOC: Plans of the promenade and lounge decks, showing the hotel-block superstructure layout and distribution of public facilities throughout the uppermost hull deck.

(Author)

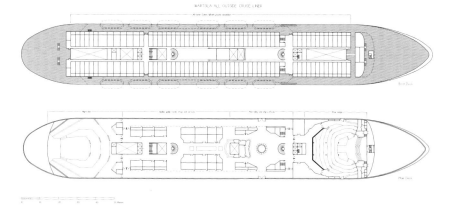

cally at least, the resulting decrease in superstructure width and lowering of the significant combined weight of the lifeboats, their davits and launching gear by several decks would improve an AOC-concept ship's seakeeping characteristics and inherent stability.

A similar approach was at the time also taking shape under the completely different circumstances of yet another daring new cruise-ship scheme, this one from Knut Kloster's bold thinking. In a bid to build upon the impact of his restoration of *France* as *Norway*, the visionary Norwegian struck upon the idea of converting one of the huge supertankers then laid up in a fjord near Andelsnas into a cruise ship. As it turned out the supertanker adaptation would have been impractical for various technical reasons. Instead, the underlying concept of this vast floating city was translated into his ponderous 250,000-ton megaship *Phoenix*. However, both in the idea of the tanker conversion and its newbuilding successor, the design was based on cabins being housed entirely in superstructure blocks above the public spaces.

A similar approach to the *Phoenix* plan's, first four and later three, superstructure blocks was proposed by Aalborg Wærft to offer greater proportions of outer cabins for other large cruise-ship schemes. Called the 'square root' system, this featured a diagonal cabin plan with the superstructure sides deeply serrated to accomplish the essence of Kloster's separate towers, while at the same time retaining continuity along each deck near the centreline. This offered various possibilities for atria, spiral staircases and glass-sided lifts at the centres of each connected node or pods with its surrounding cabins.[5]

Like any radically new idea, this rather startling reallocation of space and function was not without its compromises. The issues were more acute in the instance of AOC, which was more closely related to conventional ship scale and proportions. There was the problem of what to do with the air-conditioning and ventilation machinery, usually located atop the superstructure or along the centreline core of the uppermost hull decks. For example, *Tropicale*'s air-conditioning and ventilation plants were located on her accommodation decks within the hull, while *Song of America*'s layout favoured a bridge-deck placement between the lifeboats, following the example of *Finnjet*.

The solution adopted for AOC was to a great degree an amalgamation of both schemes. These installations were in effect moved up with the cabins into the superstructure. Here the AOC plan offered the major advantage that the air-conditioning plant rooms could be constructed as integral casings several decks high. This became possible by virtue of the accommodation being above the strength deck, where the demands for structural rigidity would be less onerous. Thus the creation of such large structurally void machinery spaces served to further lighten the superstructure weight. The air-conditioning units themselves could be up-ended from their usual shipboard arrangement and slotted very efficiently into these spaces. The remaining centreline space would be taken up, as usual, with the necessary stairs, lifts and service accesses,

the funnel casings, and, of course, air intake and outlet shafts.

Any temptation on the designers' part to use a single centreline passage arrangement, as tried in *L'Atlantique* and *Stockholm*, was effectively thwarted by this arrangement. Levander's people were probably already aware of the irregularities of plan inherent in centre-passage cabin arrangements anyway, and of the added costs of their construction. Instead, an utterly functional and straightforward Scandinavian-style liner plan with two parallel passages was adopted, with absolutely rectangular, and for the most part uniform-sized, rooms arranged along the outer sides of the passages. The final advantage of this arrangement was that the topmost deck was left virtually clear of air-conditioning and ventilation equipment of any kind, except for the funnel and a tidy cluster of air intakes and outlets. There was thus more topsides space for passenger enjoyment, as well as the structural expediency of being able to accommodate the swimming pool tanks into the centreline spaces left above the air-conditioning plants.

Despite the originality of the AOC design, it was ingeniously worked in with other already-proven Wärtsilä advances in passenger-ship design. Most significantly was AOC's adoption of *Song of America*'s provisions handling and general workflow patterns. AOC's cabin areas and public rooms would likewise be serviced from two vertical cores, each with its own lifts and connected at the bulkhead-deck level with a wide service artery equipped with electric fork-lift vehicles. A new feature added in AOC was double height shell hatches with moveable ramps, capable of handling a wide range of pier heights. What little information was given on propulsion of the AOC ship indicated again use of the Wärtsilä 'gold-standard' geared four-engine diesel approach.

Partial deck plans, detail cabin layouts and various artist renderings were prepared, illustrating the AOC concept as it might possibly be built. This would have been a 1,500-passenger ship of PANAMAX width and about 225m length overall with eleven decks, probably of around 55,000 tons. To the best of my knowledge no model was ever built of this prototype, nor was there any need for one, as the concept sold quite quickly. However, the illustrations showed the possibility of building such a ship, not only with all outside cabins, but with each having its own private balcony. Also discernible, albeit perhaps only to the more experienced eye, was the stark reality of the superstructure being absolutely rectilinear. This consequence of structural economy was somewhat skilfully camouflaged by the addition of *Song of America*-style verandas forward, and an attractive sweep of terraced decks aft.

An article on AOC design was being prepared for the Royal Institution of Naval Architects' Journal *The Naval Architect* in 1981, when an urgent telephone call from the Helsinki yard's managing director Martin Saarikangas asked that its publication be halted only days before going to press. Wärtsilä had by then already entered into critical negotiations with British shipowners who, for competitive reasons, did not want details of the design made public. When a paper on ideas for a new generation of large cruise ships was read at a November

1981 meeting of the Royal Institution of Naval Architects by P&O's Southampton general manager, David McKee, there was little doubt left in anybody's minds as to who that British shipowner might be.

Although the Wärtsilä AOC proposal was not disclosed, British shipbuilders were subsequently invited to submit design proposals and to tender their building prices to P&O for a large cruise ship of advanced design. The most original of these came jointly from the design teams of Vickers of Barrow and Swan Hunter of the Tyne, coincidentally the same corporate consortium which had submitted the winning bid to build Cunard's Q3, before that project was cancelled in 1961. However, the Vickers/Swan Hunter price in sterling of £120 million was substantially higher than Wärtsilä's American-dollar quote of $150 million. At about Canberra's size of 45,000 tons, this would be the largest British-flag passenger ship built since QE2, and it was a bitter blow to the British shipbuilding industry that the order was won abroad on the basis of price.

The new ship was ordered for America-based service of the P&O subsidiary Princess Cruises of Los Angeles. Princess at that time was operating a fleet of three 1960s-class cruise ships in the range of 16,000 to 20,000 tons, namely Sun Princess, Island Princess and Pacific Princess. Like other cruise operators catering to American clientele, Princess was forced to also follow the progression of NCL, Carnival, RCCL and others towards larger and more spectacular tonnage. P&O's 1960s-generation Oriana and Canberra were then still among the world's largest liners and, thanks to their superb original design, had retained much of their attractive modernity. However, both ships were solidly committed to meeting the needs of P&O's British and Australian cruise trades.

Could Oriana and Canberra have been made available to Princess, they were already known to be the wrong ships for the American cruise market, as had already been learned from trying Canberra in the New York-based cruise trade in 1973. Nearly a decade later, Americans would be even less inclined to book either ship's vast quantities of tourist-class cabins lacking private toilet facilities. Yet another consideration of differing and indeed evolving shipboard lifestyles was that of entertainment facilities. Americans had become accustomed to professional cabaret-style entertainment on cruise ships ever since the proper facilities had been worked into QE2's original design. Virtually none of the public rooms aboard either ship was suitable for such entertainment, lacking the necessary proscenium-style stages and built-in lighting and sound systems. Although Canberra's stadium area had been made into a makeshift theatre of sorts, it was not satisfactory, being both too small and still essentially no more than an enclosed deck area lacking air conditioning.

Where Kloster had succeeded so eminently with France, of nearly the same age as Canberra, was that the elite French ship had been built with private toilet facilities attached to all passenger cabins, and with an immense theatre, already suitable for staging live entertainment. Like Carnival, RCCL and

Holland America, P&O was forced to build anew from the keel up. Where the British shipowners felt that they had gained a great marketing advantage in their choice with Wärtsilä was that it offered something completely new, if not in its basic idea, at least in the design approach offered. Furthermore, P&O had managed to secure secrecy of the plan, which the builders had scarcely had time to circulate among other prospective buyers.

When the announcement was made in February 1982 that an order had been placed in Finland, it was only stated that the ship would be of a revolutionary new design. A 'decoy' artist's rendering of a very sleek and minimalist-looking ship appeared first in Lloyd's List, and was for a long time the only material available on the new ship. Size was initially stated to be 40,000 tons, placing her third in the P&O fleet, following Canberra and Oriana respectively.

Meanwhile, away from the public eye, and perhaps also unobserved by competitors of the owners and builders, the original AOC brainchild was shaped into the mould of Princess Cruises' requirements and the constraints of the contract price. The Knud E Hansen office was appointed to work with P&O's regular in-house consultant naval architectural firm, Three Quays of London. In view of the design's originality, engagement of the Danish firm was no doubt based on their extensive involvement with recent cruise-ship designs as well as their long-standing association with Wärtsilä. The two consultancies jointly represented P&O for design and drawing appraisal as well as building supervision for the ship herself.

At essentially the same overall length as the concept design, yard number 464, as the ship was originally identified, would be somewhat smaller, with a width of 29.2m and a double-occupancy passenger capacity of 1,200. Nonetheless this transformation of abstract conception into commercial reality did produce a remarkably close adaptation of the original brainchild.

Royal Princess: The 'decoy' rendering, released when the then still un-named ship was ordered, with minuscule lifeboats seeming to float freely at the superstructure's sides.

(Wärtsilä, neg WHT82-88)

Royal Princess: **The photographs of the model gave a first impression of what the ship would actually look like, although the reason for the large windows in the hull was still not explained.**

(Wärtsilä, neg WHT82-672)

One of the things which would no doubt have appealed least to Princess Cruises was the layout of the AOC-concept standard cabins. Albeit these were rectangular hotel-style rooms, the high passenger capacity claimed of the design could in reality only be achieved with rather narrow rooms. At a width of only 2.45m, these were not much wider than the first-class compartments of the European international-service EUROFIMA railway coaches, which measure up to 2.322m in width. Although entirely satisfactory for an arrangement of seats opposite each other for daytime use aboard a train, these dimensions presented difficulties in the arrangement of AOC's cabins. With the greater amount of space required for full-size beds and the need to provide veranda access, neither the *wagon-lit*-style parallel bed arrangement nor the *Sea Venture*-type L-plan arrangements could be used. However, thanks to the greater room depth of 6.25m afforded by the AOC-concept superstructure, Wärtsilä's designers were able to arrange both beds end-to-end along one wall of the room, a workable, although not entirely satisfactory, arrangement sometimes to be found ashore in urban European hotels.

Obviously P&O and Princess cruises realised that a European planning expediency of this type was not going to sell in the luxury sector of the American cruise market, which this revolutionary new ship was destined to serve. The concept plan was reworked, no doubt involving a change to the structural frame spacing, to provide for a slightly greater standard room width of 2.52m. This allowed for a more standard Holland America-type arrangement of parallel beds against the opposite side walls. Where verandas were attached to standard-size rooms, which in 464 was only done on the decks above the lifeboats, the added width allowed space for the necessary balcony door between the beds. Of course this solution precluded use of the Carnival/RCCL moveable-bed trick to instantly form double beds whenever called for.

Another change which the owners wanted was a switch from the shower-only outfit of standard cabins in the concept design to full tub-baths with shower nozzles for all standard rooms. Both the generic AOC plan and the actual realisation of 464 called for use of prefabricated bathroom units from Wärtsilä's own accommodation works at Piikkiö in western Finland. The wider bath-equipped module would not have allowed enough room for the cabin door to also be accommodated in the passage-side wall. This was overcome by using an angled cabin entrance. The bathroom units were essentially rectangular with one corner 'cropped' at about 20 degrees to give the impression of added space in the cabin itself. The cabin entrances in the new P&O ship were set at 90 degrees to this angled wall, itself containing the bathroom door, at the end of short beamwise passages bypassing the inner parallel-sided ends of the modules. It was an effective solution which provided the added few hundred millimetres of wall space needed, as well as yielding an architectural illusion of greater spaciousness in the rooms themselves. To some extent this scheme represented a scaled-down and simplified version of the 1966 *Kungsholm*'s cabin layout.

Another change in plan was brought about as a result of 464's narrower beam. This reduction of overall width by some 3m only left sufficient room for cabin balconies on those decks above the lifeboats, their davits and other equipment. Thus the lower three decks of the 464 superstructure were entirely slab-sided, with the cabins at these levels having large rectangular windows only. Throughout the full length of the fifth deck and the forward half of the sixth decks, balconies were fitted for 152 standard cabins, deluxe rooms and suites. Here too, the original AOC design was scaled down from its original conception of five full superstructure accommodation decks.

In order to accommodate the 600 rooms needed for 464's double-occupancy capacity of 1,200, thirty-eight standard cabins had to be located in the hull below the main run of public rooms. These too were outer rooms at the ship's sides, their location made possible in part by confining the double-height show lounge of the original AOC design to a single deck in 464. Accommodation was also provided forward of the show lounge for fourteen musicians and performers, each berthed in single outside cabins with private toilet facilities.

Against the trend towards low-speed twin diesels for new cruise tonnage, 464 would also be powered by a quadruple aggregate in favour of its intrinsic operational flexibility. In this case a further developmental step was taken towards the modern power station approach, with the main engines also providing the principal source of electrical power. Four Strömberg generators, each capable of meeting the ship's entire hotel load, were coupled to the main gearboxes.

With the ship expressly designed for optimum efficiency at a cruising speed of 18kts rather than her 22kt contracted maximum, it was possible to sustain normal operation with only one engine in each geared pair running and but one of the four main generators online. An additional generator only needed to be brought online for running the bow thrusters while manoeuvring in and out of ports. The electrical system

A young Princess Diana at the naming ceremony of the ship which was named to honour her.

(Princess Cruises)

was therefore provided with full backup redundancy, with only half of its generating capacity ever having to be used under any circumstances. Because of the intrinsically higher operating temperatures of the medium-speed diesels, this extremely versatile power package was also capable of meeting the ship's needs for steam through reclaimed exhaust gases and engine-block cooling water.

With the added electrical load, proportionally larger and more powerful engines were needed than had been previously used in installations of this type. Wärtsilä-built Pielstick machines were ultimately chosen in preference to the Sulzer Z40 motors preferred by the builders since their success with *Finlandia* nearly twenty years earlier. At about 45,000 tons, and with a downrated cruising performance similar to that of *Song of America*, 464's engines were specified with nearly double the power of the slightly smaller Norwegian-owned ship. According to Alsthom Atlantique, under whose license 464's engines were built, this was to be the most powerful Pielstick installation to go into a single hull up to that time.

The four main generators were housed in a separate compartment aft of the principal machinery space. Apart from coinciding with the layout of 464's fourteen watertight bulkheads, isolation from the heat and fumes of the diesel machinery was expected to ensure the best performance and reliability of the electrical plant. The gearing for each pair of engines thus had the double function of reducing the engine crankshaft speed of 400rpm to 125rpm at the propeller shaft, as well as independently stepping it up fourfold to the generator speed of 1,200rpm.

The total-economy approach to AOC's realisation also involved optimisation of the hull form for the completed ship's foreseen actual service conditions. This was refined to conform with the machinery and propeller optimum per-

formance at 18kts. Tank testing at the Copenhagen and Trondheim model basins was used to determine the best seakeeping characteristics at this speed. The owners were particularly concerned about avoiding slamming under the conditions tested. With a design draught of more than 0.5m deeper than that of *Tropicale*, *Nieuw Amsterdam* and *Song of America*, the final hull form showed no sign of this tendency in simulated wave conditions of up to 5m, or about Beaufort force 8.[6]

By the time actual building work commenced on 11 November 1982 the owners had decided to name their new ship *Royal Princess*, in line with existing Princess Cruises' nomenclature. This choice also honoured the then recent marriage of Prince Charles to Lady Diana Spencer, an event of enormous public appeal both in Britain and overseas. It was rumoured that P&O wanted to name the ship specifically after the young bride, but that Buckingham Palace would not acquiesce to this since the building contract had been awarded outside Britain. Nonetheless, the ship's connection with the princess was made by way of the specially commissioned portrait which adorns the main foyer, and by her participation in the naming ceremony at Southampton. Cruise ships are very seldom named for living personages outright, with even an implied reference such as this being rare. It is a worthy tribute to her tragically short life that Diana was so honoured as a young woman, only twenty-three years of age when the ship was named in late 1984. Indeed, this was an association which, although never stated, appears to have captured the romantic and stylishly modern spirit which the name Princess Cruises itself endeavour to convey.

Building of *Royal Princess* generally followed Wärtsilä's practice of lightweight construction, using comparatively shallow frames and deck beams set at a shorter spacing interval than commonly used for larger ships. Special consideration was also given to minimising structural weight in the superstructure. The lower lifeboat location and the central multiple-

Royal Princess: **The ship as built, with only some slight variation from the model in the detail of the top deck arrangement.**

(Wärtsilä, neg WHT84-1232)

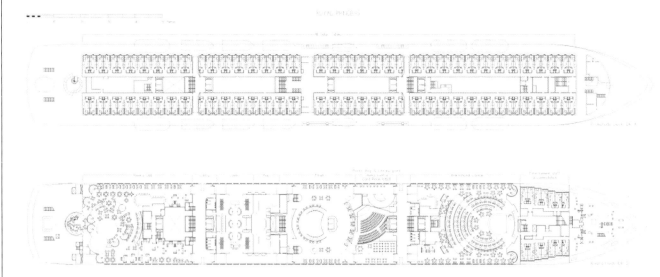

deck void spaces for air-conditioning units were advantages towards this end already inherent in the AOC concept itself. *Royal Princess* was built with a completely rectilinear super-structure in the interest of limiting the amount of structural steelwork to only what was absolutely necessary to house the cabins and services. However, as in the original visualisation of AOC, lightweight verandas and fairings were added to both ends of the otherwise unsightly deckhouse in the interest of appearance.

The drive for structural economy also precluded use of Wärtsilä's own manufactured cabins, as the supporting frames for the modules themselves would have added extra structural weight. Bathroom units were the only prefabricated items to be supplied from the Piikkiö plant, with the cabins being built up around them using Swedish-made Stockfors bulk-head panels. The ready-made bathrooms were rolled into place on removable castors before the final sections of each deck were welded into place. The remaining wall sections were built up after completing the outer enclosure of each deck, using a system of vibration-absorbing floor channels. The balconies fitted to the upper two levels of cabins were in reality a lightweight appendage welded to the superstructure shell in much the same manner as the verandas and fairings forward and aft.[7] The balustrades of the private balconies continued the line of the uppermost forward fairings along the ship's sides to the aft veranda decks. Oblique-lined steel pro-files were used to join the two lowermost fairings forward and aft of the lifeboats.

Combined with the balconies and fairings at either end of the superstructure, these trimmings were very effective in conveying at least the impression of a more traditional curvi-linear liner look. Indeed without them *Royal Princess* would have appeared with about as much aesthetic charm as a North Sea oilfields accommodation barge.

Another special structural consideration of *Royal Princess*'s design was that of the windows needed for the public rooms being in hull plating rather than the deckhouses. A row of

Royal Princess: **Plans of the Promenade and Riviera decks, showing the relationship of the finally realised plan to its first conceptualisation as illustrated earlier.**

(Author)

large openings thus had to be cut into the hull plating imme-diately below the strength deck, at a very critical stress area of the entire ship. The openings themselves each spanned the width of three hull frames, allowing only each fourth frame to reach the strength deck uninterrupted. The intervening frames had to be cut short at a juncture with a horizontal truss or frame beneath the window sills. This structural com-promise was overcome by using special high-tensile steel in the upper strake of the hull plating and in the first level of the

Royal Princess: **A view of the double-height foyer, whose overall plan would eventually evolve into the elaborate atria of later ships. Note the portrait of the late Diana, Princess of Wales on the forward wall near the lift enclosure.**

(Wärtsilä, neg WHT84-1481)

superstructure shell. Supporting columns at the line of the superstructure's outer shell were also rooted two decks deep into the hull for added strength and rigidity. To some extent these were similar to measures taken earlier in the lightweight construction of P&O's first *Oriana* and Cunard's *QE2*. However, in *Royal Princess*'s case, the builders were not burdened with the added concerns of a difficult bi-metallic joint between the hull and superstructure. This time P&O wanted all-steel construction.

Interior design of the ship's public rooms was given over to the specialists in that field after their extent and overall layout had been extruded from the concept design's realisation. As already mentioned, the forward show lounge was relegated to a single deck height. The centreline promenade in the midships area of the AOC lounge deck was also done away with, leaving the two outer promenades at the ship's sides as the main thoroughfares and accesses to the smaller rooms amidships. The concept of the original main lobby was kept, and somewhat enhanced with the addition of a central double-height well, extending to the deck below and flanked by two curved stairways. This furnished an attractive and effective link with the dining room beneath. In its own right it was the first vestige of larger and more elaborate atria to be featured in future ships.

P&O had in fact wanted to extend this space fully up through the superstructure to a dome above in a somewhat scaled-down seagoing rendition of New York's Guggenheim Museum. The idea was for this to be a central focal point for each deck in somewhat the same manner as *Rotterdam*'s double main staircases. Unfortunately this was dropped owing to the vicissitudes of obtaining United States Coast Guard approval for so large an open space aboard ship.

Apart from the double-height central lobby, the designers were left with a succession of wide and uniformly low-ceilinged spaces to work with. Contracts for this task were awarded to the Los Angeles firm Hirsch-Bedner and to Njål Eide of Oslo. Hirsch-Bedner, which had no prior shipboard experience but a well-established reputation in the hotel design field, were to develop the overall design scheme. According to then P&O Cruises chairman Dr Rodney Leach, their brief was to 'Create the ambience of a well-to-do California home'. Njål Eide's was to apply his extensive ship-design experience to executing the detailed design work. The final result was the creation of a single design theme throughout the vessel as was being done by VFD for Holland America or Joseph Farcus in his work for Carnival, rather than the integration of various individual architects' schemes as used, for instance, in *Song of America*.

The California styling of *Royal Princess*'s interiors was achieved through an underlying style of stark elegance, primarily emphasising a fairly neutral colour palette of pastel tones. The most prevalent colour throughout the scheme was peach in various hues. This represented a minimalist and unobtrusive styling which had become popular ashore during the 1980s, and had been widely tried in various high-grade

commercial interiors and hotels. In its rarefied shoreside form it was perhaps too bland for cruising, where it had to compete with, or at least stand up against, the far stronger natural influence of tropical seas and skies in their deep and varied hues, and where passengers must live with the scheme continuously for a week or more. Accordingly, the ship's California palette was enriched with the widespread use of traditional shipboard materials such as teak and brass. Contrasts in texture were also used where, for instance, fossilised stone would be juxtaposed against brightly polished metals. Taking perhaps a leaf from the example of VFD's then recent work for Holland America, innovative lighting and the liberal use of artwork were used to full advantage.

As construction of *Royal Princess* progressed and details of her design were gradually released, she met with enormous public appeal and enthusiasm. Her maiden voyage, a transatlantic positioning, was completely sold out within only three hours of being made available for bookings. A follow-on transit of the Panama Canal and the first of her subsequent Los Angeles-based regular cruises were likewise quickly filled up. The commercial option of being able to effectively sell all 600 outside cabins at premium rates was taken up with the per diem rate for each passenger. This was initially set at $330 for the standard cabins and higher for the larger rooms and suites with private balconies. The only concession to cheaper fares was made in the case of those cabins where the view was partially obscured by the lifeboats and their davits. *Royal Princess*'s fares were thus twenty-five per cent higher than those of other Princess ships and thirty per cent above the American cruise fleet average at the time.

Measured at 44,348 tons as completed, *Royal Princess* emerged into P&O's fleet between *Canberra* and *Oriana* as the Line's second-largest ship. However, *Canberra* and her tenure among the world's largest passenger ships would be short-lived, as the 45,000-ton class was soon to become very much more populated. The first of Carnival's three *Holiday*-class was due for delivery within six months. During the following four years these would be joined by ships of similar size for NCL and Home Lines.

Indeed much was expected of *Royal Princess*, both on the part of her builders and owners, as well as Princess Cruises, the P&O subsidiary which would actually operate her. When she was delivered in October 1984, Wärtsilä's Martin Saarikangas believed that she was the world's most modern cruise vessel. He expressed the deep emotion often felt by shipbuilders when handing over a new vessel to her owners, saying that as *Royal Princess* departed from Helsinki to the patriotic strains of Sibelius's *Finlandia*, 'a part of my heart left with the ship'. P&O's Dr Rodney Leach accorded her the optimistic accolade of 'a twenty-first-century ship'. Meanwhile Princess Cruises' sales literature had by then for some time been enthusiastically declaring that she was 'destined to become a legend'.

At the time of *Royal Princess*'s completion, P&O had options with Wärtsilä for two further ships of the same

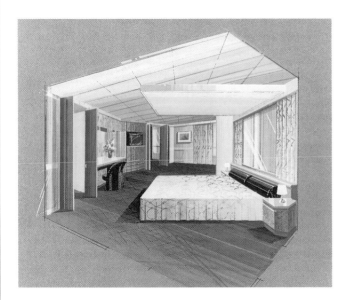

***Crystal Harmony*: Artist's rendering showing the bedroom from one of the Crystal Penthouse suites.**

(Crystal Cruises, Los Angeles)

design. Two years earlier, when *Canberra* was engaged in the Falkland Islands conflict, there had been some speculation, or perhaps wishful thinking on the part of some, that one of these options might be exercised as a replacement for *Canberra*. Indeed, if she were either lost or returned in such a condition as to preclude the viability of her return to regular commercial service, this would have been P&O's most likely choice at the time.

CRYSTAL AND OTHER AOC VARIATIONS

Once the time had expired for P&O to exercise their further AOC options, which it eventually did, Wärtsilä was once again free to promote the design on the open market. Although *Royal Princess* was a success in her own right, her example did not however engender any great rush of enthusiasm for larger exclusively AOC tonnage. By that time Princess's own experience in operating the ship had shown that there was insufficient demand for her all-premium-priced accommodation, and fares eventually had to be brought down into line with the rest of their fleet.

What had perhaps been overlooked in the AOC approach was that the trade tends to demand a wider variety of accommodation options, particularly in larger ships. For instance, there are people who want the choice of being able to book at bargain lower rate, and who are quite prepared to accept some compromise in luxury and service to do so. Also those spending larger sums of money for top-grade facilities would expect some degree of individuality in their chosen space. These passengers would probably not be too keen to find once aboard that they had booked one of several hundred

identical suites. Other owners subsequently investing in large luxury cruise ships have tended to offer a wider range of cabin types, with the choice of standard rooms being extended from 'inside or outside' to 'inside, outside or outside with veranda'. *Crystal Harmony*, completed five years later in Japan for the Nippon Yusen Kaisha–backed Crystal Cruises, bore the closest resemblance to *Royal Princess*'s AOC concept in her further development of a similar overall layout. Slightly larger than the P&O ship, though with accommodation for a mere 960 passengers, the Japanese ship featured a greater diversity both of public rooms and cabins, including even a few inside rooms. She offered her passengers the choice of eight cabin types as opposed to *Royal Princess*'s four, excluding the two 'Royal' suites.

For the longer voyages on the high seas which would make up her worldwide cruising programme, *Crystal Harmony* was designed with more of the structural stamina of, for instance, Hapag-Lloyd's *Europa*. This was achieved by way of a longer and lower profile, to minimise pitching on Pacific crossings and better resist wind forces against the ship's sides. The superstructure was one deck lower than that of *Royal Princess*. Apart from their affect on performance, these features contributed significantly to *Crystal Harmony*'s aesthetic appearance. The flare lines of the bow and stern form were also given a fairly full form as added protection for the ship.

Crystal Harmony's builders, Mitsubishi Heavy Industries, appear to have found particular favour with the AOC superstructure's practical approach to offering a high proportion of passenger cabins with balconies, even in considerably smaller ships. They subsequently demonstrated this in the design of *Frontier Spirit* and *Asuka*, delivered in 1991 and 1992 respectively.

At 28,717 tons, the 604-passenger *Asuka* featured the added luxury of balconies for 102 of her 292 all-outside cabins. The AOC/*Royal Princess* approach was adapted to the ship's smaller scale using a *Finnjet*-style vertical division

***Crystal Harmony*: Seen at speed on the high seas, where the longer and lower profile is of benefit to her performance especially on ocean crossings.**

(Mitsubishi Heavy Industries, Kobe)

Frontier Spirit: **An artist's rendering shows the same arrangement with veranda cabins above an open promenade, in this instance reduced to the scale of a Yachtcruiser class of ship.**

(Mitsubishi Kobe Shipyard)

between the public rooms and sleeping accommodation. The cabins were thus forward on seven decks, of which the lower three were in the hull. The balconies belonged only to those rooms on the topmost three superstructure decks, where they were forward of the lifeboats. All four superstructure decks also featured single centreline passages. The accommodation in the hull was arranged either side of two parallel passages, with the centreline space being taken up with various plant rooms and other services.

In *Frontier Spirit* the basic AOC concept was distilled down into the yet smaller scale of a Yachtcruiser-type design. By the time of her delivery, Wärtsilä's aspirations to fill that market-gap niche had already materialised in the form of *Sea Goddess*, as discussed later. *Frontier Spirit* was one of several variations of the Yachtcruiser concept to have subsequently materialised. Her eighteen veranda rooms set an unprece-

dented standard for the Yachtcruiser class where, hitherto, *Oceanic Grace* of Japan's Showa Line had led the field with her nine deluxe veranda suites.

The sister ship for *Crystal Harmony*, envisaged from the outset by Crystal Cruises, was not realised until five years later. While it was generally expected that NYK would also have awarded the building contract to Mitsubishi, or at least to another Japanese yard, the ship was ultimately built in Finland. As successors to *Royal Princess*'s builders Kvaerner Masa-Yard got the job. Named *Crystal Symphony*, the similarly sized ship was designed for the same number of passengers and with a similar range and layout of public facilities.

The building of the second Crystal ship showed a number of minor differences, reflecting the differing building practices of Mitsubishi and Kvaerner Masa-Yard. For instance, the hull of the newer ship is shorter by 2.9m and wider by 0.6m than that of her Japanese-built sister. One major difference in the actual building process was Kvaerner Masa's use of prefabricated accommodation throughout the ship, with the exception only of the two ultra-deluxe Crystal penthouse suites.

In view of the cabin space available, owing to the small passenger capacity for the ship's size, some of these were the largest ready-made cabins to be produced by the yard's Piikkiö plant. The quality of finishing demanded by Crystal's deluxe-market trade also brought these units up to an unprecedented standard of quality for manufactured accommodation. Where Wärtsilä had been thwarted in their aspirations to use Piikkiö ready-made cabins in *Royal Princess* by concerns over topsides weight economy, the reduced superstructure height of *Crystal Symphony* solved the problem for Kvaerner Masa-Yard almost precisely a decade later. However, the inevitably higher degree of standardisation imposed by using manufactured cabins was probably the reason for eliminating the attractive pie-slice shaped rooms housed in the semi-circular aft superstructure wall on *Crystal Harmony*'s promenade deck. Also dropped from the newer ship's plan, no

Crystal Symphony: **The ship appears remarkably similar to *Crystal Harmony* although they were built half way around the world from each other.**

(Kvaerner Masa-Yards, New Shipyard, Turku, no TUT 95-123D)

Crystal Symphony: **Palm Court, showing the effective use of skylights in this bright and airy top-deck room.**

(Gero Nylius; copyright INDAV Finland, no TU T95-68 E O)

doubt in support of the builders' patent AOC design approach, were the few inside rooms offered on the earlier Japanese-built Crystal ship.

Other changes in layout were introduced by the owners, following their service experience with *Crystal Harmony*. These included a horizontal doubling of the atrium area, emphasising more strongly its function as a focal point of circulation among the ship's principal public areas. The alternative Japanese and Italian speciality restaurants introduced in the lido-deck plan of the earlier ship were relocated to the main lounge deck aboard *Crystal Symphony*, allowing for an expanded version of the more informal Lido Café above. Also relocated from the lido deck was the Palm Court Entertainment Lounge, turning up amidships in the Finnish-built ship as the Starlight Club.

These show a more experienced approach in establishing the most appropriate adjacencies for cruise-ship public spaces, based on their preferred use for either daytime or evening activities. For instance, experience in cruise-ship operations show that passenger lifestyles of the 1990s tend to stress a resort-style preference for light and informal buffet-style breakfast and daytime dining in the pool and lido vicinities, with most passengers seeking more formal *à la carte* dining in the evening. Thus the newer ship's design achieved a more definite delineation between daytime and evening activities, relegating each more precisely to their own decks. While passengers would naturally gravitate towards the topmost sun and lido decks from early morning until dinner time, the relocation of *Crystal Harmony*'s Palm Court Lounge's function to the main run of public rooms aboard *Crystal Symphony* brought it into the centre of the ship's nightlife.

With the public room adjacencies more tightly integrated by their function within the programme of daily activities, there would be less chance of entertainment and spending opportunities being missed owing to having a less-than-ideal location. Operationally, this sort of segregation of day- and night-time activities proved itself advantageous in that it allowed the under-used daytime parts of the ship to be effectively shut down at dinner time, freeing service staff to minister more effectively to the needs of what had effectively become the concentrated hub of nocturnal revelry. Considering these refinements of the public area plan, *Crystal Symphony* probably can be said to represent the ultimate expression of the original AOC design, appropriately also rendered by the successors of its original proponents.

From among these examples, *Royal Princess* remains a pivotal element in passenger-ship design history, not so much for its original AOC brainchild as from the design's by-product feature of providing an abundance of ship's rooms with private verandas. After all, from the passenger standpoint, anyone paying the premium for an outside cabin was only getting something that had always been available, and he or she could not care less whether or not the ship also offered rooms without windows. However, a room with its own patch of private deck space was a definite and tangible status symbol, some-

thing that few liners of the past could offer in any number.

Prior to *Royal Princess*, the 1928-built Italian Cosulich liners *Saturnia* and *Vulcania* had the distinction of offering the greatest numbers of veranda cabins. Each had forty-two first-class cabins with verandas arranged below their main promenades on what outwardly appeared to be ordinary open stretches of the weather deck. This remarkably straightforward approach resulted in a very pleasing aesthetic outer appearance, uncompromised by this deck's division into private spaces. Notable later examples from the 1930s, albeit each with smaller numbers of veranda rooms, included Matson's *Mariposa* and *Monterey*, P&O's 'Straths' and, of course, *Normandie* with twenty-four hotel-style rooms, each having its own stretch of the glass-enclosed promenade deck, and the quarter-circle private decks attached to her superlative five-room Deauville and Trouville suites.

In ship design of the 1950s and 1960s private verandas generally fell victim to the rationale of fully air-conditioned, and hence fully enclosed, ocean-going interiors. Among the few exceptions were the Messageries Maritimes' *Viet Nam* trio, Grace Line's *Santa Paula* and *Santa Rosa* as well as Home Lines' *Oceanic*. The 1962-built *France* was particularly notable for her unusual arrangement of eight top-deck cabins around a common central court open to the sky above. It was only in 1974 that this feature of resort hotel design began to return to favour, when a ready-made two-deck appendage was hoisted atop *QE2*'s superstructure containing twelve veranda suites of which two featured two-storey layouts. However, even in the ultra-deluxe category, accommodation of this sort was then still very much an elitist exception to the general rule.

As still more cruise ships were being planned to follow *Royal Princess*, *Crystal Harmony*, *Asuka* and others into service during the 1990s, cabin verandas had become probably *the* most sought-after feature in shipboard accommodation since private en-suite bathrooms had become the cabin innovation of the 1920s. In the evolution of sophisticated modern lifestyles, which stress ever-greater personal privacy, the private veranda has given passengers a new opportunity to make their experience of being aboard a cruise ship something very special. The private veranda gave them their only opportunity to really experience being at sea by actually letting its breezes and the sounds of its wake against the hull inside their own living space. Elsewhere onboard the ship, inside and outside worlds would remain entirely isolated, one from the other, by the sealed 'envelope' of the air-conditioning systems. Even venturing onto the open decks of many modern ships, one tends to be thwarted from any direct communion with nature by the presence of full-height glass windscreens intended to keep the ravages of wind and salt spray at bay.

Breakfast and lunch could be served on the veranda in the fresh sea air against the backdrop of changing tropical scenery or a panoramic seascape of animated cloud, light and reflection. A romantic evening could likewise be discretely spent under the stars in the enjoyment of a bottle of champagne or perhaps in fond embrace. Finally, upon retiring to bed at the end of the day, the veranda door might be left ajar to enjoy the real sensuality of being at sea on a great ship. These at least were the images of an elitist lifestyle conveyed, both directly and subliminally, through advertising to those who would book a veranda room or suite for their cruise.

The view of engineering and deck departments aboard ships with veranda cabins was no doubt less romantic. Day-to-day cleaning and maintenance of the private verandas and their furnishings inevitably fell to the hotel department, adding to the cabin steward or stewardess's work. If a rain squall or thunderstorm suddenly was to come up, the cabin staff had to quickly stow the chaise-longue and chair cushions, requiring quick entry to dozens of cabins where passengers might have been in various stages of undress, relaxing or sleeping. Structural maintenance of the veranda areas and their usually teak-planked decks remained with the deck crew. They too had to be given access to each cabin, with their work mostly restricted to the already busy turnaround time between cruises. From the standpoint of the engineering department, there was the concern of extra loads on a ship's air-conditioning and ventilation systems. Obviously passengers were going to keep their veranda doors open for hours at a time, probably without switching off the air conditioning.

For many years ships' cabin doors have been fitted to leave a gap of a centimetre or so under their bottom edges, allowing for equalisation of air pressure between the individual cabins and the 'common element' of passages, stairways, etc. These had become the contemporary alternative to the jalousie or vent fitted in the cabin doors aboard liners before the age of manufactured or prefabricated accommodation. In the case of the modern veranda cabin this raised concerns not only about air conditioning but also of fire safety, where open veranda doors could cause dangerous flame-fanning drafts in alleyways and stairwells, even when the air-conditioning and ventilation systems would be completely shut down.

The technical and operational considerations of veranda cabins are myriad, yet their immense popularity with passengers has proven to be such that there is no turning back. From the cruise operator and shipowner standpoints, veranda cabins offer the potential for greater revenue. The higher per-person fares which veranda accommodation can command at least compensate for the added operating costs incurred. For example, at the time of writing, the fare for a minimum-grade veranda room was about $50 per day more than the highest-grade room without a veranda on a European cruise aboard *Crystal Harmony* or *Crystal Symphony*.

SEAWARD AND ROYAL VIKING SUN

Meanwhile, Wärtsilä's experience prior to the Kværner Masa-Yard's building of *Crystal Symphony* had been to build *Seaward* for Norwegian Caribbean Line and *Royal Viking Sun* for Royal Viking Line, both of which were delivered in 1988.

Although themselves not full embodiments of the AOC plan, these, like a great many other cruise ships built elsewhere, could hardly escape its influence altogether.

The NCL ship was in reality a provisional measure to bridge the tonnage gap in the Line's fleet between their White Fleet and *Norway* with a ship capable of competing in the league of Carnival's *Holiday*. Knut Kloster by this time already had his sights resolutely fixed upon realisation of *Phoenix*. *Seaward* was planned around proven elements from Wärtsilä's experience with *Song of America* and *Royal Princess*. After tailoring the various components of these two designs into an amalgam which would meet RCL's immediate needs, the ship could be completed in the comparatively short time of only fifteen months.

A hybrid juxtaposition of *Song of America* and *Royal Princess*'s accommodation plans was devised to gain the greatest advantages of both layouts. Up to the strength deck *Song of America*'s plan was closely followed to achieve the higher population density wanted by the owners. With all principal public spaces other than the dining rooms relegated once again to the superstructure decks, one more hull deck was made available for sleeping accommodation than the AOC approach would have allowed. Upwards from the public rooms, the rationale of *Royal Princess*'s narrower AOC-style superstructure prevailed. Here three levels of cabins were laid out either side of triple-height air-conditioning and ventilation casings. No private balconies were fitted to *Seaward*'s cabins. The economy in structural weight that this alone realized was sufficient to permit the building economy of using fully prefabricated Piikkiö cabin modules.

In addition to her *Royal Princess*-style atrium joining the main and international decks, *Seaward*'s designers also opened up her stairway arrangement on the cabin decks above to make it more attractive. Instead of the single staircases placed oppo-

Seaward: **Seen here in Finnish waters as a somewhat bulkier and rather austere amalgam of elements from *Song of America* and *Royal Princess*.**

(Wärtsilä)

Royal Viking Sun: The ship on trials off the coast of Finland, bearing a rendition of her owners' original fleet image tempered with elements of *Royal Princess* and *Crystal Harmony*.

(Wärtsilä)

site each bank of lifts as aboard *Royal Princess*, double stairways were arranged either side of *Seaward*'s lift ensembles, extending the functional areas of the deck lobbies outwards beyond the cabin passageways. Here the outside superstructure walls were opened up into wide window bays of floor-to-ceiling bonded-in tinted glass in the two main vertical rises through the three cabin decks. With the addition of occasional furniture in these areas, they were transformed into additional usable public areas suitable as informal meeting places or for relaxation.

The value of these areas was that they gave the same sense of orientation to the cabin decks that the atrium had in the public areas below. Here the opened-up deck lobbies more appropriately made reference to outside points, where the interior was instead made up of numerous private spaces rather than the open expanses of large lounges and other communal spaces. Thus such things as the boat-deck railings, the lifeboats and davits themselves, as well as the direction of the ship's wake, gave the passenger bearings in terms of knowing which side of the ship he or she might be on, and whether at the boat-deck level or one or two levels above it. The presence of two such lobbies also served to indicate clearly whether one's cabin might be in the forward, central or aft fire zones, a helpful fact of orientation, which otherwise most passengers would no doubt have found beyond their normal perception of layout. Although less spectacular than the atrium, this arrangement was nonetheless, for its own special purposes, no less effective.

At about the same time Wärtsilä also built *Royal Viking Sun*, on a similarly cost-effective basis and tailored to the higher standard of luxury expected by Royal Viking Line's luxury market clientele. A larger adaptation of the original *Royal Viking Star* hull was developed, incorporating *Song of America*'s workflow rationale into an otherwise classic Royal Viking internal layout with larger cabins. The public rooms were arranged throughout the lower two decks of a *Royal Princess*-style superstructure placed within the confines of the

lifeboat davits also at its base. Throughout the two decks above these, and forward of the pool lido and sun decks still higher up, there were 140 outside cabins and suites with private verandas. This figure amounted to thirty-nine per cent of the ships 384 cabins, of which ninety-six per cent were outer rooms. The deckhouse structure above the public rooms was similar to that of *Royal Princess* in that the cabin verandas were welded to its outer shell and a limited use was made of multiple-height air-conditioning casings in its forward end.

However, the ship's overall weight distribution and centres of buoyancy and gravity allowed for use of prefabricated cabins throughout. These were of a remarkably high decorative standard, being no doubt the most luxurious units of their type produced by Wärtsilä's accommodation subsidiary up to that time. *Royal Viking Sun* was among the first cruise ships to feature walk-in wardrobes as a standard cabin feature. The public rooms, designed by Njål Eide, were of a likewise high decorative standard, stressing the use of high-quality and durable materials and fittings to minimise maintenance and replacement expenses over the ship's expected lifespan.

A common design feature of both ships, despite their different market-sector orientation, was the prominence given to their atria. In both instances the atrium was planned as a central focal point of the main public areas, providing passengers with a sense of their whereabouts in relation to the ship's main lounges and dining room. The relatively low location of public rooms resulting from the AOC-inspired superstructure and lifeboat arrangements of these ships also brought the atrium area conveniently into the proximity of each ship's main entrance, allowing it to serve also as the main lobby. These atria were also given a sense of function of their own by housing the purser's and other offices, shops, hairdressing salon and other such services. The whole functional integration of public areas, ship's offices and shopping arcade was made possible by these atrium plans.

This in effect overcame the long-standing ship-design problem of embarkation lobbies, with their attached offices

Nordic Empress: **The high-tech styling of the ship which still displayed the futuristic character of her original design conception as** *Future Seas.*

(Royal Caribbean Cruise Lines)

and services being often too far out of the way. The upper-deck locations of public rooms stressed in traditional liner design approach often made any integration of main lobby with other communal areas difficult, owing to its need to be properly positioned for pierside gangway access. Dining rooms were all too often located two or more decks below this level, also preventing the main lobby from doubling as a restaurant foyer. The problem persisted to some degree even in the design of some larger cruise ships with public rooms on their uppermost decks such as Carnival's *Tropicale* and *Holiday*, ships which were at the same time also much admired for some of the more traditional aspects of their design. This particular shortcoming was overcome in the still larger *Fantasy* class introduced in 1990 by merely extending the atrium, a seven-deck-high affair, down to the embarkation lobby.

In *Royal Viking Sun*, the owners still wanted their main foyer in the hull, as aboard their earlier ships. Here too the sense of focus set by the atrium was retained by extending its central well through the two top hull decks. With the diversity of their application in so many ships of the mid 1980s period, both the veranda cabin and the atrium, which were originally only by-products of the original AOC idea, had arrived to stay. Come to think of it, was not the phonograph in fact an offshoot of something else Thomas Edison was trying to invent, which nobody seems to remember much about any more?

OTHER DEVELOPMENTS

From these ideas other inspirations and innovations soon began to take root. Other owners and builders seemed buoyed by the examples of what they were seeing, and confident enough to let their designers proceed in similar directions. Other new ideas in internal layouts and atria were tried along with some more progressive expressions in exterior aesthetics.

Starting with a similar general arrangement to that of *Seaward*, *Future Seas* was among the first to present a radically new high-tech external appearance. Originally ordered from France's Chantiers de L'Atlantique by Admiral Cruises, this ship was completed in 1990 as *Nordic Empress* for Royal Caribbean Cruises after the lines merged in 1988.

The superstructure lines were smoothed out, with an obliquely raked front bulwark, effectively encasing two *Song of America*-style forward-facing deck galleries. A less protracted treatment of the afterdecks helped to create an overall impression of at least a more plastic, if not entirely aerodynamic form. The application of dark-blue ribands in the paint scheme surrounding the public-room windows of the uppermost hull deck, and to the cabin fenestration on the decks above, was used to diminish the expression of detail and offer a more clean-lined external appearance.

On the upper decks glass was featured extensively, in a manner similar to that of the much larger *Sovereign of the Seas*, which had already been delivered a year earlier by the same yard. The glazing here too was in the same green tint which had been used on the Line's larger ship. However, its extension fully forward over the navigating bridge in this example helped to solidify the sense of ultra-modern plasticity which the design as a whole conveyed.

The interior layout stressed many of the same design features of rival NCL's Finnish-built *Seaward*, including the arrangement of public rooms and emphasis of superstructure-sited cabins, as well as a sophisticated indoor/outdoor resort-style pool area and lido plan. The by then *de rigueur* atrium and *Seaward*-style upper-decks stairway approach were amalgamated to form an open vertical space passing through six decks. This featured glass lifts and a dome above its central light shaft. The atrium space itself was enclosed in fire-resis-

Windward: **Seen departing from Vancouver, her high-tech styling makes her appear a much smaller ship that she actually was.**

(Jack McCarthy, Vancouver)

Dreamward: The Dreamward Terraces Dining Room, looking forward towards the port side and showing the two upper terraces and a liner-era stairway configuration.

(Norwegian Cruise Line, Miami)

tant glass at all levels, thereby separating it from the deck lobbies, and complying with the United States Coast Guard fire safety regulations.

The design of this ship was also notable for its well-articulated main-deck plan in which the show lounge and dining room were located at its fore and aft extremities respectively. Both were double-height rooms, although the dining room was rooted one deck lower than the show lounge, with the result that both spaces only had common access along the main deck. The interspersing midships spaces included, apart from the atrium, a notable innovation in the casino design. This space rose in three stages beamwise from the main deck to the level above. The inspired combination of the atrium and casino brought about a close vertical relationship between these two principal entertainment decks. In addition to the fore and aft relationship of the dining room and show lounge, the whole scheme gave rise to an unencumbered natural flow of movement about the length of both decks, ensuring the maximum usage of centrally located rooms, as well as the casino and shops with the spending opportunities they offered.

In late 1992 Chantiers de L'Atlantique delivered *Dreamward*, the first of two near-identical sister ships, to NCL. She and her later running mate, *Windward*, were of similar exterior design expression to the *Future Seas/Nordic Empress* concept.

The smooth-lined expression of hull and superstructure form of these ships was strengthened by the inclusion of a partial whaleback over the forward mooring deck. Basically a low-angle extension of the forward superstructure wall over the bow mooring deck, this helped to form a strong sense of cohesion between the hull and superstructure. Its effect was best perceivable when seen from above, a view which, apart from brochure and publicity photography, passengers seldom have the chance to experience.

Another noteworthy detail of *Dreamward*'s exterior design was the arrangement of stairways ascending the flight of terraced aft deck and from the navigating bridge to the top of the superstructure forward. These were placed at the corners of each deck, and arranged in such a way that the superstructure's shell formed their outer sides and bannisters. Indeed such an arrangement has the effect of imparting an outstanding impression of the ship's characteristics to those aboard. As one ascends or descends from deck to deck in this manner, aboard any ship so arranged, the maximised visual impressions of the superstructure and decks are sure to create a very strong impression of the ship as a whole – far more so than if the stairs pass through the deck plating, which is more often the case.

The interior layout of *Dreamward* and *Windward* was of an entirely different rationale from that of most other ships of her time. It was in some respects similar to the Line's earlier *Southward*, but rendered more on the scale of P&O's first *Oriana*. However, the layout was perhaps only a throwback to earlier thinking in that it lacked the modern focal element of an atrium, which could well have helped unravel the inherent complexities of *Dreamward*'s own special features.

Terracing of the floors was used extensively throughout these interiors to gain the maximum advantage of the ship's many large windows. The two dining rooms, both located fully aft, were terraced, one directly above the other, to maximise the view over the ship's stern. Each room was arranged on three levels, rising in one-metre steps from their aft ends. The lower dining room was given direct access to the ship's aft swimming pool, while the upper facility was arranged adjacent to the midships pool by way of a wide passage bypassing the aft stairtower and funnel casing. This ingenious layout gave both dining rooms access to the ship's more informal centres of daytime activity around the pools and lido areas, as well as retaining good proximity to the evening entertainment centres, including the show lounge, casino and night club. This effectively eliminated the need to cater separately for passengers' daytime and evening dining preferences, with one or other facility being underused, if not entirely vacant, at various times of the day.

The midships-sited main lounge, although given a maximum height of two decks, was in reality fitted out as a single-deck area, also with tiered seating. The pool lido area above was similarly terraced, but in the opposite direction, achieving an essentially wedge-shaped lengthwise cross section in the show lounge. The higher end of the show lounge was at its stage end, with decreasing headroom towards the back wall. Here, as in the dining rooms aft, large windows were used to their greatest advantage in creating a sense of openness and space. Despite its obviously entertainment-orientated design, this room's contact with, and views of the outside world made it also more suitable than most of its kind for alternative daytime uses.

In fact, the show lounge and forward-facing observation lounge atop the navigating bridge were designed to do alternative duty as conference and meeting rooms. Both of these areas were fitted with retractable partitions allowing them to be divided into two separate rooms for such purposes. These, as impromptu additions to a purpose-designed conference room, provided *Dreamward* and *Windward* with one of the more extensive conference facilities available in her class of cruise ship.

The overall design rationale of *Dreamward* and *Windward* achieved remarkably high accommodation standards for ships of their class. At about the same size as the Line's *Seaward*, individual cabin areas were built to match those of *Norway*'s more generously proportioned rooms, with only a slight reduction in lower-berth capacity to 1,450 from the 1,548 figure of the Finnish-built ship. Still more remarkably, the proportion of outside rooms, including those with verandas was eighty-five per cent, the figure striven for as the ideal by *QE2*'s designers in the 1960s. This feat was to some extent achieved in *Dreamward* and *Windward* by arranging crew cabins inboard of the passenger accommodation on the lower decks.

The cabins were quite highly standardised, with little deviation of plan to create suites or other variations. However, a degree of highly practical versatility was reached by fitting moveable walls between thirty-nine pairs of rooms, allowing them to be combined into larger U-shaped suites suitable either for family use or as hospitality/working accommodation for business travellers. The king-size beds in either side of the suite would be folded away into the wall, with their place being taken by a fold-out table, suitable for dining or as a working space. Further flexibility was provided in all cabins by way of convertible settees, which could accommodate a third person.

A similar approach to *Dreamward*'s layout also emerged in the near-total rebuilding of *Sally Albatross*, an already-converted Baltic cruise ship which had started her life as the 1980-built ferry *Viking Saga*. After being virtually gutted by fire while undergoing a refit in Stockholm *Sally Albatross* was rebuilt from the hull up, retaining her original nested lifeboats, but taking on a similar superstructure arrangement to *Dreamward*,

Dreamward: **A view of connecting cabins, in which a wall between the sitting areas slides out of sight behind the beds. Note the frame above the bed in the foreground which allows it to fold flush into the wall when the rooms are used as a business or hospitality suite.**

(Norwegian Cruise Lines)

with public rooms concentrated on the uppermost decks. Within the smaller scale of *Sally Albatross*, the interleaved mid-ships plan of the show lounge and open-air sun terraces above was foregone in favour of an all-weather pool and spa area covered by a glass roof with opening sections. The space below was taken up with a conference complex and casino, while a Carnival-style show lounge was situated at the forward end of these two decks. Dining facilities were situated aft, but again without the terracing used in the larger NCL ships.

AIDA

A few years later, when the Rostock-based cruise Line Deutsche Seetouristik were looking to launch a new cruise venture, they investigated the possibility of purchasing *Sally Albatross*. The ship was again for sale, following a grounding off the coast of Finland. Deutsche Seetouristik eventually decided that she was too small for their purposes and ultimately ended up placing an order with Kværner Masa-Yard for a larger new ship based on her overall layout.

Named *Aida*, this ship was planned specifically for their idea of 'clubship cruising'. The concept of this was developed from the idea of the sophisticated all-inclusive resort and sport hotels in Tunisia and Turkey and from the later growth of the same concepts at Bavaro Beach and Punta Cana in the Dominican Republic. Originally, the idea of bringing together people with similar interests in sport, recreation and gastronomy was promoted by the exclusive Spa Hotels in Germany and other European countries which catered to the wealthy. Organisations such as Wandervogel, White Bears, Boy Scouts, Girl Guides, and, in the 1930s, the programmes of the Kraft durch Freude in Germany brought the same sort of pleasures to young people as well. It was, after all, the KdF's *Wilhelm Gustloff* and *Robert Ley* which had taken these same concepts to sea in such remarkable scale during the late 1930s. Post-World War II prosperity and mobility led to the founding of Club Olympique and the later development of Club Med. The evolution of a far more fitness-conscious society since the 1980s has brought the whole idea once again more upscale to the level of the Bavaro Beach resorts.

The problem in taking the club-type resort holiday experience to sea was that people still believed there had to be a far more structured way of doing things, particularly of feeding passengers, within the confines of a ship. Long after the need for the regimented catering services of the multi-class liner has disappeared, cruise passengers have still tended to remain confined to rigid meal times and specific seating assignments. Informal and alternative dining continued to be stressed mainly as daytime options, with the main evening meal often being offered only on the basis of a formal liner dining experience. While some newer ships have started to offer open seating and more flexible dining hours, many remained firmly locked into the old two-sitting arrangement. The result was that the more spontaneous opportunities of meeting people at meal times the way that one does in a resort or club holiday ashore were not realised and the whole experience remained less flexible and informal. Without the resort-style spontaneity of interaction between passengers, particularly around the social opportunities offered by the dining experience, it becomes very difficult to make the club-holiday concept work properly aboard ship.

What the *Aida* clubship experience endeavoured to do was to remove many of the old protocols and traditions which have stood in the way of opening up cruise-ship lifestyles to the standard of the modern resort. This is accomplished by amalgamating an expanded adaptation of the informal alternative dining experience of the regular cruise ship with a likewise more free-form *haute cuisine* main dining option based on the popular European Mövenpick-style Marché restaurants. The significance of specific meal times and regimented seating is diminished by making the service available virtually around the clock on a come-and-go basis, with passengers having the flexibility to sit where and with whom they please at any time.

The *Sally Albatross* style of layout, which gathers all public amenities together, rather than segregating them to individual strata of more liner-like evening spaces and less-formal day-time recreational facilities on the upper decks, was thought to suit the clubship idea ideally. The 38,000-ton *Aida*'s plan closely integrated her entire range of public spaces, both indoor and out, throughout the uppermost decks. Open planning was stressed, with the various areas appearing more to dissolve one into the other, rather than being separated by lobbies and vestibules. The entire midships area of deck 9 formed a vast integrated recreation area, serving the needs of everything from an indoor lido lounge with entertainment and dancing, to fitness and aerobic spaces and the beauty salon. The asymmetrical plan oriented those more active areas to port side and the quieter activities to the starboard side. This created two rooms, the Laguna and Winter Garden, divided by the pool tank of the deck above and by a fireproof bulkhead. Despite the necessary bulkhead's intrusion, a strong sense of cohesion was achieved by a 400mm-high railed foot-bridge joining the two along the port side.

Design played an important role in setting the informal and active mood of *Aida*'s cruise programmes. As Kai Bunge of Hamburg-based Partner Ship Design said of his interior design work here, 'This is not [for] "I want to be entertained" passengers, but rather "I want to participate" passengers'. Features of the deck-9 areas included faux-rock caves, simulated weather effects and special lighting. Illumination which simulated daylight in the Laguna changed at dusk, with the area's palm trees being illuminated from below as is done in many European tropical resorts. One idea put forward for the show lounge, where few changes in approach might be expected, was for the front few rows of seats to be backless with the notion of encouraging passengers to come up on stage and join in the activity.

The operation of *Aida*'s dining facilities was styled along the lines of Marché restaurants. A wide variety of international specialities, emphasising the places visited on each cruise, were offered on a mostly self-service basis. The experience stressed freshness and high quality of food, with much of its preparation being done in view of passengers. The Markt and Karibik restaurants, on seperate decks above could seat about 1,000 passengers when in full operation at peak times. For those who still preferred the traditional shipboard dining experience, the 120-seat Restaurant Maritim offered a full *à la carte* dinner service from either a standard or surcharge menu.

Part of the clubship concept was to give passengers the flexibility to eat when they were hungry rather than to confine them to a rigid schedule of meal times. Nonetheless, there had to be a specific order to the day, with breakfast running from 7am to 10am with earlybird coffee and croissants available from 6am, lunch from 12.30pm to 2pm, *Kaffestunde* (coffee and cakes) from 3.30pm to 4.30pm and dinner between 7pm and 9pm. Food preparation and cooking was basically centred around these fairly traditional meal times. A greater selection of items were produced than would normally be required for a traditional shipboard operation based on table service, and the schedule provided for a number of items to be offered in sufficient quantities to last through the between-meals periods. A cook in the Karibik restaurant would be kept on duty between lunch and dinner, and sometimes even up to midnight to provide to order meals which might be requested at these times. Otherwise, the main galley and food preparation areas were essentially to be in operation from 1am, when the bakers started their day's work, until the end of dinner service at 10pm.

Operationally, the Karibik, Markt and Maritim restaurants were all served from a central galley located starboard side on deck 8. This adjoined the Markt and Maritime restaurants directly, and the Karibik restaurant by way of its own pantry and service core immediately above. Food preparation facilities, including the bakery, butcher's and confectioner's shops, were centred around the crew galley below on deck 3. The officers' staff and crew dining rooms were forward of this on the port side, and the storage area's cool rooms and larders were astern. This arrangement coincided with the service rationale which was developed by Kvaerner Masa-Yard's predecessor entity Wärtsilä in the early 1980s with *Song of America*, and applied throughout much of the industry ever since.

Food preparation was put under the direction of a *Kuchenchef* (chef de cuisine) with three sous-chefs in charge of the main galley, the Karibik restaurant, and the food preparation facilities/crew galley on deck 3. The *Kuchenchef*'s department would be staffed by about eighty-six people, more or less evenly distributed among these three areas. The restaurants themselves were managed by an executive *maitre*, with twelve stewards and utilities in the Karibik and an additional sixteen people divided between the Markt and Maritim restaurants. Apart from the complimentary wine and beer provided in the Karibik and Markt facilities, Maritim was to

be the only restaurant to offer a wine list and bar service. Here the wine/bar steward would offer service from the nearby Aida Bar. This style of operation offered great economy through the reduced need for service personnel, amounting to a saving of some 200 crew positions. *Aida*'s total crew complement was 320, with the ship being able to operate fully booked with as few as 309, realising a crew-to-passenger ratio of 1:4, which would be quite remarkable for *Aida*'s upper-middle-market status.

Externally, *Aida* was created as a very attractive ship, with a good fifty-fifty balance of her hull and superstructure and a graceful yacht-like stance about her. While the influence of *Sally Albatross* was discernible in her oblique stern lines and the continuous bands of upper-decks glazing, she distinctly carried her own identity. The red kissing lips and mascara-highlighted brown eyes supergraphics, painted as a late-delivered surprise by German artist Feliks Büttner, clearly bespeak the young-at-heart image of *Aida* cruising, even though they may take a little getting used to by some of the older salts.

1   Kai Levander, *The Viking Saga Series – Tailor-Made by Wärtsilä*, p 20.
2   Kai Levander, *Increased Profitability for Passenger Ships*, p 15.
3   Kai Levander, *Increased Profitability for Passenger Ships*, p 15.
4   *The Naval Architect*, London, January 1985, p E35.
5   Bent Hansen, 'Ship Design for the Further Development of the Cruise Market', *Cruise & Ferry* 85, p 6.
6   *The Motor Ship*, December 1984.
7   *The Naval Architect*, January 1985, p E3

CHAPTER 10

TOWARDS SIX FIGURES

Progress towards the 100,000-ton ship

The problem with being 'number one' is that everyone else wants to upstage you. Kloster became number one as owner of the world's largest cruise ship, *Norway*, in 1980. He had been fortunate enough to purchase the laid-up *France* at a bargain price, and was able to convert her for cruising for much less than it would have cost to build outright such a large and prestigious ship. *France* had no comparable running mate and *QE2*, the only other passenger ship then in the exalted over 60,000-ton-plus class, was still in service and not likely to be sold. By virtue of *QE2*'s entirely different services and clientele, Kloster had the cruise industry's truly large-ship prestige and trading advantage virtually to himself – at least until someone else took the bold step of building so large a ship to compete with *Norway*.

Having already progressed to larger ships for competition with NCL, Royal Caribbean Cruise Line and Carnival were the most likely opponents to take such a step. It was just a matter of which would go first. Kloster, however, seemed confident that by the time *Norway*'s rival materialised he would have moved on to something much larger, in the form of his own 250,000-ton *Phoenix* project.

It was in fact RCCL which made the first move to counter Kloster's success with *Norway*, which in turn began the development of ever larger ships.

SOVEREIGN OF THE SEAS

In 1983, shortly after *Song of America*'s delivery, RCCL started investigating their further development plans in terms of a 70,000-ton cruise ship with accommodation for 2,200 passengers. *Norway* at the time was registered at 69,300 tons and had also 2,200 passenger berths. After conducting their own market and surveys to determine that there was sufficient potential for still further growth in the cruise industry, RCCL entered into a design study with Wärtsilä's Helsinki shipyard.

A project group consisting of representatives from RCCL's three owning companies, along with the heads of the Line's operating departments and their management, met with Wärtsilä's technical staff, headed by Kai Levander. The group was at first divided into three separate committees to study the project's financing, market research and technical design. Once the basic feasibility of the ship had been ascertained, RCCL's delegation regrouped into a steering committee, chaired by Gotaas-Larsen's co-managing director, Richard Fain, and made up of representatives from the three owning companies along with RCCL's technical superintendent, Olav Eftedal, and Skaugen's naval architect, Martin Hallen. These men were all seasoned hands at new buildings, having been involved in the entire fleet's creation.

In line with this group's responsibilities, an inspection team was also organised comprising the proposed ship's desig-

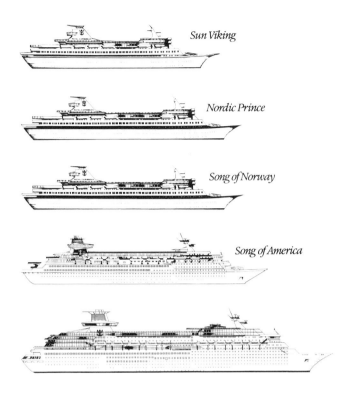

Sun Viking

Nordic Prince

Song of Norway

Song of America

A progression of scale: profile drawings showing *Sun Viking*, representing the original scale, her lengthened sisterships *Nordic Prince* and *Song of Norway*, *Song of America*, and the then still un-named new high-economy-of-scale ship.

(Royal Caribbean Cruise Line, Miami)

nated captain, staff captain, chief engineer and a combined ventilation and air-conditioning officer. Both groups worked closely with Kai Levander's design team at Wärtsilä to produce the ship's detailed specifications and the technical drawings on which the building contract would be negotiated. A comprehensive model testing programme was also carried out at the Marintek test basin in Trondheim so that the proposed ship's performance in service could be accurately foreseen before its construction was contracted.

Unfortunately for Wärtsilä, the contract was awarded instead in France to Chantiers de L'Atlantique at St Nazaire. Wärtsilä lost out as there was no government subsidy for shipbuilding in Finland as there was in France. The French yard's bid to build the ship was $180 million, only $30 million more than Wärtsilä's bid for building the considerably smaller *Royal Princess* three years earlier. It was also somewhat ironic that the ship to challenge *Norway*'s position was to come from the same yard which had delivered her as *France* twenty-one years earlier. Another twenty-seven years before that, French Line's *Normandie*, held by many to be the greatest liner ever built, had left the same yard to pursue her illustrious but tragically short service career. Before the new RCCL ship's name, *Sovereign of the Seas*, was announced, some had speculated (or maybe it was only wishful thinking) that the name *Nor-*

mandie would be chosen in honour of the great French liner of the 1930s.

With the design process so far advanced when the contract was signed in July 1985, Chantiers de L'Atlantique was able to commit to delivering the ship only twenty-nine months later. Construction could be started almost immediately. Throughout the building of the ship and her entry into regular service, the steering committee and the inspection team remained intact to oversee the process, right down to the smallest details. They met monthly to review progress and to resolve executive and management issues, while the inspection team effectively became part of the shipyard retinue, living nearby, and eventually taking up residence aboard their ship.

From the standpoint of overall layout, the design created between RCCL and Wärtsilä was essentially a further development of the *Song of America* plan. Martin Hallen's first visualisation of the new ship was a '*Song of America* facsimile, that accommodating 2,600 passengers would require an additional fire zone'.[1] Indeed, with a waterline length 55m longer than that of the earlier RCCL ship, she would need the extra fireproof subdivision along with its own ventilating system, stairways and deck accesses. This would in effect be sandwiched in between the public rooms and the forward cabin block of the *Song of America* plan. The 3.8m increase in width allowed room for one additional cabin in each of the side-to-side rows of inside rooms. The added length and breadth of the hull also would allow for two more decks each in the hull and superstructure. Thus, progressing from *Song of America*'s design, *Sovereign of the Seas* would feature a greater proportion of cabin accommodation above the public rooms as in the more recent example of *Seaward*.

The task of nearly doubling *Song of America*'s passenger capacity was of course to a great extent determined by the sheer cubic volume inside a hull whose dimensions and geometry had been determined by concerns of hydrostatics, seaworthiness, and so on. However, that was only the easy part. The question of servicing all those additional souls with food, drink, entertainment, and basic creature comforts such as air conditioning, light, running water, toilet facilities and whatever else human cargo will demand, called for a lot more than merely increasing the sizes of the public rooms and service areas proportionally. Some details of planning, perhaps long taken for granted, had to be completely rethought.

One such detail was how best to feed 2,600 passengers without giving the impression of 'messing' aboard a troop ship. When even greater numbers of people travelled in a single ship during the liner era, they were invariably divided among two or more classes, with each dining separately. The large ferries being built for the Helsinki–Stockholm run while *Sovereign of the Seas* was being planned also differed. Their added-cost catering usually offered a choice of restaurants on a continuous open-seating basis throughout the evening. With the responsibility of feeding all passengers for a week at a time within the fares they had paid, cruise-ship

The difference in scale between *Sun Viking* and *Sovereign of the Seas* becomes far more dramatic seen in the three-dimensional context of the two same-scale builders' models.

catering could not be so flexible. The designers had to take into consideration the logistics of feeding large numbers of people at fixed times. While a two-sitting service was still considered to be acceptable in the mass market, the dining room needed would be required to seat 1,300 passengers at a time, making it difficult to design creatively and still harder to cater adequately.

The steering committee decided to have two dining rooms, one above the other, each being served by its own galley, and each room having to seat around 650 people on a two sitting basis. The designers could create a more intimate and comfortable atmosphere, and eliminate the long walks to and from the serveries for the waiters. The galleys, aft of the dining rooms, were each fully self-contained and capable of functioning independently of one another. Each had identical food preparation, serving, and dish-washing facilities. However, they were organised functionally to work together,

***Sovereign of the Seas*: A cut-away diagram of the ship, showing her 'over-and-under' dining rooms located directly aft of the atrium at its lower levels.**

eliminating duplication in such specialised items as meat cutting and baking.

The lower galley was organised to handle the preparation for both dining rooms for those dishes which could be cooked on a mass-production basis, with the finishing being done in both galleys nearer serving times. It also included the bakery and other specialised services. The upper galley, which was slightly smaller, also served the crew, whose various dining rooms were grouped astern of it. Together these constituted the world's largest floating kitchen. The location of this complex aft, with no passenger spaces astern of it, made for easy and unhindered passenger circulation about the ship, without obstructing fore-and-aft access along any of the passenger decks.

Sovereign of the Seas was also outfitted with a third galley located on the sun deck at the base of the main mast, serving the two-deck high Windjammer Café and adjacent lido deck areas. The magnitude of catering to so many people is, to my mind at least, rather dramatically illustrated by the fact that the ship needed to produce seventeen tons of ice cubes per day to keep up with the demand of her eleven bars.

Use of the dining rooms was at least predictable, with a set number of passengers expected to show up at meal times. However, this was not necessarily so in other parts of the ship. To get an idea of how passengers actually used the facilities of an RCCL cruise ship Olav Eftedal posted spotters in *Song of America*'s public rooms during a cruise to do a head count every ten minutes. While this enabled him to determine the movement pattern of the 1,400 or so passengers aboard, simple arithmetic was all that was needed to project his findings to greater scale of the new ship. The steering committee and designers were thus able to determine, for instance, how many seats would be enough for the main entertainment features in the evenings, and how many others could be expected to be filled in other lounges and bars, and what level of patronage could be foreseen for the casino and discotheque.

The seating breakdown of the corresponding public rooms aboard *Song of America* and *Sovereign of the Seas* showed that there was not an exponential increase of capacity in all cases. In fact there are fewer seats in the larger ship's discotheque, as this comparison shows:.

	Song of America	*Sovereign of the Seas*
Viking Crown lounge	139	250
Discotheque	310	230
Second show lounge	564	675
Third show lounge	—	450
Main show lounge	743	1,050
Cinema/conference room	202	146 x 2

The public room arrangement of *Sovereign of the Seas* remained in principle very similar to *Song of America*'s plan, although with some reorganisation of the functions of the rooms in each location. For instance, the main show lounge was moved aft, to the corresponding location of *Song of America*'s secondary Oklahoma Lounge. The midship space, which aboard the earlier ship was occupied by the main show lounge, was appropriated aboard *Sovereign of the Seas* for a large casino, with the secondary show lounge going to the deck above, where one would have found the discotheque aboard *Song of America*. Eftedal's survey appears to have established that gambling was in reality more popular than it was foreseen to be in any of the Line's earlier ships.

The reason for locating the main show lounge aft was no doubt more a matter of structural design, motivated by a need to keep up with the pace of development, since passengers aboard as prestigious a ship as *Sovereign of the Seas* would naturally expect a Carnival-style double-height cabaret facility. Rooms of this type have to be sited at more or less either end of the ship, so as not to obstruct the free flow of movement along the full length of the lounge decks. With the boat deck's aft end location taken up with the cabaret room's upper gallery, the discotheque was pushed farther aloft to the stern of the cabin deck above.

Martin Hallen's added fire zone ahead of the public rooms gave rise to the ship's most stunning design feature. Here, a large Hyatt Regency-style hotel atrium was created extending the height of five decks, including the double-height space of the main show lounge. It rose from the foyer forward of the lower dining room to the boat deck, where it gave access to the second show lounge and to the upper galleries of the main entertainment centre farther aft as well as the open deck. With its surrounding galleries, shops and cafés, the atrium complex almost fully occupied the full length of the fire zone which housed it. Only at its lower level was its space encroached upon by cabins extending along the outside edges within the hull's shell. At the level of the upper dining room it encompassed the ship's main entrance lobby, while various shops and other smaller rooms surrounded the atrium shaft itself.

Arguably a waste of space, as open areas of this type and double-height lounges tend to be decried by their critics, *Sovereign*'s atrium was intended as a magnificent space designed to impress. It filled that function admirably, giving embarking passengers, seeing it for the first time, a real sense of the whole vast cruise ship's impressiveness. It retained the first impression of *Sovereign*'s greatness, as seen at the quayside upon one's arrival from the airport, to be savoured while aboard throughout the cruise. To fob off the paying clientele with low-ceilinged rooms and utilitarian stairways would have been to short-change them on the sensation of experiencing the world's newest and largest cruise ship. Design of the atrium, with its wide circular central well, was entrusted to Njål Eide, who rendered it as a glittering celebration of spaciousness and social ambience right at the nucleus of the ship's accommodation.

In his book *From Song to Sovereign*, commissioned by RCCL for the inauguration of *Sovereign of the Seas*, John Maxtone-Graham does justice to the atrium's point of inboard focus:

The space is called the Centrum, traditional name for the traffic core of many European cities. But *Sovereign*'s sea-going Centrum serves as a core, a vortex and celebration combined. Geographical confusion is dispelled within this inviting three-dimensional thoroughfare. One enters the vessel and is in immediate touch with its amenities. Through the Centrum one effortlessly achieves a compendium of public rooms – dining rooms, photo galleries, purser's and shore excursion desks, casino, shopping arcade, library, card room, lounge, bars and café. Traditionally, naval architects are wary of extravagant use of interior space, but Centrum's glittering reaches, centralising yet simplifying at the same time, glamorise the flow of circulating about the ship as never before.[2]

The various levels of *Sovereign*'s atrium were connected not only by wide curved sweeps of stairs, but also by two

Sovereign of the Seas: **Interior of the Centrum, featuring a degree of shipboard spaciousness not seen since the days of** *Normandie*, **although distributed in a vertical massing rather than along the horizontal lines of the earlier French liner's vast** *Salle à Manger*.

glass-walled lifts, the first of their kind to be used aboard a ship. Self-contained within the Centrum's space, and serving only those decks which it encompassed, these were popular with passengers as a means of circulating among the various services and public areas. In a small survey carried out a few years later by the marine access equipment manufacturers MacGREGOR-NAVIRE, this type of lift was shown to be effective in giving passengers a necessary sense of orientation or 'being in control'.

> ...given the choice, most people prefer using escalators for floor-to-floor transfer, next in popularity came panoramic elevators, and finally conventional elevators.

> The reason for this rating was mainly given as 'the possibility to look around while being moved' or 'the feeling of being in control'. Both arguments, in fact, are known from the airline industry where the ability to see what is happening and the feeling of being in control are the most important factors of 'psychological comfort'.[3]

Indeed *Sovereign*'s atrium has been the inspiration for other atria, which have since become a focal point of virtually all large-scale cruise ships, and have even found their way in smaller-scale renditions into the Yachtcruiser class. The fact that this, the first of the truly large and elaborate shipboard atria, was constructed by Chantiers de L'Atlantique, followed in the yard's historic reputation for structural daring of this type. The 40,945-ton *L'Atlantique*, delivered to France's Compagnie de Navigation de Sud-Atlantique in 1931, had a 140m-long interior *rue* (street), which at its centre was three decks high. *Normandie*, which was delivered four years later, featured interior spaces of legendary proportions, including her vast 100m-long first-class *salle à manger* (dining room) which was three decks high. The ritual *grande déscente* from her double-height promenade-deck lounges to the dinner table was made by a twin U-shaped progression of wide stairways encircling the ship's four massive lift towers and descending through three and a half decks, with the final flight of steps being inside the dining room entrance. Although not forming an open atrium as a whole, this arrangement featured a foyer, two and a half decks high, at its lower level and a double-height vestibule above.

Going from structural daring to structural rationale, the hull frame spacing of *Sovereign of the Seas* was predominantly 800mm, increasing to 865mm for the two frames either side of each fireproof bulkhead. This was becoming a standard technique of modern shipbuilding, where additional space would be allowed either side of these divisions so that the regular pattern of cabin assemblies would not be interrupted by the added thickness of these divisions. Apart from these periodic variations of frame spacing, which corresponded to the locations of the ship's five fireproof divisions, there was

not the traditional narrowing of the frame spacing towards the extremities of the bow and stern.

The fore-and-aft spacing of internal supporting columns was also varied along the ship's length, according to the locations of the double-height public rooms. For instance, in the region of the main show lounge, where additional structural stiffening was needed, the columns were spaced every six frames. Farther forward, where all decks up to the Windjammer Café were of normal height, there was only the need for a column every eight frames. However, spacing of the four lines of columns from the centreline was constant throughout the ship. This was arranged to correspond with the cabin layout. The outer row of columns were located so as to be along the seaward side of the two main fore-and-aft cabin passageways. The inner rows were positioned to occupy a narrow gap either side of the centre three rooms in each block of inner cabins.

Certainly the influence of Wärtsilä's initial design work was apparent in the cabin layout and its relationship to the structural grid of fore-and-aft frame arrangement and the beamwise column spacing. At approximately 16sq m each in area, *Sovereign*'s cabins were only three per cent larger than *Song of America*'s rooms. The three levels of accommodation above the public rooms were laid out in a plan very similar to that of *Royal Princess*. This also included similar use of the centreline space in the upper superstructure to house the air-conditioning plants. The cabins at these levels were thus almost exclusively outside rooms with windows.

The engine room was another area to bear the influence of Wärtsilä's design approach. Again, as in all four earlier RCCL ships built in Helsinki, a four-engine medium-speed power package was specified. The long-stroke Pielstick PC20L engines chosen were a new model, for which *Sovereign* was their first marine installation. As an improved version of the earlier PC2-6, designed for prolonged operation at part load on low grades of fuel, the new engines offered improved reliability and fuel economy. However, *Sovereign* was not engined with power-take-off generators as in other ships, but rather with a completely separate generating aggregate as in the earlier RCCL ships.

One major engineering concern in the design of *Sovereign* was that of reducing engine noise and vibration to an absolute minimum. To achieve this, each pair of main engines was in effect floated free of the ship's structure on a shock-mounted frame or 'raft'. Each raft was secured to the ship's structure with twenty-four resilient rubber pads, arranged for three-dimensional absorption of axial transverse and vertical vibration and motion. The inevitable trade-off against the advantages of this arrangement was that all connections to the engines, including fuel, coolant and lubricant lines, electrical wiring, compressed air inlets, exhaust uptakes and, alas, the drive shafts, also had to be made through flexible linkages of one kind or another. The drive connections to the hard-mounted gearboxes had to be made through special flexible couplings which would allow the continuous transmission of power even while the engines might be misaligned due to

Sovereign of the Seas: **Seen from above while at sea, the** *Song of America***-style arrangement and proportioning of her funnel conveyed a remarkably well-balanced and almost deceptive impression of her great size.**

(Royal Caribbean Cruise Line)

motion in rough seas.[4]

It bears noting that, at nearly double *Song of America*'s size in terms of gross registered tonnage, *Sovereign*'s required propulsion power was only twenty-four per cent greater. Again, as in earlier comparisons of *Song of America* with *Song of Norway*, it was through refinements in hull form, propeller design and the improved operating efficiency of modern propulsion machinery, rather than the brute force of increased motive power, that the performance required of larger ships could be achieved with ever greater effectiveness.

Externally, the completed ship presented a very handsome and well-balanced appearance. She looked very much less like an enlarged rendition of *Song of America* than might have been expected considering the approach to her design. She presented more the appearance of a liner, albeit a modern one, than did many other purpose-built cruise ships. This impression was created in part by the sweep of her bow and proportionally greater length of her forecastle deck. The rake of the bow line was less exaggerated than that of the earlier RCCL ships. Emphasis on the superstructure height was reduced by the oblique rake of its closed-in front, stepped back slightly at mid-height by the forward turn of the boat-deck promenade loop. The impression of height was further diminished by the high bulwarks surrounding the forecastle deck.

Once again RCCL retained their preference for a traditional cruiser stern. Seemingly in homage to *Normandie*, her builders' masterpiece of the 1930s, *Sovereign of the Seas* was likewise given a third anchor and a stern form similar to the great French Line ship. This also featured a chine in the shell plating above the covered stern mooring deck, where the rake of the stern form was reversed. However, above *Sovereign*'s stern the plane of the reverse-raked upper plating was in effect continued up the full height of the superstructure, where it circumscribed the progressively smaller perimeters of the upper decks.

Sovereign's oval-shaped Viking Crown lounge, repeated on the later sister ships *Monarch of the Seas* and *Majesty of the Seas*, was the last of its type. Its shape and relationship to the funnels and interior layouts of the later Vision-class ships became somewhat modified. However, in the still larger Eagle ships this trademark feature takes on a new keyhole shape surrounding the funnel.

The exterior styling of *Sovereign* required rethinking yet again about the riband which had surrounded the large superstructure windows of the line's earlier ships. The addition of a second row of dining-room windows made *Song of America*'s variable-width band impractical. The problem was somewhat aggravated by the existence also of a short row of windows to the main lobby forward of the upper run of dining-room panes, positioned slightly lower owing to varying deckhead heights within.

The *Song of Norway*'s riband approach was tried in some artistic renderings using only the upper row of windows, but this was not really to anyone's liking. Somehow its proportions on the larger ship seemed wrong and the two tiers of dining-room windows looked as though they had been forgotten. The final solution found by Per Höydahl, who styled the ship's exterior, was to paint three bands, encompassing only the three rows of large windows, creating accent stripes rather than an encircling riband. The main-lobby windows were excluded from this scheme, diminishing the visual discord of their being at a different height. Höydahl added a riband around the uppermost row of cabin windows in the superstructure above the lifeboats, creating a shadow effect under the lido-deck overhang, which served also to diminish the impression of height.

After a Christmas-time positional crossing of the Atlantic, *Sovereign of the Seas* commenced her regular service career on Saturday, 16 January 1988. The commanding presence of this vast white ship in Miami heralded the dawning of a new era in cruise shipping, when the glory of the former liner age's most celebrated leviathans would live once again in the form of a spectacular new ship, with more of her genre already on the drawing boards. While the purpose and, to some degree, the fundamental design considerations of passenger ships had changed irrevocably, what remained to be seen and beheld was that the new *Sovereign* belonged in her own right to the same league as the greatest ships ever built.

The only shadow of doubt over *Sovereign* was cast by the United States Coast Guard on the subject of fire safety. They considered the Centrum to be a 'high-risk area' on account of its open stairways in such proximity to the shops and services containing such flammable goods as alcohol, photographic film and perfumes. The Coast Guard's contention was that if a fire were to break out, passengers would be drawn to the Centrum, with only two alternative enclosed fireproof stairtowers being available. At the risk of the ship being banned from cruising from American ports, RCCL agreed to immediately install a sprinkler system in the Centrum, along with exhaust fans capable of clearing the area of smoke in ten minutes. Similar modifications were also made in the two later ships as they were being built. The Coast Guard's position was understandable as some of the worst fires aboard passenger ships have occurred in American ports and territorial waters, the *Morro Castle* and *Normandie/Lafayette* disasters being perhaps the most memorable.

Even as *Sovereign of the Seas* was being enthusiastically welcomed in Miami, other new ships in her class were already being built in France and Finland. Prior to *Sovereign*'s delivery, during 1986, Sitmar Cruises had placed an order with Chantiers de L'Atlantique for a ship of 62,500 tons, with an option for a second vessel. Carnival had, in January 1987, ordered their first 70,000-ton ship from Finland's Wärtsilä Marine, the new corporate entity to emerge from the builder's merger with Valmet.

FANTASY

While *Jubilee* and *Celebration* were still being completed at Kockums, Carnival was already considering economy-of-scale at yet a higher level. Influenced no doubt by RCCL's progress, they also sensed the strategic importance of at very least matching the competition's latest tonnage in terms of size and prestige. However, they decided to launch their greatest and newest ship into the three- and four-day cruise market, a sector which tends often to be served by a Line's older tonnage.

Originally designated by the project name *Fiesta*, the ship was named *Fantasy* at a fairly early stage of her construction.

Like RCCL, Carnival sought to replicate the already proven design success of their latest 45,000-ton *Holiday*-class ships. While Carnival would retain the distinctive exterior styling, accommodation layouts and interior styling, a number

Fiesta: **The project for Carnival's greater economy-of-scale generation was first revealed to the public in tangible terms as this artist's rendering, which was released shortly after the contract was signed with Wärtsilä.**

(Carnival Cruise Lines)

of significant technical changes were nonetheless made. The most significant of these was a switch from the direct-drive diesel propulsion introduced in *Tropicale*, to a power-plant-style diesel-electric installation of the type installed aboard *QE2* during the changing of her engines in 1986–7.

The design brief also called for a number of changes to be made in the accommodation, based on experience with the *Holiday* superliners and on the new features known of the competition's *Sovereign of the Seas*. The main points were:

Introduction of an atrium.

Introduction of a semi-dedicated bar area for the aft dining room with direct access between the bar and the dining room.

Relocation of the veranda suites from deck 11 forward to deck 6 midships.

Introduction of a demi-suite grade of accommodation with veranda.

Considerable expansion of the gymnasium and sauna area by relocating these spaces forward on deck 12. Space also to be provided for a dedicated aerobics room.

Considerable expansion of the midship lido area by careful placement of the funnel uptakes farther aft than in Carnival's earlier ships.

The hull form of the Kockums-built *Jubilee* was taken as the starting point for the larger ships. Its length and breadth were both increased, giving a better-proportioned liner-type exterior appearance. Apart from the increased overall dimensions, *Fantasy* required a fuller afterbody form to contain the two engine compartments needed for her six diesel generator sets as well as a separate space for the two drive motors. The machinery also had to be concentrated as far aft as possible to provide the additional lido space wanted topsides. The detailed hull form and locations of the propellers, rudders and thruster tunnels were determined through a detailed series of model-tank tests carried out in the Netherlands by MARIN.

Another important aspect of the model testing was to determine the best arrangement and use of manoeuvring devices. Simulated harbour manoeuvring tests of berthing and unberthing the ship at Freeport in the Bahamas were carried out using a fully operational 8.4m model of the ship. Freeport was chosen as representing one of the more difficult manoeuvring situations likely to be encountered in actual service. The entrance channel to be navigated at this port, along with the need to turn the ship within the relatively tight confines of its inner basin, would demand the interaction among all of the ship's manoeuvring devices, including her propellers, transverse thrusters and rudders.[5]

Carnival wanted *Fantasy* to be capable of berthing and unberthing herself without the aid of tugs in bad weather with winds of up to 35kts. Originally it had been thought that five thrusters, three forward and two aft, would be sufficient. The third aft unit was added as a result of the model experiments to allow the ship to move towards or away from a dock sideways without having to bring the main propellers and rudders into play. The combined use of propellers, rudders and thrusters in such situations brings about complex interactions among these devices which are not easy to predict. The testing at MARIN also showed that protective grids fitted over the thruster tunnels reduced effective performance by approximately eight per cent. It was thus decided only to fit these on the bow units, leaving the stern thrusters to the protection already offered by their location inboard of the exposed propeller shafts.

Forward, *Fantasy* was given a new-style 'gooseneck' bulbous forefoot. The bulb itself was turned upwards slightly on its supporting 'neck' rather then being straight-ahead as was the original bulb design. This was found to give the best performance in the ship's maximum speed range of 19–22kts, yet also to perform without serious degradation at speeds as low as 7 knots which were often used when making overnight transits from one island to another in regular cruise service.

Diesel-electric propulsion through variable-pitch propellers was chosen for *Fantasy*, following the successful example of its installation aboard *QE2* in her re-engining. The diesel-electric power-plant approach had in this example proven its flexibility in passenger-ship operations, with optimum performance demanded at various speeds. In *QE2*'s case these ranged from 16kts in cruise service to 28.5kts on her North Atlantic crossings, and even higher if lost time has to be made up.

However, Carnival decided in favour of cyclo-controlled drive motors, based on the operational flexibility it offered for their own operation in the short-cruise trade. Using simpler thyristor control circuitry, the cyclo-converter provided a single-step conversion of the generator AC frequency down to the lower frequency range which controls the motor speed. This allowed for a smooth and continuous adjustment of the motor speed, which in *Fantasy*'s case was from 140rpm down to zero.[6] The inevitable drawbacks of this approach were the higher initial cost of the cyclo-converters themselves and their relatively high operating temperatures.

The power plant could be readily used in various operating configurations to meet the diverse navigating circumstances underway, as well as the frequent and prolonged in-port periods common to island cruises. Also with the constantly high demand for electrical power, 3,500kW for air conditioning alone in *Fantasy*'s case, it made good sense to have a system where at least some generator sets could be kept running at optimum efficiency while in port. This in turn would ensure adequate supplies of reclaimed energy as by-product domestic steam and hot water during these periods, without the need for separate auxiliary generators and

boilers. In an analysis of a theoretical 1,400 passenger ship carried out by *Fantasy*'s cyclo propulsion drive manufacturers, ABB/Strömberg, they projected a payback of the added cost for a cyclo-regulated diesel-electric plant in as little as 1.8 years in service.[7]

Fantasy's installation was planned to meet four main service conditions:

Anticipated hotel electrical load of 7,500kW.

Propulsion power available for a maximum speed of 22.3kts with all diesel generators on-line, and a service speed of 19.5kts maintainable with one generator set off-line.

Diesel engines to be normally run at sixty to eighty-five per cent of maximum continuous rating (mcr).

Ability to sustain in-port electrical services with only two generator sets in operation.[8]

The idea of adopting a mix of two engine sizes, as in the 'father and son' pairs of larger and smaller diesels used in a number of geared and direct-drive installations, allowed a still wider diversity of generating conditions to be met in *Fantasy*. Four generator sets were powered by twelve-cylinder vee-form Sulzer ZA40s and two smaller units by eight-cylinder in-line ZA40s. Choice of the ever-popular Sulzer medium-speed engines remained a preference of Wärtsilä's design and building practice, despite the change from mechanical to electric propulsion. The two smaller diesel engines were in fact the same type used in *Royal Viking Sun*, completed by Wärtsilä a year earlier.

Fantasy's six alternator sets were arranged in three separate engine rooms, with the four larger units in two side-by-side compartments and the two smaller units in a third space ahead of these on the ship's port side. This arrangement added to the installation's operational flexibility a degree of security in that flooding, the outbreak of fire or any other such accident could be contained, leaving at least two-thirds of the ship's power-generating capacity unharmed. The two generator sets in each compartment were secured to resiliently mounted 'rafts' as in *Sovereign of the Seas*, to ensure a that minimum of noise and vibration would be transmitted to the ship's structures. Since the self-contained generator sets were each mounted as a whole in this manner, the complexity and expense of *Sovereign*'s flexible drive shaft couplings was eliminated, with the transmission of electrical power being easily made through flexible cable connections.

The drive motors themselves were located in a single separate compartment immediately aft of the twin engine rooms housing the four larger generator sets. The 14,000kW synchronous motors with double-wound stators and single rotors were about thirty-two per cent of the power of the 44,000kW units needed to propel the smaller 66,451-ton

QE2 at up to 10kts faster than *Fantasy*'s top speed. The weight of *Fantasy*'s cyclo-controlled motors was reported by their manufacturers to be about half of comparable DC-linked frequency-regulated propulsion motors.[9]

Control of *Fantasy*'s propulsion system, where even simple forward motion and speed were determined by precisely the right combination of engine revolutions and propeller pitch, demanded a systematic approach. When manoeuvring at low speeds for docking or undocking, with the complex interplay of the propellers, rudders and transverse thrusters, the task became considerably more complex, to the point of probably eluding the grasp of even the sharpest and most attuned human minds. Yet, through computerised process control and with much of its programmed intelligence gleaned from the tank testing and harbour manoeuvring simulations done at MARIN, the whole process could be packaged and automated to the point of offering full control through a single joystick-type control.

Two separate computer systems were used to control *Fantasy*'s movements. One was a vector system to keep the main motors operating at their most effective level, and the other an overall system control unit to maintain the power and shaft speed determined by the joy-stick setting on the bridge, and to ensure that a sufficient number of generators were on-line to meet the needs of that setting. The system computer was also programmed to handle special navigating situations such as regenerative feedback during ship slow-down. This can be caused by the inertia of the propellers slowing down at a more gradual rate than the drive motors, when they spin the motor armatures. This inversion of normal function results in power actually being generated by the drive motors rather than being absorbed by them. The system computer also handles a number of other operational tasks, including synchronisation of the propellers to ensure maximum power and a minimum of vibration, as well as management of performance in a number of special situations such as a crash stop.

A third computer served as a power management system, keeping the required number of generators in the ship's power plant on-line to meet the combined propulsion, auxiliary, domestic and, when needed, manoeuvring loads. This system was also programmed to handle various malfunction contingencies such as blackout and overload recovery, automatic generator-set switching when conditions such as low lubricant pressure or high coolant temperatures might be detected.[10] *Fantasy* probably had the most highly advanced automation of any merchant ship at the time of her building.

On the decks above the technological wonders of her machinery spaces, *Fantasy* represented a proportionally larger rendition of Carnival's earlier *Holiday*-class ships. Here, as in the example of *Sovereign of the Seas*, the additional hull length gave the larger ship's overall exterior profile a more balanced, classic liner appearance. The impression of greater size was to some extent diminished by the proportionally larger funnel fitted. The only other visually distinguishing feature was the extension of the *Holiday*-style enclosed pool lido overhang

down to the lounge deck below, where it formed a large window bay, in the casino on the port side and the promenade space to starboard.

Although slightly smaller than *Sovereign of the Seas* in her overall hull dimensions, *Fantasy*'s superstructure was more dominant, comprising three rather than two full-beam decks below her boat deck. *Sovereign of the Seas*, her later sister ships *Monarch* and *Majesty of the Seas*, along with *Fantasy* and the seven additional fleetmates to be built in her class over the following two decades, would be the last superliners to feature the traditional 'wedding-cake' liner-style superstructures. The upper-decks lifeboat locations with progressive narrowing and shortening of the decks above their level had the effect of visually lightening the topsides structural massing. It was precisely this quality of diminishing the impression of their vast size which made great express liners such as *Normandie*, the Cunard *Queens*, and in more recent times, *France* and *QE2*, so attractive in the eyes of the general public.

New safety regulations, as discussed later in this chapter, would ultimately mandate *Canberra*-style nested lifeboat arrangements in ships of this size. This in turn would call for a radical rethinking of exterior styling and fleet image for RCCL and Carnival, as well as drastically changed internal layouts as these Lines inevitably progressed to the planning of further tonnage. Despite their fuller hull forms and proportionally greater superstructure massing, futuristic funnels and other modern features, Carnival's *Fantasy*-class ships were the last in their size range to retain a traditional style of superstructure with an upper-decks lifeboat arrangement.

Internally, the accommodation was designed around the cabin module idea developed for the *Holiday*-class superliners. The overall cabin layout was remarkably similar to that of the *Holiday*-class ships. *Fantasy*'s additional 4.5m of beam was for the most part taken up with a centre-line core between the backs of inside cabins. This space was either used for services

Fantasy: Seen as a proportionately larger adaptation of *Holiday*'s overall arrangement, is readily distinguishable from the smaller class by the windows of the veranda suites beneath the riband surrounding the hull.

(Carnival Cruise Lines)

Fantasy: Cleopatra's Bar, had the corresponding location and function of *Holiday*'s Rick's Cafe. Another of Farcus's theatrical settings for passenger pleasure, this room shows remarkable authenticity in the integrity of its reproduction of genuine Egyptology.

(Carnival Cruise Lines)

such as air-conditioning plant rooms, deck pantries and other such facilities or by a single row of cabins, turned 90 degrees to the adjacent rooms and accessed by a corridor set to one side.

The new ship's wider beam also allowed for a deviation from this plan on deck 6 amidships, where twenty-eight deluxe suites were arranged, each with its own glass-enclosed private veranda. This lower-than-usual location for cruise-ship design recalled the classic liner practice of locating premium-grade accommodation on the upper hull decks, as in the case of *Canberra*'s deluxe rooms or *France*'s elaborate Ile de France and Normandie suites. The traditionalist wisdom of locating expensive suites closer to a ship's centres of buoyancy and gravity, where the effects of even the slightest rolling are less noticeable, makes sense. However, to the cruising public, many of whom are more accustomed to buildings than to ships, it would seem more logical for the most luxurious accommodation to be in the higher location, in keeping with popular notions of hotel and apartment block penthouses.

The public rooms also followed the same general pattern as those of the *Holiday*-class superliners, although with the singularly spectacular addition of a seven-deck-high atrium. Rooted in the main entrance lobby on deck 7, this wide vertical space reached upwards to a large glass dome at deck 13. *Fantasy*'s atrium differed from its counterpart aboard *Sovereign of the Seas* in that, although larger, it played a less significant role in the ship's overall circulation pattern. With the emphasis on a more horizontal distribution of public rooms aboard *Fantasy*, there was not the same need for open stairways in the atrium area to provide vertical access among lounges and other facilities on so many different decks. The upper reaches of *Fantasy*'s atrium passed through two accommodation levels, with the topmost deck housing the health spa and fitness centre.

The location of the spa and fitness centre in a prime area of the ship, with a forward outlook over the bow, recognised the importance that the pursuit of physical wellbeing has attained in modern lifestyles. Located above all other ship's amenities, it was also the only area to offer a forward view. The corresponding locations in ships designed ten years earlier were more apt to be allocated to observation lounges and bars. Indeed as people's life expectancy has increased, so has their interest in keeping up health and physical fitness. In addition to the usual range of saunas, massage and exercise rooms, the complex also included a separate aerobics hall and a banked outdoor jogging track encircling the main mast on the deck above.

By the time *Fantasy* was delivered in January 1990, Carnival had already taken up options with Wärtsilä for two additional ships of her class, to be named *Ecstasy* and *Sensation*. These fanciful names were the source of much levity in the cruise trade, with 'Intoxication', 'Inebriation' and even 'Copulation' being suggested as possibilities for the further propagation of the species. However, the whole *Fantasy* building programme was put in jeopardy when Wärtsilä Marine filed for bankruptcy in Helsinki on 23 October 1989 just prior to *Fantasy*'s completion. The subsequent financing of Masa-Yard by those owners left with unfinished work at the Helsinki and Turku yards allowed work on *Fantasy* to proceed with the ship completed on schedule. The contracts for the later *Ecstasy* and *Sensation* were renegotiated at slightly higher prices.

Since *Fantasy*'s delivery another seven ships of her class have followed her into service. Although Joseph Farcus has endowed each of these with its own distinct design theme and character, they nonetheless represented one of the greatest ever examples of passenger-ship class building. While it was once customary for shipping Lines to think in terms of perhaps two or three sister ships of the given design, the ever-increasing demand for cruise tonnage has produced large classes of ships. Holland America's four ship *Statendam* class is still being added to by the larger *Rotterdam* and three follow-on ships. Likewise, the 77,000-ton *Sun Princess* is being followed by three additional hulls along with two more of the 109,000-ton *Grand Princess* type.

STAR PRINCESS

During 1984, while detailed planning of Royal Caribbean's *Sovereign of the Seas* was well underway, the Vlassov family-owned Sitmar Cruises embarked upon a significant fleet expansion of their own, with plans for three 1,600-passenger ships in the 62,500-ton range. An order for the first of these was placed in June 1986 at Chantiers de L'Atlantique, with an option for a second ship to follow a year later. Construction almost immediately took over the space in the supertanker-sized building drydock vacated by *Sovereign*, as the Royal Caribbean hull moved on to the fitting-out dock. The first Sitmar ship was to be delivered in 1988.

Artist's rendering of Sitmar's new ships, showing some very progressive styling with elements of *Canberra*'s design, particularly in the streamlining of the lifeboat recesses and the plated-in deck above them.

(Sitmar Cruises)

Early artistic renderings of the first ship, released when the contract was signed, showed a very futuristic profile. It featured a three-deck-high lifeboat recess, divided along its length by an enclosed section of its upper two levels supported atop a deftly swept back shell profile. A similar profile farther forward gave support to the upper superstructure mass, where it closed off the boat recess, allowing the promenade deck beneath to join with the bow deck. There, the bulwark plating was swept upwards to the steeply raked superstructure front above the promenade deck level. Openings in the bulwarks softened the structural severity otherwise created, and reflected the lines of the shell profiles along the ship's sides. There was a wide bowed stretch of windows in the ship's sides below the break between the lifeboat recesses, its shape reflecting the circular deck, with the glass-domed lounge pavilion atop the bridge, and incorporating the curvilinear superstructure front and navigating bridge face into its perimeter.

Inside, the accommodation arrangement was based generally on *Canberra*'s plan, with the main suite of public rooms below the nested lifeboats on the promenade deck, and a second run of daytime gathering places atop the superstructure, surrounding the swimming pools and lido areas. The overall plan also integrated the contemporary rationale of *Nordic Empress*'s promenade-deck layout with the cabaret lounge forward, the dining room fully aft and a variety of smaller rooms, inside promenades and galleries between the social focal points at either end. These rooms were located near the vertical centre of the hotel block, with cabins on two decks below and four above, sparing passengers berthed on any deck the necessity of ascending or descending the entire ship's height if mustered to their lifeboat stations. There was also the advantage that in an emergency the lounges themselves, which could seat all persons aboard, would offer direct access to the lifeboats from secure, comfortable and familiar surroundings.

A return to *Canberra*'s overall internal layout, coincided

with a heightened concern for passenger-ship safety the world over. At the early planning stages, Sitmar chairman Boris Vlassov's main concern was mainly to create a well-designed ship, as had also been John West's intent in *Canberra*'s case more than twenty-five years earlier. However, as the new Sitmar ship was taking shape, the tragic loss of the ferry *Herald of Free Enterprise* in March 1987 turned the world's attention to the whole issue of shipboard safety for passengers.

Not only was the operation of passenger-carrying tonnage of all types scrutinised, with a view to avoiding the type of oversight which had caused the ill-fated ferry's car deck to flood so quickly, but the whole approach to safety-conscious design was questioned. Although this accident involved a ferry of newfangled design, it also drew attention to the modern block-principle rationale of virtually all new tonnage, including cruise ships. There were not only calls for new and more stringent Safety of Life at Sea regulations, but even questions as to the basic integrity of the naval architectural profession.

The *Canberra*-style plan emerged anew, with some variations, as the most practical solution, becoming a virtually standard layout approach for cruise ships and ferries in the over 40,000-ton range. However, changes in the style of shipboard layout since *Canberra*'s design brought about some reshaping of the overall concept. For instance, the preference for dining rooms located on the upper decks and perceived need for full-beam cabaret lounges threatened to reduce the open promenade deck to a short dog-run beneath the lifeboats, in place of the attractive superstructure-encircling loop aboard *Canberra*. Designers resorted to variations such as the *Royal Princess* approach of lowering the dining room and show lounge beneath the promenade level. Other alternatives were derived from the earlier *Willem Ruys* and *Oriana* plan with public rooms arranged on the decks immediately above the lifeboat recess. Holland America's *Statendam*-class ships and the Baltic ferry *Silja Europa* followed this approach. In other Baltic ferry examples, including *Silja Serenade* and *Silja Symphony*, dining rooms were located below the lifeboat recess and their show lounge above the forward end of its promenade loop. In all of these instances, passengers could assemble in the main public rooms in an emergency without having to endure the marathon climb through six decks, which those berthed in *Fantasy*'s lowest cabin decks might have to face.

Boris Vlassov's overseeing of the planning for Sitmar's entry into high economy-of-scale tonnage reflected a similar application of life-long experience to that which Charles Morris had brought to bear on *Oriana*'s design in the 1950s. Vlassov wanted ships which would give Sitmar thirty years or more of steady and reliable service. He believed in a precautionary redundancy factor above the computer-calculated minimum denominators of structural stamina, propulsion and auxiliary power. He opted for proven reliability and simplicity in engineering over the higher flights of technological complexity and advancement. Originally he wanted a geared steam propulsion plant, following the operational success of his only preceding newbuilding *Fairsky*, which had quietly slipped into service at the end of the early 1980s round of cruise ship building activity. The reality that few yards could still build steam-powered ships, and the increasing scarcity of engineers and ratings with steam experience, caused him to look instead to the diesel-electric re-engining of *QE2* which was being planned at the same time.

The choice finally reached by Vlassov and his technical advisors from Sitmar and Chantiers de L'Atlantique's design department was for a four-engine medium-speed diesel power plant driving CGEE Alsthom generators. The selection of engines was based on meeting the power requirements with a minimum number of cylinders, and hence also a minimum number of moving parts to be maintained. The choice of an eight-cylinder version of the nine-cylinder engines as had been specified for the *QE2* refit was purely coincidental. These were the only machines of their type which met the power criteria with as few as eight cylinders each, and which by the time of his ship's completion would have been proven their power in service aboard *QE2*.

The actual propulsion system was based on an updated version of the *Normandie* approach, using synchronous motors driving fixed-pitch propellers. However, thanks to modern electronics, the mechanical excitation switching of *Normandie*'s day, which was controlled by varying the generator speed, has since given way to computerised solid-state thyristor circuitry, powered from the constant AC voltage and frequency of the ship's power station-type generator plant. CGEE Alsthom, who supplied the motors and synchro-converter electronics for this ship, were the corporate successors to the Franco-American collaboration of the Société Générale de Constructions Electriques et Méchaniques Als-Thom and the General Electric Company which had designed and built *Normandie*'s machinery.

The specification of fixed-pitch propellers and a single rudder were likewise given on the basis of simplified running and maintenance over a long life expectancy. Although controllable-pitch screws were the preferred option for most owners, Vlassov was concerned about their higher cost, inherent complexity and long-term maintenance considerations.

Fairmajesty: Model of the ship showing the new Sitmar livery, along with a loss of the more fluid forms of line seen in earlier renderings.

(Sitmar Cruises)

Indeed his approach was similar to that of Swedish American Line in that simplicity was seen as the key to long-term reliability. The builders were already experienced with modern single-rudder passenger-ship configurations from having constructed Holland America's *Nieuw Amsterdam* and *Noordam* a few years earlier. Again, it was a question of minimising the number of moving parts to those needed for a single steering mechanism. With the superior speed control capabilities claimed of synchro-controlled motors, it was thought by both the owners and the builders that a mechanically far simpler fixed-pitch propeller could be controlled to efficiently give the necessary service, even while manoeuvring at low speed.

The builders favoured the fixed propeller for diesel-electric propulsion systems of this type as it allowed for quick reversal, when needed for a crash-stop. This could be achieved without having to allow time for the propeller's regenerative torque to diminish to less than the engine's reversing torque, as would be the case in a geared- or direct-diesel drive. Since an electric motor would be capable of retaining its maximum torque through its entire operative speed range in either direction, any such manoeuvre could be made as readily as with controllable-pitch propellers.[11]

Sitmar were to have named this ship *Fairmajesty*, following their usual 'Fair-' nomenclature. Far more appealing than this rather trite contrivance of monarchist sentiment was a change in livery, introducing some rather stunning graphic styling. The buff funnel colour and letter-V marking of the earlier Sitmar ships was replaced by a blue background colour bearing a flowing script-style white letter S, whose tail was continued into three wave-like lines underscoring the letter, the uppermost line being in red. These waves were to be repeated in red and blue on a much larger scale along the side of the hull below the funnel. They crossed the row of dining-room windows aft at promenade-deck level, and extended down well below the waterline. A model of the ship so adorned, also showed a thin blue riband around the hull at the high waterline with the submerged surfaces also to be painted white. The lowest swirl of the wave graphic reached almost as far down as the keel. The idea was that the clear tropical waters would in effect show this artwork down as far as daylight could penetrate, giving the graphic a dimension of depth and infinity.

However, the name and livery changed as the ship became the property of P&O in their acquisition of Sitmar in July 1988. P&O's Princess Cruises subsidiary was by that time beginning to fall behind in the expansion spiral, as their competitors were forging ahead with orders for larger economy-of-scale tonnage. Their own most recent ship was the 45,000-ton *Royal Princess*, and there was nothing further on the drawing boards, either for Princess or the parent Line. Quite apart from the four existing Sitmar ships with their combined capacity of 4,370 berths, the still uncompleted *Fairmajesty* and the two larger sister ships subsequently ordered from Fincantieri in Italy would quickly bring Princess Cruises up to the large-ship standards of Royal

Fairwind: **Seen here as the only real manifestation of the new livery before Sitmar was purchased by P&O. Presumably it was not practical to repaint the hull's underwater surfaces.**

(Sitmar Cruises)

Caribbean and Carnival. These three ships would increase the Line's capacity by an additional 5,200 berths. Additionally, the cost of the already-ordered new ships was twenty to thirty per cent less than it would have been if contracts had been negotiated at the time of the acquisition.

Fairmajesty was renamed *Star Princess* and was completed in regular Princess Cruises' livery. She went into service during March 1989, only slightly later than her originally scheduled debut with Sitmar. With her fully nested lifeboats and large superstructure proportions *Star Princess* presented a massive and imposing appearance. Some of the more fluid features of line and form seen in Sitmar's early artistic renderings were compromised out of existence, even before the P&O takeover. Gone altogether were the swept-back streamlining of the lifeboat recess openings and the bowed midship overhangs of the deck below. The glass dome had disappeared from the lounge pavilion atop the bridge, and the strongly styled lines of the gusset plating around the bow deck had also been diminished. Although not unattractive, the completed ship's appearance projected something of an 'engineered look' about her, bespeaking the technical rationale of her design. To my own mind this was conveyed largely by the triple-height lifeboat recesses enclosing the large overhead rail-type davits which were used.

In consideration of the ship's huge size, the circular lounge atop her bridge lacked the visual impact it perhaps should have had. During her final sea trials, with a press contingent on board, one New York reporter joked that perhaps the lounge's circular housing should be painted black so as to look like a Frenchman's beret.

The two later ships ordered in Italy showed a higher degree of styling, thanks largely to the hand of noted Genoese architect Renzo Piano. Perhaps best known at the time for his design work with the eminent British architect Richard Rogers for the glass-and-steel Centre Georges Pompidou in Paris, Piano was essentially given the same brief as James Gardner had received for *QE2*. Indeed the design problem of creating a more appropriately marine expression for so vast a mass of tonnage was similar, only this time it was somewhat more obtuse in scale.

Piano's approach was to soften the bulky masses of this ship into 'something of grace and poise'.[12] The key element of this was his creation of a huge dolphin's-head-shaped dome atop the forward end of the superstructure. The long curvilinear profile of this was arranged to rise gradually from a point aft of the main mast to the crown of the dolphin's head above the navigating bridge. The 'crown', semi-circular in plan, was brought down to the bridge level in a much steeper curve which finished at an angle to coincide with the steeply raked superstructure front. Along either side, the dome was joined flush with the superstructure's outer shell on lido-deck level. Farther aft, its glassed-in sides enclosing the lido area were turned inwards on a wide radius, providing a finishing touch consistent with the lines of the dolphin-head's crown or dome. Above, the dome's aft end terminated in a low fairing which helped to deflect winds from the open lido areas otherwise exposed to the sky. By the time these features were actually realised, their lines of form had in fact been greatly softened in comparison with the bold lines of form first visualised by Piano.

The dolphin head was potentially a massive structural load atop an already immense superstructure. It could only be rendered into reality if constructed of lightweight material. While Fincantieri would eventually use glassfibre funnels for *Costa Classica*, its use for so large a superstructure enclosure was probably considered a little too avant garde. Aluminium alloy was ultimately used, not only for the dome itself, but also for the enclosures of lido deck aft of the bridge, as well as for the funnel, the deck housing at its base and the mast. The bridge itself, at the forward end of Lido deck was constructed

Crown Princess: **Here the dolphin head and refinements to the lifeboat recesses asserted the smoothness of form lacking in the earlier ship. If the dolphin head had been lowered by one deck, with its windows forming a continuation of the lido windscreening, the overall effect would have been dramatically futuristic.**

(Princess Cruises, Vancouver)

of steel for additional strength. The 310 tons of aluminium alloy used here represented a weight economy of forty to forty-five per cent over similar structures made of steel. Construction of the dome was noteworthy in that it and the mast were completely assembled ashore as a single welded structure, and hoisted atop the ship in a single lift.

The steel superstructure front, which was windowless apart from the bridge and the observation lounge in the dome, was given very smooth and clean lines above the diminutive open bow deck. Likewise, the stern was clean-lined and simple in its geometry. Only the uppermost superstructure decks were terraced in the traditional manner. Below these the aft wall dropped to the promenade-deck level in a single angled plane, whose pitch reflected that of the hull's transom stern below.

The outward appearance of the two Fincantieri ships was also greatly improved over that of *Star Princess* in that the lifeboats and their handling equipment were contained within a double-height recess similar to that of *Canberra*. This was achieved largely thanks to the builders' choice of Italian-made hydraulic lifeboat davits which required a minimum of height. Made by Technimpianti, these offered the added safety value of being able to launch boats against greater angles of list than is possible with many other davit types. Perhaps the only disappointment was the rather small straight-lined steamer stack, which one P&O executive was overheard to deride as 'that dustbin of a funnel'.

The interior layout of the Fincantieri-built twins, ultimately named *Crown Princess* and *Regal Princess*, was similar to that of *Star Princess*, apart from the inevitable differences in cabin arrangement brought about by the smaller lifeboat recesses in the Italian-built ships. The vast interior volume of the dolphin-head dome inspired somebody at P&O to relocate *Crown Princess*'s casino to its central area. This was not a popular move, neither for the casino users and staff, nor for those who rightfully felt that the gaming facilities were an intrusion of the room's more obvious role as a daytime observation lounge.

Each of the three ships featured a triple-height atrium, connecting the promenade-deck run of main public facilities with the main entrance lobby two decks below. While the two lower levels were primarily cabin decks, the immediate atrium area was given an additional sense of functionality with the inclusion of shops and a patisserie in addition to the purser's office. At its mid-level the atrium also served as a vestibule for the theatre located amidships aft of the nearby midships stairtower. Although less awesome than Carnival's glass-domed atria, these spaces, which were nonetheless attractive in their own right, were designed with particular consideration of the strict United States Coast Guard fire regulations.

These atria were bracketed immediately fore and aft by each ship's two forward fireproof stairtowers. The attractive open-plan stairways of the atria themselves were entirely secondary in function. The entire atrium area in each ship could

be closed off without compromise of the natural lines of circulation from the lower-deck cabin areas directly to the main stairtowers. These were also the first Princess ships to feature double-height Carnival-style show lounges. Strangely, though, the upper and lower levels of these were not connected within the rooms themselves. A move from one level to the other had to be made outside the room, by way of the nearby forward stairtower.

Interior design of all three ships was co-ordinated by the California-based firm Welton Becket Associates. They were engaged by Sitmar on the reputation of their widely acclaimed hotel, corporate and commercial work. Their most noted hotel interiors at the time included the Contemporary Resort Hotel at Disney World in Florida and the recently opened Hyatt Regency Reunion in Dallas. Becket decorated *Star Princess* and the two later ships in their characteristic style of understated modern urban hotel elegance, a scheme already in keeping with Sitmar's design approach

Star Princess: **The three-deck atrium, which, though modest by *Fantasy*'s standards, has become the prototype for Princess's later *Sun Princess* class and for P&O's new *Oriana*.**

(Princess Cruises)

as shown in *Fairsky*, completed a few years earlier. For P&O this was consistent with the then still-unchanged Scandinavian-designed interiors of their *Pacific Princess* and *Island Princess*, and, at the same time, with California-inspired *Royal Princess* interiors.

Crown Princess was completed and handed over to P&O in June 1990, with *Regal Princess* following a year later, in keeping with the original delivery dates negotiated with Sitmar. Princess Cruises had by this time expanded their operations into Europe, and the interest generated in *Crown Princess's* unusual exterior look was maintained by keeping the ship in the Mediterranean for her first summer, before switching to the Caribbean in the late autumn. However, beyond their wide public appeal, these three P&O ships asserted a general prototype for the layout of most future development in large economy-of-scale passenger tonnage.

OTHER DEVELOPMENTS

As part of new IMO (International Maritime Organisation) safety resolutions added in the early 1990s to the SOLAS (Safety of Life at Sea) 1974 convention, lifeboat embarkation heights above the waterline were to be limited. Foreseeing a probable restriction of 25m, the nested lifeboat arrangements of *Canberra's* type quickly became the rule rather than the exception in virtually all new designs for larger ships in the 1990s. By that time 50,000 tons marked the low end of the economy-of-scale range. As was to be seen in the next few years *Costa Classica* and *Costa Romantica* were to emerge into this range as about the largest ships which could still be built with a conventional upper-deck lifeboat arrangement. Holland America's slightly larger *Statendam* class were built in a variation of the *Star Princess*-style layout with fully nested lifeboats. Of the larger ships in the over 70,000-ton range, only Royal Caribbean's final *Sovereign*-class vessel, and the remainder of Carnival's *Fantasy* ships were allowed to be completed under the old rules.

New entries into this size class were, without exception, forced to comply with the requirement for a lower emergency embarkation deck, and thus to follow the universal trend towards nested lifeboats. This and restrictions on atria with regard to their size and access to separate fireproof stairtowers were the two most obviously visible manifestations of the new safety rules. Other requirements for new ships of all classes carrying more than thirty-six passengers prohibited dead-end corridors and passages, and made floor-level evacuation lighting systems of the type used in airliners necessary for all accommodation areas. The extent of fireproof subdivision, including fireproof isolation of lifeboat embarkation areas, was increased while smoke alarms, sprinklers and automatic door closers for all passenger and crew cabins became mandatory.

The 1990 and 1994 resolutions amending SOLAS 1974 also updated the damage stability standards, particularly with

Legend of the Seas: **The ship photographed at sea, with the vast extent of her dining room and lobby windows visible in the lifeboat recess, and showing the redesigned Viking Crown Lounge at the base of her nearly-amidships funnel.**

(Royal Caribbean Cruise Line).

regard to the design of ferries and cargo ships with drive-on vehicle decks. The additional margin of stability required for cruise ships took into account the specific circumstances of evacuation. Under the earlier rules a passenger ship meeting the stability requirements could still conceivably capsize in a damaged condition while all her passengers were mustered on one side of the vessel when the lifeboats were turned out and if there was a strong wind blowing against the opposite side.[13] Indeed, considerations of this sort showed the vulnerability of large cruise ships with their extremely long and high superstructures, particularly where the effects of winds are concerned.

The first large cruise ships to be completed under the new rules were P&O's *Oriana* and Chandris's Celebrity Cruises' *Century*, both constructed by Meyer Werft, P&O's Princess Cruises ship *Sun Princess*, delivered by Fincantieri, Costa's *Costa Victoria* from Bremer Vulkan, and Royal Caribbean's Chantiers de L'Atlantique-built *Legend of the Seas*. With the exception of *Oriana*, which is discussed later, all of these emerged at the high end of what at the time could most appropriately be called the under 100,000-ton class. As these were being completed, work was already well in hand at Fincantieri on the world's first over 100,000-ton cruise ships.

Legend of the Seas, which came out at approximately *Sovereign's* size, showed how the earlier ship's design was effectively reworked around a nested lifeboat arrangement and other new safety requirements. Operationally, she was planned with a view to longer itineraries, and a higher speed of 24kts, making her potentially suitable for such things as longer Pacific cruises and other voyages which had long been the preserve of ships such as *Rotterdam*, *Canberra*, and *QE2*.

Legend of the Seas: **A partial view of the dining room showing the impressive expanse and vertical lines of the windows which give some impression of an opened-up rendition of** *Normandie*'**s legendary interiors.**

(Royal Caribbean Cruise Line)

However, *Legend* also incorporated other popular recent developments in passenger ship design introduced by Chantiers de L'Atlantique in the time since *Sovereign* was built. Originally code-named Project Vision, the design brief for this ship called for *Nordic Empress*'s openness of plan in an effort to create an optimum sense of orientation, both within the ship itself and beyond to her outside surroundings.

This was accomplished through integrating vast expanses of glass in the boat deck with an increased presence of the atrium, and a new adaptation of the Line's trade-mark Viking Crown Lounge, which admitted daylight and a heightened sense of one's whereabouts throughout the ship's public spaces. The vast central lobby, encompassing the atrium's expanse, and the main dining room were pushed to the full double-deck height of the lifeboat recess, with full-height windows along their sides. These huge window bays were extended outwards, breaking into the lines of lifeboats, to

offer unobstructed outlooks beyond the ship's sides. The dining room's sense of spaciousness was carried by the arrangement of its upper level as a 'flying' mezzanine, leaving the periphery areas along the window walls, as well as the room's centre, open to its full height. Were it not for the mezzanine, this room would have created an incredibly strong impression of the spectacular Chantiers de L'Atlantique upper-deck dining rooms of *L'Atlantique* and *Pasteur*.

As in Carnival's *Fantasy*-class ships, *Legend*'s atrium made the connection between the central run of public rooms and the mainly daytime recreation areas on the topmost decks. However, in the Royal Caribbean ship the atrium was surmounted by the Viking Crown Lounge rather than Carnival's Guggenheim Museum-style dome. The Line's trademark lounge pod was in effect floated above the glassed-in upper reaches of the atrium at the pool lido level. Sun and daylight filtering down from this level to the lobby below was enough to balance the openness of plan at boat-deck level with a sufficiently light and bright impression of the whole atrium shaft down through the three cabin decks.

Although the funnel lounge was not itself incorporated into the atrium proper, the two panoramic glass lifts broke through the top of the atrium, bringing the Viking Crown space more centrally into the main circulation pattern than on previous Royal Caribbean ships. *Legend*'s funnel was in fact unusually far forward, reflecting the midships location of her machinery. The Viking Crown pod was attached to its front side, as opposed to the stern location of its original manifestations on the Line's first ships. Placement of the funnel to coincide with the interior plan in this way was possible thanks to the inherent flexibility of layout allowed by the ship's diesel-electric machinery. This, Royal Caribbean's first experience with electric propulsion, was predicated, not only by the yard's success with *Star Princess*, but also by the Line's requirement for a higher cruising speed, enabling them to develop longer worldwide cruise itineraries. The synchro-controlled propulsion system with fixed-pitch propellers was similar to that of *Star Princess*.

Legend of the Seas was followed, not only by the option for a second ship being taken up with Chantiers de L'Atlantique, and yet a third ship later booked in France, but also with orders for two additional vessels from Finland's Kværner Masa-Yard. The slightly larger Finnish-built *Grandeur of the Seas* differed in that she and the later *Enchantment of the Seas* were planned for an intermediate speed of 22kts. Once again, the Line reverted to an aft machinery location. The four-engine diesel-electric plants of these ships were located three-quarters aft in a compact configuration with the diesels astern of the generators and drive motors. The exterior visual impression, and indeed the internal design advantage, of this extremely far-aft machinery installation was achieved by routing the exhaust uptakes farther astern and bringing the funnel uptake up to a position completely astern of the engine room from deck 1 upwards.

The most obvious exterior change that this brought about

in *Grandeur of the Seas* was a separation of the funnel itself from the Viking Crown Lounge. The upper-decks space between these two features was occupied by an indoor-outdoor solarium and pool attached to the adjacent fitness centre, which in the faster *Legend of the Seas* had been sited aft of the funnel. The Finnish-built ships, along with a further sister ordered in France, also differed from the original *Legend* prototype in that their lifeboats were located one deck higher up. This was brought about by a need to increase the dining room capacity to accommodate the greater passenger capacities of the aft-engined ships. At its main level the dining room was thus given the ship's full width. Apart from the loss of the closed-in deck above separating the boat recesses from the strata of verandas, this precipitated other changes of internal layout. Among these, the main show lounge was moved two decks higher up and a second show lounge was relocated aft. One consequence of this was that the double-height windows which made *Legend*'s dining room so attractive ended up being vertically divided between the corresponding room's mezzanine and a suite of smaller public spaces above in the later ships. Despite the variations in plan, both design alternatives offered the same overall feeling of spaciousness and airiness which underlay the whole original Project Vision approach.

Century, *Costa Victoria* and Princess's second *Sun Princess* were all adaptations of the original *Star Princess* layout to at least some degree. However, these were also later economy-of-scale ships, each endowed with a great deal of individuality devised to carry a specific sense of fleet identity.

The structural design and layout of *Century* and her two slightly larger sisters were firmly rooted in the proven practices emerging from examples such as *Star Princess* and Holland America's *Statendam* class. However, these ships assert a remarkable fleet image of their own, borne out of Jon Bannenberg's styling of Celebrity's earlier *Horizon* and *Zenith*. What was perhaps somewhat surprising about *Century* was that she offered far less veranda accommodation than other ships in her class. There were only two cabins with verandas, including two Royal Suites. The verandas were almost obscured from view by the enclosed lido-deck projection above, and as they were entirely white in colour were inconspicuous against the ship's bold paint scheme of two dark ribands, on of which completely engulfed the lifeboat recesses while the other encompassed a row of windows two decks below the verandas. A second row of veranda cabins was added in the two larger ships, again without detracting from the rather massive and robust appearance of these ships.

Undoubtedly the most remarkable aspect of all three *Century*-class ships is their interior design. John McNeece of London and the Athens-based husband-and-wife design team of Michael and Agni Katzourakis were once again hired by John Chandris, along with the accomplished American hotel architect Birch Coffey and a number of other noted specialist designers. To ensure a variety of experiences among the three ships, the areas assigned to each designer were var-

ied from one to the other. For instance, the main dining room aboard *Century* was designed by Birch Coffey, who in the second ship *Galaxy* was given the Café, while the main dining room on that ship was designed by the British firm United Designers. *Century*'s atrium was created by John McNeece and that of *Galaxy* by Michael and Agni Katzourakis, although McNeece was responsible for the main theatre lounges in both ships.

The dining rooms in these ships were particularly noteworthy. Adopting a double-height mezzanine plan at the stern they carried a strong 'hospitality' image, created in part by the broad expanse of windows in the ship's transom stern. From the outside these, with their double-height central panels, were to create the impression of an art-deco-style Miami hotel with a huge open and welcoming central portal. From within the outlook astern was emphasised by the room's

full-height axial central gallery lying between the port and starboard mezzanines. Birch Coffey's treatment of *Century*'s Grand Restaurant was particularly outstanding for its '*Normandie*-sque' treatment of the processional staircase connecting its two levels. As a newcomer to ship design, Coffey made an extensive study of ocean liner and cruise ship design before starting to work on *Century*'s interiors. His treatment of the dining room in particular shows a sensitive understanding of the essence of *grande luxe* shipboard elegance, bequeathed to his native New York by the great liner era, and a remarkable ability to adapt it to the modern-day cruise ship lifestyle experience.

One feature brought forward and expanded from *Horizon* and *Zenith* was their popular Rendez-Vous bars located near the dining rooms. These were spacious and versatile areas which filled the need for a gathering place for passengers to pass the time while waiting for the dining room to open at meal times. Also being part of the main run of public rooms, use of the Rendez-Vous areas was not merely limited to the immediate pre-dinner hour, as was the case when aperitif lounges of one sort or another were tried in earlier ships such as *Andes*. With a seating capacity of 418, including its sit-up bar for twenty, and space for a small band or orchestra, these rooms in the *Century* ships were versatile enough to hold their own at any hour of the day or night. Located at the mezzanine level of the dining room, the Rendez-Vous Lounge also incorporated its own twin stairways descending to the deck below for those who might prefer not to make the *grande descente* of the processional stairway in the dining room itself.

One of the more notable features of *Galaxy* is her observation lounge forward above the bridge. This room, which doubled as the discotheque after dark, had its ceiling height pushed up to 4m, which gave it an unprecedented outlook on three sides through its continuous expenses of bonded-in tinted glass. The upper half of the glazing was inclined inwards, increasing the room's sense of light and airiness and giving greater visibility of the night skies. This was one of the

Galaxy: **The added headroom given to the Stratosphere observation lounges in the second and third ships of the *Century*-class provides for spectacular outlooks forward and to either side of the room's terraced seating.**

(Celebrity Cruises)

spaces which emphasised the rather high-tech aspect of all three ships. Various computer and video technologies have been applied extensively throughout these ships as part of a business arrangement between Celebrity Cruises and the Sony Corporation of America. These facilities include interactive information systems using the cabin television sets, extensive electronic gaming facilities provided in a number of the public spaces, and entertainment enhancements which included, among other things, a 48-screen video wall in each of the show lounges.

Costa Victoria's design emerged out of an amalgam of *Classica*'s distinctive Italian styling and a project design being marketed by Bremer Vulkan. *Sun Princess* has in effect maintained the momentum already established with Fincantieri in the final two Sitmar ships which P&O acquired. Indeed the Renzo Piano styling of the earlier ships appears to have been the last of the Sitmar legacy, as *Sun Princess* has appeared without the distinctive dolphin-head dome or the somewhat derided 'dustbin' funnel. She in essence portrayed something of a larger *Star Princess* with more refined lines of form. Indeed the ownership of all these was unmistakeable at first sight, even if the name boards, funnel markings and houseflags were not to have served their identifying purposes.

Apart from being the biggest, most lavishly outfitted and most individualistic vessels of their type, they showed a turning point in design philosophy towards emphasising the cruise itself as the ultimate destination. In other words, the ship herself would be the main attraction, with the islands visited being secondary, as mere periodic diversions from life aboard. It was a move towards the philosophy of Knut Kloster's original conception of his vast *Phoenix*.

By the mid 1990s the effectiveness of economy of scale in ship design and operation had shown itself to be optimum for vessel capacities of around 2,000 passengers. Although greater numbers of berths achieved little added economy in shipboard staffing levels, and service optimisation, the major cruise Lines in this market continued to seek the prestige value and marketing economies of still larger ships. However, to progress beyond the dimensions and draught of ships such as *Century*, *Costa Victoria* or *Sun Princess* would be also to accept some compromise in operational flexibility. The greater draught of as much as half a metre would restrict the number of ports where such ships could berth alongside a pier, with tenders having to be used in many more ports, while access to others would be denied altogether. The time taken to disembark and reboard as many as 2,600 passengers by launch or tender alone would be sufficient reason to limit the number of port calls in favour of offering the passenger more options for enjoyment onboard the ship itself. Finally, the larger ships would be unable to transit the Panama Canal, curtailing not only canal cruises themselves, but also the flexibility for repositioning between the Caribbean and Pacific, as well as world cruise itineraries, which tend to become unworkable without the possibility of using the Panama Canal.

With the larger and more progressive ships of the 70,000-ton range, cruise Lines started to introduce the type of diversity of dining and entertainment options foreseen for the 100,000-tonners, as they endeavoured to maximise their onboard revenue-earning opportunities and solidify their market positions by offering more of a total-resort product. For instance, the second show lounges in *Century* and *Sun Princess* were upgraded to larger sizes and more fully equipped to function as alternative prime-time evening entertainment venues, while the range of smaller fixed-function rooms, such as *Century*'s video gaming lounge, were expanded to offer more diversity of activity. Alternative dining places such as patisseries, wine bars, pizzerias and Parisian cafés have been stressed as offering the same type of variety as one would expect of a resort complex ashore.

Sun Princess: **A cut-away diagram of the ship, showing its similarities with *Sovereign of the Seas* in regard to the dining room and atrium arrangements, but with a more extensive array of public facilities.**

(Princess Cruises)

CARNIVAL DESTINY AND GRAND PRINCESS

As the march of progress in most fields of human endeavour tends to emphasise the idea of 'bigger and better', somebody inevitably had to breech the 100,000-ton mark sooner or later. This plateau had in fact become more attainable over the years as gross register tonnage rules have changed. In broad, and perhaps oversimplified, terms greater amounts of the internal space within passenger ships has become subject to inclusion in the tonnage measure. Accordingly, the figures have risen for any given ship, so that the 100,000-ton behemoth of today would probably be not much larger than the internal volumes (of which gross register is the measure) of perhaps *Normandie* or the old Cunard *Queens*, if those ships were to be measured by today's rules.

However, these finer points of tonnage measurement are generally unknown to the travelling public. For most people the idea of a 100,000-ton cruise ship continues to hold enormous prestige value. For the first Line to put such a ship into service, it makes an important statement of being 'number one' in the field. While the volatility of the modern cruise industry can only ascribe the accolade of 'world's largest' to a ship until its size is inevitably surpassed, being the first to reach the six-figure plateau makes a historical mark which cannot be taken away.

Carnival were the first to move in this direction, placing an order in early 1993 with Fincantieri for a 95,000-ton ship ultimately to be named *Carnival Destiny*. Since tonnage figures tend to rise in any radically different ship design, as was the case in *QE2*, it was widely anticipated that this ship would be completed at something over 100,000 tons. Without any alteration to the overall dimensions of 270m length and 35m beam, the number of decks or the extent and shape of the superstructure, the tonnage could be increased as needed, merely with modifications of detail. The addition of a sliding Magrodome-type roof over one of the top-deck swimming pools and careful sizing of the veranda openings of the deluxe cabins were enough to push the gross register into six figures. The volume enclosed by the retractable glass roof, and in the private verandas thus became internal spaces subject to inclusion in the gross register tonnage reckoning.

In comparison with the 1940-delivered *Queen Elizabeth* of 313.5m length and 36.1m beam, *Carnival Destiny*'s overall statistics reflected the tendency in modern shipbuilding towards a stockier hull form. Although slightly narrower at the waterline with a beam of 35.5m, the new Carnival behemoth was considerably shorter at 372.3m overall. Length and draught tend to be circumscribed by the port facilities available to modern cruise ships, while the perhaps less restrictive beam dimension does permit for the added stability upon which to build higher up. *Carnival Destiny* would be 4m wider than Carnival's earlier *Fantasy* generation, not enough to permit an extra row of cabins and the corridor needed to access them. However, the added stability yielded by the increased beam did permit an increase of one and a half cabin decks over the four levels of accommodation in the earlier-generation ships. Any deviation from this plan would have inevitably had the undesired effect of increasing the proportion of inside cabins. While the standard cabins would offer marginal increases in size and luxury, it would be the public areas which would, in the words of Kværner Masa-Yard's Kai Levander, be 'most in pursuit of "wow"'.

Carnival Destiny would nonetheless represent a significant change in design approach over the Line's earlier *Holiday*- and *Fantasy*-class tonnage. The major difference in structural design had more to do with the new safety regulations requiring a lower lifeboat position than with the increased size and capacity of the ship herself. Essentially, Carnival's design people had to adapt to a *Star Princess*-style nested lifeboat arrangement without compromise to the popular layout and design features of the existing Fun Ships. The main concern as far as the public rooms were concerned was to retain the Line's asymmetrical plan with its starboard-side inside promenade.

This precluded a *Star Princess* type layout with the main public rooms being contained within the outer promenades at boat-deck level. Even with *Carnival Destiny*'s added beam, a plan of this type would have restricted the room dimensions too far for the 3,360 passengers who would use them. However, the ship's size and passenger capacity were both large enough to justify three full decks being allocated to the main suite of public rooms. With the usual double-height lifeboat recesses, at least one deck above or below these would have the benefit of a full-beam width, and thus space for a Carnival-style inside promenade.

Rather than go below the boat-deck promenades as was done in *Royal Princess* and a number of other modern cruise ships, Carnival brought their starboard promenade 'street' with its adjoining lounge bars, casino and other facilities up to

Carnival Destiny: **The ship fitting out at Fincantieri's Manfalcone yard in 1996, with the arrangement of her pools and terraced lido areas discernible atop the completed superstructure,**

(Andy Newman, Carnival Cruise Lines)

the deck directly above the lifeboat recess. Still in keeping with the Line's preferred ship layout, the dining rooms and lower reaches of the main show lounge were immediately below. The real difference in plan for the larger ship was that these facilities were given the full two-deck height of the lifeboat inset. The dining rooms were each arranged on two levels with a large open well and connecting processional stairways at the centre of each. The galley was sited in traditional style between the two dining rooms at their main boat-deck level. Apart from the double service escalators to the upper level of the two rooms, the space above the galley was taken up with lobbies and galleries providing passenger access to either room from the midships and aft stairtowers.

The greatest change in plan, and indeed one of the ship's most spectacular interiors, was the show lounge, which thanks to the extra deck allocated to public facilities by way of the lifeboat arrangement could be extended to a full three-deck height. Large amphitheatre-style rooms on this scale were first proposed for a number of Wärtsilä's more progressive SWATH cruise vessels of the mid 1980s, as well as, of course, for Kloster's *Phoenix*. It took both the enlarged proportions of *Destiny* and the daring of Carnival's designers to turn such a thing into a practical reality.

Without the encumbrance of a file of lifeboats along either side of her top decks, *Destiny*'s design offered an unprecedented opportunity for developing versatile all-weather daytime recreation facilities unattainable on even the largest of Carnival's earlier ships. In addition to the usual open-air midships pool, a second swimming pool was added aft of the funnel with a retractable glazed dome and nearby two-level lido restaurant. A link between the health spa,

Carnival Destiny: **Seen arriving in Miami for the first time, the ship's size substantially dwarfs the *Fantasy*-class ship seen moored in the background.**

(Carnival Cruise Lines)

which retained its pride of place forward above the bridge, was made by way of a unique sweep of sun-bathing terraces joining the spa with the midships pool one deck lower down.

Carnival Destiny's huge combined passenger-and-crew head count of over four thousand called for special consideration in complying with the 1995 amendments to the SOLAS Convention covering ships' lifesaving appliances. The standard set following the loss of the ferry *Estonia,* in which 852 lives were lost, set out that passenger ships, regardless of their size, had to be equipped so that they could be completely evacuated in no more than thirty minutes. To simplify and speed the process of mustering those aboard in an emergency, an embarkation deck was fitted inboard of the boats, allowing them to be boarded before being turned out for lowering. Time would be saved by eliminating the usual double-step operation of first turning the boats out and lowering them to the deck below for embarkation and then lowering them to the sea once filled. *Carnival Destiny*'s arrangement would allow the boats to be filled in their stowed position while they were being prepared for lowering. For passengers in particular this would alleviate the sense of fear inherent in entering a boat already suspended beyond the ship's side.

This brought about a change in Carnival's procedures for mustering passengers aboard their other ships. The Line was accustomed to following the practice of assembling passengers in the public rooms, preferred by many Lines for the flexibility it offered in directing passengers to the boats as they are readied. This has long been considered favourable to using

Carnival Destiny: **Looking more like the real thing ashore than any theatre previously to go into a ship, the Palladium Show Lounge's auditorium, complete with a chandelier, was given a full three deck height.**

(Carnival Cruise Lines)

Grand Princess: The ship as completed, showing what has to be the ultimate progression of the overall Princess design approach to the six-figure tonnage range.

(Princess Cruises)

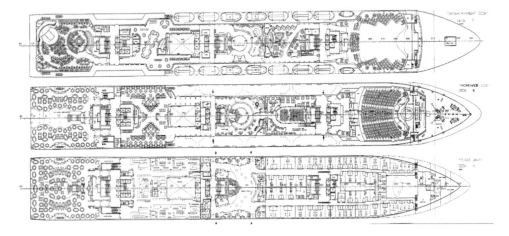

Century: Partial plan of the ship, showing a fine example of the public room layout typical to many larger, recently built luxury cruise liners.

(Princess Cruises)

specific lifeboat assignments, where the lowering of a boat can be delayed by the absence of one latecomer. *Carnival Destiny*'s evacuation procedures were centred around mustering passengers along the lifeboat embarkation deck at locations determined by cabin number, but not assigned to a specific boat. This took into account the reality of passengers arriving at their muster stations over a varied time period, during which the several boats at each location could be loaded sequentially and lowered once each was filled.

In theory at least, this should provide the most efficient way for quickly evacuating this ship's 3,300 passengers and 1,040 crew. It is, of course, to be hoped that these procedures will never have to be used in a real emergency.

P&O were quick to follow Carnival's initiative with an order for a 100,000-ton ship of their own. Given the name *Grand Princess*, she too was booked with Italy's Fincantieri, giving them the distinction of being builders of the world's largest modern cruise ships. Despite introducing innovations of her own this ship's overall design was firmly rooted in the Line's already proven design formula, dating back to *Star Princess*, and perhaps tracing its roots still farther back to *Canberra*.

1 John Maxtone-Graham, *From Song to Sovereign*, p 80.
2 John Maxtone-Graham, *From Song to Sovereign*, p 81.
3 MacGREGOR-NAVIRE, *Marine News*, May 1991, p 8.
4 Tony Newman, *The Naval Architect*, February 1988, p E66.
5 Stephen Payne, *The Naval Architect*, October 1989, pp E369-70.
6 Stephen Payne, *The Naval Architect*, February 1990, p E83.
7 *The Naval Architect*, October 1989, p 370.
8 Stephen Payne, *The Naval Architect*, March 1993, p 34.
9 *Lloyd's Ship Manager, Cruise and Ferry Quarterly Review*, February 1990, p S7.
10 *The Naval Architect*, October 1989, p E369.
11 Chantiers de L'Atlantique, *The Naval Architect*, July/August 1989, p E269.
12 *Lloyd's Ship Manager, Cruise and Ferry Quarterly Review*, London, October 1990, p S2.
13 Ulrich Jahnke, *Cruise & Ferry Info*, No 5, 1994, p 4.

ALTERNATIVES OF SCALE

Ascendency towards the 20,000-ton yacht

Large economy-of-scale ships are not to everyone's liking, neither from the passenger's point of view nor, in many cases, from that of the owner or cruise operator. Consequently various alternatives have either continued to flourish or have been introduced as new vessel types. The eternal 20/20 (20,000-ton/20kt) ship has retained its popularity, no longer as the mainstay size and speed standard, but certainly as the still-preferred option for a number of cruise Lines. From its proven example a smaller variation was derived which could handily accommodate a jumbo-jet load of passengers, offering operators fly-and-cruise possibilities involving the charter of a single airliner. Also to emerge as an alternative-of-scale option has been the Wärtsilä vision of the ultra-deluxe Yachtcruiser and Windcruiser, which would provide the intimacy of superlative luxury of cruising aboard a private yacht in conjunction with the entertainment and service offered by larger full-fledged commercial cruise ships.

THE 20,000-TON/20KT STANDARD

Long since the early-1970s completions of Royal Viking's original three Wärtsilä-built luxury sister ships, several Lines have shown a continuing preference for vessels in their size and performance range. During the early 1980s, at a time when Lines such as Carnival and Royal Caribbean were following Kloster's trend towards larger tonnage, the domestic German company Hadag made their own bid to enter the deep-sea cruise market with an 18,835-ton ship ordered from Howaldtswerke-Deutsche Werft's Hamburg yard for completion at the end of 1981, about the same time as *Europa*'s delivery.

Named *Astor*, she was in many regards a smaller rendition of the Hapag-Lloyd ship, being of a perhaps less ostentatious scale for the number of passengers to be accommodated. While the original design as conceived by the owners was for a capacity of only 450 passengers, the progress of detailed planning with the builders ultimately revealed a figure of around 600 to be optimum for the ship's size. With slightly more than the 21,000-ton *Royal Viking Star*'s 559 berths, this would still provide the level of luxury and comfort which Hadag wanted to offer their passengers.

The completed ship's style and onboard character was very much akin to that of *Europa*. This was particularly evident in the yard's own interior design and decoration of the public rooms, reflecting the same elegantly low-key approach taken by Joachim Buchwald and Wilfred Köhnemann in the Hapag-Lloyd ship. However, *Astor*'s plan was simpler in that it followed the traditional horizontal liner layout approach, with the great majority of public spaces concentrated along the length of a single deck, rather than being vertically divided following the *Finnjet* example as had been done in *Europa*.

In this regard *Astor*'s design was more akin to that of the

The first *Astor*: Her design combined the human scale of the original Royal Viking Line ships with *Europa*'s style of modern German cruise ship design.

(Airphoto HADAG LFA HH 1393/81)

Royal Viking ships, to those prestigious 1960s liners such as *Sagafjord* and *Kungsholm*, which had made a profound impression on the development of modern cruising. *Astor* thus has asserted these characteristics as the basis of other designs in her general size range which have since followed.

Her own tenure in the service of her original owners was short-lived, with the ship being sold in 1984 to Safmarine, South Africa's counterpart of Union Castle Line. The Line's managing director Marmion Marsh was keen to reinstate the liner service between Cape Town and Southampton which had been closed with the withdrawal of *S A Vaal* and *Windsor Castle* in the late 1970s. He believed that there was still sufficient demand for the line service and high-season domestic cruise service to sustain a single ship of intermediate size and capacity.

However, despite her seemingly ideal size and capacity, as well as a purchase price of only $50 million, *Astor* was not the right ship, particularly for long trans-equatorial voyages to and from Britain. Having been designed primarily for seven-day cruises in the Baltic and Mediterranean, she lacked the degree of spaciousness which Union Castle and Safmarine passengers were accustomed to. The ship had no hold for passengers' baggage and insufficient storage space in her cabins. To help resolve this problem all passenger beds were raised a few centimetres to provide enough space underneath them for stowing suitcases.[1] Indeed, in regard to these things she was clearly more a 'lightweight' product of the *Royal Viking Star* cruise era than of the dual role into which ships such as *Sagafjord* and *Kungsholm* had been cast.

The more serious side to *Astor*'s shortcomings in Safmarine's service was that her power, bunker storage and fresh-water generating capacities were barely sufficient for the long periods at sea. *Astor*'s tight schedules and extended periods of sustained running at near full speed resulted in difficulties with her mechanical systems. No doubt for the same reasons, the ship also suffered a number of electrical failures. While

there was little which could be done to overcome these shortcomings in the existing ship, Safmarine decided to build a replacement of similar overall design, but with the additional size and stamina needed for a regular liner service.

Astor was sold to the German Democratic Republic for state-run workers' cruises, under her new name *Arkona*. This netted a profit of $3 million for Safmarine on their original purchase, enabling them to order a new vessel from the same builders. Also named *Astor*, the replacement ship was of near-identical configuration and layout, with approximately the same passenger capacity.

	First *Astor*	Second *Astor*
Length oa	164.35m	176.50m
Length bp	140.00m	151.90m
Beam	22.60m	22.60m
Draught	6.12m	6.10m
Power output	4 x 3,300.00kW	2 x 3,300.00kW
	—	2 _ 4,400.00kW
Service speed	18.0kts	17.8kts
Maximum speed	20.0kts	21.0kts
GRT	18,835.0	20,159.0
Passenger capacity	638	656
Crew	210	250

In addition to the increased bunker and fresh-water capacities, as well as an added margin of reserve propulsion power, with a slightly higher top speed, the new ship's passenger facilities were also improved. This included a higher proportion of deluxe cabins and suites as well as the addition of a casino and more extensive health and fitness facilities. The new ship was registered in Mauritius and, nominally at least, run by a British cruise operator in a bid to avert disfavour in world cruise markets arising from South Africa's policy of apartheid. It was hoped that she would attract the same type of loyal following as *Andes* had done in her day.[2] However, this venture suffered from light bookings, particularly on the line voyages, and was eventually wound up with the ship being sold to the Soviet Union's Morflot, becoming *Fedor Dostoevsky*.

Both ships have fared well in these subsequent careers, which has seen them both return to the type of cruise service for which the original *Astor* was designed. In the eternal chess game of world shipping, both have since operated under charters to German tour operators. Since the German reunification in 1990, *Arkona* has been owned by Rostock-based Deutsche Seetouristik, and her cruises marketed through Germany's largest cruise operator, Seetours International. The later ship, which continues to be operated by the Black Sea Shipping Company of the Ukraine, has retained a solid German following in her worldwide cruises. Both ships have in effect found their mark in a particular niche market sector which caters to a largely European clientele and offers a wide range of more unusual destinations. It is a trade which does

Shin Sakura Maru: **This view shows her original cargo/pas-senger configuration which allowed her to be used for the Japan Industry Floating Fair.**

(Yoshiho Ikeda, Osaka)

not support the vast numbers of passengers served in the economy-of-scale Caribbean, Mediterranean and Alaska trades.

On the opposite side of the world, a similarly specialised indigenous cruise market was at the same time beginning to emerge in Japan. Here too the 600-passenger ship was seen as the ideal entity. While at one time Japan maintained a fairly large fleet of passenger liners on various worldwide services, modern cruising has been slow to come to the Land of the Rising Sun.

As in Germany, Japan's indigenous cruise market is more deeply rooted in the nation's own culture and has likewise developed as a separate entity from the vast 'melting pots' of the European and North American trades. A further similarity between the two nations also lay in the fact that neither sustained the rebirth of their respective merchant passenger fleets following World War II, as did nations such as Britain, Italy, France, the Netherlands and the United States. Thus Japan lacked a similar surfeit of existing tonnage and supporting infrastructures for any larger-scale transition to cruise operations from line services.

Of the few post-war Japanese passenger-carrying vessels, Mitsui-OSK's 1950s-built *Brazil Maru* and *Argentina Maru* were in reality large combination cargo/passenger liners, providing extensive emigrant-type accommodation on their services to South America. While *Brazil Maru* took up a static role as a floating museum and restaurant at Kobe when the service was discontinued in 1974, *Argentina Maru* became one of three international exhibition ships for Japanese trade and industry. Renamed *Nippon Maru*, she joined the purpose-built *Sakura Maru* and *Shin Sakura Maru*, which had been completed in 1962 and 1972 respectively. *Nippon Maru* was in fact more like the newer *Shin Sakura Maru*, which was also designed with conventional cargo holds forward of a half-length superstructure. *Shin Sakura Maru*'s cargo spaces were designed to also be used as exhibition halls, with cabins being

provided in the superstructure for ninety-two exhibitors and industry representatives.

Cruising was tried on a limited scale aboard *Nippon Maru* and *Shin Sakura Maru* during the 1970s. In 1982 *Nippon Maru* was sold to the People's Republic of China, becoming *Ziluolan* in cruise service there. At about the same time *Shin Sakura Maru* was extensively rebuilt as a permanent cruise ship, with her superstructure greatly extended forward over the original cargo/exhibition spaces. She was given accommodation for 556 passengers and a fairly extensive range of Japanese-style public facilities, including two auditorium-style double-height multi-purpose rooms.

With good trading results and a steadily growing interest in cruising an order was placed for a second Mitsui-OSK ship, ostensibly replacing the earlier *Nippon Maru*, to be named *Fuji Maru*. Reflecting the somewhat cautious nature of Japanese expansion into cruising, the new ship was designed to provide general training for young people and company employees in an informal sea-going atmosphere through special events planned during many of these voyages. Expressed in the words of a release published in a Japan Ship Exporters' Association newsletter, this auxiliary role was for *Fuji Maru* to serve as a 'ship for youth to promote friendship and to train young people'.[3] Since most employees in Japan tend to receive comparatively short annual holidays, and that the time other workers would spend aboard for training trips would likewise be short, the ship was planned for sea voyages normally of not more than seven days. These were to be operated on a fly-cruise basis in the Pacific islands, Australia and New Zealand, with the long stretches between the voyage areas and Japan being covered by air.

While the accommodation of the old *Nippon Maru* and *Shin Sakura Maru* were more akin to British and Australian

Shin Sakura Maru: **After being rebuilt for full-time cruising, the ship's still attractively functional lines retain a remarkably long freighter-like foredeck. Aft of her is the newer Japanese cruise ship *Fuji Maru*.**

(Yoshitatsu Fukawa, Hiratsuka)

character, a higher standard was set for the new ship in a bid to eventually secure a more diverse and up-scale clientele, both in Japan and possibly elsewhere too. Unlike the older ships, all cabins aboard the new *Fuji Maru* were to feature private en-suite toilet facilities. By following a general layout with all cabins in the superstructure above the public rooms, it was possible to also provide windows in all rooms. However, one concession to the younger clientele foreseen was that 119 of the ship's 164 cabins were fitted with fold-away pullman berths for third and fourth passengers in each room.

The cabins were of a generally international standard for modern cruise ships, apart from the inclusion of so many pullman berths. However, the public rooms were of a decidedly more Japanese character. For instance, the two-deck-high Pacific Hall located at the forward end of the ship had more the appearance of a hotel convention hall than its Las Vegas cabaret counterparts aboard the majority of America-based cruise ships. With its flat floor and exclusive use of moveable and stackable chairs and other portable furnishings, the room offered the flexibility of being usable for stage presentations of one sort or another, lectures and training assemblies, as well as other activities such as sporting events and indoor games. This space, with its shallow mezzanine was similar to the 'assembly halls' aboard *Shin Sakura Maru*, the earlier *Nippon Maru* and a number of the larger and more sophisticated ferries being introduced into some of the longer domestic routes.

Japanese cruise passengers tend to prefer the diversity of shipboard facilities also enjoyed by their British and European counterparts, as opposed to the fewer and larger spaces which appeal to American passengers. Consequently *Fuji Maru's* range of public facilities, extending through the uppermost hull deck and the superstructure's base level, was quite varied for a ship of her size. These included the formal Sakura Saloon, the Emerald Lounge as a ballroom and alternative entertainment facility with its own stage, a veranda lounge, bar, library, shops and other services, as well as informal enclosed promenade areas of the *Kungsholm* and *QE2* type on A deck (lettered decks started with A above the upper deck, increasing up to F deck atop the navigating bridge). Immediately below on the hull's Upper deck were the main dining room, a smaller 'special' saloon, the main entrance foyer, with its open stairwell and cluster of ship's offices rounding off this ensemble of public spaces, assembled aft of the Pacific Hall's lower level.

In addition to the usual arrangement of swimming pools, lido areas and informal public spaces on the uppermost decks, *Fuji Maru* also offered the traditional communal baths which are a significant part of the Japanese lifestyle. Indeed these are as essential to a Japanese ship as are the saunas to Scandinavian ferry and cruise tonnage.

Even before *Fuji Maru* was delivered, an order was placed for a sister ship of near-identical technical specifications. While this vessel was ostensibly to serve the same market as *Fuji Maru*, changes introduced into her design showed ten-

Fuji Maru: **Taken while running her sea trials, this photograph shows the unusual superstructure arrangement at her funnel base, and a remarkable adaptation of the *Royal Princess*-type forward veranda treatment which endeavours to reflect the lines of the bow.**

(Japan Ship Exporter's Association, London)

dencies towards the American market standard of near-exclusive double-occupancy accommodation. Named *Nippon Maru*, her layout was altered to offer the same number of beds with a greater emphasis on double-occupancy cabins. Thus the number of rooms was increased to 200, with only nineteen of them having additional upper berths.

This change was accomplished through adapting the overall plan to emphasise a concentration of the public spaces towards the ship's stern and distribution of the cabins over five decks, primarily in the forward part of the ship. This was in reality an adaptation of the *Finnjet*-style vertically segregated plans adapted in Hapag-Lloyd's *Europa* a decade earlier. The upper-deck plan was essentially similar to the earlier ship with regard to the arrangement of the central main lobby, with the dining room galley and crew mess rooms farther aft. The forward space on this and E deck above was, however, appropriated for cabins, with the Main Hall being relocated two levels higher up to the superstructure's aft end on B and C decks. The remaining lounges, saloons and other facilities were arranged through the aft half of C and D decks. The Main Bar was sited at the forward end of C deck, providing *Nippon Maru* with the type of observation lounges which were very popular with Japanese passengers, and featured in the plans of many domestic ferries.

Although of similar design and technical specifications, and to some degree in the image and character expressed by their exterior appearances, the two ships were nonetheless quite easily distinguishable one from the other. *Fuji Maru* featured a Viking Crown Lounge-type enclosure at the base of her funnel, which unlike the freestanding appearance of the Caribbean prototype was supported by four angled buttresses. Straddling a pair of lifeboats at their bases, these gave the ship and her funnel a rather heavy structural appearance. In *Nippon Maru* this was changed in favour of a less dominant-looking deckhouse enclosure forward of the funnel somewhat resembling the upper deck's treatment of the attractive American Grace Lines ship *Santa Rosa* of the 1950s.

Two more ships of the 20/20 type were introduced in the early 1990s, showing in their design and character a steady progression towards greater luxury and comfort, approaching the international luxury-market standards of NYK's *Crystal Harmony*.

	Fuji Maru	*Orient Venus*	*Asuka*
Length oa	167.00m	174.00m	192.82m
Length bp	147.00m	155.00m	160.00m
Beam moulded	24.00m	24.00m	24.70m
Draught	6.33m	6.30m	6.60m
Service speed	20.00kts	21.00kts	21.00kts
Maximum power	15,750.00kW	13,636.00kW	17,300.00kW
GRT	23,340.0	21,906.0	28,717.0
Passengers	603	606	604
Number of cabins	165	195	282
Crew	135	120	243

About the time of *Nippon Maru*'s completion in 1990, *Orient Venus* was delivered by Ishikawajima-harima Heavy Industries' Tokyo yard to Nihon Cruise Line. She was designed for a 'space charters' role similar to that of *Fuji Maru* and *Nippon Maru* for Japanese companies wanting to send their employees on educational and recreational 'incentive' voyages, with space not taken up by the Line's corporate customers being available for individual bookings. Here too, a large auditorium was provided along with two additional conference rooms.

The majority of *Orient Venus*'s public rooms were laid out on a horizontal plan, occupying the full-beam width of the lowest superstructure deck. The layout of these spaces in fact quite closely followed *Astor*'s plan, with the main lounge forward, main dining room aft and smaller spaces amidships. The greatest difference from the German ship here was the galley's location starboard side, where it also served a smaller secondary dining room, rather than being fully astern. The full-beam extension of the superstructure upwards above the boat deck aft had a similar appearance to *Europa* and *Astor*, with the added internal volume of *Orient Venus*'s interiors at these levels enclosing her Main Hall and other business facilities. In providing the special features of Japanese cruising, an outlook over the bow was offered from the *Nippon Maru*-style Forward Saloon immediately beneath the navigating bridge, while the communal baths and spas were relegated to an inside location deep within the hull, where they unfortunately lacked the outlook offered aboard *Nippon Maru*.

From the standpoint of styling and image, *Orient Venus* presented a softer curvilinear expression of form, apart from the rather angular mass of her aft superstructure elements. With the widely bowed superstructure front, extended up beyond the boat deck, and the more generous than usual pro-

portion of her forward mooring deck, this ship presented something of a retrospective 1960s liner look.

Nearly two years after *Orient Venus*'s completion NYK's *Asuka* emerged from the Nagasaki yard of Mitsubishi Heavy Industries at 28,717 tons as the largest ever cruise ship built for domestic service. *Asuka*'s size also eclipsed that of the two 27,500-ton express liners *Kashiwara Maru* and *Izumo Maru* laid down in 1939 for a 25kt express trans-Pacific line service, but never completed as such owing to the circumstances of World War II. Forseen as a possible fleet mate for NYK's America-based Crystal Cruises subsidiary.

As discussed earlier, *Asuka*'s accommodation layout stressed the *Europa*-type vertical approach, adapted to also uphold the All Outside Cabins feature as seen in *Crystal Harmony*. Her passenger facilities were otherwise of the same standard of those aboard *Crystal Harmony*, with the same architects co-ordinated by Sweden's Robert Tillberg who was responsible for their design and decoration. With the owners' requirements that, although destined for their own home market, the ship had also to meet international luxury market standards, a number of compromises and trade-offs had to be taken into consideration. For instance, the Japanese market would not demand a casino, whereas they would expect their special baths and a wider range of smaller and more fixed-purpose public spaces.

Asuka's spa and fitness centre was thus designed with Japanese baths as well as the jacuzzis, saunas and cold-water plunge baths demanded by Western lifestyles. While the Grand Hall's tiered cabaret-lounge seating arrangement has more permanently set the room's function primarily as an entertainment venue, the cinema complex three decks higher up has been arranged to double as a flexible conference and meeting facility. Directly opposite these areas the English-style Asuka Lounge was positioned to serve both as the ship's formal lounge or as a reception room for business activities if needed as such. On the uppermost deck, the Vista Lounge filled the need for a forward observation area although, in a characteristically more Western style, its location was above the navigating bridge rather then below it. The Las Vegas Corner adjacent to the Piano Bar and Grand Hall was created as a small space for the slot machines and other automated gaming amusements enjoyed by Japanese passengers, yet was spacious enough to be able to alternatively accommodate several 'live' gaming tables.

Design of the cabins was given very careful consideration. These were designed by Professor Vittorio Garroni Carbonara, who was also responsible for *Crystal Harmony*'s passenger accommodation. One of the most contentious issues concerned the choice of shower units or full-sized tub baths for *Asuka*'s standard rooms. With a slightly smaller 17.0sq m area as opposed to *Crystal Harmony*'s 18.4sq m standard cabin area, there was indeed a case in favour of the more compact shower units. However, with a little ingenious reworking of his angled entry plan for the larger ship's rooms, an oblique bathroom plan was devised which could accommodate the

***Asuka*: Her profile is seen here in home waters at Kobe. The functions of the accommodation within can be easily read by the location of verandas and cabin windows in the forward part of the ship, larger windows for the public rooms, windscreened decks aft and an observation lounge atop the bridge.**

(Yoshitatsu Fukawa, Hiratsuka)

full-size baths which the owners thought appropriate for the luxury they wanted to offer. While showers were considered acceptable for the younger Japanese people taking educational and incentive cruises, NYK was clearly interested in promoting *Asuka*'s cruises to the still largely untapped wealthy executive and retiree markets. In line with this image, the ship was also first to provide TV sets and mini-bars, not just in the deluxe state rooms and suites, but in all passenger cabins.

Following her delivery in October 1991, *Asuka* was slow to build up a following, to the point of nearly being transferred to Crystal Cruises. She has gradually carved herself a niche in the Japanese cruise market which places her on somewhat the same level as *Europa*'s enviable reputation in the German-speaking world. However, the continuing phenomenon of the 20/20 ship has not been confined only to special niche markets such as Germany, South Africa and Japan. It still manages to hold a segment of the mainstream American market.

Not all operators, even in the mass-market sector, want to or even believe that they can fill several thousand berths every week of the year. At the same time, not all passengers want to travel in such huge packs as those aboard, for instance, *Norway* or *Fantasy*. One of the foremost practitioners of this approach in the Caribbean trade emerged from a number of mergers and other business moves as Crown Cruise Line. The origins of this venture can be traced back to the formation of Miami-based Commodore Cruise Lines in 1967. Starting up with chartered tonnage, Commodore became part of the Sally Line and eventually was merged with the EffJohn consortium, while continuing to build their trade and their fleet on second-hand tonnage. These traced their origins to the 1950s-built former Greek Line flagship *Olympia*, and the Moore McCormack twins *Argentina* and *Brasil*, ending up with the

names *Caribe 1*, *Enchanted Isle* and *Enchanted Seas* respectively.

EffJohn's original plans for new tonnage called for a single larger 37,000-ton ship to be booked with Astilleros Espanoles and placed under the Commodore houseflag. Deciding eventually to stay in the same size range of their existing fleet, EffJohn placed orders for two ships of this class with Union Naval de Levante yard in Valencia, for delivery in 1992 and 1993. The builders already had an order in hand for a slightly smaller cruise ship for Grundstad Maritime Overseas-owned Crown Cruise Lines. EffJohn acquired a fifty per cent interest in Crown Cruise Line and entered into an arrangement to operate all three new ships under their own houseflag. In this way the problems of integrating new tonnage into the existing Commodore fleet were avoided entirely.

While the Grundstad-ordered *Crown Monarch* was slightly smaller and differed in some details of her plan from the two EffJohn sisters, named *Crown Jewel* and *Crown Dynasty*, all three ships were of essentially the same class and character.

	Crown Monarch	*Crown Jewel/Dynasty*
Length oa	150.72m	163.81m
Length bp	125.10m	139.83m
Beam	20.60m	22.80m
Draught	5.40m	5.40m
Power output	4 x 3,100.00kW	4 x 3,280.00kW
Service speed	20.0kts	19.5kts
GRT	15,271.0	19,200.0
Passenger capacity	556	916
Crew	210	304

These ships entered service between 1991 and 1993 as something of a throwback to the charm and human scale of passenger and cruise motor-ships built in the 1960s and 1970s. Incorporating, of course, the latest advances in marine engineering, workflow optimisation and service rationalisation, they also retained the abject simplicity and straightforwardness of the traditional horizontal approach in the planning of the public spaces. Like *Astor*, *Fuji Maru* and *Oceanic Grace*, the three *Crowns* were small enough so that the latest safety regulations still accorded them the inherent design simplicity of allowing their lifeboats to be 'topsides' rather then fully nested as in most of the new economy-of-scale ships. Even with the full-beam enclosed lido areas above the lifeboats there was still a strong sense of the more classic style of passenger ship. The lack of hundreds of upper-deck veranda cabins, and in *Crown Monarch* even of an atrium with glass elevators, contributed greatly to their charm and individuality rather than creating any impression of detracting from their acceptability in the mass market.

Crown Jewel and *Crown Monarch* were especially attractive, with their softer and less angular superstructure lines. Long sweeping curves were used in the detailing of the lido area windscreens and in the forward deck openings at either side of the main lounge. The promenade-deck plan was particularly

Crown Dynasty: **The ship visits Vancouver while under charter to Cunard. Contrary to Eric Th. Christiansson's ideas on aesthetics, this ship does have a 'back side' in that the large atrium window aft of the lifeboats is not repeated on the port side, seen here.**

(Captain Jack McCarthy, Vancouver)

well articulated, providing ample space for the various lounge bars, shops and other facilities all surrounded by a wide open promenade completely encircling the ship. The show-lounge plan, which featured a beamwise arrangement of its tiered seating and production stage, was particularly notable in showing that facilities of this type can be accommodated within the space surrounded by the promenade. The widely bowed side walls of this room added architectural interest and diversity to its interior, as well as to the open deck spaces outside. An asymmetrical arrangement of the smaller midships interior spaces and arrangement of a five-deck atrium at the starboard side with a triple-height panoramic window added not only diversity but also a sense of greater spaciousness.

THE YACHTCRUISERS

The concept of the Yachtcruiser class of ship (a name coined by Wärtsilä), in one sense brought the whole idea of cruise shipping full-circle, back to Albert Ballin's original vision of *Prinzessin Victoria Luise* as a luxury cruising yacht. In his 1982 'Increased Productivity for Passenger Ships' paper presented for the Hellenic Institute of Marine Technology, Wärtsilä's Kai Levander identified a 'market gap' for smaller cruise ships complementing the economy-of-scale alternative. As explained:

The cruise market today shows a very evident gap and demand for high-class cruise vessels for 50 to 200 passengers. Some people find the existing bigger cruise liners too crowded or the ports visited uninteresting and spoiled by excessive touristic exploitation. On the other hand, the yachts that can be chartered and taken

to unspoiled islands do not offer the comfort, service and safety that many passengers wish to have. Today there is great interest in both sailing and motor cruise liners for this gap between the big and the small.

Explaining the economic potential from this alternative of scale, his paper went on to point out:

The profitability depends on the economy of scale. For a small vessel this means that it has to be special or attractive in some distinctive way to justify the higher ticket prices. Technical or operational explanations will not be accepted by the passengers. A small ship must offer the 'consumer' something he or she wants and cannot get on a bigger ship.[4]

While Wärtsilä's Yachtcruiser and Windcruiser were in themselves new ideas, various other ideas had already started to materialise in the gap between the 600-passenger *Royal Viking Star* prototype and the smaller privately chartered vessels catering to as many as twenty-five people. A number of shipping Lines had tried smaller ships in the under 10,000-ton category based on the notion of being able to convey a jumbo-jet load of passengers to offshore points from which they would cruise to some of the more exotic and out of the way destinations beyond the reach of most Europe- or America-based circuits. Holland America's 9,000-ton *Prinsendam* and Royal Cruise Line's slightly larger *Golden Odyssey* were both products of the early 1970s with accommodation for about 400 passengers each. This figure coincided more or less with the capacity of the Boeing 747 airliner in the high-density cabin configurations used for charter flights.

Prinsendam was originally intended for cruising in the Indonesian Archipelago, catering to an American clientele who would be flown to and from the ship as part of the

Prinsendam: **Manoeuvring in the care of a tug at Kobe in October 1976, the scale of the ship can be seen as that of a modern cruising yacht. Her lines of form were to be the harbinger of later Holland America developments in their early-1980s economy-of-scale tonnage.**

(Yoshiho Ikeda, Osaka)

whole cruise package. *Golden Odyssey* was likewise planned to offer Mediterranean, European and other more distant itineraries at the far end of overseas flights originating in the United States. Although attractive enough in their own right, neither of these ships offered anything above the standard levels of luxury and service provided in the home-based Caribbean and Alaska trades. Their more exotic ports and the added convenience of the air travel being packaged as part of the cruise were the only factors which placed them in the elite class. However, the ships themselves did not offer any added attraction or distinction to otherwise justify the higher ticket prices. *Prinsendam* ended up serving the more affordably reached summertime Alaska market for a number of years before her loss in 1981, while *Golden Odyssey* ended up likewise largely relegated to seven-day operations directly served by the domestic airline network.

An alternative to the *Prinsendam* and *Golden Odyssey* type of cruise offering had also emerged a few years earlier as the yet smaller 'expedition'-type ships. These were capable of navigating in polar waters and other out-of-the-way and environmentally sensitive areas such as Mauritius, the Easter Islands and the Galapagos. They were extremely rugged vessels built to the highest possible ice-class registry standards and equipped with special rafts and other equipment allowing landings to be made in the complete absence of even the most basic docking facilities.

The first of these to be built was *Lindblad Explorer*, a minuscule vessel of only 2,500 tons delivered by the Finnish yard Nystads Verv AB. She carried about 100 passengers in comfortable, though rather basic, accommodation and had an unrestricted cruising range of more then 6,000 nautical miles. Every conceivable need of modern life was ingeniously packed into her modest dimensions, including a hospital and dispensary, a hairdresser's salon, and a remarkably extensive galley and bakery. She carried a cruise director as well as expert guides and lecturers on the lands to be visited. In addition to the dining room, public facilities included a forward-facing observation lounge and an auditorium, both capable of seating all passengers at the same time, as well as an outdoor swimming pool. A most unusual feature of this and a number of later ships of the same class, was the addition of a small enclosed viewing platform in the main mast.

Certainly these ships offered a truly exceptional cruising and lifestyle experience which more than justified the higher prices which had to be charged. Several other ships of similar design have been either new-built or converted from other vessels since *Lindblad Explorer* made her debut. These included the slightly larger 1974-built polar-class *World Discoverer* and the *Santa Cruz*, built in 1979 exclusively for year-round service in the Galapagos region.

However, despite the success of these remarkable little ships in their own niche market, they did not offer the big-ship amenities and services which Levander envisaged for his Yachtcruiser and Windcruiser designs. For Wärtsilä's purposes, these were too rigidly committed to the 'exploration' aspects

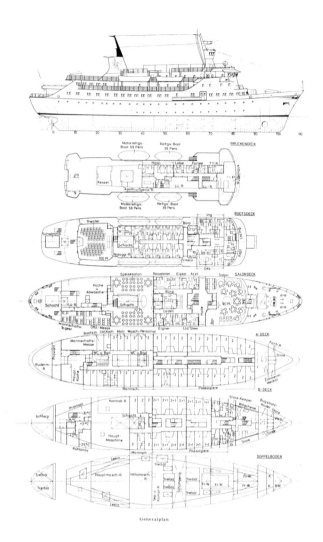

Lindblad Explorer: **General arrangement plans, showing the remarkable completeness of this very small long-range ship's facilities.**

(Schiffahrts-Verlag 'Hansa', Hamburg)

of their cruises, failing to offer their passengers the alternative diversions of deck sports, dancing, shooting craps in a casino or, in other words, having some fun too. In fact, as the Yachtcruiser idea has subsequently materialised and gained popularity, the expedition ship has become a specialised variant of its development.

The inspiration for large modern yacht-type cruise tonnage can, no doubt, be attributed in part at least to the completion of several very large and prestigious state yachts in the early 1980s. The Saudi Arabian royal yacht *Abdul Aziz* and the *Al Mansur*, owned by the government of the Republic of Iraq, and obviously outfitted for official service, were both in reality constructed as scaled-down deep-sea liners. VIP facilities aboard *Abdul Aziz* consisted of a state apartment, with adjacent ladies' suite and accommodation for two children,

Al Mansur: **On sea trials in Finnish waters, she appears in many regards as the prototype of Wärtsilä's Yachtcruiser design, although her large lounge-deck windows denote a horizontal plan, rather than the vertical arrangement of Yachtcruiser.**

(Wärtsilä, Turku)

and twenty-eight double guest cabins. *Al Mansur* offered twin two-room state suites and twelve double guest cabins. Additionally, both ships had numerous other staff and crew cabins for their total complements of about 300 persons each.

With *Al Mansur* having been built by Wärtsilä, it seems likely that her example might have inspired some of the thinking which went into Yachtcruiser the way that *Hohenzollern* had inspired Ballin's plans for *Prinzessin Victoria Luise* more than eighty years earlier. For obvious reasons of security, both of these remarkable ships were built under a heavy veil of secrecy and few, other than those directly involved in their design and building, have had the opportunity to learn anything of their internal layouts, architectural design and outfitting. Those who have seen them from afar at sea will attest to their being two of the most beautiful passenger ships ever built. Their interiors indeed did justice to their outer aesthetics.

At its early conceptual design stages, Wärtsilä's Yachtcruiser showed some similarity to *Al Mansur*, particularly with regard to its two-thirds-aft arrangement of the lifeboats at either side of the funnel which allowed for greater flexibility of plan in the forward part of the ship. The plan also included a similar engine arrangement, consisting of twin geared diesel. However, the accommodation plan differed considerably, in view of the need to emphasise luxury suites for 120 passengers, rather than the maximum of 36 provided for under the certification rules covering yachts such as *Abdul Aziz* and *Al Mansur*. Thus the exterior profile of Yachtcruiser also took on a heavier and more massive proportion, since inside the cabin accommodation would be a far more dominant feature than the public areas. While *Al Mansur*'s public rooms occupied the full length of the superstructure in traditional liner fashion, Yachtcruiser's layout would stress passenger suites in the forward part of the ship, with the communal areas surrounding

the funnel uptake aft and central vertical access cores.

This adaptation of Wärtsilä's original *Finnjet* plan was in fact all but necessary. In Yachtcruiser's 5,000 tons size range, only the uninterrupted stretches of space forward of the funnel casing offered the possibility for a completely standardised luxury cabin layout for the higher numbers of rooms needed. The more traditional layout of small cabins following the *Prinsendam*, *Golden Odyssey* or *Lindblad Explorer* examples would not have been acceptable in this instance. For the Yachtcruiser market nothing short of the full-size *Europa*-style deluxe state room would suffice. Consequently, the relatively narrow beam of less than 15m made a centre-corridor plan necessary. To be wholly effective, this had to be rendered without the added complexity and loss of space inherent in working around engine casings, stairtowers and other working parts of the ship.

Vertical plans of this kind have remained the standard for most developments in the Yachtcruiser field, even in its bigger and later manifestations approaching true liner tonnages. One notable exception in motor Yachtcruiser design were the twin *Lady Diana* and *Lady Sarah*, built by Flender Werft in 1989, where the public rooms were laid out horizontally on the upper deck above the two strata of cabins for each ship's sixty-four passengers. The state rooms were nonetheless forward of the main vertical cores, including a divided engine exhaust uptake straddling the centre passage at its aft-most end. The smaller spaces astern were taken up with such facilities as the entrance lobby, exercise room and saunas. The realisation of Wärtsilä's Windcruiser, as discussed later, also stressed a horizontal layout with public rooms in the superstructure and two levels of cabins on the hull decks below. It made more sense for the public rooms and other spaces which had to be custom built anyway to be worked in around these features. The cabins could thus be either erected from standard wall sections and ready-made bathroom modules or could be completely prefabricated.

The unfortunate consequence of this type of rationale was that the exterior lines of Yachtcruiser took on a much stockier appearance than those of *Abdul Aziz* and *Al Mansur*. Also the regular arrangement of cabin windows on three decks was less attractive than *Al Mansur*'s liner-style riband of large lounge-deck windows ahead of her lifeboat recess. Coincidentally, *Abdul Aziz* was in fact also of a vertical plan, with most of her communal spaces aft, though less noticeably so as she featured open decks surrounding her superstructure and giving a more horizontal look. Nonetheless Yachtcruiser's exterior appearance became the prototype for this class of ship as built in many variations which followed Wärtsilä's own rendering of it into reality as the twin Sea Goddess ships.

These were ordered in May 1982 from Wärtsilä by Norwegian-owned K/S A/S Norsk Cruise, to be operated on one- and two-week cruises by a new Line named Sea Goddess Cruises Ltd, a subsidiary company also based in Oslo. The basic premise of the venture was that there would be a sustained interest in higher-priced cruises for individual passen-

Sea Goddess I: **A later rendering of the design as modified to the owners' requirements, showed an interesting, though ultimately unworkable, adaptation of *Al Mansur*'s lifeboat arrangement.**

(Sea Goddess Cruises, Oslo)

Sea Goddess I: **The interior of the main lounge shows a successful rendition of large-ship contemporary luxury on the considerably smaller scale of the Yachtcruiser genre.**

(Wärtsilä, neg WHT 84-462)

gers and companies based on per-diem fares of $500 per person. With the mass market then sustaining rates from $150–250 a day, these would be among the most expensive cruises available anywhere. Reviving the long-forgotten term 'members', perhaps unknowingly so, for his clientele, Sea Goddess's president Ron Kurtz explained that:

> Guests will be made to feel like members of a private yacht club, and there will be no bar bills and no gratuities.

In a modernised conception of the type of service which ships such as *Prinzessin Victoria Luise* and *Stella Polaris* offered in their day, Sea Goddess's passengers would enjoy the informal ambience, including the free run of virtually the whole ship, and personal service of these great classic cruise yachts. Advancing to the modern lifestyle conveniences beyond the days of these early yachts, Narstad's passengers would also enjoy fully stocked mini-bars and video cassette players in their own accommodation, along with free round-the-clock room service. When making their bookings, 'members' would indicate their favourite types and brands of liquor and their preferences for either single or double beds so that the cabins could be made up accordingly with the bar units custom stocked.

The cruises themselves were to stress island hopping with daily calls at one or more locations. These were to be the smaller and more exclusive resorts, beaches and other locations which the larger cruise ships could not reach. They were to be directed towards the more active type of clientele who might already be members of yacht clubs and who would be most likely to enjoy activities such as swimming, windsurfing, snorkelling and scuba diving. The idea was that they would be given ample opportunity to pursue such activities at the resorts the ships would visit. Additionally, each Yachtcruiser

would have its own watersports platform and equipment. Since these ships could get much closer to the shoreline, and could do so away from commercial harbours, these activities could be enjoyed directly from aboard, as, for instance Aristotle Onassis might have taken his morning swim from his own yacht *Christiana*.

These pleasures would be rounded out to include the big-ship cruising experiences of *haute cuisine* dining, live entertainment and casino gaming. The main dining room and lounge would each have sufficient seating capacity for all aboard. Meal service was planned on an open-seating basis, with members not being limited to specific meal times or table assignments. In addition to a day lounge, piano bar, casino and library, a compact gymnasium with adjoining sauna and massage room would complete the full range of cruise-ship facilities to be expected in the luxury market.

Travel agents were instructed to be selective as to the type of people to whom they should sell Sea Goddess cruises. Members were to be affluent and active people who would be most likely to mix well in the more intimate environment of a yachtcruiser-type experience – no couch potatoes, please, and definitely only gentlemen not possessing dinner jackets, thank you. The reality of selling these cruises eventually boiled down to accepting just about anyone holding a valid credit card with a sufficiently high credit limit.

The ships themselves, unimaginatively named *Sea Goddess I* and *Sea Goddess II*, were each of 4,253 tons, with sixty-one suite-style cabins accommodating a total of 121 passengers and a crew complement of 71 persons. Although considerably smaller than the 7,359-ton *Al Mansur*, the well-articulated *Sea Goddess* plan appeared remarkably spacious. The public spaces were in reality only two-thirds aft, being for the most part arranged between the funnel uptake and the forward accommodation block. The principal passenger and service stairways were offset to the port side, with the space opposite being taken up with the entrance lobby, purser's office, shops and other smaller facilities such as the library and hospital. The dining room, main lounge and day lounge with its adjoining bar and casino were farther aft in a full-beam space between the stairs and the funnel casing on the three members' accommodation decks.

The open lido deck with its swimming pool and access to the watersports platform were the only passenger facilities aft of the funnel, with primary access being by way of a stretch of open deck starboard side only, bypassing the main lounge. Other deck areas included an open space ahead of the gymnasium, itself incorporated into the base of the funnel as a gazebo-like enclosure accessible from the outside only. Wärtsilä even managed to uphold its standard of providing a walk-around open promenade at this level, with the unusual feature of its forward end looping around the front of the navigating bridge. An open sports deck was also to be found atop the superstructure.

Sea Goddess I went into service in May 1984, first making a series of summer Mediterranean cruises followed by a transatlantic positioning cruise, before taking up a full-time programme of seven-day eastern Caribbean circuits. The delivery of *Sea Goddess II* followed a year later without any significant change of plan or outfitting. In fact the introduction of these two ships engendered a spate of further interest in smaller high-luxury ships ordered from a number of other European yards.

Among those most like the original *Sea Goddesses* were a fleet of eight Renaissance Cruises ships, serially named *Renaissance I* to *Renaissance VIII*. These originated with an Italian design by Dr Adolpho Nertollotti for Yachtcruiser-type vessels inspired by Adnan Kashoggi's private yacht *Nabila*. With backing from three groups of investors, including Fearnley and Eger, proposals were made to the Italian government for their backing on a similar basis to that behind the Sitmar and Costa newbuilding programmes. The subsidy was

Oceanic Grace: **Representing Japan's interpretation of the yacht cruising idea, she presents an attractive modernistic flare all of her own.**

approved for eight ships, four to be built by Cantiere Navale Ferrari in Albiano Magra and four by Nuovi Cantieri Aquania in Marina de Carrara. Following the financial failure of the original conglomerate entity Yachtship Cruise Line, the venture was restructured and operated by Fearnley and Eger, appropriately under the new name Renaissance.

With internal layouts very similar to the *Sea Goddesses*, the Renaissance ships differed in the arrangement of their funnel casings. Located farther forward than those of the Wärtsilä-built ships, these were offset to the starboard side of the centreline so as to allow an L-shaped arrangement of the public room layout. In addition to overcoming the difficulty of being left with unworkably small spaces to either side of a centre casing in a plan of this scale, the offset also allowed the centre access plan of the cabin area to be continued through the communal areas. These ships also featured open decks surrounding the superstructure accommodation in a manner

Sea Goddess I: **The completed ship, looking remarkably like the original design concept.**

(Wärtsilä, neg WHT 84–538 V)

similar to *Abdul Aziz*, giving their outward appearance a more horizontal expression of line and form.

Also noteworthy was the single Japanese Yachtcruiser *Oceanic Grace*, delivered to Showa Line in 1989 from NKK Corporation's Tsu works. Although generally similar to *Sea Goddess* in design concept and outfitting, this ship was first to introduce a choice of cabin types in her class. The original idea of the Wärtsilä Yachtcruiser was that all accommodation would be of exactly the same standard, supporting the notion of cruise members being of equal standing in their enjoyment of so unique and luxurious a cruise. *Oceanic Grace*'s four cabin categories included an owner's suite with private veranda, eight additional deluxe state rooms with verandas, with the remainder being made up of standard accommodation without private deck space and one cabin equipped for handicapped travellers. Although of similar length to *Sea Goddess*, *Oceanic Grace* had the benefit of an additional 0.8m of beam which contributed remarkably to her sense of spaciousness aboard. Also noteworthy was the modern angular styling of the Japanese ship exterior, which, along with her *Renaissance*-style side-by-side funnels, gave her a rather high-tech appearance.

In Yachtcruiser-type tonnage as in the larger economy-of-scale domain, sizes inevitably increase as competing interests try to find bigger and better ways of doing things. Indeed, by the time the first *Renaissance* ships were being commissioned Yachtcruisers began to eclipse *Al Mansur*'s size. The first of these were the *Seabourn Pride* and *Seabourn Spirit* built in Germany by Schichau Seebeckwerft AG for Norwegian industrialist Atle Brunstad's Seabourn Cruise Line.

	Al Mansur	Sea Goddess	Seabourn Pride
Length oa	121.00m	105.00m	133.80m
Length bp	96.50m	93.00m	112.40m
Beam moulded	17.50m	14.60m	19.00m
Draught	5.51m	4.30m	5.00m
Service speed	20.00kts	17.50kts	19.30kts
Maximum power	8,822.00kW	3,540.00kW	7,280.00kW
GRT	7,359.0	4,253.0	9,975.0
Passengers	300★	120	212
Crew	n/a	71	112

★Total complement

At about twice the size of *Sea Goddess I* and *II*, *Seabourn Pride* and *Seabourn Spirit* were large enough to contain the necessary accommodation and services within the more sleek-lined and less angular-looking enclosure which had characterised the *Al Mansur* and *Abdul Aziz* image. Continuous stretches of bonded-in reflective glass were used in the superstructure forward of the lifeboats to create a riband effect which would convey the long horizontal expression of *Abdul Aziz*'s open decks surrounding her state and guest accommodation. The semi-circular superstructure front was also given the same deeply raked profile as that of the Arabian yacht, thanks to her added size which could sustain such extravagance of form. Also noteworthy was the recessed lifeboat arrangement, following *Al Mansur*'s example. In ships of this class the main reason for nested boats was to increase the amount of topsides deck space available for passenger recreation. While some early renderings of the Wärtsilä Yachtcruiser *Sea Goddess I* showed a similar approach, it was not carried through.

Seabourn Pride came closer than other Yachtcruisers in

Seabourn Spirit: Seen underway in German territorial waters, the ship illustrates the Yachtcruiser genre's progression to a large enough scale to permit a refinement even of *Al Mansur* or *Abdul Aziz*'s sleekness of line.

(p. a. kroehert, Bremerhaven, neg 89161-29; courtesy of Schichau Seebeckwerft AG)

Seabourn Spirit: Standard accommodation looking from the sitting room and picture window towards the sleeping area, where the bathroom and walk-in closet are visible. The suite's entrance is to the right of the open closet door beyond the writing table.

(Author)

World Discoverer: **The proportions of this ship were ideally suited to rare cruises of the Great lakes, where she is seen in transit of the Welland Canal in August 1975.**

(Gordon Turner, Toronto)

Seabourn Spirit; **The observation lounge, its restrained nautical theme featuring a globe, as seen in the foreground, and the electronic display board in the rear to the right of the room's entrance.**

(Author)

combining the ambience of an exclusive yacht-club lifestyle with a truly large-ship sense of luxury, spaciousness and diversity throughout her accommodation. For the first time, a cruise-liner style show lounge was featured with terraced seating and a wide multi-function stage. Other large-scale features included a four-deck atrium with double curved staircases, a forward-facing observation lounge atop the bridge and a liner-style dining room on the bulkhead deck beneath the passenger cabin block. While most of the upper-decks public rooms were at least partially enclosed by the curvilinear lines of the superstructure, giving a sense of Yachtcruiser scale to the ship, her dining room in the hull's midbody was far more reminiscent of a deep-sea liner.

Cabin accommodation aboard *Seabourn Pride*, which generally followed *Europa*'s mini-suite plan with separate sleeping and sitting areas, was among the most luxurious and best out-fitted accommodation to be found on any modern cruise ship, regardless of tonnage and capacity. With a floor area of 26sq m, these exceeded the 21sq m size of *Europa*'s standard rooms and were the match of premium-grade accommodation aboard much larger new ships such as *Royal Viking Sun*. Arranged either side of a single central corridor on each of the three cabin decks, the rooms were a revival of the 1966 *Kungsholm* plan, with their entrances being at the ends of short beamwise corridors bypassing the line of passage-adjacent bathrooms and walk-in wardrobes. One thus entered directly into the spacious rectangular volume of the room proper, which was divided equally between its daytime and nocturnal functions. In a reversal of the *Sea Goddess* cabin plan, the sleeping area was innermost, adjacent to the bathroom and wardrobes, while the outer half was furnished as a sitting room in front of an enormous 1.5m-wide picture window.

The interior finishing of the cabins was carried out by the German firm Oldenburger Möbelwerkstätten GmbH, a workshop specialising in high-quality handcrafted furnishings

and fittings. A distinctly shipboard ambience of quiet under-stated elegance and luxury was achieved with top-quality materials, superb craftsmanship and a strong passion for detail. The furniture and related fittings were finished in oak, with marble inlays used for the working surfaces such as the vanity unit surfaces and table tops. Vertical strips of mirrored glass were set into the corner pilasters of the rooms to give an illusion of even greater spaciousness. Other elements such as soft furnishings, artwork and lighting were all carefully integrated into the complete design scheme to enhance overall appearance and comfort. The lighting scheme in particular was perfected to make the accommodation look as attractive after dark as in daylight.[5] The mini-bar, television set and video cassette player were housed inside the cupboards, so that their presence could be concealed when not being used. Another thoughtful feature was the adjustable-height coffee table, which could be raised to serve as a dining or writing table.

Seabourn introduced a number of remarkable shipboard technical features for the enjoyment of their passengers. The larger size of these Yachtcruisers made them suitable for worldwide service, with rolling schedules allowing passengers to combine consecutive seven- or fourteen-day cruises into longer voyages of up to sixty days. Consequently the owners sought to offer a greater variety of diversions. Sensing that Yachtcruiser passengers would be likely to have some of the same scientific interests as those accustomed to the expedition-type experience offered by *Lindblad Explorer* and *World Discoverer*, an observatory pod was installed above the top deck. Passengers could climb into its eight adjustable seats, each with its own viewing port, binoculars and celestial charts were provided to learn of the visible areas surrounding their ship's position at any location about the globe. These facilities turned out to be most effective only while in port, when the ship was stationary.

The bright and spacious forward observation lounge, with

its ample seating and bar, was also furnished with a console housing an auxiliary set of bridge navigating instruments including a radar monitor for passengers to follow the ship's progress. A custom-designed computerised wall map display was also fitted, showing the ship's actual position and voyage track, ports of call with arrival and departure times and information about future voyage itineraries. The display information could be controlled by passengers, by the use of a built-in push-button keypad.

The Nautilus Room at the bottom of a downward extension of the atrium staircases was designed and equipped as an underwater viewing station. Up to sixteen passengers could be seated surrounding a wide porthole in the bottom of the hull to view the seabed and marine life beneath the ship. Powerful spotlights incorporated into the viewing port's perimeter were focused to illuminate the seascape below and to attract fish and other creatures into view. A television camera also served to broadcast these scenes via the closed-circuit cabin television system.

The most spectacular of *Seabourn Pride*'s facilities was the self-stowing marina and watersports outfit carried in the stern of the hull. This consisted of a retractable floating swimming pool assembly with fold-up side platforms for watersports and tender embarkation extending about 10m aft from the stern when in use. The bottom-hinged stern door, in effect a small-scale adaptation of the linkspan ramps of a ro/ro ferry or cargo ship, formed the threshold area of the marina when lowered to its open position. A telescopic centreline rail with a moveable trolley was fitted to deploy this entire structure, along with two covered tenders from what was in effect a boathouse inside the ship. Shell doors in the stern quarters provided folding landing stages to port and starboard for water-skiing and windsurfing. The equipment itself was stowed in the areas to either side of the marina and tenders when underway.

Seabourn Pride and *Seabourn Spirit* set a standard of their own in the Yachtcruiser, or perhaps more appropriately stated, mega yacht category. Not only did their larger size accord them a more aesthetically pleasing appearance, and a far greater cruising range, but also allowed them to offer special features such as the observatory and watersports facilities which would make travelling aboard these ships a unique experience. Seabourn, however, did not exercise their option with Schichau Seebeckwerft for a third ship. It was in effect taken up by Royal Viking Line, who wanted to diversify their offerings to include also the ultra-deluxe mega yacht experience for their clientele. Named *Royal Viking Queen*, she was of near identical design, although lacking some of Seabourn's more exotic features such as the observatory, Nautilus Room and the double washbasins fitted in the cabin bathrooms.

Two other ships which were planned, although unfortunately not built, were to have been operated by a revitalised Swedish American Cruises through Minneapolis-based Radisson Group. Orders placed with *Renaissance*'s builders, Cantiere Navale Ferrari, were cancelled before construction

Silver Cloud: **The Show Lounge represented a masterful adaptation of the Carnival-style double-deck facility to the scale of a large Yachtcruiser.**

(Silversea Cruises, Miami)

work had commenced. At about the same size as the Seabourn ships, these were to have featured an unusual accommodation layout. The 116 suites in each ship would have featured entirely separate and enclosed bedrooms, in addition to the spacious bathroom, dayroom and entrance hall. The plan, which placed the bathroom between the dayroom and bedroom, made extremely good use of the greater depth of these suites inboard from the ship's sides. It would have brought to the cruise ship for perhaps the first time a real sense, not just of a hotel room, but rather of an ocean-going adaptation of the modern urban apartment or condominium.

Considering the 21.1m beam of these ships, this type of layout offered new possibilities of being adaptable to larger luxury tonnage as a simplified *Stockholm*-type centre corridor plan. With the addition perhaps of verandas at the higher levels, the idea could have worked well for such newbuildings as these in the 50,000-ton range then being planned for Costa, Holland America and P&O.

Inevitably, the mega yacht has progressed to still larger sizes to the point of approaching the 20/20 liner ideal. Monte Carlo-based V-Ships, who had sold their Sitmar operation to P&O in 1988, re-entered the cruise business with two ultra-deluxe ships based essentially on the *Seabourn Pride* plan. Planned at 13,000 tons, these offered accommodation for 317 passengers in 157 suites, of which all but those on the lowest deck were to have private balconies. The overall dimensions of 155.8m in length and a 23.4m beam qualified the ships for a double-height show lounge, which was difficult to render within their scale without looking contrived. These conveyed a great sense of spaciousness throughout, as was especially evident in such areas as the cabin passageways, deck lobbies, vestibules and other circulation areas.

Named *Silver Wind* and *Silver Cloud* these measured 15,000 tons as completed. One cannot help but wonder if in reality they do not really belong to the big ship league, although on a very exclusive platform of their own. Certainly the two following ships of 23,000 tons each ordered at the beginning of 1995 do bring this class of sophisticated modern *grande luxe* cruising up to the deep-sea liner size category.

The collapsible marina outfit of the Seabourn ships was not repeated, with the watersports equipment instead being brought ashore for use from the beaches at which the ship would anchor. In the early design stages a self-stowing river-boat-type bow gangway of the type used in many American coastal and river cruise boats had been planned for landings of this type. However, the idea was dropped, no doubt on account of the ship's greater size.

Two other ships in this overall category, notable for their special combination of the Yachtcruiser idea and the expedition prototypes, were *Society Adventurer* and *Frontier Spirit*, both completed in the early 1990s. While generally following the Yachtcruiser design formula, these were also given 'ice-class 1A Super' strengthened hulls for navigation in polar regions and exceptionally high environmental protection devices enabling them to venture into ecologically sensitive areas such as the Easter Islands and the Galapagos. Instead of the windsurfing and water skiing facilities of their tropical counterparts, these ships were equipped with Zodiac-type excursion craft needed to make expeditions ashore to uninhabited areas both in tropical latitudes and the polar seas.

The forward-facing observation lounges on both ships were fitted with terraced seating for all passengers aboard, and equipped with audio/visual facilities for the extensive destination lectures which are an important aspect of expedition cruising. Another notable aspect of *Society Adventurer* was her long operational range of 8,500 nautical miles. This was supported by large stores capacities along with sewage and refuse containments capable of holding an accumulation of waste for up to twenty-five days.

THE WINDCRUISERS

Of the product line developed by Wärtsilä's passenger ship research and development department, Windcruiser was a personal favourite of Kai Levander's. He even modified his own sailboat to create a scaled-down working model of the concept. As a sailor and yachtsman himself, he had a profound understanding of sail and a passion for its use in cruising. As a naval architect of remarkable perception of both the technical and business sides of actually rendering such a ship into reality, he saw it as a means of attracting new passengers to modern and comfortable cruise ships. The thrust of his Windcruiser design was market driven to appeal to the travelling public at large, rather than merely to nostalgic romantics or sailing aficionados. Nor was it offered on the primary basis of being more environ-

mentally friendly or less expensive to fuel than Yachtcruiser or other ships with engines.

Fuel still had to be considered in the cost of operating Windcruiser, as she was to be both wind and machinery powered, with neither option being auxiliary to the other. Thus the ship would offer the flexibility to run a precise seven-day schedule without time being lost to being 'becalmed' with a lack of wind. A fairly substantial power-generating capacity was also needed to sustain services such as light, air conditioning, cooking and refrigeration, sanitation and sewage handling and a fully automated sailing rig. Without this automation the sailing crew would need to increase which was not an option in the operational costs.

The prospects of actually building Windcruiser began to solidify in 1984, when Karl Gösta Andern, Åland-born owner of New York's Circle Line, approached Wärtsilä in Helsinki with his own ideas for a modern sailing-ship cruise operation. What Andern wanted, however, was a larger ship, with more sail area and the addition of a few traditional touches such as a sheered foredeck and a bowsprit. As the custom design work for these features was to be done at Andern's expense, he reserved the right to seek tenders from other yards for building his windship. Unfortunately for both Levander and Wärtsilä, the owner was able to secure a better price and financing terms from the small specialist French yard Société Nouvelle des Ateliers et Chantiers du Havre (ACH) near the French port of Le Havre.

Further refinements were made to the Wärtsilä design, for which they also received a royalty fee in addition to payment for the work done for Andern, which included widening of the hull to improve stability and the addition of fin stabilisers into a space created at the middle of the bilge keels. Meanwhile Andern's venture had incorporated itself as Windstar Cruises and had hired as the Line's president Jean-Claude Potier, former US manager for French Line, and later chief executive officer of Sun Line.

French-born Potier's vision of cruising was one of luxury, cast in a new mould rather than ossifying in the past glories of the liner era, even in its most modern manifestations such as *France* and *QE2*. His belief was that there was no premise for Caribbean cruises to be rooted in liner traditions and staged aboard converted deep-sea tonnage. He believed that even the larger purpose-built cruise ships of the 1970s and early 1980s were too heavily committed to traditional notions of liner design with their hotel and resort interior décor, and their dogged adherence to such liner institutions as captain's cocktail parties, theme nights with singing waiters in the dining rooms and bingo. He wanted a more genuinely maritime milieu with a naturally leisurely lifestyle topsides in the public spaces and a unique sense of place in the cabins below. Rather than having the mainly closed-in feel of the converted liners and economy-of-scale cruise ships, *Wind Star*, as the first ship would be named, was to be 'Open to the sea, the wind and the sky.'[6] It was against this background that Potier chose a fellow Frenchman, the Parisian architect and industrial designer Marc Held, to do the interior design.

Although Held had no earlier experience with passenger-ship design, like Le Corbusier and many others in his profession, he had a professed life-long fascination with ships and their workings. His sensitivity to the special considerations of ship-design work were expressed in a collection of letters exchanged with the noted American biologist and writer Gerald Weissmann and published in his own book, *Lettres à Gerry*:

If the hulls are gentle to the sea, the belly of a boat must be soft to the touch of man's fragile skin. Whether at rest, or in rolls, or in surf, every bump becomes an aggression. The angles and edges round off into the form of a palm. The pulleys, the rails, the bars become moulded like all floating wood. An aesthetic of gentleness, of overcoming wear and tear is born of these arrangements, and evokes an unconscious sensitivity. The disappearance, perhaps temporarily of the sailing merchant marine has not really interrupted the tradition. Metal boats, propulsed by powerful motors, haven't dominated the sea. They have had to continue to 'court' her so as not to lose themselves.

In his conclusion to this letter, entitled '*Bateaux*' ('boats', which in French is more liberally used to include ships in preference to the terms *paquebot* or *navire*) Held expressed an optimistic view of better things to come in cruise ship design:

An unexpected renaissance has come, from the old country that France is. At first hidden in remodelled garages, far from the technocrats, the speculators and the philosophers, the sea-lovers have taken up the torch with the means available to them. Here, there is invention in every sense. Faithful to the spirit of the old days but not inhibited by it. Bright young men with strong arms reinvent the art of sailboating. A fine example of our world of architecture, stifled by speculation, facility, dogmatism and consolidation. It is, indeed, a question of giving all their importance to the plurality of experience, to invention. It is within a solid anchorage in the traditions of know-how, of quality, of clarity and of sensuality that these bases of a renewal are to be found. Attitudes that are innovative, but still not merely entranced with novelty, these are what we need to enrich the heritage that has been bequeathed us. Civilization's works see the light in a spirit of courage, humanity, respect for men and for the environment.[7]

In the hands of her creators, particularly Potier and Held, who shared the common bond of their French nationality, language and culture, *Wind Star* had progressed from the more basic type of craft first visualised by Kai Levander to a larger and more luxurious vessel more akin to the standards of *Sea Goddess*. She had progressed to the class of being a fully fledged *grande luxe* Yachtcruiser endowed with the added attraction of being a modern sailing ship.

Wind Star was completed and handed over to her owners in late 1986. She was the first of three near-identical ships, with *Wind Song* and *Wind Spirit* following in 1987 and 1988 respectively. The option for a fourth ship was not taken up. With an overall length of 134m, *Wind Star* emerged as the

Wind Star: An early rendering by Yannick Manier, shows the vessel's openness to the seas and skies. Ironically, various elements of styling added later would ultimately give a more closed-in impression.

(Windstar Sail Cruises, Miami)

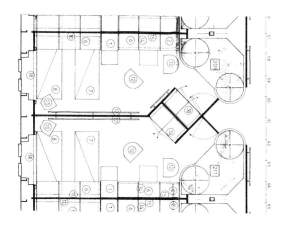

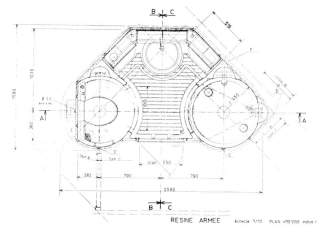

RESINE ARMEE   échelle 1/10   PLAN n°B.1356 indice C

Wind Star: **Plans of the cabin interior in which the angled entrance arrangement offers a welcome variation of the absolutely rectangular plan of most ships' cabins.**

(ACH, France)

longest sailing ship ever built. Her hull dimensions compared with a length of only 85.3m for *Cutty Sark* and 114.45m for the Soviet school ship *Kruzenstern*, the world's largest modern-day tall ship. In the cruising field, *Sea Cloud* (originally *Hussar*, a private yacht) came closest at a measure of 2,323 tons and a length of 96.3m.

Wind Star's sailing outfit was designed around a four-masted jib rig, using four main jib sails, a flying jib and a mizzen sail or spanker as it is sometimes called. The sails were constructed of a lightweight and strong Dacron polyester sail-cloth especially selected for the Windstar ships. The six triangular sails of each ship amounted to a total area of 1,997.35sq m, slightly under two-thirds that of the twenty-nine sails comprising *Sea Cloud*'s barque rig. The rig was designed to be operated directly from the bridge and were under computerised control.

This was accomplished by way of roller-furling the sails around their forestays. The hydraulic control equipment was mounted on horizontal sail booms pivoted beneath the

forestays and capable of being swung to either side of the ship from their opposite ends. These functioned so that the shallow-draught hull, which was designed without a deep sailing-boat type of keel, would not slide away from the wind. Complete furling or sheeting (rolling up and unrolling) of all sails could be accomplished in as little as two minutes. The control system was designed to keep the heeling of the ship to a maximum of eight degrees from vertical. This had been determined as the psychological point beyond which passengers would feel uncomfortable and disoriented. Arguably this gave *Wind Star* a rather unusual vertical stance for a sailing yacht, perhaps taking something away from the real experience of sailing aboard a traditional ship such as *Sea Cloud*. However, *Wind Star* was intended from the outset to offer more of a modern *grande luxe* experience than of a true return to traditional sailing-yacht living.

Control was by way of a Hewlett-Packard computer using software specially written for Windstar by the shipyard. The system provided for either direct control from the bridge or operation of the sails in conjunction with the engines. Environmental factors such as wind direction and speed also served to regulate the sails to maintain the selected course and speed. Also, the computer system controlled the stabiliser fins and anti-heeling tanks to maintain the angle of heel under sail within the limits.

At a modest 12kts, *Wind Star*'s maximum cruising speed under sail in ideal wind and sea conditions was in fact more than adequate for her style of operation. Her itinerary had been planned to stress the pleasures of 'cruising before the mast' on a leisurely island-hopping circuit. She was intended to operate under sail alone for most of her sea time. Requiring service speeds which were often of well below 10kts, her schedules could be easily maintained with sufficient reserve speed if needed.

Alternative diesel-electric propulsion was provided by a single 1400kW Jeumont Schneider motor, yielding a maximum speed of 12kts. The added manoeuvrability needed for docking was derived from a 350kW bow thruster. Both of these devices were driven from the ship's diesel power station powered by three Normed-Wärtsilä generator sets, which also satisfied her domestic power requirements. With the flexibility accorded by a diesel-electric power link to the propellers, the generator sets could be sited forward, allowing for a reversal of the usual Yachtcruiser accommodation layout with cabins forward and public rooms aft. A tall white winged funnel was incorporated into the main mast located behind the navigating bridge.

The passenger accommodation could thus follow a more traditional horizontal layout with cabins below decks and public spaces above in the superstructure. A vertical division was retained, in this instance segregating the passenger areas to the midships and aft areas of *Wind Star* and the crew living quarters and the service areas to the forward-most third of the hull's length. At the principal public level, this resulted in a *QE2*-like plan with the galley forward of the main

Wind Star: **The remarkably liveable cabin corridor offered elegant Wagon Lits touches, such as the protective metal trim and corner bumpers, and the added luxury of the artwork.**

dining room. Its location also coincided with the position of engine uptakes, allowing them to also carry waste gases and steam aloft via the main mast.

The décor of the passengers' quarters lived up entirely to everything that Marc Held professed to stand for in maintaining a uniquely environmentally hospitable and appropriately sensual expression of modern shipboard design within the context of his perception of a renaissance in sail-ship design. The seventy-five passenger state rooms were outstanding for the manner in which they conveyed the look and feel of a fine yacht rather than of nondescript rectangular economy-of-scale cabins with square windows. The portholes, the handrails, the rich burled maple cabinetry and wall panelling were absolutely ship-shape. The addition of overhead storage compartments into the vanity and entertainment fitments and above the heads of the beds was reminiscent of traditional yacht outfitting.

The rooms were of a smaller size than those of *Sea Goddess*. Full advantage was taken of their reduced scale to equal the functionality and liveability of other Yachtcruiser cabins, and to heighten the sense of compactness and versatility of a truly well-devised ship's plan. On the other hand, the large queen-sized beds (separable as twin beds if desired), televi-

sions with video players, mini-bars and international satellite telephones were there to pander to even the most discriminating urban cruise passenger. Potier had insisted on the telephones, arguing that anyone paying $300 per day for a cruise in the late 1980s would insist on one.[8]

The cabins were arranged either side of a central passageway along the passenger area of the two lower passenger decks. The entrance to each was set at an angle to provide an added measure of privacy and a sense of spaciousness. This was achieved thanks to a clever arrangement of the cabin bathroom units and the wardrobes. The arrangement also made a welcome change from the perfectly rectangular shape of most modern cruise ships. The bathroom modules, which were essentially triangular in plan, allowed for the angled wall at the cabin's inner end to be curved around them to form an extremely attractive panelled entry to the cabin proper. Even the central corridor itself was refreshingly elegant. The curvilinear recesses at the entrances to each pair of cabins with their dark polished wood panelling added a sense of texture and depth to the passage. A carefully chosen selection of attractive framed prints showing old sailing ships adorned the lighter intervening expanses of wall, giving this all-too-often utterly utilitarian circulation space something of the richness of a wagon-lit sleeping coach from the Orient Express.

The cabins were complemented by an elegant suite of public rooms on the upper two decks. These comprised a restaurant and main lounge, each capable of accommodating all 150 passengers. In addition to the main lounge aft, there were a number of smaller rooms including a pool bar, veranda, entrance foyer, library and casino. Elsewhere on the ship there was a gymnasium, sauna and the watersports platform of the type featured aboard *Sea Goddess*.

The ceiling and walls of the restaurant were panelled in stained pine, giving this essentially modern and functional room a touch of sailing-ship tradition. As the word 'restaurant' implies, traditional seat assignment and regimentation of meal times were dispensed with in favour of an 'open' seating arrangement available over extended meal periods.

The main lounge was lighter and brighter in character. It was one of those shipboard rooms which brings the inside and outside worlds together. In addition to the vistas provided by the large windows flanking this room, there was a view of the billowing sails above through a large central skylight. The skylight and its effect on the room's natural lighting lent a traditional touch, somewhat reminiscent of the charm of Edwardian passenger-ship interiors.

The slightly smaller veranda, one deck higher, was similar in character. However, here the glazed walls on three sides of the room were retractable, giving unrestricted access to the open deck. This room was equipped for daytime meal service, while at night it was to serve as the ship's discotheque. Of the other smaller rooms, the tiny casino with its two gaming tables and dozen or so slot machines was particularly attractive. The walls and ceiling were covered with fabric reflecting the pattern of the gaming tables. Perhaps one of *Wind Star*'s

Wind Star: A view of the casino, which was a surprisingly charming space in the small scale demanded by the ship's passenger count.

(Author)

most remarkable interiors was her circular entrance lobby, which featured a shallow ceiling rotunda, painted to represent the night sky and illuminated by tiny bulbs arranged to represent stars. This seemed most appropriate for a sailing yacht where the passenger becomes more accustomed to looking up to the skies, the sails and at night the heavenly bodies.

	Sea Cloud	*Wind Star*	*Club Med 1*
Length oa	96.31m	134.00m	187.20m
Length bp	?	110.00m	162.00m
Beam moulded	14.93m	15.80m	20.00m
Draught	5.03m	3.90m	5.00m
Service speed	15.00kts	12.00kts	14.30kts
No of sales	29	6	7
Sail area	3,158.00sq m	1,997.35sq m	2,500.00sq m
Auxiliary propulsion	4,473.60kW	1,400.00kW	3,080.00kW
GRT	2,323.0	5,307.0	14,475.0
Passengers	80	150	425
Crew	65	75	183

The design success of these ships has since resulted in two larger versions of their type being built by ACH for Club Méditeranée. These were more than double the size of the Windstar ships, having, apart from the inevitable increases of length and beam, an extra superstructure deck along with an additional mast and sail. The rig, alternative propulsion system and overall layout were otherwise generally similar to that of the earlier ACH-built sailing ships.

The accommodation of the Club Med ships was in fact more basic, in line with Club Med's shoreside resorts, bringing the idea of Windcruiser back to its original conception in Kai Levander's mind of being perhaps closer to Windjammer Barefoot Cruises-style adventure for a younger clientele.

Wind Star: The ship's entrance lobby, featured a distinctive celestial ceiling dome and the un-embellished nautical touches of portholed doors and metal handrails.

(Author)

Although each cabin had its own washroom with shower and washbasin, a single toilet cubicle was shared between each pair of rooms. The extent of public facilities was more extensive, with a full-beam main lounge amidships and the dining room repositioned forward with a view ahead over the bow.

OTHER DEVELOPMENTS

There have been countless other adaptations of smaller liner-style designs, Yachtcruiser and Windcruiser variations and even modern replications of more traditional sailing ships. Not to be overlooked among these was the SWATH, which apart from other proponents of catamarans was most avidly promoted by Wärtsilä. The Finnish builders offered various configurations ranging from high-speed car ferries through handy Yachtcruiser-sized variants up to a 2,000-passenger behemoth with an immense triple-height dinner theatre in its midbody. Only one prototype of SWATH has been realised so far for cruise service. Delivered to Diamond Cruise Oy of Helsinki in 1992 from the Finnyards Rauma facility in their adaptation of the idea as *Radisson Diamond*, the 20,300-ton ship went into Caribbean service under management of the Minneapolis-based Radisson Hotels.

Radisson Diamond offered Yachtcruiser luxury to 354 passengers berthed in exclusively outside cabins, the majority of which included private verandas. The cabins were arranged at either side of the ship above her two hulls, with the public spaces and services occupying the centre part of the 32.03m-beam ship's superstructure. The most outstanding of these was a six-deck-high central atrium, encompassing the main entrance lobby and various other smaller spaces. Forward and aft of this on decks 8 and 9 were the double-height main lounge and dining room, with outstanding views both fore and aft. The beam, which was about the same as that of *QE2*, provided also for a well-articulated layout of informal public spaces, recreation and sports areas and open decks above. With the deckhouses at these upper levels generally confined to the width of the central public areas on the accommodation decks below, unusually wide open deck areas, with the proportions of Orient Line's liners of the 1960s, were made available for passenger enjoyment.

One of the ship's most outstanding technical features was a watersports platform stowed aft on deck 6, and fitted with hydraulic gear for lowering it down to water level between the two hulls. Access to this in its lowered position was by way of an elevator and stairway descending to deck 4, where a shell door was fitted in the inner side of the starboard hull. This location of the watersports centre also no doubt had the effect of thwarting attempts by daredevil boaters with water skiers in tow from speeding between the hulls as though through a tunnel.

Development of these various smaller ship types has been difficult as their owners have found that no matter how exclusive their offerings might be, they were still handicapped by not having the bulk purchasing powers, national and global marketing and reservations infrastructures and the airline support of the major league players such as Carnival, RCCL, and Klosters. Indeed the lack of air-sea packages was a problem for operations such as Sea Goddess, Windstar and Seabourn. The final solutions for these Lines were through their absorption into Cunard, Holland America and Carnival respectively. These enabled the larger Lines to expand their offerings into this elite market niche by way of their existing business and operations infrastructures. For Renaissance, not without their own troubles, the solution seems to have been found in building up a larger fleet themselves, while the owners of *Silver Wind/Cloud* opted for larger ships, and thus a greater economy-of-scale in its own right.

Radisson Diamond: **This model of the ship shows the arrangement of decks and of the water-sports platform made possible by her catamaran hull configuration**

(Rauma yard Oy, Rauma)

1   George Young, *South Africa on World Sea Lanes*, pp 93-4.
2   Stephen Payne, *The Naval Architect*, January 1987, p E19.
3   *Sea-Japan*, No 208, Feb-Mar 1988, p 2.
4   Kai Levander, 'Increased Profitability for Passenger Ships', 1982, p 11.
5   'Seabourn Pride', *Hansa*, No 3/4, 1989, p 184.
6   Joseph Novitski, *Wind Star*, pp 112-13.
7   Marc Held, *Lettres à Gerry*, pp 81-90.
8   Joseph Novitski, *Wind Star*, p 6.

CLASSICAL RENAISSANCE

Inspirations anew from the liner era

As design trends usually run in cycles, so too the march of progress in cruise shipping eventually had to come full circle to re-examine some of the original considerations of traditional liner design. By the late 1980s many cruise operators found themselves to be competing on very similar itineraries, and in need of being able to reach out farther to new and more distant destinations so as to offer their clientele something different. As it had once been in the liner era, speed would again become a consideration in passenger-ship design. This time the object was not to shorten the voyage time, but rather to widen its range within the same time frame. Cruise duration had by that time been well determined by the market itself. While the luxury sector would continue to sustain itineraries of from fourteen days up to three months for round-the-world cruises, the veritable 'gold standard' of the mass mainstream market was seven days.

At the time a number of Lines were faced with the eventual inevitability of having to replace purebred deep-sea express tonnage such as *Rotterdam*, *Canberra*, and *Eugenio Costa*. These already had the speed and range to serve the extended itineraries, as well as the stability and structural stamina to comfortably make crossings of the Atlantic and Pacific Oceans in world-cruise service. Holland America, P&O and Costa were looking at how these characteristics could be replicated in new forms consistent with modern cruise shipbuilding practice.

Even Cunard, who have spent vast sums of money keeping their prestigious *QE2* up to the very latest standards, have discreetly investigated contingencies for her eventual replacement.

To satisfy both the extended range of requirements for the seven-day market and to uphold the existing standards of speed and comfort in the long-range luxury market, a combination of traditional liner power and a modern shallow-draught hullform would be needed. The increase in performance actually sought in the instances of the seven-day ships was more of a return to sustained running at 20kts from the 'de-rated' 16–18kt service speeds of many ships delivered in the early 1980s. While this could easily be accommodated with existing design techniques, the higher speeds needed for longer-range operations in Holland America and P&O's cases presented a far more onerous challenge. Here a compromise would have to be struck between the fine-lined deep draught and inherently more stable hullforms of either Line's existing deep-sea tonnage and the modern cruise-ship rationale of shallower-draught and fuller-form hulls.[1]

Quite apart from the technical aspects of speed and stability, however, Lines such as Costa, Holland America and P&O were acutely aware of the immense popularity of the more classic design features of their remaining liners. Consequently, they have striven to preserve these qualities within the modern rationale of new classes of ships designed to take up where the liners would eventually leave off.

COSTA CLASSICA AND STATENDAM

As medium-size cruise tonnages crept inevitably up from the 40,000-ton-plus figure to the over 50,000-ton mark, owners sought greater individuality and diversity of design to establish their own unique fleet identities. This is perhaps most dramatically illustrated in the case of two orders placed by Costa Cruises and Holland America with Italy's Fincantieri shipyards in the late 1980s. Both Lines had their own ideas of retaining a traditional yet modern image inspired by the success of existing liner flagships. Costa's *Eugenio Costa* (originally *Eugenio C*) and Holland America's *Rotterdam* epitomised the best of 1950s and 1960s design, and remained perennial favourites among each Line's loyal followings.

The builders based their bids for both Lines on the same overall concept. Yet, through the ensuing detailed design and building processes, these originally identical plans evolved into ships of entirely different styles being tailored for each owner. While there remained commonality in various aspects of structural design and overall plan, the completed ships differed remarkably in the detailed layout of their passenger facilities, interior décor, lifeboat arrangements and even in the fundamental choice of propulsion machinery. To see them without knowing of their singular origins, one would have no idea that they bore any relationship to each other whatsoever. Their radically different superstructure designs alone obscured the fact that they were even of similar size, as one had a far more massive appearance than the other.

Costa was one of several Mediterranean-based Lines to build new ships of the medium-tonnage range in the 1980s. Home Lines had ordered a running mate for their *Atlantic*, in the form of the 42,092-ton *Homeric*, delivered by Germany's Meyer Werft in 1986. Four years later the same yard handed over the slightly larger *Horizon* as the first-ever new vessel for Chandris, with a second hull, *Zenith*, to follow two years later in 1992. Although impressive in their own right, these were of fairly conventional design concepts, with the modest atria, superstructure dining room locations and distinctive exterior livery of the Chandris ships showing among their more progressive features.

Following their 1986 conversion of the former Lloyd Triestino liner *Guglielmo Marconi* as *Costa Riviera*, Costa Crocieri (Costa Cruises) proceeded with a four-ship fleet modernisation programme worth $850 million.[2] Two of these were to be the under-30,000-ton *Danae/Daphne*-style rebuildings *Costa Marina* and *Costa Allegra*, carried out by the Officine Marieotti in Genoa. Two larger newbuildings of 50,000 tons each, to be named *Costa Classica* and *Costa Romantica*, were booked with Fincantieri's Marghera yard near Venice. As in the container-ship conversions, performance of the new ships would be based on an intermediate service speed of 19.5kts, provided by a geared medium-speed four-engine aggregate driving twin controllable-pitch propellers. Design of *Costa*

Classica was carried out between the owners and builders in 1986 and 1987, with construction commencing in 1989.

Part of Costa's business plan was to integrate its Europe- and America-based fleets into a completely interchangeable operation with all ships being able to serve either market, which company president Dr Nocola Costa pointed out were not 'easy to blend together'. In reference to the diversity of his European sector alone, which is not as homogenous as its American opposite number, Dr Costa went on to explain at the time of the ship's completion:

> We are trying to blend together the Italians, the French, the Spanish, the 'Latin' Europeans. The Germans come too, because they like Italy... . We are working with four different languages, sometimes five. For the crew dealing with passengers this is not easy... . It means, for instance (sic) we need to translate all official documents.[3]

Costa's directive for the aesthetics of these ships, both inside and out, called for international European styling rather than exclusively Italian design, as a more universal approach was thought to be most in demand by the substantial American proportion of their expected clientele.[4] Additionally, the designers were challenged to create a unique image with worldwide public appeal. It was to be high-tech and modern, yet also evocative of the classic ocean-liner image, featuring such traditionally nautical details as round portholes, open deck railings, ventilator cowls and tall cylindrical steamship-style stacks. The interiors were to stress light and brightness as well as a clear sense of orientation. Kitsch and over-wrought decorative styling were to be avoided absolutely in favour of a contemporary European expression.

This brought about a veritable renaissance in Italian passenger-ship design which, despite any intention of being more international than Italian, would reintroduce a characteristic contemporary individuality of the nation's passenger tonnage started as far back as the 1930s. Costa's own *Eugenio C*, delivered in 1966, well represented the later developments of the art as one of the last examples from that earlier era of Gustavo Pulitzer-style liner chic so much admired in its time. While fundamentally creating an appropriately updated and upgraded *Eugenio C* aesthetic for a more sophisticated 1990s-generation clientele, features of Pulitzer's 1930s work were to re-emerge too. For instance, the portholes in the interior walls of the shopping arcades were distinctly reminiscent of his *Oceania* design which was shown at the Milan Trienalle in 1933.[5]

In *Costa Classica* and *Costa Romantica* these design elements made a significant reference to an earlier age, before today's hermetically sealed ships' interiors, when one was allowed to be more conscious of the unique milieu of the ship, and when the technical vicissitudes of the shipbuilders' art were permitted to co-exist with interior spaces which also had their references to shoreside architecture. For instance, the

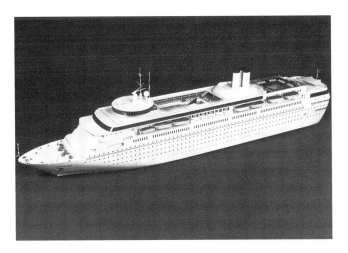

Costa Classica: **The builders' model showed the Gregotti styling with its clustered steamer funnels, café awning, open deck railings and cabin portholes. These were juxtaposed against the more modern elements of the terraced lidos and the circular observation pod supporting the main mast.**

(Gregotti Associati, Milan)

cabin porthole bespoke the notion of seaworthiness and structural strength, albeit perhaps only subliminally. Likewise the presence of unshorelike objects such as lifeboat davits and ventilator cowls, along with those upward vistas of the super-structure decks edged with their deftly nautical-looking open steel railings, and of the vast steamer funnels above, projected a sense of the technical magnificence of the ship's structure in harmony with its aesthetic attraction. Many modern cruise ships and ferries have since become so closed in that those upward vistas of lifeboats, decks and funnels were no longer to be enjoyed, short-changing the passenger's perception of the ship herself with only views of the passing seascape seen through rectangular building-like windows cut in the steel shell of the hull and superstructure.

Two of the most powerful examples of steamship imagery created by the Milan firm Gregotti Associati, commissioned for the design of the ships, were to be found in the atrium and the canvas awning rigged above the open-air café. The atrium, which extended up through five decks, was 'grounded' in the main entrance lobby, located in traditional fashion deep in the hull on deck 5. Above the large rectangular foyer, which gave access to the embarkation doors, twin cabin passages and a third centreline hallway joining the two main stairway and lift groupings farther forward and aft, the atrium itself rose as a square shaft or trunking through two cabin decks and two levels of public rooms farther up. At the cabin levels this shaft was enclosed on all four sides with marble, while on the lounge levels above it was open, with only ship's deck railings surrounding it. Whether viewed from above or below, it echoed the structure of the ship herself, with the enclosed levels representing the hull and the upper two tiers the railed open decks above. While the sky was in reality still a

farther two decks above this, the atrium was given a brightly illuminated ceiling, creating the impression at least of round-the-clock daylight.

A cantilevered staircase floating in the space between the two lounge levels added a perhaps surreal touch of liner design eclecticism, representing the typical railed companionways which connected the open decks of a traditional steamer to each other. In a perhaps less romantic context, the atrium could be viewed as a stylised hold or cargo hatch, rising through the hull's centre to the open decks above. The 'trunkway' of its passage through the two cabin decks was slightly wider at the lower level, in the way that such things usually are in reality. Even to those perhaps unfamiliar with holds and cargo hatches, this particular image still carried a powerful notion of the ship's working in at least an abstract manner.

This atrium did its job of providing a focal point and sense of orientation about the ship, and succeeded eminently in doing so in an entirely appropriate nautical context, without recourse to inappropriate artiness and kitsch. The fact that it in effect bypassed the two cabin decks, which its closed trunkway impaled, was insignificant. Atria can only really provide a focal point on the lounge decks, where they can be made more visible through the larger rooms and more open planning of these decks. The atrium's effectiveness was in this regard also strengthened through its direct relationship to the two principal stairways. Although widely spaced forward and aft, these were in effect brought into more or less direct contact with each other in the layout of public rooms at the two upper levels as well as to the central foyer passage at its lowest level. The stairways themselves also reflected something of the atrium's openness. The four main staircases, two in each stair-tower, were arranged in an L-shaped plan with the inside of

Costa Classica: **The Piazza Navona looking forward along the starboard side of the atrium which passes through its centre and is connected with the deck above by the suspended stairway seen at mid left.**

(Costa Cruise Lines)

the L open through the full height of each stairtower. This in itself provided a sense of orientation in allowing one to judge their location relative to the ship's height. This was in fact a feature of classic liners such as *Conte de Savoia*, *Constitution/Independence* and latterly *QE2*.

Although a much simpler thing than the atrium, the Alfresco Café awning was in its own right every bit as effective. It was a single large canvas sheet suspended across a tubular frame attached atop six metal tripod pylons surrounding the café's centre buffet area. Inclined upwards slightly towards the higher decks forward, it could be viewed both as a modern-day manifestation of the awnings which were once rigged across *Conte de Savoia*'s open decks as protection against the hot tropical sun, and as a somewhat stylised representation of a ship's sail. Seen either way, it was an appropriately nautical touch which provided a special sense of being aboard ship.

However, one unexpected aspect of this well-articulated plan was that the open deck spaces beneath the lifeboats, which are normally a major promenade space, were closed to passengers except for emergency use. These spaces had been reduced to a bare minimum, owing to the emphasis of interior space. Nonetheless their being declared out of bounds to passengers seemed to be rather at odds with the basic design objective of evoking the liner era, when the open decks played a very important role not only socially, but also in forming the passengers' image and impressions of their ocean-going surroundings. *Costa Classica*, and later, *Costa Romantica*'s passengers could only venture outside the superstructure's enclosing shell on the upper decks, where their outward impressions of being aboard ship would be formed by the more modern thinking in pool and lido deck layouts, without those upward vistas of lifeboats, davits, superstructure and so on.

The atrium and café awning are but two examples of the entire design theme of the so aptly named *Costa Classica*, both inboard and out. Her exterior profile was essentially traditional, although possessing a quality of timelessness. Where many ships of her size were by that time being built with nested lifeboat arrangements of one type or another, *Costa Classica* retained a conventional topsides outfit, albeit with a fully enclosed lido deck cantilevered above the boats. Two-thirds aft atop a moderately proportioned fanhouse there was a trio of tall cylindrical funnels, described by the designers as 'a redesigned quotation of the typical shapes of passenger shipping's golden age'.[6] The massif of this was balanced forward against a circular glass-enclosed observation pod supporting the main mast and its array of antennae, satellite navigation domes and other communications paraphernalia. Following the modern rationale of gaining the maximum amount of revenue-earning interior space, the superstructure extended fully aft at the boat deck level, with full-height windows surrounding the stern in an updated rendition of *Oriana*'s Stern Gallery of 1960.

The overall lines of form were strong and angular, sug-

gesting a sense of modernity in a somewhat softened adaptation of the rectilinear ferry and cruise-ship styling of the early 1980s. Looking farther back, these forms also recalled the aesthetics of Harland & Wolff's early enclosed superstructures as first seen in the example of Holland America's *Rotterdam* of 1909. Indeed the return to portholes for *Costa Classica*'s cabin decks was a classic touch which made this sort of historical connection. With a horizontal division between the hotel block and the public rooms, virtually all cabins, except for ten deluxe suites with private verandas, were relegated to the four hull decks beneath the main suite of lounges. Thus the classic approach of portholes for cabins and larger rectangular windows for the public rooms above could be clearly applied to great effect.

Costa Classica's cabin portholes were enlarged to a diameter of 700mm, and were appropriated one to a cabin. The larger size appeared definitely modern, while the grid plan of the cabins themselves created an absolutely regular pattern of openings in the shell plating, clearly bespeaking the modern rationale of the ship's internal layout. Above the cabins, where the shell plating was continued in a single plane up to the boat deck, the tall lounge windows were arranged to fit within each alternate pair of structural frames. While these windows were arguably too narrow, their outer appearance conveyed the sense of structural strength and integrity already suggested by the portholes. This was again an element of highlighting the technical magnificence of the ship's structure in harmony with its aesthetic public appeal.

Despite her expression of ocean-liner classicism, *Costa Classica* was, in reality, of greatly advanced technical and structural design. The basic hull form and overall structural arrangement were developed by the noted Italian naval architect F Cernobori, who had designed many of the most noted Italian passenger liners of the 1960s.[7] For *Costa Classica* he created a fairly full hull form with moderate flare in the bow lines, formed to provide a good margin of stability on a relatively shallow draught of 7.6m. Because of the upper-decks location of the public rooms and their wide use of heavy decorative materials, weight economy became an important consideration. Aluminium alloy was used for much of the upper part of the superstructure, above the boat deck. As a further weight-saving measure the three funnels were made from fibreglass.

The internal layout of the ship was of equal design significance, as it had been carefully planned to arrive at the most efficient accommodation plan possible. This was achieved largely by way of a frame spacing interval of 700mm, which was relatively small for larger passenger ships. Each fourth frame formed part of a transverse web for additional strength. The web interval provided a convenient cabin width spacing of 2.8m.

The web-frame spacing was thus wide enough to allow the interior designers sufficient latitude to produce luxury cabins with the beds being oriented hotel-style across the width of the rooms, or fore-and-aft in relation to the ship's dimensions. Four rows of supporting columns were laid out along the line of each alternate web frame. These were arranged to coincide with a location near the adjacent bathroom modules of each pair of cabins so that an absolutely consistent room arrangement was possible throughout each deck. The overall layout was devised to follow the virtually standard large-ship cabin plan with two parallel fore and aft passages flanking a double row of back-to-back inner rooms.

This in effect brought the standardised approach to cabin plans of the German KdF ships of the 1930s to its logical conclusion. Instead of planning the accommodation around a somewhat arbitrary frame interval determined by a particular yard's established practice, Cernobori had planned *Costa Classica* around the revenue-earning hotel rooms which would be their commercial lifeblood, indeed the embodiment of the ideal of form following function.

The cabins themselves were no doubt one of *Costa Classica*'s distinguishing design elements. Crisp and high-tech, almost to the point of being too spartan, they fulfilled the notion of efficient and well-appointed luxury shipboard accommodation rather than the ideal of resort hotel rooms scaled down to the proportions afforded by a seaworthy steel hull. Writing later, at the time of *Costa Romantica*'s completion, Gregotti Associati's Pierluigi Cerri explained of his work:

> The image we searched for was excellent comfort and high homogeneity. This is why we opted for a special plastic laminate that is a picture-perfect replica of pearwood throughout. We wanted to create a classic yacht stateroom, not a hotel room. The entire design seeks to give those aboard the impression that they are taking a sea journey.[8]

Costa Classica: **As standard cabin set up for twin-bedded occupancy, viewed from inboard towards the vanity unit and bathroom. Note the unusual placement of the television set.**

The layout of the public rooms on the decks above was simple, straightforward, and to some extent modularised by the same regular pattern of the secondary and web-frame spacing. The overall concept followed the plan of *Nordic Empress* and the ex-Sitmar design of P&O's much larger Fincantieri-built *Crown Princess*, with amphitheatre-style show lounge fully forward, dining room aft, and casino and other rooms amidships. The atrium featured prominently at the centre of both levels and in their overall circulation plan, yet without dominating the scheme. Unlike *Nordic Empress*, the P&O ships and others of similar plan, Costa's designers situated the galley fully aft of the dining room, in the interest of avoiding awkward asymmetrical plans with midships-located galleys on the lounge deck or the complexity of escalator service from facilities on the deck below. The stern vista which this arrangement denied to the dining room was offered instead from the deck above, where the full-beam ballroom was given panoramic full-height windows both sides and astern.

The décor of the spaces was refreshingly modern throughout, with much of the furniture and other fittings specially designed for the ship. The overall sense of luxury and elegance owed much to the careful selection of materials, some being modern and nautical in character and others more traditional and shore-like, but rendered seaworthy through new treatments. Again, Pierluigi Cerri explained:

> Once we had uniformly defined the inner skin from the constructional and the modular viewpoints, we began diversifying by working on the fittings. This is one of the chief differences from overseas naval architecture criteria; they establish remarkable differences between each exceptional spot on board (the discotheque, the ballroom, the theatre, the casino, the shopping centre). Each is treated like a separate startling stylistic situation in accordance with a special marketing philosophy. All the secondary areas are nondescript. On the contrary, our design calls for continuous forms and spaces. As concerns the materials, one must distinguish between the supports and the coverings. The former, mounted on the skeleton of metal tubing, used to consist of fireproof 'Navilite' panels. Now they are being superseded by aluminium honeycomb or by thin sheet metal and rock wool. Some of the cladding is of building materials (marble, mosaics and stones); other materials are traditional, yet they have been modified, like light marble only 3 to 5mm thick mounted on honeycomb panels. And some materials have been reinvented, like plastic laminates. Silk screening has become so sophisticated that the final appearance is hyper-realistic. In addition we tried to maintain some specific naval materials: teak gratings and a special canvas. Also some design elements hark back to previous naval memories (like the stern cable-suspended tent

Costa Classica: **The completed ship seen on her maiden visit to Venice in November 1991, contrasting a modern expression of classic marine design with the enduring classicism of the city's waterfront architecture.**

(Costa Cruise Lines)

Costa Romantica: **One of the forward-facing deluxe suites added to the second ship's range of accommodation. The view is essentially that seen from the navigating bridge, only from the vantage point of one deck higher up.**

(Costa Cruise Lines)

construction which was made to resemble an awning).[9]

In November 1991 *Costa Classica* appropriately made her public debut against the classical backdrop of Venice's waterfront architecture. After an extensive promotional programme in southern European waters she commenced her commercial service with a positioning voyage to the Caribbean. Initially her time was to be divided between serving her American clientele during the winter months and the Mediterranean-based European market for the high-season summer months. As she made her initial cruises her operation was carefully studied in order that as much as possible could be learned and applied, if necessary, to the refinement of *Costa Romantica* outfitting, since the second ship's delivery was due in September 1993.

Indeed a number of changes were introduced into *Costa Romantica*'s detailed planning and layout. Perhaps most significant among these was the appropriation of the enclosed lido deck's most forward spaces for additional deluxe suites. Whenever a fairly homogeneous cabin plan is devised for a passenger ship, no matter how good that plan is, there always seems to be a later desire (probably on the part of the marketing people) for more diverse deluxe accommodation. For example, 'penthouse' suites were added to both *QE2* and *Finnjet*, while the rational planning of *Royal Princess*'s accommodation yielded somewhat to the offering of a greater range of room types on the Japanese-built *Crystal Harmony*. Unfortunately, *Costa Romantica*'s added suites, which were of the glass-walled type housed in the two decks added atop *Norway*, took away her only enclosed public space with an unob-

structed forward view over the bow. Thankfully this change did not take anything away from the ship's external appearance as completed.

The public room plan was reworked to incorporate a circular 'Piazzetta' as the sort introduced in the second container ship conversion, *Costa Allegra*. This went into the space occupied by the casino in *Costa Classica*, eliminating the casino in the earlier ship's plan with but a handful of 'one-armed bandits' remaining. The change effectively designated the second ship to favouring the lifestyle of the company's European clientele, for whom gambling is a less important pastime.

Another change introduced was the universal rearrangement of the standard cabin layout to the industry-preferred

Costa Romantica: **The fitness spa, although displaced by the new suites, still retained pride of place on the Monte Carlo deck adjacent to the pool lido.**

(Costa Cruise Lines)

beamwise bed layout of *Royal Princess* and most other new ships. The fore-and-aft bed arrangement of *Costa Classica*'s plan had in fact turned out to be rather awkward owing to its relationship with the cabin entrance. The arrangement of the en-suite bathroom modules and wardrobe fittings at either side of the entry vestibule brought one into the cabin proper at a point some three-quarters of a metre from the nearest side wall, directly in front of the foot-ends of the beds. Despite the clever and unusual arrangement of a settee and room divider surmounted by a swivel-based television set, the need to walk around the ends of the beds was not well received. The television's awkwardly contrived location was in fact an unfortunate intrusion into the very heart of the living area.

A better solution might have been to adopt the cabin plans of Hapag-Lloyd's 1981-completed *Europa* or P&O's *Star Princess*, where the wardrobes and bathroom were at the same side of the entrance, effecting a corner entry to the cabin proper. This approach brings one into the room at a point beyond the ends of the beds, and has the advantage of asserting the greatest impression of spaciousness.

Speaking to the press at *Costa Romantica*'s introduction in Venice, architect Ciugi Cerri said of the ship's essentially high-tech design:

> The ship makes the transition from the technical to the emotion, creating an ambience which does not give way to technology.

Costa's new ships carried out to sea and into their commercial services a philosophy of design renaissance which has breathed new life into Italian passenger shipping. As one critic expressed it:

> Sailing in the wake of *Rex* and *Conte di Savoia*, these ships had a great tradition to live up to.

Holland America Line, by comparison, had merely to continue their on-going fleet renewal programme and existing philosophy of retaining their outstanding design reputation. Holland America had started preliminary planning for their next generation of ships shortly after taking delivery of *Nieuw Amsterdam* and *Noordam* in 1983 and 1984. It was standard practice for many shipping Lines to upgrade their fleets on a ten year cycle. The newest ships would be placed in the premiere service, between Europe and New York for instance, relegating the former generation's tonnage to a secondary service, perhaps a colonial run. The ships formerly catering to the secondary service would then usually be retired and scrapped, giving the average liner a lifespan of from twenty to twenty-five years. Starting with Cunard's building programmes of the 1880s and 1890s, the regularity of this pattern through the twentieth-century histories of most Lines was somewhat upset by both world wars, in which virtually two decades were lost to fleet reconstructions. The 1960s repre-

sented the last generation of newbuilding for many of those Lines whose traditional services had survived that long.

As this cycle had set the pace of development in the liner era, so too in the cruise industry there was the perceived need to catch up with the greater sizes and prestige of the competition's newer ships. By 1988 Holland America had signed a letter of intent with *Europa*'s builders, Bremer Vulkan of Bremerhaven, for two 60,000-ton ships. With the completion of these anticipated a year apart in April of 1991 and 1992, this would have continued the Line's fleet-renewal cycle. The 1938-completed *Nieuw Amsterdam* had languished through the war-torn 1940s to set the pace for the 1950s. In 1959 *Rotterdam* was commissioned as the Line's standard-bearer of luxury and elegance through the 1960s. Then the little *Prinsendam* had been perceived as the modern direction in cruising for the 1970s. The sister ships *Nieuw Amsterdam* and *Noordam* had reinstated the larger liner image for the 1980s, with the planned Bremer Vulkan ships to surpass their already high standards with an anticipated sense of the luxury and splendour ultimately to be expected of the 1990s and on into the dawning of the twenty-first century.

As explained by Holland America's chairman and chief executive officer, Nico Van der Vorm:

> The new ships will be built in the up-market style of the mainstream vessels of the present fleet, *Nieuw Amsterdam* and *Noordam*.

These would have been, in effect, double-sized renditions of the 1980s ships, at 60,000 tons each and with a service speed of 21kts. The main and promenade decks of the earlier *Nieuw Amsterdam/Noordam* would have each been doubled, creating a two-level dining room with a central well and a greatly extended range of public facilities above, throughout two decks rather than one. The public-room plan would have featured a double-height show lounge, ingeniously set at an oblique angle allowing for an increased width of the stage proscenium. The remaining public spaces aft of this were similar in plan and concept to those of *Nieuw Amsterdam* and *Noordam*, building on the success of those ships. The asymmetrical six-sided cinema and the lido café, with its wide buffet counters, were immediately recognisable elements of the earlier ships.

Aft, on the upper level of public rooms, there was to have been what amounted to a greatly expanded rendition of *Rotterdam*'s elegant Ritz Carlton ballroom. Here the semi-circular mezzanine of the *Rotterdam* plan would have been expanded to a completely encircling gallery, retaining as a central feature the wide curved sweep of stairs so admired in the 1959-built flagship. Anticipating a good share of the growing business and conference market, the plan also included an extensive suite of meeting rooms as well as two large 'hospitality suites' on the uppermost deck.

Before these plans could be realised, Holland America Line was absorbed into the Carnival Cruises empire in 1989, acquiring Carnival ownership but retaining its own unique identity as an autonomous subsidiary. The contract with Bremer Vulkan was not finalised as Carnival's technical department and consultant naval architects, Technical Marine Planning, reassessed Holland America's direction in light of Carnival's own eminently successful design and building formulae. Some feared for the spread of the Fun Ship cascading show lounge windows and huge gull-winged funnels to the new subsidiary's planned tonnage.

Indeed changes were made to the rather austere liner look of the proposed Bremer Vulkan ships, appearing in some respects rather like *Oranje* in her final modernised form as *Angilena Lauro*. Gone were the unrealised plan's strong references to Holland America's earlier ships, being replaced by a new and entirely businesslike rationale of operational efficiency. There was also no reference to the Fun Ship eclectic, but rather a proven design concept developed out of Carnival's Fun Ship success and well suited to the upper market sector which the Dutch-traditioned subsidiary would continue to serve.

At a smaller size of 50,000 tons, and with a 1,717-person lower-berth capacity lowered to 1,266, the Carnival design was considered to be more effective. The design of these ships for longer cruises in Holland America's established market was in reality the realisation of Carnival's own *Tiffany* project to diversify themselves into the prestige cruise sectors above their mainstream Fun Ship trade. Acquisition of Holland America had enabled Carnival to enter this market with an existing loyal clientele, ready-made product and fleet of ships which only needed to be expanded in their own inimitable fashion of aggressive business development. This approach embodied the design concept of *Tiffany* as the starting point, with Holland America to be involved in the later stages of detailed planning and in supervision of the building.

After preliminary discussions had been held with a num-

Statendam: **Derived from the same conceptual beginnings as** *Costa Classica*, **and of similar tonnage to the Italian ship, she had a far more massive appearance owing to her nested lifeboats.**

(Holland America Line)

ber of builders, orders were finally placed in November 1989 with Fincantieri for three ships of 50,000 tons to be built at their Monfalcone yard near Trieste. Fincantieri was well positioned to fill this order as they already had *Costa Classica's* design in hand as a suitable prototype which could be adapted to the specific needs of Holland America. The Costa hull form and overall structural design were taken as the starting point of the Holland America contract. The time needed for initial designing was thus reduced to a point where delivery dates near those planned with Bremer Vulkan could still be met. Names of the ships were to be of Holland America's choice. *Statendam*, *Maasdam* and *Ryndam* were chosen in order of their 1992, 1993 and 1994 completions respectively. In company and shipyard language, they became known by the rather militaristic pseudonym, the 'S-class'.

Bearing little resemblance to their Italian half-sisters from the Marghera yard, the new Holland America ships took on a massive profile of their own, with *Canberra*-style nested lifeboats and two tiers of open cabin verandas along the upper decks. Inside, the proven Carnival design rationale for optimum service and efficiency was brought into full force, for the first time beyond the confines of the parent line's rapidly growing Fun Ship fleet. Holland America's house design firm, De Vlaming, Fennis, Dingemans – Interiors BV (VFD), was engaged to impart their uniquely European *Rotterdam*-inspired fleet image and feel. The new ships were to continue the approach the designers had already developed with the *Nieuw Amsterdam* and *Noordam* and with the lengthening of *Westerdam*.

Up to this time F W De Vlaming had done the ship work, leaving F C J Dingemans and H M Fennis to run the practice at home in the Netherlands, where there were a variety of shore-based projects in hand. Dingemans understudied with De Vlaming, whom he regards very highly as a teacher and indeed a mentor. Dingemans worked with De Vlaming on *Statendam*, but with a greater degree of independence. He has since taken over major responsibility for the later S-class ships following De Vlaming's retirement.

VFD were teamed up with Kym Anton for the cabin design and Carnival's Joseph Farcus, who was brought into the team to adapt his own special expertise in designing the entertainment facilities. Farcus was given responsibility for the show lounge and for the top-deck observatory. Carnival thought that the longer itineraries of their Holland America subsidiary's cruises warranted the design diversity that would be achieved by using more than one design firm. Indeed this was a combination which brought together two design forces of great individuality from the diametrically different viewpoints on design held by Carnival and Holland America.

Dingemans believed that the intentions or 'statement' which designers wish to express in a ship should be clearly evident in the way she is moulded and shaped. For example the dolphin-head domes of P&O's *Crown Princess* and *Regal Princess* endeavour to make a point of expressing the relationship of these ships to their natural element of the sea. If the owners had kept the originally much stronger lines of form, which also expressed something of the dolphin's tail too, the effect would have been far more dramatic.

The ships of Carnival and Holland America each externally express their intentions. Carnival's image is that of the 'Fun Ships' to be aboard, while Holland America makes a singularly stronger statement about the ships themselves, with emphasis on the more traditional deep-sea liner attributes of greater power strength and seaworthiness. This is of course not to say that Carnival's tonnage lacks these essential qualities, but merely that they are not in themselves strongly expressed by the exterior styling. However, with passengers typically being aboard the Holland America ships for longer cruises, the image of the ship and of being at sea is intrinsically stronger and is justifiably expressed as such in the exterior styling. Summed up in Dingemans' own words: 'One should be able to "read" the purpose of the design from the outside.'

From the standpoint of interior design, the Carnival and Holland America requirements are practically poles apart from each other. In Joseph Farcus's work for Carnival's *Fantasy*-class ships, which are for short three- and seven-day cruises, the philosophy is: 'Forget about home: Enjoy yourself'.

In his approach to the *Statendam*, and even more so the later S-class ships, which cruise the globe on longer itineraries, Dingemans acknowledged that passengers would be aboard for greater periods of time, that they would be visiting many different and unfamiliar ports, and that therefore they would expect the ship itself to make them feel at home in a cultural atmosphere which they would already be familiar with.

Passenger profiles differed greatly between Carnival and Holland America, as was reflected by the design approach of the two fleets. Farcus realised that aboard his *Fantasy*-class ships he only had their hearts and minds for a few days, which is not long enough for them to get to know such a huge ship. The layouts thus had to be simple and straightforward, with a strong emphasis on the 'arterial' promenades. Passengers could walk this route or strip as though on a familiar stretch of Fifth Avenue or the Champs Élysées and choose the places or attractions which appealed to them most.

Conversely, the Holland America passenger, particularly aboard one of the newer S-class ships, tended to have far more time to become familiar with the ship. The asymmetrical public room deck layout, with its diagonal orientation of traffic flow, was becoming a veritable trade-mark of the Holland America shipboard architecture. It originated with some of VFD's work ashore in the Netherlands, where rooms of varying sizes were needed for banking and other commercial offices. Asymmetrical elements of the *Rotterdam*, and earlier-refitted *Statendam* public room plans, were more coincidental than influential. *Nieuw Amsterdam* and *Noordam* were the first Holland America ships to adopt VFD's asymmetrical approach. Its advantage in shipboard plans was that it offered a greater variety of both larger and smaller meeting places than might otherwise be achievable. As Dingemans explained:

It creates a contradiction between the collective part of being in a ship with many others and the individual part of being on one's own or in a smaller group. Passengers want to have some of the cruise's experiences together as well as to enjoy others alone or in more intimate company, or to be able to reflect on them individually.

As one might expect, Holland America tended to host a greater proportion of older people than those attracted to Carnival. They would be well seasoned to life's experiences, and less apt to be impressed with the high-tech and high-fantasy effects which appeal to the younger set. These people were more likely to be very focused on how they have to function in society.

Many have chosen a Holland America cruise to relax and enjoy themselves after having already served society in their lifetime's work or professions, their roles as parents and as educators of the younger generations and so on. These people wanted a rather different experience than would be offered to their offspring aboard a Carnival ship. They wanted a greater emphasis on the destinations and on the learning that goes with a more diverse itinerary, as well as the enjoyment of less structured social activities, which afforded the opportunity for more personal interaction. Traditional shipboard rituals, such as dressing formally for dinner and making the processional *grande descente* to the dining room 'to be seen' by those already seated, were spontaneous accessories to the cruise experience as a whole.

In the initial stages of structural and technical design some refinement of Fincantieri's Costa hull form was needed for Holland America's purposes. Since Carnival did not want to use aluminium in the superstructure or moulded fibreglass funnels as Costa had done, a slightly fuller form and the addition of 3m to the waterline length were needed, increasing the waterplane area to maintain the same degree of stability. Another change which required some refinement of hull appendage placement and form was the owners' choice of Heinze flap-type rudders for improved manoeuvrability. Additional model testing had to be carried out at the Vienna Model Basin and at MARIN at Wageningen, the Netherlands, to accommodate these changes.

The structural arrangement of the S-class hulls, with respect to watertight subdivision along with the overall layout of machinery and service spaces, closely followed the original Costa plan, with only slight variation as necessary to accommodate Carnival's choice of diesel-electric propulsion for the new Holland America ships. This was to be a further-optimised adaptation of the integrated power plants used in Carnival's larger *Fantasy*-class tonnage.

Plans of the lower four decks of both the Costa and Holland America ships were otherwise quite similar. One of the main differences was the inclusion of a large Carnival-style baggage handling area ahead of the ship's stores and their handling space on B deck of the Holland America ships. The two decks above were devoted almost exclusively to passenger accommodation, of near-identical layout both in the Holland America and Costa ships, the main difference being the presence of an atrium at these levels on the Italian ships. Above these was the strength deck, and from that point up the two Lines' ships were of radically different design.

The adoption of a nested-lifeboat plan for the S-class was new to both Carnival and Holland America. This influenced the creation of a *Canberra*-style accommodation layout with the cabin block divided at its vertical midpoint by the main run of public rooms. However, the principal suite of communal spaces were located above the lifeboat recess rather than within its confines, in a scheme more reminiscent of the P&O flagship's 1960 fleetmate *Oriana*, or the still earlier example of Rotterdamsche Lloyd's 1947 *Willem Ruys*. This gained the advantage of using the full beam of the ship for the lounges and offering commanding views from full-height windows.

The upper level of the main show lounge and dining room, along with several other lounges, the casino, library and card room were thus located on the upper promenade deck of each S-class ship. The upper lifeboat-recess space immediately below on the promenade deck, which in ships of this type has always been difficult to use as windows tend to be obstructed by the boats and their handling equipment, was given over to those rooms where vistas of the outside world are not so important anyway. These included the conference centre shops and other services. Also on this deck were the lower levels of the dining room and the main show lounge. The names of these two decks was rather euphemistic, as in fact neither offered a ship's promenade in the conventional sense of the word. On the lower promenade deck, where a traditional *Canberra*-style teak-planked deck surrounded the

superstructure beneath the lifeboats, the inboard space was taken up by a third level of cabins, continuing the lower accommodation block up above the strength deck.

Despite the higher location of the public rooms in relation to *Canberra*'s layout, the more modern design approach, stressing larger and taller superstructures, nonetheless allowed for an upper accommodation block on two decks above. These levels housed deluxe cabins and suites with private verandas. A fully enclosed lido and pool area with a Magrodome-style sliding roof was yet above these, with a forward-facing observation lounge still one deck higher up.

The approach taken by VFD to the layout of public rooms on the upper promenade deck was distinctly Holland America, both in conception of the plan and in decorative styling of the spaces themselves. First VFD stressed an expanded rendition of their original asymmetrical *Nieuw Amsterdam/Noordam* scheme. The S-class layout featured an essentially S-shaped circulation pattern encompassing the atrium lobby adjacent to the main show lounge, crossing the ship's centreline to the starboard windows in the vicinity of the large portside casino, where there were a number of other smaller rooms on its starboard side, and then turning back again towards the centreline near the funnel casing and aft stairways. From this point aft a pair of parallel passages provided access to the upper level of the main dining room located fully astern.

An asymmetrical circulation scheme was also followed within the narrower confines of the deck below, where the conference rooms and other smaller spaces were arranged inboard of the lifeboat recesses. As in its earlier rendition aboard *Nieuw Amsterdam* and *Noordam*, the plan's overall effect again gave the impression of a still larger ship, despite the real increase in size of the S-class. However, the expanded scale of *Statendam* and her two later sisters did allow for the creation

Statendam: **The Carnival-style show lounge in a very successful adaptation without the cascading-effect windows which have become a trademark feature of the parent company's fleet.**

(Holland America Line)

Statendam: **The writing room, which again shows the use of artistic touches, with additions of the sculpture in the corner at the left and the antique-style desk lamps. These created a rich and luxurious feel of an otherwise essentially modern space.**

(VFD Interiors BV, Utrecht)

Statendam: A view of one of the private dining rooms adjacent to the main facility. This clearly shows VFD's speciality of achieving a sense of luxury through the adornment of a simple space with high-quality furnishings and fittings. Note the ornately-framed painting, classic style of the patterned carpet and chairs.

(VFD Interiors BV, Utrecht)

of a great variety of small and intimate passenger spaces, recalling the many such nooks and corners to be found in the Line's still earlier *Nieuw Amsterdam* of 1938 as well as their much-loved flagship *Rotterdam*.

Once again, VFD succeeded in imparting a distinctive sense of luxury through their eminently effective rationale of economical and durable modernity. As in their earlier Holland America designs, this was achieved through the use of durable plain wall and floor coverings and quality stock furnishings, enlivened with carefully selected works of art and imaginative lighting. Its basic formula unchanged, the scheme was enriched and extended in these larger and more prestigious new ships, particularly through its broadened use of antiques, artifacts and other art objects throughout the public and circulation areas. Fibre-optic lighting was extensively used to illuminate these items to their greatest effect. The great advantage of this type of lighting in such applications lay in its ability to be delivered wherever needed in a vitrine or display case without generating heat and with no need for the display enclosure to be opened for replacement of light bulbs. The light source, usually a single low-voltage quartz-halogen lamp, was housed in a black box outside the display, usually beneath the enclosure out of sight.

From the standpoint of interior design and decoration, the S-class introduced a number of design features which were new to Holland America. *Statendam* was the Line's first ship to feature an aft superstructure location for the main dining room. This was two decks high, its upper level forming a mezzanine similar in plan to *France*'s original Versailles dining room. However, the two broad stairways joining both levels of *Statendam*'s Rotterdam dining room and the panoramic sweep

of windows surrounding both levels on three sides added a whole dimension of spaciousness and brightness to the scheme. In one respect the dining room could perhaps be seen as substituting in a modern and rationalised context the two-deck-high elegance of the Ritz Carlton lounge of the flagship *Rotterdam*, from which the room took its name

Statendam was also the first Holland America ship to follow the contemporary trend of featuring an atrium. As in the prime instance of *Royal Princess*, this was confined to the height of the lounge and dining-room levels, three decks in *Statendam*'s case. In keeping with the asymmetrical layout of these decks, the atrium itself was also offset from the centre-lines slightly towards portside.

Despite the ravages of an engine-room fire which put the ship's delivery in jeopardy and threatened to delay her first cruises, *Statendam* went into service as scheduled on 25 January 1993. Her first-season itinerary started with two trans-Panama Canal cruises, taking the ship to Los Angeles and back again to Florida. After making several Caribbean circuits, she again crossed the Atlantic on a cruise voyage as the first leg of a thirty-five-day 'Grand European Tour'. *Statendam*'s maiden call at Amsterdam on 1 June was a veritable 'homecoming' for Holland America, after an absence of some twenty years from European waters. Although the word 'Tiffany' had effectively disappeared from Carnival's corporate lexicon with their acquisition of Holland America, this occasion of the Line's return to Amsterdam represented fulfilment of the Tiffany Project's mission of establishing a worldwide luxury-cruise operation for Carnival. In effect the essence of Tiffany was embodied under the well-established tradition and reputation of the Holland America houseflag.

In an interview granted to me by VFD's Mr Dingemans at his Utrecht studio in 1995, I asked if Holland America, or indeed VFD, had found it necessary to make special provision for the differing tastes and expectations of the S-class ships' American and European clientele. Explained in his own words:

Europeans think that these interiors are reflecting an American way of life, while Americans feel that the atmosphere is decidedly European.

When I asked what about possible future trends of his work for Holland America, Dingemans merely said: 'It is difficult to outgrow the Holland America image'.

The five Italian-built Costa and Holland America ships of this class were jointly bringing the world of cruising together for their respective owners. Costa's new fleet was amalgamating their once completely separate European and American operations with a renewed sense of the company's former international line services. Holland America, after concentrating almost entirely on their Caribbean and Alaska markets for twenty years, was inaugurating a new manifestation of their once worldwide presence. Apart from the great diversity of design throughout the whole cruise industry's new ships, the

Statendam: **This was the first Holland America ship to introduce an atrium. Note the escalators at the lower left which connect this space with the embarkation deck below.**

(Holland America Line)

renewed worldliness of these two Lines was in effect restoring something of the international character of the liner era – Costa with the flair of their distinctly Italian style, and Holland America in their characteristic Dutch way of doing things.

Costa have since progressed to larger German-built tonnage in a continuation of their fleet expansion. Holland-America have added a fourth Fincantieri ship to their original S-class. A larger and faster fifth ship, known to her creators as *Super Statendam* or *Fastdam*, was completed as the Line's new flagship *Rotterdam*, their sixth ship to bear this name.

ORIANA

With as long a history as any shipping Line, P&O also found themselves to be in the position of looking beyond the future of an aging and much-loved flagship. While the limelight of the P&O Group's newbuilding progress had been taken by developments in their Princess Cruises division, the parent firms' British operation was still being primarily serviced by *Canberra*. This valiant ship had more than lived up to her claim of being 'the ship which shapes the future' and had magnificently performed the unexpected task of serving as a troop, hospital and prisoner-of-war ship during the 1982 Falkland Islands conflict. Her outstanding reputation in both these regards clearly bespoke the excellence of her well-conceived original design and solid top-quality construction. From the viewpoint of *Canberra*'s loyal passenger following, her sense of timelessness, reflecting P&O's own long-standing traditions of service, had rightfully earned her a very special place in the hearts of many ordinary Britons.

Be that as it may, the hard reality of cruise shipping by the late 1980s seemed to show *Canberra* in a somewhat less favourable trading position. Several breakdowns of her aging turbo-electric machinery, along with her high fuel consumption of as much as 400 tons per day, had become the major sources of concern. P&O had for a number of years been upgrading the ship's accommodation during her annual overhauls in an effort to keep pace with their newer tonnage. Here a major concern was to provide a greater proportion of the original tourist-class accommodation with en-suite toilet facilities, despite the fact that there seemed always to be enough demand for these cabins at the inexpensive rates they fetched without their own lavatories. All in all, the ongoing costs of keeping the ship running were mounting to the point of making her replacement seem at least commercially prudent, even if not emotionally so.

Project Gemini was inaugurated by P&O in the late 1980s to study the possibilities of building a large new cruise ship, destined specifically to service the special needs of the British market. It was also foreseen that, even if not immediately so, this ship would be an eventual replacement for *Canberra*. Little information was released about the project, although it was rumoured that the *New Canberra*, as the ship was called in some informed circles, might be the first to eclipse the 100,000-ton mark in a bid to assert an appropriate sense of prestige to the flagship's eventual successor. Negotiations were held with Lloyd Werft in Bremerhaven, resulting in preliminary design work being done by the German yard. However, the cost of preparing a contract design alone ultimately proved to be prohibitive, and the project seemed to be doomed as P&O again re-examined the future of *Canberra*.[10]

The demise of Project Gemini, at least as a German-built ship, seemed apparent when Bremer Vulkan later released a project design for a large cruise ship at the 1991 Cruise & Ferry Conference in London. The work done by Lloyd Werft, itself an operating division of the Vulkan Group, appeared to have passed into the hands of the parent yard as the basis of this design. Within the envelope of some rather avant-garde oblique-lined exterior styling, deck plans of this ethereal ship revealed the familiar names of *Canberra*'s public rooms.[11]

In January 1992, when everyone's attention was focused on the imminent placing of an order for another Princess-

Project Gemini: The
Bremer Vulkan cruise ship
design which emerged from
the work originally done
with Lloyd Werft towards
an eventual replacement
for *Canberra*.

(Bremer Vulkan AG, Bremen)

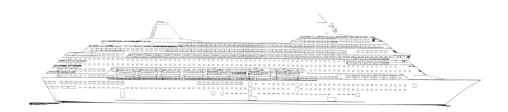

style ship with Fincantieri, Germany's Meyer Werft emerged as a 'dark horse', securing the order for the exclusively British-market ship. The owners already fully understood the indigenous differences in their diverse American, Australian and home British markets, as learned through efforts over the years to interchange P&O and Princess tonnage. As discussed earlier, *Canberra* did not meet American cruise-accommodation standards in the 1970s, while towards that decade's end *Kungsholm*'s adaptation as *Sea Princess* was perceived in Australia as being too American in character. The more European nature of *Sea Princess* has ultimately served her well as a suitable fleetmate for *Canberra*.

P&O's intention to make their new ship distinctly British was clearly asserted by their early choice of the name *Oriana*, clearly identifying her as an intended running mate for *Canberra*. The special nature of the new ship was to be such that P&O took the unusual step of defining her interior spaces in far greater detail than is normally specified in the building contract. A total of twenty-six public rooms, including the atrium and dining rooms, were specified in preference to the emphasis on larger spaces shown in America-based ships. Also taken into account was the home market demand for a larger variety of cabin accommodation, including four-berth rooms which could be sold on a shared basis, and for larger-than-usual open deck spaces, totalling 1,022sq m in area.

Based on the passenger profiles of *Canberra* and *Sea Princess*, later renamed *Victoria*, P&O could expect for *Oriana*

Oriana: An early rendering of the ship ordered from Meyer Werft, still un-named, but already showing the adaptation of *Canberra*'s elegantly subtle streamlining to the far greater bulk of her modern economy-of-scale design approach.

(P&O Group)

a nearly ninety-nine per cent British clientele on Southampton-based Mediterranean, Red Sea, Caribbean, Atlantic, Baltic and British Isle itineraries. For the annual round-the-world voyages, the mix could be expected at around seventy-eight per cent British, with the remainder being Australian, North American and South African.[12] By comparison, *Europa*'s German-speaking patronage amounted to between eighty-five and ninety per cent, while *QE2*, marketed as a British ship, has always catered to a larger proportion of American passengers.

Scaled down somewhat from the 100,000-ton vision of Project Gemini, the new ship was to be of 67,000 tons with a passenger capacity of 1,975 and a relatively high service speed of 24kts. This made the new ship about one and a half *Canberra*'s size and slightly larger than *Star Princess*.

	Canberra (1961)	Oriana (1995)	Star Princess (1989)
Length oa	249.93m	260.00m	246.60m
Length bp	224.05m	225.55m	201.00m
Beam moulded	31.09m	32.20m	32.30m
Draught	9.91m	7.90m	7.70m
Service speed	27.50kts	24.00kts	21.00kts
Maximum power	63,410.00kW	47,750.00kW	24,000.00kW
GRT	44,807.0	69,153.0	63,254.0
Passengers	1,700	1,975	1,600
Crew	802	760	600
No of public rooms	21	26	15

The precedents for *Oriana*'s planning were to originate not only from the more contemporary European examples of *Europa* and Holland America's newest tonnage, but largely from a profound appreciation of what had made *Canberra* so eminently successful in the British cruise market for more than a quarter of a century.

When *Canberra*'s plans started to take shape in the late 1950s, someone coined the phrase 'The ship which shapes the future' in recognition of her many innovative design features. It was a neat piece of marketing jingoism for its day, which seemed to strike the right chord in people's anticipation of the revolutionary superliner, with engines and tanker-style funnels aft and a progressive architectural design approach which endeavoured also to anticipate her role as a cruise ship. Indeed, *Canberra* lived up to the promise of shaping the future, being considered by the time of *QE2*'s debut at the decade's close as a ship already ten years ahead of her time. Going well beyond the normal P&O-fleet life expectancy of some twenty to twenty-five years, *Canberra* retained a unique sense of still being able to influence things to come well into her third decade in service. Perhaps it was also the case of *Canberra* having shaped the future of the British home cruise market itself as much as she had already influenced world cruise-ship design as a whole.

Quite apart from the elements of layout, design and styling which *Canberra*'s example has imparted to the cruise industry, she has also promoted an image and great sense of public appeal. In point of truth, the travelling public is not generally concerned about anything going on lower down than the dining room floors, in the engine rooms and other working areas of the ship. Machinery, auxiliary systems of one sort or another, stevadorage and provisions handling are of little concern in choosing the right ship for one's dream cruise, as long as these things all work properly. Passengers are not interested in the rationalisation of layouts to any point beyond easily finding their way about the ship. Then as now, for all the average passenger cares about machinery, the ship could be powered by anything as long as it is not nuclear. What they want, and are alone prepared to pay for, is something with a reputation and an image that fires their imaginations.

This was precisely the quality that made *Canberra* so outstanding, not as anyone's individual brainchild, but rather as an amalgam of many progressive ideas. Each in itself was already proven in some previous manifestation, and all were assembled together as a 'total design solution'. It is in this regard that *Canberra* has ultimately proven her worth as the first modern ship in which naval architecture, marine engineering, industrial design, architectural design and interior decoration were all brought together at a very early stage of planning. The design of *Canberra* in effect took in everything, from the hull and the boilers right through to such things as the dining-room crockery and glassware. Virtually nothing was left untouched, or perhaps more accurately stated, undesigned.

As far as the importance of public appeal was concerned, *Canberra* portrayed an overall comprehensible impression of finesse and clean-lined modernity which bespoke the progressive and greatly optimistic times of her creation. Her exterior lines represented an updated impression of the classic liner image. A consistent image was carried throughout *Canberra*'s interiors and right down to the most minute details of her furnishing and outfitting. In other words, the 'packaging' of the ship and her service as a whole created an attractive signature image.

P&O's first *Oriana*, which predated *Canberra* by only a matter of months, made a noteworthy point of comparison. Naval architecture, rather than a sense of public appeal or market image, had been the predominant force in her design. The rationale of *Oriana*'s superstructure lines had to do with ease of manoeuvrability, and that of her two dissimilar funnels had more to do with function than form. Much loved as this great ship was in her own right, she probably suffered more from critics unfamiliar with these matters then she deserved to.

When Project Gemini was launched in 1988 as the genesis planning for a new, exclusively-British, cruise ship, *Canberra* was carefully studied from the standpoint of the type of cruise experience and service she offered. Her twenty per cent share of all cruises sold in Britain, accounting for forty-five per cent of those starting and ending in Britain, were business factors to be reckoned with.

What the Project Gemini people learned was that *Canberra* had become something of an institution, having taken on a club-like atmosphere in which a growing core of 'regulars' welcomed the intake of newcomers as a private club might foster its membership. In Germany the same phenomenon was also to be found with *Europa*'s loyal following, while in Japan *Asuka* started to foster a similar niche in the emerging Japanese luxury cruise market. What P&O had to do was to preserve the unique atmosphere of *Canberra*, with her own special features and atmosphere, and at the same time bring it forward into the context of a larger and more up-to-date ship. While much of the accommodation layout was still current with the trends which *Canberra* herself had helped to form, the newer behind-the-scenes operational rationale developed through modern economy-of-scale thinking would have to be worked into the plan as well.

The new *Oriana* was likewise to offer a wide range of cabin grades, including a larger-than-usual number of four-berth rooms offering the flexibility expected by Britons travelling in groups or individually in shared accommodation. The accommodation in all grades was to be generally improved over the earlier ship's standards in its size, amount of storage space, facilities and fittings, as well as inclusion of private lavatories for all rooms. The top-grade accommodation, comprising eight named suites and sixteen deluxe suites, was on a par with its counterpart amenities on the latest America-based luxury cruise ships, such as those of Holland America and Princess. All twenty-four suites and an additional ninety-four standard cabins were to offer verandas.

A noteworthy feature of *Oriana*'s cabin design was that the ship's planned annual three-month world cruises set the standard for storage space in rooms at all categories. Each was outfitted with a generous amount of wardrobe space with separate full-height sections for long items such as dresses, gowns and coats, as well as half-height rails for suits, shirts, blouses and skirts. A minimum of twelve drawers was provided in each room's bedside cabinets and dressing-table fitments, with storage space for suitcases and other bulky items being provided beneath the lower beds.

However, *Oriana* sadly lacked anything as original as *Canberra*'s and the earlier *Oriana*'s attractive 'court' cabin arrangements. This unusual feature, shared by only a very few other ships, had the attraction of also offering periodic glimpses of natural daylight admitted to the long passages of the cabin

Oriana: **Examples of the ship's wide range of accommodation grades, showing the standard outer cabin (left), and a larger deluxe suite with veranda (right).**

(Meyer Werft, Papenberg)

decks, a refinement lacking in the modern rationale of ruthlessly standardised economy-of-scale accommodation planning. Also not to be found was the single centre passage plan which the court cabin groupings made possible in the forward part of the earlier ship. Nonetheless, *Oriana*'s overall cabin layout was well orientated around a simple arrangement of twin parallel passages throughout.

A wide variety of public rooms was also offered, reflecting *Canberra*'s diversity of facilities. However, the one item to be specifically excluded was the Las Vegas-style theatre/lounge, indigenous to virtually all new America-based tonnage. This was considered to be neither consistent with the entertainment preferences of British passengers nor with the club-like onboard atmosphere to be retained. The main show place would instead be a true theatre auditorium, with full production facilities for the music-hall-style variety shows, plays and other features which P&O's own clientele had become accustomed to. Two alternative lounges were also to be equipped for professional production facilities for night-club and more intimate cabaret-style revues, as well as daytime musical recitals and for dancing. In addition to a wider range of entertainment expected, dancing has also become an important aspect of British cruising lifestyle. Apart from ballroom dancing and elaborate programmes of daytime dance instruction, 'synchronised dancing' has become a staple P&O Cruises feature, where passengers can themselves perform for their shipmates.

The two secondary show lounges also had to do daytime duty as places for handicrafts classes and for bridge tournaments and whist drives, as well as for traditional British shipboard horse racing. The new *Oriana* would also need a separate daytime drawing room for English afternoon tea and for classical music recitals, replicating the primary function of *Canberra*'s much-admired Meridian Room. A separate cinema/auditorium would also be needed for film shows and for

the cruise port lectures which, like their German counterparts aboard *Europa*, British cruise passengers tend to take fairly seriously. Finally, P&O could also expect their home clientele to demand a variety of smaller and more specialised bars and club rooms, spacious and well-appointed libraries and card rooms as well as children's playrooms.

However, the new *Oriana*'s plan was not merely to ossify in the mould of *Canberra*'s glory, but also to incorporate various features either lacking or not as well developed in the existing flagship. These included the addition of a modern health spa, prominently positioned in a forward-facing location atop the ship with windows forward, port and starboard. The universal modern-day cruise lifestyle demand for alter-

Oriana: **The very complete range of public rooms included a separate cinema, augmenting the theatre for film shows, lectures, business assemblies and other functions.**

(Meyer Werft)

native informal daytime dining was met with a *Royal Princess*-style facility located around the base of the funnel. Also included was a full-scale casino with a separate arcade for slot machines. All of these were facilities not included in *Canberra*'s original plan, but which were worked into the layout one way or another over the years as the need for them arose.

Perhaps most importantly of all, *Canberra*'s well-articulated overall plan and its especially free flow of movement among the ship's public spaces, cabin areas and open deck areas was reproduced and improved upon wherever possible. This enduring quality of *Canberra*'s design was particularly remarkable in view of the fact that she was built as a two-class ship with provision for being opened up in cruise service. As in the case of Holland America's *Rotterdam*, very little needed to be done to adapt the ship for permanent cruising service.

The back-to-back arrangement of *Canberra*'s purser's offices and other ship's services in the middle of the promenade deck was perhaps a little awkward in her cruise role, as were the partial-height stairways accessing her cinema tucked away amidst the cabin block on the two decks above. In the new *Oriana*, the corresponding site of *Canberra*'s purser's lobbies was opened up, and in effect turned inside out, around the atrium's central focal point. Thus the ship's offices and services formed a periphery element surrounding the key hub of circulation at the centre of things. The cinema was integrated into the main assembly of public spaces, and the dining rooms were close at hand, being but one deck below the main lounges. Three stairtowers of near-identical plan provided access to all decks, keeping the lines of vertical circulation simple and direct. The detailed design work which was carried out among the owners, builders and interior designers has done great justice to the influence of *Canberra*. It has brought the essence of her outstanding original design ahead by at least two generations.

The new *Oriana*'s profile was considerably heavier and her lines of form stockier in concession to the vast volume of internal space needed for the economy-of-scale proportions of larger cabins, extended public spaces and more supporting services of one kind or another. The need of economisers and energy-reclaim facilities for economical running and of silencers and filters to satisfy stringent environmental protection measures has made a thicker funnel necessary. *Oriana* was formed with perhaps more the stature of a Bentley or Rolls Royce than a Ferrari.

Yet in these lines of form and scale of proportion, *Oriana* has undoubtedly materialised as a descendent of *Canberra*. The plated-in deck with its regular-sized cabin windows above the lifeboat recess gave a similar visual balance of masses between the open and closed-in areas of the superstructure as contributed so successfully to the earlier ship's distinctive image. The swept-back form of the lifeboat openings themselves were a direct copy of *Canberra*'s attractively subtle streamlining. The funnel has been skilfully contoured to give the impression of *Canberra*'s immediately-recognisable twin stacks. It is only when *Oriana* is viewed either head on or from astern that one sees how the two profiles are joined or 'webbed' to form the single stack of required girth.

As in *Canberra* the massif of the funnel and its base structure was visually balanced against the mast and a corresponding extension of the forward part of the superstructure. The pavilion-style enclosure forward on the sun deck, service enclosure above it on the observation deck and the health spa below at lido deck level to some extent replicated the earlier ship's four-deck bridge structure. *Oriana*'s superstructure front is also stepped back at these levels, not only identifying her with *Canberra*'s appearance, but also providing a similar forward-facing open deck. However, except for the fanhouse on the observation deck, the enclosed spaces are for passenger use rather than officers' accommodation as on the earlier ship. The bridge is below, and farther forward in the superstructure proper.

The arrangement of the lido deck, with its glassed-in

Oriana: **Running her trials in the North Sea, the unquestionably *Canberra*-inspired arrangement of her upper decks is clearly visible. Note the inset of the windscreening along the top deck and above the navigating bridge, one of the finer points retained from the earlier ship's design.**

(Meyer Werft)

promenade encircling the health spa, reflects an up-to-date adaptation of *Canberra*'s top-deck windscreening with an outer promenade area. While the forward superstructure enclosure of the health spa extended to the full beam of the ship, with enclosed promenades at either side, the set-back glass windscreens were repeated forward of it, providing both protected and exposed open deck areas overlooking the ship's bow. The retention of this unique refinement of the earlier ship was in consideration of the fact that British passengers prefer a far greater contact with the elements than do their counterparts from across the pond. While American cruise patrons traditionally tend to prefer exposure, primarily to the tanning rays of the sun, from above only, Britons still want to be able to feel the sea air and salt spray in their hair and faces.

Although concealed at its forward end within the superstructure plating, the main open promenade-deck loop five decks lower down, beneath the lifeboats, was carried all the way around the ship as was *Canberra*'s. Once again, the main public rooms were located at this level, although in their greater scale and numbers they were extended to much of D deck above, between the boats themselves. Carnival-style single indoor promenade passages along the port side of both decks provided access to these and with the linking element of the four-deck high atrium at its uppermost two levels.

Many of the rooms themselves echoed *Canberra*'s corresponding spaces in their function and character. The interior designers' brief called for a British character with a capital B. Nowhere was this more apparent perhaps than in the Lord's Tavern, a friendly cricket-theme rendezvous place in character with *Canberra*'s always well-patronised Cricketer's Tavern. John McNeece, whose office was responsible for most of *Oriana*'s public interiors, drew his inspiration for this room's decoration from the Lord's Cricket Ground at St John's Wood, near his own home in London.

Slightly larger than *Canberra*'s Cricketers, *Oriana*'s Lord's was given a more open expression, with one of the longer sides of its L-shaped plan exposed to the promenade deck with five large windows and double doors opening the space up to a deck café area. A central feature of the room's interior was the bar with its overhead awning styled after the canvas canopies atop the Mound Stand stadium at Lord's. As in its prototype aboard *Canberra*, the room's decoration was made up largely of genuine cricket artifacts and memorabilia.

Apart from the technical sophistication of its fittings, particularly the millwork, bar handrail details and picture framing, the scheme was rendered with a sense of humour too. One wall was covered with a life-size *trompe l'oeil* depicting a cricket match in progress at Lord's, from a viewpoint behind the backs of a number of spectators standing at the edge of the pitch. Part of the idea of this was that wives could photograph their husbands from behind as though they too would be watching along with the painted figures on the wall. The room's green carpeting was specially woven to give the 'lined' appearance of a freshly rolled cricket pitch when seen in varying lighting conditions about the room. Real cricket balls were fitted into the ends of the bar handrail sections, as details intended to be 'discovered' by passengers while they became more intimately familiar with the room during a cruise. Also waiting to be discovered were the 'awful' ham-and-eggs team colours of the MCC (Marylebone Cricket Club), which were featured in the bordering of the window blinds.

The Anderson Room, named after the Peninsular Steam Navigation Company's founder Arthur Anderson, was another room with a distinctively British character. It was unashamedly based on a traditional London club theme, with a marble-topped bar, classical paintings hung on richly panelled walls, ornate carpeting and opulent period-style furniture, including winged club chairs. This room too offered its own sense of humour. The contents of the large breakfront cabinets were not real, but rather exquisite *trompes l'oeil* of antique books and china artifacts, concealing the modern amenities of large-screen televisions which would otherwise be out of place in those surroundings. Nonetheless the televisions are there for occasions such as the FA Cup finals and Wimbledon, when British passengers would consider them not only appropriate but essential in any surroundings. The lower doors of these cabinets conceal the required firefighting equipment. A little fun was had here at the expense of the regulatory authorities, with the obligatory letter F also being scribed into the decorative scrollwork of the door handles.

In McNeece's opinion, the Harlequin Room was *Oriana*'s most difficult interior to design. The room had to be different things at various hours around the clock: a ballroom for dancing or alternatively cabaret lounge during the evening hours, a night club or discotheque late at night, as well as a multifunction lounge during the daytime. The morning and afternoon roles alone involved such diverse activities as dance instruction, crafts classes and tournament play. A large floor area was needed for ballroom, line and synchronised dancing, as well as for cutting bolts of cloth needed for handicrafts and arranging tables for bridge and whist. Alternatively a smaller space was required for the discotheque and night club. McNeece resolved this dilemma by way of a spacious rectangular floor with an elliptically-shaped compass rose pattern set into its centre. This provided enough visual delineation of the space so that furniture could be moved onto the periphery area surrounding the central ellipse when the larger seating capacity and smaller dancing space were needed.

Illumination also played an important role in the transformation of Harlequin to its disco role, with a colonnade of focused lights surrounding the disco dance floor. Passengers stepped through this 'barrier' of luminescence to cross between the dance floor and the rest of the room. Harlequin's good appearances were retained at other times of the day by concealing the disco lighting above a reflective ceiling made of one-way mirrored solar glass above the dance floor, reflecting the elliptical shape of its smaller elliptical central area.

Harlequin and the Pacific Lounge both replicate *Canberra*'s central William Fawcett room as alternative night-time entertainment or dancing venues which also had to work well as

Oriana: Harlequin's, where John McNeece and his staff tackled the age-old ships' interior design problem of making a room to equally well serve various and differing functions at different hours of the day and night. The high emphasis on special entertainment lighting and production effects in a modern cruise ship makes the task more challenging than ever.

(Meyer Werft)

bright and airy daytime lounges that would not be overburdened with the presence of entertainers' paraphernalia standing idle during those hours. Although the Curzon Room was created as *Oriana*'s worthy equivalent to *Canberra*'s elegant Meridian Room, it unfortunately lacked its openness of plan.

The Peter Pan's playroom for children, one of several interiors designed by Robert Tillberg, provided *Oriana* with among the best facilities for youngsters aboard any modern cruise ship. This attractive, bright and spacious room, with its own kitchen and toilet facilities, was spacious enough to provide separate areas for various activities such as painting and drawing, games and various other amusements. In addition to the numerous toys provided, there was a play house with its own garden, a Lego table, and computer and video games for the older children. The facility, staffed by two full-time children's hostesses, was an unqualified success in keeping the little ones happy and amused throughout the day, to the point that they were seldom to be seen wandering about the ship for want of ways to pass the time.

Apart from the 'processional' staircases joining the various levels of *Oriana*'s atrium, a small spiral stairway was also added nearby to connect to the Selfridges shopping area's two levels. This was at least a noble gesture towards replicating *Canberra*'s most admired architectural feature, her dramatically lighted spiral ascent from the Meridian Room to her Crow's Nest four decks higher up. While *Oriana* was given a wider range of public rooms, her designers managed to maintain a general feeling of intimacy and human scale throughout. This was an important aspect of maintaining *Canberra*'s acquired club-like atmosphere on the new ship's larger scale. *Oriana*'s architects resisted any urge to glorify the expression of vastness in favour of expressing elegance and good taste.

The fine example of P&O's second *Oriana* clearly showed that, despite the criticisms of modern naval architecture often made by traditionalists, worthy new fleetmates and eventual successors could be built for such famed and well-loved ships as *Canberra*. As the fifth *Europa* has retained Hapag-Lloyd's rich sense of tradition and classic sense of timeless onboard elegance, and Holland America's *Statendam*-class ships have upheld *Rotterdam*'s sense of superb comfort and luxury, so too has *Oriana* retained P&O's unique image so meticulously created with her earlier namesake and with *Canberra*. In all of these examples the new rationale of optimised workflows, centralised and integrated services, and structural bulk needed to enclose the necessary revenue-earning payloads, have been contained within functional forms and with internal styling which at least endeavour to uphold the existing and well-known fleet images of which they have become a newer manifestation.

The influence of the original Project Gemini work done with Lloyd Werft was certainly evident in the layout of *Oriana*, as built. Bremer Vulkan's project plans which once bore public room names such as Ocean Room, Meridian Room and Century Bar, have evolved further, and ultimately into the realisation of yet another cruise ship of great individuality. An alternative interior layout, featuring a near-absolute horizontal division between cabin and public spaces two decks above the lifeboat recess, formed the basis of the yard's 1,800- and 2,300-PAX designs.

It was this that formed the basis of a contract signed for first one, and then two, large ships in the 70,000-ton range. The name *Costa Germanica* was first mooted

Costa Victoria: **An imposing ship of massive proportions which bring her into the truly big-ship league. Nonetheless, she still possesses the clean-lined businesslike look of the liner, as prescribed by Costa's design philosophy.**

(Cost Cruise Lines)

in early 1994, with the ship eventually being laid down as *Costa Victoria*. The general arrangement, featuring an upper-decks concentration of the public spaces, coincided with the design approach of the existing *Costa Classica/Romantica* and with the two smaller converted ships. With the same 'retrospective' styling of their design approach, these ships, which were under construction at the time of writing, showed promise of exhibiting a rich sense of individuality. Some of their more notable features included a forward-sited atrium with an outlook over the bow from three decks, as well as the unusual location of an indoor swimming pool and health spa complex at the promenade-deck level beneath the lifeboats.

Following the yard's closing after *Costa Victoria*'s delivery the second hull was purchased by NCL and renamed *Norwegian Sky*. Somewhat restyled by Tillberg Design this ship is to emerge with a unique identity all her own. With her bridge lowered two decks and elimination of some of the Costa ship's uppermost deckhousings, she will present a longer and sleeker look with the addition of two strata of cabin verandas.

Despite the great diversity of cruise ship designs already proven in service, the latest Costa newbuildings seemed to show the boundless possibilities for creativeness in ship design which the human mind can render.

1   Stephen M Payne, *Cruise & Ferry Info*, No 2, 1994, pp 18-19.
2   *Lloyd's List*, November 19, 1992, p 7.
3   *Lloyd's Ship Manager, Cruise and Ferry Quarterly Review*, November 1993, p 34.
4   *Lloyd's Ship Manager, Cruise and Ferry Quarterly Review*, February 1992, p S9.
5   Georgio Ciucci, *Passegna*, December 1990, p 37.
6   *Lloyd's Ship Manager, Cruise and Ferry Quarterly Review*, February 1992, p S12.
7   Tony Newman, *The Naval Architect*, January 1992, p E40.
8   Pierluigi Cerri, *Domus*, p 54.
9   Pierluigi Cerri, *Domus*, p 54.
10 Tony Newman, *The Naval Architect*, January 1991, p E31.
11 *The Naval Architect*, May 1991, p E213.
12 David Tinsley, *Lloyd's List*, 7 April 1993, p 7
13 Stephen M Payne, *Cruise & Ferry Info*, No 2, 1994, pp 18-19.
14 *Lloyd's List*, November 19, 1992, p 7.
15 *Lloyd's Ship Manager, Cruise and Ferry Quarterly Review*, November 1993, p 34.
16 *Lloyd's Ship Manager, Cruise and Ferry Quarterly Review*, February 1992, p S9.
17 Georgio Ciucci, *Passegna*, December 1990, p 37.
18 *Lloyd's Ship Manager, Cruise and Ferry Quarterly Review*, February 1992, p S12.
19 Tony Newman, *The Naval Architect*, January 1992, p E40.
20 Pierluigi Cerri, *Domus*, p 54.
21 Pierluigi Cerri, *Domus*, p 54.
22 Tony Newman, *The Naval Architect*, January 1991, p E31.
23 *The Naval Architect*, May 1991, p E213.
24 David Tinsley, *Lloyd's List*, 7 April 1993, p 9.

EPILOGUE

During the two years leading up to the publication of this book, the constant pace of cruise shipping development seems boundless. Ever more tonnage and products of great individuality are coming on-stream and are planned for the dawning years of the new millennium.

Robert Tillberg believes that the present boom in passenger ship building will continue for at least the next ten years, and feels that there probably will be no end in sight even after that. Yet he believes that there is not likely be any great revolution in marine design bringing about any radically new ship types, but rather a sustained evolution of new ideas. Indeed, with Disney's entry into the field and Cunard's plans for new tonnage, there is, if anything, a heightened sense of regard for the still enormously powerful classic image of the ocean liner.

Without doubt, THE most significant new ship to enter service in 1998 is *Disney Magic*. Apart from the many other features which make her unique, she was particularly noteworthy as being the first cruise ship to be specifically designed to also provide for families with children.

The Walt Disney Company's announcement in 1992 that they would enter the cruise field was met with some scepticism within the industry, that a billion-dollar project was being mounted by a company with no deep-sea shipping experience. Yet this remarkably progressive organisation has applied their vast experience of running theme parks and resorts, and operating the supporting infrastructures which transport, feed, lodge and entertain the people who visit them, in ways which are in many regards new and refreshing. Where special expertise was needed in fields such as naval architecture, marine engineering, design and other technical and supporting functions, Disney succeeded in assembling, to use their own preferred term, a 'cast' from some of the industry's most prominent people and organisations.

In line with their extensive architectural work ashore, which consistently stresses a clarity of its various styles and an appropriate regard for historical authenticity, Disney asked that their ships be created as 'modern classics'. Based on a concept developed by Njål Eide, with additional work done by Robert Tillberg and the American industrial design firm, frogdesign, *Disney Magic* was given a contemporary interpretation of the child's story-book image of a great ocean liner. With two stylised steamship funnels above a snowy white superstructure, itself atop a dark hull, the ship created a dramatically classic impression.

Disney Magic's substantial size of 83,338 tons, was skilfully down-played in her exterior appearance by the use of a number of techniques which tend more to emphasise the proportions of a classic liner. The hull was painted in Anthracite, a colour whose thirteen per cent blue content is less severe than absolute black. While nested lifeboats have become the standard for ships of this size, Njål Eide had the idea to create the attractive visual effect of a traditional outfitting of upper-deck lifeboats, by arranging the lido-deck windows in stylised 12m bays corresponding to the location of the lifeboats four decks lower down.

The bow plating was extended upwards to create a fully-enclosed forward mooring deck covered by a modified whaleback. This effectively gave the impression of a low, and long, superstructure. The three strata of cabin verandas above the lifeboats were arranged with openings corresponding to the boat locations, surrounding groups of five verandas each at the first two levels, and a continuous line of open verandas above. This too helped to diminish any excessive impression of height and also gave the visual effect of 'floating' the lido-deck window bays above the superstructure sides.

The ship's design combined modern forms and ideas with the more traditional elements. While visually complementing the classic semi-circular superstructure front, *Disney Magic*'s ultra modern double-height navigating bridge introduced a contemporary sense of the scientific and technological installations at Disney's EPCOT (Experimental Prototype Community Of Tomorrow) theme park in Orlando. Apart from the bridge's space-age interior, other influences of the Walt Disney Company's ever-resourceful Imagineering department were to be found in the Oceaneer Club and Lab areas exclusively for children, as well as the Animator's Palate restaurant – a remarkable restaurant which changed itself from a completely black-and-white scheme to full colour during the course of the dinner service.

The exclusively-for-children Mickey's Kids' Pool was shaped to look like the famed and beloved little cartoon mouse, which Walt Disney himself created in 1928, and which launched his phenomenal world-wide success. Mickey Mouse's colour yellow was used for the lifeboats and a riband just below the boat deck. The ship's rounded stern was adorned with a 4-metre sculpture of Disney's Goofy, poised precariously with paint bucket and brush as though touching up the filigree work.

Disney Magic was built to also cater to an adult clientele, as are the Disney resorts and many of the attractions at the theme parks ashore. The entire forward section of Deck 4's public areas were designated for exclusive use by grown-ups. Various architectural styles were used throughout the ship's public spaces, ranging from the whimsical to the elegantly formal. The Lumière's Restaurant successfully recreated the dining ambience of a French- or Italian-Line Atlantic leviathan, while the adults-only Palo restaurant aft on Deck 10, with its outlook over the ship's stern, was distinctly reminiscent of Normandie's famous Café Grill. The design scheme for the Disney Theatre and its adjoining lobby bar have emerged in the art-deco style of New York's Radio City Music Hall. The main atrium lobby was given a Grand Hotel feel, perhaps reminiscent more of a Mississippi River Boat, depending perhaps on one's point of view or sense of imagination.

The cabin accommodation was created to present a more timeless nautical feel, particularly in the rooms which had large porthole rather than a veranda. A notable feature of the rooms in most grades was the inclusion of convertible settees, allowing a family of four to be comfortably accommodated in a single stateroom. A most thoughtful detail in planning for family living was the division of the en-suite bathroom into two separate areas, one with a toilet, the other with bath or shower, and a washbasin in both. This was

a planning detail originating with Disney's family resorts ashore.

P&O/Princess's *Grand Princess* also took to the seas during 1998, as the world's largest and most expensive cruise ship thus far, at 109,000 tons. Designed by Gionfranco Bertaglia, she too was created as a modern classic in her own right, drawing on an amalgam of nautical, non-nautical, classic and contemporary influences. The semi-circular superstructure front and the soft lines of the bow, incorporating a unique walk around the promenade, were, as in the Disney example, inspired by the illustrious era of the great ocean liners.

The transom and aft quarters were designed as a modern representation of a seventeenth-century sailing galleon's high stern, complete with protrusions representing the immense lanterns of these ancient ships. The galleon effect was also stressed through a progressive increase of the superstructure height towards the stern. This was achieved, not only by the addition of a quarter deck, but also by the inclined lines of the retractable dome ahead of the funnel, and an inclined gallery accessing the ship's unique lounge pod fully aft.

In complete contrast with this idea and with the otherwise nautical expression of the ship, the 'lantern protrusions' were topped off by a wide lounge pod in the form of an automotive ground spoiler, housing the ship's discotheque and night club. This, to some degree, reflected the shape of the fully-enclosed navigating bridge forward. In an early visualization of his galleon concept, Bertaglia had wanted to construct the 'lanterns' of glass, using them to house panoramic lifts accessing the lounge pod above.

The idea of the spoiler-shaped pod had to do with creating an image of the style and stability of fast cars and asserting an expression of the ship's own 'directionality'. The change of expression from *Grand Princess*'s gentler curvilinear, and unquestionably nautical, bow and forward superstructure forms, to the stronger lines and juxtaposition of marine and non-marine idiom astern as the ship passes, was truly remarkable. One wonders, though, if the travelling public grasped and understood the sailing galleon references.

Like *Disney Magic*, *Grand Princess* was intrinsically a ship of prodigious height. Yet the impression of this, with as many as five tiers of cabin verandas above the lifeboats, avoided an overbearing appearance. The verandas at the lower two levels were extended farther out above the lifeboats than those of the decks above them. This had the effect of reducing the impression of the ship's sheer height when viewed from near or afar.

Whilst *Grand Princess* was designed with some unique spaces of her own, the scale of these individually tended to avoid celebrating the ship's size in the way that, for instance, larger and more open areas were featured in *Carnival Destiny*. Aboard *Grand Princess*, Genoese architect Giacomo Mortola, and Princess's own Theresa Anderson have continued to express some of the more traditional liner elegance of the fleet's interior architecture.

Beyond these latest deliveries already in service, Disney's second ship, *Disney Wonder* is scheduled to sail in mid 1999. Already Carnival has ordered four more vessels in their Destiny class, while *Grand Princess* is to be joined by a pair of near-identical sisters in her class.

The largest vessels to be ordered thus far are Royal Caribbean's three Project Eagle vessels at a colossal 136,000 tons each. The most outstanding design feature of these is to be a high horizontal atrium extending along the centre of each, for much of the entire superstructure's length. First introduced on a smaller scale in the 1990-delivered Baltic ferry *Silja Serenade*, this feature's rendition on the Eagle ships will likewise feature inside cabins with a view into the atrium. Other novelties will include a dining room three decks high and the industry's first ever ocean-going ice-skating rink and rock-climbing wall. The exterior appearance will be fairly conventional, presenting a taller and heavier impression of the Line's Vision class, with the Viking Crown Lounge once again attached to the funnel.

While these already bring the number of ships in the 100,000-ton-plus category to eleven, Carnival, Celebrity, Costa and Royal Caribbean have each also ordered more vessels in the 85,000-ton range, which has now become the second level in the economy-of-scale hierarchy.

The slightly smaller *Superstar Leo* and *Superstar Virgo*, which were completed at Meyer Werft for Singapore-based Star Cruise in 1998 and 1999 respectively, will debut as the first ships designed specifically for the rapidly-growing Asian cruise market. The points of reference for Star Cruises are quite different from most American- and European-based lines. They are more hotel oriented and stress a greater range of interior themes, reflecting various atmospheres from various parts of the world.

In the Japanese restaurant there are to be genuine tatami and tapenyaki rooms. Star Cruises will offer the largest Chinese restaurants afloat, each of which will feature three intimate VIP rooms. They are also moving in new directions for alternative informal dining, with the Blue Lagoon dining areas offering Oriental and 'Hawkers' fast food. The lido areas will be themed on Singapore's colonial Raffles feel. The ten deluxe suites are named after Asian cities such as, Tokyo, Shanghai, Taipai, Hong Kong and Singapore, with the decoration endeavouring to capture the spirit of each.

There is a general trend towards the visual contrasts of bright and vivid colours, lacquered surfaces and patterned fabrics. The design scheme also has to recognise a great diversity of cultural background. For instance, Chinese people tend to love the European influence of wealth and opulence, with Palladian themes and elements of Wren, Wedgewood and Adams. Malaysians prefer to have more things from their own culture with some European influence, but with their own points of reference.

While Renaissance and Silverseas have each extended their original Yachtcruiser-style products up to a second generation of ships in the over 20,000-ton range, other new yachts have entered the ultra-exclusive under 5,000-ton opposite to economy-of-scale. Among these are *Mystique Princess* (1996) and *Le Levant* (1998), both of which offer superb accommodation and service on voyages to exotic destinations beyond the reach of many larger vessels.

Looking to a perhaps more distant horizon, Cunard's recently announced Project Queen Mary shows great promise of introducing a new generation of ocean liners. This is being planned not merely as a cruise vessel capable of making occasional crossings, but as a true deep-sea superliner with the structural stamina and reserves of power required for regular Atlantic service, with cruise facilities of the highest standard added. Since Cunard is now owned by Carnival Corporation, it is unlikely that only one such ship will be built or that it will be under 100,000 tons in size. Certainly the far horizons of cruise shipping are wide and bright.

APPENDIX A

Ships' specifications

ANDES (AS BUILT 1939)

Owners	Royal Mail Lines Ltd, London, England
Registry	Great Britain
Classification	Lloyds Register 100 A 1 and British Board of Trade survey
Service	Atlantic service between Southampton, Santos, Bahia, Rio de Janeiro, Montevideo and Buenos Aires. Later adapted for worldwide cruising.
Builders	Harland & Wolff, Queen's Island, Belfast
Contract price	£1.36 million
Hull number	1005
Delivery date	24 September 1939
Length oa	204.00m
Length bp	192.02m
Beam, moulded	25.40m
Draught, maximum	8.92m
Height, to strength deck	14.48m (C dk)
GRT	25,689
Service speed	21.0kts
Propulsion power	22,368Kw (ind)
Passenger capacity	607
Crew	451
Number of decks	7
Watertight subdivision	11 transverse bulkheads
Main machinery	2 sets of triple-expansion steam turbines driving twin fixed-pitch 3-bladed screws through single-reduction gearing. The machinery was of Parsons design, built by Harland & Wolff. Steam was provided by Babcock-Johnson superheat watertube boilers.
Auxiliaries	3,000kV of electric power at 220DC, generated by 3 turbo-alternator sets, augmented by 2 diesel generators for use in port.
Manoeuvrability	Single rudder
Stabilisers	Denny-Brown fin stabilisers were fitted later in the ship's career.
Structural design	Royal Mail with Harland & Wolff
Interior design	Heaton Tabb & Co with Hampton and Sons

ASTOR (FIRST SHIP)

Owners	Hadag Cruise Line GmbH, Hamburg, Germany
Registry	Germany
Classification	Germanische Lloyd +100 A4 E1 'Mit Friebord 2,005m' Fahrgastschiff MC E 1 Aut
Service	7-day cruises
Builders	Howaldtswerke-Deutsche Werft AG, Hamburg, Germany
Contract price	US$55 million
Hull number	165
Delivery date	23 December 1981
Length oa	164.35m
Length bp	140.00m
Beam, moulded	22.60m
Draught, maximum	6.12m
Height, to strength deck	16.05m (Prom dk)
GRT	18,835
Service speed	18.0kts
Propulsion power	14,200kW (ind)
Passenger capacity	638
Crew	210
Number of decks	9
Watertight subdivision	12 transverse bulkheads
Main machinery	4 x 6-cylinder, 4-stroke M A N 6-L-40/45 medium-speed diesel engines, connected in pairs through Lohmann & Stolterfoht GVA 1500 8/So reduction gearing to 2 skew-back KaMeWa propellers of 4.3m diameter driven at 155rpm. The engines were of 400mm bore and 480mm stroke.

Auxiliaries	2,800kW of electric power generated by 2 alternators driven by the main engines. Backup/redundancy power of 6,000kW provided by 4 additional alternators, each driven by a M A N 9-AS-2-25/30 medium-speed diesel engine.
Manoeuvrability	2 rudders, 1 900kW bow thruster
Stabilisers	AEG/Denny Brown fin stabilisers
Structural design	Howaldtswerke-Deutsche Werft
Interior design	Howaldtswerke-Deutsche Werft

ASUKA

Owners	NYK (Nippon Yusen Kaisha) Line, Tokyo, Japan
Registry	Japan
Classification	NK (NS★ 'Passenger Ship', NMS★ MO B), USCG
Service	Worldwide cruising
Builders	Mitsubishi Heavy Industries, Nagasaki, Japan
Contract price	US$86 million
Hull number	?
Delivery date	19 April 1989
Length oa	192.00m
Length bp	160.00m
Beam, moulded	24.70m
Draught, maximum	6.60m
Height, to strength deck	15.95m (Main dk)
GRT	28,717
Service speed	21.0kts
Propulsion power	17,300kW (ind)
Passenger capacity	604
Crew	243
Number of decks	11
Watertight subdivision	? transverse bulkheads
Main machinery	2 x 7-cylinder medium-speed Mitsubishi-M A N, B & W 7-L58/64 diesel engines, direct driving twin Lips controllable-pitch propellers through reduction gearing at a maximum of 138rpm. The propellers were of 4.6m diameter.
Auxiliaries	3,400kW of electric power generated by 2 alternators driven by the main engines. Backup/redundancy power of 5,100kW provided by 3 additional alternators, each driven by a Daihatsu 8DL-28 medium-speed diesel engine.
Manoeuvrability	1 spade-type rudder, 1 x 1,450kW bow thruster
Stabilisers	Sperry folding-fin stabilisers
Structural design	Mitsubishi Heavy Industries
Interior design	Co-ordinating architect, Robert Tillberg

ATLANTIC (1982)

Owners	Home Lines Cruises Inc, New York, USA
Registry	Liberia
Classification	American Bureau of Shipping +A1 E (hull) +AMS (machinery), SOLAS 1974, US Coast Guard and Health regulations
Service	Tropical cruising
Builders	Constructions Navales et Industrielles de la Mediterranee (CNIM), La Seyne, France
Hull number	1432
Delivery date	March 1982
Length, overall	204.70m
Length between perpendiculars	172.00m
Beam, moulded	27.35m
Draught, maximum	7.38m
Height, to strength deck	22.75m (Belvedere dk)
GRT	30,262
Service speed	21.0kts
Propulsion power	22,064kW (ind)
Passenger capacity	1,306
Crew	490
Number of decks	9
Watertight subdivision	transverse bulkheads
Main machinery	2 low-speed 10-cylinder GMT B.600.10 diesel engines, direct driving twin skew back propellers.
Auxiliaries	6,800kVA of electric power generated by 4 separate diesel alternator sets.
Manoeuvrability	Single rudder, 1 thruster fwd
Stabilisers	Fin stabilisers
Structural design	Home Lines/CNIM
Interior design	Studio de Jorio

CANBERRA

Owners	P&O-Orient Lines Limited, London, England
Registry	Great Britain
Classification	Lloyds Register of Shipping +100A1 and Recommendations of the Ministry of Transport.
Service	Line service between Britain and Australia with provision also for worldwide cruising.
Builders	Harland & Wolff, Queen's Island, Belfast
Contract price	GB£16 million
Hull number	1621
Delivery date	19 May 1961
Length oa	249.93m
Length bp	225.55m
Beam, moulded	31.08m
Draught, maximum	9.91m
Height, to strength deck	20.88m (Promenade dk)
GRT	44,807
Service speed	27.50kts
Propulsion power	63,410kW (ind)
Passenger capacity	2,238
Crew	960
Number of decks	14
Watertight subdivision	15 transverse bulkheads
Main machinery	2 AEI turbo-alternator sets, each comprising a 17-stage, single-cylinder

steam turbine driving a 32,200kVA alternator producing 6,000V AC at 51.5Hz max. Each set switchable to either or both double 42-pole synchronous motors, direct-driving a 4-bladed 6.24m diameter fixed-pitch propeller. Steam raised by 4 Foster Wheeler type ESD boilers at 53kg/cm² @ 515°C.

Auxiliaries	4 x 1,500kW AEI turbo alternators feeding a 440V 60Hz bus, with power for domestic use stepped down by transformers to 230V AC.
Manoeuvrability	single rudder, 1 x 597kW thruster fwd
Stabilisers	Denny-Brown fin stabilisers
Structural design	John West with BTH Ltd (machinery) and Harland & Wolff
Interior design	Co-ordinating architect, Sir Hugh Casson

CARNIVAL DESTINY

Owners/operator	Carnival Cruise Lines, Miami, USA
Registry	Liberia
Classification	Lloyds Register +100A1 + LMC, UMS, SOLAS 1990, US Coast Guard and Health regulations
Service	Caribbean cruising
Builders	Fincantieri Narghera Yard, Venice, Italy
Contract price	US$400 million
Hull number	?
Delivery date	late 1996
Length oa	272.00m
Length bp	?m
Beam, moulded	38.00m
Draught, maximum	8.25m
Height, to superstructure	?m
GRT	100,000
Service speed	21.0kts
Propulsion power	63,400kW (ind)
Passenger capacity	3,360
Crew	1,040
Number of decks	14
Watertight subdivision	18 transverse bulkheads
Power Plant	Integrated power plant comprising 6 diesel alternator sets, powered Sulzer driving ABB/ Strömberg 3-phase synchronous generators through elastic couplings. Power generated at 6,600V 60Hz 3-phase AC, and distributed through a common busbar to meet propulsion and hotel loads. Two main motors, controlled through thyristor cyclo-converters, each motor direct-driving a high-skew controllable-pitch propeller.
	Domestic power stepped down from the main busbar to 440/220/110V
Manoeuvrability	2 rudders, 6 thrusters (3 bow, 3 stern)
Stabilisers	Active-fin stabilisers
Structural design	Technical Marine Planning, London,

	consultants to the owners, Elomarine Ltd, Raisio, Finland, consultants to builders
Interior design	Joseph Farcus, Miami, USA

CARONIA (1949)

Owners	Cunard White Star Line, Liverpool, England
Registry	Great Britain
Classification	Lloyds Register and British Board of Trade survey
Service	North Atlantic service between London and New York, and worldwide cruising
Builders	John Brown and Company (Clydebank) Ltd, Glasgow, Great Britain
Hull number	635
Delivery date	January 1949
Length oa	217.94m
Length bp	202.70m
Beam, moulded	27.74m
Draught, maximum	9.14m
Height, to strength deck	21.41m (Promenade dk)
GRT	34,183
Service speed	21.0kts
Propulsion power	0kW (ind) (?)
Passenger capacity	932
Crew	587
Number of decks	10
Watertight subdivision	10 transverse bulkheads
Main machinery	2 sets of triple-expansion steam turbines, HP, and IP/LP turbines running at 3,686 and 1,990rpm respectively. Driving twin fixed-pitch 4-bladed screws of 5.715m diameter at 140rpm through double-reduction gearing. Steam raised by 6 watertube boilers at 462.2°C.
Auxiliaries	4,400kV of electric power at 224V DC, generated by 4 turbo-alternator sets built by W H Allen & Sons Ltd, plus 2 x 175kVA diesel alternators providing 220V three-phase AC at 50Hz for fluorescent lighting.
Manoeuvrability	Single rudder
Stabilisers	None
Structural design	Cunard & John Brown Ltd
Interior design	Cunard & John Brown Ltd

COSTA CLASSICA
(NEAR-IDENTICAL SISTERSHIP COSTA ROMANTICA COMPLETED 1993)

Owners/operator	Costa Crociere SpA, Genoa, Italy
Registry	Italy
Classification	Registro Italiano Navali (100 A1.1 notation) American Bureau of Shipping +100 A1 Passenger Vessel with IAQ1 and AACU for unmanned engine room.
Service	Worldwide cruising
Builders	Fincantieri Narghera Yard, Venice, Italy
Contract price	US$283.3 million (L365 billion).
Hull number	5877
Delivery date	November 1991

Length oa	219.30m
Length bp	182.00m
Beam, moulded	30.80m
Draught, maximum	7.60m
Height, to superstructure	19.18m (Genoa dk 7)
GRT	52,926
Service speed	19.5kts
Propulsion power	21,200kW (ind)
Passenger capacity	1,904
Crew	607
Number of decks	12
Watertight subdivision	15 transverse bulkheads
Main machinery	4 x 4-stroke 8-cylinder Fincantieri-Garandi Motori/Sulzer ZA40S medium-speed diesel engines, connected in pairs through Renk Tacke reduction gearboxes, driving 2 Lips controllable-pitch 4-blade propellers of 5.2m diameter at 139.36rpm.
Auxiliaries	14,540kW of electric power at 6,600V three-phase AC at 60Hz, generated by 4 Fincantieri-GMT 12-cylinder A320 Series 4-stroke diesel alternator sets. Power is stepped down to 440/220/110V for hotel and domestic services.
Manoeuvrability	2 rudders, 3 x 950kW thrusters (2 fwd, 1 aft)
Stabilisers	Fincantieri folding-fin stabilisers
Structural design	Hull design by F Cernobori
Interior design	Gregotti Associati International srl Milan, Italy

CROWN MONARCH

Owners	Crown Cruise Line, Palm Beach, USA
Registry	Panama
Classification	Det Norske Veritas +1A1 Passenger Ship MV Ice Class 1C, SOLAS 1990, US Coast Guard and Health regulations
Service	Caribbean cruises
Builders	Union Naval de Levante, Valencia, Spain
Contract price	US$95 million
Hull number	185
Delivery date	November 1990
Length oa	150.72m
Length bp	125.10m
Beam, moulded	20.60m
Draught, maximum	5.40m
Height, to strength deck	?m
GRT	15,271
Service speed	20.0kts
Propulsion power	12,400kW (ind)
Passenger capacity	556
Crew	210
Number of decks	8
Watertight subdivision	14 transverse bulkheads
Main machinery	4 x 6-cylinder, Bergen BRM9 medium-speed diesel engines, connected in pairs through Lohmann & Stolterfoht Navilus GVE1200 reduction gearing to 2 Ulstein

	controllable-pitch of 4.0m diameter driven at 165rpm.
Auxiliaries	5,250kVA of electric power generated at 440V three-phase AC at 60Hz by 2 Strömberg alternators driven by the main engines. Backup/redundancy power of 5,250kVA provided by 2 additional alternators, each driven by a Bergen BRG6 medium-speed diesel engine.
Manoeuvrability	2 rudders, 2 x 430kW bow thrusters
Stabilisers	Sperry fin stabilisers
Structural design	Union Naval de Levante
Interior design	Yran & Storbraten

CROWN PRINCESS
(NEAR-IDENTICAL SISTERSHIP REGAL PRINCESS COMPLETED 1991)

Owners/operator	Astramar, SpA, Italy, leased to P&O Group (Princess Cruises), London, England
Registry	Italy
Classification	Registro Italino Navali, Lloyds Register +100A1 + LMC, UMS, SOLAS 1990, US Coast Guard and Health regulations
Service	Worldwide cruising
Builders	Fincantieri Monfalcone Yard, Trieste, Italy
Contract price	US$276.8 million
Hull number	5839 (5840)
Delivery date	May 1990
Length oa	245.00m
Length bp	204.00m
Beam, moulded	32.25m
Draught, maximum	7.85m
Height, to superstructure	20.03m (Promenade dk)
GRT	69,845
Service speed	19.5kts
Propulsion power	24,000kW (ind)
Passenger capacity	1,748 (1,900 max)
Crew	650
Number of decks	14
Watertight subdivision	15 transverse bulkheads
Power Plant	Integrated power plant comprising 4 diesel alternator sets, powered by 8-cylinder M A N, B&W type 8L 58/64 4-stroke medium-speed motors driving Cegelec 3-phase generators. The generator sets each rated at 9,420kW, feed the main switchboard at 6,600V 60Hz 3-phase AC to meet propulsion and hotel loads. Propulsion by 2 Cegelec 12,000kW 24-pole synchronous motors running at a stepless variable speed of up to 145rpm, regulated by 12-pulse static-frequency synchrconverter. Each motor direct-driving a Lips fixed-pitch 6-bladed propeller.
	Domestic power stepped down from the main busbar to 440/220/110V
Manoeuvrability	Single rudder, 3 thrusters (2 fwd, 1 aft)
Stabilisers	Fin stabilisers and Frank Mohn tank heeling control system

Structural design	Charles Arkinstall, Monaco, naval architect to the owners), Exterior styling of ship rendered by Renzo Piano, Genoa, Italy
Interior design	Welton Becket & Asociates, Santa Monica, USA

DISNEY MAGIC (1998)
(NEAR-IDENTICAL SISTERSHIP DISNEY WONDER COMPLETED 1999)

Owners/operator	Disney Cruise Line, Celebration, USA
Registry	Bahamas
Classification	Lloyds Register +100A1 Passenger Ship IWS, US Coast Guard and Health regulations
Service	Caribbean cruising
Builders	Fincantieri Marghera Yard, Venice, Italy
Contract price	US$350 million
Hull number	5989
Delivery date	July 1998
Length oa	294.06m
Length bp	263.32m
Beam, moulded	32.35m
Draught, maximum	7.60m
Height, to bulkhead deck	13.85m (upperdeck)
GRT	83.338
Service speed	21.5kts
Propulsion power	38,000.00kW (ind)
Passenger capacity	1,750 (2,400 max)
Crew	915
Number of decks	14
Watertight subdivision	16 transverse bulkheads
Power plant	Integrated power plant comprising 5 diesel alternator sets powered by 16-cylinder GMT Sulzer 1640S medium-speed motors driving GE generators each rated at 11,200kW, 2 GE 19 MW double-wound synchronous main motors driving a Lips Italia fixed-pitch 6-bladed propeller of 4.87 metre diameter. Domestic power stepped down from the main busbar to 440/220/110V
Manoeuvrability	2 Becker-type rudders, 3 x 1,800kW thrusters (2 bow, 1 stern)
Stabilisers	Atlas fin stabilisers
Structural design	Delatmarin (consulting naval architects), frogdesign (industrial design)
Interior design	Design Continuum, Nial Eide, Yran & Storbraten, Robert Tillberg, The Rockwell Group, Wilson & Associates, Walt Disney Imageering

EUROPA (1981)

Owners	Bremer Schiffsvercharterungs AG, Bremen (leased to Hapag-Lloyd)
Registry	Germany
Classification	Germanische Lloyd 100 A4 E1 (fahrgastschiff + MC, E1 Aut 24/24)), SOLAS 1974, US Coast Guard and Health regulations
Service	Worldwide cruising
Builders	Bremer Vulkan AG Schiffbau und

	Maschinenfabrik, Bremen-Vegesack, Germany
Contract price	DM176.3 million
Hull number	1001
Delivery date	5 December 1981
Length oa	199.92m
Length bp	170.50m
Beam, moulded	28.50m
Draught, maximum	7.85m
Height, to strength deck	18.96m (Haupt dk)
GRT	33,819
Service speed	22.0kts
Propulsion power	21,280kW (ind)
Passenger capacity	600 (758 max)
Crew	295
Number of decks	12
Watertight subdivision	11 transverse bulkheads
Main machinery	2 x 2-stroke, 7-cylinder, crosshead M A N K7 SZ 70/125 B diesel engines, direct driving twin Ostermann fixed-pitch propellers at a maximum of 145rpm. The engines were of 700mm bore and 1,250mm stroke, and the 5-bladed propellers were of 4.75m diameter.
Auxiliaries	5,000kVA of electric power generated by 2 thyristor-regulated Siemens alternators direct driven from the main engines. Additional 10,525kVA power is provided by 5 MWN type TB1 510-6 medium-speed diesel engines driving Siemens alternators. All power generated at 440V 3-phase AC at 60Hz.
Manoeuvrability	single semi-balanced rudder, 1,250kW thruster fwd
Stabilisers	Denny Brown/AEG fin stabilisers type E/h 12s with hydroplane area of $9.1m^2$
Structural design	Hapag-Lloyd and Bremer Vulkan
Interior design	Joachim Buchwald and Wilfred Köhnemann, with further academic advice and council being rendered by Professor Arno Votteler of the Akademie der Bildenen Künste in Stuttgart

FANTASY
(SEVEN NEAR-IDENTICAL SISTERSHIPS COMPLETED BETWEEN 1991-97)

Owners/operator	Carnival Cruise Lines, Miami, USA
Registry	Liberia
Classification	Lloyds Register +100A1 + LMC, UMS, SOLAS 1990, US Coast Guard and Health regulations
Service	Caribbean cruising
Builders	Wärtsilä/Masa-Yard, Helsinki, Finland
Contract price	US$210 million
Hull number	479
Delivery date	26 January 1990
Length oa	260.60m
Length bp	224.00m
Beam, moulded	31.50m
Draught, maximum	7.85m

Height, to superstructure	24.90m (Empress dk)
GRT	70,367
Service speed	21.0kts
Propulsion power	28,000kW (ind)
Passenger capacity	2,634
Crew	920
Number of decks	13
Watertight subdivision	18 transverse bulkheads; longitudinal bulkhead between port and stbd engine rooms
Power Plant	Integrated power plant comprising 6 diesel alternator sets, 4 powered by 12-cylinder vee-form and 3 x 8-cylinder in-line type Sulzer ZA40S medium-speed engines driving ABB/ Strömberg 3-phase synchronous generators through elastic couplings, The 2 larger generator sets each rated at 7,920kW and the 4 smaller units at 5,280kW. Power generated at 6,600V 60Hz 3-phase AC, and distributed through a common busbar to meet propulsion and hotel loads. 2 ABB/Strömberg 14,000kW double-wound synchronous main motors operated at 50–140rpm, controlled through thyristor cyclo-converters, varying the power frequency from 0–14Hz, each motor direct-driving a KaMeWa type 144XF3/4W high-skew controllable-pitch 4-bladed propeller of 5.2m diameter.
	Domestic power stepped down from the main busbar to 440/220/110V
Manoeuvrability	2 Mariner-type semi-balanced rudders, 6 x 1,500 kW thrusters (3 bow, 3 stern)
Stabilisers	Brown Brothers active-fin stabilisers
Structural design	Technical Marine Planning, London, consultants to the owners, Elomarine Ltd, Raisio, Finland, consultants to builders
Interior design	Joseph Farcus, Miami, USA

FUJI MARU

Owners	Mitsui-OSK (Osaka Shosen Kaisha) Lines (Passenger) Ltd Tokyo, Japan
Registry	Japan
Classification	NK (NS★ 'Passenger Ship', NMS★ MO B)
Service	Worldwide cruising
Builders	Mitsubishi Heavy Industries Shipbuilding and Engine Works, Kobe, Japan
Contract price	US$63.5 million
Hull number	1177
Delivery date	19 April 1989
Length oa	167.00m
Length bp	147.00m
Beam, moulded	24.00m
Draught, maximum	6.33m
Height, to strength deck	13.50m (Upper dk)
GRT	23,340
Service speed	20.0kts
Propulsion power	15,750kW (ind)
Passenger capacity	603

Crew	135
Number of decks	8
Watertight subdivision	11 transverse bulkheads
Main machinery	8 x 2-cylinder, crosshead Mitsubishi 8 ECU 52 LA diesel engines, direct driving twin KaMeWa controllable-pitch propellers at a maximum of 133rpm. The four-bladed propellers were of 4.6m diameter.
Auxiliaries	3,200kW of electric power generated by 2 alternators driven by the main engines. Backup/redundancy power of 5,100kW provided by 3 additional alternators, each driven by a Daihatsu 8DL-28 medium-speed diesel engine.
Manoeuvrability	1 spade-type rudder, 1 bow thruster
Stabilisers	Sperry folding-fin stabilisers
Structural design	Mitsubishi Heavy Industries
Interior design	

GRIPSHOLM (1957)

Owners	Svenska Amerika Linien, Göteborg
Registry	Sweden
Classification	Lloyds Register Class A100 (ice strengthened), Registro Italiano Navali, American Bureau of Shipping
Service	dual-purpose, North Atlantic service between Göteborg and New York and worldwide cruising
Builders	Ansaldo S.A., Genova, Italy
Hull number	1500
Delivery date	May 1957
Length oa	192.32m
Length bp	67.85m
Beam, moulded	24.90m
Draught, maximum	8.25m
Height, to strength deck	15.37m (Upper dk)
GRT	23,191
Service speed	19.0kts
Propulsion power	14,762.88kW (ind)
Passenger capacity	842
Crew	364
Number of decks	7
Watertight subdivision	12 transverse bulkheads
Main machinery	2 x 2-stroke single-acting 9-cylinder crosshead Götaverken diesel engines, direct driving twin fixed-pitch propellers at 112rpm. The engines were of 760mm bore and 1,500mm stroke.
Auxiliaries	4,375kVA of electric power at 440V three-phase AC at 60Hz, generated by 5 ASEA diesel alternator sets. Power is distributed at 440, 220 and 24V for domestic, galley and all other auxiliary equipment. 3 exhaust-gas boilers and 2 oil-fired boilers to provide steam for domestic load at 4,000K/hr.

Manoeuvrability	Single rudder
Stabilisers	Denny-Brown fin stabilisers
Structural design	Eric Th Christiansson
Interior design	Svenska Amerika Linien

HOLIDAY

(SLIGHTLY LARGER SISTERSHIPS *JUBILEE* AND *CELEBRATION* COMPLETED BY KOCKUMS, SWEDEN, IN 1986 AND 1987 RESPECTIVELY)

Owners	Carnival Cruise lines, Miami, USA
Registry	Panama
Classification	Lloyds Register +100A1 + LMC, UMS, SOLAS 1974, US Coast Guard and Health regulations
Service	Caribbean cruising
Builders	Aalborg Wærft A/S, Aalborg, Denmark
Contract price	US$170 million
Hull number	246 (Kockums no 596, 597)
Delivery date	20 June 1985
Length oa	222.56m (223.37)
Length bp	183.00m
Beam, moulded	27.00m
Draught, maximum	7.50m
Height, to strength deck	21.05m (Upper dk)
GRT	46,052 (47.262)
Service speed	19.5kts
Propulsion power	23,520kW (ind)
Passenger capacity	1,794 (1,896)
Crew	660 (670)
Number of decks	12
Watertight subdivision	15 transverse bulkheads
Main machinery	2 x 2-stroke, single-acting 7-cylinder, crosshead Sulzer 7RLB66 diesel engines, direct driving twin KaMeWa controllable-pitch propellers at a maximum of 140rpm. The four-bladed propellers were of 5m diameter.
Auxiliaries	6,620kVA of electric power generated by 2 Siemens IFJ5802-6TA-82-Z alternators direct driven from the forward ends of the main engines through Pneumaflex type KAB 430 clutch couplings. Backup/redundancy power of 9,930kVA provided by 3 additional alternators, each driven by a 12-cylinder Wärtsilä Vasa 12 R 32 medium-speed diesel engine through Lohmann & Stolterfoht IMA 800 B two-stage step-up gear boxes.
Manoeuvrability	2 rudders, 4 thrusters (2 x 894KW fwd, 2 x 746kW aft)
Stabilisers	Howaldtswerke-Deutsche Werft AG fin stabilisers
Structural design	Technical Marine Planning, London (consulting naval architects to the owners)
Interior design	Joseph Farcus, Miami

KUNGSHOLM (1953)

Owners	Svenska Amerika Linien, Göteborg
Registry	Sweden
Classification	Lloyds Register Class A100 (ice strengthened)
Service	dual-purpose, North Atlantic service between Göteborg and New York and worldwide cruising
Builders	Koninklijke Mij de Schelde, Flushing, The Netherlands
Hull number	273
Delivery date	October 1953
Length oa	182.87m
Length bp	161.60m
Beam, moulded	23.47m
Draught, maximum	8.02m
Height, to strength deck	14.88m (Main dk)
GRT	21,141
Service speed	19.0kts
Propulsion power	13,048kW (ind)
Passenger capacity	802
Crew	418
Number of decks	6
Watertight subdivision	10 transverse bulkheads
Main machinery	2 x 2-stroke double-acting 8-cylinder Burmeister and Wain diesel engines, direct driving twin fixed-pitch Lips propellers of 5.18m diameter at 115rpm. The engines were of 720mm bore and 1,250mm stroke.
Auxiliaries	4,250kW of electric power at 220V generated by 6 diesel alternator sets for domestic, galley and all other auxiliary equipment. 3 Cochran auxiliary boilers installed to provide steam for domestic load.
Manoeuvrability	Single rudder
Stabilisers	Anti heeling tanks?
Structural design	Eric Th Christiansson
Interior design	H P Mutters & Zoon with Inge Westim

KUNGSHOLM (1966)

Owners	Svenska Amerika Linien, Göteborg
Registry	Sweden
Classification	Swedish Board of Shipping, Lloyds Register Class A100 (ice strengthened)
Service	dual-purpose, North Atlantic service between Göteborg and New York and world cruising
Builders	John Brown & Co (Clydebank) Ltd, Glasgow, Great Britain
Contract price	GB£7 million
Hull number	728
Delivery date	April 1966
Length oa	201.17m
Length bp	173.73m
Beam, moulded	26.52m
Draught, maximum	8.08m
Height, to strength deck	17.95m (Upper dk)
GRT	26,678

Service speed	21.0kts
Propulsion power	22,368kW (ind)
Passenger capacity	750 Atlantic service
	450 cruising
Crew	438
Number of decks	10
Watertight subdivision	11? transverse bulkheads
Main machinery	2 x 2-stroke, single-acting 9-cylinder, crosshead Götaverken VG-9U diesel engines, direct driving twin fixed-pitch propellers at a maximum of 124rpm. The engines were of 760mm bore and 1,500mm stroke.
Auxiliaries	4,000kW of electric power at 440V three-phase AC at 60Hz, generated by 5 ASEA/Ruston and Hornsby diesel alternator sets for domestic, galley and all other auxiliary equipment. 2 Marshall & Anderson exhaust-gas boilers and 2 oil-fired units of the same make provided a total of 16,100Kg/hr steam for domestic load.
Manoeuvrability	Single rudder
Stabilisers	Denny-Brown fin stabilisers
Structural design	Eric Th Christiansson
Interior design	coordinated by Robert Tillberg

MONTE SARMIENTO

Owners	Hamburg Südamerika Dampfschiffahrts Gesellschaft
Registry	Germany
Classification	Germanische Lloyd Class +100A A (E) mit Freibord
Service	emigrant and seasonal farm labourer trade to South America, also used for cruising
Builders	Blohm & Voss, Hamburg
Hull number	407
Delivery date	November 1924
Length oa	159.70m
Length bp	151.50m
Beam, moulded	19.95m
Draught, maximum	7.10m
Height, to strength deck	15.30m (C dk)
GRT	27,288
Service speed	14.20kts
Propulsion power	5,219.20kW (ind)
Passenger capacity	1,010 in cabin berths
	1,460 in open berths
	2,470 total
Crew	239
Number of decks	7
Watertight subdivision	8 transverse bulkheads
Main machinery	4 x 2-stroke, single-acting 6-cylinder crosshead MAN diesel engines of 600mm bore and 700mm stroke. These were coupled in pairs through single-reduction gearing to twin four-bladed variable-pitch propellers of 5.4m diameter. The engine speed of 215rpm was reduced to a

	propeller speed of 77rpm.
Auxiliaries	1050kW of electric power for auxiliary equipment, galley appliances, lighting and other domestic needs were provided by 3 diesel alternator sets.
Structural design	Blohm & Voss
Interior design	Blohm & Voss

NIEUW AMSTERDAM (1983)
(NEAR-IDENTICAL SISTERSHIPS NOORDAM, COMPLETED 1984)

Owners	Holland Amerika Lijn, Rotterdam
Registry	Netherlands Antilles
Classification	Lloyds Register Class + 100 A1/UMS, SOLAS 1974, US Coast Guard and Health regulations
Service	Worldwide cruising
Builders	Chantiers de L'Atlantique, St. Nazaire, France
Contract price	US$150 million
Hull number	V27
Delivery date	July 1983
Length oa	214.65m
Length bp	181.60m
Beam, moulded	27.20m
Draught, maximum	7.40m
Height, to strength deck	21.91m (Main dk)
GRT	33,930
Optimized cruising speed	18.0kts
Propulsion power	21,600kW (ind)
Passenger capacity	1,374
Crew	599
Number of decks	11
Watertight subdivision	? transverse bulkheads
Main machinery	2 x 2-stroke, single-acting 7-cylinder, C C M Sulzer 7RLB66 diesel engines, de-rated to 10,8000kW at 135rpm for optimum fuel economy. Direct driving twin Escher Wyss 4-bladed controllable-pitch propellers of 5m diameter. The engines were of 660mm bore and 1,386mm stroke.
Auxiliaries	4,800kW of electric power generated by 2 Alsthom-Unilec alternators driven at 1,200rpm by the main engines through Lohmann & Stolterfoht gearboxes. Backup/redundancy power of 4,4000kW provided by 2 additional alternators of the same type, both driven by a single C C M Sulzer 4RLB56 low-speed diesel engine through similar step-up gearing.
Manoeuvrability	Single rudder, 2 x 750kW thrusters. (1 fwd, 1 aft)
Stabilisers	Sperry Girofin stabilisers
Structural design	Holland Amerika/Chantiers de L'Atlantique
Interior design	de Vlaming, Fennis, Dingemans BV, Utrecht

ORIANA (1960)

Owners	P&O-Orient Lines Limited, London
Registry	Great Britain
Classification	Lloyds Register of Shipping +100A1 and Recommendations of the Ministry of Transport
Service	Line service between Britain and Australia with provision also for worldwide cruising
Builders	Vickers-Armstrong Ltd, Barrow in Furness
Contract price	GB£14.7 million (approx)
Hull number	1061
Delivery date	15 November 1960
Length oa	245.05m
Length bp	225.55m
Beam, moulded	29.57m
Draught, maximum	9.63m
Height, to strength deck	20.96m (B dk)
GRT	41,923
Service speed	27.50kts
Propulsion power	59,680.00kW (ind)
Passenger capacity	2,184
Crew	899
Number of decks	15
Watertight subdivision	15 transverse bulkheads
Main machinery	2 sets of Vickers/PAMETRADA triple-expansion steam turbines driving twin 4-bladed fixed-pitch screws of 6.09m diameter at 147rpm through double-reduction gearing. Steam raised by 4 Foster Wheeler type ESD boilers at 53 kg/cm² @ 515°C.
Auxiliaries	4 x 1,750kW turbo generators yielding 220V DC, plus 3 x 250kW diesel alternators providing 230V three-phase AC at 50Hz for fluorescent lighting.
Manoeuvrability	Single rudder, 4 x 410kW thrusters. (2 bow, 2 stern)
Stabilisers	Denny-Brown fin stabilisers
Structural design	Charles F. Morris with PAMETRADA (machinery) and Vickers-Armstrong
Interior design	Co-ordinating architects Brian O'Rorke and Prof. MIsha Black

ORIANA (1995)

Owners/operator	P&O Cruises, London
Registry	Great Britain
Classification	Lloyds Register +100A1 + LMC, UMS, Ice Class D, SOLAS 1990, US Coast Guard and Health regulations
Service	Worldwide cruising
Builders	Meyer Werft, Papenberg, Germany
Contract price	GB£280 million
Hull number	636
Delivery date	2 April 1995
Length oa	260.00m
Length bp	224.05m
Beam, moulded	32.20m
Draught, maximum	8.20m
Height, to superstructure	20.40m (Promenade dk)
GRT	69,153
Service speed	24.0kts
Propulsion power	24,000kW (ind)
Passenger capacity	1,975
Crew	760
Number of decks	14
Watertight subdivision	15 transverse bulkheads
Main machinery	4-engine father-&-son M A N /B&W medium-speed aggregate comprising 2 x 9-cylinder and 2 x 6-cylinder L58-64s connected in pairs through Valkan-Ratio couplings and Renk Tacke double-reduction gearboxes with take-off couplings. These generators switchable to also serve as auxiliary propulsion motors. 2 Lips type 4C18 controllable-pitch 4-blade propellers of 5.8m diameter driven at 127.6rpm.
Auxiliaries	31,500kVA of electric power at 6,600V three-phase AC at 60Hz, generated by 2 alternators driven through the main-engine gearing and by 4 auxiliary units driven by M A N /B&W 6L40/45 diesels. Power is stepped down to 660V for auxiliary engine room loads by 4 transformers, and to 440/220/110V for hotel and domestic services by 8 additional transformers.
Manoeuvrability	2 rudders, 3 Lips 1,500kW bow thrusters (2 bow, 1 stern)
Stabilisers	Brown Brothers fin stabilisers
Structural design	Charles Arkinstall, Monaco, (consulting naval architects to the owners)
Interior design	Robert Tillberg, Viiken (Sweden), Petter Yran, Oslo, John McNeece and John Picken, London

PRINZESSIN VICTORIA LUISE

Owners	Hamburg-Amerika, Hamburg
Registry	Germany
Classification	Germanische Lloyd See-berufsgenossenschaft
Service	worldwide cruising
Builders	Blohm & Voss, Hamburg
Hull number	144
Delivery Date	19 December 1900
Length oa	135.94m
Length bp	121.92m
Beam, moulded	14.33m (Spar dk)
Draught, maximum	5.03m
Height, to strength deck	9.07m
GRT	4,409
Service speed	15.0kts
Propulsion power	2,684.2kW (ind)
Passenger capacity	200
Crew	n/a
Number of decks	4
Watertight subdivision	8 transverse bulkheads

Main machinery	2 x 4-cylinder triple-expansion reciprocating steam engines, driving twin fixed-pitch propellers at 123rpm. The high, first and second intermediate, and low pressure cylinders were of 484, 700, 1000 and 1450mm. These were connected to a 4-section crankshaft at angles of 65, 94, 107 and 94 degrees to each other. Steam generated by 4 single-ended coal-fired boilers, each having 3 furnaces.
Auxiliaries	Electric lighting was provided throughout the accommodation and decks, comprising a very modern installation for its time.
Manoeuvrability	Single rudder
Stabilisers	None
Structural design	Blohm & Voss
Interior design	Blohm & Voss

QUEEN ELIZABETH 2 (AS BUILT)

Owners	Cunard Line Limited, Liverpool
Registry	Great Britain
Classification	Lloyds Register and British Board of Trade survey
Service	North Atlantic service between London and New York, and worldwide cruising
Builders	John Brown and Company (Clydebank) Ltd, Glasgow, Great Britain
Contract price	GB£25.4 million
Hull number	736
Delivery date	18 April 1969
Length oa	293.57m
Length bp	269.75m
Beam, moulded	32.00m
Draught, maximum	9.91m
Height, to strength deck	n/a (see text)
GRT	65,862
Service speed	28.5kts
Propulsion power	82,060kW (ind)
Passenger capacity	1,025
Crew	906
Number of decks	13
Watertight subdivision	14 transverse bulkheads
Main machinery	2 sets of John Brown/PAMETRADA double-expansion steam turbines, HP and LP turbines running at 5,207rpm. Driving twin controllable-pitch 6-bladed screws of 5.79m diameter at 174rpm through double-reduction gearing. Steam raised by 3 Foster Wheeler type ESD boilers at 60KG/CM² @ 510.2°C.
Auxiliaries	16,500kV of electric power at 3,300V AC, generated by 3 John Brown/AEI turbo-alternator sets. Power is distributed through step-down transformers at 415 and 240V for most domestic loads.
Stabilisers	2 pairs of Denny Brown AEG folding-type fin stabilisers

Structural design	Dan Wallace, Tom Kameen
Interior design	Co-ordinating architects, James Gardner and Dennis Lennon

ROBERT LEY

Owners	Deutsche Arbeitsfront, Berlin
Registry	Germany
Classification	Germanische Lloyd Class +100A See-berufsgenossenschaft
Service	worldwide cruising, with a 12,000 nautical mile range (equivalent to a voyage from Hamburg to Yokohama)
Builders	Howaldtswerken A-G, Hamburg
Hull number	754
Delivery date	24 March 1939
Length oa	203.80m
Length bp	190.00m
Beam, moulded	24.00m
Draught, maximum	7.56m
Height, to strength deck	20.70m
GRT	27,288
Service speed	15.5kts
Propulsion power	6,561.28kW (ind)
Passenger capacity	1,774
Crew	435
Number of decks	9
Watertight subdivision	12 transverse bulkheads
Main machinery	Diesel electric, driving twin 3-bladed fixed-pitch propellers at 121rpm directly from two Siemens 48-pole synchronous motors. Speed between 14.5 and 16kts controlled by varying motor AC line frequency between 44 and 48.4Hz. Main source of electrical power for motors and auxiliary services delivered from 6 M A N /Siemens alternator sets generating 9,000KvA at 2300V.
Auxiliaries	Auxiliary power stepped down from main switchboard to 220/380V for distribution to auxiliary and hotel services including boilers for domestic hot water.
Stabilisers	Frahm anti heeling tanks
Structural design	Howaldtswerken A-G
Interior design	Professor Woldenar Brinkmann, Munich

ROTTERDAM (1959)

Owners	Nederlandsche-Amerikaansche Stoomvaart Maatschappij, Rotterdam, The Netherlands
Registry	The Netherlands
Classification	Lloyds Register of Shipping +100A1 with freeboard
Service	Line service between Rotterdam and New York with provision for worldwide cruising
Builders	De Rotterdamshe Droogdok Mij N V, Rotterdam
Contract Price	NLG100 million (US$26.25 million)
Hull number	300

Delivery date	September 1959
Length oa	228.12m
Length bp	198.12m
Beam, moulded	28.65m
Draught, maximum	9.00m
Height, to strength deck	21.96m (Prom dk)
GRT	38,650
Service speed	20.50kts
Propulsion power	28,332.80kW (shaft)
Passenger capacity	1,456
Crew	776
Number of decks	13
Watertight subdivision	13 transverse bulkheads
Main machinery	2 sets of De Schelde triple-expansion steam turbines driving twin 3-bladed fixed-pitch screws of 6.1m diameter at 135.5rpm maximum through double-reduction articulated gearing. Steam raised by 4 De Schelde V2M boilers at 50kg/cm^2 @ 460°C.
Auxiliaries	5,400kW6, 749kVA at 440V three-phase AC at 60Hz generated by 4 Werkspoor/Smit Slikkerveer turbo alternator sets, plus a 350kW gas-turbine alternator set for emergency power.
Manoeuvrability	Single rudder
Stabilisers	Denny-Brown fin stabilisers
Structural design	New Building Department of NASM in Collaboration with the builders
Interior design	J A van Tienhoven, H P Mutters, Mutero NV L W Wirtz and others

ROYAL PRINCESS

Owners	P&O Cruises, London, England
Registry	Great Britain
Classification	Lloyds Register of Shipping +100A1, British Ministry of Transport and US Coast Guard and Health regulations
Service	Tropical cruising
Builders	Oy Wärtsilä Ab Helsinki Shipyard, Finland
Contract price	US$150 million
Hull number	464
Delivery date	30 October 1984
Length oa	231.00m
Length bp	196.50m
Beam, moulded	29.20m
Draught, max	7.80m
Height, to strength deck	19.40m (dk 4)
GRT	44,348
Trial speed	22.30kts
Optimized cruising speed	18–19kts
Propulsion power	28,160.80kW (brake)
Passenger capacity	1,260 (incl 60 upper berths)
Crew	500
Number of decks	9
Watertight subdivision	14 transverse bulkheads
Main machinery	4 x 4-stroke 8-cylinder Wärtsilä/Pielstick 6PC4-2L medium-speed diesel engines, connected in pairs through Gieslinger

elastic couplings and Wichita 248 MLI clutches to Royal Schelde gearboxes with step-up power take-off couplings. 2 highly-skewed KaMeWa controllable-pitch 4-blade propellers of 5.2m diameter driven at 125rpm.

Auxiliaries	30,000kVA of electric power at 6,600V three-phase AC at 60Hz, generated by 4 Strömberg alternators driven through step-up gearing from the each pair of main engines. Standby power generated by 2 Wärtsilä Vasa 6R22/Strömberg alternator sets rated at 950kW each. Power is stepped down to 440/220/110V for hotel and domestic services.
Manoeuvrability	2 rudders, 2 x 750 kW thruster fwd
Stabilisers	1 pair Sperry Gyrofin 13.5m^2 stabilisers
Structural design	Wärtsilä and P&O with Knud E Hansen as owners' consultant naval architects
Interior design	Overall scheme by Hirsch-Bedner with Njål Eide, as principal executing architect

ROYAL VIKING STAR
(NEAR-IDENTICAL SISTERSHIPS ROYAL VIKING SKY/SEA)

Owners	Bergensk Dampskibsselskab, Bergen, Norway
Registry	Norway
Classification	Det Norske Veritas + 1A1 EO and Norwegian Skibscontrollen rules, SOLAS 1967, US Coast Guard and Health regulations
Service	Worldwide cruising
Builders	Oy Wärtsilä Ab Helsinki Shipyard, Finland
Hull number	395
Delivery date	26 June 1972
Length oa	177.74m
Length bp-	150.48m
Beam, moulded	25.20m
Draught, at summer WL	7.45m
Height, to strength deck	15.20m (A dk)
GRT	21,847
Service speed	21.50kts
Propulsion power	13,420.80kW (brake)
Passenger capacity	559
Crew	326
Number of decks	11
Watertight subdivision	11 transverse bulkheads
Main machinery	4 x 2-stroke 9-cylinder Wärtsilä/Sulzer 9ZH 40/48 medium-speed diesel engines, connected in pairs through Pneumaflex KAE 360 high-elastic friction clutches to Lohmann & Stolterfoht GVA 1400 H double-reduction gearing. 2 controllable-pitch propellers of 4.3m diameter driven at 155rpm. The engines were of 400mm bore and 480mm stroke.
Auxiliaries	6,000kVA of electric power at 450V three-phase AC at 60Hz, generated by 6 x 4-stroke 8-cylinder Wärtsilä 824 diesel engines driving Strömberg HSSTL

Stabilisers	11/755 B16 alternators. Sperry Gyrofin fin stabilisers
Structural design	Based on Knud E Hansen concept, developed by owners and builders
Interior design	Principal designer, Finn Nilsson, Oslo

SAGAFJORD

Owners	Den Norske Amerikalinje A/S, Oslo
Registry	Norway
Classification	Det Norske Veritas +1A1
Service	dual-purpose, world cruising and occasional North Atlantic crossings between Oslo and New York
Builders	Forges et Chantiers de La Méditerranée, La Seyne, France
Contract price	GB£6 million
Hull number	1366
Delivery date	18 September 1965
Length oa	188.97m
Length bp	167.64m
Beam, moulded	24.99m
Draught, maximum	8.23m
Height, to strength deck	?
GRT	24,002
Service speed	20.0kts
Propulsion power	17,894.40kW (brake)
Passenger capacity	800 Atlantic service 450 cruising
Crew	350
Number of decks	9
Watertight subdivision	11 transverse bulkheads
Main machinery	2 x 2-stroke, single-acting 9-cylinder, Sulzer-type RD68 diesel engines, direct driving twin fixed-pitch propellers at 150rpm. The engines were of 680mm bore and 1,250mm stroke.
Auxiliaries	4,000kW of electric power at 440V three-phase AC at 60Hz, generated by 6 NEBB/Bergen diesel alternator sets. Power is distributed at 440, 220 and 24V for domestic, galley and all other auxiliary equipment. 2 Spanner Swirlyflo boilers provided steam for domestic load.
Manoeuvrability	single rudder, bow thrusters
Stabilisers	Denny-Brown-AEG fin stabilisers
Structural design	Kaare Haug
Interior design	coordinated by Frichjof Platou and Njal Eide

SEABOURN PRIDE
(NEAR-IDENTICAL SISTERSHIP SEABOURN SPIRIT)

Owners	Seabourn Cruise Line, Oslo
Registry	Norway
Classification	Det Norske Veritas +1A1 Ice C, NAUT-B, E0, US Coast Guard and Health regulations
Service	Worldwide cruising
Builders	Schichau Seebeckwerft AG, Bremerhaven
Contract price	US$50 million
Hull number	?
Delivery date	18 November 1989
Length oa	133.80m
Length bp	112.40m
Beam, moulded	19.00m
Draught, maximum	5.00m
Height, to strength deck	12.40m (dk 5)
GRT	9,975
Service speed	19.3kts
Propulsion power	7,280kW (ind)
Passenger capacity	212
Crew	112
Number of decks	9
Watertight subdivision	8 transverse bulkheads
Main machinery	2 x 12-cylinder, Bergen-Diesel KVMB-12 and 2 x 8-cylinder Bergen-Diesel KRMB-8 medium-speed diesel engines, connected in father-&-son pairs through Lohmann & Stolterfoht reduction gearing to high-skew LIPs BV propellers of 3.2m diameter driven at 200rpm.
Auxiliaries	3,000kVA of electric power at 440V three-phase AC, 60Hz, generated by 2 AEG alternators, each driven by a Bergen-Diesel KRG-6 medium-speed diesel engine.
Manoeuvrability	1 semi-balanced rudder, 1 Burnvoll 590kW bow thruster
Stabilisers	B+V fin stabilisers
Structural design	Schichau Seebeckwerft AG, Bremerhaven
Interior design	Petter Yran, Oslo

SEA GODDESS I
(NEAR-IDENTICAL SISTERSHIPS SEA GODDESS II)

Owners	K/S A/S Norsk Cruise, Oslo
Registry	Norway
Classification	Det Norske Veritas +1A1, E0, US Coast Guard and Health regulations
Service	7-14-day tropical cruises
Builders	Wärtsilä Shipbuilding Division, Helsinki Shipyard
Contract price	US$34 million
Hull number	466
Delivery date	21 March 1984
Length oa	105.00m
Length bp	93.00m
Beam, moulded	14.60m
Draught, maximum	4.30m
Height, to strength deck	8.70m (Main dk)
GRT	4,253
Service speed	17.5kts
Propulsion power	3,540kW (ind)
Passenger capacity	120
Crew	71
Number of decks	6
Watertight subdivision	6 transverse bulkheads
Main machinery	4 x 12-cylinder, vee-form, four-stroke Wärtsilä Vasa 12V22HF medium-speed diesel engines, each connected through Valmet reduction gearing to a high-skew

Hjelset propeller of 2.7m diameter driven at 210rpm.

Auxiliaries	1,860kVA of electric power generated by 3 alternators, each driven by a Wärtsilä Vasa 4R22HF medium-speed diesel engine.
Manoeuvrability	1 semi-balanced rudder, 1 Ulstein 250kW bow thruster
Stabilisers	Sperry fin stabilisers
Structural design	Wärtsilä Shipbuilding Division
Interior design	F S Platou, Oslo

SEA VENTURE
(NEAR-IDENTICAL SISTERSHIP ISLAND VENTURE)

Owners	Norwegian Cruiseships A/S, Oslo, Norway
Registry	Norway
Classification	Det Norske Veritas NV + 1A1 and Norwegian Sjøfartsdirektoratet safety rules, SOLAS 1967, US Coast Guard and Health regulations
Service	7-day cruises in American West Coast waters and Caribbean
Builders	Rheinstahl Nordseewerke GmbH, Emden, Germany
Hull number	411
Delivery date	9 May 1971
Length oa	168.76m
Length bp	145.00m
Beam, moulded	24.60m
Draught, maximum	7.70m
Height, to strength deck	15.15m (A dk)
GRT	19,903.10
Service speed	21.50kts
Propulsion power	13,420.80kW (brake)
Passenger capacity	767
Crew	317
Number of decks	11
Watertight subdivision	12 transverse bulkheads
Main machinery	4 x 4-stroke 10-cylinder Fiat C. 4210 SS medium-speed diesel engines, connected in pairs through Pneumaflex KAE 340 high-elastic friction clutches to Lohmann & Stolterfoht GVA 1400 H double-reduction gearing. 2 four-bladed controllable-pitch propellers of 3.95m diameter driven at 185rpm. The engines were of 420mm bore and 500mm stroke.
Auxiliaries	5,700kVA of electric power at 450V three-phase AC at 60Hz, generated by 3 Fiat B 308 and 1 Fiat B 306 4-stroke inline diesel engines driving synchronous alternators.
Stabilisers	Denny Brown AEG fin stabilisers
Structural design	Knud E Hansen ApS consulting naval architects to the builders
Interior design	Robert Tillberg coordinating architect with Finn Nilsson and Karen Margrethe

Heyerdahl of Oslo and Mildred Masters of New York

SKYWARD (1969)

Owners	Klosters Rederi A/S, Oslo
Registry	Norway
Classification	Det Norske Veritas + 1A1 for unrestricted international service, SOLAS 1966, US Coast Guard and Health regulations
Service	medium-range international cruise service in tropical waters
Builders	AG Weser Seebeckwerft, Bremerhaven, Germany
Hull number	942
Delivery date	21 December 1969
Length oa	160.00m
Length bp	n/a
Beam, moulded	22.80m
Draught, maximum	6.27m
Height, to strength deck	13.90m (A dk)
GRT	16,254.00
Service speed	21.50kts
Propulsion power	12,958.53kW (brake)
Passenger capacity	927
Crew	246
Number of decks	7
Watertight subdivision	11 transverse bulkheads
Main machinery	2 x 4-stroke 16-cylinder V-form M A N V8V 40/54 diesel engines, driving twin controllable-pitch propellers through single-reduction gearing at 225rpm. The engines were of 400mm bore and 540mm stroke.
Auxiliaries	3,325kW electric power at 440V three-phase AC at 60Hz, generated by 5 x 4-stroke Bergens Mekaniske Verksteder diesel alternator sets. Power is distributed at 220V for domestic, galley and domestic use.
Stabilisers	Fin stabilisers and anti-heeling tanks
Structural design	Knud E Hansen ApS
Interior design	Mogens Hammer

SONG OF AMERICA

Owners	Royal Caribbean Cruise Lines, Miami, U S A
Registry	Norway
Classification	Det Norske Veritas + 1A1 EO and Norwegian Skibscontrollen rules, SOLAS 1967, US Coast Guard and Health regulations
Service	Caribbean cruising
Builders	Oy Wärtsilä Ab Helsinki Shipyard, Finland
Contract price	US$130 million
Hull number	431
Delivery date	9 November 1982
Length oa	214.50m
Length bp	181.20m
Beam, moulded	28.40m
Draught, max	7.00m

Height, to strength deck	17.40m (Main dk)
GRT	37,584
Trial speed	21kts
Optimized cruising speed	17kts
Propulsion power	16,470.80kW (brake)
Passenger capacity	1,575 (incl 161 upper berths)
Crew	501
Number of decks	10
Watertight subdivision	14 transverse bulkheads
Main machinery	4 x 4-stroke 8-cylinder Wärtsilä/Sulzer 8ZL 40/48 medium-speed diesel engines, connected in pairs through pneumatically-operated elastic friction clutches to Lohmann & Stolterfoht double-reduction gearing. 2 KaMeWa controllable-pitch propellers of 4.45m diameter driven at 145rpm. The engines were of 400mm bore and 480mm stroke.
Auxiliaries	10,750kVA of electric power at 450V three-phase AC at 60Hz, generated by 5 x 8-cylinder Wärtsilä Vasa 6R32 diesel engines driving Strömberg alternators.
Manoeuvrability	2 semi-balanced rudders, 2 x 710 kW controllable-pitch bow thrusts
Stabilisers	1 pair fin stabilisers 1 pair Heeling tanks
Structural design	Based on Knud E Hansen concept, developed by owners and builders
Interior design	Principal designer, Mogens Hammer, Njål Eide, Finn Nillson

SONG OF NORWAY
(NEAR-IDENTICAL SISTERSHIPS NORDIC PRINCE, SUN VIKING)

Owners	Royal Caribbean Cruise Lines, Miami, U S A
Registry	Norway
Classification	Det Norske Veritas + 1A1 and Norwegian Skibscontrollen rules, SOLAS 1967, US Coast Guard and Health regulations
Service	Caribbean cruising
Builders	Oy Wärtsilä Ab Helsinki Shipyard, Finland
Hull number	392
Delivery date	5 October 1970
Length oa	168.30m
Length bp	137.33m
Beam, moulded	24.00m
Draught, at low W L	6.30m
Height, to strength deck	14.20m (A dk)
GRT	18,416
Service speed	21kts
Propulsion power	13,420.80kW (brake)
Passenger capacity	870
Crew	300
Number of decks	9
Watertight subdivision	11 transverse bulkheads
Main machinery	4 x 2-stroke 9-cylinder Wärtsilä/Sulzer 9ZH 40/48 medium-speed diesel engines, connected in pairs through Pneumaflex KAE 360 high-elastic friction clutches to Lohmann & Stolterfoht GVA 1400 H

	double-reduction gearing. 2 controllable-pitch propellers of 4.0m diameter driven at 155rpm. The engines were of 400mm bore and 480mm stroke.
Auxiliaries	5,640kVA of electric power at 450V three-phase AC at 60Hz, generated by 6 x 8-cylinder Wärtsilä 814Tk diesel engines driving Strömberg alternators.
Stabilisers	Sperry Gyrofin fin stabilisers
Structural design	Based on Knud E. Hansen concept, developed by owners and builders
Interior design	Principal designer, Mogens Hammer, Kobenhavn

SOUTHWARD (1971)
(SISTERSHIP SEAWARD COMPLETED AS SPIRIT OF LONDON for P&O)

Owners	Klosters Rederi A/S, Oslo
Registry	Norway
Classification	Det Norske Veritas + 1A1 for unrestricted international service, SOLAS 1966, US Coast Guard and Health regulations
Service	medium-range international cruise service in tropical waters
Builders	Cantieri Navali del Tirreno e Riuniti (CNTR) Genoa, Italy
Hull number	288
Delivery date	December 1971
Length oa	163.30m
Length bp	137.00m
Beam, moulded	22.80m
Draught, maximum	6.50m
Height, to strength deck	16.55m (Boat dk)
GRT	16,600.00
Service speed	21.50kts
Propulsion power	13,420kW (brake)
Passenger capacity	928
Crew	302
Number of decks	7
Watertight subdivision	11 transverse bulkheads
Main machinery	4 x 4r-stroke 10-cylinder Fiat C. 4210 SS medium-speed diesel engines, connected in pairs through Pneumaflex KAE 340 high-elastic friction clutches to Lohmann & Stolterfoht GVA 1400 H double-reduction gearing. 2 CNTR KaMeWa controllable-pitch propellers driven at 225rpm. The engines were of 420mm bore and 500mm stroke.
Auxiliaries	4,160kVA electric power at 440V three-phase AC at 60Hz, generated by 5 x 4r-stroke Bergens Mekaniske Verksteder RSGN8 diesel alternator sets. Power is distributed at 220V for domestic, galley and domestic use.
Stabilisers	Sperry Gyrofin stabilisers
Structural design	Knud E. Hansen ApS
Interior design	Mogens Hammer

SOVEREIGN OF THE SEAS
(NEAR-IDENTICAL SISTER SHIPS *MONARCH OF THE SEAS* AND *MAJESTY OF THE SEAS*, DELIVERED 1991 AND 1992)

Owners	Royal Caribbean Cruise Lines, Miami, USA
Registry	Norwegian International Offshore Register (NIS)
Classification	Det Norske Veritas +1A1 + EO, SOLAS 1974, US Coast Guard and Health regulations
Service	Caribbean cruising
Builders	Alsthom-Chantiers de L'Atlantique, St Nazaire, France
Contract price	US$185 million
Hull number	A29
Delivery date	23 December 1987
Length oa	268.30m
Length bp	236.00m
Beam, moulded	32.20m
Draught, maximum	7.55m
Height, to strength deck	15.12m
GRT	73,192
Service speed	21.0kts
Propulsion power	20,480kW (ind)
Passenger capacity	2,694
Crew	780
Number of decks	14
Watertight subdivision	18 transverse bulkheads
Main machinery	4 x 9-cylinder SEMT-Pielstick PC20L in-line medium-speed diesel engines, connected in pairs through pneumatically-operated elastic friction clutches to Lohmann & Stolterfoht gearboxes. 2 KaMeWa 132XF1/4 controllable-pitch 4-bladed propellers of 4.9m diameter driven at 142.5rpm.
Auxiliaries	15,090kVA of electric power at 6,600V three-phase AC at 50Hz, generated by 6 x 8-cylinder Wärtsilä Vasa 6R32 diesel engines driving Unilec alternators. Power for hotel and domestic services stepped down by transformers to 440, 220 and 110V.
Manoeuvrability	2 Becker flap-type rudders, 2 x 1,250kW bow thrusts
Stabilisers	2 pairs of Sperry fin stabilisers
Structural design	Based on RCCL/Wärtsilä concept, developed by owners and builders
Interior design	Principal designers, Njål Eide, John McMeece, Robert Tillberg and Petter Yran

STAR PRINCESS
(LAUNCHED AS *FAIRMAJESTY* FOR *SITMAR CRUISES*)

Owners/operator	P&O Group (Princess Cruises), London, England
Registry	Liberia
Classification	Lloyds Register +100A1 + LMC, UMS, SOLAS 1974, US Coast Guard and Health regulations
Service	Worldwide cruising
Builders	Alsthom-Chantiers de L'Atlantique, St Nazaire, France
Contract price	US$200 million
Hull number	B 29
Delivery date	4 March 1989
Length oa	246.60m
Length bp	201.00m
Beam, moulded	32.30m
Draught, maximum	7.70m
Height, to superstructure	20.48m (Promenade dk)
GRT	63,524
Service speed	21.0kts
Propulsion power	24,000kW (ind)
Passenger capacity	1,600 (1,740 max)
Crew	600
Number of decks	13
Watertight subdivision	15 transverse bulkheads
Power Plant	Integrated power plant comprising 4 diesel alternator sets, powered by 8-cylinder M A N B&W type 8L 58/64 4-stroke medium-speed motors driving CGEE-Alsthom 3-phase generators. The generator sets each rated at 9,420kW, feed the main switchboard at 6,600V 60Hz 3-phase AC to meet propulsion and hotel loads. Propulsion by 2 CGEE-Alsthom 12,000kW 24-pole synchronous main motors running at a stepless variable speed of up to 145rpm, regulated by 12-pulse static-frequency synchrconverter. Each motor directly driving a LIPs fixed-pitch 4-bladed propeller.

Domestic power stepped down from the main busbar to 440, 220 and 110V |
Manoeuvrability	Single semi-balanced rudder, 3 thrusters (2 bow, 1 stern)
Stabilisers	Fin stabilisers and Frank Mohn tank heeling control system
Structural design	Charles Arkinstall, Monaco, naval architect to the owners,
Interior design	Welton Becket & Asociates, Santa Monica, USA

STARWARD (1968)

Owners	Klosters Rederi A/S, Oslo
Registry	Norway
Classification	Det Norske Veritas + 1A1 'car ferry', SOLAS 1966, US Coast Guard and Health regulations
Service	medium-range international cap-passenger service to be marketed as point-to-point voyages or cruises
Builders	AG Weser Seebeckwerft, Bremerhavn, Germany
Hull number	935
Delivery date	29 November 1968

Length oa	160.00m
Length bp	n/a
Beam, moulded	22.80m
Draught, maximum	6.20m
Height, to strength deck	13.90m (A dk)
GRT	13,108.00
Service speed	21.50kts
Propulsion power	12,958.53kW (brake)
Passenger capacity	736
Crew	225
Number of decks	7
Watertight subdivision	11 transverse bulkheads
Main machinery	2 x 4-stroke 16-cylinder V-form M A N V8V 40/54 diesel engines, driving twin controllable-pitch propellers through single-reduction gearing at 225rpm. The engines were of 400mm bore and 540mm stroke.
Auxiliaries	2,625kW electric power at 440V three-phase AC at 60Hz, generated by 5 x 4-stroke Bergens Mekaniske Verksteder diesel alternator sets. Power is distributed at 220V for domestic, galley and domestic use.
Stabilisers	Fin stabilisers and anti-heeling tanks
Structural design	Knud E Hansen ApS
Interior design	Mogens Hammer

STATENDAM
(NEAR–IDENTICAL SISTERSHIPS VERNDAM, RYNDAM AND VEENDAM COMPLETED 1993/4)

Owners/operator	Holland America Line, Seattle, USA
Registry	Bahamas
Classification	Lloyds Register +100A1 + LMC, UMS, Ice Class D, SOLAS 1990, US Coast Guard and Health regulations
Service	Worldwide cruising
Builders	Fincantieri Monfalcone Yard, Trieste, Italy
Contract price	US$180 million
Hull number	5881 (5882, 5883)
Delivery date	11 December 1992
Length oa	219.30m
Length bp	185.00m
Beam, moulded	30.80m
Draught, maximum	7.60m
Height, to superstructure	19.18m (Promenade dk)
GRT	55,451
Service speed	20.0kts
Propulsion power	24,000kW (ind)
Passenger capacity	1,266 (1,629 Max)
Crew	602
Number of decks	12
Watertight subdivision	15 transverse bulkheads
Power Plant	Integrated power plant comprising 5 diesel alternator sets, 2 powered by 12-cylinder vee-form and 3 x 8-cylinder in-line type Sulzer ZA40S medium-speed motors driving ABB/ Strömberg 3-phase

synchronous generators through Gieslinger flexible couplings. The 2 larger generator sets each rated at 12,200kVA and the 3 smaller units at 8,200kVA. Power generated at 6,600V 60Hz 3-phase AC and distributed through a common busbar to meet propulsion and hotel loads. 2 ABB/Strömberg 12,000kW double-wound synchronous main motors running at between 50 and 144rpm, controlled through thyristor cyclo converter units, regulating the power frequency from 0–14Hz, each direct-driving a KaMeWa controllable-pitch 4-bladed propeller of 5.3m diameter.

Domestic power stepped down from the main busbar to 440/220/110V

Manoeuvrability	2 Heinze flap rudders, 3 x 1,720kW thrusters (2 bow, 1 stern)
Stabilisers	Fincantieri Riva Trigoso fin stabilisers
Structural design	Technical Marine Planning, London (consulting naval architects to the owners)
Interior design	de Vlaming, Fennis, Dingemans BV, Utrecht with Joseph Farcus, Miami

STELLA POLARIS

Owners	Det Bergensk Dampskibsselskab, Bergen, Norway
Registry	Norway
Classification	Det Norske Veritas and Lloyds Register
Service	worldwide cruising
Builders	Götaverken, Göteborg
Contract price	SEK4 million
Hull number	n/a
Delivery date	Jan 1927
Length oa	136.85m
Length bp	109.73m
Beam, moulded	15.42m
Draught, maximum	5.36m
Height, to strength deck	9.14m
GRT	5,020
Service speed	15.5kts
Propulsion power	2,982kW (ind)
Passenger capacity	198
Crew	n/a
Number of decks	5
Watertight subdivision	8 transverse bulkheads
Main machinery	2 x 4-stroke 8-cylinder Götaverken-Burmeister & Wain diesel engines, directly driving twin fixed-pitch propellers. The cylinders were of 550mm bore and 1,000mm stroke distance.
Auxiliaries	500kW of electric power for auxiliary equipment, galley appliances, lighting and other domestic needs were provided by 5 diesel alternator sets.
Stabilisers	?
Structural design	Götaverken

Interior design	Götaverken

STOCKHOLM (1938–41)
(THE COMPLETED REPLACEMENT SHIP)

Owners	Svenska Amerika Linien, Göteborg
Registry	Sweden
Classification	not classified for intended service
Service	dual-purpose, North Atlantic service between Göteborg and New York and worldwide cruising
Builders	Cantieri Riuniti dell'Adriatico, Monfalcone, Italy
Hull number	1203
Delivery date	October 1941
Length oa	205.60m
Length bp	190.50m
Beam, moulded	25.10m
Draught, maximum	8.70m
Height, to strength deck	n/a
GRT	30,390
Service speed	19.0kts
Propulsion power	14,688.08kW (ind)
Passenger capacity	1,350 Atlantic service 640 cruising
Crew	n/a
Number of decks	10
Watertight subdivision	11 transverse bulkheads
Main machinery	3 x 2-stroke double-acting 10-cylinder CRDA-Sulzer diesel engines, direct driving triple fixed-pitch propellers at 115rpm. The engines were of 720mm bore and 1,250mm stroke.
Auxiliaries	4,250kW of electric power at 220V generated by 5 Polar diesel alternator sets for domestic, galley and all other auxiliary equipment. 3 Cochran auxiliary boilers installed to provide steam for domestic load.
Stabilisers	Frahm anti-heeling tanks
Structural design	Eric Th Christiansson
Interior design	Decoration by various Swedish artists

ST. SUNNIVA

Owners	The North of Scotland & Orkney & Shetland Steam Navigation Company, Aberdeen
Registry	Great Britain
Classification	Lloyd's Register
Service	Shetland and Orkneys cruising
Builders	Hall Russell, Aberdeen
Hull number	n/a
Launch date	24 March 1887
Delivery date	May 1887
Length oa	n/a
Length bp	71.62m
Beam, moulded	9.14m
Draught, maximum	n/a
Height, to strength deck	6.70m
GRT	864
Service speed	15.5kts

Propulsion power	141kW (ind)
Passenger capacity	142
Crew	n/a
Number of decks	3
Watertight subdivision	n/a
Main machinery	1 x 3-cylinder triple-expansion reciprocating steam engine, driving a single fixed-pitch propeller at 96 rpm. The cylinders were of 609.6, 914.4 and 1,600.2mm diameter and 914.4mm stroke distance. Steam generated by two double-ended coal-fired boilers
Auxiliaries	Auxiliaries providing for electric lighting and call bells in the accommodation.
Stabilisers	None
Structural design	Hall Russell
Interior design	Hall Russell

SUNWARD (1966)

Owners	Klosters Rederi A/S, Oslo
Registry	Norway
Classification	Det Norske Veritas + 1A1 'car ferry', SOLAS 1966, British MoT regulations
Service	medium-range international cap-passenger service to be marketed as point-to-point voyages or cruises
Builders	A/S Bergens Mekaniske Verksteder, Bergen, Norway
Contract price	GB£2.5 million
Hull number	?
Delivery date	July 1966
Length oa	139.42m
Length bp	122.50m
Beam, moulded	20.80m
Draught, maximum	5.50m
Height, to strength deck	13.27m (Promenade dk)
GRT	8,666.08
Service speed	20.75kts
Propulsion power	9,841.92kW (brake)
Passenger capacity	558
Crew	n/a
Number of decks	6
Watertight subdivision	12 transverse bulkheads
Main machinery	2 x 2-stroke 12-cylinder crosshead Burmeister & Wain 42VT2BF-90 diesel engines, direct driving twin 3-bladed, fixed-pitch LIPs propellers of 3.7m diameter at 217rpm. The engines were of 420mm bore and 900mm stroke.
Auxiliaries	2,500kVA of electric power at 380V three-phase AC at 60Hz, generated by 4 Thrige/B&W diesel alternator sets. Power is distributed at 220V for domestic, galley and domestic use. 1 Lindholmen oil-fired boiler provided domestic steam.
Stabilisers	Fin stabilisers and anti-heeling tanks
Structural design	Knud E Hansen ApS, & C Barclay
Interior design	Mogens Hammer

TROPICALE

Owners	AVL Marine Inc, Monrovia. (leased to Carnival on 5-year hire-purchase plan)
Registry	Liberia
Classification	Lloyds Register +100A1 + LMC, UMS, SOLAS 1974, US Coast Guard and Health regulations
Service	Caribbean cruising
Builders	Aalborg Waerft A/S, Aalborg, Denmark.
Contract price	US$100 million
Hull number	234
Delivery date	4 December 1981
Length oa	204.00m
Length bp	177.00m
Beam, moulded	26.30m
Draught, maximum	7.00m
Height, to strength deck	18.10m (Upper dk)
GRT	36,600
Service speed	21.0kts
Propulsion power	19,832.96kW (ind)
Passenger capacity	1,396
Crew	491
Number of decks	11
Watertight subdivision	15 transverse bulkheads
Main machinery	2 x 2-stroke, single-acting 7-cylinder, crosshead Sulzer 7RND68M diesel engines, direct driving twin KaMeWa controllable-pitch propellers at a maximum of 150rpm. The 4-bladed propellers were of 5m diameter.
Auxiliaries	6,620kVA of electric power generated by 2 Siemens IFJ58066 alternators driven by the main engines through Tacke SH11-1600QS gearboxes. Backup/redundancy power of 9,930kVA provided by 3 additional alternators of the same type, each driven by a N A N -B&W-Holeby 16U28LH4 medium-speed diesel engine.
Manoeuvrability	1 spade-type rudder, 1 bow thruster
Stabilisers	Denny Brown AEG fin stabilisers
Structural design	Technical Marine Planning, London (consulting naval architects to the owners)
Interior design	Joseph and Carole Farcus, Miami

VICTORIA
(ORIGINALLY BUILT AS DUNNOTTAR CASTLE, 1936)

Owners	Incres Steamship Company Ltd. Monrovia
Registry	Liberia
Classification	Lloyds Register +100A1, SOLAS 1948
Service	converted for New York-based Caribbean and tropical cruises of 12–18 days
Builders	Harland & Wolff, conversion carried out by Wilton Fijenoord of Schiedam, the Netherlands
Hull number	959 (Harland & Wolff)
Delivery date	December 1959
Length oa	174.80m

Length bp	161.40m
Beam, moulded	21.79m
Draught, maximum	7.95m
Height, to strength deck	12.25m (Main dk)
GRT	14,917
Service speed	18.0kts
Propulsion power	14,017.30kW (ind)
Passenger capacity	615
Crew	300
Number of decks	7
Watertight subdivision	9 transverse bulkheads
Main machinery	2 x 2-stroke turbocharged 7-cylinder Fiat type-C757S diesel engines of 750mm bore and 1,320mm stroke; direct driving twin 4-bladed fixed-pitch LIPs propellers of 4.75m diameter at 132rpm.
Auxiliaries	1,400kVA of electric power at 220V, generated by the ship's original four Harland & Wolff diesel generator sets. A 120kVA three-phase AC Lehmeyer/MAM alternator was added to handle the fluorescent lighting installed throughout the accommodation.
Stabilisers	n/a
Structural design	Wilton Fijenoord
Interior design	Gustavo F Pulitzer

VISTAFJORD

Owners	Den Norske Amerikalinje A/S, Oslo, Norway
Registry	Norway
Classification	Det Norske Veritas +1A1
Service	dual-purpose, world cruising and occasional North Atlantic crossings between Oslo and New York
Builders	Swan Hunter Shipbuilders Ltd, Neptune Yard, Wallsend, England
Hull number	n/a
Delivery date	18 September 1965
Length oa	191.08m
Length bp	167.64m
Beam, moulded	24.38m
Draught, maximum	8.25m
Height, to strength deck	16.76m (Upper dk)
GRT	24,291
Service speed	20.0kts
Propulsion power	17,894.40kW (brake)
Passenger capacity	800 Atlantic service 550 cruising
Crew	390
Number of decks	10
Watertight subdivision	10 transverse bulkheads
Main machinery	2 x 2-stroke, single-acting 9-cylinder, Clark-Sulzer RD68 diesel engines, direct driving twin 4-bladed fixed-pitch propellers at 150rpm. The engines were of 680mm bore and 1,250mm stroke.
Auxiliaries	4,140kW of electric power at 440V three-phase AC at 60Hz, generated by 6

NEBB/Bergen diesel alternator sets. Power is distributed at 440, 220 and 24V for domestic, galley and all other auxiliary equipment. 4 exhaust-gas boilers and 2 Spanner Swirlyflo boilers provided steam at 5,500Kg/hr for domestic load.

Stabilisers	Denny-Brown-AEG fin stabilisers
Structural design	Kaare Haug
Interior design	coordinated by Frichjof Platou and Njal Eide

WILHELM GUSTLOFF

Owners	Deutsche Arbeitsfront, Berlin
Registry	Germany
Classification	Germanische Lloyd Class +100A *See-berufsgenossenschaft*
Service	worldwide cruising, with a 12,000 nautical mile range (equivalent to a voyage from Hamburg to Yokohama)
Builders	Blohm & Voss, Hamburg
Hull number	511
Delivery date	15 March 1938
Length oa	208.50m
Length bp	195.00m
Beam, moulded	23.50m
Draught, maximum	6.50m
Height, to strength deck	17.25m
GRT	25,484
Service speed	15.5kts
Propulsion power	7,083.20kW (ind)
Passenger capacity	1,465
Crew	426
Number of decks	8
Watertight subdivision	12 transverse bulkheads
Main machinery	4 single-acting, two-stroke, airless-injection 8-cylinder M A N diesel engines of 520mm bore and 700mm stroke distance. These were geared in pairs to twin fixed-pitch propellers through single reduction gearing, reducing the engine speed of 220rpm to the shaft speed of 105rpm. The four-bladed propellers were of 5m diameter and of 15.43 tonnes weight each.
Auxiliaries	3,420kW of electric power at 220V for auxiliary equipment, galley appliances, lighting and other domestic needs, provided by 9 diesel alternator sets in three separate compartments.
Stabilisers	Frahm anti-heeling tanks
Structural design	Blohm & Voss
Interior design	Professor Woldenar Brinkmann, Munich

WIND STAR
(NEAR-IDENTICAL SISTERSHIPS *WIND SONG, WIND SPIRIT*)

Owners	Windstar Cruises, Miami
Registry	Bahamas
Classification	Bureau Veritas 1 3/3 E, Pass Ship/EWAP, Deep Sea STB-CSA-F, AUT, US Coast

	Guard and Health regulations
Service	Worldwide cruising
Builders	Société Nouvelle des Ateliers et Chantiers du Havre (ACH), Le Havre
Contract price	US$33 million
Hull number	269
Delivery date	19 October 1986
Length oa	134.00m
Length bp	110.00m
Beam, moulded	15.80m
Draught, maximum	3.90m
Height, to strength deck	9.60m (dk 3)
GRT	5,307
Service speed	12.0kts
Number of sails	6
Sail area	1,997.35m^2
Propulsion power	1,400kW (ind)
Passenger capacity	150
Crew	112
Number of decks	5
Watertight subdivision	8 transverse bulkheads
Sailing rig	4-masted jib rig, using four main jib sails, flying jib and mizzen sail. Automated roller furling is used under a computer control system.
Power Plant	Integrated power plant comprising 3 diesel alternator sets, powered by Wärtsilä-Vasa/MORMED 6R22D medium-speed engines driving Jeumont Schneider generators. These produce a total of 3,705kVA of electrical power. Alternative propulsion is provided by a single Jeumont Schneider motor rated at 1,400kW, driving a single 2.4m-diameter propeller at 1,200rpm.
Manoeuvrability	1 rudder, 1 x 350kW bow thruster
Stabilisers	Aerofin stabilisers and an active anti-heeling tank system
Structural design	Wärtsilä/ACH, Helsinki/Le Havre
Interior design	Marc Held, Paris

APPENDIX B

Industrial and Interior Designers

Anton, Kym – USA

1992   *Statendam* class of four ships (with de Vlaming, Fennis Dingemans and Joseph Farcus); interior design of passenger cabins.

Bannenberg, Jon – London, England

1969   *Queen Elizabeth 2* (under Dennis Lennon & Partners); interior design of Double Room, card Room, indoor pools and some first-class cabins.

1990   *Horizon* (under coordinating designers Michael and Agni Katzourakis with Patricia Hayes & Associates, Jon Bannenberg and John McNeece); exterior styling of ship.

1992   *Zenith* (under coordinating designers Michael and Agni Katzourakis with Patricia Hayes & Associates, Jon Bannenberg and John McNeece); exterior styling of ship.

1996-99   *Century, Galaxy, Mercury*, exterior design and styling of ships.

Bernadotte, Count Sigvard Oscar Frederik – Stockholm, Sweden

Noted Swedish industrial designer of glass, porcelain, silverware, textiles, etc. Awarded Gold Medal, Silver Medal and Diploma at the Milan Triennale.

1966   *Kungsholm* (with Robert Tillberg); interior design of the Forward Lounge and its adjoining verandah lounges.

1996-9   *Century, Galaxy, Mercury*; exterior design and styling of ships

Bidnell, Michael – London, England

1990   *Nordic Empress* (with Njål Eide, Per Höydahl and Peter Yran); interiors of casino, Viking Crown Lounge, shops and conference centre.

Black, Professor Misha – London, England

Noted for his corporate interior design work for companies such as Olivetti and Time-Life, Professor Black also served as design consultant to British Airways, (then BOAC) and the British Transport Commission. He has served his profession as a member of t7he Council of Industrial Design and as President of the Society of Industrial Artists.

1960   *Oriana* (with Design Research Unit Ltd); coordinated interior design of passenger accommodation in collaboration with Brian O'Rorke and R D Russell & Partners,

1969   *Queen Elizabeth 2* (under Dennis Lennon & Partners); interior design of ship's synagogue.

Brinkman, Professor Woldenar – Munich, Germany

1938-9   *Wilhelm Gustloff/Robert Ley*; supervised the interior design of public rooms aboard both ships.

Buchwald, Joachim – Hamburg, Germany

Buchwald is a noted industrial designer, whose involvement in ship design work started in 1952. This included the interiors for the 1959 conversion of the French liner *Pasteur* as *Bremen*.

1981   *Europa* (with Wilfred Köhnemann); interior design of all passenger and crew cabins, as well as the lido bar and adjacent areas.

Buzas, Stefan – London, England

1969   *Queen Elizabeth 2* (under Dennis Lennon & Partners); interior design of 736 Club and art gallery.

Canalli, Guido – Italy

1990-92   *Costa Marina/Costa Allegra*; interior design of accommodation.

Casson, Sir Hugh – London, England

Well-known English architect and industrial designer, Knighted for his design work for the Festival of Britain 1951. A number of prominent buildings in England with Casson, Conder and Partners. Previous ship work, interiors of state suites for Royal Yacht *Britannia*.

1961   *Canberra* (Casson, Conder and Partners); coordinated interior design of all passenger accommodation with collaborating designers John Wright, Barbara Oakley. Himself designing the first-class public rooms. Also worked with P&O naval architect John West on exterior styling of the ship.

1969   *Queen Elizabeth 2* (under Dennis Lennon & Partners); supervised design of the childrens' and teenagers' rooms which were carried out by his students at the Royal College of Art, Elizabeth Beloe and Tony Heaton.

Crosby, Theo – London, England

1969   *Queen Elizabeth 2* (Crosby, Fletcher, Forbes, under Dennis Lennon & Partners); interior design of Look Out lounge and all graphic design and sighnposting throughout the ship, as well as menu cards, cabaret notices, stationery, etc.

De Jorio, Giuseppe, 'Studio De Jurio srl' – Italy

Educated at the University of Naples, Giuseppe de Jorio founded the Studio in Rome during 1955, specializing in building and transport-media design. Among his early ship design commissions were interiors of the Lloyd Triestino liner *Guglielmo Marconi* in 1961. Early conversions planned by de Jorio include the first *Angelina Lauro* and *Achille Lauro*. Apart from many cruise ships, the Studio has also rendered the Grimaldi ferries *Majextic* and *Splendid* as well as general plans for Adnan Kashoggi's yacht *Nabila*. Other transport work has included schemes for British Rail and the Finnish State Railways. Architectural works include public, commercial and residential buildings in Italy and Europe. Dr de Jorio is joined in the practice by his two sons Vittorio and Marco.

1982   *Atlantic*; interiors of public rooms.
1984   *Ausonia*; refurbishment of ships' interiors.
1985   *Costa Riviera*; complete design scheme for refurbishing of public rooms in refit of the former Lloyd Triestino ship *Guglielmo Marconi* for Holland Amerika cruising.
1987   *Eugenio Costa*; refurbishment of ships' interiors.
1990   *Angelina Lauro*; design scheme for conversion of the former ferry *Narcis* as a cruise ship.
1994   *Italia Prima*; design scheme for conversion of the former passenger/cargo liner *Stockholm* as a cruise ship.

Eide, Njål – Oslo, Norway

1959   *Rotterdam* (under Van Teinhoven); interiors of public rooms.
1966   *Sagafjord* (with Finn Nilsson under F S Platou); Saga Dining Room, main staircase, main lobby and one deluxe suite on Upper deck with F Platou.
1973   *Vistafjord*; interiors with Finn Nilsson and Kay Korbing.
1982   *Song of America* (under coordinating designer MOgens Hammer); aft show lounge, night club and funnel lounge.
1984   *Royal Princess*; execution of design schemes developed by Hirsch-Bedner of Los Angeles.

1987   *Sovereign of the Seas* (with John McNeece, Robert Tilberg and Petter Yran); Atrium, Viking Crown Lounge, casino Music Man show lounge, Finian's Rainbow music lounge.
1988   *Royal Viking Sun*; interiors of public rooms.
1990   *Nordic Empress* (with Per Höydahl, Michael Bidnell and Peter Yran); interiors of the Atrium, Broadway Theatre, forward show lounge and dining room.
1991   *Viking Serenade* (with Joyce Snoeweiss); refurbishment of existing public spaces of former *Stardancer*, (built 1982 as superferry *Scandinavia* for DFDS) and design of new public spaces added at base of funnel.
1995-8   *Legend of the Seas* class (with Per Höydahl, Yran & Storbraaten); majority of public interiors, including the Viking Crown Lounge and Atrium.
1995-8   *Sun Princess, Dawn Princess, Sea Princess*; exterior design concept end interior design with Giacomo Mortola and Theresa Anderson.
1998   *Disney Magic*; exterior design concept with Robert Tillberg and Frogdesign.

Farcus, Joseph – Miami, USA

1978   *Festivale*; restyling of existing public spaces and decoration of new rooms added in conversion of ship, formerly Safmarine's *S A Vaal*.
1981   *Tropicale*; interior of all accommodation, styling of funnel and other exterior elements.
1985   *Holiday* class of three ships; interior of all accommodation, styling of funnel and other exterior elements.
1990-98   *Fantasy* class of eight ships; interior of all accommodation, styling of funnel and other exterior elements.
1992   *Statendam* (with Kym Anton and de Vlaming, Fennis. Dingemans); interior design of main show lounge and Observatory lounge.

Gardner, James – London, England

Started as a jewellery designer, progressing into the exhibition field in which he was appointed as a C.B.E. (Commander of the Order of the British Empire) for his work on the British exhibits at the Brussels World Fair, 1956. Later responsible for the *Britain To-Day* exhibits at Expo 67 in Montréal.

1969   *Queen Elizabeth 2*; joint design co-ordinator with Dennis Lennon & Partners for entire ship. Gardner was responsible for the exterior styling of the ship with Cunard naval architect Dan Wallace.

Garroni Carbonara, Vittorio 'Garroni Associati' – Genoa, Italy

Founded in 1971 as Studio Garroni Associati with partners M. Musio-Sale and M.G. Robbiano. The firm specialized originally in the design of private yachts and other specialized work in the naval fiels. Professor Vittorio Garroni Carbonara himself is a professor of naval design, having in 1991 founded a design school associated with the Genoa State University specialising in international boat and ship design in the 'Italian style'.

1990   *Crystal Harmony* (under Robert Tillberg with Alastair Fletcher, Mogens Hammer); interior design of passenger cabins.
1991   *Frontier Spirit* (with Robert Tillberg); interior design of public spaces and passenger cabins.
1991   *Asuka* (under Robert Tillberg with Kenmoti Design); interior

1993   *Italia* 'steamship retrospective'; exterior styling and interior designs scheme for cruise ship conversion of former *Stockholm/ Volkerfreunsdchaft* (scheme unrealised).

1995   *Crystal Symphony* (under Robert Tillberg with Alastair Fletcher, Mogens Hammer); interior design of passenger cabins.

Gregotti Associati International srl – Milano, Italy

Gregotti Associati was founded in 1974 by Augusto Cagnardi, Pierluigi Cerri and Vittorio Gregotti, specializing in urban planning, architecture and graphic design. Cerri, who has been primarily responsible for the firm's graphic work, including interior designs for commercial and retail spaces, has also executed the studio's ship design work, He also brought to these projects a diverse experience in furniture and lighting design as well as extensive exhibition and graphic work.

1991   *Costa Classica*; exterior styling of ship and complete interior design of accommodation.

1993   *Costa Romantica*; exterior styling of ship and complete interior design of accommodation.

1996   *Costa Victoria*; exterior design of ship and interior design of accommodation with Robert Tillberg.

Grung, Geir –

1970-72   *Song of Norway, Nordoc Prince, Sun Viking*; exterior styling of ship and layout of passenger decks.

1982   *Song of America*; exterior styling of ship and layout of passenger decks.

Heikkinin, Lasse – Helsinki, Finland

1988   *Sally Albatross*; interior design of modified public areas and of cabins for conversion of the former Baltic Ferry *Viking Saga* as a cruise ship.

1992   *Sally Albatross*; interior design of all public spaces for ship's rebuilding after destruction in drydock by fire.

Hammer, Mogens – Copenhagen, Denmark

1966-69   *Sunward, Starward, Skyward*; interiors of public rooms, cabins and crew accommodation.

1070   *Song of Norway, Nordoc Prince, Sun Viking*, Interiors of public rooms cabins

1982   *Song of America*; coordinating designer (over Njål Eide, Finn Nilsson), also executed main show lounge, cinema, piano Bar, inside and outside cabins with parallel bed arrangement.

1990   *Crystal Harmony*; (with Robert Tillberg, Alastair Fletcher, and Garroni Carbonara.

Held, Marc – Paris, France

Marc Held formed his own practice as an architect and industrial designer in 1974. His product designs range from wrist watches and ski equipment to tableware and furniture. He has also designed displays and exhibitions for various international design shows and museums, including remodelling of the Pavillon de Marsan at the Louvre in Paris. His architectural work has covered both the residential and commercial fields, including several prestigious buildings for IBM in France. In the hospitality field includes the Beverly Wilshire Hotel in California as well as the Frantel in Riems.

1986   *Wind Star*; complete interior design scheme.

Heyerdahl, Karen Margrethe (Mrs) – Oslo, Norway

1971-72   *Sea Venture/Island Venture*; selection of colour schemes and textiles suitable to American passenger taste with Mildred Masters of New York.

Heyes, Patricia & Associates – New York, USA

1990   *Horizon* (under coordinating designers Michael and Agni Katzourakis with Jon Bannenberg and John McNeece); design of health and recreation facilities on decks 11 and 12.

1992   *Zenith* (under coordinating designers Michael and Agni Katzourakis with Jon Bannenberg and John McNeece); design of health and recreation facilities on decks 11 and 12.

1996   *Atlantic/Oceanic*; refurbishmant of interiors for Premier Cruises.

1996   *QE2*; refurbihment of cabin soft furnishings.

Hisrch-Bedner & Associates – Los Angeles, USA

Noted Americal hotel design firs, whose most prestigious project at the time of their first cruise ship contract was the Hyatt hotel on Maui, Hawaii.

1984   *Royal Princess*; overall interior design scheme for passenger public spaces, executed by Njål Eide of Oslo.

Höydahl, Per – Oslo, Norway

1990   *Nordic Empress* (with Njål Eide, Michael Bidnell and Peter Yran); exterior styling of ship, arrangement and design of deck and recreation areas.

1995   *Legend of the Seas* (with Njål Eide, Lars Iwdal and Yran & Storbraaten); exterior styling of ship, arrangement and design of deck and recreation areas.

Inchbald, Michael – London, England

Earlier ship-design work included the tourist-class Smoking Room, Bar and Rotunda aboard Union Castle's *Windsor Castle* of 1960 as well as modernizations of Cunard's *Carmania* and *Franconia*.

1969   *Queen Elizabeth 2* (under Dennis Lennon & Partners); interior design of Queens Room and Quarter Deck Library.

Katzourakis, Michael and **Agni** – Athens, Greece

This husband-and-wife team started in the graphic design field during the early 1970s. Their ship design career started when they were invited in 1973 by Panogopoulis to design graphics for his first cruise ship *Golden Odyssey*.

Since then A&M Katzourakis have been involved in design work for more then 45 cruise ship newbuildings and conversions.

1988	*Aegean Dolphin*; design scheme for conversion of the former ro/ro cargo ship *Narcis* as a cruise ship.
1990-2	*Horizon, Zenith*; interior design of passenger accommodation.
1992	*Appolon*; design scheme for conversion of the former Japanese ferry *Wakashio Maru* as a cruise ship.
1992	*Royal Majesty*; complete interior design scheme of all public rooms.
1993	*Marco Polo*; design scheme for conversion of the former passenger liner *Alexandr Pushkin* as a cruise ship.
1995-7	*Century, Galaxy, Mercury* (with John McNeece and Birch Coffey); interiors of all standard passenger cabins, the business centre and aperitif bar along with deck layout and planning of the pool and lido areas.

Köhnemann, Wilfred – Hamburg, Germany

Köhnermann is an architect and furniture designer, as well as an author and television program moderator on design issues.

1981	*Europa* (with Joachim Buchwald); interior design of all public rooms (excluding the lido bar and adjacent areas), all stairways, passages and other linking elements as well as the ships offices and other service areas.
1991	*Society Adventurer*; interiors of public rooms.

Korbing, Kay – Copenhagen, Denmark

1966	*Sagafjord* (under F. S. Platou of Norway); North Cape Bar, Library and Library Lounge and one deluxe suite on Upper deck.
1973	*Vistafjord*; Norse Lounge and card room.

Kukkasniemi, Arto and **Ritta 'Sistem Oy'** – Helsinki, Finland

1989	*Delfin Clipper*; interiors of public rooms.
1990	*Delfin Caravelle*; interiors of public rooms.

Lennon, Dennis – London, England

Well-known English architect whose earlier work included the Cumberland Hotel, 32 restaurant interiors for J Lyons & Co, remodelling of auditorium and crush bar for the Rome Opera House and an entire housing scheme for Camden Borough Council.

1969	*Queen Elizabeth 2* (Dennis Lennon & Partners); joint design co-ordinator with James Gardner for entire ship. Lennon was responsible for interior design of all passenger and crew accommodation with principal collaborating designers, Jon Bannenberg, Stefan Buzas, Sir Hugh Casson, Theo Crosby, Michael Inchbald. Jo Patrick and Gaby Schreiber. Himself designing the restaurants and grill room, Theatre Bar, Midships Bar, first-class luxury suites, captain's quarters, main entrance lobby and all linking elements including corridors, stairways, etc.
1977	*Queen Elizabeth 2*; interior design of the Queen Mary and Queen Elizabeth suites added atop the superstructure.
1983	*Fairsky*; interior design of dining rooms, Veranda Lounge, cinema and shopping gallery.

Masters, Mildred (Miss) – New York, USA

1971-72	*Sea Venture/Island Venture*; selection of colour schemes and textiles suitable to American passenger taste with Karen Margrethe Heyerdahl of Oslo.

McNeece, John – London, England

John McNeece founded his own architectural practice in the early 1960s. He was selected by Lady Brocklebank to work on Cunard's *Q4*, project following the success of his progressive modern design of a county administration building in Lanarkshire. While other choices of designers were ultimately made for QE2, McNeece gained early ship design experience included interior design work for Caledonian MacBrayne Ltd. Other more recent ferry work has included a number of large and prestigious ships, among them *Norsea*.

1987	*Sovereign of the Seas* (with Njål Eide, Robert Tilberg and Petter Yran); main lobby and reception area, champaign bar, French café, shops, conference room, card room, discotheque.
1988	*Crown Odyssey* (with John Terzoglou and Michael Katzourakis); 12 deluxe cabins, à-la-carte restaurant, art gallery, casino, shops, cinema/theatre, show lounge and bar, Panorama Lounge, discotheque.
1990	*Cunard Countess/Princess*; refurbishment of ships' cabins and public interiors, including lounge bars, indoor/outdoor cafés casinos and stairways.
1990	*Horizon* (under coordinating designers Michael and Agni Katzourakis with Patricia Hayes & Associates and Jon Bannenberg); interior design of show lounge, shopping arcade, casino and night club, as well as graphic design for public-room signage.
1992	*Zenith* (under coordinating designers Michael and Agni Katzourakis with Patricia Hayes & Associates and Jon Bannenberg); interior design of show lounge, shopping arcade, casino and night club, as well as graphic design for public-room signage.
1994	*Queen Elizabeth 2*; Project Lifestyle refit (with Met Studio), interior refurbishment of all cabins, show lounge (former Double Room), English Pub (former Theatre Bar), Mauretania dining room (former Columbia dining room), Queens Grill and Queens Grill Lounge. Interior design of new elements including Lido Restaurant, cabins for handicapped persons. Graphic design for onboard directional, public-room identity, life-saving and safety signage, secondary signage
1995	*Oriana* (with Robert Tillberg, and Petter Yran); interior design of Anderson's lounge, Harlequin's Lounge, Pacific Lounge, Lord's Tavern, casino and slot-machine gaming room, shops and Mall, graphic design for onboard directional, public-room identity, life-saving and safety signage, secondary signage and design of all ship's crockery.
1995-7	*Century, Galaxy, Mercury* (with A&M Katzourakis and Birch Coffey); interior design of atrium, main theatre lounge and observation lounge/discotheque.

Mutero, N V Interieurarchitecten – Rotterdam, The Netherlands

1959	*Rotterdam*; interiors of Ritz Carlton Room, libraries, Sunroom and Skyroom.

Mutters, H P and **Zoon** – The Hague, The Netherlands

1953   *Kungsholm*; interiors of public rooms with the builders, and with Inge Westin, responsible for the Drawing Room.

1959   *Rotterdam*; interior design of Promenade-deck Lounge and Ocean Bar, execution of Mutero's Promenade-deck library design.

Nilsson, Finn – Oslo, Norway.

1966   *Sagafjord* (with Njål Eide under F. S. Platou of Norway); coordinated Interiors of public rooms and passenger cabins, with collaborating designers, George Peynet, van Teinhoven and Kay Korbing. Ballroom and one deluxe suite on Sun deck designed by Nilsson.

1971-72   *Sea Venture/Island Venture*; interiors of public rooms with Robert Tillberg.

1973   *Royal Viking Sea/Royal Viking Sky*; interiors of public rooms and some cabins.

1973   *Vistafjord*; interiors with Finn Nilsson and Kay Korbing.

1982   *Song of America* (under coordinating designer Mogens Hammer); main entrance lobby, dining rooms, outside cabins with L-shaped bed arrangement.

Oakley, Barbara – London, England

1961   *Canberra* (under Sir Hugh Casson); design of passenger and crew cabins, as well as the linking elements including corridors, stairways, etc.

O'Rorke, Brian – London, England

Established a reputation for outstanding modern shipboard interiors when commissioned to design the first-class accommodation of Orient Line's *Orion* in 1936. Subsequently designed interiors of pre-war *Oronsay* and post war liners *Orcades*, *Oronsay* and *Orsova*.

1960   *Oriana* (with Misha Black, R. D. Russell & Partners); in collaboration with Design Research Unit, responsible for passenger and crew cabins.

Patrick, Jo (Mrs) – London, England

1969   *Queen Elizabeth 2* (under Dennis Lennon & Partners); Supervised design of officer and crew accommodation as well as ship's hospital.

Peynet, George – France

1966   *Sagafjord* (under F.S. Platou); cinema interior.

Piano, Renzo – Genoa, Italy

Renzo Piana is an internationally-acclaimed architect, whose innovative use of glass and steel in large structures brought him great recognition. Among his best-known projects are the Centre Georges Pompidou in Paris (co-designed with British architect Richard Rogers) and the Kansai International Airport, built on a manmade island in Osaka. Other work in the transport field includes the Genoa Metro system which renewed; "the

feeling of adventure and excitement which men and women have long felt for travel."

1990-91   *Crown Princess/Regal Princess*; exterior styling of ships with distinctive dolphin-head profile and 'retrospective' steamer funnels.

Platou, Frichjof S – Oslo, Norway

1966   *Sagafjord* (with Njål Eide); coordinated Interiors of public rooms and passenger cabins, with collaborating designers, George Peynet, van Teinhoven and Kay Korbing. Saga Dining Room, main staircase, main lobby and one deluxe suite on Upper deck with Eide.

1987   *Queen Elizabeth 2*; interior design of the penthouse suites added to superstructure as part of the re-engining refit.

1984   *Sea Goddess I/Sea Goddess II* (designs executed by Peter Yran); interior design of all passenger accommodation.

Pulitzer, Gustavo F – Milano, Italy

Prominent Italian architect, interior and industrial designer, most noted for his outstanding hotel and ships interior designs over the period from the 1930s to the 1960s. Among his most noted ship interiors from the liner era were the Lloyd-Triestino *Victoria* and Italia *Conte de Savoia* of the early 1930s.

1959   *Victoria*; interior design of passenger accommodation in the rebuilding of this former Union Castle ship for cruising.

Schreiber, Gaby – London, England

1969   *Queen Elizabeth 2* (under Dennis Lennon & Partners); design of theatre, conference rooms and some first-class Cabins.

Tillberg, Robert 'Tillberg Design' – Viken, Sweden

Robert Tillberg gained early ship experience during the 1950s with interior designs for a number of Scandinavian ferries and freighters. On the same level as his widely acclaimed cruise-ship work, he ferry designs range from short-haul day vessels to the world's largest cruise ferries. Other projects include designs of terminal facilities and of his own unique studio complex in Viken.

1966   *Kungsholm*; coordinated interior design of public rooms and passenger cabins with Clas Feder, R. Aberg and Count Bernadotte. The main lounge, cocktail lounge and library were designed by Tillberg himself. Interior decoration of the ship was supervised by Tabb Haslehurst Co. Ltd of London, who provided all working drawings to the yard.

1971-72   *Sea Venture/Island Venture*; interiors of public rooms with Finn Nilsson.

1986   *Homeric*; interior design of public spaces and passenger cabins.

1987   *Sovereign of the Seas* (with Njål Eide, John McNeece, and Petter Yran); interior design of the dining rooms and Windjammer Café.

1988   *Seaward* (with Petter Yran); interiors of principal lounges and restaurants located on International deck.

1990   *Crystal Harmony*; coordinating designers with Alastair Fletcher, Mogens Hammer and Garroni Carbonara.

1991   *Frontier Spirit* (with Garroni Carbonara); interior design of public spaces and passenger cabins.

1991   *Asuka* (coordinating designer, with Garroni Carbonara and Kenmoti Design); interior design of public spaces and passenger cabins.

1995   *Vistafjord*; refurbishment of ships' cabins and public interiors.

1995   *Oriana* (with John McNeece and Petter Yran); interiors of main entrance lobby and reception area, dining rooms, Theatre Royal, Curzon Room, library and card room, cinema, children's and teenagers' rooms, health club, lido restaurant, observation lounge and adjacent rooms.

1995-8   Legend of the Seas class (with Njål Eide, Lars Juidal and Per Höydahl, Yran & Storbraaten); dining rooms, Windjammer Café, card rooms, shops, library.

1996   *Costa Victoria* (with Gregotti Associati); interior design of forward atrium, main restaurant, upper deckpool, lido and café areas.

1998   *Disney Magic*; exterior design and styling of the ship with Njål Eide and frogdesign, cabin interiors with Yran & Storbraaten and Susan Orsini, Palo Restaurant with Dorf Associates.

van Bommel, Jan – Rotterdam, The Netherlands

1959   *Rotterdam*; interior design of main vestibule on Promenade deck and adjoining Lynbaan shopping arcade, as well as Café de la Paix and Veranda on the same deck.

van Tienhoven, Han – Amsterdam, The Netherlands

1966   *Sagafjord* (under F. S. Platou of Norway); Polaris Nightclub, dance studio, shopping arcade and one deluxe suite on Sun deck.

van Tienhoven, J A – Amsterdam, The Netherlands

1959   *Rotterdam*; interior design of main staircase and vestibule, passenger dining rooms and Ambassador Room.

VFD de Vlaming, Fennis Dingemans - Interiors BV – Utrecht, The Netherlands

Dutch architectural and interior design firm whose shoreside work has included the design of commercial buildings, private houses and villas, bank and office interiors, tunnel and roadway installations, etc. The firm became Holland Amerika's house architects following their first shipboard work with *Veendam*.

1974   *Veendam*; design scheme for refurbishing of public rooms in refit of the former Moore-McCormack ship *Argentina* for Holland Amerika cruising

1983/4   *Nieuw Amsterdam/Noordam*; interior design and decoration of public rooms and passenger accommodation. Their own hallmark asymmetrical layouts with a diagonal circulation pattern were introduced with these ships.

1990   *Westerdam*; refurbishment of existing public spaces of former *Homeric*, (built 1987 and sold to Holland America) and design of addition rooms in new midship section added in rebuilding for new owners.

1993   *Statendam* class of four ships (with Kym Anton and Jseph Farcus); interior design and decoration of public rooms and passenger accommodation. Their own hallmark asymmetrical layouts with a diagonal circulation pattern were expanded and refined with these ships.

Westin, Inge –

1953   *Kungsholm*; interior of Drawing Room with H P Mutters & Zoon and the builders.

Wright, John – London, England

1961   *Canberra* (under Sir Hugh Casson); design of tourist-class public rooms.

Yran, Petter, 'Yran & Storbraaten' – Oslo, Norway

1984   *Sea Goddess I/Sea Goddess II* (under F S Platou); concept development and interior design of all passenger accommodation.

1986   *Explorer Starship*; complete design scheme for conversion of the former ferry *Guglielmo Begonia* as a cruise ship.

1988-89   *Seabourn Pride/Seabourn Spirit*; concept development and complete design scheme for ships and their interiors.

1988   *Seaward* (with Robert Tillberg); interiors of informal upper decks, public spaces, swimming pool and lido areas on Pool deck.

1990   *Nordic Empress* (with Njål Eide, Michael Bidnell and Per Höydahl); interiors of all passenger cabins and suites.

1992-3   *Crown Jewell/Crown Dynasty*; interior design of public spaces and passenger cabins.

1992-3   *Dreamward/Windward*; complete interior design scheme for all public spaces and cabins.

1994   *Silver Cloud/Silver Wind*; complete interior design scheme for all public spaces and cabins.

1995   *Leeward;* conversion of Sally Albatross for tropical cruising.

1995-8   *Legend of the Seas* class(with Njål Eide, Lars Iwdal and Per Höydahl); interiors of all passenger cabins, excluding the suites, and all crew cabins and communal spaces.

1998   *Disney Magic/Disney Wonder*; GA plan development and architectural design of public rooms with Disney Imagineering Dept and various American designers.

BIBLIOGRAPHY

PERIODICALS

'1987 The Centenary of the 'First' Cruise Ship', Alastair Wm McRobb, *Fairplay Cruise Review* (London, 1987) pp 5-8

'A Caribbean Cruise Ship; *Victoria ex-Dunnottar Castle*', *Shipbuilding and Shipping Record* (London, January 21 1960) pp 75-77

'A diesel electric relaunch for *QE2*', *Marine Engineering Review* (New York, August 1986)

'All cruise markets are not created equal', Bruce R J Miller, *Fairplay Cruise Review* (London, 1987) pp 31-35

'Amid-Ships', Stephen Garrett, *The Architectural Review* (London, September 1961) pp 155-58

'A Ship is an Island', Sir Hugh Casson, *The Architectural Review* (London, June 1969) pp 399-408

'*Astor* (Mk 2) aims at European market', *The Naval Architect* (London, March 1987) pp E95-97

'Caribbean bound *Dreamward* Delivered to kloster' *Lloyd's Ship Manager, Cruise and Ferry Quarterly Review* (London, November 1992) pp S10-13

'Carnival passes the dream limit', Klas Brogren, *Cruise & Ferry Info* (Halmstad, No1, 1994) pp 26-27

'Carnival's 'funship': The superliner *Fantasy*', *The Naval Architect* (London, February 1990) pp E80-84

'*Club Med 1*', *The Naval Architect* (London, June 1990) pp E273-74

'Commitment expands cruise ship fleet', Tony Wilson, *The Motor Ship* (London, May 1995) pp 48-62

'Concept to Cunarder', Kenneth Agnew, *The Architectural Review* (June 1969) pp 411-20

'Conversions', Klas Brogren and Stephen Berry, *Guide 1986* (Halmstad, Sweden) pp 41-55

'*Costa Allegra*', *Lloyd's List* (London, November 19, 1992) pp 7-10

'*Costa Classica*', Tony Newman, *The Naval Architect* (London, January 1992) pp E38-45

'Cruise and ferry vessels built in France', *Hansa* (Hamburg, Nr 9/10 1989) pp 645-51

'Cruise lines look beyond Panamax', *Marine Log* (New York, February 1995) pp 31-34, 38

'Cruise Ship Cavalcade', Tony Newman, *The Naval Architect* (London, January 1991) pp E30-36

'Cruise Ships for the Future', Stephen Payne, *The Naval Architect* (London, January 1987) pp E17-28

'Cycloconverter - the propulsion reality behind the "Fantasy"'. *The Naval Architect* (London, October 1989) pp E369-70

'Das KdF-Flaggschiff *Robert Ley*', Dipl-Ing R Keine, *Schiffbau, Schiffahrt und hafenbau* (Berlin, 1939) pp 209-22

'Der Schnelldampfer Bremen', Paul Biedermann, H Hein, *der Zeitschrift des Vereins Deutscher Ingenieure*, No 21 (Berlin, 1930) pp 1-60

'Die Doppenschrauben-Fracht- und Passagier-Motorschiffe *Monte Sarmiento* und *Monte Olivier*', Dittmer und Muller, *Werft & Rederei & Hafen*, Heft 22 (Hamburg, 22 November 1924) pp 613-35

'Die electrische Antriebsanlage der KdF-Schiffes *Robert Ley*', Dipl-Ing Th Deeg, *Schiffbau, Schiffahrt und hafenbau* (Berlin, 1939) pp 223-29

'Diesel-electric propulsion chosen for *Fantasy*', *Lloyd's Ship Manager, Cruise and Ferry Quarterly Review* (London, February 1990) pp S7-10

'Diesel-electric propulsion: still an attractive option', *The Naval Architect* (London, February 1992) pp E77-79

'D S S *Rotterdam*', *Schip en Werf*, special souvenir edition (Rotterdam, September 1959) pp 1-98

'Ethics and Fashion in Design', K J Rawson, *The Naval Architect* (London, February 1990) pp 1-27

'European Passenger Liner Construction', *Marine Engineering and Shipping Review* (New York, June 1940) pp 59-60

'*Fahrgastschiff Hamburg*', *Hansa* (Hamburg, No 6, 1969) pp 389-425

'*Finlandia*, New Vehicle-Carrying Passenger Liner', *Shipping World & Shipbuilder* (London, September 1967)

'*Finnjet*, A Finnish Shipbuilding Innovation', Kai Levander, Göran Damström, *Navigator*, Nor-Shipping '77 Special issue 4 B/77 (Helsinki) pp 18-19

'*Finnjet*, Ein neues Konzept für schnelle Fährschiffe', *Hansa*, No 13 (Hamburg, 1977) pp 1229-42

'Fit for a Princess', *The Naval Architect* (London, January 1985) pp E35-42

'Fixed pitch propellers and diesel-electric propulsion', Chantiers de L'Atlantique, *The Naval Architect* (London, July/August 1989) pp E269-71

'From *Charlston Star* to *Horizon*', Peter C Kholer, *Guide 91* (Halmstad, Sweden) pp 59-69

'From the Golden Fleet to the Fun Ships', Lawrence Miller, *Fairplay Cruise Review* (London, 1987) pp 17-22

'From *Tropicale* to *Fantasy*', Stephen M Payne, *The Naval Architect* (London, March 1993) pp 25-36

'*Frontier Spirit*', Akio Miura, *Designs 90* (Halmstad, Sweden) pp 90-91

'Further Details of the 27-Knot Orient Liner', *Shipbuilding and Shipping Record* (London, 17 January 1957) pp 82-83

'Greek Cruise', David Glass, *Guide 89* (Halmstad) pp 63-67

'gts *Finnjet*', Olavi Pylkkänen, Kai Westerlund, *Navigator*, Nor-Shipping '77 Special issue, 4 B/77 (Helsinki) pp 14-16

'gts *Finnjet*, first gas turbine driven passenger ferry in the world', *Schiff & Hafen / KommandobrÜcke*, Heft 6 (Hamburg, 1977) pp 553-59

'Gustavo F Pulitzer and the Ship as an Aesthetic Fact', Georgio Ciucci, *Passegna* (Bologna, December 1990) pp 30-39

'*Hamburg*', *Shipbuilding and Shipping Record* (London, 2 May 1969) pp 611-14

'Hamburg-South America Liner *Monte Rosa*', J H Isherwood, *Sea Breezes* (Liverpool, July 1986) pp 464-68

'Hapag Lloyd's new *Europa*', *The Naval Architect* (London, January 1982) pp E8-11

'Holland America Liner *Nieuw Amsterdam*, of 1938', J H Isherwood, *Sea Breezes* (Liverpool, June 1982) pp 293-99

'Holland America's *Nieuw Amsterdam*', *Fairplay* (London, 14 July 1983) p 11

'Home Lines', Stephen Berry, *Guide 87* (Halmstad) pp 23-27

'Hope for a revival in the order book', *The Naval Architect* (London, May 1991) p E213

'Informality in Ship Furnishing', *Shipbuilding and Shipping Record* (London, 26 December 1935) pp 711-12

'Italian ship conversions', *The Naval Architect* (London, July/August 1990) p E347

'Japan re-enters the luxury cruise vessel market', *Lloyd's Ship Manager, Cruise and Ferry Quarterly Review* (London, September 1989) pp S5-7

'Jewel of the Crown', James L Shaw, *Designs 91* (Halmstad, 1991) pp 92-97

'Kreuzfahrtschiff *Astor*', *Hansa*, No 6 (Hamburg, 1982) pp 369-86

'Kreuzfahrtschiff *Europa*', *Hansa*, Special edition *Europa* (Hamburg, November 1981)

'Kreuzfahrtschiff *Oriana*', *Hansa*, No 4 (Hamburg, 1995) pp 22-34

'Kreuzfahrtschiff *Oriana*', *Hansa*, No 5 (Hamburg, 1995) pp 75-80

'*L'Atlantique*', *Shipbuilding and Shipping Record* (London, 1 October 1931) pp 426-38

'Lloyd's Ship Manager', *Cruise and Ferry Quarterly Review* (London, February 1992) pp S9-11

'Looking at a Queen', Lawrence Dunn, *Shipbuilding and Shipping Record* (London, 28 September 1967) pp 437-40

'Looking over the horizon', *Lloyd's Ship Manager, Cruise and Ferry Quarterly Review* (London, November 1993) pp 34-35

'Luxuskreuzfahrtenschiff *Skyward*', Dipl-Ing A Schlenker, Ing F Künker, *Hansa*, No 10 (Hamburg, 1970) pp 851-59

'Luxuskreuzfahrtenschiff *Starward*', Dipl-Ing A Schlenker, Ing F Künker, G Henschel, *Hansa*, No 4 (Hamburg, 1969) pp 269-87

'Manoeuvring simulations with Carnival Cruise Lines' *Fantasy*', Stephen Payne, *The Naval Architect* (London, October 1989) pp E373-79

'Modifications to QE2 enhance her role as a cruise ship', *Shipping World & Shipbuilder* (London, February 1873) pp 221-22

'Nave da Crociera *Costa Romantica*', Pierluigi Cerri, *Domus* (Milan, Italy) pp 46-55

'New System of Passenger Accommodation for Ships', *Marine Engineering and Shipping Age* (New York, April 1927) pp 211-15

'*Nieuw Amsterdam* A Floating Palace of Art', *The Studio* (London, July 1938) pp 3-17

'Off on *Holiday*', Stephen M Payne, *The Naval Architect* (London, October 1985) pp E411-16

'Onboard Report (*Oriana*)', Stephen Barry, *Designs 95* (Halmstad, 1995) pp 15-49

'Passenger Ship Safety', Ulrich Jahnke, *Cruise & Ferry Info*, No 5 (Halmstad, 1994) pp 4-8

'P&O Newcomer takes tips from a veteran', David Tinsley, *Lloyd's List* (London, 7 April 1993) p 7

'P&O Order 45,000-Ton Liner from Harland & Wolff', *Shipbuilding and Shipping Record* (London, 31 January 1957) pp 145-47

'P&O's *Crown Princess* is the first Heir in Fincantieri's new passenger rule', *Lloyd's Ship Manager, Cruise and Ferry Quarterly Review* (London, October 1990) pp 52-4

'P&O's *Oriana*', *Marine Engineer's Review* (London, May 1995) pp 18-26

'Pleasure Cruising Motorship *Stella Polaris*', *Shipbuilding & Shipping Record* (London, 10 March 1927) pp 282-83

'QE2: Design for future trends in world travel', Kenneth Agnew, *The Architects' Journal* (London, 9 April 1969) pp 985-91

'*Queen Elizabeth 2* A Ship With a Past...and a Future', *Shipbuilding and Shipping Record* (London, 31 January 1969) pp 145-64

'*Queen Elizabeth 2* now in service', *Shipbuilding and Shipping Record* (London, 2 May 1969) pp 601-03

'RMS *Andes*: Ship of Three Worlds', Stuart Nicol, *Ships Monthly* 9-part series (London, March-November 1971)

'*Romantica* Joins Costa Family', *Lloyd's Ship Manager, Cruise and Ferry Quarterly Review* (London, January 1994) pp 17-19

'*Royal Princess*', *The Motor Ship* (London, December 1984)

'*Royal Viking Star*', *Shipping World & Shipbuilder* (London, August 1972)

'*Sagafjord*', *The Motor Ship* (London, November 1965) pp 342-56

'*Sagafjord*-The owners' Aims', Hans Chr Henriksen, *The Motor Ship* (London, November 1965) p 340

'*Seabourn Pride*: Ein Luxus-Kreuzfahrer der Extraklasse', *Hansa*, No 3/4 (1989) pp 173-187

'*Sea Venture Island Venture*', *Hansa* Special Issue (Hamburg, undated)

'Ship Interiors', Misha Black, *Shipbuilding and Shipping Record*, International Design and Equipment issue (1959) pp12-16

'*Silver Cloud*', *Cruise & Ferry Info*, No 8 (Halmstad, 1994) pp 19-20

'*Silver Moon & Silver Cloud*', *Cruise & Ferry Info*, No 2 (Halmstad, 1993) pp 14-15

'Sitmar Line', Peter Plowman, *Ships Monthly*, 3-part series (London, October-December 1988)

'Some Considerations in the Design of Modern Ships', George G Sharp, *Transactions of the Society of Naval Architects and Marine Engineers* (New York, 1947) pp 447-91

'*Southward* Cruise ship built by Cantieri del Tirrenio E Riuniti', *Shipping World & Shipbuilder* (London, February 1972) pp 278-80

'*Sunward* Design Considerations', C Barclay, *Shipping World & Shipbuilder*, Annual Review Issue (London, 19 January 1967)

'*Sunward*', *Shipping World & Shipbuilder* (London, August 1966) pp 235-41

'The 15,000-ton liner *Dunnottar Castle*', *The Motor Ship* (London, August 1936) pp 170-76b

'The Centralized Machinery Control System in the *Sagafjord*', M P Perrin, *The Motor Ship* (London, November 1965) p 355

'The Cruising Liner', Keith P Lewis, *Sea Breezes* (Liverpool, February 1950) pp 82-89

'The Evolution of the Modern Cruise Liner', Stephen M Payne, *The Naval Architect* (London, May 1990) pp 163-88

'The Interior Design of Passenger Ships', Sir Colin Anderson, *Journal of the Royal Society of Arts* (London, May 1966) pp 477-93

'The jewel of the Viking crown', Tony Newman, *The Naval Architect* (London, February 1988) pp E62-69

'The Motorship *Wilhelm Gustloff*', *The Shipbuilder and Marine Engine Builder* (London, November 1928) pp 608-15 (December 1938) pp 649-52

'The passenger motorship *Venus*', *The Shipbuilder and Marine Engine Builder* (London, June 1931) pp 530-37

'The Passenger Ship: Backward or Forward', *The Architectural Review*
    (London, November 1960) pp 362-67
    The Pride of Seabourn's fleet, *Lloyd's Ship Manager, Cruise and Ferry
    Quarterly Review* (London, February 1989) pp vi-xi
'The return of the true liner', Stephen M Payne, *Cruise & Ferry Info*, No 2
    (Halmstad, 1994) pp 16-17
'The *Rotterdam*', *Shipbuilding and Shipping Record* (London, 8 October 1959)
    pp 270-76
'The Traveller and his Stateroom', *Shipbuilding and Shipping Record* (London,
    27 December 1934) pp 688-90
'The Wind Blows Free', J B Boothroyd, *Punch* (London, 31 May 1961)
    pp 832-33
'Three Notable Ships', C M Squarey, *Shipbuilding and Shipping Record*
    International Design and Equipment issue (London, 1961) pp 2-4
'To Sea With *Seaward*', Tony Newman, *The Naval Architect* (London,
    September 1988) pp E259-67
'*Tropicale*', *The Motor Ship* (London, March 1982) pp 53-58
'Twins', Klas Brogren, *Designs 86* (Halmstad, 1986) pp 59-61
'Twin Screw Pleasure Yacht *Prinzessen Victoria Luise*', *Marine Engineering*
    (New York, September 1901) pp 262-66
'Umbau *Queen Elizabeth 2*', *Hansa*, No 12 (Hamburg, 1987) pp 725-754
'Viking Visionaries', Peter T Eisele, *Steamboat Bill*, No 114 (New York,
    Summer 1970) pp 86-89
'*Vistafjord*', *The Motor Ship* (London, July 1973) pp 181-186
'*Wind Star*', *The Naval Architect* (London, February 1987)
    pp E77-78

TECHNICAL AND COMPANY PAPERS, MANUSCRIPTS, ETC

Brown, David T, *A history of the Sulzer los-speed marine diesel engine*
    (Gebruders Sulzer, Winterthur, Switzerland, 1984)
Caronia Britain's Wonder Ship of 1949, Cunard White Star Line publicity
    brochure (Liverpool, 1949)
Finnlines, Cases in the Wake of a Finnish Shipping Line, company publication,
    (Helsinki, 1980)
Hansen, Bent, 'Ship design for the further development of the cruise
    market', Cruise & Ferry 85, conference paper (London, May 1985)
Hapag-Lloyd, 100 Jahre Kreuzfahrten 1890-1990, company publication
    (Bremen, 1990)
Hopkins, J, S Payne and D Storer, 'Design and optimization of Holland
    America Line's new *Statendam*', Cruise and Ferry 93 conference paper
    (London, May 1993)
Levander, Kai, 'Wärtsilä, *Increased Profitability for Passenger Ships*' (Hellenic
    Institute of Marine Technology, Athens, Greece, 1982)
Levander, Kai, 'Wärtsilä, *The Viking Saga Series - Tailor-Made by Wärtsilä*',
    (Helsinki, Finland, 1980)
MacGREGOR-NAVIRE, 'Passenger and baggage handling', *Marine News*
    company magazine (London, May 1991) pp 8-9
Musio-Sale, Massimo, Garroni Associati, 'Interior/exterior design –
    Restyling a 1950s liner', Cruise & Ferry 93, conference paper (London,
    May 1993)
Schmid, H, *Versatility with economy for cruise ship propulsion*, (Gebruders Sulzer,
    Winterthur, Switzerland, April, 1986)
'You can call me Al', *100A1*, the magazine of Lloyd's Register (London,
    1994) Issue 4, pp 23-26

BOOKS

Bel Geddes, Norman, *Horizons* (Little, Brown and Company, Boston, 1932)
Bent, Mike, *Coastal Express* (Conway Maritime Press, London, 1987)
Bushell, T A, *Royal Mail; Centenary History of the Royal Mail Line* (Trade and
    Travel Publications Ltd, London, 1939)
Cormack, Alastair and Anne, *Days of Orkney Steam* (Kirkwall Press, 1971)
    Carnival Cruises (Ed) *The SuperLiner Holiday* (Sterling Publications Ltd,
    London, 1985)
Dawson, Philip S *British Superliners of the Sixties* (Conway Maritime Press,
    London, 1990)
Dawson, Philip, *Canberra: In the wake of a legend* (Conway Maritime Press,
    London, 1997)
Donaldson, Gordon, *Northwards by Sea*, 2nd Ed (Paul Harris Publishing,
    Edinburgh, 1978)
Hardy, A C, *History of Motorshipping* (Whitehall Technical Press Ltd,
    London, 1955)
Held, Marc, *lettres à gerry* (L'Equeirre, Paris, 1986)
Howarth, David and Stephen, *The Story of P&O* (Weidenfeld and Nicolson,
    London, 1986)
Huldermann, Bernhard, *Albert Ballin*, transl by W J Eggers (Cassell and
    Company Ltd, London, 1922)
Keilhau, Wilhelm, *Norway and the Bergen Line* (AS John Griegs Boktrykkeri,
    Bergen 1953)
Kludas, Arnold, *Die Großen Passagierschiffe der Welt* (Gerhard Stalling Verlag,
    Hamburg, 1974)
Ikeda, Yoshiho, *Large Ferries in the World* (Privately published, Osaka, 1978)
Ingells, Douglas J, *747, Story of the Boeing Super Jet* (Aero Publishers,
    Fallbrook, California, 1970)
Maxtone-Graham, John, *From Song to Sovereign* (Book Division of Passenger
    Cruise Network, Stamford Conneticut, 1988)
Maxtone-Graham, John, *Liners to the Sun* (Macmillan, New York, 1985)
Miller, William H, *German Ocean Liners of the 20th Century* (Patrick Stephens
    Ltd, London, 1989)
Morris, Charles F, *Origins, Orient and Oriana* (McCartan & Root,
    New York, 1980)
Novitski, Joseph, *Wind Star* (Macmillen Publishing Company,
    New York, 1987)
Ovstedal, Barbara, *Norway* (B T Batsford Ltd, London, 1973)
Payne, Stephen M, *Grande Dame: Holland America Line and the ss Rotterdam*
    (RINA Ltd, London, 1990)
Potter, Neil, and Jack Frost, *Queen Elizabeth 2* (George G Harrap & Co Ltd,
    London, 1969)
Prager, Hans Georg, *Blohm+Voss; Ships and Machinery for the World* (Koehlers
    Verlagsgesellschaft GmbH, Herford, 1977)
Quartermaine, Peter, *Building on the Sea* (Academy Editions/National
    Maritime Museum, London, 1996)
Vernon Gibbs R N, Commodore C R, *The Western Ocean Passenger Lines and
    Liners* (Brown Son & Ferguson Ltd, Glasgow, 1970)
Williams, David L and Richard P de Kerbrech, *Damned by Destiny* (Teredo
    Books Ltd, Brighton, 1982)
Worker, Colin F *The World's Passenger Ships* (Ian Allan, London, 1967)
Young, George, *South Africa on World Sea Lanes* (Marine Underwriters of
    South Africa, Cape Town, 1991)

INDEX

Page references in italics refer to illustrations.

'A boats' 30, 32
A & J Inglis 20
A/S Bergens Mekaniske Werksteder 79
Aalborg Waerft 117, 123, 158
ABB/Strömberg 181
Abdul Aziz 202–3, 206
ACH *see* Société Nouvelle des Ateliers et Chantiers du Havre (ACH)
Achille Lauro 146
Admiral Cruises 169
AF Klaveness & Co A/S 90, 91, 129
AG Weser 84, 95, 98
Aida 8, 172–3; *270, 271*
Akademie der Bildenen Künste 103
Al Mansur 202–3, 204, 206; *203*
Alcantara 25, 30, 33
Alexandr Pushkin class 44, 156
Alexandra 19–20; *19*
Alexandra of Britain 20
Almanzora 33
Alsthom Atlantique 110, 161
Amazon 14
Amelio de Mello 135 *see also Ithica*
American International Travel Service (AITS) 115, 116, 117
Ancon class 69
Andern, K G 209

Anders Wilhelmsen 88
Anderson, A 231
Anderson, T 236
Anderson, Sir C 70
Andes (1913) 28
Andes (1939) 30–4, 37, 38, 52, 135, 136, 137, 139, 140, 190, 196, 237; *30, 31, 33*
Angelina Lauro 147, 222 *see also Oranje*
Annie Johnson 152 *see also Costa Allegra*
Ansaldo 48
Anton, K 222, 256
AOC 8, 155, 156–69; *156, 157*
Aquitania 28, 76
Araguaya 33
Arandora 28 *see also Arandora Star*
Arandora Star 28–30, 38, 135; *28, 29 see also Arandora*
Arcadian 24, 28 *see also Asturias* (steamer)
Architectural Review, The 77
Argentina 51, 52, 62, 67, 69, 89, 94, 111, 138, 200 *see also Enchanted Isle*
Argentina Maru 197 *see also Nippon Maru*
Ariadne 83–4 *see also Patricia*
Arison Shipping Company 83
Arison, M 117
Arison, T 82, 83, 84, 88, 95, 115, 116, 117, 119
Arkona 196 *see also Astor* (1981)
Arosa Star 83 *see also Puerto Rico*

Astilleros Espanoles 200
Astor (1981) 195–6, 198, 200, 237–8; *196 see also Arkona*
Astor II 196
Asturias (1927, motorship) 25, 30, 33
Asturias (steamer) 24 *see also Arcadian*
Asuka 164, 166, 199, 200, 228, 238; *200*
Ateliers et Chantiers de Bretagne 110
Atlantic (1953) 108
Atlantic (1982) 99, 105–10, 113, 114, 115, 117, 118, 216, 238; *106, 107, 109*
Atlantic Container Line 94
Atlantic Crown class 94
Atlantic Cruise Lines 84
Atlantis 28–30, 33; *28 see also Andes* (1913)
Atlas 135 *see also Ryndam*
Auguste Victoria 15
AVL Marine Inc 117
Axel Johnson 152 *see also Regent Sun*
Bahama Star 83
Ballin, A 15–16, 19, 201, 203
Bannenberg, J 151, 190, 256
Barclay, C 79, 80, 81
Bates, Sir P 34
bcd-Programm system 99–101
Begonia 146 *see also Explorer Starship*
Berbice 14
Bergen Line *see* Det Bergenske Dampskibsselskab

Bergensfjord 48
Berlin 53, 105, 131 *see also Gripsholm* (1928)
Bernadotte, Count S 52, 256
Bertaglia, G 235
Bibby Line 140
Bibby-style cabins 29, 31, 43, 50
Bidnell, M 256
Biedermann, P 25
Bilu 82, 83
Birch Coffey 190
Bitsch-Christiansen, A 53
Black, Prof M 68, 71, 74, 256
Black Prince 82
Black Sea Shipping Company 57, 88, 97, 196
Black Watch 82
Blohm & Voss 16, 19, 39, 40, 53, 55, 89
Blue Star Line 28
'Blue Train' 81; *81*
Boheme 88
Bommel, J van 261
Borge, V 88
Brasil 51, 52, 62, 67, 69, 89, 94, 111, 138, 200 *see also Enchanted Seas*
Brasil (1948) 105 *see also Drottningholm*
Brauer, M 53
Brazil Maru 197
Bremen (1930) 25–6, 29, 43, 47, 55, 997, 103, 105
Bremen (1959) 53, 57, 97, 101–2, 103, 105 *see also Pasteur; Regina Magna*

Bremer Vulkan 98, 99, 150, 188, 191, 221, 222, 232
Breschag Bremer Schiffsvescharterungs AG 104
Brinkmann, Prof W 41–2, 256
Britannic 34
British India Line 140
Brocklebank, Sir J 73
Brostrom, D 45
Brostroms 45, 105
Brunstad, A 206
Buchwald, J 103, 195, 256
Bunge, K 172
Büttner, F 173
Buzas, S 256
Calgaris 24
Cambodge 135, 138–9, 152; *139 see also Stella Solaris*
Cammell Laird 34, 82
Canadian Pacific 27, 53, 115
Canalli, G 152, 256
Canberra 7, 32, 48, 54, 58, 64, 65–72, 86, 91, 96, 103, 106, 119, 121, 122, 123, 124, 133, 141, 148, 157, 159, 163, 164, 182, 183, 184, 187, 188, 194, 215, 222, 224, 226, 227, 228, 229, 230, 231, 232, 238–9; *66, 67, 68, 69, 70*
Cantiere Navale Ferrari 205, 208
Cantieri dell'Adriatico 87, 106
Cantieri Navali del Tirreno e Riuniti (CNTR) 86
Cantieri Riuniti del'Adriatico 45
Cap Arcona 30, 31, 40, 41, 69, 91; *39, 43*
Carbonara, Prof V G 199
Caribbean 136 *see also Dunnottar Castle*
Caribe 146
Caribe I 153, 200 *see also Olympia*
Caribia 37 *see also Caronia*
Carinthia 144 *see also Fairsea*
Carmania 115, 117
Carnival Cruises 8, 10, 64, 107, 109, 112, 115, 116, 117, 118, 119, 120, 121, 122, 123, 124, 125, 126, 127, 128, 129, 141, 142, 144, 145, 147, 153, 154, 159, 160, 163, 167, 169, 172, 174, 176, 180, 181, 182, 183, 186, 187, 188, 189, 192, 193, 194, 195, 214, 221–2, 224, 225, 231, 236 *see also 'Fun Ships'*

Carnival Destiny 23, 192–4, 236, 239; *192, 193, 275, 276*
Carnivale 116, 120 *see also Queen Anna Maria*
Caronia 30, 32, 34–7, 38, 52, 66, 73, 76, 104, 190, 196, 239; *34, 36 see also Caribia*
Casson, Sir H 68, 71, 74, 103, 122, 257
Celebration 123–4, 127, 180; *123*
Celebrity Cruises 188, 190, 191, 236
Century 188, 190; *194*
Cernobori, F 218, 219
Cerri, P 219–20
CGEE Alsthom 185
Chandris 65, 97, 153, 188, 216
Chandris, J 190
Chantiers de l'Atlantique 110, 111, 169, 170, 175, 178, 180, 183, 185, 188, 189; *112*
Château de Chambord 60
Chimborazo 14
China National 110
Christiana 204
Christiansson, E Th 44–52, 61, 77, 89, 107, 156
Chusan 49
Circle Line 209
Clemens, S *see* Twain, M
Clipper Line (Rederiaktiebolaget Clipper) 23
Club Med I 213
Club Méditerranée 213
Cockerill-Ougree 83
Commodore Cruise Lines 200
Compagnie de Navigation de Sud-Atlantique 101, 178
Compagnie Française de Navigation 110
Compagnie Générale Sudatlantique 46
Compagnie Générale Transatlantique *see* French Line
Constitution 218
Constructions Navales et Industrielles de la Méditerranée (CNIM) 106, 110
Conte di Savoia 32, 138, 218, 221
Copenhagen 88 *see also Odessa*
Cormack, A & A 15
Costa, Dr N 216
Costa Allegra 152, 216, 219; *152, 153 see also Annie Johnson*
Costa Classica 152, 186, 188, 191, 216–21, 222, 233, 239–40; *217, 219, 220, 278*

Costa Line 65, 96, 152–3, 188, 205, 208, 215, 216, 223, 224, 225, 226, 232, 236
Costa Marina 152, 216; *152 see also Regent Sun*
Costa Riviera 153, 216 *see also Guglielmo Marconi*
Costa Romantica 152, 188, 216–21, 233; *220*
Costa Victoria 190, 191, 233; *233*
Cosulich 166
Council of Industrial Design 74
Crosby, T 257
Crown Cruise Line 200
Crown del Mar 144 *see also Las Palmas de Gran Canaria*
Crown Dynasty 200–1; *201*
Crown Jewel 200–1
Crown Monarch 200–1, 240
Crown Princess 187–8, 219, 222, 240–1; *186*
Crystal Cruises 164, 165, 199, 200
Crystal Harmony 164–7, 199, 219; *164*
Crystal Symphony 165–7; *165*
Cunard 7, 12, 13, 15, 24, 25, 27–8, 30, 32, 34, 35, 37, 44, 45, 72, 74, 77, 78, 92, 96, 104, 108, 115, 139, 144, 147, 150, 151, 159, 163, 182, 192, 214, 215, 221, 234
Cunard Adventurer 88, 95; *87*
Cunard Ambassador 88, 95
Cunard Countess 95, 96
Cunard Princess 95
Cutty Sark 211
Damned by Destiny 47
Danae 152, 216; *152*
Daphne 152, 216
Days of Orkney Steam 15
De Jorio, G 257
De Porceleyne Fles 64
De Rotterdamsche Droogdok Mij NV 59
Del class 69
Del Mar 61
Del Norte 61
Del Sud 61
Delta Line 61, 69
Denis Lennon and Partners 74
Design Research Unit 68, 71
Det Bergenske Dampskibsselskab (Bergen Line) 15, 19, 21, 22, 23, 82, 90–1
Deutsche Arbeitsfront (German Labour Front) 39

Deutsche Atlantik Line *see* German Atlantic Line
Deutsche Seetouristik 172, 196
Deutsche Werft 40
Deutschland 135 *see also Victoria Luise*
DFDS ship 22
Diamond Cruise Oy 214
Diary of a Voyage from Cornhill to Grand Cairo 10
Dickinson, R 116
Dingemans, F C J 222, 223, 225
Disney Magic 234–6, 241
Disney Wonder 236
Dolphin IV 135 *see also Ithica*
Domino 13
Donghia, A 145
Doric (1920s) 24
Doric (1973) 57, 106, 107, 108 *see also Hanseatic*
Drapeau, J 142
Dreamward 146, 170–1; *170, 171*
Drottningholm 105 *see also Brasil* (1948)
Dubigeon 110
Dunera 140
Dunnottar Castle 136 *see also Caribbean*
Dunnottar Castle (1936) 135, 136, 138; *136, 137 see also Victoria* (1959)
Dutch West Indies Company 111
Eastern Shipping Corporation 88
Ecstasy 183
Edward VII of Britain 20
EffJohn 200
Eftedal, O 174, 176–7
Eide, N 131, 133, 163, 168, 176, 234, 257
El Djezair 67, 68
Elsinor 21, 22
Empress of Britain 26, 27, 29, 37, 116, 144
Empress of Canada 115, 116; *116 see also Mardi Gras*
Empress of Scotland 53 *see also Hanseatic*
Enchanted Isle 200 *see also Argentina*
Enchanted Seas 200 *see also Brasil*
Enchantment of the Seas 189
Ericsson, L 79
Estonia 193
Etruria 25
Eugenedes, N V 53, 106

Eugenides, E 105, 139
Eugenio C(osta) 55, 91, 106, 123, 215, 216
Europa (1929) 25–6, 299, 43, 47, 55, 97, 103, 105; *97*
Europa (1965) 97, 102; *97 see also Kungsholm (1953)*
Europa (1981) 9, 10, 16, 37, 96–105, 107, 108, 111, 113, 114, 128, 129, 131, 147, 164, 195, 198, 199, 200, 203, 206, 221, 229, 232, 241; *97, 98, 100, 103, 104, 105, 267*
Explorer Starship 146 *see also Begonia*
Fain, R 174
Fairfield Shipbuilding & Engineering 28, 83
Fairline Shipping Corporation 141
Fairmajesty 185; *185 see also Star Princess*
Fairsea 144 *see also Carinthia*
Fairsky (1964) 141, 185, 188 *see also Oxfordshire*
Fairsky 118
Fairstar 141
Fairwind 144; *186 see also Sylvania*
Fantasy 121, 125, 126, 169, 180–3, 184, 188, 189, 192, 200, 223, 241–2; *180, 182, 183, 271*
Farcus, C 116, 122, 123
Farcus, J 116, 117, 122, 123, 125–6, 127, 133, 154, 163, 183, 222, 223, 257
Fascination 279
Fearnley & Eger 88, 93, 205
Fedor Dostoevsky 196
Fennis, H M 222
Ferrier, G 28
Ferris, T 38
Festivale 116, 117, 118, 122, 124, 141, 144, 153; *268 see also S A Vaal*
Fincantieri 185, 186–7, 188, 191, 192, 194, 216, 219, 222, 223, 226, 227
Finlandia 82, 87, 88, 89, 125, 129, 131, 161
Finnhansa 83, 88
Finnjet 98, 111, 112, 129, 130, 131, 133, 154, 158, 164, 195, 198, 203, 220
Finska Angfartygs 82 *see also Oy Finnlines*
Flagship Cruises Ltd 93, 95
Flender Werft 203

France 32, 54, 58, 64, 72, 73, 75, 84, 96, 109, 110, 117, 119, 121, 125, 131, 142, 143, 144, 145, 146, 147, 152, 158, 159, 166, 174, 175, 182, 183, 20, 225; *141 see also Norway*
Franconia 115, 117
Frankfurt Express 102
Fred Olsen Line 82
French Line 12, 13, 22, 30, 32, 45, 72, 110, 142, 143, 175, 179, 209
Fritz Heckert 43–4
frogdesign 234
From Song to Sovereign 177
Frontier Spirit 164–5, 208; *165*
FS Platau 91
Fuji Maru 197–8, 199, 200, 242; *197, 198*
'Fun Ships' 8, 10, 116, 222, 223
Furness Withy & Company 27, 31
Future Seas see Nordic Empress
Galaxy 190; *191, 273*
Galileo Galilei 153
Gardner, J 54, 74, 77, 89, 150, 186, 257
Garonne 14; *14*
Garroni Carbonara, V 257–8
Gebrüder Sulzer 89, 113, 118, 128, 147, 161
General Electric Company 185
George V of Britain 19–20
Georgic 34
German Atlantic Line (Deutsche Atlantik Line) 53, 56, 57, 90
Gibbs, W F 58
Golden Odyssey 201–2, 203
Gotaas-Larsen Group 88, 174
Goulandris family 116
Grace Line 27, 138, 166, 199
Grand Princess 183, 192–4, 235–6; *194*
Grandeur of the Seas 189–90
Greek Line 116, 120, 144, 153, 200
Green Goddess see Caronia
Gregotti Associati 217, 219
Gripsholm (1928) 29, 45, 46, 49, 53 *see also Berlin*
Gripsholm (1957) 32, 48–51, 52, 61, 64, 66, 69, 75, 77, 86, 89, 91, 107, 156 *see also Regent Sea*
Grundstad Maritime Overseas 200
Grung, G 89, 90, 131, 132, 133, 258

Guglielmo Marconi 153, 216 *see also Costa Riviera*
Haakon VIII 20
Hadag 195
Hall Russell and Company 11
Hallen, M 89, 90, 174, 175, 176
Halve Maan 64
Hamburg 52–7, 86, 89, 93, 96, 97, 98; *53, 54, 56 see also Maksim Gorkij*
Hamburg Amerikanische Paketfahrt Aktien-Gesellschaft (HAPAG) 13–14, 15, 16, 17, 19, 39, 40, 53, 84, 96, 104, 135 *see also Hapag-Lloyd*
Hamburg Atlantic Line 106
Hamburg Südamerika Line 30, 39, 40, 41, 91
Hammer, M 80, 89, 131, 133, 258
Hanseatic 53, 106 *see also Empress of Scotland; Doric* (1973)
Hansen, K E 22
Hapag-Lloyd 16, 37, 96, 97, 98, 99, 100, 102, 103, 104, 105, 107, 115, 127, 146, 164, 195, 198, 221, 232
Hapag-Lloyd Werft (Lloyd Werft) 146, 147, 226, 232
Harland & Woolf 30, 31, 32, 66, 67, 136, 218
Harsia, P 155
Held, M 209–10, 212, 259
Hellenic Institute of Marine Technology 134, 155, 201
Helsinki Express 83 *see also Nili*
Herald of Free Enterprise 184
Heikkinin, L 258
Heyerdahl, K M 258
Heyes, P 258
Himalaya 49
Hirsch-Bedner 163
Hitler, A 38, 42
Hohenzollern 15, 16, 17, 203
Holiday 122, 123–9, 147, 167, 169, 180, 182, 183, 192, 243; *124, 125, 126, 127, 128, 268*
Holland America Line 15, 45, 59, 60, 62, 64, 71, 96, 103, 107, 109, 110, 111, 112, 113, 114, 115, 116, 117, 125, 131, 135, 146, 151, 156, 159, 163, 183, 184, 185, 188, 190, 201, 208, 214, 215, 216, 218, 221, 222, 223, 224, 225, 226, 227, 228, 230, 232 *see also New Building Department*

Home Lines 53, 57, 65, 84, 87, 93, 96, 99, 105–6, 108, 109, 110, 113, 115, 117, 118, 139, 156, 163, 166, 216
Homeric (1920s) 24
Homeric (1955) 106 *see also Mariposa*
Homeric (1986) 110, 216
Horizon 190, 216
Howaldtswerke Deutsche Werft AG 39, 40, 53, 55, 102, 153, 195
Höydahk, P 179
Hudson, H 64
HW Metallbau 128
Iberia 65, 66
IM Skaugen A/S 88, 89, 174
Inchbald, M 258
Incras Steamship Company Ltd 136
Independence 218
International Maritime Organisation (IMO) 188
Ishikawajima-harima Heavy Industries 199
Island Princess 94, 159, 188; *93 see also Island Venture*
Island Venture 88, 92, 93–5; *93 see also Island Princess*
Israel Car Ferries 82
Italia 53, 87, 105 *see also Kungsholm (1928)*
Italian Line 58, 84, 109, 138
Ithica 135 *see also Amelio de Mello; Dolphin IV*
Izumo Maru 199
Jamaica Queen 83 *see also Nili*
Japan Ship Exporters' Association 197
Jarvis, H 32
Jerusalem 83 *see also Miami*
John Brown & Co (Clydebank) Ltd 34, 74, 77
Jonstorp 45
Jubilee 123–4, 127, 180; *123, 128*
Jungstedt, K 47
Jupiter (1920s) 21
Jupiter (1966) 82
K/S A/S Norsk Cruises Ltd 203–4, 214
Kaiser Wilhelm der Grosse 122–3
Kaiser Wilhelm II 15
Kaiser Wilhelm of Germany 16, 19
Kashiwara Maru 199
Kashoggi, A 205
Katzourakis, A 190, 258–9
Katzourakis, M 190, 258–9

Kawasaki Heavy Industries 116, 117
Kerbrech, R De 47
Khalkis yard 152
Kingo, J 155
Kioscoglou, H 139, 140, 141
Klosowski, A 104
Kloster, K U 799, 82, 83, 84, 86, 87, 88, 95, 96, 115, 117, 129, 141–2, 146, 158, 159, 167, 174, 191, 193, 195
Kloster Rederi A/S 79, 83, 86, 92, 95, 115, 214
Kloster Sunward Ferries 79, 81
Knud E Hansen 22, 79, 80, 82, 84, 86, 87, 88, 89, 93, 141–2, 159
Kockums 123, 180; 123
Köhnemann, W 103, 195, 259
Kommandittselskapet Cruise Venture A/S & Co 93
Kommandittselskapet Sea Venture A/S & Co 93
Korbing, K 259
Kraft durch Freude (KdF – Strength through Joy) 39–44, 45, 50, 52, 55, 115, 148, 172, 219
Kronprins Olav 22
Kronprinsessan Victoria 121, 125
Kruzenstern 211
Kukkasniemi, A 259
Kungsholm (1928) 25, 26, 27, 29, 30, 37, 45, 46, 47, 49, 51, 119 see also Italia
Kungsholm (1953) 48–51, 52, 61, 64, 66, 67, 75, 77, 89, 107, 156, 243; 49, 51, 97 see also Europa (1965)
Kungsholm (1966) 45, 48, 50, 51–2, 55, 84, 86, 91, 92, 95, 118, 119, 160, 196, 198, 207, 227, 243–4 see also Sea Princess
Kurtz, R 204
Kvaerner Masa-Yards 156, 165, 172, 173, 189, 192
L'Atlantique 30, 46, 55, 110, 156, 158, 178, 189
La Marseillaise 30, 49 see also Maréchal Petain
La Playa 40
Lady Diana 203
Lady Sarah 203
Lafayette 180
Lancastria 24
Laos 139
Las Palmas de Gran Canaria 144 see also Crown del Mar

Latsis Group, The 116
Laurentic 24
Leach, Dr R 163
Le Corbusier 209
Leda (1920s) 21
Leda (1950s) 91
Legend of the Seas 188–90; 188, 189
Leipziger Illustriete Zeitung 9
Leith & Clyde Shipping Company 10
Le Levant 236
Lennon, D 74, 94, 259
Leonardo da Vinci 32, 66, 72, 84, 109, 124
Lettres à Gerry 209–210
Levander, K 154–5, 156, 157, 174, 192, 201, 202, 209, 210, 213
Lindblad Explorer 202, 203, 207; 202
Lindholmens 45
Liners to the Sun 36, 112
Lloyd's List 159
Lloyd Triestino 22, 87, 91, 138, 153, 216
Lloyd Werft see Hapag-Lloyd Werft
Loewy, R 62, 69, 90
Louis Cruises 140
Lubecker Flenderwerft 82
Lunn, Dr 13
Maasdam 135 see also Stefan Batory
Maasdam (1993) 222
MacGREGOR-NAVIRE 178
Magrodome roofs 93, 98, 106, 146, 151, 192, 224; 93
Majesty of the Seas 179, 182
Maksim Gorkij 57, 97 see also Hamburg
Malolo 27, 108; 27 see also Matsonia
Manner, G 57
Mardi Gras 115–16; 116 see also Empress of Canada
Maréchal Petain 30 see also La Marseillaise
MARIN 180, 181, 223
Marine Engineering and Shipping Review 46
Mariposa 27, 106, 166 see also Homeric (1955)
Marsh, M 196
Massachusetts Institute of Technology 155, 157
Masson, B 127
Masson, G 127
Masters, M 95, 259

Matson Line 27, 106, 108, 166
Matsonia 27 see also Malolo
Matthias-Thesen-Werft 43
Maud of Norway 20
Mauretania 28
Mauretania (1939) 34, 122–3
Maxtone-Graham, J 36, 112, 177
McCuaig, A 150, 151
McDonald, S 96
McKee, D 159
McNeece, J 120, 150, 190, 231, 259
Mercury 272
Meridian 153
Messageries Maritimes 30, 49, 135, 138, 166
Met Studio 150
Meteor (1904) 19; 19
Meteor (1950s) 91
Meyer Werft 188, 216, 227, 236
Mezzani 152
Miami 83 see also Jerusalem
Michelangelo 7, 54, 58, 84, 109, 121
Mikhail Lermontov 141
Milne Mitchell, P G 30
Ministry of Transport 140
Mitsubishi Heavy Industries 164, 165, 199
Mitsui-OSK 197
Monarch of Bermuda 27, 31
Monarch of the Seas 179, 182
Monchy, W de 60
Monte Sarmiento 88–9, 244
Monterey 27, 166
Moore McCormack Line 51, 62, 67, 89, 94, 111, 138, 200
Morflot 196
Morris, C F 66–7, 71, 184
Morro Castle 180
Mortola, G 236
Mutero NV Interieurarchi-tecten 63, 259
Mutters, H P 260
Mystique Princess 236
Nabila 205
Nagler, N 64
Narstad 204
Nassau 136
National Bank for Reconstruction 62
Naval Architect, The 158
Navy Club 152
Nazis 23, 38, 39, 44, 147
Neckermann 57
Nederland Line 113
Neptunia 87
Nertollotti, Dr A 205

Nevasa 140, 141
New Building Department 62
Nieuw Amsterdam (1938) 7, 47, 55, 59, 61, 63, 6, 103, 110, 225; 59
Nieuw Amsterdam (1983) 107, 110–14, 115, 128, 131, 147, 154, 161, 185, 221, 222, 223, 224, 244; 110, 111, 112, 113, 114
Nihon Cruise Line 199
Nili 82, 83; 83 see also Helsinki Express; Jamaica Queen
Nilsson, F 91, 94, 95, 131, 133, 260
Nippon Maru 197, 198, 199 see also Argentina Maru; Ziluolan
Nippon Maru II 198
Nippon Yusen Kaisha 164, 165, 199, 200
NKK Corporation 206
Noordam 1077, 110–14, 128, 131, 185, 221, 222, 223, 224
Norddeutscher Lloyd see North German Lloyd
Nordenfjeldske Dampskibssel-skab 15, 20, 90, 91
Nordic Empress 169, 170, 184, 189, 219; 169
Nordic Prince 86, 88, 89, 90, 95, 129; 175
Normandie 7, 12, 22, 26, 29, 31, 47, 55, 59, 62, 69, 75, 110, 121, 142, 144, 145, 146, 148, 166, 175, 178, 179, 180, 182, 185, 192
Norske Sprinkler A/S 82
North Atlantic Blue Riband 62
North German Lloyd (Norddeutscher Lloyd) 13, 15, 25, 26, 43, 45, 52, 53, 57, 96–7, 103, 104, 146 see also Hapag-Lloyd
North of Scotland & Orkney & Shetland Steam Navigation Company ('The North Company') 10–11, 12, 13, 15
Norway 117, 123, 124, 125, 129, 141–6, 158, 167, 171, 174, 175, 200; 143, 269 see also France
Norwegian America Line 37, 50, 79, 92
Norwegian Caribbean Lines (NCL) 83, 84, 86, 87–8, 91, 95, 96, 105, 119, 124, 143, 146, 159, 163, 167, 169, 170, 171, 172, 174, 233

Norwegian Cruise Line *see*
Norwegian Caribbean Lines
(NCL)
Norwegian Cruiseships A/S 93
Norwegian Sky 146, 233
Nuovi Cantieri Aquania 205
NV Koninklijke Mij De
Schelde 32, 48, 61
Nystads Verv AB 202
Oakley, B 70, 71
Ocean Monarch 31
Oceania (1930s) 31, 216
Oceania (1950s) 87
Oceanic 55, 84, 87, 91, 93,
105, 106, 107, 108, 109,
110, 139, 166
Oceanic Grace 165, 200, 206;
205
Odessa 88 *see also Copenhagen*
Officine Marieotti 216
Oivind Lorentzen 93
Ojjeh, A 1442
Oldenburger Möbelwerkstätten
GmbH 207
Olympia 153, 200 *see also
Caribe I*
Olympic 31
Onassis, A 204
Oppenheimer, Sir D 74, 150
Oranje 45, 46, 67, 101, 147, 222
see also Angelina Lauro
Orcades 47
Oriana (1960) 58, 64, 65–72, 77,
87, 96, 101, 106, 108, 124, 141,
146, 159, 163, 170, 184, 188,
218, 224, 228, 245; *65, 69*
Oriana (1995) 226–32, 245;
227, 229, 230, 232, 280
Orient Express 10, 29, 81
Orient Line *see* Orient Steam
Navigation
Orient Steam Navigation
(Orient Line) 13, 14, 26,
47, 65, 66–7, 68, 71, 86, 113,
138, 141, 214
Orient Venus 199
Oriental Queen 141
Orion 26–7, 47, 68; *26*
Oronsay 65, 66
O'Rorke, B 26, 68, 71, 260
Orsora 72
Oscar II of Norway 14
Oslofjord 48, 66
Oxfordshire 140, 141 *see also
Fairsky* (1964)
Oy Finnlines 83, 87 *see also
Finska Angfartygs*
Oy Wärtsilä AB 45, 82, 86, 87,
88, 89, 90, 91, 95, 128, 129,

131, 134, 146, 152, 154, 155,
156, 157, 158–9, 160, 161,
163, 164, 165, 167, 168, 173,
174, 175, 178, 180, 181, 183,
193, 195, 201, 202, 203, 205,
206, 209, 214
Pacific Princess 159, 188; *94 see
also Sea Venture*
PAMETRADA 73
Pan American Cruise Line 83
Panama Canal 9, 104, 163,
191, 225
Panama Railway Company 69
Parama 139
Partner Ship Design 172
Pasteur 30, 31, 53, 57, 60, 97,
101, 110, 189 *see also
Bremen* (1959)
Patria 40, 49
Patricia 82 *see also Ariadne*
Patrick, J 260
Peninsular and Oriental Steam
Navigation Company
(P & O) 10, 13, 14, 15, 32,
47, 65, 66, 67, 68, 70, 71, 72,
87, 96, 113, 123, 138, 140,
141, 146, 159, 160, 161, 163,
164, 166, 170, 185, 186, 187,
188, 191, 194, 208, 215, 219,
221, 222, 224, 226, 227, 228,
229, 231, 232, 235 *see also*
Trident; Princess Cruises
Penttinen, I 155
Perowne, Mr 13
Peynet, G 260
Phoenix 158, 167, 174, 191, 193
Piano, R 186, 191, 260
Platou, F S 91, 260
Port Line 152
Port Melbourne 152
Port Sydney 152
Potier, J-C 209, 210, 212
Premier Cruises 106, 114
President Jackson class 61, 69
Prince Olav see Prins Olav
Princess Cruises 96, 141, 159,
160, 161, 163, 185, 186, 187,
188, 190, 226, 227, 228,
235–6
Princessa Victoria 140 *see also
Victoria* (1959)
Prins Olav 19–23, 79, 90, 135;
20
Prinsendam 110, 111, 112,
201–2, 203, 221; *201*
Prinzessin Victoria Luise 8, 15–19,
20, 21, 23, 38, 108, 201, 203,
204, 245–6; *16, 17, 18*
Project Eagle 236

Project Gemini 226–8, 232;
227
Project Lifestyle 150–2
Project Qqueen Mary 236
Project Vision 189–90, 236
Puerto Rico 83 *see also Arosa Star*
Puerto Rico Steamship
Company 83
Pulitzer, G 138, 216, 260
Q3 72, 73, 74, 76, 77, 159
Q4 73, 74, 77
Quaker City 10
Queen Anna Maria 116, 120,
144 *see also Empress of Britain;
Carnivale*
Queen Elizabeth 7, 34–5, 192
Queen Elizabeth 2 7, 8, 99, 34,
35, 36, 37, 41, 44, 53, 54, 56,
58, 64, 72–8, 86, 89, 91, 92,
93, 94, 96, 102, 103, 108, 120,
121, 123, 133, 139, 142,
146–52, 159, 163, 166, 171,
174, 180, 181, 182, 185, 186,
188, 192, 198, 209, 211, 214,
215, 218, 220, 227, 228, 246;
*73, 74, 75, 76, 77, 146, 148,
149, 150, 151 see also* Project
Lifestyle
Queen Mary 7, 26, 31, 34, 35,
36, 5, 72, 74, 142
Queen of Bermuda 27, 31
Queens 7, 12, 36, 72, 73, 77, 78,
152, 182, 192
R D Russell and Partners 71
Radisson Diamond 214; *214*
Radisson Group 208, 214
Raffaello 7, 54, 58, 84, 109, 121
Raymond-Whitcomb 22–3
Rederi A/B Swedish Lloyd 82
Rederiaktiebolaget Clipper *see*
Clipper Line
Regal Princess 187–8, 222
Regent Sea 52 *see also Gripsholm*
(1957)
Regent Sun 152 *see also Axel
Johnson; Costa Marina*
Regina Magna 97 *see also
Bremen* (1959)
Renaissance 110
Renaissance Cruises 205,
214, 236
Renaissance I–VIII 205–6, 208
Rex 221
Rheingold train service 29
Rheinstahl Nordseewerke
GmbH 93, 94
Robert Ley 38–44, 45, 46, 49,
55, 69, 93, 115, 147, 156, 157,
172, 246; *41, 44, 45*

Röda Nejlikan-type lounges
121, 125
Rogers, R 186
Rome 14; *14*
Rothschild, Baron 13
Rotterdam 7, 9, 32, 48, 54, 58,
59–64, 66, 67, 68, 69, 71, 75,
77, 84, 93, 103, 106, 109, 110,
111, 112, 121, 123, 125, 133,
139, 141, 142, 163, 183, 188,
215, 216, 218, 221, 222, 223,
225, 230, 232, 246–7; *60, 61,
62, 63, 265, 266*
Rotterdam VI 226
Rotterdamsche Lloyd 30, 61,
113, 224
Royal Caribbean Cruise Line
86, 88, 89, 90, 91, 92, 95, 96,
105, 119, 129, 130, 131, 133,
154, 159, 160, 169, 174, 175,
176, 177, 178, 179, 180, 182,
183, 185–6, 188, 189, 195,
214, 236
Royal Cruise Line 95, 201
Royal Institution of Naval
Architects 158–9
Royal Mail Line 13, 14, 24, 25,
28, 30, 32, 33, 34, 37, 136
Royal Odyssey 95 *see also Royal
Viking Sea*
Royal Princess 123, 156–63,
164, 165, 166, 167, 168,
175, 178, 184, 185, 188,
192, 220, 221, 225, 230,
247; *160, 161, 162*
Royal Society of Arts 70
Royal Viking Line 37, 88, 89,
90, 91, 92, 93, 95, 96, 99, 105,
119, 129, 139, 167, 168, 195,
196, 208
Royal Viking Queen 208
Royal Viking Sea 91, 95, 96,
129; *90, 91, 267 see also
Royal Odyssey*
Royal Viking Sky 91, 95; *91, 92
see also Sunward* (1980s)
Royal Viking Star 91, 95, 139,
142, 168, 195, 196, 202,
247–8; *92 see also Westward*
Royal Viking Sun 37, 167–9,
181, 207; *168*
Ryndam 135 *see also Atlas*
Ryndam (1994) 222; *279*
S A Vaal 116, 141, 153, 196 *see
also Festivale; Transvaal Castle*
Saarikangas, M 158, 163
Sabaudia 45 *see also Stockholm*
Safety of Life at Sea (SOLAS)
regulations 184, 188, 193

Safmarine 116, 196
Saga 82
Sagafjord 37, 48, 50, 75, 82, 84, 89, 91, 92, 94, 95, 196, 248
Sakura Maru 197
Sally Albatross 171–2, 173 see also Viking Saga
Sally Line 200
Santa Cruz 202
Santa Paula 138, 166
Santa Rosa 27, 138, 166, 199
Saturnia 166
Scandinavian Song 95 see also Sunward (1966)
Scharnhorst 26
Schichau Seebeckwerft AG 206, 208
Schreiber, G 75, 260
Scythia 27
Sea Cloud 211, 213
Sea Goddess I 13, 23, 165, 203–5, 206, 210, 212, 248; 204, 205
Sea Goddess II 13, 23, 165, 203–5, 206, 210, 212
Sea Princess 52, 96, 227 see also Kungsholm (1966)
Sea Venture 88, 92, 93–5, 107, 139, 142, 160, 249; 94 see also Pacific Princess
Seabourn Cruise Line 206, 207, 208, 209, 214
Seabourn Pride 10, 23, 206, 207, 208, 248–9
Seabourn Spirit 23, 206, 208; 206, 207
Seabourn type 13
SeaEscape 95
Seaward 86, 87, 88 see also Spirit of London
Seaward (1988) 167–8, 169, 171, 175; 167
Seetours International 196
Sensation 183
Shalom 53, 54, 106, 107, 110
Sharp, G G 62, 69
Shaw Savill 67
Shin Sakura Maru 197, 198; 197
Shipbuilding and Shipping Record 26
Showa Line 165, 206
Silja Europa 184
Silja Line 110, 125
Silja Serenade 184, 236
Silja Symphony 184
Silver Cloud 208, 214; 208, 278
Silverseas 236
Silver Wind 208, 214
Silvia Regina 112, 125, 129

Sitmar Cruises 65, 96, 116, 118, 141, 144, 180, 183, 184, 185, 186, 187, 188, 191, 205, 208, 219 see also Fairline Shipping Corporation
Skaugen, S 89
Skyward 84–8, 249; 85, 87
Sloman, R M 9, 10
Smallpiece, Sir B 74
Société Générale de Constructions Eléctriques et Méchaniques Alsthom 185
Société Nouvelle des Ateliers et Chantiers du Havre (ACH) 209, 213
Society Adventurer 208, 209
Solent 14
Somerfin SA 82, 83
Song of America 114, 129–34, 154, 155, 158, 161, 163, 167, 168, 169, 173, 174, 176–7, 178, 179, 249–50; 129, 130, 132, 175
Song of Norway 86, 88, 89, 90, 95, 129, 130, 132, 133, 179, 250; 175
Sony Corporation 191
Southern Cross 67, 68
Southward 86, 87, 170, 250; 87
Sovereign of the Seas 23, 147, 169, 174–80, 181, 182, 183, 188, 189, 251; 176, 177, 179
Soviet Merchant Marine 57
Spero 82
Spirit of London 87 see also Seaward
Squarey, C M 66, 67
St Ninian 15
St Rognvald 10–15
St Sunniva 10–15, 23, 253; 11, 13
St Sunniva Chronicle 12 see also The Deeds of the St Sunnivites
St Sunnivites 13, 18 see also St Sunniva Chronicle; The Deeds of the St Sunnivites
Star Cruises 236
Star Princess 183–8, 189, 190, 191, 192, 194, 221, 227, 251; 187, 272 see also Fairmajesty
Starship Atlantic 114 see also Atlantic (1982)
Starward 84–8, 251–2; 87
Statendam 109, 111, 116, 117, 125, 183, 184, 188, 190
Statendam (1992) 222, 223–6, 232, 252; 222, 224, 225, 226, 280
Stefan Batory 135 see also Maasdam

Stella Maris 139, 140
Stella Oceanis 139, 140
Stella Polaris 19–23, 28, 34, 38, 79, 90, 204, 252; 22
Stella Solaris 138–40; 139 see also Cambodge
Stephen, E 88, 90
Stockholm (1938) 44–5, 48, 51, 55, 56, 253; 45
Stockholm (1939) 45–8, 49, 50, 55, 69, 253; 46, 47, 48, 51
Stockholm (1948) 47–8, 156, 158, 208
'Straths' 66, 166
Suez Canal 9, 72
Sun Lines 116, 139, 209
Sun Princess 159, 83, 188, 190, 191; 191, 274
Sun Viking 88, 89, 90, 95; 90, 175, 176
Sun Viking type 8
Sunward (1966) 79–80, 81, 82, 83, 84, 86, 89, 991, 92, 95, 99, 115, 253; 80, 81, 87 see also Scandinavian Song
Sunward (1980s) 95, 146 see also Royal Viking Sky
Superstar Leo 236
Superstar Virgo 236
Svea (1966) 82
Svea (1985) 45
Svea Corona class 110
Svenska Amerika Linen see Swedish American Line
Swan Hunter 73, 159
SWATH (small water-plane area twin hull) 156, 193, 213, 214
Swedish American Cruises 208
Swedish American Line (Svenska Amerika Linen) 25, 29, 37, 44, 45, 46, 47, 48, 50, 52, 58, 79, 86, 89, 91, 92, 97, 101, 105, 107, 117, 142, 185
Swedish Lloyd 22, 83 see also Rederi A/B Swedish Lloyd
Sylvania 73, 144 see also Fairwind
T Mariotti 152
Tagus 10; 265
Technical Marine Planning 117, 222
Technimpianti 187
Teinhoven, J A van 62, 63
Thackeray, W 10
The Deeds of the St Sunnivites 13 see also St Sunniva Chronicle

The Innocents Abroad 10
The Scotsman 10
Thomas Cook Company 10, 13, 15
Tienhoven, H van 261
Tienhoven, J A van 261
Three Quays of London 159
Tiffany 222
Tillberg, R 52, 94, 95, 199, 232, 234, 260–1
Tillberg Design 233
Transvaal Castle 116, 136, 153 see also S A Vaal
Travel Weekly 83
Trident 67
Tropicale 102, 107, 112, 114, 115–23, 124, 127, 128, 129, 131, 134, 142, 145, 154, 158, 161, 169, 180, 254; 118, 119, 120
Trygge, B 155
Twain, M 10
Uganda 140, 141; 140
Umbria 25
Union Castle Line 81, 116, 135, 136, 153, 196
Union Naval de Levante 200
United Designers 190
United Fruit Company 40
United States 7, 58, 62, 72, 73
United States Line 58
Universal Line SA 37
V-Ships 208 I Sitmar Cruises
Valmet 180
Vaterland 39
Vectis 14, 135; 14
Veendam 111, 146
Venus (1932) 21–2, 91
Venus (1966) 82
Vereins Deutscher Ingenieure (VDI) 18
Viceroy of India 66, 78
Vickers Armstrong 65, 66, 67, 73, 159
Victoria 84
Victoria (1931) 22, 31, 91, 138
Victoria (1959) 136–8, 139, 140, 254–5; 136, 137, 138 see also Dunnottar Castle (1936); Princessa Victoria
Victoria and Albert 20
Victoria Luise 135 see also Deutschland
Victoria Steam Ship Company 84
Viet Nam 139, 166
Viking Line 154–5
Viking Saga 154, 171 see also Sally Albatross

Ville d'Alger 26
Vistafjord 37, 48, 50
Vlaming, F W de 222
Vlaming, Fennis, Dingemans –
    Interiors BV (VFD) 111,
    112, 163, 222, 223, 224, 225,
    261
Vlassov, B 184, 185
Volendam 109, 111, 146
Vorm, N Van der 221
Votteler, Prof A 103
Vulcania 166
Vulkan Group 226
Wallace, D 73, 74
Wallenins Group 88
Walt Disney Company 234–6
Wandborg, T 141–2, 144
Warwick, Capt W(illiam) 78
Warwick, W(alter) C 33
Weber, H 126
Weissmann, G 209

Welton Becket Associates 187
West, J 67, 68, 70, 184
Westin, I 261
Westward 95 *see also Royal
    Viking Star*
White Fleet 167
White Star Line 24, 31 *see also*
    Cunard
White Vikings 95
Wigham Richardson 73
Wild, Capt G A 71
Wilhelm Gustloff 38–44, 45, 46,
    69, 93, 115, 156, 157, 172,
    255; *39, 41, 42, 44*
Wilhelmsen, G 90
Willem Ruys 30, 45, 61, 77,
    101, 147, 184, 224
Williams, D 47
Wilson Line 13
Wilson Line 82
Wilton Fijenoord 136, 141

Wind Song 210
Wind Spirit 210
Wind Star 23, 209, 210–11,
    212–13, 255; *210, 211, 212,
    213, 277*
Windcruiser 156, 195, 209–13
Windjammer Barefoot Cruises
    213
Windsor Castle 66, 72, 106, 116,
    136, 196
Windstar Cruises 209, 211,
    213, 214
Windward 146, 170–1; *169*
Wirtz, C L W 63
Witts & Borgen 82
World Discoverer 202, 207; *207*
World War I 20, 24, 62, 89,
    135
World War II 21, 23, 30, 34, 41,
    44, 46, 47, 52, 55, 58, 59, 64,
    105, 136, 142, 147, 172, 197,

199
Wright, J 71, 261
Yachtcruiser 156, 165, 178,
    195, 201–9, 210, 211, 212,
    213, 214, 236; *203, 204,
    205, 208*
Yachtship Cruise Line 205
Yao Hwa 110
Yarmouth 83
Yourkevitch, V 38
Yran, K 93
Yran, P 261
Zenith 190, 216
Zim Israel Navigation
    Company (Zim Line) 53,
    83, 106, 107, 110
Zim Line *see* Zim Israel
    Navigation Company
Zonis, M 95, 116, 117